# Psychology and Effective Behavior

## L. N. Jewell, Ph.D.

**WEST PUBLISHING COMPANY**

ST. PAUL • NEW YORK • LOS ANGELES • SAN FRANCISCO

*Cover art:* "Ideal Couple" by Max Papart, Nahan Galleries, New York
*Cover design:* Diane Beasley
*Copy editor:* Sharon Sharp
*Art work:* Rolin Graphics
*Compositor:* The Clarinda Company
*Interior design:* Roslyn Stendahl, Dapper Design

COPYRIGHT ©1989    By WEST PUBLISHING COMPANY
                   50 W. Kellogg Boulevard
                   P.O. Box 64526
                   St. Paul, MN 55164-1003

96  95  94  93  92  91  90  89        8  7  6  5  4  3  2  1  0

**Library of Congress Cataloging-in-Publication Data**

Jewell, Linda N.
   Psychology and effective behavior.

   Includes index.
   1. Psychology.   2. Adjustment (Psychology)
I. Title.
BF121.J48   1989        150         88-33766
ISBN 0-314-27033-7

## Fine Art and Photo Credits

**Part I,** page **2,** "Girl Before a Mirror" by Pablo Picasso, Museum of Modern Art, New York. Reproduced for chapter opening art for chapters 1 and 2.

**Chapter 1**
**5,** Earl Dotter/Archive Pictures; **8,** Jeffry Myers/Stock Boston; **10,** Lionel J-M. Belevigne; **12,** J. Berndt/Stock, Boston

**Chapter 2**
**23,** Jeffry W. Myers/Stock, Boston; **33,** G. Goodwin/Monkmeyer Press Photo Service; **40,** David Powers/Stock, Boston; **46,** Audrey Gottlieb/Monkmeyer Press Photo Service

**Part II,** page **53,** "Ideal Couple" by Max Papart; Nahan Galleries, New York. Details reproduced for chapter opening art for chapters 3, 4, and 5

**Chapter 3**
**64,** George Malave/Stock, Boston; **65,** Ethan Hoffman/Archive Pictures; **71,** Gerard Fritz/Monkmeyer Press Photo Service

**Chapter 4**
**80,** Stock, Boston; **85,** Elizabeth Crews/Stock, Boston; **95,** Kirk Schlea/Berg & Associates; **99,** Margaret C. Berg/Berg & Associates

**Chapter 5**
**106,** Frances M. Cox/Stock, Boston; **110,** Michael Hayman/Stock, Boston; **113,** Elizabeth Crews/Stock, Boston; **116,** Rhoda Sidney/Monkmeyer Press Photo Service; **118,** Hazel Hanrin/Stock, Boston

continued on page 458

*For My Family*

*May you live all the days of your life.*

Jonathan Swift

# Contents in Brief

v

# Contents

**PART 2: YOU: A UNIQUE INDIVIDUAL**    **53**

---

---

## APPENDIX A: BEHAVIOR MODIFICATION: THE SELF-MANAGEMENT OF BEHAVIOR    431

---

## APPENDIX B: A SAMPLE MARRIAGE CONTRACT    439

# Preface

## PERSPECTIVE

When I was a young graduate student in psychology, it was fashionable to stay up late into the night debating the relative merits of pursuing knowledge about human behavior for its own sake versus pursuing this knowledge with the specific goal of applying it to make the world a better place. Looking back, I believe that I lost a lot of sleep to no purpose; this debate is now (and probably was then) a theoretical one. Psychologists who pursue research careers without specific interest in application expect that others will use what they learn. Applied psychologists who try to help people solve problems without specific interest in research (and many conduct research as well) are nevertheless aware that research is the foundation of their practice.

The academic subject usually called the psychology of adjustment extends the interrelationship between the search for knowledge about human behavior and the application of that knowledge to the individual level. Courses in this area are for the purpose of helping people who are not psychologists to understand themselves and other people better and to use psychological theory and research to help them manage their own lives and their own problems more effectively. The challenge to those of us who author textbooks for such courses is to demonstrate this applicability to a wide audience while remaining faithful to the integrity of a scientific discipline.

In this vein, I see *Psychology and Effective Behavior* as a bridge. This bridge gives students a way to get from one place to another. From knowledge to application. From understanding human behavior and the world a little better to being able to use this knowledge to manage and control their own lives more effectively. To the extent that students can indeed cross this bridge successfully, I have met the challenge inherent in writing this book to my own satisfaction.

## PLAN OF THIS BOOK

*Psychology and Effective Behavior* has five parts. The first part is introductory; Chapter 1 is an introduction to the book and the subject matter of the course. Chapter 2 is an introduction to the broad categories of personal and environmental factors that interact to produce human behavior.

Part 2 expands upon the personal factors affecting human behavior. Chapter 3 is an overview of human cognitive, emotional, and moral development. Chapter 4 begins the examination of that complex concept we call personality;

this discussion is completed in Chapter 5 with a detailed look at the self, self-concept, and self-esteem.

Part 3 expands upon the social environmental factors affecting human behavior. Chapter 6 explores the social worlds of attraction and friendship. Chapter 7 narrows the view to examine sex and sexual relationships, and Chapter 8 narrows it still further to focus on the very special relationships of love and marriage. In Chapter 9 the perspective is opened up again as we take an overview of the two worlds in which most of us spend most of our time—the worlds of education and work.

Part 4 of *Psychology and Effective Behavior* is devoted to basic life coping skills that everyone may use to improve the quality of day-to-day life. Chapter 10 examines communication and communicating. Chapter 11 looks at decisions and decision making, and Chapter 12 is devoted to stress and stress management. This is, if you will, an applied section dedicated to that majority of people who are getting along pretty well already; it also serves as a foundation for the discussion of specific adjustment problems to be found in the next section.

Part 5 focuses on the kinds of problems that traditionally have formed the core of courses in psychology of adjustment. Personal behavior and life-style problems, such as weight control and substance abuse are discussed in Chapter 13. Chapter 14 is about social relationship problems, such as peer pressure, loneliness, and divorce. Chapter 15 examines more individual personal emotional and psychological problems. Part 6, Chapter 16, helps students explore the variety of resources available if they find they need help in managing their own lives effectively.

## LEARNING FEATURES

The structure of *Psychology and Effective Behavior* incorporates several features designed to help the student master this material. In each chapter, bold-faced type is used to alert the student to terms or concepts that are central to the material in that chapter. A few definitions are set entirely in bold-faced type; this signals the student that this definition is central to the subject matter of the entire book.

Bold-faced terms appear in the list of *Key Words and Phrases* at the end of each chapter together with other words and phrases that incorporate central ideas from the chapter (as distinct from actual definitions). When used as outlined in Chapter 1, *Key Words and Phrases* serves as a study outline for the chapter.

Terms appearing in italics in each chapter are the more important terms and ideas that should come to mind when the student considers a key word or phrase. For example, *proximity, similarity,* and *complementarity hypothesis* are among the concepts that should come to mind when the student checks his or her understanding of the term **interpersonal attraction** (Chapter 6).

Students also may find summaries helpful as study aids. *Summing Up* is an interim summary that appears whenever there is to be a significant change of topic within a chapter. An example is when Chapter 3 shifts from a discussion of cognitive development to a discussion of emotional development. *Summing Up* helps students change mental gears; it also provides a forum for commentary that may be useful in helping to put the topic into perspective.

Some chapters have an end-of-chapter feature called *Putting it All Together* as well as interim summaries. As the name suggests, *Putting it All Together* helps students integrate material that is conceptually all of a piece although the pieces have been presented separately for clarity. For example, a number of personality theories are presented in Chapter 4; *Putting it All Together* helps students see the relationships among these theories and how all relate to the broader question of the meaning and measurement of personality.

In addition to these basic structural learning aids, a number of regular learning features appear in each chapter in *Psychology and Effective Behavior*. *Face of the Future* is a discussion based on new research or thinking about a chapter-related topic. This "cutting edge" feature is a supplement to the chapter material; it also may serve as a stimulus to, and foundation for, student research reports or papers.

Most chapters in *Psychology and Effective Behavior* have a self-test on one or more chapter-related topics. As the title of this feature suggests, the tests in *Test Yourself* have been chosen for their ability to help students gain *self-knowledge* or insight. Tests that commonly are given in formal counseling situations, and tests that require professional interpretation, do not appear in this feature.

If I have a personal favorite among the various features in this book, it is *For Discussion*. This feature asks questions based on presented facts and/or major conflicting viewpoints about a chapter-related topic. It is intended to stimulate student thinking and class discussion about an important, and often controversial, issue. Not all of these issues are new; the debate about legalizing marijuana that is summarized in the *For Discussion* section of Chapter 13 has been going on for a generation at least.

The last of the regular chapter learning features is *Read On,* an annotated list of selected books for further reading on various major chapter-related topics. Most of the books in *Read On* are available in paperback at the major book store chains; a few are textbooks included because I believe that their excellence outweighs the difficulty some students may have locating them. Both students and professors are encouraged to add to the lists in *Read On* by sharing the titles of personal favorites.

## ACKNOWLEDGEMENTS

No one writes a textbook alone. We get help from publishing staff, from reviewers, from colleagues, from preparation assistants, and often from family and friends as well. I would like to acknowledge the assistance I have received from many such individuals, beginning with West Executive Editor, Peter Marshall, Developmental Editor, Rebecca Tollerson, and Production Editors Tamborah Moore and Stacy Lenzen. Copy editor Sharon Sharp also is to be commended for her fine work.

I especially want to thank the many reviewers who contributed their ideas, suggestions and comments to the various stages of this manuscript.

My sincerest thanks also are due to Sheila Fleishell, a paragon among research assistants. Finally, my wholehearted thanks to William Goodyear who gave me the technical assistance and confidence I needed to give up my beloved typewriter and confront the modern world of word processors.

## Reviewers

**W. B. Apple**
Private practice—Princeton, NJ
(formerly) University of South Dakota

**Mary Bayless**
Brevard Community College

**Morton Berger**
Nova Community College

**Steve Coccia**
Orange Coast Community College

**Robert DaPrato**
Solano Community College

**Marc DesLaurier**
Kansas City Community College

**Ronald Evans**
Washburn University

**Angela Gonzales**
Miami Dade Community College

**John Hall**
University of Houston-Downtown

**Thomas Harris**
University of Wisconsin-LaCrosse

**Dr. Rob Heckel**
University of South Carolina-Columbia

**Gary Johnson**
Normandale Community College

**Warren Jones**
University of Tulsa

**Mary Kelso**
Antelope Valley College

**Terry Knapp**
University of Nevada

**Robert Koettel**
University of Nevada-Las Vegas

**Fred Medway**
University of South Carolina-Columbia

**Jeanne O'Kon**
Tallahassee Community College

**David Pancoast**
Old Diminion University

**Ralph Pifer**
Sank Valley College

**Christopher Potter**
Harrisburg Area Community College

**Dr. Juan Ramirez**
University of Northern Colorado

**Jack Shilkret**
Anne Arundel Community College

**Don Stanley**
North Harris Community College

**Kenneth Steere**
Manchester Community College

**Robert Tomlinson**
University of Wisconsin-Eau Claire

**Max Trenerry**
University of Wyoming

# Introduction and Foundation of Behavior

**W**elcome to *Psychology and Effective Behavior*. That is the title of the first section in Chapter 1 of Part 1 of this textbook about you and your life. It also serves as a good summary of Part 1, which is intended to introduce you to the subject matter of this course and the major themes of this book and to stimulate your interest in the 14 chapters to follow.

The major topics in Chapter 1 are descriptions of what you can expect this book to do (and not to do) for you, an overview of the subject matter of this course you are taking, and a brief discussion of the sources from which the material in this book has come. Effective behavior is defined, and the theme of personal control, which most psychologists believe is central to achieving such behavior, is introduced.

Chapter 2 presents an overview of the factors that psychologists find constitute the three major influences on human behavior. Personal factors, the physical environment, and the social environment are each discussed in an overview section. Each of these discussions is then followed by a more detailed examination using a specific example. The basic theme of this chapter is that human behavior is complex, and oversimplified explanations do not work in favor of understanding yourself or others better. This theme, like that of control, will underlie every chapter in *Psychology and Effective Behavior*.

The more psychologists and others learn about human behavior, the more they realize that all of it is the result of a complex interaction between a person and his or her physical and social environments. This may make understanding behavior more difficult, but it also opens up multiple avenues for those of us who might wish to change something about ourselves or our behavior; in other words, if you have some understanding of it, the very complexity of human behavior can work in favor of personal control and more effective behavior.

# Introduction

## WELCOME TO *PSYCHOLOGY AND EFFECTIVE BEHAVIOR*

Y ou are embarking upon an exploration of the most fascinating subject in the world—yourself. This is a book about your behavior, your emotions, your personality, your interests, your health, your goals, your friends, your loves, and your problems. It is about making decisions and communicating with others and going to college and having a career and handling stress and being in close relationships and many other aspects of your day-to-day life. Its purpose is to help you learn more about yourself and your world and to use what you learn for more effective behavior.

Of course, *you* is a subject you have been studying all of your life. What can you learn here? The answer to this question is important because if you have expectations that can't be met, you will be disappointed. If you are disappointed, your interest and motivation to learn will be reduced. So let's take a brief look at some of the things this book can and can't do for you.

## Unrealistic Expectations: What This Book Can't Do for You

Unlike the textbooks you use in many of your college courses, the subject matter of this one is very personal. Because of this, your expectations for acquiring knowledge that will be both interesting and useful are high, and that is as it should be. Experience suggests, however, that some students, particularly those who are taking their first psychology course, have expectations that can't be fulfilled.

■ *This book won't make you an expert on human behavior.* In the chapters to come, you'll learn terms, be introduced to theories, read about research, and get a look at some of the directions in which the exciting field of psychology is moving. In the process, you should come to understand yourself and those around you better, but you won't be an expert. In fact, if this book and this course do their jobs, one of the things you will learn from them is how much more there is to learn. Whether your subject is yourself or others, there is always more to learn about human behavior.

■ *This book won't support all of your beliefs.* It is safe to say that no other field of study generates the volume of "pop" literature there is in psychology. When it comes to human behavior, everyone seems to have a theory—even characters on television shows. You have been exposed to such material all of your life, and you are very unusual if you have not acquired some erroneous beliefs along the way. Many of these ideas are harmless enough, but they have no foundation in fact.

A good example of a relatively harmless belief is the popular conviction that to change someone's behavior, you must change an underlying attitude. This simply is not true. Attitudes influence behavior, but so do a great number of other factors. There are many avenues open if we want to change behavior, and it usually is unnecessary to try to change attitudes. In fact, over 50 years of research suggest that things often are the other way around; it may be necessary to change behavior first if we want to change an attitude (Erlich, 1969).

Some of the popular "facts" about human behavior are more dangerous because believing them can keep people from doing things they need to do to make their lives better in some way. A good example is the idea that problems can be avoided or solved by thinking positively.

There are two reasons for not placing too much reliance on the power of positive thinking. First, we get the things we want or change the things we don't like by doing, not by thinking. Sad to say, wishing does not make it so. Second, thinking *realistically* is crucial to managing our lives effectively, and sometimes this means facing unpleasant truths. If we try to avoid doing so in the name of positive thinking, we make it much more difficult to solve our problems or reach our goals (Goodhart, 1985).

■ *This book won't solve your problems.* Reading a book won't solve your problems any more than positive thinking will, and any book that promises to do so is misleading you. This is an objection that many psychologists have to some of the personal self-help books you see in bookstores or find at your local library; they promise things they can't deliver.

Most self-help books contain a good idea or two, but the tone of many is unrealistic and oversimplistic. Some are little more than collections of trendy terms. These may be fun to toss around in conversation, but they don't help you understand yourself any better and they certainly don't solve your problems. A few of these books also have a "me-first" tone that is both offensive and misleading; each of us must adapt to others in the process of trying to get what we want or need in life.

Not all self-help books suffer the problems described; there are some very useful ones available. Some of the better ones are listed in the *Read On* feature

A book can't solve your problems, but it can help you to learn to solve your own more effectively.

that follows most chapters in *Psychology and Effective Behavior*. Most of these are available in paperback at your local bookstore. By all means, look into these books if you are interested. They may be useful to you in your *own* efforts to solve your problems and control your life, although they can't do these things for you.

## Realistic Expectations: What This Book Can Do for You

This book won't support all of the beliefs you brought into this course, and it won't solve your problems or make you an expert on human behavior; but it can do some very important things.

■ *This book can give you information.* The background of *Psychology and Effective Behavior* is the knowledge that psychologists and others have acquired about human behavior. Selected information from that body of knowledge is presented as appropriate to the subjects under discussion. Some of this may not be new to you, especially if you have taken related high school or college courses. Some will be new; and even if there seems to be no immediate use for the information in your life, it should be interesting in its own right since it is about that endlessly fascinating subject—human behavior.

■ *This book can help you achieve insight.* It has been said that knowledge is power, and the power of information about yourself and your behavior can be considerable. For one thing, having facts about disturbing problems (depression is a good example) gives you a perspective that makes them less frightening. For another, information about the range of reactions people have to various situations (such as sexual relationships) can help you evaluate your own responses more realistically; we often worry unnecessarily about things that seem unusual to us but are perfectly normal.

Finally, knowledge can help you attain insight into your own behavior and that of others. **Insight is understanding that goes beyond the obvious or simple assumptions or value judgments.** The idea that other people (or we ourselves) do stupid or hurtful or self-defeating things because they (or we) are "bad people," "lack will power," or just do so "for no reason at all" makes it very difficult to deal with these behaviors. **The more you understand about yourself and about human behavior, the less frustrating life tends to be.**

■ *This book can give you some skills for managing your life more effectively.* A book cannot solve your problems, but it can give you information, ideas, resources, techniques, and ways of thinking about things that can help *you* solve them. For instance, this book cannot tell you how to communicate better with your particular boss, child, or special friend, but it can make you aware of some of the more common barriers to effective communication. It also can describe techniques that have helped others to overcome such barriers and may help you.

In short, this book is a resource to help you work toward effective behavior. Since that is the goal, it is time to take a closer look at just what this term means.

Knowledge is power.

*Francis Bacon*

## WHAT IS EFFECTIVE BEHAVIOR?

The word *effective* is an evaluation and, like all evaluative terms, it must have some reference point. The question is; effective according to what standard? Is your behavior effective when you are happy, when you are accomplishing personal goals, when you are making a contribution to the world, when you are behaving as others believe you should, or when you don't have any problems?

All of these standards have been used at one time or another to evaluate whether or not an individual's patterns of behavior are effective, but all present difficulties. The obvious choice would seem to be happiness, but *happiness* is very difficult to define, even for ourselves, and researchers find few people who say that they are happy all of the time (Diener, 1984). Similarly, the accomplishment of personal goals and the ability to make a positive contribution to the world go up and down over the course of life.

The idea that effective behavior can be defined by the standards of others is unsatisfactory as well. What others want or expect from us can be unacceptable or make us feel hemmed in and miserable. As for "no problems," how many people do you know who have no problems? If this were the standard, few of us could be said to measure up.

Another basic difficulty with the standards for effective behavior described is that they concern themselves with the *outcomes,* or end results, of your day-to-day actions and decisions. Yet outcomes are affected by many things, some of which you can't control. As a result, such standards may underestimate considerably your ability to manage your own behavior effectively. In addition, some of the outcomes of your actions and decisions won't be known for a very long time. How do you evaluate the effectiveness of your behavior in the meantime?

For a number of reasons, it seems to make sense to look at effective behavior in the context of your general approach to life on a day-to-day basis and whether this is working for you. From this perspective, effective behavior is defined in terms of an ongoing process rather than an end result and in terms of your own standards, rather than the standards of others.

**Effective behavior is flexible, controlled, and productive behavior that allows you to feel good about yourself and others as you move toward understanding yourself and achieving realistic personal goals and good relationships.**

This definition, which we will return to many times, incorporates the factors most psychologists believe are important measures of effective behavior (Atkinson, Atkinson, & Hilgard, 1983). It is relatively complex, so let's look at the various components more closely.

- *Flexible behavior.* You have your own plans and goals and your own accustomed patterns of behavior, but you are not rigid about them. You recognize the necessity of being able to adapt to changing conditions, and you do not become upset or unable to function when you have to do so.

- *Controlled behavior.* You may act impulsively from time to time, but you have confidence in your ability to control your own behavior. If you don't conform to social norms or the expectations of others, it is because you have made a choice, not because you "couldn't help yourself."

- *Productive behavior.* You have enthusiasm and energy for life and channel it into productive activities, such as education, work, relationships, and hobbies. You don't have to drive yourself to meet the ordinary demands of daily life.

- *Self-esteem and self-acceptance.* You have a sense of your own worth and feel accepted by others around you. You are comfortable in most situations and generally feel able to behave spontaneously rather than trying to be what others want or expect in the situation.

- *Self-knowledge.* You make a conscious effort to increase your awareness of your own feelings, motives, and behavior and to avoid hiding things from yourself.

- *Realistic personal goals.* You are able to be fairly realistic in judging your own capabilities and reactions. You don't consistently tackle things you can't accomplish or take the easy road and shy away from challenges. In addition, you are realistic in interpreting what is going on around you, and you do not consistently misperceive what others say and do.

- *Good relationships.* You are able to form close and satisfying relationships with other people. You are sensitive to the feelings of others and don't make excessive demands or try to manipulate others solely to gratify your own needs or prove to yourself that you are worthwhile.

Most psychologists probably would agree that the closer you come to having these characteristics, the easier it will be for you to be satisfied with the

> We're just here for a spell, so get a few laughs and do the best you can.
>
> *Will Rogers*

way you are managing your own life. Like the perfect weight, however, these measures are ideals. There is no sharp line differentiating people who meet these standards from those who don't. Each of us is somewhere on a continuum from very close to very far away from each of these effective behavior criteria.

It also is necessary to recognize that not everyone has the interest or motivation to strive for more effective behavior. People who do sometimes find themselves frustrated by the fact that people who don't are blocking their progress. For example, you may want to improve the quality of your relationship with your girlfriend, boyfriend, or spouse, but the desire does not seem to be mutual. He or she just won't try to open up and help the two of you achieve more honest communication. So, rather than working toward what you believe to be something better, you find yourself trying to adjust to the situation as it is.

## The Psychology of Adjustment

Each of us lives with constraints that put limits on our opportunities and our freedom of action. Some of these **constraints on behavior** stem from something about ourselves or our situation that we can't change. If you are short, you probably are not going to be a basketball star. If you come from a very large family, you may have less money to spend for clothes or entertainment than your college roommate. If the high school you went to was not academ-

Most psychologists consider good social relationships an important part of effective behavior.

ically sound, you may have to work harder in your classes than others. If you are a single working parent, it may take you much longer to attain your college degree than it would otherwise.

In addition to such personal constraints, the world we live in also puts limits on us; you are not free to do exactly what you want to do. There are laws that say you can't smoke in a movie theater or drive your car 70 mph on a residential street. Other laws say you have to pay taxes on the money you earn and pay for the items you want to take out of a store. Rules and regulations say you have to do certain things before you are entitled to drive a car or get married or enter this college or graduate from it.

Unwritten rules, called **norms,** also place limits on our behavior. There is no law that says you have to wait your turn in line at the grocery store, but there is likely to be some unpleasantness if you try to break in at the front. It just "isn't done." You don't have to take a shower every day or comb your hair or wear shoes if you don't want to either, but you will be very out of place and conspicuous in some settings if you don't, and some people will avoid you.

The wishes and expectations of others also prevent us from doing exactly what we might want to do. Even though you are very tired and want only to collapse in front of the television set, you take your children to a movie because you promised them you would. Or you clean up the apartment because you know your roommate likes it clean and you want to maintain your good relationship. Or you don't go to a party you want to attend because your girlfriend or boyfriend or spouse can't go and would be hurt if you went alone.

The constraints presented by our personal characteristics and life situations, laws, rules, norms, and the desires and expectations of others are factors to which most of us must adjust as we go about our business of trying to lead satisfying lives. For this reason, the subject matter of this course often is called the **psychology of adjustment.** Although each of us must adjust to a unique personal situation, we also face certain common adjustment issues. Here are a few that you are facing now or may expect to face in the future.

- *Changing-sex role expectations.* The last 20 years have seen a tremendous upheaval in traditional male and female roles, and so far these have not recrystallized into the clear and generally accepted sex role expectations of former times. There is more variability in expectations about appropriate male and female behavior now than at any time in history, and *flexibility* seems to be the key to adjustment in this area for some time to come.

- *Continual progress.* To anyone born before 1960, one of the most characteristic features of the last quarter-century has been the astonishing rate of scientific and technological advancement. All indications are that this is only the beginning, so even if you take the current state of the world for granted, at some point it will begin to change faster than you would like. You must adjust both to these changes and to the knowledge that things will go on changing.

- *Advancing medical knowledge.* The medical and biological sciences are opening up vistas for human health, appearance, recovery from injuries, and longevity scarcely dreamed of a generation ago. Babies are being "grown" in tubes, surgeons are transplanting live human hearts from one body to

A changing world requires adjustment.

another, men are being transformed surgically into women, and people who have lost both legs can get artificial ones so sophisticated that they can walk, dance, and ski.

These advances are exciting and mean better lives for many people and longer lives for others. They also mean that you may face difficult choices that your parents and grandparents did not have to make. Among these choices are deciding whether or not to have a family, commit yourself to donating an organ to someone else in the event of your premature death, or try to improve on nature with cosmetic surgery.

■ *A more dangerous world.* Many of the changes that are occurring in today's world are for the better, but you also must adjust to some negative aspects. Both crime and terrorism are on the increase world wide, and the arms race proceeds despite widespread concern. We have polluted our air and our water and upset the balance of nature to a serious degree in some areas. And we are spreading new diseases, such as the acquired immunodeficiency syndrome (AIDS), to replace the ones medical science has conquered.

Opinions vary widely as to what is behind this period of social, political, and environmental deterioration; where it will end; and what might be done to stop it. Some believe that there is no hope. Others believe that enough concerned individuals can turn things around. For this generation as for no other, it may be that "if you aren't part of the solution, you are part of the problem."

Whether you choose to be active in trying to change the world or not, you must live in it. Both its dangers and its changes are challenges to your adjustment. They are also stressors that can get you down and seem just too much at times. Perhaps you don't have much control over these aspects of your life, but you have a great deal over other aspects.

# The Psychology of Effective Behavior

As it is defined here, effective behavior is an *active* concept, and there are many aspects of your life in which you can take the initiative and exert this active control.

- *Finding your own values.* Values are learned as we grow up and experience life. You have to live with the value choices made by others, but you are free to choose your own. Some of these will be shared with other people, of course. For example, many people in our society value freedom, friendship, and enjoying life. Some values are more individual in nature. For example, some people seem to place a positive value on taking risks and "living dangerously," whereas most do not.

   Whether they have much or little in common with the values of others, your values are your own. No one else can tell you what you do or do not consider important (although they may try to tell you what you *should* consider important). These values may shift over time, but they are always central to your life.

- *Choosing a career.* The world and the people around you place certain constraints on your choice of a way to spend your working life, but you still have a wide range of choices within these constraints and those imposed by your own abilities. It is possible to make this choice in a reactive manner by drifting into whatever line of work is convenient, but you have the alternative of exploring possibilities, making an active choice, and changing that choice if it turns out not to suit you.

- *Choosing a life style.* Closely related to value and career choices is the matter of choosing a life style. Do you want to be a career-oriented single person living in a condominium and driving a BMW or a family-oriented married person with children, a house in the suburbs, and a station wagon? Do you want travel and excitement or roots and tradition? Do you want to be a big fish in a little pond or a little fish in a big pond? Or maybe you won't settle for less than being a big fish in a big pond.

   The list of possible ways to live is quite long despite constraints that may be imposed by your own abilities and life situation. The key is *choice*. When you seek out your own information about alternatives and make a choice based on your own values, you feel in control of your own life.

## Effective Behavior and a Sense of Control

Psychologists and other mental health professionals increasingly are impressed with the role that a sense of **personal control** plays in physical and mental health and general satisfaction with life. Feelings of being manipulated by others, of being a victim of forces beyond control, of lacking the ability to cope with life's demands, or simply of not understanding what is going on are turning out to be central to a great many different kinds of problems, such as

- Anger
- Anxiety
- Obesity

- Depression
- Alcoholism
- Job dissatisfaction
- Relationship problems
- Negative stress reactions
- Debilitating premenstrual syndrome
- Premature death among geriatric or critically ill patients

Psychologists call your belief in your ability to control your own life and cope with your own problems **perceived self-efficacy** (Bandura, 1977). This belief develops over time as you accumulate experience in meeting (or not meeting) your own goals and standards for behavior. To the extent that this experience is positive, you become more confident that you can continue to master whatever situations you may meet in the future. Studies of this belief find that greater perceived self-efficacy seems to be associated with better self-management of particular problems, such as weight control (e.g., O'Leary, 1985), as well as with better general psychological adjustment (e.g., Heppner & Anderson, 1985).

People with a history of *not* meeting their goals or living up to their own standards may come to believe that they have no control over what happens to them. Seligman (1974) called this acquired sense of having little or no control over one's fate **learned helplessness.** The passive, "not trying" approach to life that can follow from such a belief is characteristic of people who suffer from severe, chronic depression.

Learned helplessness has been demonstrated frequently in laboratory studies with animals (e.g., Seligman & Maier, 1967), and a number of researchers have produced similar reactions in human subjects. In one study, for example, subjects who previously had been given a series of unsolvable puzzles to work made no attempt to terminate a loud, unpleasant noise that later was set off by the experimenter. By contrast, subjects who had been given no puzzles, or puzzles that could be solved, learned quickly what they could do to stop the noise (Hiroto & Seligman, 1975).

Learned helplessness seems to be cumulative as the effects of giving up control in more and more situations add up. The less control a person exercises over his or her own life, the less likely it is that what happens will be what he or she wants. The less that what happens is what a person wants, the more helpless he or she is likely to feel. During this process, other responses that interfere with effective coping (thinking negative thoughts about one's worth as a person, for example) may be learned as well (Abramson, Seligman, & Teasdale, 1978).

Belief in your ability to control your own life is a central theme of this book because it is a central aspect of effective behavior. This book is a resource to help you increase that control, and before closing this introductory chapter the sources of the material offered in this resource will be reviewed briefly.

For many people, maintaining a desired weight is an important part of feeling in control of their own behavior.

# THE SCIENTIFIC STUDY OF HUMAN BEHAVIOR

If this is your first course in psychology, you may be expecting to read mostly about personality and abnormal behavior and psychotherapy. These are the topics many people think of when they hear the word *psychology*. Certainly they are important in this field, but they tell only part of the story. Psychologists also study perceptual processes (such as vision and hearing); the functioning of the brain; job performance; group behavior; human sexuality; marriage, family, and other human relationships; child development; communication; exercise and sports; drug addiction; and a large number of special interest subjects.

Material from almost all of these areas of psychology will appear in the chapters to come. You also will hear from biologists, chemists, physicians, sociologists, and others, as well as psychologists. What all of these people have in common is that they share a scientific approach to the study of human behavior. Unlike writers, painters, philosophers, religious leaders, and others who interpret human behavior on the basis of their personal experiences and feelings, psychologists and other scientists study it within a particular framework called the scientific method.

## The Scientific Method

The **scientific method** is a cyclical process of investigation that is guided by defined rules and logic and is characterized by commonly understood terminology and methods. A diagram of this basic process is shown in Figure 1–1.

As you study this figure, you can see that the scientific method is a cyclical process (follow arrows) that begins with a question. For example, a psycholo-

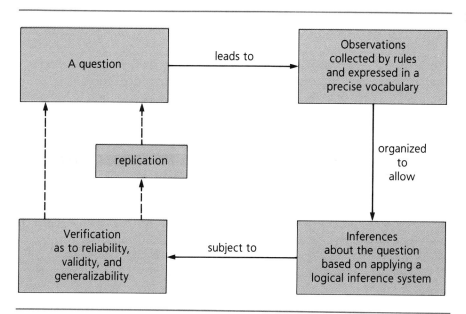

Figure 1–1   **The Scientific Method.**

gist might be interested in whether or not marriages are happier if the partners are older when they marry. As a first step to answering this question, the psychologist would make relevant observations (collect data). One way to do this would be to give questionnaires about marital satisfaction to selected samples of couples, some of whom were younger than a defined age when they were married and some of whom were older than this age.

Based on an analysis (usually statistical in nature) of the different patterns of answers received from couples who were younger when they married versus couples who were older, the psychologist would draw a tentative conclusion. This conclusion, which is called an **inference,** might be that couples who wait to marry until they are older seem to be more satisfied with their marriages.

This inference would remain very tentative while our researcher sought verification of his or her initial results. Would the same pattern emerge if the study were done again (replicated) with different subjects? That second study might support the first but reveal the possibility that the level of education of the people involved makes a difference. Our psychologist then would want to collect more data, make new and possibly more specific inferences, do additional verification, and so on around the cycle.

At appropriate points along the way, our investigator might publish his or her research results to date in a professional journal. As you may know already, most of the names and dates that you find in parentheses in this and other texts refer to such publications. You also will find many statements that begin something like "In general, researchers find that . . ." This statement refers to the collected published research of a number of people investigating the same or a similar question.

To continue with age at marriage as an example, you may read that "in general, researchers find that divorce rates are higher for couples who marry young." This simple statement reflects the efforts of many people who have carried out many studies into the relationship between age at marriage and divorce. These researchers have communicated with one another through professional conferences and scientific journals and have built upon and refined one another's work on this same question.

Much of what you find in this book is the result of the process just described. Some questions have been around the cycle many times; the relationship between age at marriage and divorce is an example (e.g., Carlson & Stinson, 1982). Other lines of investigation are newer and conclusions are more tentative. In both cases, the fact that all of the work is done within the accepted scientific method makes it possible to compare results and, where appropriate, to integrate them into general conclusions.

The scientific method is the standard for research in all of the sciences, not just in psychology. Without such a common approach it would be impossible to "know what we know" in any discipline, because everyone would be working in individual ways and results could not be compared meaningfully. Because it is so important to the advancement of science, it is worth taking a closer look at the major characteristics of the scientific method.

■  *The scientific method uses precise terminology.* A common vocabulary of precise terms is the means by which different researchers in an area of study communicate with one another. This vocabulary ensures that everyone who uses a term—*attitude,* to take an example—is talking about the same

Life is like riding a bicycle. You don't fall off unless you stop pedaling.

*Claude Pepper*

thing. Learning this special language is one of the first steps to acquiring knowledge in any field.

- *The scientific method has rules for collecting information.* These are rules about the nature and number of observations (data), the conditions under which they will be made, and how they will be measured. For example, you might "study" the behavior of children on a playground by stopping each afternoon to watch them for a few minutes on your way to this class.

  In contrast to your informal approach, the scientific method would require you to specify (a) what aspects of the children's behavior you are observing, (b) how you are going to measure these aspects, (c) how many times you plan to make your observations, and (d) whether there is anything special about the time of day that you observe (relative to other times of the day you might observe). Without these rules, it would be difficult for you to draw valid conclusions about your observations. It also would be impossible for others to replicate your study to see how your observations and conclusions compare with their own.

- *The scientific method uses a system of logic to draw conclusions* (make inferences). A scientist in any field wants to know that what he or she has observed is not the result of some chance combination of factors before adding an inference to the pool of knowledge about a subject. In scientific terminology, we say that he or she wants to know that a particular result is *significant*. The system of logic used to help make this decision usually is statistical in nature. As long as the rules for making observations are followed, there are many statistical tools available to help determine the significance of observations.

- *The scientific method requires verification of its conclusions.* To the scientist, nothing is ever proven; it simply is supported or not supported by the weight of the evidence at a particular time. In psychology, this evidence accumulates at an increasing rate. Sometimes, this means that previous ideas and conclusions must be discarded. For example, the hypothesis that "a happy worker is a good worker" has not stood up to scientific examination (e.g., Fisher, 1980).

  The weight of the evidence for other theories is just the opposite. In some cases, confirmation has been so consistent and strong that we speak of a "law" of human behavior. One example is the "law of effect," which states that behavior is modified by its outcomes or consequences. Psychologists think it is unlikely that this basic principle of behavior will be challenged in the future, but they must remain open to the possibility.

## A Word about Theories

As you followed the discussion of the scientific method, you may have found yourself wondering where scientists get the questions that start the cycle. There are a number of possible sources. One is just plain old curiosity. Isaac Newton is said to have been stimulated to formulate his theory of gravity by his curiosity about why an apple fell down from a tree (and onto his head).

Some questions are suggested by the work of other scientists, either individually or as a group. For example, the persistent failure of researchers to come up with clear support for the commonsense idea that "a happy worker is a good worker" led psychologists Porter and Lawler (1968) to wonder if everyone was getting it backwards; perhaps a good worker is a happy worker? In case you are curious, this idea does hold up better, but the matter is not really that simple either (Cherrington, Reitz, & Scott, 1971).

Many research questions come not from individual curiosity or the research of others, but from theories. A **scientific theory** is a unified account of some limited range of phenomena (Anderson & Borkowski, 1978). Examples of phenomena relevant to this book are personality, alcoholism, moral development, and self-concept.

To get good marks *as a theory,* a theory must be open to test. This is accomplished by putting questions generated by the theory through the scientific method process shown in Figure 1–1. This is where a great many of the questions that psychologists investigate come from—theories about one or another aspects of human behavior.

Not all theories can be tested in their entirety, and some cannot be tested even in part. Freud's theory of personality is a good example of a theory that defies the scientific method to a substantial degree. You probably already know something of the enormous influence that Sigmund Freud has had on the world, so you know that resistance to scientific test does not make a theory useless. At the same time, it is important to remember that no matter how accepted they are or how much sense they seem to make, the principles of such theories are untested assumptions.

A final note before we leave theories behind. The reason we have theories is that we want or need explanations for things. If a theory has been so thoroughly tested for so long that there seems no possibility that it will ever be disproved, we speak of a *law,* such as the law of gravity (or the law of effect that was mentioned earlier). Many human behavior phenomena, however, are a very long way from this level of confirmation. As a result, psychologists are still in the stage of having a number of theories about them, all of which are being tested or awaiting test. They can't all be included in a book such as this, so let's look briefly at how the theories that do appear were chosen.

In some areas we will be considering, there is a leading theory and one or more lesser theories; the question of how human cognitive abilities develop is a convenient example. When we come to these areas, the leading theory is reviewed as this is the theory that most investigators take as the standard against which to evaluate other theories.

In other instances, as when we examine personality, there are several competing theories of about equal status, and it is impossible to select one as the most influential or accepted. In such cases, there is an overview of the major approaches to the question.

Finally, there is the case of the traditional theory and what we might call the revolutionary theory. In this instance, a theory long believed to be resistant to attack suddenly is thrown into question by new research. This is the "cutting edge" of psychological research, and we will meet it a number of times (in the discussion of the causes of obesity, for example).

## In Conclusion

The purpose of this discussion of theories and the scientific method is to give you a perspective on the material in the chapters to come. Unless it is stated as such, this material is *not* personal opinion. Psychologists check and recheck and check again, and still they present their findings as somewhat tentative; new research may shed new light on the question.

The conservatism that characterizes the scientific study of behavior can be very frustrating when you want an answer to a question about your life. Should you wait a few years to get married or not? Without more information about you and your life, all that most psychologists would be willing to tell you is that your chances of being divorced probably are lower if you delay marriage until you are out of your teens.

Although a scientific approach to the study of behavior can be frustrating at times, it also protects you. This is a book about you and your life. You want it to be based on a solid foundation, not on untested personal opinions and ideas. You want your individuality respected; what is true "in general" may not be true for you.

So, read *Psychology and Effective Behavior* with an understanding that psychologists have used the conservative scientific method to build an impressive body of knowledge about human behavior. This knowledge can be of enormous value to you as you work toward fuller self-knowledge and a life that is satisfying to you. But psychologists cannot give you a formula for achieving the good life. You must work that out for yourself.

## Summary

This is a book about you and your life. Its purpose is to help you learn more about yourself and your world and to offer you some skills for using this knowledge to achieve more effective behavior. Effective behavior is behavior that allows you to feel in control of yourself and your life, to be flexible and productive, to like and accept yourself, to set and achieve realistic goals, and to enjoy good relationships. It is an active concept that includes (but is not limited to) adjusting to the constraints set by others and by your own situation.

To achieve this purpose of helping you increase your knowledge of yourself and your world, research and practice in psychology and many other fields, including medicine, biology, anthropology, and sociology, are surveyed. Those who work in these fields are dedicated to the scientific method of investigation, which is a conservative cyclical process in which all conclusions are subject to modification by new information.

The scientific method is not the only approach to the study of human behavior. Painters, writers, musicians, philosophers, religious leaders, and others also have something to say about the human condition, and from time to time we will hear from them as well. But science, in particular the science of psychology, remains the foundation for this text.

## STUDY SUGGESTIONS

If you are to benefit from the store of scientific knowledge that is provided for you here, it is necessary that you study it. You may have a strategy for doing this already. Many students seem to find it useful to read a chapter once for

EXHIBIT 1–1
## Three Suggestions for Studying *Psychology* and *Effective Behavior*

### Read the Chapter Outline First
Moving from one chapter to the next requires you to change mental gears rather sharply. Reading through the outline helps take you out of the last chapter and into the current one before you begin to read. It also gives you a mental framework into which to fit the various topics as you come to them.

### Don't Skip the "Summing Up" Sections
These are found within chapters when there is a significant shift in topic or emphasis. Like chapter outlines, they help you to make the transition more smoothly. And unlike the usual chapter summaries, they often contain new material or commentary that will be useful in putting things into perspective.

### Use the "Key Words and Phrases" as a Study Guide
This section is intended to give you a means for a quick review of your understanding of the chapter. To use it to help you study, do the following:

1. Define the term.
2. State at least two facts about it and more if you can.
3. If you cannot do *both* 1 and 2, go back to the relevant part of the chapter and review the material.

You are more likely to benefit from this procedure if you make the effort to write your answers down or say them aloud. The difference between thinking to yourself, "Oh, I know that one," and being able to define the term on a test can be considerable.

meaning, go back through it a second time to underline or highlight the most important parts, and then review the highlighted material. Some also make outlines. Whether you take this approach or some other, the suggestions in Exhibit 1–1 should help round out your study plan. These suggestions are based on the structure of this particular book but apply equally to any textbook that has similar features.

## ■ *KEY WORDS AND PHRASES*

| | | |
|---|---|---|
| constraints on behavior | learned helplessness | psychology of adjustment |
| effective behavior | norms | scientific method |
| inference | perceived self-efficacy | scientific theory |
| insight | personal control | |

**■ READ ON**

*Dictionary of Psychology* (2nd ed.) by J. P. Chaplin. New York: Dell, 1985. A standard paperback reference book that provides up-to-date definitions of terms from psychology and related disciplines in clear, jargon-free language. Encyclopedia-type entries are provided for central concepts, theories, and significant individuals in the field.

*How to Think Straight about Psychology* by K. E. Stanovich. Glenview, IL; Scott, Foresman, 1986. An up-to-date discussion of what psychology is and is not and how it relates to science in general.

*Psychology* (3rd ed.) by J. P. Dworetzky. St. Paul, MN: West, 1988. If this is your first course in psychology, you might find it both interesting and useful to look through a current introduction to this field, such as this up-to-date volume by Dworetzky. Your instructor can offer other suggestions.

**■ REFERENCES**

Abramson, L. Y., Seligman, M. E. P., & Teasdale, J. (1978). Learned helplessness in humans: Critique and reformulation. *Journal of Abnormal Psychology, 87;* 49–74.

Anderson, D. C., & Borkowski, J. G. (1978). *Experimental psychology: Research tactics and their applications.* Glenview, IL: Scott, Foresman.

Atkinson, R. L., Atkinson, R. C., & Hilgard, E. R. (1983). *Introduction to psychology* (8th ed.). New York: Harcourt Brace Jovanovich.

Bandura, A. (1977). Self-efficacy: Toward a unifying theory of behavioral change. *Psychological Review, 84;* 191–215.

Carlson, E., & Stinson, K. (1982). Motherhood, marriage timing, and marital stability: A research note. *Social Forces, 61;* 258–267.

Cherrington, D. J., Reitz, H. J., & Scott, W. E., Jr. (1971). Effects of contingent and non-contingent reward on the relationship between satisfaction and performance. *Journal of Applied Psychology, 55;* 531–536.

Diener, E. (1984). Subjective well-being. *Psychological Bulletin, 95;* 542–575.

Erlich, H. J. (1969). Attitudes, behavior, and the intervening variables. *American Sociologist, 4;* 29–34.

Fisher, C. P. (1980). On the dubious wisdom of expecting job satisfaction to correlate with performance. *Academy of Management Review, 5;* 607–612.

Goodhart, D. E. (1985). Some psychological effects associated with positive and negative thinking about stressful event outcomes: Was Pollyanna right? *Journal of Personality and Social Psychology, 48;* 216–232.

Heppner, P. P., & Anderson, W. P. (1985). The relationship between problem-solving self-appraisal and psychological adjustment. *Cognitive Therapy and Research, 9;* 415–427.

Hiroto, D. S., & Seligman, M. E. P. (1975). Generality of learned helplessness in man. *Journal of Personality and Social Psychology, 31;* 311–327.

O'Leary, A. (1985). Self-efficacy and health. *Behavior Research and Therapy, 23;* 437–451.

Porter, L. W., & Lawler, E. E. (1968). *Managerial attitudes and performance.* Homewood, IL: Irwin.

Seligman, M. E. P. (1974). Depression and learned helplessness. In R. J. Friedman and M. M. Katz (Eds.), *The psychology of depression: Contemporary theory and research.* New York: Wiley.

Seligman, M. E. P., & Maier, S. F. (1967). Failure to escape traumatic shock. *Journal of Experimental Psychology, 74;* 1–9.

# You and Your Environment: The Foundations of Behavior

On July 18, 1984, an unemployed security guard named James Huberty shot and killed 21 of the customers in a McDonald's restaurant in southern California. Seventeen other people were wounded. All of the victims were strangers to Huberty. In the days and weeks that followed, just about everyone seemed to be speculating about what could have caused this outburst of violent behavior.

The most popular explanation for Huberty's behavior was that he was mentally ill. A related theory was that he was under the influence of drugs at the time. Some were sure that he was simply a "bad apple" with a love for violence that finally got out of control. Others believed that his unhappy marriage must have been behind it all.

In the news media much was made of Huberty's unemployed status; it was suggested that being unemployed had so damaged his self-esteem that he felt the need to commit an act that would make people sit up and take notice of him. Some writers speculated that television and movie violence may have overstimulated Huberty in his vulnerable state. A few seemed inclined to blame this incident, like similar ones in the past, on the easy availability of hand guns in this country.

Huberty is dead, shot down by police at the scene of the killings, so we never will know what reasons he might have given for his behavior. Two years later, however, his widow came up with a theory different from any that had been proposed. She brought suit against McDonald's Corporation on the grounds that food additives used by the fast-food chain acted on Huberty's brain in such a way as to trigger the violent behavior that culminated in his death.

Is Mrs. Huberty "crazy" too? Emphatically not. Her allegations have not been proven, but the premise that what people take into their bodies in the form of food or drink affects their behavior, sometimes in extreme ways, is sound. For example, you may have heard of hyperactivity (the popular name for what psychologists call attention-deficit disorder), a childhood disorder characterized by a short attention span, a low tolerance for frustration, and verbal and physical aggression. The causes of this disorder are not agreed upon, but parents and teachers have reported that the symptoms of some of its young victims appear to be aggravated by the chemicals in "junk food."

A more common example of the fact that what is eaten or drunk may affect behavior is to be found right in your own home if you are a coffee drinker. Many people feel lethargic and unable to think clearly in the morning until they have had a cup or two of coffee; caffeine energizes them. Others drink caffeine at night to help them concentrate on mental work longer. And of course, some people don't drink it at all; it makes them nervous and jittery. In all of these instances, biological processes (reactions to caffeine) are affecting behavior, just as Mrs. Huberty claimed that reactions to food additives affected her late husband's behavior.

Psychologists, biologists, physicians, and others interested in human behavior long have known that biological factors have effects on behavior as well as on human development. Only recently, however, have they begun to appreciate the astonishing range and complexity of these effects, especially when they interact with other, nonbiological, factors. For a long time, psychologists and other scientists tended to take one side or the other in what has been called the nature-nurture controversy.

## THE NATURE-NURTURE CONTROVERSY

**Psychology is the study of human behavior.** It has a long-standing tradition of emphasizing the role that individual personal characteristics, especially inherited ones (such as sex, race, and brain functioning), play in determining behavior. As research began to demonstrate how much our characteristics and behaviors are influenced by our environments, however, some psychologists began to rethink this position. They came to believe that experience with the environment after birth ("nurture") must override all but the most extreme inherited differences between people.

The more traditional psychologists and scientists did not agree. Biology, they said, is and always will be the very foundation of behavior. If you want to understand people, you must look to "nature." This debate between the traditional position and newer ideas about the determinants of behavior became known as the nature-nurture controversy.

## Nature *and* Nurture

**The nature-nurture controversy is a debate among scientists and others as to whether heredity or environment plays the greater role in human development and behavior.** This debate is not dead yet, although most psychologists no longer take sides in it since research evidence has made it clear that the controversy is meaningless (e.g., Reinisch, 1986).

Most scientists now agree that both heredity and environment influence behavior and it isn't possible to select one set of factors as *the* most important. In the last analysis, it is the *interaction* of these influences that leads to any particular act or pattern of behavior. Let's return to James Huberty's extremely aggressive behavior to illustrate this very important point.

For the sake of argument, let's assume that Huberty may have been unusually sensitive to certain food additives (a biological factor, probably inherited). If this were true, eating too much food that contained these additives may indeed have altered his brain functioning, *but there were many possible behavioral effects this might have had.* When we go on to consider that Huberty also was unemployed (a fact about his life), was able to get to McDonald's (a fact about his physical environment), was able to own a gun (a fact of his social environment), and had held a number of jobs (including security-guard work and army duty) that required him to be able to use it (a learned personal skill), we begin to see more clearly how the specific behavior of that terrible July day might have come about.

This discussion of Huberty is entirely speculative; we probably never will know the whole truth about his murderous rampage. What we can say is that it was *not caused* by something so simple as food additives. Scientists are learning more all the time about the ways that biological processes may affect behavior. In the chapters to come, you will learn of possible links with depression, schizophrenia, alcoholism, debilitating reactions to stress, and overeating. But the biological factors are not *direct* causes in the sense that a person who has the particular biological characteristic is destined to follow the behavior pattern.

Most of the research to date suggests only that certain patterns of individual biological makeup can create a predisposition toward certain behavior patterns. This means that one person may be more likely than others (with a different biochemistry) to exhibit certain behavior *if* environmental and other

Scientists know that what we eat can affect behavior through a complex interaction of biological processes and environmental influences.

personal characteristics are compatible. Thus, one individual might be more inherently vulnerable to the negative effects of stress than most people, but if he or she is relatively happy with life (and/or not exposed to many stressors), these effects may not appear. At the same time, this person might be affected far more negatively by any stress that does occur than seems reasonable to most people.

## Summing Up ■

The nature-nurture controversy as it relates to the causes of behavior has been discussed in some detail for several reasons. First, most non-scientists still think in terms of one or the other when they are trying to explain behavior. Most of the explanations offered for Huberty's actions, for example, emphasized something about Huberty personally (e.g., he was crazy) *or* something about his environment (e.g., guns are too easy to get).

A basic theme of this book is that all behavior is understood only in terms of personal factors (which include, but are not limited to, biological factors) *and* environmental factors. Furthermore, the various factors relevant to any particular behavior interact with one another, and this interaction can change the effect of any particular one of them. For example, in the discussion of the effects of age on behavior, you will learn that older people make more errors on some kinds of work tasks than younger people. If the older people are more experienced, however, they will perform better despite their age. In other words, the *interaction* of two personal factors (experience and age) changes the effect that one alone (age) has on work performance.

To further complicate matters, it must be noted that behavior itself interacts with the factors that influence it to change the picture. There is evidence, for example, that making a conscious effort to arrange your face (a behavior) so that you look angry, depressed, sad, or happy can trigger corresponding internal changes so that you actually feel this way (McDermott, 1986).

In summary, both personal and environmental factors affect behavior, and these factors interact with one another and with the behavior they cause so that new influences on future behavior are created. This complexity of interactions is where personality, self-concepts, relationships, accomplishments, decisions, problems, and all of the other topics considered in this book originate.

In the remainder of this chapter we take a closer look at just what is meant by personal and environmental influences on behavior. We survey each category of influences and examine in detail one example from each category. By themselves, these examples offer you much interesting and useful information, but it is together that they make the main point of this chapter: *Human behavior is complex and its causes are multiple and interrelated.*

The purpose of this chapter is to help you learn to think of "the cause" of any particular behavior as being made up of a complex interaction of factors. This way of thinking seems to be easier for most people if they can sort the various factors that might be relevant into broad categories. When you finish this chapter, you should be able to understand and differentiate between the three categories that are relevant to understanding human behavior: (1) the person, (2) his or her physical environment, and (3) his or her social environment.

Although the various influences of human behavior are discussed separately in this chapter, you should not lose sight of the fact that this separation is artificial. It bears repeating that all of the factors that influence behavior operate in an interactive fashion, and it seldom is possible in real life to make a clear separation of influences. For this reason, most psychologists are reluctant to speak of "the cause" of any particular instance of behavior, such as the random killings by James Huberty. Instead, they speak of causal factors—the major personal and environmental factors that contribute to any instance of behavior.

How old would you be if you didn't know how old you are?

*Satchell Paige*

## PERSONAL FACTORS AND BEHAVIOR

Conception occurs when an ovum is fertilized by a sperm. At this moment your eye color, your brain structure, your body build, your susceptibility to certain diseases, and a host of other *genetic* personal characteristics are determined by the genes contributed by your two natural parents. Age, while not inherited through genes, is determined at this time as well (with some variation allowed for the gestation period).

Once you are born, you embark upon the acquisition and development of a multitude of *acquired* personal characteristics, including personality, skills, attitudes, values, and interests. Together, this mix of genetic and acquired personal characteristics makes up the **personal factors** that affect behavior.

Personal factors, both inherited and acquired, influence your behavior at every stage in your life. Some of these influences are direct. Some are indirect. Of the various possibilities that are available, chronological age has been selected as a means of exploring the concept of direct and indirect influences of personal factors on behavior.

The choice of age was dictated by a number of considerations. First, everyone ages and the measurement of age is standardized. Second, many of the other possibilities, such as sex and personality, are discussed in detail in later chapters. Finally, age lends itself more gracefully to a clear discussion of a complex concept than do many of the alternative choices.

## Example: Age and Behavior

Age and aging fascinate almost everyone sooner or later, and psychologists are no exception: chronological age has one of the thickest research files of all the personal characteristics that influence behavior. Its direct effects on behavior are relatively easy to demonstrate for the simple reason that there is a direct relationship between your age and what you are physically (and to some extent mentally) *capable* of doing. There also is a direct, if more variable, relationship between age and life experience, and this has significant effects on behavior as well.

## Direct Effects of Age on Behavior

The simplest example of how your age affects your behavior may be seen by looking at the earliest years of your life span. As an infant, you could open and close your eyes, suck on objects placed in your mouth, eliminate waste, move your head, and jerk your arms and legs. If someone stroked your foot, your toes would fan out and your big toe would flex. This was about the extent of your behavioral capabilities.

Things changed very quickly as you began the process of becoming an independently functioning human being. Much of this process involved learning to use your body and to coordinate your movements with one another and with objects and space in your environment. Figure 2–1 summarizes the milestones of this *motor development* from birth to about 15 months of age.

**Figure 2–1  Milestones in Motor Development: Birth to Fifteen months.**

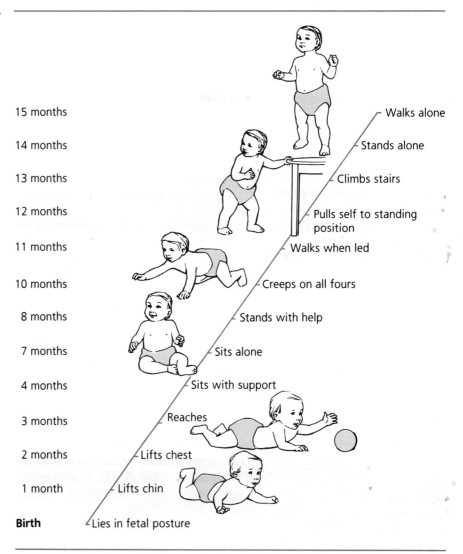

|  |  |
|-----|-----------|
| 15 months | Walks alone |
| 14 months | Stands alone |
| 13 months | Climbs stairs |
| 12 months | Pulls self to standing position |
| 11 months | Walks when led |
| 10 months | Creeps on all fours |
| 8 months | Stands with help |
| 7 months | Sits alone |
| 4 months | Sits with support |
| 3 months | Reaches |
| 2 months | Lifts chest |
| 1 month | Lifts chin |
| **Birth** | Lies in fetal posture |

The most important aspect of Figure 2–1 is the *sequence* of events. The ages are based on average data from studies of child development, such as the classic work by Shirley (1931) and the many researchers who followed her (e.g., Ridenour, 1978). A particular child may develop at a faster or slower rate and so pass each of these milestones at an earlier or later age. For example, it is not correct to say that a child should be walking by 15 months. Children walk when they are good and ready, and an important part of this readiness is being physically mature enough. The same is true for learning other skills, such as how to use a spoon, read, write, and play with other children. In the early years, then, your age had a great deal of direct influence on your behavior through the process of physical maturation.

The influence of age on behavior through the process of maturation continues into the teenaged years. As you grew older, the repertoire of things you were capable of doing or learning continued to expand. Your adolescence was marked by a more refined eye-hand coordination (which affects the learning of certain skills, such as tennis), substantial muscular development, and increases in overall physical strength.

During this period, marked sex differences in developmental patterns also began to appear. Males are only a little stronger than females before the age of 12, for example. But between 12 and 17, most become progressively stronger than their female friends (Malina, 1979). You may want to check out these strength differences for yourself in the brief physical fitness test presented in *Test Yourself.* You also may want to think about what factors, besides basic differences in anatomy, would account for such differences.

## TEST YOURSELF
## Are You as Fit as a Twelve-Year-Old?

In late 1984, the American Athletic Union made public the results of a study of physical fitness among youth in America. Results were not encouraging; two out of three young people in the study could not pass basic physical fitness tests. Could you? Below is a sample of the tests for 12-year-olds. If you have no health problems or physical disabilities, give them a try.

| Test | Males | Females |
|------|-------|---------|
| Bent-knee sit-ups in 1 minute | 38 | 33 |
| Push-ups in 2 minutes | 30 | 40 (modified*) |
| Long-jump | 5'4" | 4'11" |
| Mile run | 8 min., 42 sec. | 10 min., 18 sec. |

*Push-up from a hands-and-knees position.

How did you do? if you failed the test despite being older (and stronger) than a twelve-year-old, it may be time to make a physical fitness program part of your schedule. Be *sure* to have a physical checkup before beginning any new exercise program, especially if you have ever had any health problems or you currently lead an inactive life.

Adolescence also brought about all of those changes in behavior that tend to accompany puberty, the biological change from sexual immaturity to the ability to reproduce. Even if people do not become sexually active until much later, puberty tends to mark a shift away from childhood concerns and toward the social interests of adult men and women.

Although they occur throughout life, the effects of physical and biological age-related changes on behavior are most obvious in people under 20 and over 40. As we have seen, these effects are dramatic in the early years as maturation expands behavioral potential rapidly. Things tend to level off in the middle years, but connections between age and behavior become quite obvious again sometime around the age of 40. The ability to party all night and be 100 percent at work the next day seems to slip away, for example, and many people have to eat less and exercise more to remain at the same weight.

Such changes occur because a number of physical and physiological functions begin to deteriorate around the age of 40. (There is considerable individual variation in the actual age, but this happens to everyone sooner or later.) Vision, hearing, reaction times, and other faculties become less efficient, and these changes affect behavior in a number of ways. To select one example, many researchers have reported studies that find older workers to be slower and/or to make more errors on some kinds of work tasks than younger workers (e.g., Czaja & Drury, 1981). Most such differences are not due to motivation problems or a lack of work commitment or other psychological variables, but to the direct effects that aging can have on many work-related skills.

Not all researchers who have studied differences between older and younger workers have found that the younger ones perform better. Giniger, Dispenzieri, and Eisenberg (1983) reported that experienced workers performed better in their study than inexperienced ones, regardless of age. In some aspects of life, then, getting older means getting better. For every year that you live, you can experience and learn more about the world, life, your job, and other people.

Not much has been said about the effects of age on mental behavior to this point, beyond a mention that mental skills are tied to maturation in the early years. Do these skills deteriorate with age, as do physical skills and bodily functioning? For a long time, it was taken for granted that they did. Most people believed that deterioration of such mental skills as memory, the ability to solve problems, and the ability to learn new things is an inevitable part of the aging process. Scientists now are beginning to think otherwise.

People who study the brain and intellectual functioning have accumulated a considerable body of research on the subject of age-related changes. In this literature are many studies that suggest that certain of the *behaviors* that tend to go along with advancing age may be as much (or more) responsible for reductions in mental functioning as age itself. Examples are tendencies to become rigid in behavior patterns, to give up intellectually stimulating activities (working crossword puzzles, for example) for unchallenging ones (watching television, for example), and to stop practicing problem-solving skills (Schaie, 1984).

One eminent brain researcher has summarized the results of her acclaimed work in this area as follows:

> I found that people who use their brains don't lose them. It was that simple (Diamond, 1984).

**Note:** Reprinted with special permission of NAS, Inc.

Whether it is actually as simple as that remains to be demonstrated conclusively, but so far the evidence seems to support Diamond's position. Certainly, this research leaves no doubt that there is still much scientists don't know about the effects of age on mental abilities and performance.

Although we have scarcely scratched the surface of the subject, this discussion serves to illustrate the basic point about the direct effects of age on behavior. Throughout your life there have been and will be things that you do or don't do (or do more or less well) because of the age that you are at the time. The idea that age is a matter of attitude is not completely true by any means.

## Indirect Effects of Age on Behavior

Aging, from the moment of conception on, means change. A great many of these changes involve basic physical and, perhaps, mental abilities. There also are changes in outward physical appearance that seem to be built in by nature. Like other age-related changes, these follow a fairly predictable pattern.

Among the physical changes that most women are likely to notice once they pass 40 are drier skin, a redistribution of body fat, and a loss of skin tone. Many find their hair going grey, and it may be thinner. Developmental bone loss (called *osteoporosis*), more severe in women than in men, begins about this time as well. Most men are not affected seriously by this problem until about age 70. By contrast, women as young as 30 may notice such symptoms as their front teeth beginning to cross over one another as a result of bone loss in the jaws.

Men also change in appearance as they age. Wrinkles and deep facial lines appear, and by age 50 the skin on the neck and in the cheeks begins to loosen and sag. Many middle-aged men develop a "beer belly" even though they remain slim in other areas. Hair often begins to go grey by age 40, and hair loss, if there is to be any, accelerates. (For more detail on how men and women age, see *Read On*.)

The appearance changes that begin in middle age aren't very attractive to many people. As a result, a great deal is said and written in our culture about ways to "fight growing old." A great deal also is sold to promote attempts at staying young. The following are among the products that Americans spend billions of dollars on each year.

- Antiwrinkle creams (you are throwing your money away)

- Hair-restorer creams and other preparations (ditto)

- Injections of megavitamins (large doses of some vitamins endanger health)

- Body wraps to restore skin tone (a temporary improvement, if any)

- Cosmetic surgery to remove lines, wrinkles, and bags (may work, but all surgery involves some risk and the benefits of cosmetic surgery aren't permanent—it has to be done again)

As the sample list makes clear, most of the common "remedies for aging" don't bring about any permanent change or don't work at all. Some are dangerous. Why, then, are so many people willing to spend so much money on them? In the answer to this question lies an excellent example of an indirect effect of age on behavior.

For at least a generation, we in the United States have lived in a culture that places great value on being young. Being young cannot last, but the desire to do so (or a least to look so) does for a great many people, so they do things they probably would not do if they lived in another time or place. They dye their hair, use antiwrinkle cream, and wear clothes in unflatteringly youthful styles, to select three examples. Not all of this is for the sake of vanity, however. Our *youth culture* has affected employment opportunities and relationships as well. Some people who are experienced and competent in their chosen occupations are genuinely fearful of being replaced or passed over in favor of someone younger if they begin to show visible signs of age. There are many husbands and wives who are equally fearful that the great emphasis on youth will lead a spouse to look around if they don't keep battling "bag and sag."

There are, then, a number of possible reasons we might be concerned with physical appearance changes as we grow older. There also are some effective ways to slow down many of the more visible of these changes. As described in Exhibit 2–1, these ways have two things in common. First, they are preventative, not curative. Second, they don't cost a dime. If looking young is important to you, now is the time to start following these suggestions, whatever your age.

Spending a great deal of money and time in an effort to look younger is one of the most common indirect effects of age on behavior. An interaction of a personal characteristic (chronological age) with the social environment (value our culture places on youth) leads to behaviors we call "trying to look younger." There are many other relationships between age and behavior that seem to stem from the same source. For example, it is a fact that most first-time smokers are under the age of 21. If you haven't started by then, you probably won't. There is no known biological basis for this phenomenon; the source seems to lie in the fact that younger people are more likely to be concerned with being cool and doing something they believe is "adult" (and perhaps with defying their parents) and less likely to be concerned with the possibility of eventual health problems (which at that age often seem very far away).

## EXHIBIT 2–1

## Some Hints for Slowing Down the Effects of Physical Aging

### Exercise

Begin now to get regular, vigorous cardiovascular exercise, such as swimming, walking, or jogging. In addition to increasing stamina and lung capacity and keeping the pulse rate down, cardiovascular exercise will help to combat the tendency of the heart to become less muscular and more clogged with useless connective tissue with age. It also will help to tone your muscles and keep you looking, as well as feeling, fit.

### Don't Smoke

In addition to increasing your risk of lung cancer and heart disease enormously, smoking puts lines in your face and makes your teeth and breath unattractive.

### Have Regular Physical and Dental Checkups

Both physicans and dentists emphasize that many "normal" physical signs of aging, such as tooth loss, aren't normal at all; they are the result of neglect or failure to detect early symptoms. Learn to think of these visits as preventive maintenance, not something you have to do when something goes wrong. Many people find it helps the memory to schedule such appointments in the month of their birthdays.

### Drink Alcohol Only In Moderation

Like smoking, alcohol has effects that show on your face, and these are cumulative. If you drink alcohol, drink it in moderation. You can't undo the effects of 20 years of hard drinking when you are 40 even if you stop using alcohol completely at that time.

### Protect Yourself From the Sun

"Catching rays" is the major cause of the skin's aging appearance as well as of skin cancer. Again, effects are cumulative, and now is the time to cut down. Work and play in the sun normally, but wear a sun block and don't lie in the sun for hours just to tan your skin. If you are fair and/or burn easily, you'll look better longer and reduce your chances of skin cancer (which are greater than those of your friends with darker skin) if you also cover up. White cotton clothing works well, and a hat will protect your face. (A special note to women on the subject of your skin: Don't *ever* go to bed with makeup on. No matter how tired you are, remove it first; this will pay big dividends as you age.)

### Develop Good Eating Habits

Just as your nutrition as a child had a significant impact on your development and current health, so what you eat now affects how you will look and feel 20, 30, and 50 years in the future. Doctors and nutritional researchers are learning more all the time about the role of diet in making you look and feel better (and possibly in preventing disease). You don't have to be a health-food nut. Just learn the basic food groups, balance your diet, "unlearn" your taste for empty calories and salt, and start now to eat more fruits, vegetables, and fish and less fat and red meat.

*Note:* From a variety of sources on age and aging

**Summing Up** ■

Chronological age was used to illustrate the point that personal characteristics have both direct and indirect effects on behavior. A similar discussion might have been developed for sex, race, intelligence, personality, interests, or any of the other personal attributes of an individual. What is important is that you start moving toward an understanding of the multiple and complex causes of behavior and away from the kinds of oversimplified explanations that characterized reactions to the James Huberty case. The next section continues to develop this theme, although we will be looking not at personal factors, but at environmental factors.

## THE ENVIRONMENT AND BEHAVIOR

Mary and Elizabeth are identical twins. Until they went to college, both lived at home with their parents and a younger brother in a midwestern state. They were healthy, attractive girls who did well in school, sang in the church choir, and had many friends. Now, at 28, Mary is a fourth-grade teacher in her hometown. Her husband is a self-employed mechanic, and they have one son, aged three. They spend their vacations at a nearby lake in a cottage owned by Mary's parents.

Elizabeth is a successful model and promising actress in Los Angeles. She has appeared on several television shows and in two movies and has been praised for her dramatic good looks and natural acting ability. She travels extensively in her work, returning home occasionally to visit her parents for a few days. Her name has been linked with many men in the Hollywood gossip columns, but she has no plans for marriage in the near future.

Unlike most of the rest of us, Mary and Elizabeth are not totally unique individuals, because they share an inherited genetic structure. They look alike, wear the same size in clothes and shoes, have almost identical scores on intelligence tests, are the same blood type, and even have similar dental records. How could two people so alike have become so different?

A substantial part of the answer to this question may be found in Mary and Elizabeth's environments. Although these would seem to have been the same for the first 18 years, closer examination reveals that this was not so. The physical environment was, in fact, about the same for both girls, but there were significant differences in their social environments. Although they were in the same grade at school, for example, Mary and Elizabeth were encouraged by their parents and teachers to have separate friends.

Through their friends, Mary and Elizabeth were exposed to a variety of different life-styles and interests. The mother of one of Elizabeth's friends had been a professional dancer, and Elizabeth and her friend loved to pretend that they too were on the stage. Eventually, Elizabeth was able to persuade her own parents to let her have dancing lessons. Mary was given the same opportunity, but declined. Her best friend had a horse, and Mary spent all of her free time at the stables. Her best friend also had a brother who loved to tinker with cars and eventually became a mechanic.

Identical twins share the same heredity, but environmental influences can make them different in many other respects.

Upon graduation from high school, both Mary and Elizabeth went to college. Elizabeth got a scholarship and went to a university in California that had a good dance and drama program. Mary was in love with her friend's brother by then and didn't want to go so far away, so she attended the local branch campus of a state university. At this point, the sister's physical environments became as different as their social ones.

Mary and Elizabeth are fictitious, but their stories illustrate a fundamental point about human development and behavior: Our inherited/biological characteristics form the foundation, but our physical and social environments play a significant role in what kind of people we become and how we behave on a day-to-day basis. These environments, the physical and the social, are the second and third of the categories into which factors influencing behavior may be sorted.

## The Physical Environment and Behavior

Your **physical environment** consists of aspects of your surroundings that you can see, smell, feel, and hear. This includes objects, temperatures, odors, lighting, color, air, and noise. It also includes other people as physical objects; a crowd you must push through to reach your gate at an airport or your seat in a large lecture hall are examples that may be familiar to you.

Unless conditions are extreme, most of us seldom give much thought to the ways that our physical environments affect our behavior. Nevertheless, these factors have a full role to play. Temperature, to take one example, affects how you feel and what you wear and what you do outside, but it also has effects on how well you perform mental tasks such as studying. When the thermometer goes over about 80° Fahrenheit, you are likely to make more errors (Fine & Kobrick, 1978).

Temperature also can affect the way you behave toward others. Extreme heat seems to be associated with more aggressive behavior (e.g., Rotton & Frey, 1985), whereas extreme cold may have the opposite effect and even make people more willing to help each other (e.g., Bennet, Rafferty, Canivez, & Smith, 1983).

Noise affects behavior as well. *Noise* is sound that is very loud, unpredictable, uncontrollable, or undesired. If it is excessive or just goes on too long, it can damage your hearing. Ordinary stereo headphones have been found to create temporary hearing loss after three hours (Gilbert, 1985). Eight hours of close-up exposure to live rock music will damage your hearing permanently. To help those who may be concerned about this potential problem, the *decibel* (dB) ratings (the standard measure of loudness) and maximum safe-exposure levels to a number of common sources of sound are presented in Table 2–1.

Although noise can damage your hearing, not all of its effects are physical. Noise has been found to affect a variety of behaviors, such as learning and performance in school. In one well-known study, children in school classes that faced a noisy train track were found to be reading at levels from three

Table 2–1  **Safe Exposure to Noise**

| Source | dB | Maximum Safe-Exposure Time* |
|---|---|---|
| Whispering | 30 | Unlimited |
| Quiet office | 40 | Unlimited |
| Refrigerator | 45 | Unlimited |
| Normal conversation | 60 | Unlimited |
| Washing machine | 65 | Unlimited |
| Car | 70 | Unlimited |
| Vacuum cleaner | 70 | Unlimited |
| Heavy traffic | 80 | Unlimited |
| Factory | 85 | Approximately two 8-hour shifts |
| Motorcycle | 90 | 8 hours |
| Live rock music (distance) | 90 | 8 hours |
| Subway train | 100 | 8 hours |
| Power mower | 105 | 1 hour |
| Riveter/jack hammer | 110 | 30 minutes |
| Auto horn | 120 | 7 minutes |
| Amplified rock music (up close) | 130 | 20 minutes |
| Gun firing | 140 | Danger at any exposure |

*This is the safe *physical* exposure; psychological stress may occur after much shorter periods of time.

**Note:** From a variety of sources, including the Better Hearing Institute months to a full year behind their peers who were in quieter classrooms in the same building (Bronzaft, 1981). Two years after a 10 percent noise-reduction program was put into effect, all of the children were reading at or above grade level.

The purpose of this brief introductory section about some of the effects of temperature and noise on behavior was to encourage you to begin thinking in a conscious fashion about your physical environment and how it affects you. Now that you are focused, we will take a closer look at one feature of this environment (as we did with one personal characteristic) and consider what psychologists know about how it can affect behavior.

## Example: Physical Space and Behavior

There are several aspects to the study of the ways that physical space influences behavior. One has to do with what psychologists call personal space. **Personal space** is an area surrounding the body that we feel belongs to us. Its boundary is invisible, but each of us knows where our own lies, and we feel uncomfortable when someone comes too close *(invades our space)*.

How close is too close? This depends to a considerable extent on the nature of the relationship between the people involved. Hall (1966) found that people in this country tend to utilize four different categories of personal space, depending on this relationship. These different *personal distances* are described in Exhibit 2–2. Many researchers have noted that these typical American distances do not hold in other parts of the world; Arabs, to take one example, tend to have much closer zones and prefer to interact and communicate with almost everyone at close, touching range.

In addition to situational and cultural differences in preference for personal distances, there are sex and age differences (Sherrod, 1982). Children get closer together than do adults, and men tend to prefer more space than women. Men and women also are sensitive to different kinds of invasions of personal space. Men react most negatively when someone comes too close

## EXHIBIT 2–2
## Personal Space Zones

### Zone 1: Intimate Distance
From 0 to 1½ feet is reserved for intimate relationships and contacts, such as intimate conversation, lovemaking, and comforting another person.

### Zone 2: Personal Distance
From 1½ to 4 feet is the "conversational zone" for conversations between friends or acquaintances.

### Zone 3: Social Distance
Four to 12 feet is the distance for formal, impersonal, and business encounters, such as a discussion with a bank officer.

### Zone 4: Public Distance
Distances of over 12 feet are preferred for public speaking.

*Note:* Based on *The Hidden Dimension,* by E. T. Hall, 1966, New York: Doubleday.

from the front; women, when someone comes too close from the side (e.g., Fisher & Byrne, 1975).

What do people do when they feel that their personal space has been invaded? Most of us will reduce or avoid eye contact with the invader and shift our own position or, if that isn't possible, our body orientation. If the invader is a stranger and circumstances permit, we often will leave the area altogether (Patterson, Mullens, & Romano, 1971).

Many people also take steps to avoid personal space invasion in the first place. Look around you the next time you are in any waiting area. Unless it is very crowded, you probably will observe that people leave seats between themselves and the next person and often put personal belongings in the empty seats to discourage new arrivals from sitting there. Look around in your library as well. If it has a table study arrangement, you probably will see the same spacing.

The physical space between us and others serves both to protect our privacy and to communicate with others about the way we see our relationship with them. Sometimes, however, the density with which an area is populated makes it impossible to defend our personal space. *Density* refers to the number of units in a given space. When there are too many of these units, be they people or other objects, we may feel *crowded*.

Feeling crowded is a stressful state that can have a number of negative effects. Among these are anxiety, frustration, decreased satisfaction with social relationships, and even a greater susceptibility to physical illness (Rohe, 1982). A series of well-known studies of crowding in a college dormitory also found feelings of being crowded to be associated with (a) a tendency to find other people less compatible and (b) a tendency to withdraw from socializing with others (Baum & Valins, 1977).

Although people tend to exhibit similar patterns of behavior when they feel crowded, there are substantial individual differences in whether or not they react this way to density. The form of the density also seems to make a difference. There seem to be more negative effects associated with density in living quarters, for example, than with outside density (e.g., Galle, Gove, & McPherson, 1972).

Psychologists, sociologists, and others interested in physical space are learning more all the time about what space means to people and how it affects their behavior. As they do so, they are helping architects, engineers, and city planners to appreciate that physical environments create psychological and social environments that must be considered when designing buildings and other spaces for human use. More on this may be found in *Face of the Future*.

*Face of the Future* illustrates the fact that research into the effects of physical environmental variables on behavior has uses that are very practical. Although you probably are not an architect or a builder, you can use this research to increase your own personal health, productivity, and satisfaction. Here are just a few examples of how you might apply the results of the investigations just described.

- When studying, try to do so in a cool, comfortable place.
- Try to cut down on the noise in your life, especially if you are "addicted" to loud music as a background for all activities.

## FACE OF THE FUTURE:
Creating Social Environments with Physical Space

There is a famous news photograph that shows an award-winning St. Louis urban renewal housing project deliberately being dynamited less than 20 years after it was built. When it opened in 1955, the Pruitt-Igoe project, which consisted of 33 high-rise buildings, was hailed as a milestone in safe, attractive housing for low-income families. Within a few years, it was a wreck. There was garbage and litter everywhere, the halls had been vandalized beyond all repair, and many windows were boarded over to cover broken panes.

Pruitt-Igoe was not only ugly, it was dangerous. Assault and rape, most often committed by residents, were frequent. No one dared to use the elevators or to go into the central stairway. Frightened, the residents began to move out; when the vacancy rate had risen to 70 percent, the city voted to tear down the project.

The Pruitt-Igoe project is a classic lesson in the relationship between physical and social environments. Although buildings and apartments were clean, functional, attractive, and efficient, they had no character. Each one looked like all the others, and residents had no sense of belonging to a particular unit; the physical environment fostered anonymity. It also fostered isolation, because there were no places for neighbors to meet informally. As a result, few residents made any friends; investigators looking into what went wrong at Pruitt-Igoe found no sense of neighborhood or community.

The housing project in St. Louis was built with the very best of intentions, but those who designed it did not understand the effects that the physical environment can have on behavior. The new high-rise buildings looked like a great improvement over the slums they replaced; anyone should have been happy to live there. They weren't, and the same thing has been found in other projects. Slums may be ugly, inefficient, and lacking in physical amenities, but sociologists find that they often offer a strong sense of community. Perhaps because the insides of slums are so dreary, people congregate outside. Privacy is lacking, so people become involved with, keep an eye on, and help one another. This "neighboring" (Ottensmann, 1978) seems to create a sense of belonging that discourages antisocial behavior, such as vandalizing.

The lessons of Pruitt-Igoe and other high-rise housing projects for low-income families have led planners to rethink the issues, and few such buildings are erected these days. The trend is toward low-rise (four to six stories) or garden-type apartments oriented around common green areas. The Martin Luther King Village in Atlanta has gone further, offering attractive townhouse-style units that look like much more expensive housing.

There seems little doubt that piling people's homes on top of one another while simultaneously isolating them from one another, creates an undesirable social environment. But there is more to the question of the relationship between physical and social environments as may be seen in another architectural experiment that seems to be going wrong—the open-plan office.

An open-plan office has no walls to divide the workspace of individual employees from one another. This plan has become very popular in the last 10 years or so. Accountants like it because it is flexible and economic. Managers like it because they can see what is going on. Psychologists thought

*Continued*

### Continued

it would allow co-workers a greater opportunity to get to know one another, communicate with one another, and have a sense of belonging to a team. If the lessons from housing studies have any bearing, employees should find this a more pleasant work environment.

They don't. Employee reactions to the open-plan office have been consistently unfavorable (Oldham & Brass, 1979). In one series of studies, investigators found that all employees, regardless of the nature of their work, preferred individual offices (Sundstrom, Burt, & Kamp, 1980). The open-plan arrangement was associated with lower satisfaction with the work environment, lower job satisfaction, and, in some cases, lower job performance.

Taken together, the problems with high-rise housing and open-plan offices make it clear that the balance of human social needs and needs for physical and psychological privacy is a delicate one that easily is tipped too far one way or the other by the physical environment. As sociologists, environmental psychologists, and other researchers come to understand the significant impact of this environment on the behavior of those who occupy it more fully, architects, engineers, planners, and others are responding. When it comes to the design of physical space, the face of the future looks like a much more human one.

- When choosing a place to live, try to find one that offers personal privacy but has areas that allow you and your friends/neighbors to interact with one another naturally.

### Summing Up ■

The physical environment is what most people think of when they hear the word *environment*. Various aspects of this environment, such as temperature, noise, and physical space, affect both your physical condition and a wide variety of your behaviors. These variables also can affect your social environment, as the discussion in *Face of the Future* illustrates.

It should be noted that it isn't necessary to look to something as dramatic as a huge public housing project or as formal as the layout of an office to see the interaction between physical and social environments and how this can affect people. If you live with someone, you encounter this phenomenon frequently. For example, temperature seems a relatively objective physical environmental variable until you must negotiate your temperature preference with others who have different ideas. The same is true for noise, lighting, and even furniture arrangement; all play a part in the nature of your home social environment. It is to the social environment that we now turn our attention.

## The Social Environment and Behavior

Although physical environmental influences on behavior are important, most people seldom think much about them. The same is not true for the social environment, a set of influences on behavior of which most people tend to be very aware.

**The social environment consists of other people, our relationships with them, and the laws, rules, and norms that regulate our interactions with them.** This environment has many segments, each of which may be a little different. There is a social environment at home, one at school, one at work, one that characterizes the region of the country we live in, and one that is the broad *culture* of the United States of America. The various small groups we belong to, such as a sorority, a church, a sports team, or a club, also have their own social environments.

To a considerable degree, each of us creates our own social environments through our choices of where we live, what people we associate with, and how we spend our time. We also have some day-to-day influence on many of our various social environments through suggestions and changes we might make and through our very presence. Unless you live alone, for example, the place you live is not the same social environment it would be if you moved out and someone else moved in. In other words, social environments are not something uncontrollable like the weather. They are social creations, and they are always changing.

Each of these dynamic social environments of which you are a part has an influence on your behavior and a role in shaping the kind of person you are at any point in time. Your social environments affect what you *can* do, what you are *expected* to do, and what you *want* to do. If you work, your company (a social environment) has certain rules that affect what you can and can't do. It also has a job description for your job that outlines what you are expected to do. Finally, the rewards that go with successful performance in your company may affect what you want to do; you may decide that you will work hard, perform well, and get ahead, for example.

Similar statements could be made about every social environment in which you operate. Because these social influences have such a major impact on your behavior, the three most important sources of this influence will be reviewed; these are the presence of others, norms, and expectations.

> I am I plus my circumstances.
> *Jose Ortega y Gasset*

## The Presence of Others and Behavior

Because you live in a social world as well as a physical one, much of what you do is done in the presence of others—family, friends, acquaintances, and strangers. If you take a moment to think about it, you will see that there are many things you would do when you are alone that you wouldn't do when these others are present. For example, you might sing in the shower, but not in front of anyone else. You might put your feet up on your desk at work if you are alone and the door is closed, but you wouldn't think of it if there was a possibility that someone might see you.

The fact that people behave differently when they are alone and when others are present is one of the oldest findings in the area of social psychology. Sometimes, as in the examples, they just behave differently. Sometimes, they do what they are doing better if other people are around, especially if it is something they know how to do well. The ability of others to bring out the best in our behavior, whether in working, playing sports, or just telling a joke, is called the **social facilitation effect.**

Psychologists have been studying the social facilitation effect since the 1890s (Triplett, 1989). Over time, they have found that it is not quite as simple as it first appeared. In a classic study, Pessin (1933) discovered that sometimes the mere presence of other people interferes with what we are trying to do. Instead of producing social facilitation, there is a **social inhibition effect.** This effect is especially noticeable if we are trying to learn to do something new. You may have seen this the first few days on a new job or when you were taking tennis lessons with good players watching.

Whether or not the presence of other people interferes with what you are doing depends to a considerable extent on how well you already know how to do it. If you are an experienced driver, for example, you probably would not be nervous if someone asked you to give a lift to a friend you did not know personally. On the other hand, if you've just learned to use the word processor in your library's resource center and are trying to finish up a paper in the presence of several other students waiting to use the machine, you may find yourself making mistake after mistake.

Social inhibition also seems to be greater if the people around you appear to be paying attention to what you are doing and you think they may be evaluating it in some way (Cottrell, Wack, Sekerak, & Rittle, 1968). Many students feel this effect when it comes their turn to make a class presentation, for example. If the opinion of others watching you is important to you, there may be even greater inhibition (Gross, Riemer, & Collins, 1973).

In summary, the mere fact that other people are around changes your behavior. It may be different from what it would be if you were alone, or it

The presence of others facilitates the performance of certain kinds of well-learned behaviors.

may be the same, but done better or worse than if you were alone. You can think of many examples of all three effects in your own life.

## Norms and Behavior

**Norms are unwritten rules for behavior that grow out of social interaction.** They exist in all social environments right on up to the level of society in general. For example, calling new acquaintances, the parents of your friends, and even strangers with whom you are doing business on the telephone by their first names is an American social norm. This behavior, common in most parts of our country and most (but not all) segments of our society, is unthinkable in other cultures.

There also are norms that are specific to certain parts of the country, to particular educational institutions, to work organizations, to sports teams, to groups of friends, and even to families. These include expectations about how to dress; how to communicate with others; what time to get to parties; how much working or studying to do; how to behave in a restaurant, bank, or other public place; and so on down a long list. These expectations aren't written down as are laws, and they can look rather ridiculous if they are. Consider, for example, the following norm that is widespread in our society: "Look at the floor indicator, not at the other passengers, when riding in an elevator."

The fact that norms are unwritten and can look pretty silly if you do write them down in no way decreases the enormous influence they have on our behavior. Most of us know and conform to (abide by) the norms of our various social environments, even though they are not rules or laws and no one has been given any authority to make us follow them.

The penalties for violating norms are almost all social. (Occasionally we hear of a street gang or other group that has harmed a member physically for not conforming to expected behavior, but that is the exception.) If you violate the strong norm our society has about not making a scene in public, for example, people around you will look at you with disapproval and whisper among themselves. Unless you actually harm someone or damage property, however, you won't be arrested; at worst, you will be asked to leave the "scene of the scene."

Although some norms appear pretty pointless, most serve important purposes.

1. There are few laws for how we speak to and interact with others, and life would be pretty chaotic and confusing without some standards for this interaction.

2. Within small groups, norms help keep the group together and set it apart from other groups (Jewell & Reitz, 1981).

3. Norms help groups get things done. For example, a norm of friendly competition within a group of unpaid volunteers collecting for a charity might help the fundraisers go beyond their financial goal.

The number of norms you encounter as you go about your daily life is enormous; look at the settings in *Test Yourself* to see how many you can think of now. There is an example in each category to help you get started.

## TEST YOURSELF
## What Are the Norms that Influence Your Behavior?

*Instructions:* For each category below, think of as many "unwritten rules" as you can for behavior that you personally follow. Try to think of norms that are specific to the category and that you wouldn't follow in a different social setting. (For example, everyone at school wears jeans, but you don't wear them to work, where the norm is for neat, businesslike clothing.) Use a separate sheet of paper if necessary.

ENVIRONMENT: School
*Example:* Talk about what a bore classes are (even if you really like them).

_____
_____
_____
_____
_____

ENVIRONMENT: Work
*Example:* Get to work a little bit early.

_____
_____
_____
_____
_____

ENVIRONMENT: Clubs or social organizations
*Example:* Wear Nike brand exercise clothing to the health club.

_____
_____
_____
_____
_____

ENVIRONMENT: Friends
*Example:* When eating out together, pay for your own food.

_____
_____
_____
_____
_____

ENVIRONMENT: Home
*Example:* Fill up the ice tray if you take the last few cubes.

_____
_____
_____
_____
_____

If you put thought into this exercise, the results should be both interesting and surprising. Most people tend to overestimate the influence that laws and rules have on their behavior and to underestimate the extent to which they voluntarily do things they might not do otherwise (or *not* do things they might do otherwise) in conformity to norms.

## Expectations and Behavior

Norms are general standards for behavior in certain situations and groups. No one person "sets" them, and, in most cases, no one person has any authority or particular responsibility for seeing that people conform to them. Norms are about things it is understood are and aren't done; they grow and develop over time out of social interactions among groups of people. By contrast, expectations, as the term is used here, are specific to two people.

**Expectations** are beliefs about how another person will, or should, behave. Here are some examples of expectations other people who are important in your life might have for your behavior.

- Your father expects you to finish college.
- Your mother believes you have exceptional art talent and expects you to pursue an art-related career.
- Your boyfriend/girlfriend expects you to date only him/her.
- Your spouse expects you to spend every Christmas at the home of his/her mother.
- Your grandmother expects you to write or call her once a week.
- Your son expects you to attend all of his Little League baseball games.
- Your professor expects you to do better work with each assignment.
- Your boss expects you to be a top performer because you have such a good school record.

Most of us have people in our lives who have such expectations. Whether you actually conform to them or not, they affect your behavior just because they are there. If you do conform, you may do things that you really don't want to do (or *not* do things that you really *do* want to do). If you don't conform, there may be serious consequences. Your boyfriend or girlfriend may stop seeing you, for example, or you might lose your job.

Even if failing to conform to the expectations of others does not lead to serious negative consequences, you still may feel guilty at letting someone down. You also may feel angry because he or she has put you in this position, and this, in turn, can affect the way you interact with the person involved.

Sometimes, there is no problem about conforming to the expectations that one person has for you, but this can put you in the position of failing to meet the expectations of another person. Unfortunately, the expectations that others have for us often collide.

- Your parents want you to take a job in your hometown; your girlfriend or boyfriend wants you to go to another state.
- Your boss encourages you to go to night school under the company's employee tuition support program; your children want you at home at night.

■ Your friends expect you to show up for the Saturday workout at the health club; your spouse looks forward to weekends as your exclusive time together.

Things are pretty complicated at this point, but it gets more so because it isn't just the expectations of others that affect your behavior. Your expectations for others affect interactions as well. You can see this in many small examples all around you. Remember when a friend got upset because you went to a new movie with a different friend? You were very surprised by this because you were sure the first friend would not be interested in this kind of movie. In other words, your expectations for the way he or she would react to an invitation led you not to make it.

Psychologists have studied the effects of our own expectations about the behavior of others in a wide variety of settings. They find that the influence of our expectancies is strong; we do tend to behave toward others in a way that is consistent with what we expect them to do. A classic illustration of this principle, and its surprising results, is reported in Exhibit 2–3.

At Oak School, the beliefs of teachers about the intellectual potential of certain students led them to treat those students as bright. They gave them more help and positive attention, and the children responded by *being* bright. The teachers had created what psychologists call a self-fulfilling prophecy.

A **self-fulfilling prophecy** is the achievement of a particular outcome because one expects it to occur and so behaves in ways that make it "come true." Any reasonably nice restaurant will serve to illustrate this concept. Many waiters and waitresses expect women to be poorer tippers than men. When a woman is seated at their station, therefore, they are likely to provide indifferent service, because they don't expect to receive a good tip no matter what they do. The woman customer responds to this poor service with the poor tip it deserves, and, presto, the server's prophecy has come true.

Of course, the woman in question may be aware of this general expectation and leave a large tip just to disprove the belief that women are stingy tippers. In this case, her expectations about the expectations of someone else influenced her behavior; she gave a server who had not earned it a large tip. Clearly, expectations are strong and complex influences on behavior. Nor do theses influences end with your interactions with others. Your own expectations for yourself also have a significant effect on your behavior. There is a leading theory of work motivation, for example, that stresses the role that an employee's belief about his or her ability to perform well plays in how much effort (motivation) is put into the job (Nadler & Lawler, 1979). This general expectancy theory of work motivation predicts that people who believe they will perform well if they make the effort work harder (and so are likely to perform better.)

Research into this theory of work motivation confirms a connection between performance and beliefs about performance. In one experiment, for example, subjects who were to perform an experimental task were told either that (a) they could expect to do very well or that (b) they could expect to do very poorly on this task (Arvey, 1972). Those who were told that they could expect to do very well did well; those who were led to expect that they would do poorly did poorly. In fact, the task was so simple that almost anyone could do it well.

**EXHIBIT 2–3**

## Expectations and Behavior: Pygmalion in the Classroom

In *Pygmalion,* a famous play by George Bernard Shaw, a speech professor transforms a London flower seller into a lady who can pass for a duchess by teaching her to walk, dress, and talk like a lady. As this transformation takes place, others begin to *treat* Eliza like a lady, and as a result, she comes to *feel* like one on the inside as well as to behave like one on the outside. In the years since this play (later made into a movie musical called *My Fair Lady*) was first presented, the word *pygmalion* has come to be synonymous with bringing about change in someone through the way they are treated. Psychologist Robert Rosenthal (Rosenthal & Jacobson, 1968) studied this phenomenon in a very different setting—the grade school classroom.

Rosenthal gave children at a school called Oak School a phony intelligence test, which he said would enable the school to identify children who would be showing sudden spurts of intellectual ability within the next year. Then he *randomly selected* 20% of the children who had taken the test and identified them by name to their teachers as "spurters." What he predicted would happen as the result of this experiment was the following:

1. Teachers would expect "spurters" to bloom intellectually during the year.
2. Because they expected something special from these children, the teachers would treat them differently; specifically, the teachers would give the children more help, positive attention, and challenging assignments.
3. Because the children were treated differently, they would, in fact, develop intellectually during the year to a greater extent than the other children.

Were Rosenthal's predictions borne out? Absolutely. In every one of the six grades involved, "spurters," as a group, showed greater gains on an I.Q. test given at the end of the year than the other children (previous scores on this legitimate I.Q. test were on record). The change was particularly dramatic in the first grade, where spurters gained an average of almost 15½ points over other children.

Rosenthal's phony spurters also got better grades in reading and were rated as being more intellectually curious, better adjusted, and happier than the other children. The expectations of others can be powerful indeed. By affecting the way those others treat us, they change our social environments and so influence our own behavior.

The fact that people can create their own self-fulfilling prophecies should not be taken as evidence for the power of positive (or negative) thinking on success or failure. It is the effect of such beliefs on behavior that makes the difference. Subjects in the Arvey study did not do well because they expected to do well; they did well because expecting to do well led them to put more effort into the task. The other subjects put forth so little effort that they managed to perform poorly on an exceptionally easy task.

Real-life situations are more complex than experimental ones, and usually you have more information about how well or poorly you might do something than what you are told by one other person. If all of this information (what you know about the task at hand, how you have done in the past, and so on) suggests that you should do well at something, one message of self-fulfilling prophecies is to let yourself believe this. Expectations do influence behavior, and you may remember from Chapter 1 that psychologists believe realistic expectations influence it in the direction of more effective behavior.

## The Social Environment in Action: An Example

Three sources of social environmental influences on your behavior have been reviewed. We have been discussing these as if they were separate influences, but of course they are not. As you go about your day-to-day activities, you are being affected by the presence of others, norms, and expectations from yourself and others simultaneously. Other aspects of the social environment, such as rules and laws, are active as well. By way of illustrating how this multitude of forces can affect individual behavior, let us travel to the physical environment of a large American city.

An important way in which large cities differ from other communities is in the "cover" that they provide for the individual. The more people there are in any given space, the less likely it is that the behavior of any particular one of these people will attract attention. Even if it does, the likelihood that those who are noticing will know the person is greatly reduced. This is *anonymity*, the condition of being unknown to those around you.

One effect of the greater anonymity in our larger cities is that people are less likely to be caught if they commit a criminal act. Social psychologist Phillip Zimbardo (1969) conducted a classic experiment on the possible relationship between anonymity (condition of social environment) and crime (behavior). He arranged for automobiles to be abandoned in two communities, one in New York City and one in the California suburb of Palo Alto. At the end of a 64-hour observation period the New York car had been vandalized 24 times, and all that remained was a useless shell.

The population density in a large city creates anonymity, which can lead to social indifference.

The Palo Alto car was undamaged. Only one person went near it at all and that was to put the hood down when it began to rain. According to Zimbardo, the high probability of being recognized (low anonymity) was a crucial factor in keeping the Palo Alto citizens honest. In terms of the current discussion, we might say that anonymity seems to reduce the power of norms and laws, such as respecting the property of others.

Anonymity definitely appears to be a contributing factor to antisocial behavior, such as vandalizing an automobile. On the other hand, freedom from being recognized is very attractive to many people who would not think of doing such a thing. Being able to come and go without everyone in the community knowing and discussing the details is a major benefit of city life for some people. Paradoxically, the presence of so many people offers a sense of personal privacy that may be entirely lacking in smaller communities, and behavior is influenced accordingly.

You may be one of those to whom privacy is very important, but if you are like most people, you don't wish to be ignored completely. Unfortunately, this is another risk of living in a large city. Social indifference can be the price you pay for freedom from prying friends/family and gossipy neighbors.

**Social indifference** refers to a general lack of interest in, and concern for, others in a social environment. It is manifested in our cities in a variety of ways. Some are merely annoying; the well-dressed young woman does not apologize even though she realizes she has just driven the sharp heel of her shoe into your unprotected toe. Others are appalling; some years ago, a young woman was murdered in full view and/or hearing of 38 people. Not one tried to help or even called the police.

The circumstances of Kitty Genovese's murder in New York City in 1964 were shocking and the implications horrifying. By all accounts, this young woman did not have to die. Could it really be possible that people in cities are so callous? If it is, how does this happen? Psychologists Latane and Darley (1970) set out to find the answers to these questions. In a series of experiments they discovered that the witnesses to Genovese's death were not unique, but merely an example of what they called the bystander effect. The term *bystander effect* refers to an inverse relationship between the number of people who are around when someone is in trouble and the likelihood that this person will get help.

Latane and Darley found that in many situations, the more people there are present, the less likely it is that a person will get help. This finding has been confirmed many times since. Individual callousness is not an adequate explanation for why it happens, although it may be a factor in some cases. Norms also play a role. Staying out of things going on between people we don't know is a strong norm in our society; *I didn't want to get involved* was heard more than once in the investigation of the Genovese murder.

Norms or no norms, the number of people who will watch someone being murdered and do nothing is small. Research tells us, however, that the number who take no action in an emergency because they assume someone else must have done so may be quite large. The presence of others tends to reduce feelings of individual responsibility. Psychologists call this *diffusion of responsibility,* meaning that responsibility gets "spread around" through the group. If the group is large enough, individual responsibility may get spread so thin that no one person takes any action. Each one is operating on the assumption that others have done what should be done. If what should be done is to call for help, many find the thought of being the second or the tenth caller about an incident embarrassing.

Uncertainty about what really is going on also seems to be a factor in producing the bystander effect. In another widely publicized incident, the 25 people who watched a young woman being raped on an adjacent rooftop explained that the roof had been used for sexual encounters by others in the past. Despite the woman's screams, they were not *sure* that the man was not her boyfriend and this was some kind of game they played. As a result of this uncertainty, they did nothing to help. Here again, we can see norms about minding our own business and diffusion of responsibility in a crowd in action.

The bystander effect is an unfortunate product of the social environment. Norms, the presence of others, expectations about how these others will act, and personal concern about looking foolish to others combine to produce behavior that most people would say they are incapable of before it happens.

You don't have to be in a large city to see social indifference in action. You can observe the patrons of a small-town bar watch two men beating each other up and do nothing to stop it. You can read stories of the people in a quiet suburb who watched a neighbor's house being burglarized and didn't ask any questions or call the police. You might even be involved yourself. Did you ever see a classmate copying from another classmate's exam and say nothing, telling yourself that you didn't know the person whose paper was being copied so it was none of your business (or perhaps you convinced yourself that someone else would report the incident)?

The fact that our complex social environments can create social indifference is not an inescapable fact of life. Social concern, like social indifference, is made up of individual decisions about behavior. More on this issue is to be found in *For Discussion*.

## Summing Up ■

Your social environment is created by other people, your relationships with them, and the laws, rules, norms, and expectations that govern your interactions with them. This environment is a dynamic one with many segments. Work, school, family, society, groups, friends, clubs, and so on all have their own characteristic social aspects. As a result, the influence of the social environment on behavior is both enormous and complex.

Psychologists have studied the effects of many aspects of the social environment on a wide variety of behaviors. Here, the influence of the presence of others, norms, and specific expectations about how people will or should behave were reviewed. By way of illustrating the interaction of these forces, the particular social environment created by the dense population of a large city's physical environment and the forces in this environment that can create social indifference to the welfare of others were examined.

## FOR DISCUSSION:
## ARE YOU YOUR NEIGHBOR'S KEEPER?

The communities we live in are not nearly so safe as most of us would like. Many people, however, are reluctant or afraid to get involved in trying to solve the problem. The "moving van caper" is a good illustration of the kind of results this reluctance or fear can have. Hundreds of times a day in this country, thieves pull a moving van into a driveway, fill it with the contents of a house, and drive away in full view of the neighbors and anyone else who happens to be passing by.

Why don't the neighbors do anything? Some say that they assumed the occupants of the house had decided to move and had not told anyone. Others say they were afraid that they would suffer in some way if they reported the van. Some simply shrug and say, "It's none of my business, and anyway they have insurance."

Uncertainty, fear of reprisal, apathy, and concern for looking foolish are the enemies of responsible social concern and the aids of those bent on criminal acts. Many have even come to count on this social indifference. Said one burglar of his so-called daring daylight adventures, "There was nothing daring about them. In the daytime, if people see you coming or going from a place, they figure it's O.K. and ignore you. At night, if they hear a noise or see a light, they get up to in-vestigate or call the police" (personal communication).

One approach to breaking down reluctance to being "our brother's keeper" when it comes to a crime is a program called Crime Stoppers. Crime Stoppers is an incentive program to encourage citizens to report what they may have seen or what they might know about unsolved offenses. These are described to the public by local newspapers and radio and television stations in cooperation with the police. Anonymity is guaranteed, and if the information leads to arrest and conviction or recovery of stolen property the citizen receives a monetary reward of up to $1,000.

Forty-eight of our 52 states now have Crime Stopper programs, and the results are impressive. By February of 1985, citizen tips were estimated to have helped police solve some 70,000 crimes and to recover almost $350 million worth of stolen property and narcotics (Rosenbaum & Lurigio, 1985). Despite this success, Crime Stoppers is controversial. Many people object strongly to the idea of paying people to do their civic duty. Unfortunately the very success of Crime Stoppers makes it clear that many people do not do this duty without incentive. Figures available also make it clear that this program saves society far more than it costs.

Others object to Crime Stoppers on the grounds that it encourages people to spy on one another, creating a police-state mentality that might prejudice individual freedom. Individual freedom is violated very time a crime is perpetrated against a citizen, however, so watching out for the other person's property and safety may as easily be seen as a protection of this freedom.

The one fact no one disputes is that there are not enough police officers to do what has to be done. Since 1960 the number of police has declined more than 50% relative to the number of crimes. This is not going to change. When it comes to combating crime, accepting some responsibility for being our brother's keeper may be the only hope. Paying people to do so is one approach. Alternatively, we could try to make social responsibility a norm rather than a violation of one. Why do you think people resist "getting involved" when they know they could be the next victim? Do you know of any citizen groups who seem to be successful in combating this traditional norm? What kinds of programs do they have? How might wider use be made of their approach?

## SUMMARY

When psychologists study the causes of behavior, they look first to the individual and his or her personal inherited and acquired characteristics. Then, they examine the environment of the individual, both the physical environment and the social environment, because *all* behavior is the result of an interaction of these factors.

The purpose of this chapter was to give you an appreciation, by example, of how various factors can affect behavior by themselves and how interactions can change the nature of these influences. If all of this seemed complex to you, you got the correct message. There is little, if anything, as difficult to determine with any certainty as the causes of any particular behavior.

---

## ▪ KEY WORDS AND PHRASES

| | | |
|---|---|---|
| direct effects of age on behavior | norms | self-fulfilling prophecy |
| expectations and behavior | personal factors | social environment |
| indirect effects of age on behavior | personal space | social facilitation effect |
| nature-nurture controversy | physical environment | social indifference |
| | psychology | social inhibition effect |

---

## ▪ READ ON

*How a Woman Ages* by R. M. Henig and the Editors of *Esquire* magazine. New York: Ballentine Books, 1985. This may be the best single source available to the nonscientist on the subject of the physical, physiological, and psychological changes that occur as a woman ages. The writing style is easy to read, and you'll learn what is normal, what is reversible, what is correctable, and what women probably just will have to live with.

*How a Man Ages* by C. Pesman and the Editors of *Esquire* magazine. New York: Ballentine Books, 1984. This is the companion book to *How a Woman Ages,* and it is every bit as good. The author has included interesting anecdotes about some famous men, and he reviews research that may be changing how men age.

*The Sense of Place* by F. Steele. Boston: CBI Publishing, 1981. Places have "personalities," just as people do, and this text explores how a place comes to have a sense of itself and what effects this has on the behavior of those in it.

*When Prophecy Fails* by L. Festinger, R. H. Riecken, and S. Schachter. Minneapolis: University of Minnesota, 1956. If your campus or local library has this classic, you'll find the account by three social psychologists of what happened to a group of people who predicted the end of the world (and acted on their belief) fascinating. This is a readable, real-life example of the enormous influence that a particular social environment can have on what we think of as "reality."

---

## ▪ REFERENCES

Arvey, R. D. (1972). Task performance as a function of perceived effort-performance and performance-reward contingencies. *Organizational Behavior and Human Performance, 8;* 423–433.

Baum, A., & Valins, S. (1977). *Architecture and social behavior: Psychological studies in social density.* Hillsdale, NJ: Erlbaum.

Bennet, R., Rafferty, J. M., Canivez, G. L., & Smith, J. M. (1983). *The effects of cold temperature on altruism and aggression.* Paper presented at the annual meeting of the Midwestern Psychological Association.

Bronzaft, A. L. (1981). The effect of a noise abatement program on reading ability. *Journal of Environmental Psychology, 1;* 215–222.

Cazja, S. J., & Drury, C. G. (1981). Aging and pretraining in industrial inspection. *Human Factors, 23;* 485–494.

Cottrell, N. B., Wack, D. L., Sekerak, G. J., & Rittle, R. H. (1968). Social facilitation of dominant responses by the presence of an audience and the mere presence of others. *Journal of Personality and Social Psychology, 9;* 245–250.

Diamond, M. C. (1984). A love affair with the brain. *Psychology Today, 18;* 62–73.

Fine, B. J., & Kobrick, J. L. (1978). Effects of altitude and heat on complex cognitive tasks. *Human Factors, 20;* 115–122.

Fisher, J. D., & Byrne, D. (1975). Too close for comfort: Sex differences in response to invasions of personal space. *Journal of Personality and Social Psychology, 32;* 15–31.

Galle, O. R., Gove, W. R., & McPherson, J. M. (1972). Population density and pathology: What are the relationships for man? *Science, 176;* 23–30.

Gilbert, S. (1985). Noise pollution. *Science Digest, 93;* 28.

Giniger, S., Dispenzieri, A., & Eisenberg, J. (1983). Age, experience, and performance on speed and skill jobs in an applied setting. *Journal of Applied Psychology, 68;* 469–475.

Gross, A. E., Riemer, B.S., & Collins, B. E. (1973). Audience reactions as a determinant of the speaker's self-persuasion. *Journal of Experimental Social Psychology, 9;* 246–256.

Hall, E. T. (1966). *The hidden dimension.* New York: Doubleday.

Jewell, L. N., & Reitz, H. J. (1981) *Group effectiveness in organizations.* Glenview, IL: Scott, Foresman.

Latane, B., & Darley, S. M. (1970). *The unresponsive bystander: Why doesn't he help?* New York: Appleton-Century-Crofts.

Malina, R. M. (1979). Secular changes in growth, maturation, and physical performance. *Exercise and Sport Science Reviews, 6;* 203–255.

McDermott, J. (1986). Face to face, it's the expression that bears the message. *Smithsonian, 16;* 113–124.

Nadler, D. A., & Lawler, E. E., III (1979). Motivation: A diagnostic approach. In R. M. Steers and L. W. Porter (Eds.), *Motivation and work behavior* (2nd ed.). New York: McGraw-Hill.

Oldham, G. R., & Brass, D. J. (1979). Employee reactions to an open-plan office: A naturally occurring quasi-experiment. *Administrative Science Quarterly, 24;* 267–284.

Ottensmann, J. R. (1978). Social behavior in urban space: A preliminary investigation using ethnographic data. *Urban Life, 7;* 2–22.

Patterson, M. L., Mullens, S., & Romano, J. (1971). Compensatory reactions to spatial intrusion. *Sociometry, 34;* 114–121.

Pessin, J. (1933). The comparative effects of social and mechanical stimulation on memorizing. *American Journal of Psychology, 43;* 263–270.

Reinisch, J., reported in Hall, L. (1986). New directions for the Kinsey Institute. *Psychology Today, 20;* 33–39.

Ridenour, M. V. (1978). Contemporary issues in motor development. In *Motor development: Issues and applications.* Princeton: Princeton Book Co.

Rohe, W. M. (1982). The response to density in residential settings: The mediating effects of social and personal variables. *Journal of Applied Social Psychology, 12;* 292–303.

Rosenbaum, D. F., & Lurigio, A. J. (1985). Crime stoppers: Paying the price. *Psychology Today, 19;* 56–61.

Rosenthal, R., & Jacobson, L. (1968). *Pygmalion in the classroom: Teacher expectation and pupil intellectual development.* New York: Holt, Rinehart, & Winston.

Rotton, J., & Frey, J. (1985). Air pollution, weather and violent crimes: Concomitant time-series analysis of archival data. *Journal of Personality and Social Psychology, 49;* 1207–1220.

Schaie, K. W. (1984). Midlife influences upon intellectual functioning in old age. *International Journal of Behavioral Development, 7;* 463–478.

Sherrod, D. R. (1974). Crowding, perceived control, and behavioral aftereffects. *Journal of Applied Social Psychology, 4;* 171–186.

Shirley, M. M. (1931). *The first two years: A study of twenty-five babies: Vol. 1: Postural and locomotor development.* Minneapolis, MN: University of Minnesota Press.

Sundstrom, E., Burt, R. E., & Kamp, D. (1980). Privacy at work: Architectural correlates of job satisfaction and job performance. *Academy of Management Journal, 23;* 101–117.

Triplett, N. (1897). The dynamogenic factors in pacemaking and competition. *American Journal of Psychology, 9;* 507–533.

Zimbardo, P. G. (1969). The human choice: Individuation, reason, and order versus deindividuation, impulse, and chaos. In W. Arnold and D. Levine (Eds.), *Nebraska symposium on motivation.* Lincoln, NE: University of Nebraska Press.

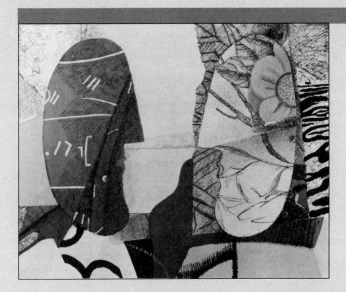

# You: A Unique Individual

It is said that every person has a double somewhere in the world; but unless you happen to be a twin, you probably never have seen anyone who looked exactly like you. There is always something a little different. The other person has a larger nose, blue eyes instead of brown eyes, or long legs and arms instead of short ones.

Even if you meet someone who resembles you to a considerable degree, what about that person's likes and dislikes, skills and knowledge, opinions and values, interests and behavior? When you take these characteristics, as well as physical appearance into consideration, it is clear that you do not have a genuine double. You are unique.

In Part 2 of *Psychology and Effective Behavior*, some of the processes and characteristics that make every person in the world unique are examined. Chapter 3 reviews human, cognitive, emotional, and moral development. Chapter 4 examines the fascinating concept of personality and personality development with a focus on those theories that emphasize what you appear to be like to other people. This discussion is continued in Chapter 5, but the emphasis is shifted to self and self-concept—how you look to yourself.

Read Part 2 in the light of your own history. Think about the characteristics you were born with. Everyone says you are the image of your mother, but isn't that your father's determined chin? Think about how such factors may have affected who you are and what you do today. Think also about your development and how this has been affected by your environment. Were you reading when you started school, perhaps because so much emphasis was placed on books and reading in your home? Did you become an accomplished pianist after your Aunt Jane gave you a piano when you were nine?

Finally, think about the effects of your own behavior and decisions on what you are like today. Do you find yourself fascinated by history and planning to make it your major after signing up for an introductory course on a whim? Or perhaps you aspire to become a physician as a result of doing volunteer work in a local hospital for several summers while you were in high school.

As you read Part 2 and think about the complex set of forces that have played a role in who you are today and what you plan to do tomorrow, resolve never to take yourself for granted again. Remind yourself also that no matter how old you are, you never will be "finished." Life is process, and you will continue to change over the course of it as you interact with your environment. You are not a passive pawn in these changes, however; a basic message of *Psychology and Effective Behavior* is that you have considerable control over what direction they take.

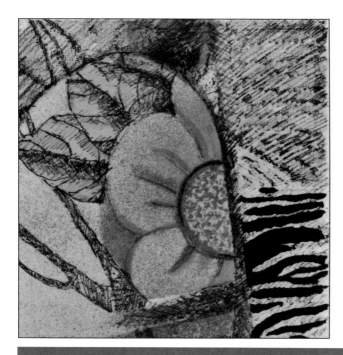

# Your Cognitive, Emotional, and Moral Development

**N**ot too long ago, two children were found living in an abandoned school bus. The children were filthy and undernourished, but otherwise their physical development appeared to be normal. Neither one could make human sounds, however, even though the older child was 8 years old.

These children had been deprived from birth of the social stimuli that are needed if human speech is to develop. By contrast, a 6-year-old boy in another part of the country became the youngest subject ever to be implicated in a narcotics investigation. The child, fluent in both English and Spanish, is said to be very knowledgeable in the language of drug negotiations and to have acted as an interpreter in a cocaine sale.

These stories are true. The extreme variation in the language development of the children involved is variation in one aspect of cognitive (mental) development. This development, in turn, is one of the important influences on behavior that belongs in the personal factors category. In this chapter, we begin Part 2's exploration of some of the major personal factors in more detail. In addition to cognitive development, we will consider emotions and emotional development and values and morals.

The task of this chapter is a large one that requires compressing a great deal of information from three separate and distinct areas of psychological study and research into a relatively few pages. Do not be disheartened by this; the purpose of this chapter is not to make you an expert in developmental psychology. Rather, it is to offer you ideas, theories, and research that are interesting in themselves and also will help (a) to "raise your consciousness" of the developmental processes that had so much influence on who you are and what you do today and (b) to increase your understanding and appreciation of the ongoing nature of human development.

The theories presented in this chapter provide frameworks to help you organize your thinking about some complex developmental processes. As you go along, you will be able to apply much of this material in a personal way to your own life, and you are encouraged to do so. Keep in mind, however, that the theories described are much too general to tell you if your own development was "normal." When psychologists observe individuals, they find that some people go through proposed developmental stages very quickly, some very slowly, and some do not go through all of the stages at all. Inherited biological factors have much to do with this rate of progression, and the environment may either encourage or retard it. In some cases, as the stories related at the beginning of this chapter demonstrate, the environment in which an individual is raised can introduce so much variation that the word *normal* loses its meaning.

## COGNITIVE DEVELOPMENT

The word *cognitive* is related to the verb *know*. **Cognitive development** refers to the development of your abilities to think, learn, solve problems, adapt to your environment, and be creative. If this development occurs especially early (compared with most people) and/or reaches a very sophisticated level (compared with most people), we speak of high intelligence.

*Intelligence* and *cognitive development* do not mean the same thing. People develop cognitively, whatever their level of intelligence, just as they develop physically, whatever their level of attractiveness. Cognitive development is development of the mind. It goes on in the brain by processes that are very complex and by no means completely understood. Scientists discover something new about the brain and its functioning almost every day. If you would like to learn more about this subject, *Read On* at the end of this chapter will be helpful. Here, we move on to consider the leading theory of cognitive development.

## A Theory of Cognitive Development

The most famous theory of how cognitive development proceeds in the early years of life was put forth by a Swiss biologist and naturalist, Jean Piaget. Curiously, Piaget became interested in human thought processes through his work with an aquatic animal called the mollusk. He noticed that mollusks are able to use their experience to adjust to their environments, and he became curious about how this process might work in humans.

Piaget's curiosity led him to a lifelong study of children (in which his own child played a major role). This study brought him to the conclusion that humans go through a predictable series of cognitive changes as they grow (Piaget, 1952). The major stages of this development are shown in Table 3–1. These stages are not based on differences in how much children at different ages know. It is the thinking process itself that differs from one stage to the next. Older children and adults don't have just more to think about; they also think about things differently.

To illustrate this idea that it is the thought processes themselves that change from one stage to the next, let's go back for a moment to the early

For me, an experiment is successful when I find something unexpected, totally unanticipated. That's when things become interesting.

*Jean Piaget.*

**Table 3–1  Piaget's Stages of Cognitive Development**

| Stage | Age Range | Sample Cognitive Characteristic(s) | Example |
|---|---|---|---|
| **Sensorimotor motor** (sensing and reacting) | To one month | ▪ Reflex | ▪ Sucks |
| | 1–4 months | ▪ Self-investigation | ▪ Plays with toes |
| | 4–8 months | ▪ Reaching out | ▪ Shakes a rattle |
| | 8–12 months | ▪ Goal-directed | ▪ Moves object to get to another object |
| | 12–18 months | ▪ Experimentation | ▪ Drops object over and over to see what happens as result |
| | 18–24 months | ▪ Problem-solving | ▪ Looks for object removed from sight |
| **Preoperational** (simple reasoning with symbols and language) | 4–7 years | ▪ Inductive reasoning | ▪ My cat has four legs so animals with four legs are cats. |
| **Concrete operations** (dealing with the here and now) | 7–11 years | ▪ Concrete rule formation | ▪ 6 objects are 2 groups of 3 objects |
| **Formal operations** (reasoning with logic) | 11 + years | ▪ Hypothetical problem solving ▪ Cause-effect relationships | ▪ Understands/solves abstract problems such as those in algebra |

stages of what Piaget called the *sensorimotor period*. At this stage, a toy you could not see no longer existed for you; it was a true case of "out of sight, out of mind." As your cognitive development continued, however, you developed a sense of object permanence—the ability to understand that objects continue to exist even when they are out of sight. At this point, you understood that the toy still existed even though you could not see it.

When you reached this stage, you would search for a toy that had been taken away from you. At first, you looked only where you last had seen the toy. As your cognitive development proceeded, however, you began to understand that it could be other places. (For example, you might have gone to your toybox and looked there because that is where you often found your belongings.) At a still more advanced stage of development, you came to understand that objects you *never* had seen existed, so you begged your parents for a toy like the one your playmate bragged about.

Piaget believed that all children go through his stages in the same sequence. Although a child may exhibit characteristics of two stages during a transition period, he or she does not skip a stage. This is because each stage is built upon the last one. Just as you had to learn to walk before you could run, so you had to be able to understand concrete objects you could see and touch before you were ready to think in abstract hypothetical terms.

Although Piaget's stages of cognitive development are built upon one another, the ages at which they occur can vary considerably from one person to another. As in all areas of development, each of us develops to our own degree on our own timetable, and both the extent and the pace of development affect behavior. Trying to learn algebra before developing to Piaget's formal operations stage, for example, would be difficult. The child would be unlikely to do well, might feel frustrated, and possibly could develop a permanent dislike for math.

As the example of the child who takes algebra too early illustrates, cognitive development affects an individual in ways that go beyond the content of what he or she is able to master in school. Anyone, child or adult, who has not developed to the formal operations stage will have difficulty dealing with life issues and problems that require thinking beyond the concrete here and now. Failure, frustration, and a tendency to avoid thinking about these areas are likely results, and none of these is helpful when it comes to the goal of achieving effective behavior.

Piaget lived a long life and he spent 50 years of it developing, refining, and revising his theory. His work, like that of pioneers in almost any area of study, has had many critics, but it remains the standard against which other ideas about early cognitive development are compared. Meanwhile, other scientists are becoming increasingly interested in cognitive development in later life. In particular, they are beginning to question the assumption that cognitive abilities must deteriorate in old age. More on this may be found in *Face of the Future*.

## Learning

**Learning is a relatively permanent change in behavior or behavior potential that comes about through interaction with the environment.** This definition goes far beyond what is learned in a classroom, although it certainly applies to that situation. When you take a college course such as this one, for example, you are interacting with an aspect of your environment, and you come out of this situation changed in some way.

Perhaps you come out of this course being able to do something you couldn't do before, such as explain to a friend the advantages and disadvantages of various birth control methods. Or perhaps you have added to your store of potential behavior; for example, you now have some ideas of what to do if you should find yourself feeling depressed. These are relatively permanent changes in your capabilities; they will remain unless they are forgotten by disuse or they are replaced by new learning about these things.

There is much that each of us must learn to become functioning independent individuals. Some of these things—standing, walking, feeding ourselves—are governed to a considerable degree by maturation. Other tasks, including talking, reading, writing, getting along with others, distinguishing right from wrong, avoiding personal danger, and acquiring knowledge and specific skills, such as driving a car, don't come so naturally.

### Classical Conditioning

Psychologists and other scientists who study learning distinguish among several basic types of learning processes. The simplest of these is called classical conditioning. **Classical conditioning** comes about through the pairing of a

# FACE OF THE FUTURE:
## Slowing Down "Mental Aging"

Biologists tell us that every organ in our bodies begins wearing out virtually from the day we are born. As a result, vision, hearing, digestion, limb movement, eye-hand coordination, and most other physical and bodily functions are far less efficient at 60 than at 20.

The brain is a bodily organ, so it also ages: older people have a measurable reduction in number of brain cells compared with younger people. Because the brain is the site of cognitive functioning, it would seem to make sense that it would become less efficient as it loses cells. Certainly, we can see some evidence for this around us. Some elderly people have difficulty learning complex new skills (such as speaking a foreign language), experience memory losses (some temporary, some apparently permanent), take longer to say or write their thoughts, and exhibit occasional confusion about people and events.

For a long time, this reduction in cognitive functioning was taken for granted as an inevitable part of the natural aging process. Scientists now are beginning to think otherwise. Many factors have stimulated new research. One is the development of increasingly sophisticated methods for studying the brain. These techniques also have opened up exciting new possibilities for treating disorders, such as Alzheimer's disease, that are characterized by sudden mental deterioration.

Another factor leading many to question the inevitability of mental aging is the ever-increasing number of elderly citizens who show few signs of it. Examples include Ann Landers (in her 60s), Ronald Reagan (in his 70s), B. F. Skinner (in his 80s), and George Burns (in his 90s), as well as many people who are not well known.

Such people have always been around, of course, but never before in such numbers. Psychologists, doctors, and biologists and gerontologists (scientists who specialize in the study of aging) have had unparalleled opportunities to compare these fully functioning senior citizens with peers who show "typical" signs of cognitive deterioration, and they are coming up with very similar conclusions. "Use it or lose it," as the physical fitness buffs say.

As an example of the research on which this rather revolutionary inference is based, consider Schaie (1984), who studied over 100 people from the time they were in their midforties until they were in their midsixties. Schaie found that those people who maintained a high level of cognitive functioning in later life had several things in common.

- They had remained flexible in their behavior and attitudes.
- They had remained involved in a broad range of intellectually stimulating activities.
- They continued to practice their problem-solving abilities.

So far, there is little to contradict such findings as those of Schaie and many others. The face of the future is shaping up to be a time of unparalleled opportunity for tomorrow's senior citizens, who may be able to avoid much of the "natural" deterioration of mental abilities of yesteryear by maintaining good health and getting plenty of mental and physical exercise.

natural response with a stimulus that previously had no connection with the response.

What is learned in classical conditioning is an association between two things that previously were not associated. The most famous demonstration of such learning occurred in the late 1800s when Russian psychologist Ivan Pavlov reported an experiment in which he "taught" a dog to salivate at the sound of a bell. He did this by ringing the bell each time food was presented, a time at which dogs salivate naturally. Eventually, the dog would salivate when the bell was rung, even though no food was presented.

Learning theorists have special terms for the events that occurred in Pavlov's laboratory. The event that elicits a natural response, such as food, is called an **unconditioned stimulus** (UCS). The natural response, such as the dog's salivation, is called an **unconditioned response** (UCR). The "unnatural" event with which it becomes associated, such as the bell ringing, is a **conditioned stimulus** (CS). When the natural response (UCR) is made to the conditioned stimulus (CS), it is called a **conditioned response** (CR). (It is exactly the same response, but it is made under *learned* conditions.)

Classical conditioning is not something that happens only in a scientific laboratory. We all have some patterns of behavior learned this way. For example, driving by your favorite pizza restaurant may give you that hollow feeling and slight stomach contractions known as hunger even though you weren't thinking about food at the time. In fact, you may even have found yourself, like Pavlov's dog, salivating a little when you read the word *pizza*.

Salivation is a simple physiological behavior, but classical conditioning is not limited to such uncomplicated responses. Attitudes, fears, and other emotional responses may be learned through essentially the same process. In Table 3–2, you see an outline of the classical conditioning process by which an individual might learn to dislike or even fear going to see medical doctors.

In a fashion similar to that outlined in Table 3–2, people can learn a variety of emotional and psychological reactions to a wide variety of other events, objects, or conditions. Can you think of an example from your own life? Can you can fill in the squares in the table appropriately to see how this learning might have come about?

---

## Table 3–2   The Classical Conditioning Process

| ORIGINAL SITUATION: | UCS ⟶ (physical pain) | UCR (worry/anxiety) |
|---|---|---|
| ASSOCIATION: | CS ⟵- - - - - - ⟶ (medical office, staff) | UCS (physical pain) |
| CONDITIONING: | CS ⟶ (medical office, staff) | CR (worry/anxiety) |

## Operant Conditioning

Classical conditioning is a very simple learning mechanism. More of what you learn occurs by what learning theorists call operant conditioning (sometimes called instrumental conditioning). **Operant conditioning** comes about through the pairing of some behavior with what happens afterwards. It is based on the *consequences of behavior* rather than on *associations between events*.

To help you understand this idea if it is new to you, let's go back to your first class at this college or university. We'll assume that you were excited and looking forward to this new experience and that you were very careful to set out for the class in plenty of time to get there when it started. When you arrived at a few minutes before the scheduled time, you found to your dismay that the classroom was packed. There were no seats left and no place to put a chair even if you could have found one, so you had to sit on the floor for an hour. This made it difficult to see and hear the professor and was very uncomfortable as well.

You learned from this experience that the consequences of being on time for class were unpleasant (punishing), so you decided that you would get to all of your classes early in the future (your behavior changed). You did so and found that some of these classes were overcrowded, as the first had been, but others were not; so you learned that you had to get to some classes early if you wanted a seat, but that it was safe to arrive at others at the scheduled time. This is an example of **discrimination learning.** You learned to discriminate (tell the difference) between which classes you had to get to early and which you did not.

By the end of your first year of coursework, you realized that there was a pattern to this business of overcrowded classrooms. In particular, night classes and classes that started between the hours of 9 A.M. and 2 P.M. usually were crowded; those that started early in the morning or late in the afternoon almost never were. This is an example of **generalization learning;** you learned to generalize from particular stimuli (individual classes on a case-by-case basis) to others that had the same properties (classes that started at particular times).

In this example, you learned to make connections between your behavior and what happened to you as a result of it; this is operant conditioning. You learned that if you did not arrive well before the scheduled time for certain classes, you could not get a seat and you felt left out of the class. Such unpleasant consequences of behavior are called **punishers.** With **punishment** you are less likely to repeat the punished behavior under similar conditions in the future; this behavior has been *weakened.*

By contrast with punishers, **reinforcers** are rewarding consequences of behavior that make it more likely that the same behavior will be repeated in the future. If the reinforcer is of a positive nature, we say the behavior has been *strengthened* through **positive reinforcement.** Much of your early language learning occurred this way. Your first tentative voicing of *mama* was greeted with cries of delight, and you were the center of attention. This was powerful reinforcement, and you repeated the sound over and over until the novelty wore off and those around you ceased to respond so enthusiastically. Then you tried out *dada* and the process began again.

Not all of the rewarding consequences of behavior are of the positive type described. Some reinforcement occurs in a different way. For example, you

Intelligence is quickness in seeing things as they are.

*George Santayana*

may have formed the habit of doing all of your studying in the library during the day so you can avoid your spouse's and your children's complaints that you are ignoring them when you try to study at home at night. When behavior *stops* something that we find unpleasant, or keeps it from happening at all, we say the behavior has received **negative reinforcement.**

Negative reinforcement is not the same as punishment for two reasons. First, in negative reinforcement, the unpleasantness occurs before the behavior. (In the example, you received complaints, which made you unhappy. You stopped them by changing your behavior.) In punishment, by contrast, it occurs after the behavior. Second, the effects of punishment and negative reinforcement on the associated behaviors are quite different. Punishment makes it less likely that the behavior will be repeated in the future. Negative reinforcement makes it more likely; like positive reinforcement, *negative reinforcement strengthens the behavior it follows.*

To summarize to this point, reinforcement makes associated behaviors more likely to occur again, and punishment makes them less likely to occur again (at least in the same circumstances). Not all reinforcers are positive; some are negative in that they stop or avoid something unpleasant or disliked. It also should be noted that some punishment consists of a reinforcer being withheld or taken away rather than of something unpleasant being done or presented. The temporary suspension of driving priviledges by a parent or a court is an example. It is not standard practice for psychologists to distinguish between these two punishment situations. You may find it less confusing, however, to think of the withholding or stopping of something desirable (such as driving privileges) as "negative punishment," whereas the presentation or occurrence of something unpleasant (having to sit on the floor) is "positive punishment." This distinction is depicted in Table 3–3.

Sometimes the consequences of behavior aren't really either rewarding or punishing. Suppose, for example, that you decided to tune in to a highly advertised new television program. You watched it for the hour it was broadcast and decided that it was okay but not great, and maybe you'd give it another chance. After two more episodes, you gave it up. It wasn't painful to watch, but it wasn't good to watch either; you'd just as soon do something else with

## Table 3–3   Relationship between Different Forms of Reinforcement and Punishment

|            | Presented                    | Taken away (stopped) or Avoided |
|------------|------------------------------|---------------------------------|
| Reinforcer | Positive Reinforcement       | (Negative) Punishment           |
| Punisher   | (Positive) Punishment        | Negative Reinforcement          |

**Note:** This table is based on suggestions by T. Knapp, University of Nevada at Las Vegas. Thanks to T. Knapp for suggestions.

that hour. What has happened here is **extinction of a behavior** (watching that particular television show). That particular behavior has left your repertoire.

Although extinction sounds a bit like what happens when behavior is punished, there is an important difference. Punishment makes it less likely that a behavior will occur again under similar circumstances, but it usually does not make the behavior disappear. For example, a person who receives a speeding ticket in the little town he or she must pass through on the way to work is unlikely to speed in that town again. We could make a good guess, however, that he or she has not given up speeding altogether.

This example illustrates why, as a general rule, punishment is not a very good way to change behavior. If you punish your child for saying a word that you don't think children should say, for example, what you most likely are teaching him or her is not to say the word in front of *you*. Look out the next time grandma babysits!

The principles of operant conditioning tell us that you will be more effective in erasing this unbecoming behavior by ignoring it (neither reinforcing nor punishing it) so that eventually it will extinguish. This, of course, is easier said than done, as any of you who are parents will recognize immediately. It may be a little easier if you also can provide consistent positive reinforcement for a related desirable behavior while ignoring the undesired one. For example, each time such an incident occurred, you might focus attention on another word the child has used right before or after the one you don't like and compliment him or her on knowing it or using it correctly. Over time, the combination of ignoring the undesired word and reinforcing vocabulary development (or some other positively valued behavior) should accomplish your purpose.

Together, the three different possible outcomes of behavior and how they affect that behavior make up what psychologist E. L. Thorndike (1905) called the **law of effect.** This law tells us that those relatively permanent changes in behavior or behavior potential we call *learning* come about in a systematic way based on experience with the environment.

The process of learning through operant conditioning is a continuous one that goes on simultaneously in many areas and at many levels with a complex interplay of reinforcement and punishment and extinction. To help you appreciate this point, consider a few hours in the life of a student we'll call Jeff. (To keep it simple, we'll consider only reinforcers and punishers and avoid the complex issue of extinction.) Poor Jeff got up late this Monday morning and so did not have time to eat breakfast before his first class (a punisher). Trying to make up for lost time, he drove too fast on the way to the campus and was stopped by a police officer and issued a traffic citation (a punisher).

Jeff now was later than ever, but when he got to the parking lot for the building his class was in, a car pulled out of a spot right by the front door (a reinforcer). He raced into the classroom 10 minutes late and tried to slip into a seat without being noticed. It didn't work; the professor stopped the lecture, glared at him, and made a negative comment about students who can't get to class on time (punishers). Jeff sat down quickly and concentrated on trying to catch up with the lecture.

After class, another student stopped Jeff to say that he collected Jeff's paper when they were returned at the beginning of the class (a reinforcer). When Jeff thanked him, the second student reminded him that Jeff had done the

Unplesant outcomes of behavior, called punishment, are not all administered by other people; some occur as the direct result of behavior itself.

same for him once last term. Jeff took his paper, which he had worked extra hard on, and saw a grade of *A* at the top (a reinforcer). Whistling, he headed for the cafeteria to try to get a quick bite to eat before his next class. He felt so much better now that he smiled at the attractive girl next to him in the cafeteria line. She smiled back (a reinforcer), they began talking, and the girl invited him to sit with her (another reinforcer).

We'll leave Jeff at the cafeteria with his new friend, as he's served his purpose. In the course of a few short hours, he has experienced the consequences, both reinforcing and punishing, of a variety of behaviors. As a result, he has learned a number of important things. If you asked him to tell you what these were, he might reply that he has learned that (a) a few minutes of extra sleep aren't worth the price; (b) he shouldn't be late to his Monday morning class, because this professor minds even though others in the past haven't seemed to notice; (c) doing favors for people can have unexpected positive outcomes; (d) working hard on a paper pays off; and (e) taking a chance on being rebuffed by someone he finds attractive can work out okay.

Of course, as time goes on, Jeff may have new experiences that modify or change in some way what he says he learned that Monday morning. Indeed, some of what he says he learned may not have been learned at all in the sense that it brought about a relatively permanent change in his behavior. (He may have to miss many more breakfasts before he gives in and buys an alarm clock, for example.) And some of what he learned may not hold the next time similar circumstances hold. For example, he may rebuffed the next time he approaches an attractive girl who is a stranger to him.

This brings us to a final note about operant conditioning, one that has to do with the relationship between the *frequency* with which reinforcing consequences follow behavior and how strong that behavior becomes. Some of the behaviors you have learned through positive (or negative) reinforcement are rewarded every time you make them. For example, you may have gotten into the habit of recommending books for your mother to read because every time you do, she thanks you and tells you how much she enjoyed your choice. Behaviors that receive **continuous reinforcement** in this way extinguish very quickly if reinforcement stops. It may take only one incident of your mother telling you that she didn't much like a book you recommended for you to stop making these suggestions.

Other behaviors are reinforced only occasionally. You may find a letter (as opposed to bills and advertising material) in your mailbox only once in a while, but the possibility that today might be the day keeps you heading straight for the mailbox as soon as you get home. This occasional reward for a behavior is called **intermittent reinforcement,** and the associated behavior takes much longer to extinguish than when reinforcement is continuous.

The different effects of continuous and intermittent reinforcement on behavior have important implications for bringing about learning or changes in behavior in ourselves or others. In general, the most stable learning occurs when continuous reinforcement in the early learning stages (for quicker learning) is gradually reduced to intermittent reinforcement (for slower extinction) once the behavior is well established.

In this complicated world, much of what we learn comes from watching others.

## Social Learning

Both classical and operant conditioning are forms of learning based on direct experience. You know, however, that you also learn from others, both from what they say and from what you see them do. This learning from others is called **social learning** (Bandura, 1977).

In its simplest form, social learning occurs merely by observing what someone else (called a *model*) does and copying the behavior if the outcome seems to you to be reinforcing to the model in some way. This simple *observational learning* might be the way you learned how to behave at your first major formal dinner party, for example. When you did what the others did, no one paid any attention to your eating behavior (which was reinforcing, because you didn't feel embarrassed as you had feared you might).

Not all social learning can be explained by the simple process of watching what a model does, observing that it is reinforced, and copying it. People may imitate the behavior of others when no reinforcement of any kind can be identified. On the other hand, the mere imitation of others does not necessarily mean that learning has taken place. Sometimes it only means that a person is falling in with what are perceived to be the social requirements of a situation. True social learning requires four conditions (Bandura, 1971).

Children have more need of models than of critics.

*Joseph Joubert*

1. *The learner must be paying attention to the modeled behavior and recognize its distinctive features.* If you are trying to learn to give better oral presentations in class by watching another student you think is good, you must pay attention to the presentation and figure out which parts of it are critical (e.g., enthusiastic voice tone) and which aren't (e.g., what the speaker wears).

2. *The learner must retain what he or she has observed.* When you go home to practice the observed behavior in front of a parent, a friend, the dog, or a mirror, you must be able to remember the important aspects of the behavior.

3. *The learner must be able to reproduce the behavior.* Being able to remember a particular pattern of behavior does not necessarily mean that you can copy it. Social learning is limited by the extent of a person's capacity to imitate. For example, perhaps your voice is small and weak, and no matter how hard you try, you simply cannot project it in the way that you recall the effective speaker doing.

4. *The learner must be motivated to display the behavior.* Whether it comes from within the learner him- or herself (self-administered reinforcement), from the outcome of modeling the behavior (direct reinforcement), or just from what happened to the model (vicarious reinforcement), Bandura recognized that some form of reinforcement is necessary for social learning to occur.

To continue with our example, you aren't likely to be motivated to make a permanent change in your class presentation methods on the basis of what someone else did (social learning) unless the person you copy got a good grade (vicarious reinforcement), you felt really good about how you sounded when you imitated his or her style (self-administered reinforcement), or you got a good grade yourself when you imitated it (direct reinforcement).

The ability to learn from others vastly increases your ability to master your environment. No one has time to learn everything that must be learned through direct experience. Social learning also helps us to avoid some of the punishing consequences that almost always go along with the more trial-and-error operant conditioning process. For example, you did not have to learn through your own direct experience that if you take an exam without studying for it, you are likely to fail. Over the years you have seen this happen to others many times.

**Summing Up** ■

Classical conditioning, operant conditioning, and social learning account for a great deal of your behavior potential as well as your actual behavior, but learning theorists aren't sure they tell the whole story. For example, none of these processes explains the behavior we call *creative* very well. By definition, creative behavior is original. It gives us books, music, art work, toys, gadgets, and scientific theories we haven't had before.

Psychologists know that there are things we can do to encourage and stimulate creative behavior; to take a simple example, you can give a child a box of crayons and a pile of paper. We also can reinforce creativity when it occurs; if the child produces a pleasing drawing, you can offer praise and show the drawing proudly to others or display it in a prominent place.

Psychologists also have developed tests to measure creative potential, but many people with high scores on such tests would not be described as creative. What brings such behavior out in the first place? The question becomes even more puzzling when we remember that creative behavior begins appearing in some people at such an early age that they scarcely have had time to learn the basics of living. Some of the great classical musicians, for example, were as 6-year-olds composing musical works that still are performed today. However much we know at this time, it is clear that there still is much to be learned about learning.

## EMOTIONAL DEVELOPMENT

**Emotions** are states of feeling characterized by internal bodily changes that arise in response to imagined or actual events or experiences. Some of these events or experiences elicit such common feelings that the emotion seems to be instinctive, or "programmed in" to people. Fear of falling is one example. In more cases, however, experienced emotions depend on a person's *assessment of the event or experience*. Your friend may feel strong fear at the mere sight of a snake encountered as the two of you walk in the woods, whereas you have no such emotion because you know that there are only harmless snakes in this area. You, on the other hand, may become anxious the moment a test is announced, whereas that same friend is unmoved by this event.

Different people experience different emotional reactions to the same events and experiences, and they display these to others in different ways as well. The range of possibilities is very rich, yet psychologists believe the actual number of human emotions is limited. Table 3–4 presents two researcher's lists of what they believe to be the primary human emotions. As you can see, there is a difference of opinion as to how many basic emotions we experience and what they are, but both of the lists are rather short. You also probably noticed that there are some surprising omissions. Where are the familiar feelings of anxiety, hate, grief, and love? Most researchers believe that these are complex combinations of more basic emotions. Anxiety, for example, seems to be part fear, part guilt, and part anger (Smith & Ellsworth, 1984). What combinations would you think make up hate? Grief? Love?

Some specific emotions, such as love and anxiety, and how these affect our lives are discussed in later chapters. Here, a more general look at emotions and emotional development is taken. Our discussion begins with the curious question of how it is that you know what you are feeling.

## Emotional Experience: How Do You Know What You Feel?

Internal bodily changes are part of all emotion, and if you have thought about it at all, you probably have assumed that these responses are caused by the emotion. A friend you have not seen for over a year shows up at your door unannounced one evening. What a surprise! How exciting! You believe that these emotions—surprise and excitement—cause the variety of internal reactions you are experiencing. The adrenalin pumps, your heart beats a little faster, your breath comes a little quicker, and you feel energized; you smile, you exclaim, and you rush here and there asking questions and trying to make your guest comfortable.

This commonsense theory of emotions describes this sequence: event (friend at door), emotions (surprise, excitement), bodily reactions (increased heart rate and faster breathing), actions (smile, ask questions, hug, and so on). Most psychologists don't believe this is what happens, however. Current ideas

---

### Table 3–4   Two Views of the Basic Human Emotions

| | |
|---|---|
| Anger | Anger |
| Joy | Joy |
| Fear | Fear |
| Disgust | Disgust |
| Surprise | Surprise |
| Contempt | Acceptance |
| Shame | Sadness |
| Guilt | Anticipation |
| Interest-Excitement | |
| Distress | |

**Note:** List in column 1 from *Human emotions* by C. E. Izard, 1977, New York: Plenum. List in column 2 from "A Language for the Emotions" by R. Plutchik, 1980, *Psychology Today, 14,* 68–78.

about emotion are based on a different sequence: event, bodily reactions, emotion, action.

In this current view of emotions, the emotion does not cause the bodily reactions, the reactions cause the emotion. Furthermore, it is possible that this reaction is merely a general state of internal physiological arousal that we have learned to give different "emotion names" to depending on the circumstances at the time they occurred (Schachter & Singer, 1962).

The idea that you have to learn to label your emotions may not make much sense to you. Fear is fear, isn't it? And love is love? Well, not necessarily. Psychologists have considerable evidence that even as adults people sometimes mistake one emotion for another. A well-known study of fear and sexual attraction is a good example.

Two Canadian psychologists conducted an experiment in which they arranged for male subjects to be interviewed by a woman interviewer on a swaying bridge some 230 feet over a rushing river (Dutton & Aron, 1974). Others were interviewed by the same woman on a low, fixed bridge. Still others were interviewed on these bridges by a male interviewer. After their interviews, the subjects were asked to write stories based on ambiguous pictures. Relative to the stories written by other subjects, those written by subjects who had been interviewed on the high swaying bridge by the woman contained a much higher sexual content. In addition, significantly more of these subjects took advantage of the opportunity to call the female interviewer after the experiment was concluded than did other subjects.

The researchers who carried out this study explain their results in terms of subjects' interpretations of the internal arousal that resulted from the settings of the interviews. Men interviewed by a woman on the high, swaying bridge interpreted their feelings as being caused by the attractive interviewer rather than by the fearful aspects of their surroundings. Men interviewed by men on the same bridge interpreted the cause of their internal arousal as a response to possible physical danger, that is to fear, not sexual attraction.

Not all psychologists would accept this explanation, but there is a considerable body of research to support the basic premise that people describe similar bodily reactions in considerably different ways depending on the context in which they occur. Psychological processes also can affect the experience of emotions. For example, some psychotherapists believe that much depression is really anger turned inward by people who have been taught that anger is not an acceptable feeling.

What does all of this tell us about the development of our emotional selves? First, if emotions are based on physiological arousal, it seems likely that you felt most or all of the ones you feel now at an early age, although you didn't call them anything. Second, if what you *do* call them depends on the context in which they occur, then healthy emotional development may depend to some extent on the degree to which these associations are made in a realistic fashion. A recent theory of the stages of emotional development illustrates this idea.

## A Theory of Emotional Development

The idea that we all pass through a similar sequence of physical and cognitive development stages has been understood and accepted for some time. Psychologists have been slower to define emotional development stages, but there

---

Table 3–5   **Emotional Milestones to Age 4**

STAGE 1. Children learn to calm themselves and to express their "personalities" through the preference they show for certain kinds of experiences (such as being held). This stage lasts about 3 months.

STAGE 2. This is described as a time for "falling in love," a time when infants learn the joys of interaction with humans. It lasts until about age 7 months.

STAGE 3. From about 3 until 10 months, infants are learning to communicate with others so that those others can interpret their needs and wants.

STAGE 4. In this important stage, which lasts from about 9 to 18 months, children are beginning to figure out how to match up their behavior and their feelings.

STAGE 5. In this period, from 1½ to 3 years, children begin to have mental images of emotional experience and to express emotions in words as well as in behaviors, like crying.

STAGE 6. Between the ages of 2½ and 6, children make significant progress in "emotional thinking." They learn to distinguish between different feelings and between what they feel or want and reality.

---

**Note:** Summarized from "Team Maps Children's Emotional Milestones" by C. Cordes, 1985, *APA Monitor*, March, 32–33.

---

is a new model based on 8 years of intensive research and clinical work with children (Greenspan & Greenspan, 1986). The six proposed stages of emotional development from birth to age 4 are summarized in Table 3–5.

As with Piaget's stages of cognitive development, the Greenspans' stages of emotional development are built upon one another. The authors of this theory believe that there are important long-term consequences for children whose development at any stage is faulty and that parents (or other caretakers) are a critical factor. Among the problems they believe can develop if adults fail to respond to children appropriately at the various stages of development are (a) difficulty understanding and accepting reality, (b) a limited range of emotional responses, (c) a reduced capacity for love, and (d) an inability to control rage.

The Greenspans' theory is new, and we will want much more data before drawing any firm conclusions about how parents should go about helping their children to develop into emotionally healthy adults, but it is a beginning. For example, the theory suggests that if the only way an infant can communicate his or her needs successfully (stage 3) is by screaming, the child may fail to learn more subtle ways (than anger) to get attention. This implies that parents who do not respond to a child's more positive communication attempts may be assisting the development of a limited range of emotional responses.

## The Concept of Emotional Maturity

One implication of a theory of emotional development, such as that of the Greenspans, is that somewhere down the line there is a maturity stage. It would be nice if there were a list of the characteristics that define such a stage, but there are some obstacles to creating such a list. First, we must ask if *emotional maturity* refers to the feelings we have or to the way we express them.

To most people, emotional maturity probably is a concept that has more to do with the way we express our feelings than with the feelings themselves. For example, you probably would see nothing amiss when a 2-year-old expressed anger by throwing a tantrum. By contrast, this same behavior in your girlfriend, boyfriend, or spouse would be labeled *immature*, although perhaps you wouldn't deny him or her the right to feel angry. On the other hand, perhaps you might if you thought that what the adult was feeling angry about was trivial and "childish."

This brings up a second problem with the concept of emotional maturity. To say that an adult who throws a temper tantrum is immature is to make a value judgment. All societies make such judgments about the appropriate expression of certain emotions. In our culture, it is fair to say that most people consider it more acceptable to express positive emotions than negative ones. Many people also believe that adults should control *all* strong feelings in public, and some still believe that men should not express certain emotions (e.g., sadness) in certain ways (e.g., crying) at any time. Can you think of other examples of values our culture places on emotions and emotional expression? If you come originally from another country, can you see any important differences between your country and the United States on this issue?

Many psychologists and other mental health professionals believe that these traditional norms, which emphasize keeping a lid on negative emotions and expressing others in socially approved ways, do not promote mental health. They also believe that labeling emotions as positive/negative, appropriate/inappropriate, or mature/immature is, by itself, promoting unhealthy attitudes (e.g., Rogers, 1966).

From this point of view, all feelings are valid and it is important both to try to *know* what they are and to *accept* them for what they are. It helps in this second regard to keep in mind that feeling is not doing. There are many actions that are not acceptable for one reason or another (laws, norms, your own values), but having feelings that could lead to such actions does not make you guilty of the actions. Former President Jimmy Carter didn't commit adultery, but he admitted openly that he had "lusted in his heart."

It also is important to be able to *own* your own feelings, that is, to be able to understand the difference between the behavior of others and your own feelings. For example, if you own your feelings in an argument about the amount of time your girlfriend, boyfriend, or spouse spends at work, you will say something like, "I feel neglected when you spend so much time away from me," not "You obviously don't enjoy being with me anymore." Owning your own feelings requires you to recognize and accept that they *are* your feelings and that they are not necessarily deliberately caused by, understood, or even recognized by others.

What about *expressing* your feelings? Most psychologists probably would agree that it is not healthy to bottle up feelings or to try to deny that you have them; but there are no guidelines about expressing them, because the range of possible situations is so great. In some cases it seems best to tell another person of your feelings, either positive or negative; in others this may not be such a good idea. For example, if you really need your job, you probably shouldn't

Emotions are powerful forces, but psychologists have research to suggest that we must learn what to call these feelings on the basis of the situations in which they occur.

tell a disliked supervisor what you think of him or her, but you can express your feelings or work off the tension they have created in other ways.

- You can hold imaginary conversations with this person in which you say exactly what you think of his or her behavior and how it makes you feel.
- You can say these same things to a sympathetic friend.
- You can work off your emotional steam in exercise of some sort, by playing tennis or mowing the lawn, for example.
- You can make a conscious effort to quit dwelling on the matter and relax with a book, a hobby, or a long soak in the tub.
- If the situation is very bad, you could express your feelings by quitting your job.

Recognizing, owning, accepting, and allowing yourself to express your emotions in a nondestructive way are important to your emotional well-being, but there are no objective standards for what you should feel under certain circumstances or how you should express these feelings. This means that the issue of what constitutes emotional maturity must be left somewhat open. A guideline that is useful, however, lies in the concept of control. Self-control is considered by most people to be one of the basic dimensions on which adults and children differ emotionally. The emotional maturity of people who know that their own emotional behavior frequently is out of their control (or who get consistent feedback from others that they lack control) is open to some question. Such people often benefit from exploring this issue with a professional counselor.

## Summing Up ■

Emotions are reactions to events or experiences characterized by bodily changes that produce a state of arousal. There is some evidence that we must learn to interpret this arousal according to the situation in which it occurs. A recent theory of emotional development suggests that this learning about emotions begins early in life and that important people in an infant's world can assist or retard it in ways that have long-term consequences for emotional well-being.

Emotional maturity is a difficult concept to define, both because of some conceptual confusion between the experience of emotions and the expression of emotions, and because definitions of emotional maturity are highly dependent on cultural values. Many psychologists believe that this value dependency results in standards that run counter to emotional health, which they believe requires identifying, accepting, owning, and expressing one's feelings.

## MORAL DEVELOPMENT

**Moral** means "of or relating to right and wrong" (Stein, 1982). How do we know what right and wrong are? As with standards for the appropriate expression of emotions, standards for right and wrong are defined to a considerable degree by the values of a culture. This is logical in the sense that all societies must depend upon general conformity to understood standards of conduct for survival. You can see this in the list of a few basic rights and wrongs in our society in the last half of the 20th century in Table 3–6. It is obvious that observing these "rights" would make for a more harmonious society, but you know from experience that the difference between right and wrong is not always as sharp and clear as this list implies. The following are just a few of many grey areas.

- It is right to tell the truth and wrong to lie, but what is simply not volunteering information or telling all you know when asked a question?

- It is wrong to kill, but what if a doctor follows the request of a patient who made a "living will" asking not to be connected to any artificial life-support system?

- It is right to help people in trouble, but what if this puts someone else in jeopardy? Should a father of three small children risk drowning in an attempt to save a stranger?

> Doing what's right isn't the problem. It's knowing what's right.
>
> *Lyndon B. Johnson*

## Moral Dilemmas

The situations just described, along with countless others that people face every day, are moral dilemmas. A **moral dilemma** arises when opposing standards for right and wrong are dictating contradictory behaviors. (People who have no sense of right and wrong do not have moral dilemmas.) The Bible, the Koran, various philosophers and prophets, organized religions, parents, friends, and even psychologists are among those offering definitions of right and wrong behaviors that may create such dilemmas.

Frank Herbert, author of the popular *Dune* series of books, believes that most moral dilemmas can be resolved by means of the Golden Rule: Treat other people the way you would want them to treat you. Herbert writes:

> The most common excuse is to say someone else shaves a moral corner, so what you're doing is diluted by numbers. My response to this cop-out is to say: All it takes is two people, each using the other as an excuse, and your society can degenerate into moral chaos.
>
> Yes, there are people who will try to take advantage of you if you live this way, but they do more harm to themselves than they do to you (Herbert, 1984, p. 9).

### Table 3–6  Some Common Moral Standards in Our Society

| Right | Wrong |
| --- | --- |
| Telling the truth | Lying |
| Respecting the property of others | Stealing or vandalizing |
| Helping people in trouble | Ignoring other people's problems |
| Respecting life | Taking life |
| Sharing with others | Being selfish |
| Obeying laws | Breaking laws |

Herbert describes the moral decisions each of us must make each day as a constant "battle between good and evil." This description implies that we know and understand that certain actions can be called good and others cannot, as, indeed, most of us do. Where does this knowledge come from? We certainly are not born knowing the difference between right and wrong.

## A Theory of Moral Development

The most well known theory of how we come to develop a sense of right and wrong is that proposed by psychologist Lawrence Kohlberg (1969). Kohlberg believed that there are three levels of moral development with two separate stages at each level. The first level, called the *preconventional level,* lasts from birth until about the age of 9.

At stage 1 of the preconventional level, a child's ideas about right and wrong begin to develop on the simple principle of avoiding punishment. For example, you may have learned that it was wrong to hit your baby sister because you got a spanking every time you gave in to this impulse. A little later on, at stage 2, you began to think of right in terms of being rewarded; being nice to your sister was right because it brought you praise or treats from your parents.

You can see that the preconventional level of moral development is not based on any fundamental ideas of right and wrong, but on the consequences of behavior. A broader conception of right and wrong, based on an understanding of the need for an orderly society, develops at the *conventional level* of moral development. During stages 3 and 4 at this level, moral decisions are based on a respect for authority and a desire to do one's duty.

Somewhere around the age of 16, Kohlberg believed, we all have the potential to develop our concepts of moral principles and to evaluate right and wrong in terms of these principles. This *postconventional level* of moral development is based first (stage 5) on taking a broad view of the situation. The last stage (6) is based on the idea of *conscience.*

At stage 6 in Kohlberg's formulation, you don't cheat on a test even though you know you won't get caught. You don't cheat because cheating is wrong, not because you would be punished if you did get caught (preconventional level) or because cheating is against the rules (conventional level). Kohlberg's full sequence of moral development is illustrated in Table 3–7 by means of the reasons six different 17-year-olds might give for smoking or not smoking marijuana, an illegal substance. This particular example is used to illustrate an important point; people do not necessarily go through all the stages of moral development. Like the hypothetical teenagers in the table, they may go through life operating at any level in the sequence.

Kohlberg's theory of moral development has been controversial (as indeed Kohlberg himself was controversial). He modified his ideas somewhat in response to the criticisms (Levine, Kohlberg, & Hewer, 1985), but it probably still is fair to say that his theory is not accepted to nearly the same degree as the theory of Piaget, upon which it is based. Nevertheless, it is a useful framework for thinking about this complex subject, and its very lack of general acceptance serves to stimulate other research in this important area. For example, some child development researchers have found evidence they believe invalidates Kohlberg's premise that moral development depends on the ability to think and reason. More on this may be found in *For Discussion.*

> Today we've got this view that people are only human when they act like utter fools. What's human is what's highest in us. It's not what's lowest or what's weakest.
>
> *John Maher*

## Table 3–7 Kohlberg's Theory of Moral Development

| Level | Stage | Basis for Moral Judgement | Example |
|-------|-------|---------------------------|---------|
| I | 1 | Desire to avoid punishment | "If I smoke pot and get caught, I'll be in big trouble." |
| | 2 | Expectation of reward | "If I smoke pot, I'll have more friends." |
| II | 3 | "Good-boy" orientation | "I'm a good student and an athlete, and people like me don't break laws." |
| | 4 | Respect for law, authority | "I don't really see anything wrong with it; but it is against the law, and where would we be if everyone just ignored laws?" |
| III | 5 | Weighing personal needs with situation | "The laws are quite clear about smoking pot, but it helps me relax, and no one is going to get upset about the occasional smoke." |
| | 6 | Personal moral principles | "I know everybody does it; but it is wrong, and if my friends don't like my decision that's just too bad." |

## FOR DISCUSSION:

## Is Moral Behavior Thinking or Feeling?

*Honesty, justice, fairness, mercy, kindness, concern for the feelings of others*—these are the words and phrases most of us would come up with if asked to define moral behavior. Most of the theories about how people come to behave in these ways assume that they must be learned. The basic assumption is that moral behavior is based on understanding the concepts of right and wrong and applying this knowledge to decisions about behavior.

Understanding and using principles of right and wrong seem to require fairly sophisticated reasoning, reasoning that is beyond most young children. Therefore, most theories of moral development are tied to cognitive development. As we learn to think in more complex ways, this argument goes, we are able to grasp more complex ideas about moral behavior. Some of these ideas must wait until adolescence, because certain kinds of reasoning abilities do not appear until then.

This view has been accepted for some time. Developmental psychologists have been studying the behavior of young children in some new ways,

however, and some now believe that these children can, in fact, make moral judgments. Says Radke-Yarrow, one of these researchers,

In the early years of childhood we see expressions of empathy and sympathy and also serious attempts to help, share, protect, and comfort. If that's not moral behavior, then I guess I'm in the wrong field of study (Alper, 1985, p. 74).

The psychologist who made that statement, along with others working in this same line of research, believe that moral development does not start with understanding what moral behavior is, but with the emotion of empathy. Furthermore, they believe that **empathy,** the ability to feel what others are feeling, is an *innate* emotion. To support this belief, they offer a variety of observations, including many examples of situations in which infants become distressed when they seem to sense distress in others.

The suggestion that any form of human behavior is instinctive is always highly controversial, and the theory

that moral behavior rests on an instinct is not going to be an exception. This isn't a bad thing for our knowledge of human behavior, because controversy stimulates investigation. This one may generate especially hot debates, because the idea itself is so appealing.

It is . . . attractive to speculate that an innate behavior, empathy, is central to behavior so crucial to human civilization—subjugating one's own needs, interests, and desires to those of society . . . Alper (1985, p. 76).

What is your opinion? Can you remember any of your earliest experiences of moral behavior on your own part or that of others? Have you observed any examples of such behavior in your children, younger brothers and sisters, or the children of others? If the basis for moral behavior is actually innate rather than learned, how would you explain the large number of people who apparently fail to develop to any level of moral maturity (people who are dishonest, unfair, cruel, have no concern for others, etc.)?

## Values

We couldn't have a discussion of moral development without a discussion of values. **Values** are those aspects of life and living that are important to us personally. Values are individual, but most of us have certain ones in common—although we may differ considerably in the priorities we place on them. You may find it interesting in this regard to compare yourself with a sample of adults in the state of Washington who responded to one survey about value priorities by filling in the form in *Test Yourself.* But whatever your particular values and the priorities you give them, your values are useful to you in many ways (Rokeach, 1973).

## TEST YOURSELF
## Your Value Priorities

A few years ago three sociologists designed a television program called *The Great American Values Test* in order to conduct an experiment into the influence of television on values. To take their test, place a number to the left of each value that describes its importance to you (1 = most important; 18 = least important). The actual ranks of a preselected sample are listed at the bottom.

| Rank | Value | Rank | Value |
|---|---|---|---|
| ____ | Beautiful world | ____ | National security |
| ____ | Comfortable life | ____ | Pleasure |
| ____ | Equality | ____ | Recognition from others |
| ____ | Exciting life | ____ | Salvation |
| ____ | Family security | ____ | Self-respect |
| ____ | Freedom | ____ | Sense of accomplishment |
| ____ | Happiness | ____ | True friendship |
| ____ | Inner harmony | ____ | Wisdom |
| ____ | Mature love | ____ | World peace |

**Note:** List of values and ranking from "The Great American Values Test: Can Television Alter Basic Beliefs?" by S. J. Ball-Rokeach, M. Rokeach, and J. W. Grube, 1984, *Psychology Today, 18,* 34–41. (Ranking by sample, top to bottom, left and then right columns: 15, 8, 12, 17, 1, 3, 5, 11, 14, 13, 16, 18, 10, 4, 7, 9, 6, 2)

- *Values serve as goals and guidelines for action.* If you value accomplishment and success, you probably will be a career-oriented self-starter and a hard worker who seeks a job with challenge and opportunity for growth and advancement. If you place a higher value on leisure time and social activities with your friends, you are more likely to seek jobs that will give you enough money to meet your basic needs without requiring too much involvement.

- *Values help you to make some tough decisions.* Values are another tool to help you through moral dilemmas. If you give a high priority to the value of honesty, you don't have to agonize over what to do with the wallet containing $150 in cash that you found while jogging. You call the owner if there is identification and turn the wallet—with the cash—over to the police if there isn't. Similarly, a high value placed on health and physical fitness may make it easier to decide not to give in to peer pressure to smoke cigarettes.

■ *Values are part of what define you as an individual.* Values are not personality traits, as psychologists use that term, but they are used in much the same way when we describe ourselves or other people describe us. Power-mad, money-grubbing, liberal, family man, and daredevil are a few examples of adjectives derived from value priorities. Using your own values and priorities as a standard, what terms would you use to describe yourself?

## Changes in Values

Your values are learned, and anything that is learned can be changed or modified. It is not at all uncommon for people to become dissatisfied with the results of adhering to one set of values. When this happens, they often find themselves temporarily disoriented while they search for meaningful new ones. This seems to happen quite often in the middle years of life, and the pattern has added its own term to our vocabulary—*middle-aged crazy.*

Of course, it isn't only people in their 40s who become disenchanted with values. In the 1960s a substantial part of an entire age group (late teens to early 20s) seemed to suffer a value crisis at the same time. In this case, it was not their own values they were rejecting but those they believed typified a flawed society.

Questioning values, other people's or your own, or even being unsure as to exactly what your own values are, is entirely normal. People in their late teens and mid-40s seem to be especially vulnerable, but such questioning or uncertainty can happen at any age. There also are certain life events, such as going away to college, taking a first big job, and having children that tend to stimulate an examination of values. Finally, the mere fact of moving through the life-span stages can produce shifts in values, or at least in priorities. It may help you to see this in your own life if you go back to *Test Yourself* and do the exercise again using your memory of your value priorities at a significant earlier time in your life (e.g., when you were still in high school, before you had children, before you embarked upon your chosen career).

**Summing Up** ■

Right and wrong are concepts that are determined partially by society and partially by individual values. The ability to use a broad set of moral principles to distinguish between right and wrong develops over time, and some people never reach this stage of moral development. (In extreme cases, we call such individuals *antisocial personalities.*)

Values are personally important standards that serve as goals, guidelines to action, standards for decisions, and expressions of your individuality. Most people have certain values in common with other people, but there can be substantial differences, both in values and in priorities. In addition, values may change or shift in priority at any stage of life.

## ■ KEY WORDS AND PHRASES

classical conditioning

cognitive development

conditioned response

conditioned stimulus

continuous reinforcement

discrimination learning

emotions

emotional maturity

empathy

extinction of behavior

generalization learning

Greenspan theory of emotional development

intermittent reinforcement

Kohlberg's theory of moral development

law of effect

learning

moral

moral dilemma

negative reinforcement

operant conditioning

Piaget's theory of cognitive development

positive reinforcement

punishers

punishment

reinforcers

social learning

unconditioned response

unconditioned stimulus

values

## ■ READ ON

*Emotion in the Human Face* by P. Ekman. New York: Cambridge University Press, 1982. An interesting discussion of how we use facial expressions to express emotions and how we "read" the emotions of others.

*The Brain* by R. M. D. Restak. New York: Bantam Books, 1984. A little book that is full of facts about this organ, which weighs less than three pounds and can store more information than all of the libraries in the world combined.

*Beyond Freedom and Dignity* by B. F. Skinner. New York: Knopf, 1971. A classic (and controversial) work from the leading spokesperson for the operant conditioning view of human development and behavior. Here Skinner turns his attention to making the world a better place by applying the principles of operant conditioning. It is fascinating reading that should stimulate your thinking about your own values even if, like many, you don't agree with Skinner.

## ■ REFERENCES

Alper, J. (1988). The roots of morality. *Science '85, 3;* 70–76.

Bandura, A. (1971). *Psychological modeling: Conflicting theories.* New York: Lieber-Atherton.

Bandura, A. (1977). *Social learning theory.* Englewood Cliffs, NJ: Prentice-Hall.

Dutton, D. B., & Aron, A. P. (1974). Some evidence for heightened sexual attraction under conditions of high anxiety. *Journal of Personality and Social Psychology, 30,* 510–517.

Greenspan, S., & Greenspan, N. T. (1986). *First feelings.* New York: Viking Press.

Herbert, F. (1984). How to win the battle between good and evil. *Family Weekly,* p. 9.

Kohlberg, L. (1969). *Stages in the development of moral thought and action.* New York: Holt, Rinehart, & Winston.

Levine, C., Kohlberg, L., & Hewer, A. (1985). The current formulation of Kohlberg's theory and a response to critics. *Human Development, 28,* 94–100.

Piaget, J. (1952). *The origins of intelligence in children* (2nd ed.). New York: International University Press.

Rogers, C. R. (1966). A theory of therapy, personality, and interpersonal relationships as developed in the client-centered framework. In S. Koch (Ed.), *Psychology: A study of a science,* Vol. 3. New York: McGraw Hill.

Rokeach, M. (1973). *The nature of human values.* New York: Free Press.

Schachter, S., & Singer, J. E. (1962). Cognitive, social, and physiological determinants of emotional states. *Psychological Review, 7,* 463–478.

Schaie, K. W. (1984). Midlife influences upon intellectual functioning in old age. *International Journal of Behavioral Development, 7,* 463–478.

Smith, C. A., & Ellsworth, P. C. (1984). Patterns of cognitive appraisal in emotion. *Journal of Personality and Social Psychology, 48,* 813–838.

Stein, J. (Ed.). (1982). *The Random House college dictionary* (rev. ed.). New York: Random House.

Thorndike, E. L. (1905). *The elements of psychology.* New York: Siler.

# Personality: You as Others See You

Pat is one of the most popular students in your class. Talkative and outgoing, she always has a smile, a wisecrack, or a cheery "How's it going?" for everyone. Pat is an average student, although the professor believes she could do better if she wanted to. She asks good questions in class and speaks up clearly and confidently when asked a question herself.

By contrast with Pat, Lee seems very withdrawn from things. He sits in the back of the room and does not speak unless someone speaks to him first; then he replies in a low voice while looking down at the desk and toying with his pen. Lee does well on tests but seems uncomfortable in discussions. During class breaks he is to be found sitting at his desk reading rather than socializing with others.

You probably would describe the differences between Pat and Lee as differences in personality. Pat is outgoing; Lee is shy. Have you ever wondered how people who seem to have so much in common could be so different? Lee and Pat are the same age, they come from very similar backgrounds, and they go to the same school. Why do the Pats walk in and take over the spotlight so effortlessly, whereas the Lees seem to wish they were invisible?

No matter how much they may have in common with others, Pat and Lee, like you, are unique. The distinctive face presented to the world, which people call personality, reflects these differences. *Personality psychology* is an area of study in psychology devoted to describing, measuring, and discovering the sources and meaning of differences in personality.

In this chapter the concept of personality is examined in some detail. We'll consider several theories about the process that leads you to be such a distinctive person in the eyes of others, even if, like Pat and Lee, you seem to have much in common with them.

79

## WHAT IS PERSONALITY?

One leading personality psychologist has noted that there may be as many definitions of the term *personality* as there are people studying it and writing about it (Mischel, 1981). He pointed out, however, that there is a common theme running through all of these definitions:

> 'Personality' . . . refers to the distinctive patterns of behavior (including thoughts and emotions) that characterize each individual's adaptations to the situations of his or her life (1981, p. 2).

In more everyday language, personality is the way we describe a person, what he or she is "like." We may use different words among ourselves to make this description, but most of us would be in general agreement about the meaning of these words. Whether Pat is described as extraverted, bubbly, outgoing, or social, we all will get about the same idea of her.

Personality psychologists would want to go beyond such descriptions. We all can see that Pat and Lee behave differently in the classroom, but how did these different patterns of behavior develop? What do they mean? Do they extend to situations other than the classroom? Have Pat and Lee always been different in this way? Will they continue to be such opposites?

There are many theoretical approaches to answering questions like these. This can be frustrating when you are trying to learn more about yourself. It seems that there should be a truth somewhere about the nature of people; but if there is, psychologists have yet to discover or agree upon it. One psychologist describes the problem as follows:

> No theory . . . can both comprehensively and empirically account for the wholeness, for the uniqueness, and for the universality of human propensities, foibles, drives, abilities, desires. The person represented in a scientifically testable way is not the real person demanded by common sense (Monte, 1980, p. 18).

What Monte is saying is that the scientific study of personality is not quite up to the complex nature of its subject matter. Nevertheless, theories of personality are very useful. They have served as guides for research, psychological therapy, and self-understanding for psychologists and others for a long time.

In this chapter, three of the major approaches to the study of personality are reviewed: trait theories, the psychodynamic approach, and behavior theories. A fourth approach, humanistic personality theory, is discussed in the next chapter. This division reflects only the close ties between some of the central ideas of humanistic approaches to personality and self-concept, the subject of Chapter 5. It does not imply anything about the relative importance of humanistic personality theory in the field.

The world *personality* serves us as a shorthand description of the way other people appear to us.

## TRAIT THEORIES OF PERSONALITY

Earlier, we described Pat as outgoing and Lee as withdrawn. A psychologist probably would use the terms *extraversion* and *introversion* to describe the same patterns of behavior. Lee, the introvert, is quiet and studious. Pat, the extravert, is easygoing and prefers the company of others to her own. She is bright but makes little effort to excel intellectually.

Swiss psychiatrist Carl Jung believed that introversion and extraversion are fundamental personality traits and that all people are basically either introverts or extraverts (Fordham, 1953). A different position was taken by American psychologist Gordon Allport (1961), who believed that your personality is described more accurately in terms of whatever different traits are most characteristic of *you,* not in terms of how much or how little of some predetermined trait you have.

According to Allport, your personality traits predispose you to respond to situations in certain ways, but not all traits are equal in terms of their influence on your behavior. *Cardinal traits* are so general that almost every act of an individual seems to stem from them; so-called religious fanatics often illustrate such a trait. Allport believed that such pervasive traits are very rare and are not to be seen in many people.

*Central traits* are less overwhelming, but still quite general, and often are called into play in guiding behavior. For example, we might say that *sociability* is one of your central traits if you approach most new situations as an opportunity to talk to and get to know others.

Central traits are highly characteristic of an individual, and Allport believed that the number of such traits it would take to describe a person accurately is very small, maybe even as few as five. Less important—both to an accurate description of a person and to the influence they have on behavior—are the *secondary traits* which predispose you to behave in very particular ways in very particular situations that may arise very infrequently.

Allport placed great emphasis on the individuality of personality. Since no two people are exactly alike, it follows that no two people can be described in exactly the same terms. Psychologists and others use a wide variety of words to help them with this description; some years ago it was estimated that there were at least 5,000 English words that could be used to describe traits of personality (Allport & Odbert, 1936).

Charm is a way of getting the answer yes without having asked any clear question.
*Albert Camus*

## The Meaning and Measurement of Traits

Formal trait theories of personality, like that of Allport, begin with the assumption that **personality traits** are predispositions to behave in certain ways. Trait theorists further assume that traits can be measured with appropriate tests and that different people have different "amounts" of any particular trait. In other words, every personality trait is a *dimension* of personality. If you give many people a test for the trait, you will find their scores make up a continuum, not a dichotomy of have/have not.

Assume, for example, that you gave a very large number of people a test for friendliness. Some would get very high scores (extremely friendly), some very low scores (not at all friendly), and most would lie somewhere in the middle on this dimension. Most contemporary views of trait psychology are consistent with this picture. All of us have some amount of many traits, although we will have so little of some that they would not be used to describe our personalities.

There are many tests intended to measure the degree to which a particular person possesses one or more personality traits. Some of the more well known of these are described briefly in Exhibit 4–1. These tests should be given only by a psychologist or other trained professional who can help you understand the results. If you are interested in taking one or more of them, see your professor or your college counseling service for more information.

One personality trait that many psychologists believe is important in explaining differences in behavior between people is called locus of control (Rotter, 1966). **Locus of control** is a term used to describe an individual's basic belief about where control over his or her life is located. People who believe that what happens to them is primarily a matter of what they themselves do are said to have more of an *internal locus of control*. Those who believe that what happens to them is largely due to chance factors beyond their control are said to have more of an *external locus of control*. You can get an idea of where you fall on this continuum by answering the questions in *Test Yourself*.

Rotter's "I-E" (for internalizer-externalizer) scale, as it often is called, is used primarily in research, rather than in counseling (which is why you can

## TEST YOURSELF
## Are You an Internalizer or an Externalizer?

*Directions:* For each of the following pairs of statements, place a check mark by the one statement with which you most agree. The statements that indicate a greater internal locus of control are listed in *Summing Up* at the end of this section. The more of these statements you agreed with, the more you lean toward the internalizer end of the scale.

1. a____ Many of the unhappy things in people's lives are partly due to bad luck.
   b____ People's misfortunes result from the mistakes they make.
2. a____ One of the major reasons why we have wars is because people don't take enough interest in politics.
   b____ There will always be wars, no matter how hard people try to prevent them.
3. a____ In the long run people get the respect they deserve in this world.
   b____ Unfortunately, an individual's worth often passes unrecognized no matter how hard he [she] tries.
4. a____ Without the right breaks one cannot be an effective leader.
   b____ Capable people who fail to become leaders have not taken advantage of their opportunities.
5. a____ No matter how hard you try some people just don't like you.
   b____ People who can't get others to like them don't understand how to get along with others.
6. a____ I have often found that what is going to happen will happen.
   b____ Trusting to fate has never turned out as well for me as making a decision to take a definite course of action.
7. a____ Becoming a success is a matter of hard work; luck has little or nothing to do with it.
   b____ Getting a good job depends mainly on being in the right place at the right time.
8. a____ The average citizen can have an influence in government decisions.
   b____ This world is run by the few people in power, and there is not much the little person can do about it.
9. a____ When I make plans, I am almost certain that I can make them work.
   b____ It is not always wise to plan too far ahead because many things turn out to be a matter of good or bad fortune anyhow.
10. a____ In my case getting what I want has little or nothing to do with luck.
    b____ Many times we might just as well decide what to do by flipping a coin.

11. a_____ Who gets to be the boss often depends on who was lucky enough to be in the right place first.

   b_____ Getting people to do the right thing depends upon ability; luck has little or nothing to do with it.

12. a_____ As far as world affairs are concerned, most of us are the victims of forces we can neither understand, nor control.

   b_____ By taking an active part in political and social affairs the people can control world events.

13. a_____ Most people don't realize the extent to which their lives are controlled by accidental happenings.

   b_____ There really is no such thing as "luck."

14. a_____ It is hard to know whether or not a person really likes you.

   b_____ How many friends you have depends upon how nice a person you are.

15. a_____ In the long run the bad things that happen to us are balanced by the good ones.

   b_____ Most misfortunes are the result of lack of ability, ignorance, laziness, or all three.

16. a_____ With enough effort we can wipe out political corruption.

   b_____ It is difficult for people to have much control over the things politicians do in office.

17. a_____ Many times I feel that I have little influence over the things that happen to me.

   b_____ It is impossible for me to believe that chance or luck plays an important role in my life.

18. a_____ People are lonely because they don't try to be friendly.

   b_____ There's not much use in trying too hard to please people; if they like you, they like you.

19. a_____ What happens to me is my own doing.

   b_____ Sometimes I feel that I don't have enough control over the direction my life is taking.

20. a_____ Most of the time I can't understand why politicians behave the way they do.

   b_____ In the long run the people are responsible for bad government on a national as well as on a local level.

---

take it here on your own). If your professor is willing, your class might want to let him or her collect everyone's scores and arrange them on a continuum so that you can see how your own orientation compares with this group. When this process is carried out formally by those who construct a test, the results are called *test norms*. These norms, like social norms, serve as reference points for typical behavior. In psychological testing, the behavior is a score on a particular test, and test norms are used to help people understand where their scores fall relative to other people who take the test.

## Traits and Behavior

Personality tests are used for research purposes, for clinical diagnosis, for executive personnel selection, and for vocational guidance. All of these uses are based on the assumption that there is some relationship between traits and behavior. It also is assumed that traits are consistent; the related behavior, therefore, should be relatively consistent.

Is it true that measured personality traits are stable? Reviews of the research evidence tend to support this assumption (e.g., Peele, 1984). In one long-term study, for example, measures of certain traits remained quite similar over the course of 45 years (Conley, 1984).

What about the relationship between personality traits and behavior? Here, too, there is evidence that such relationships exist. For example, scores on the I-E scale (see *Test Yourself*) have been found to be related to a number of behaviors. *Internalizers* (people who score more toward the internalizer end of the scale) tend to show greater academic achievement than *externalizers* (Findley & Cooper, 1983), to take one example. Internalizers also have been found to prefer to study in quiet, isolated areas of the school library, whereas externalizers seek out locations full of people and noise (Campbell & Hawley, 1982).

## EXHIBIT 4–1
## A Sample of Personality Tests

### The Minnesota Multiphasic Personality Inventory
A 550-item true-false, paper-and-pencil test measuring 10 factors, among which are *hypochondriasis* (preoccupation with bodily processes and fear of disease); *depression, hysteria* (tendency to have symptoms without any medical cause), *masculinity–femininity, paranoia* (systematic delusions), *hypomania* (mild form of manic reaction), and *social introversion* (shy, withdrawn, inhibited behavior). This test has been around for many years, has an extensive literature of related research, and is widely used in clinical practice. It takes about 90 minutes. (Published by the University of Minnesota Press)

### Myers-Briggs Type Indicator
A 126- to 166-item (depending on the form given) paper-and-pencil test of four typologies of personality: *introversion/extraversion, sensing/intuition, thinking/feeling,* and *judging/perceptive.* This test is based on psychodynamic theorist Carl Jung's theory of personality types. It takes about 25 minutes. (Published by Consulting Psychologists Press, Inc.)

### Sixteen Personality Factor Questionnaire
A 105- to 187-item (depending on the form given) paper-and-pencil test of 16 primary personality traits, including *level of assertiveness, warmth, sensitivity, emotional maturity,* and *impulsivity.* This test is used in a wide variety of settings, including business and industry, school counseling centers, and diagnostic and/or therapeutic settings. It takes about 45 minutes. (Published by Institute for Personality and Ability Testing, Inc.)

### California Psychological Inventory
A 480-item paper-and-pencil test of 18 personality factors, including *sociability, social presence, self-acceptance, sense of well-being, responsibility, socialization, self-control, tolerance, good impression, intellectual efficiency, flexibility,* and *femininity.* This test emphasizes social interaction behavior skills. It takes about an hour. (Published by Consulting Psychologists Press, Inc.)

### Edwards Personal Preference Schedule
A paper-and-pencil forced-choice test of the relative importance to a person of 15 personality factors, including *achievement, order, autonomy, affiliation, dominance, heterosexuality,* and *aggression.* This test has been widely used for some time for personal counseling and personality research. It takes about 45 minutes. (Published by The Psychological Corporation)

# Where Do Traits Come From?

The heart of the approach to personality that we are examining is that traits are the fundamental units of personality. Where do these traits come from? How does a person come to be introverted, extraverted, friendly, aloof, reliable, or persistent? Is he or she born that way?

Most trait theorists believe along with Allport that traits are developed over time in conjunction with certain basic inherited biological attributes. Let's suppose, for example, that you are known for your happy disposition. You were not born this way, but you *were* born with particular biological functioning patterns that affected your early behavior. If your particular patterns resulted in your being an alert baby who cried infrequently and was responsive to those around you, you probably got quite a lot of positive attention.

One result of this positive attention was that you came to see the world around you as a source of pleasure, and you expressed this pleasure, as babies do, by smiling, gurgling, and wriggling around. This made the people around you happy, and they responded to you in kind. If this benign circle continued, you were well on your way to your happy disposition.

Not all babies have such a smooth infancy. Some have "colic," cry frequently, and have difficulty eating and sleeping on a regular schedule. As a

Most psychologists believe that your very earliest behavior and the way others react to it has an important influence on the development of your personality.

result, they are a source of worry and uncertainty, and some parents will respond with impatience, irritation, and perhaps, with less physical affection. In a circular fashion similar to the pattern just described, some of these infants may become fretful, anxious, or insecure children.

The process described is oversimplified, but not inaccurate. Your personality, according to trait theorists, developed over time as you interacted with your environment. You will remember that most psychologists believe that your cognitive, and perhaps your emotional and moral, characteristics develop in this way. Since all of these developmental processes (including personality development) were occurring simultaneously, they also were influencing (and being influenced by) one another.

## Personality Traits and Personality Types

The idea that your personality traits are based partially on your physical/biological nature is a very old one. Hippocrates, an ancient Greek physician, believed that this nature was the primary determinant of personality. He postulated that people are born with a basic *temperament* that is determined by the balance of certain bodily substances and that all people could be classified as one of four *personality types* on this basis.

According to Hippocrates's system, the *choleric* personality, believed to have too much "yellow bile" in the body, is characterized by irritability. The depressed *melancholic* has too much "black bile," and the optimistic *sanguine* type, too much blood. Finally, Hippocrates believed that the calm, listless *phlegmatic* personality suffered from an excess of bodily phlegm.

Hippocrates's personality typology is of only historical interest to most people, but personality typologies are still very much with us. A **personality typology** is a system for dividing people into a few categories on the basis of some dominant personality trait. Most of the modern typologies have only two categories, rather than Hippocrates's four.

One of the first of the modern personality typologies is Jung's introversion-extraversion distinction. Although Jung himself emphasized that there are degrees of these traits, in practice the tendency is to label people as one or the other and to assume that this label is critical to understanding their behavior. There is more on this assumption and on one of the newest personality typologies in *For Discussion*.

The idea that people fall into one of two personality categories is an appealing one to many people. You can see why. The labels are convenient. In addition, it is much easier to explain differences in the behavior of two people on the basis of a simple category system (e.g., one is an optimist and one is a pessimist) than to have to go through the long person/environment interaction explanation that characterizes the scientific study of behavior.

The two-category personality typology is so popular that it has turned into something of a free-for-all. In addition to introversion/extraversion, optimist/pessimist, Type A/Type B, we have idea people/feeling people, people people/thing people, idealists/realists, and a host of others. To end this discussion on a light note, here is psychologist Paul Chance's ultimate personality typology:

> I've come up with my own theory. I propose that there are two kinds of people in the world: those who believe there are two kinds of people in the world and those who don't (1988, p. 19).

## FOR DISCUSSION:

## PERSONALITY TYPOLOGIES AND LABELING

Yes   No

_____   _____   Are you always trying to fit more activities into your life?
_____   _____   Do you seek out opportunities to compete with others?
_____   _____   Do you tend to talk, eat, and move rapidly?
_____   _____   Do you get upset when you have to wait for service?
_____   _____   Do you often ask people to "get to the point" in conversation?
_____   _____   Does it seem you never have enough time to do what you want to do?
_____   _____   Are you often upset by the way other people on the road drive?
_____   _____   Do you have nervous habits, such as drumming your fingers?

These questions are typical of those used to measure what is being called **Type A behavior.** The more yes answers you give, the more hurried, driving, and compulsive your behavior, and this behavior, according to a team of medical researchers, is a pattern characteristic of the lives of many patients before they suffer coronaries (Rosenman, et al., 1966). The late former president Lyndon Johnson has been described as an extreme "Type A individual." By contrast, Ronald Reagan is said to exhibit classic **Type B behavior,** showing a sense of perspective about his life and his work and a clear notion of what is and what isn't worth getting upset about.

The Type A–Type B distinction has interested many researchers. As suggested by the preceding questions, they find the Type A person to be obsessed with time, less tolerant of the behavior of others, and more responsive to challenge than the Type B person. These characteristics appear to make them more vulnerable not only to coronary attacks but also to physical illness in general (Woods & Burns, 1984). There is also some evidence that Type A's are more physically aggressive toward others (Strube, et al., 1984).

Interest in the Type A–Type B distinction is widespread and not limited

to psychologists and doctors. A recent cartoon shows a woman asking the man ahead of her in the grocery check-out line, "Do you mind if I go ahead of you? I'm a Type A." And there is at least one computer dating service using this typology as a basis for potential matches between its male and female clients.

This labeling aspect of personality typologies disturbs some people. They point out that very few of us are pure introverts or extraverts or optimists or pessimists or any of the other popular distinctions, including Type A–Type B. You probably found this out for yourself if you answered the preceding questions; some of the characteristics described you and some didn't. You also may have found it difficult to give one answer; circumstances alter cases, and most so-called Type B's exhibit Type A behaviors upon occasion.

Those opposed to personality typologies believe that no useful purpose is served by encouraging people to label themselves in this way. For one thing, there seems to be one type in every typology that is viewed by most people as positive (e.g., extravert, Type B) and one that is viewed as negative (e.g., introvert, Type A). So strong are these values that the words for the negative types have come to be common verbal insults in arguments

between people—"You're always such a pessimist!" or "Well, at least I'm not a pathetic introvert like some people I know!"

The values attached to personality typologies mean that labeling someone with the negative type can damage self-esteem. Labeling also works against understanding behavior because it can serve as a substitute for efforts to understand: for example, "He's doing poorly at work because he's a Type B. You know how lazy they are." In the same vein, it can produce a feeling of helplessness in individuals who might want to change some aspect of their behavior. Personality labels have a "well, that's just the way I am" determinism about them that does not encourage efforts to be different.

What do you think about this issue? How many examples of personality-type labeling can you find in conversation, the funny papers, or on television in the space of one day or one week? Do you find yourself tending to label others with personality-type labels? Do you think this affects the way you treat these people? How do you feel about having others stick such labels on you? Does this affect the way you see yourself? Do you have an example you can share with the class?

## Summing Up ■

The trait approach to understanding personality is based on the idea that your personality is made up of patterns of traits, which are relatively stable and which serve as guidelines for behavior. Psychologists have some evidence for these assumptions, but there also are many inconsistencies in human behavior. You've seen the honest person who lies to avoid hurting someone's feelings and the timid, docile person who becomes aggressive when pushed too far.

Situations cause people to behave "out of character," but trait theorists do not argue with this. They stress *relative consistency* and *most likely* behavior, terms that are difficult to define scientifically but do allow for the influence of the environment (situation) on behavior. The trait approach to the study of personality has been around a long time, and it is still an active area of research. (By the way, the internalizer answers from *Test Yourself* are as follows: *b, b, a, b, b, b, a, a, a, a, b, b, b, b, b, a, b, a, a, b.*)

This approach has a strong appeal for the nonscientist as well; when we describe personality, most of us do so in traits. This, according to some other personality theorists, is the major problem with trait theories. They argue that such theories *describe* personality without explaining it (Pervin, 1985). A very different approach is seen when the focus is shifted to psychodynamic theories of personality.

## PSYCHODYNAMIC THEORIES OF PERSONALITY

From a trait theory perspective, your personality is made up of traits that develop over time and serve to organize your behavior in a relatively consistent fashion. Psychodynamic theories of personality, the first and most famous of which was proposed by Sigmund Freud, focus on postulated internal psychological forces rather than on traits.

Freud was a physician working in Vienna, Austria, at the turn of the 20th century. His personal psychological writings fill 24 volumes, and his many followers (including his daughter Anna) have filled many more as they have modified and expanded his theory. Here, we must settle for a brief overview of Freud's basic ideas, which have remained a major influence on personality theory and research and on the practice of psychotherapy.

I was born modest; not all over, but in spots.

*Mark Twain*

## Personality According to Freud

Freud viewed personality as being a set of psychological forces that he called the id, the ego, and the superego. The **id** is the core and includes everything of a psychological nature that is present at birth. Here lie all of the inherited human instincts (of which sex and aggression are the most important) that Freud believed provided the energy for the entire personality system. The id is in close contact with bodily processes and finds any tension (e.g., hunger) in this system intolerable. Because avoiding pain and achieving pleasure (by reducing tension) are vital to the id, it is said to operate on the *pleasure principle*. It is characterized by a seeking after immediate gratification of desires.

Of course, none of us can have everything we need to keep tension at a low level by having all of our desires fulfilled immediately; reality just isn't like that. The **ego** is the part of the personality system that responds to this constraint. By suspending the pleasure principle until an appropriate means to satisfy a need has been found, the ego operates on the *reality principle.* This temporary overriding of the pleasure principle has been described as keeping a "lid on the id."

The third component of personality, and the last to develop, is the **superego**—the moral aspect of personality. It judges right and wrong on the basis of ideals and standards taken in (internalized) from society in general and parents in particular. Things believed to be wrong are taken into the conscience (one part of the superego), whereas things believed to be right become part of the ego-ideal (the other part of the superego). *Perfection* is the basic operating principle of the superego.

In a very broad sense, you might think of the id as the biological component of personality, the ego as the psychological component, and the superego as the social component (Hall & Lindzey, 1978). The following "conversation" may help to clarify the nature of the relationship between these three psychological forces.

> ID: *Boy, I think I'll have a big slice of that cake my wife bought at the bakery.* (instinct for immediate gratification)
>
> EGO: *You can't do that; you're on a diet, remember?* (reality)
>
> SUPEREGO: *Anyway, your wife asked you to leave the cake alone; it's for your father's birthday dinner tonight.* (conscience)
>
> ID: *I don't care! I'm hungry. I have to do something.*
>
> EGO: *Well, why don't you take a walk around the block? You sure could use the exercise!*
>
> SUPEREGO: *Yes, and you did promise your doctor that you'd exercise every other day. You know you're too fat.* (ego-ideal)

Of course, the id, ego, and superego aren't real and they don't talk to one another, but Freud did believe that they worked together as a team, as our imaginary conversation suggests. In this little scenario the tension created by the id's desire for immediate gratification of hunger was reduced by the ego's discovering an acceptable way to reduce the tension (walking) that was approved by the superego.

In Freud's terms, the tension that was created by hunger was displaced. **Displacement** refers to the reduction of tension through a means other than the original choice (in this case, walking for eating). Freud believed that substitute means for reducing tension are rarely as satisfying as the original choice would have been, so displacement leaves a residue of undischarged tension. Over time, displacement of many urges builds up a reservoir of undischarged tension (energy) that is a permanent motivating force for behavior. Freud believed that this was the basic mechanism accounting for the rich variability of human behavior.

## Behavior Versus Personality

A critical and unique feature of the psychodynamic personality theory of Freud is that he believed personality development is complete by age 5 or 6. Behavior seen beyond those ages reflects this development, however it may have progressed. Your observable traits and behavior patterns as an adult are merely manifestations of unconscious dynamics in your personality that have existed since you were a child.

Being entirely honest with oneself is a good exercise.

*Sigmund Freud*

The significance of this important distinction may be clarified by considering a person who consistently behaves in a passive, easy-to-please way. A trait theorist would take this to mean that passivity was one of this individual's basic personality traits. Not so the psychodynamic theorist. From a psychodynamic viewpoint, consistent passive behavior may be a socially acceptable cover-up for underlying aggression or anger rather than true passivity. In other words, this behavior pattern may mean simply that the ego/superego team is winning the struggle with the id's instinctive aggressiveness, at least for the time being.

As a result of this position, theorists who take the psychodynamic view of personality put little faith in the face you present to the world, and they are not interested in measuring personality traits. They believe that your real personality must be uncovered through methods that probe the unconscious, where the important dynamics are at work. One such method is called a projective test.

A *projective test* consists of ambiguous pictures or other visual stimuli onto which a person *projects* his or her hidden motives and conflicts. It takes many years of training to learn to use and interpret projective tests, but you can get an idea of how this method works by looking carefully at the "pictures" in Figure 4–1. What would you reply if you were asked to say what one represents? Is it a leaf? A butterfly? A heart? An uncut gemstone? A picture of a brain? Something else? Those who use projective tests believe that clues to the real you are revealed by the answer you give. It is through tests such as this and other indirect methods, such as the analysis of your dreams, that your real personality is uncovered.

You also give clues to your pesonality through certain kinds of behavior mistakes, such as the famous Freudian slip. An example is provided by a middle-aged man whose wife had left him for someone much younger. Now remarried himself, the man found himself repeatedly "slipping up" and saying to relatives, friends, and acquaintances; "I'd like to introduce you to my first wife."

**Figure 4.1   Ambiguous stimuli similar to those found on a projective test of personality.**

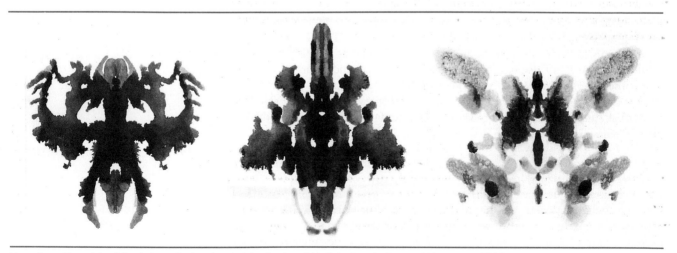

Note: From *Essentials of Psychology: Exploration and Application,* 4th ed. by Dennis Coon, 1988, West Publishing Company, p. 472.

What this man believed he wanted to say was, "I'd like to introduce you to my new wife." His slip of the tongue was embarrassing to all concerned. From a psychodynamic viewpoint, however, it wasn't a mistake at all. The man was revealing his true wish to have his first wife back, a wish that could not be expressed directly because it would hurt his second wife's feelings.

As you can see, one difficulty with Freud's theory so far as understanding your own personality is concerned is that you need the help of someone who is trained in interpreting your behavior. In sharp contrast to other views of personality, this behavior cannot be taken at face value. This leaves you in a position of having to go "into analysis" with a trained psychoanalyst if you want to understand yourself, a process that often takes years.

This reliance on people who are trained to interpret dreams, projective tests, behavior mistakes, and free association (random-thought monologues in which the patient says whatever comes to mind) remains true of psychodynamic theories of personality, although later theorists have modified Freud's ideas considerably. We will look briefly at one of these—the psychosocial theory of Erik Erikson.

## Erikson's Psychosocial View of Personality

It is far easier to describe the components of personality as Freud viewed them than it is to describe the development of a particular personality (remember those 24 volumes!). As mentioned, Freud believed this development is complete by age 6 at the latest, and you probably already are aware to some extent that he believed sexual instincts play the most important role in this development.

Erik Erikson (1963), one of the most influential of Freud's followers, agrees with Freud that biological development is the fundamental basis for personality development. He does not agree, however, with the premise that sexual urges are all-important. Erikson places much more emphasis on the role of social factors, and for this reason his approach often is called a *psychosocial* theory of personality as compared with Freud's *psychosexual* theory.

According to Erikson, people pass through eight definable stages of personality development, with new forms of behavior appearing in response to maturation and environmental (social) forces at each stage. Each stage is built on earlier ones in the same way that later cognitive development is believed to be built on earlier stages. These eight critical stages in the development of personality are described briefly in Table 4–1.

If you look carefully at the table, Erikson's sequence concept should be clear. You can see, for example, that you could not be ready to plan and pursue goals (stage 3) until you had acquired will and self-control (stage 2). If you came out of stage 2 with too much doubt about your ability to function independently, you would have too little of this autonomy to build upon. That is why Erikson called each of the stages a *crisis*. Personality development can go either way at each stage, and the outcome is critical to what happens next.

A particularly interesting aspect of Erikson's theory is his insistence that the successful resolution of the conflicts at each personality crisis requires achieving a mixture of the positive and negative aspects of the conflict. For example, you should come out of stage 1 as a basically trusting person who keeps some mistrust in reserve. You will be ill-equipped to deal with the real-

## Table 4–1 Erikson's Stages of Psychosocial Development

| Stage | Age (in Years) | Conflict to Resolve | Desired Outcome of Conflict |
|---|---|---|---|
| | | | *Infancy* |
| I | 1 | Trust vs. Mistrust | *Hope:* Belief in being about to achieve wishes and desires |
| II | 2–3 | Autonomy vs. Doubt | *Will:* Determination to have free choice as well as self-control |
| | | | *Childhood* |
| III | 4–5 | Initiative vs. Guilt | *Purpose:* Capacity to plan and courage to pursue goals |
| IV | 6–12 | Industry vs. Inferiority | *Competence:* Use of skills and intelligence to complete tasks |
| | | | *Adolescence* |
| V | 13–18 | Role Identity vs. Role Confusion | *Fidelity:* Ability to sustain loyalties and live out core identity |
| | | | *Adulthood* |
| VI | 18–35 | Intimacy vs. Isolation | *Love:* Achievement of mutual devotion |
| VII | 35–65 | Generativity vs. Stagnation | *Care:* Achievement of concern for the generation to follow, not just for self |
| VIII | 65 + | Integrity vs. Despair | *Wisdom:* Concern for life in the face of own death |

**Note:** Based on the discussion in *Childhood and Society* (2nd ed.) by E. H. Erikson, 1963, New York: W. W. Norton.

ities of the world if you are completely trusting of everyone. This same idea of balance is true for each of the other stages; in the long-run it is the *ratio* of the two aspects of each personality development conflict that is important. The ratio Erikson believed to be desirable at each stage is described in one word. For example, he called what he believed to be the desirable outcome of trust versus mistrust (stage 1), *hope.*

Erikson's ideas, as summarized in Table 4–1, offer one of the clearer examples of how theoretical ideas may be useful in a practical sense to people who are not scientists. An example of how Erikson's theory might offer parents some clear guidlines for helping children develop strong and healthy personalities is presented in Exhibit 4–2.

## The Identity Crisis

If you looked carefully at Table 4–1, you noticed that Erikson's stages of development take a lifetime. He does not accept Freud's idea that personality is totally developed in infancy and young childhood. Rather, he sees it as always developing and changing. The ages shown in the table are approximate; to Erikson, each individual marches to his or her own drummer, and it is impossible to specify an exact duration for each stage.

As he himself has aged, Erikson has become very interested in the later years of life. In his more recent writings he has emphasized the concept of a

## EXHIBIT 4–2
## Personality Theory and Parenting

To many people, there could seem little that would be of less down-to-earth day-to-day use to them in raising their children than a theory of personality. And, where some theories are concerned, they probably would be right. On the other hand, there are theories that offer some very practical guidelines, and you don't have to be a psychologist to understand or implement them. The developmental stage theory of Erik Erikson is one example.

As an example of how a psychodynamic theory of personality that is based on the work of Freud can be useful to a parent, consider stage 3 from Figure 4–2. According to Erikson, a child who is 4 or 5 years old is faced with the crisis of learning to take initiative and pursue his or her own ends. Erikson believes that the most desirable outcome of this crisis is the *"courage to envisage and pursue valued goals uninhibited by the defeat of infantile fantasies, by guilt, or by the foiling fear of punishment"* (Erikson, 1964, p. 22).

Most parents will be in favor of helping their children develop a basic sense of initiative, although many are not at all clear on how to go about it. One way, according to Erikson, is to be very careful to encourage, rather than belittle, a child's plans and goals and to praise successful accomplishment. For instance, the decision to spread out and sort by suit all 52 cards in a deck of playing cards may seem a childish waste of time to the parent. But the parent isn't doing it; the child is. To a 4-year-old it is a challenge. If he or she succeeds, the results of this activity will be a visible accomplishment of which to be proud.

Many parents faced with this situation would be inclined to fuss about the mess made by the cards or to make fun of the child for the silly way he or she chooses to spend time. The parent who wants to help the child develop initiative will compliment the organization and concentration that went into this task. Both guilt over choice of pastime and fear of punishment (for the mess) will inhibit the development of initiative. The child will feel less confident next time about striking out in a new direction and more inclined to expect the parent to guide play activities.

complete human life cycle, rather than any particular stage (Erikson, 1983). In most of his writings, however, if he emphasizes any particular stage, it is adolescence.

*Adolescence* is the time during which a person changes biologically from child to adult. The conflict at this stage is between role identity and role confusion. During adolescence, you must work through a transition period between your established role identity as "child of your parents" and one of the bewildering variety of adult roles available to you. This **identity crisis,** with its uncertainty, confusion, and anxiety, is undoubtedly the most familiar of Erikson's concepts.

Erikson believes the outcome of the identity crisis is critical because an individual's whole future depends upon its successful resolution. In former generations, it generally was true that this process would be complete (more or less) by age 18. In today's society, the identity stage of personality development appears to be getting longer and longer.

Today, increasing numbers of young people are choosing the partially or completely dependent status of student and/or are continuing to live at home well into their 20s. To date, there is no evidence that this choice has a negative effect on adjustment to life. If we take Erikson's perspective, it may be that the opposite is the case.

Acceptable roles for men and women in our society are multiplying and changing more rapidly today than at any other time in this country's history. An extended period of time during which a young person does not yet have the full responsibilities of adulthood may be a positive force in helping him or her resolve the identity crisis in the mature direction Erikson believes is critical to later development.

## Summing Up ■

There are many psychodynamic theorists other than Freud and Erikson, although Freud is the most widely known and Erikson may have the most influential theory at the current time. Like Erikson, most of those who followed Freud put more emphasis on the social environment and the ego and less upon instincts and sexual conflicts. What all of these theories have in common regarding personality, however, is the idea that it is shaped through the interaction of internal psychological forces and external events.

The psychodynamic approach to personality is fascinating to many people. Its language is colorful and its concepts mysterious. At the same time, we can recognize ourselves or people we know in some of its descriptions. Many of us know what it is to stifle an impulse at an inappropriate time. We remember going through an identity crisis or at least observing someone else's (such as a friend's or a child's). The belief that early life experiences have negative effects on life in the present also seems to be confirmed from time to time.

Despite this appeal, the psychodynamic view of personality is controversial in psychology and psychiatry. Although there is a great deal of research on its various tenets, critics say this has done little to confirm (or disconfirm) them (Mischel, 1981). The problem is that those same concepts that are so interesting to discuss and seem to fit with some of our experiences so well are impossible to define and measure in a way that meets the criteria of the scientific method.

# BEHAVIOR THEORIES OF PERSONALITY

So far, two views of personality and how it develops have been examined. To a psychodynamic theorist, your personality has developed as the result of various dynamics involving internal psychological forces and the outside world. In this view, much of what makes you tick is unconscious, and your behavior does not necessarily reflect your true personality.

To a trait theorist, your personality consists of a relatively stable set of traits that guide your behavior so that it is consistent and others know what to expect of you. These traits develop over time as the result of an interaction between you and your environment. The behavioral view of personality shares this interest in your environment and your experience with it but does not accept the concept of traits.

Behavior theories of personality focus on what you do; *your personality is your behavior.* The inner drives, conflicting forces, instincts, and basic traits of the other personality theories are left behind. If your behavior is consistent, it is because you have been rewarded consistently for behaving in certain ways, not because you have certain traits. If the rewards for a behavior stop, the behavior (and so your personality) will change.

## The A-B-C Paradigm

Those who take a behavioral view of personality examine it in terms of what you do, the conditions prevailing when you do it, and what happens as a result. These three variables are called behavior, antecedents, and consequences; since the antecedents occur first, this analysis is known as the **A-B-C paradigm.**

The *antecedents of behavior* are the conditions that prevail prior to the behavior. In ordinary terms, we could say that they are the sum total of the situation, or context, in which behavior takes place. This idea will become clearer when we look at an example of the development of a personality "trait."

The *consequences of behavior* are what happens after behavior occurs. Positive consequences of behavior make it more likely that this same behavior will occur again under similar conditions (antecedents). In this case, we say that the behavior has been reinforced. As you may remember from Chapter 3, **positive reinforcement** occurs when a desired state of affairs is brought about as a result of the behavior (e.g., you got an *A* on the test after studying harder than was your usual practice).

**Negative reinforcement** occurs when a behavior stops something undesirable or keeps it from happening in the first place (e.g., you banged on the wall, and your neighbor turned the stereo down). Like positive reinforcement, negative reinforcement makes it more likely that the behavior will occur again.

When your behavior gets you something you want, you are likely to keep doing it.

By contrast, negative consequences of behavior, which we call **punishment,** make it less likely that the behavior will be repeated.

These statements you have just read do not constitute a behavior theory of personality. In fact, it is not really accurate to refer to them as a theory; they are well-established principles of learning based on extensive research going back to Pavlov and Thorndike. These principles have been applied to a wide variety of contexts, of which the study of personality and its development is one. The *theory* part, then, comes in the speculation that personality develops in accordance with these learning principles. (For this reason, this approach sometimes is called learning theories of personality or behavior learning theories of personality.) To illustrate how this might work, let's consider a young man we'll call Chris.

## Example: Becoming a "Punctual Person"

Chris's parents place a high value on punctuality. To help develop this behavior in their children, they made certain rewards (positive outcomes) *contingent* (dependent) on punctual behavior from the time the children were quite small. If Chris and his brothers were on time for dinner, they got dessert; it they were late, they didn't. If their homework was completed by the specified time, they could watch TV; if not, no TV. Chris became so used to such rules that he hardly ever gave them a thought, much less resented them.

The pattern continued as Chris grew older. He was allowed to borrow his mother's car so long as he returned home promptly at the agreed-upon time, and the same conditions held for going out with his friends or dating. Chris's punctuality was rewarded by others as well. The supervisor at his after-school job gave him raise after raise. The work was so easy that almost anyone could do it, but Chris stood out among the other employees because he could be counted on to show up—and on time.

Chris's punctuality was reinforced in a more general way by his environment, as well. Leaving home in plenty of time for the movie meant that he was admitted to the showing he wanted. Getting to basketball games on time meant that he got to sit in his favorite section. Being on time was rewarded just about every time Chris tried it out. As a result, the stimuli for this behavior *generalized* to more and more situations; that is, **generalization learning** occurred. Sufficient generalization of the behavior "being on time" had occurred by the time he was a young man to make this behavior characteristic of Chris.

Of course, Chris is not reinforced for punctuality 100% of the time. For example, he has one friend who seldom is ready when he comes to pick her up at the time they agreed. This means that after hurrying to get ready himself, Chris has to wait while the friend gets ready to go. He also has to sit around reading uninteresting magazines almost every time he visits his dentist, and if he gets to certain classes on time, he just has to wait for the professor to show up 10 minutes late. Also, he has learned that getting to a party "on time" means being a little uncomfortable for the first hour when there are so few people that it looks as if the party might flop.

As a result of experiences such as these, Chris has learned to *discriminate* among stimuli in terms of the likelihood that his punctuality will pay off in a particular situation. This **discrimination learning** helps to make his behavior

---

A sense of humor is what makes you laugh at something that would make you mad if it happened to you.

*Anonymous*

more efficient; it is a sort of fine-tuning mechanism. This pattern of reinforcement, generalization to similar situations, and discrimination among situations that will or won't yield reinforcement for punctuality is diagrammed in Figure 4–2.

Only the broad outlines of the process just described briefly can be shown in the figure. One of the amazing things about your behavior is the vast number of fine discriminations you are able to make as you experience behavior-consequence contingencies. For example, it may be that Chris's friend is only late getting ready when she and Chris haven't made a definite plan for where they are going. If so, Chris will learn quickly to pick her up on time if they are going to a movie but not to bother if they just are going for a bite to eat.

Another thing that you can't see in Figure 4–2 is that not all of the consequences of punctual behavior were experienced by Chris firsthand. He also learned from watching others. For example, he learned from what happened to some of his friends that certain professors took a dim view of work that was turned in late. He did not have to learn by trial and error every time. In other words, what we call social learning helped to direct his behavior (and so his personality) as well.

In our story of why Chris is what a trait personality theorist would call a "punctual person," we see antecedent conditions (A) for this behavior that

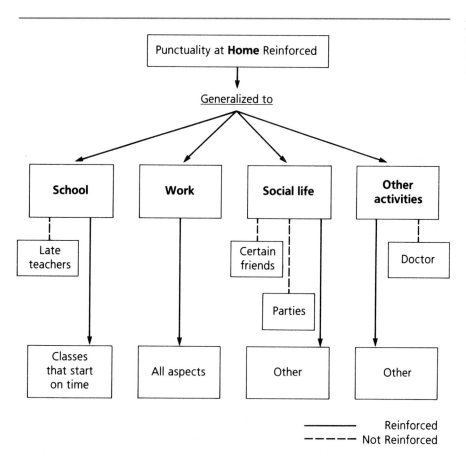

**Figure 4–2  The Role of Reinforcement, Generalization, and Discrimination in Learning to be a "Punctual Person"**

have in common a time reference point. He could be on time or late for dinner, work, class, a movie, and so on. We see that the behavior (B) we call "being on time" usually was followed by consequences (C) that were positive; it was reinforced by many people and events. As a result of this reinforcement, punctuality generalized to many situations. Sometimes, though, Chris's behavior was not reinforced, so the antecedents for punctuality gradually became more specific and less generalized. A situation with a "defined time to meet" no longer was an accurate description.

The process by which punctuality came to be a characteristic behavior of Chris's is multiplied many times over to produce other characteristic behaviors. Looked at the other way around, it is also the process by which certain patterns of behavior do *not* describe Chris. For example, he does not participate in sports, so we would not call him athletic. A behavior personality theorist would conclude that over the years, most of Chris's experiences with sports have been nonrewarding or punishing in some way.

## Reinforcers and Punishers

You've heard phrases like "different strokes for different folks," " whatever turns you on," and "one person's trash is another's treasure" many times. Such sayings reflect a basic fact of life; people are different with respect to what gives them pleasure and what they wish to avoid. Therefore, it stands to reason that they will be different to some extent with respect to what it takes to reinforce certain behaviors. You see these differences very day. Perhaps you are willing to give up some of your social activities to study hard for an *A* in this course, for example. Your best friend isn't so turned on by *A*'s—she'd rather spend more time playing tennis and take a *C* if that is how it works out.

### Learned and Unlearned Reinforcers

Both good grades in school and playing tennis are learned positive reinforcers. **Learned reinforcers** (sometimes called secondary reinforcers) are outcomes of behavior that people have learned to find personally rewarding. You have only to consider the number of people you know who tried tennis and didn't like it to realize that there is nothing intrinsically satisfying about running around trying to hit a little ball over a net. Likewise, an *A* on a report card has no meaning in and of itself. If you give one to a 2-year-old, he or she most likely will ignore it, tear it into pieces, or try to eat it.

Like tennis and good grades, much of what most of us find rewarding comes to be valued through the social reinforcement it can provide—status, praise, and recognition. Both *A*'s and playing tennis also may be the way to achieve other rewards; both, for example, might lead to a college scholarship for some high school students.

**Unlearned reinforcers** (sometimes called primary reinforcers) satisfy some biological need without the necessity for learning. Food is a familiar example of such an unlearned reinforcer. We have a wide choice of foods that will satisfy this need, however, and the choices most adults make about what to eat are learned. In fact, by the time we are adults, most of the things we find rewarding are learned. Some of these things, such as attention and acceptance by others, are reinforcing to most people. Others, such as the "high" reported to come from endangering one's life in an activity like mountain climbing or race-car driving, are more individual.

## Punishment

Punishment has not been mentioned so far in this discussion, but it is operating simultaneously with rewards to develop your behavior (and your personality). Some of these unpleasant outcomes of behavior are administered directly by other people. For example, you may have learned at an early age not to talk in class.

As a child, you like to talk in class (found it rewarding to whisper to your friends), but you were punished for it several times. Your teachers made you stay after school, and this meant that you were punished again by your parents when you got home. On the whole, these punishments were not outweighed (or even balanced out) by the enjoyment of talking during class, so you came to be a " well-behaved student".

Other kinds of punishment are natural outcomes of behavior, somewhat like unlearned reinforcers. If you tease a cat, you may be scratched. The cat isn't trying to punish you; it is trying to protect itself. You feel punished all the same and are less likely to bother the cat in the future.

Like reinforcers, much of what people find punishing is learned. Some of these things are very individual, but there is quite a lot of consistency in our culture when it comes to things of a social nature that we would like to avoid (find punishing). One of the most common is being made fun of by others. Another is having to stand up in front of a group and make a presentation or speech. In some cases, this may be fear of being made fun of; in many others, it is just a dislike for being the center of attention.

In general, the effects of punishment on your behavior are more subtle than those of reinforcement. If you wear a blue shirt to the office and receive several comments on how nice you look in blue, you are likely to reach for blue when getting dressed for your next date, dinner with your spouse, or party. When you are reinforced in some way for behavior, you tend to try it

Attention from others is one of the most powerful positive reinforcements for behavior.

out in almost any situation that has something in common with the original one; that is, to generalize it. By contrast, punishment tends to lead people to make finer discriminations between situations. For instance, a dishonest student who gets caught cheating on an exam in Professor Brown's class is less likely to give up cheating altogether than to give it up only in Professor Brown's class.

Most of those who take a behavioral view of personality development probably would agree that rewards generally have a greater influence on the development of personality than do punishers. The distinction tends to become blurred, however, both because the processes are operating simultaneously and because so many people feel punished when a reinforcer is withheld or taken away. (If you have read Chapter 3, you may recall that the term *negative punishment* was offered to you for your personal use in identifying this latter situation.)

To take only one example of this last problem, let's assume that your friend Marty is very upset at receiving a grade of *C* on a paper into which she put a great deal of effort. From her point of view, her effort has been punished. From an objective point of view, the professor, like the cat mentioned earlier, was behaving in a way that seemed appropriate in the situation (he or she thought *C* an accurate grade for the paper) and was not intending to dole out any punishment.

## Summing Up ■

Reinforcers and punishers are consequences of behaviors that follow certain antecedent conditions, and behavior theories of personality emphasize the role of these antecedent-behavior-consequence chains in developing personality. This view has proved very useful in the study of personality, especially in the study of deviant behavior. As the report in *Face of the Future* suggests, however, learning alone may not be sufficient to account for such behavior. As in many other areas, psychologists are coming to a greater appreciation of the possible role that biological factors play in personality.

Behavior theories of personality often are criticized for ignoring the inner person, especially the ability to think and to reason. This criticism is based on an erroneous understanding of this approach. It is true that some learning theorists, such as B. F. Skinner (1974), reject any explanations for behavior that rely on unseen inner states of being, such as values and attitudes. But this so-called *radical behaviorism* is not a theory of personality. In fact, Skinner rejects the entire concept of personality; he believes that psychology has no need for a separate concept to explain behavior, because it can be explained by learning.

Behavior theories of personality are founded on learning principles, but they have different goals and take a broader perspective than the radical behaviorist view of behavior causation briefly mentioned. This difference has been summed up by one personality psychologist as follows:

The individual is not a passive bundle of responses. We have long learning histories and long memories, and much of what has happened to us gets internalized and affects all our current responses and future expectations. We interpret ourselves and our behavior—we evaluate, judge, and regulate our own performance. In addition to being rewarded and punished by the external environment, people learn to monitor and evaluate their own behavior and to reward and punish themselves, thus modifying their own behavior and influencing their environment (Mischel, 1981, p. 93).

# FACE OF THE FUTURE:
## Can We Prevent the Development of the Antisocial Personality?

**Antisocial behavior** is behavior that works against the good of society as a whole. It ranges from irresponsible (such as habitually writing bad checks) to aggressive (such as physically assaulting others) to criminal (such as robbery, rape, and murder). Social workers, lawyers, judges, and parole officers long have observed a tendency for antisocial parents to have children who exhibit similar patterns of behavior. The traditional explanation for this pattern is a learning explanation. It seems logical that children who are raised by people who habitually disregard the rights of others and/or break laws will be susceptible to internalizing these values and imitating these behaviors.

Sarnoff Mednick and his colleagues are challenging this view. For over 10 years they have been studying convicted criminals and their children to determine if there could be an inherited base to what often is called the *antisocial personality*. In one 20-year study, they found that adopted children whose biological parents were convicted of crimes committed far more crimes themselves than adopted children whose natural parents had no criminal history. This was true no matter what kind of adoptive parents the children had (Mednick, 1984).

Mednick does not suggest that there are "bank robber genes" or "murder genes" that can be passed from parent to child. But many biological and neurological abnormalities *can* be inherited, and we already have evidence that such factors play a role in certain psychological disorders, such as schizophrenia (Buchsbaum, 1984). It does not seem so farfetched to suppose that some such factor may be involved in an inability to learn to abide by society's rules. Among the possible factors suggested by Mednick are abnormally slow brain-wave activity and sluggishness of the autonomic nervous system.

If scientists were able to discover a biological link to antisocial behavior, ways might be found to help affected children avoid this destructive life pattern. The feasibility of such "criminal prevention" programs already has been demonstrated at the National Center for Hyperactive Children in Los Angeles (Hurley, 1985). Hyperactivity (more accurately called attention deficit disorder) is a behavior disorder whose causes are not yet fully understood, but these children, like the children of criminals, are at high risk for exhibiting criminal behavior.

There is a long way to go yet, but any possibility of preventing the development of antisocial personalities is exciting. One thing that all professionals concerned with this problem agree upon is that it is more effective and more desirable to *prevent* the development of criminal behavior than it is to try to change it once it become a way of life.

## PUTTING IT ALL TOGETHER

Three very different approaches to the meaning and development of what we call personality have been reviewed. Each view offers ideas that make sense and that fit with our own personal observations and experiences, and none of the three necessarily excludes the others. People do have drives, such as sex, which have an influence on behavior that goes beyond learning (psychodynamic theory).

On the other hand, much of what people do clearly *is* learned. A careful consideration of your own life should make it clear that rewards and punishments have played a significant role in your characteristic patterns of behavior (behavior theory). Some of these patterns of behavior are consistent enough across time and situations to be called personality traits (trait theory). In short, all three approaches have something to offer you in the matter of trying to understand personality better—both your own and that of others.

## ■ *KEY WORDS AND PHRASES*

A-B-C paradigm

antisocial behavior

Allport

behavior theories of personality

discrimination learning

displacement

ego

Erikson

Freud

generalization learning

Hippocrates

id

identity crisis

Jung

learned reinforcers

locus of control

negative reinforcement

personality

personality trait

personality typology

positive reinforcement

psychodynamic theories of personality

psychosocial development stages

punishment

superego

trait theories of personality

Type A behavior/Type B behavior

unlearned reinforcers

## ■ *READ ON*

*The Mind Test* by R. Aero and E. Weiner. New York: William Morrow, 1981. A book of classic psychological tests that you can take and score yourself that may help you gain additional insight into yourself.

*The Life Cycle Completed* by E. H. Erikson. New York: Norton, 1983. The most influential modern psychoanalyst looks back on the human life cycle from the vantage point of 80-plus years. Erikson is the only personality theorist who has given the personality changes that occur throughout the life span a central place in his work.

*Beneath the Mask: An Introduction to Theories of Personality* (2nd ed.) by C. F. Monte. New York: Holt, Rinehart & Winston, 1980. This is a textbook that includes a collection of minibiographies of some of the most interesting people who have ever lived. Monte focuses on the people behind the theories, showing how their personal backgrounds and relationships were influential in their work, and he succeeds in bringing this material to life in a way that is unique. This book is well worth the time if you can find a copy (try your professor or your school library).

# ■ REFERENCES

Allport, G. W. (1961). *Pattern and growth in personality.* New York: Holt, Rinehart, & Winston.

Allport, G. W., & Odbert, H. S. (1936). Trait names: A psycholexical study. *Psychological Monographs, 47;* 1–171.

Buchsbaum, M. S. (1984). The Genain quadruplets. *Psychology Today, 18;* 46–51.

Campbell, J. B., & Hawley, C. W. (1982). Study habits and Eysenk's theory of extraversion-introversion. *Journal of Research in Personality, 16;* 139–146.

Chance, P. (1988). Personality's part and parcel. *Psychology Today, 22;* 18–19.

Conley, J. L. (1984). Longitudinal consistency of adult personality: Self-reported psychological characteristics across 45 years. *Journal of Personality and Social Psychology, 47;* 1325–1333.

Erikson, E. H. (1963). *Childhood and society* (2nd ed.). New York: Norton.

Erikson, E. H. (1964). *Insight and responsibility.* New York: Norton.

Erikson, E. H. (1963). *The life cycle completed.* New York: Norton.

Findley, M. J., & Cooper, H. M. (1983). Locus of control and academic achievement: A literature review. *Journal of Personality and Social Psychology, 44;* 419–427.

Fordham, F. (1953). *An introduction to Jung's psychology.* Baltimore: Penguin.

Hall, C. S., & Lindzey, G. (1978). *Theories of personality* (3rd ed.). New York: Wiley.

Hurley, D. (1985). Arresting delinquency. *Psychology Today, 19;* 62–68.

Mednick, S. (1984). Crime in the family tree. *Psychology Today, 18;* 46–51.

Mischel, W. (1981). *Introduction to personality* (3rd ed.) New York: Holt, Rinehart, & Winston.

Monte, C. F. (1980). *Beneath the mask: An introduction to theories of personality* (2nd ed.). New York: Holt, Rinehart, & Winston.

Peele, S. (1984). The question of personality. *Psychology Today, 18;* 54–56.

Pervin, L. A. (1985). Personality: Current controversies, issues, and directions. *Annual Review of Psychology, 36;* 83–114.

Rosenman, R. H., Hahn, W., Werthesseu, N., Jenkins, C., Messinger, H., Kositchek, R., Wurm, M., Friedman, M., & Straus, R. (1966). Coronary disease in the western collaborative group study. *Journal of the American Medical Association, 195;* 86–92.

Rotter, J. B. (1966). Generalized expectancies for internal versus external control of reinforcement. *Psychological Monographs, 80* (Whole No. 609).

Skinner, B. F. (1974). *About behaviorism.* New York: Knopf.

Strube, M. J., Turner, C. W., Cerro, D., Stevens, J., & Hinchey, F. (1984). Interpersonal aggression and the Type A coronary-prone behavior pattern: A theoretical distinction and practical implications. *Journal of Personality and Social Psychology, 47;* 839–847.

Woods, P. J., & Burns, J. (1984). Type A behavior and illness in general. *Journal of Behavioral Medicine, 7;* 411–415.

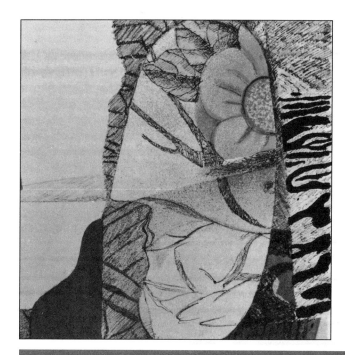

# The Self and Self-Concept: You as You See Yourself

By almost any standards, Sam is a success. He graduated from a good university with a high *B* average and quickly got a good job. His company is very pleased with his work, and he has a nice apartment and some good friends. Despite these accomplishments, Sam himself feels insecure. He believes that he had to work harder than most students for his good grades in school because he isn't "naturally bright." He says that he got his job primarily because he was in the right place at the right time, and he worries that he isn't really up to it. He doesn't share any of these doubts and worries with his family or friends, however, for fear they will think less of him.

Sam's friends describe him as bright, outgoing, persistent, and competent. He describes himself as an average person who has had a lot of luck, and sometimes he wonders how long it will be before people find out what he really is like. In other words, Sam's self-concept is quite different from the way other people see him.

You may know someone like Sam; perhaps you have had similar feelings yourself from time to time. You also may know people for whom the opposite is true; they seem to think more highly of themselves than others do or than the facts seem to warrant. Who is right and who is wrong? Which is the true person?

Who is right and who is wrong about Sam depends on your point of view. More people see Sam in a positive light than a negative one, so if we go by majority opinion, Sam clearly is wrong about himself. On the other hand, no one knows Sam as well as he knows himself. From that point of view, Sam must be right.

Your self-concept is your own view of yourself, and this is the focus of this chapter. It is this view that usually has the greatest influence on your thoughts, feelings, and behavior. We all give some weight to the opinions of others, but when these opinions are sharply at variance with our own, we are likely to discount them or to dismiss them entirely.

## WHAT IS A SELF?

In earlier chapters, the development of some of the personal characteristics that make you a complex individual with a unique combination of physical, psychological, and behavioral characteristics was reviewed. The general nature of the physical and social environments in which you live also was examined. Although you interact with these environments, you remain separate from them. You exist in, but are distinct from, the rest of the world.

Your **self** is your consciousness of being a complex entity that is separate from the world around you. It is more complex than your personality because it includes all of the other characteristics, such as the way you think and the ways that you experience emotions, that make you *you*. In other words, your personality is only one part of your self.

You were not born with any sense of self. As an infant, you didn't even understand where your physical self left off and the rest of the world began. You would suck your thumb or a toy equally happily, with no idea that one of these objects was part of your body and one was not.

Research done by psychologists who make a study of human growth and development tells us that an understanding of our separateness from our surroundings develops somewhere between ages 1 and 2. In one well-known study, for example, a 1-year-old who was placed in front of a mirror with a spot of rouge on his nose reached out and tried to touch the mirror (Brooks-Gunn & Lewis, 1975). Then he looked behind it. By contrast, a 20-month-

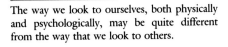

The way we look to ourselves, both physically and psychologically, may be quite different from the way that we look to others.

old looked at her reflection, reached up, and rubbed at the spot on her nose. The older child knew she was seeing herself; the younger one seemed to believe another child with a dirty face must be in or behind the mirror.

Like the child in the mirror, your earliest conceptions of *me/not me* were physical. If you were like most children, you probably drove your parents crazy for awhile with your exciting discoveries of *my foot, my eye,* and *my ear.* As you continued to grow and develop, this sense of self broadened to include nonphysical characteristics as well. The self is the *I* of *I am, I need, I want,* and *I will.* It is an integrating concept, which you use as a summary of all that you perceive yourself to be. In this chapter, self is examined as the core of a fourth approach to personality—humanistic theories of personality. We then move on to consider the more personal topics of self-concept and self-esteem.

## Self and Personality

Your self is not the same as your personality, but your personality is an important part of your self. Psychologists often call this aspect the *social self* because it consists of the face and behaviors you present to others. The *personal self* is the self seen by you alone. As we saw in the case of Sam, it may be quite similar to or quite different from your social self.

Although personality and self do not mean the same thing, there is one approach to the study of personality that views the self as the *core* of personality. **Humanistic personality theory** is the fourth major theoretical approach to the study of personality; it goes along with the trait, psychodynamic, and behavioral views examined in the last chapter. Humanistic theorists believe that an individual's own personal subjective view of being human is the most important aspect of personality. Because of this emphasis on the self and on your own view of that self, this discussion has been held for this chapter.

## THE HUMANISTIC VIEW OF PERSONALITY

As may be seen in Exhibit 5–1, humanistic views of personality differ in several important ways from the personality theories reviewed in the last chapter. To the humanistic theorist, the core of the personality is the self, and the

## EXHIBIT 5–1

### A Comparison of Humanistic and Other Views of Personality

| Theory | Personality Is: | Personality Is Studied By: | Personality Changes By: |
| --- | --- | --- | --- |
| Humanistic | Self | Self-report | Freedom from restraint |
| Behavioral | Behavior | Observation | Change in reinforcement |
| Psychodynamic | Dynamic psychological forces | Interpretation | Resolution of conflict |
| Trait | Set of traits | Measurement | Acquire new traits and/or lose old ones |

individual is the best source of information about this self. This view of your personality has been compared with a flower; your self begins as a tightly closed bud that opens up and flourishes under the right conditions and fails to bloom under the wrong ones.

The comparison to a flower captures another theme of the humanistic approach to the study of personality; like flowers, people are basically good. In the humanistic view, people are inherently motivated to grow and develop in positive ways; if they fail to do so, it is because something in their environments prevents it. Psychologist Abraham Maslow generally is given the credit for making this upbeat view of people a significant part of personality psychology.

## Maslow and Self-Actualization

Maslow (1970) believed that people are born with an active impulse to grow into healthy, happy humans. When this does not happen, it is because the environment somehow has inhibited the process, perhaps by blocking fulfillment of important human needs.

Maslow postulated two sets of these needs. The *basic needs* are physiological needs (e.g., food, shelter), safety needs, belongingness needs, needs for esteem from self and others, and a need to develop fully as a human being (self-actualization). *Metaneeds* are needs for more abstract states, such as needs for truth, justice, perfection, and beauty. Maslow thought that both sets of needs are instinctive (present at birth) and that the basic needs have a set order of importance. This is the well-known **need hierarchy,** shown in Figure 5–1.

According to Maslow, people seek to meet the needs in the hierarchy in order from bottom to top. Unmet needs lower in the hierarchy are *prepotent needs;* they exert the most influence on behavior until they are satisfied. The individual then moves on and up; when the lower needs are satisfied, higher needs emerge to exert potency. At the top of the hierarchy is Maslow's postulated need for self-actualization. (It is at this point that metaneeds, which are *not* arranged in any hierarchy, begin to emerge as influences on behavior.)

**Self-actualization** is the need to be all that you personally are capable of being as a human being. It is a growth need that encompasses, but goes beyond, satisfaction of all the needs lower in the hierarchy. This need fascinated Maslow, and he devoted many years to describing and looking for people who could be called self-actualizers. A list of what he believed to be the basic characteristics of such a person is shown in Exhibit 5–2.

Don't be concerned if you don't measure up very well to Maslow's rather intimidating self-actualizer. Maslow devoted much of his life to the search for true self-actualizers and found only one about whom he had no reservations. The personality in Exhibit 5–2 is more a description of what Maslow believed that people are capable of being than a set of standards by which we should measure ourselves. It represents the best possible outcome of that striving for good that Maslow believed we are born with.

As Maslow discovered, most people are not self-actualizers in the pure sense. Their personalities represent compromises between what they could be and what they have become through striving to meet their needs in their particular environments. Nevertheless, Maslow believed that most of us still do pretty well, and he thought it was vital that psychology develop theories of

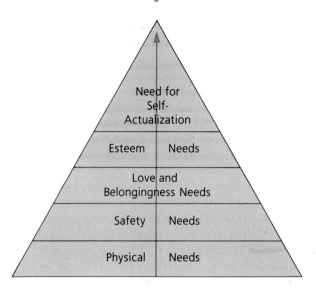

**Metaneeds:**

| | |
|---|---|
| Simplicity | Uniqueness |
| Truth | Beauty |
| Order | Perfection |
| Understanding | Justice |

**Figure 5.1 Maslow's Hierarchy of Needs**

## EXHIBIT 5–2
## Maslow's Self-Actualizing Person

According to Maslow, the self-actualized man or woman is

| | |
|---|---|
| Accepting of self | Spontaneous |
| Accepting of others | Reality-oriented |
| Creative | Self-reliant |
| Democratic | Humorous |
| Independent | Private |

He or she also

- Has a highly developed moral sense.
- Has experienced mystic states or peak experiences.
- Has a broad interest in the welfare of humankind.
- Never loses the ability truly to appreciate the wonders of life.
- Enjoys a small number of intense and intimate personal relationships.

*Note:* Summarized from the discussion in *Motivation and Personality* (2nd ed.) by A. H. Maslow, 1970 New York: Harper & Row.

personality for this majority as well as for the neurotic, inadequate, and miserable minority (as Freud focused on, for example). Although he is best known for his hierarchy of needs and for his concept of self-actualization, many psychologists think that this insistence upon a more balanced view of humankind was his greatest contribution to the field (e.g., Hall & Lindzey, 1978).

## Rogers's Self Theory of Personality

Like other humanistic theorists, psychologist Carl Rogers believed the self, not traits or psychological forces, is the core of personality. He agreed with Maslow and others that striving for self-actualization is an inherent human motive (Rogers, 1961) and believed that if you are to accomplish this you must have what he called unconditional positive regard.

**Unconditional positive regard** means receiving acceptance, love, and esteem from another without having to meet some standards that he or she imposes upon you. Such standards are called **conditions of worth;** they define the conditions (behaviors) under which another person will care for you. Conditions of worth are illustrated by the parent who says to a young child, "You're a good boy—you ate all of your vegetables," or "Only bad girls hit their brothers." To a child, statements like these attach strings to being loved and accepted. He or she comes gradually to believe that there are two sides to his or her character, what another personality theorist has called the "good me" and the "bad me" (Sullivan, 1953). Under conditions of worth, a child feels valuable and lovable only when being the "good me."

According to some personality theorists, children can learn quite early that they are only lovable when they are behaving in certain ways.

### The Good Me and the Bad Me

According to Rogers, the problem with believing in a "good me" and a "bad me" is that we begin to distort or deny having feelings or doing things that our parents (and/or parent substitutes) disapprove of (the bad me in action) because we are afraid we will lose their love if they find out. As we grow older and the world gets bigger, we generalize these conditions of worth to other relationships. For example, a woman may be afraid to express her dislike for her friend's mother for fear that he will care for her less if he learns of this "bad-me" feeling.

To Rogers, then, personality develops along lines that bring approval from people who are significant in a child's life—**significant others**—especially from parents. Since approval is very rewarding to most people, this view has something in common with behavior theories of personality. Remember, however, that behavior theorists do not accept a self as the central core of personality.

### Self Theory and the Well-Adjusted Personality

In common with the other humanistic theorists, Rogers had definite ideas about what constitutes a healthy personality. Simply stated, the fewer the conditions of worth a person has acquired, the more well-adjusted he or she is likely to be. In the absence of such constraints, the self-concept can remain unified and flexible. We don't have to twist facts or hide feelings from ourselves because we can accept all of our experiences and feelings as valid and important.

This doesn't mean that Rogers believes an embezzler or a car thief or someone who routinely cheats on exams should shrug and say, "That's just the way I am, folks!" Unlike other personality theorists, the humanistic theorists have little to say about such chronic deviant behavior. They are far more interested in the vast majority of people who do not fall into this group. To the humanistic theorist, the important thing is that we don't punish ourselves for having negative feelings and desires and for doing things that disappoint other people (a different matter from being dishonest or breaking the law). A healthy self-concept finds room for all of the feelings and experiences that are part of being human.

Rogers's beliefs about self-acceptance are at the heart of his well-known humanistic approach to psychotherapy, which he called **client-centered therapy** (Rogers, 1951). He believed that a discrepancy—which he called *incongruence*—between self-image and experience with the world lies at the heart of unhappiness and anxiety. Where there is incongruence, there is a person denying and distorting reality in accordance with learned conditions of worth.

To Rogers, a therapist's primary responsibility is to create a climate of warmth and acceptance through empathy with a client's view and experiences. By trying to see the world as the client does and communicating this understanding, the therapist creates a climate in which the individual feels safe. In this climate he or she can try to get back in touch with, express, and accept more aspects of himself/herself, thereby reducing incongruence and achieving a healthier self.

**Summing Up** ■

Your self is your awareness of being a complex entity that is separate from the world around you. It is more complex than your personality, because it includes all of the other characteristics that make you *you*, but one group of personality theorists believes that it is the core of personality. These humanistic personality theorists stress the importance of your own individual, subjective view of who you are. This is in sharp contrast to other approaches, which require measurement and/or interpretation of personality.

Humanistic personality theories also differ from the other major approaches in their definite and consistent emphasis on the positive aspects of human nature. Maslow believed that people are born with instincts to strive for health and excellence, which can be realized if the environment does not block them. Rogers was more specific about the conditions under which the human personality can flourish, emphasizing the crucial role played by significant others in a person's life.

# YOUR SELF-CONCEPT

**Your self-concept is your impression of yourself.** Most of us describe this impression in words common to personality trait theory. I might say that I am honest, hardworking, energetic, and cheerful. You might describe yourself as intelligent, outgoing, attractive, and considerate. Where do these words come from? Do they represent the "facts?" Is this what we really are like?

Impressions are perceptions or interpretations of the "facts." They may fit with reality as other people see it or they may not. For example, I describe myself as honest, yet I tell you quite openly that I always subtract 5 years when giving my age. "But that's not honest," you protest. "No big deal," I reply. "That isn't a real lie—it doesn't hurt anybody." You probably go away thinking that I have a pretty flexible definition of honesty. Rogers would say that I am distorting my dishonesty to maintain my image of myself as an honest person.

## Development of Your Self-Concept

To dream of the person you would like to be is to waste the person you are.

*Anonymous*

Where do we get these images of ourselves that are so important to protect? They come from comparing ourselves to others and from the way that we interpret others' expectations and reactions to our behavior. The process begins simply. As a very young child, your self-concept could be described in good/bad terms. Then you began to compare yourself with others. I am short (i.e., shorter than my mother and father). I am strong (i.e., stronger than my playmate next door). As you grew older, your frame of reference for drawing conclusions about yourself expanded rapidly. The most important sources of information and standards for forming impressions of yourself were your parents, your peers and friends, and society.

### Parents and Your Self-Concept

Rogers and others believe that parents (and/or parent substitutes) are the most important influences on how self-concept develops. Those who are caring for us as infants and very small children are the first sources of information and feedback we have about ourselves and our behavior. They give us this information and feedback in terms of how it compares with their own values and expectations.

Even when we grow up, become independent, and think we have substituted our own standards for those of our parents, our impressions of ourselves still tend to be influenced by their values and expectations. One 22-year-old man, for example, insists on describing himself as a sinner because he does not go to church. Despite the fact that he lives a productive life and does many things to help others, his mother's admonition that people who don't go to church are sinners still rings in his ears (or in his self-concept).

### Peers, Friends, and Your Self-Concept

If your parents are the most important influence on your self-concept, your peers and friends are not far behind. Their standards, expectations, and reactions to your behavior play an increasing role in your perceptions of yourself as you grow up. If most of your peers claim to hate studying, but you don't,

Evaluations of our behavior by our peers and friends have a strong influence on our self-concepts from an early age.

you may add the term *grind* to your self-concept description. If you are the ones your friends always turn to for ideas about what to do next, you come to think of yourself as a leader.

It is not at all unusual for information about yourself from your parents and others and information from peers and friends to conflict. For example, a child who has come to think of herself as physically delicate because her parents worry continually about her health and safety may find herself being labeled a sissy when she won't join in the rough play at school recess.

What happens when different people who are important to us have different ideas about what is desirable and acceptable behavior? According to psychologist Leon Festinger (1957), such situations create cognitive dissonance. **Cognitive dissonance** occurs when one fact or belief (called a *cognition*) conflicts with other facts or beliefs about the same subject. Festinger postulates that this condition is uncomfortable and unacceptable and people are motivated to behave in ways that will bring such dissonant ideas back into congruence.

One way out of dissonance is to twist one or more of the ideas until they fit together. The little girl might tell herself that her parents don't mean the rule about rough play to extend to school because the teacher will make sure she doesn't get hurt. In this way, she can join in the play, get rid of the sissy label, and remain her parent's delicate daughter. Alternatively, she can try to find evidence that one of the conflicting ideas is wrong. For example, she may "prove" that she isn't a sissy (even though she won't play rough games) by walking along the narrow guard rail of a high bridge.

As we grow older, our efforts to fit different ideas and perceptions into a single, consistent self-concept become more sophisticated. We get particularly good at doing this when the disagreement is between our *own* perceptions and those of others. Remember how Sam managed to resolve the conflict between his belief that he was not "naturally bright" and the fact that he got good grades at school? He concluded that he had worked harder than other students for the same grades.

## EXHIBIT 5–3
## Coping with Cognitive Dissonance: Some Examples

**Situation 1**
**Belief:** You firmly believe you are not very attractive.
**Event:** A date says, "You really look good tonight."
**Response:** You say, "It's the blue shirt. Blue makes everyone look good."

**Situation 2**
**Belief:** You believe you are a careful person.
**Event:** You don't wear your seat belt, even though you know seat belts save lives.
**Response:** You convince yourself you are guarding against getting trapped in your
    car. As you are a careful person, this is more likely than your having an accident.

**Situation 3**
**Belief:** You consider yourself very intelligent.
**Event:** You get a C on the first exam in a new course.
**Response:** When the professor refuses to raise your grade, you decide the course is
    worthless and drop it.

**Situation 4**
**Belief:** You see yourself as a good husband/wife.
**Event:** Your wife/husband threatens to leave you if you don't go with him/her to a
    marriage counselor.
**Response:** You go and explain to the counselor that this *proves* what a good husband/
    wife you are.

Some common situations creating dissonance between our views of ourselves and others' views of us and some typical resolutions are presented in Exhibit 5–3. You probably can think of others. To most of us, being confused about who we are is one of the most disturbing things that can happen, so we strive to protect our image of ourselves from conflicting information even when this image is poor.

Does distorting information to make it consistent with your self-concept have negative effects? It depends on the extent to which you do it and the degree to which you are aware of doing it. One of the dimensions of effective behavior is a realistic appraisal of one's own characteristics. A person who habitually twists any good information to fit a negative self-concept or twists any negative feedback to fit a positive one is not being realistic. Most of us fall somewhere in between these extremes. If we kid ourselves, we usually know we are doing so.

## Society and Your Self-Concept

Although it may be difficult to see how something as vague as "society" can affect the personal self-concept of one individual, examples are all around you. All societies have values, and these values affect the way their citizens see themselves. For example, getting ahead in business has been a strong American value for a long time. Therefore, if you work in a business environment but value personal family time more than getting ahead, you may come to think of yourself as lazy.

The values of a society lead to the formation of stereotypes, which can have a strong influence on individual self-concepts as well. A **stereotype** is a generalized idea about how people of a given sex, race, or other grouping do, or should, behave, think, feel, and look. For too many years, black citizens in this country saw themselves as "shiftless," because that is how society saw (and treated) them. In like fashion, many wives viewed themselves as dependent and "dumb about business," because their husbands and society treated them in this manner. These stereotypes have changed in the past 30 years or so, but stereotypes themselves persist. This may be seen quite clearly in the realm of physical appearance.

## Physical Appearance and Self-Concept

In our country today, an attractive and sexually appealing woman is slim and has long legs, a pretty face, and well-developed breasts. Her male counterpart is tall and has abundant hair, broad shoulders, and slim hips. This image is projected in the movies, on television, in magazines, and on advertising billboards, and it is used to sell everything from toothpaste to pest control services.

Many psychologists have come to believe that these stereotypes of attractiveness are very poor influences on the self-concepts of the millions of men and women who do not fit them. Although there are no statistics to tell us how many people really suffer because they don't look like movie or television stars, there is ample evidence that many try to make themselves more like this ideal. Dieting, exercise programs, makeup, fashion, and cosmetic surgery are big, big business. Is physical attractiveness really that important? Here is what two researchers in this area have to say:

> The characteristic that impresses people the most when meeting anyone from a blind date to a job applicant is appearance. And unfair and unenlightened as it may seem, attractive people are frequently preferred over their less attractive peers (Cash & Janda, 1984, p. 46).

Cash and Janda, along with a number of other psychologists, have done extensive research on physical attractiveness, and they find that your looks can affect your grades in school, selection for jobs, number of friends, and choice of a mate. Other people tend to view attractive people as more interesting, more poised, more sociable, more sensitive, and happier than less attractive people. Good-looking men are rated as more masculine and good-looking women as more feminine than men and women who do not meet our society's current standards for attractiveness.

This obsession with looks doesn't paint a very nice picture of our society, but the matter does not end here. It turns out that there are times when it *doesn't* pay to be good-looking. One of the clearest of these instances is if you are a career-oriented woman. The finding that attractive women are at a disadvantage when it comes to being selected for jobs that traditionally have been dominated by men (such as manager, police officer, or elected official) has been repeated many times.

Being an attractive women in such situations is a disadvantage that may be multiplied if a woman also looks very feminine. Cash and Janda asked some corporate personnel consultants to evaluate the characteristics of a number of businesswomen on the basis of photographs. Some of the consultants were shown photographs of women in "corporate garb" (suit, short hair, little jewelry, inconspicuous makeup).

Other consultants saw photographs of women deliberately groomed to look "feminine" (hair styled fuller and longer, sweaters and skirts, more jewelry, more obvious makeup). Both the male and the female personnel consultants rated the feminine-appearing women (relative to the corporate-appearing women) as:

- More illogical
- Less assertive
- More emotional
- Less independent
- Less self-confident
- Less interested in work
- Less financially responsible
- More likely to be flirtatious in social relationships

The really surprising thing about these results is that the women in the two groups of photographs were exactly the same women; each one had been photographed wearing two different looks. Were these findings unusual? Not at all. A number of studies have demonstrated that our society associates certain traits with femininity. These traits, which include emotionality, flirtatiousness, and dependency, are positively valued in some social settings, but they are not consistent with our expectations for businesslike behavior, and this can be a real problem.

You'll remember from earlier discussions that people tend to treat others in a way that is consistent with what they expect from those others. The businesswoman who is very feminine in appearance sets up expectations for behavior that is not businesslike. If others treat her accordingly, she may get less cooperation, fewer opportunities to excel, and less recognition for her accom-

Research finds that many people, both men and women, assume attractive, feminine-appearing women are less competent and businesslike than others.

plishments. Since messages from others are so important to self-concept, her ideas about herself and her abilities may be affected in a negative way.

The feminine-appearing businesswoman's problem is only one aspect of a broader phenomenon. As a society, we associate certain traits with femaleness in general and certain traits with maleness in general, and these traits become translated into expectations for behavior. For example, many believe that women are more sensitive than men and so should be better at caring for the sick and comforting the bereaved. By the same token, many think that men are less emotional than women and so should be better at making important decisions. These sex roles, our understanding of them, our acceptance of them, and the extent to which we conform to them have a significant impact on our self-concept.

## Sex Roles and Self-Concept

**A sex role is a collection of behaviors considered appropriate for men or women in a particular society or segment of society.** Sex roles differ considerably from one society to another and from one period of history to another. In this country today, we are in a transition period. Current sex roles are a mixture of traditional and new expectations. Here are just a few of these mixtures.

- Women are expected to have a career of some sort (new), but also to be able to cook, keep a household running smoothly, and know what to do if the baby has a fever (traditional).

- Women are expected to compete with men and to be sexually assertive (new) without losing their tactful, gentle, cooperative, and sensitive "feminine" ways (traditional).

- Men are expected to be equal partners in parenting (new) and successes in their careers (traditional).

- Men are expected to be more open and sensitive to the needs of others (new) while remaining tough and knowing what to do in a crisis (traditional).

These changing sex roles constitute an enormous challenge to today's men and women. This may be especially true if you are over **40**. Sex roles are learned, and if you are in this age group, what you learned in childhood and adolescence was considerably different from the current mixed expectations.

### Learning Sex Roles

The world begins teaching us our sex roles the day we are born. We may have to modify these lessons as the world changes, but the lessons themselves—that there are different sets of behavioral standards for males and females—are well learned.

Traditionally, girl babies are dressed in pink, treated gently, and praised for having pretty faces and delicate hands and feet. Boys are dressed in blue, praised for their strong grip, and roughhoused from an early age. Santa brings little girls dolls and pretend makeup and little boys, toy cars and pretend sports equipment. If a boy receives a doll, as some do nowadays, it will be a boy doll.

Some parents make a concentrated effort to avoid drawing sharp distinctions between "girl things" and "boy things," and the lines *have* blurred somewhat in the past 25 years or so. Much of the world is still supporting the traditional view, however. Well-meaning friends and relatives frown when a little girl gets her dress torn and dirty but remark indulgently that "boys will be boys" when her brother comes home with torn pants and dirt all over his face. Grandpa takes little Joey fishing and leaves little Sally to help Grandma fix dinner. Day-care centers make the boys shepherds and the girls angels in the annual Christmas play.

Treating boys and girls differently is part of the process of socializing them to the sex roles defined by society. **Socialization** is the process by which an individual acquires the values and learns the behaviors expected in a particular society (or subgroup of society, such as a work organization). This process is an important part of helping people acquire what psychologists call gender identity.

**Gender identity** refers to a personal sense of being male or female. It includes, but is not limited to, the physical aspects of maleness and femaleness. Gender identity also involves understanding that males and females do different things in a social context and that they have different standards applied to their behavior.

Research by developmental psychologists finds that most children have acquired some sense of gender identity by the age of 3 (Thompson, 1975). Children younger than this can tell you that they are a girl or a boy, but they don't understand why they are called that or who else falls into the same category. Furthermore, it is not for a number of years more (until about the age of 7) that they understand that being a girl or a boy is a permanent condition (Wehren & DeLisi, 1983). Dressing up in a girl's clothes won't make you a girl if you are a boy nor, as an old tale would have it, will kissing your elbow make you a boy if you are a girl.

Developing gender identity is part of adjusting to the social environment. If you were born male, for example, the world is going to expect certain things

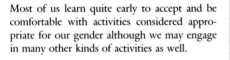

Most of us learn quite early to accept and be comfortable with activities considered appropriate for our gender although we may engage in many other kinds of activities as well.

of you. You are more likely to feel comfortable with, and accepted by, others if you conform to these expectations (at least in a general way). This is especially true in the earlier years of life when fitting in is very important to most people (Mussen, 1962). A person who fails to understand and/or rejects sex roles may find life very stressful during this time.

A few people experience difficulty with gender identity, not because they reject sex roles, but because they come to identify physically with a gender that is not their own. These individuals often make a conscious effort to look more like the sex they identify with. Such problems, like many others, exist on a continuum, ranging from a young woman going through a "tomboy" phase to people having their sexual anatomy altered surgically. The causes of the more extreme forms of cross-gender identity, or *transsexualism*, are not well understood. One reason for this is that the condition is extremely rare. Most of us have been socialized successfully to identify with our biological gender.

## Sex-Role Stereotypes

In every society in the world there always have been differences in the roles defined for the two sexes. There is no reason to believe that this will change. Men and women are fundamentally different in that women can bear children and men cannot. To many people, this difference alone—with its various associations, such as different hormones to affect behavior, the need for child care, and so on—makes it appropriate for men and women to behave in different ways. And they do. The following are among the differences researchers have found in male and female behavior that will be discussed in chapters to come.

- Men marry at a later age than women.
- Most antisocial personalities are men.
- Women form closer same-sex friendships than do men.
- Women are less accepting of their bodies than men.
- Most of the housework in our society is done by women.
- More women attempt suicide, but more men succeed in taking their own lives.
- Most of the victims of eating disorders, such as *anorexia nervosa* and bulimia, are women.
- Women are more conservative when it comes to sexual attitudes than men (although the gap is narrowing).

These and other male-female differences in behavior are real, but *indirect*. They come about because of the different ways that males and females are treated in our society and the different expectations we have for their behavior, not because of biological differences. There is another set of male-female differences in characteristics and behavior that are *not* real, but myths. The following are among the many examples that might be cited.

- Men are smarter than women.
- Women are more "social" then men.
- Women are better parents than men.

There is more difference within the sexes than between them.

*Ivy Compton-Burnett*

- Women are more dependent than men.
- Men are less emotional than women.
- Men make better decisions than women.
- Women are less achievement-oriented than men.

Beliefs about basic differences between males and females that do not hold up to scientific investigation are **sex-role stereotypes.** There may be some truth to such stereotypes in individual cases, but *there is no evidence that they are true of males and females in general.* Yet many people still treat men and women in accordance with sex-role stereotypes. As in the case of the feminine-appearing businesswoman, this can confine and restrict individual human potential and have negative effects on self-concept.

It may seem difficult to believe that sex-role stereotypes remain strong in this equal opportunity age, but such beliefs have a way of perpetuating themselves. One of the mechanisms by which this occurs is through what children are exposed to on television. As noted in *For Discussion,* television programming has changed, but there has been little fundamental change in the way men and women are portrayed in television *commercials* in 30 years.

The nature and extent of the influence that television has on our children may be a matter of debate, but there is no such disagreement about the influence that school has on their lives and their socialization to sex roles. And despite all of the social changes that have taken place in the last generation, researchers are finding that there still are strong and consistent differences in the way boys and girls are treated by their teachers. A recent study of over 100 fourth-, sixth-, and eighth-grade classes in four different states provides an example (Sadker & Sadker, 1985).

One of the most dramatic differences Sadker and Sadker found when they studied teacher behavior was the different way teachers responded to children in classroom discussion. When boys called out an answer to a teacher's question, it usually was accepted. Girls who tried to get teacher attention in this way more often were reminded to raise their hands first. Many even were reprimanded. It is not surprising, then, that the researchers found boys dominating classroom communication whatever their age and whatever the subject. They were being reinforced in a direct manner for being assertive, whereas girls were being reinforced for being passive.

Unfortunately, the line between equipping children to deal with the expectations of the world and training them to perpetuate stereotypes is a thin one. It probably is necessary to make young girls aware of the fact that many of the people they encounter in the world will expect them to be less assertive than males and to help them find ways to cope effectively with the implications of this expectation. It is another thing altogether to train them to *be* passive.

Sadker and Sadker's research results are not unique. Many other studies of student-teacher interactions in schools have found systematic differences in treatment of the sexes that perpetuate sex-role stereotypes (e.g., Hall & Sandler, 1984). These don't all favor boys, however. For example, boys usually get little sympathy if they feel sick or get hurt on the playground, whereas girls are likely to be sent to the school nurse or home for the day. Thus, the stereotype that men must be tough and rise above pain is perpetuated.

Whether your own school experiences were like these or not, you have been exposed to numerous other forms of training in sex-role stereotypes. What can be done to combat the power of these beliefs to perpetuate them-

## FOR DISCUSSION:

### TELEVISION AND SEX-ROLE STEREOTYPES

In the early days of television programming, most of the women we saw were wives and mothers who wore dresses, pearls, and high heels, even in the kitchen. They stayed home all day dispensing wisdom and home cooking. Men were husbands and fathers who wore suits and went off to work each morning. They returned home in the evening to straighten out whatever little problems the family had encountered in their absence. A single parent was always widowed, a single woman was always looking for a husband, and no one—but no one—lived together without benefit of matrimony.

Television programming has changed dramatically since the 1950s. Women have careers, and both men and women are divorced single parents. We see mixed marriages, unmarried heterosexual relationships, homosexual relationships, and a variety of other human conditions taboo on the television of 30 years ago. But things have not changed much when it comes to those insistent commercial messages.

It has been estimated that by the time he or she is 19 years old, the average American young person has spent more hours watching commercials than the average wage earner spends on the job in an entire year. And what has this young person been seeing?

- Women in the kitchen or in the bathroom squealing with excitement over a shiny floor or an odor-free toilet
- Men driving cars 100 MPH or "grabbing for the gusto" after a hard day at the steel mill
- Women dispensing soap, aspirin, and thrifty casseroles to their appreciative families, then worrying if they have gotten the wash clean enough to suit these same families
- Men giving us the latest on garbage bags, lawn mowers, and tires

A few brave advertising agencies are venturing out of these sex-role stereotypes. Ex-football player Merlin Olsen sent flowers to his friends in one commercial. Olympic gold-medal winner Mary Lou Retton roared out of a fast-food drive-in order lane in her own red Corvette in another. And in one of the most publicized commercials of all time, we heard 1984 vice-presidential candidate Geraldine Ferraro telling her daughter that she could be anything in the world she wanted to be.

Commercials that cross traditional sex-role stereotypes are in the minority, but they are a step in the right direction. Or are they? Could it be that they just are sending young viewers a new form of stereotyped message? Namely, it's okay for a man to send his friends flowers if he's tough enough. Women can speed around in their own sports cars if they are famous enough. They can even be politicians so long as, like Ferraro at the end of her message, they admit that being a mother is more important than any other achievement.

The influence of television on its viewers is hotly debated by parents, politicians, ministers, educators, television executives, and other concerned parties. Whatever the position they take, however, no one seriously suggests that it has *no* influence. So far, most of the concern has been over the issues of violence and immorality in programming. Those who seem aware of the power of commercials have focused on what they believe is the manipulation of children to get them to persuade their parents to buy certain products. But it seems entirely possible that commercials are selling people, and not just young people, views of themselves and the world as well.

What do you think? Try watching television for 3 hours one night and make notes on the commercials you see. How many sex-role stereotypes can you identify? How about other stereotypes (such as the way children, senior citizens, blacks, or teenagers are portrayed)? Are those commercials that are trying to avoid such stereotypes realistic? If you can, watch again on Saturday morning when the commercials are aimed at a young audience. Do you see any significant differences? How do you think what they see may be affecting the later attitudes and behavior of these young viewers?

selves? One answer is to educate those responsible for child care and education to the problem and how to avoid it. There is no evidence that the teachers in the Sadker and Sadker study were aware of what they were doing. Nor is it likely that most parents who treat male and female children in stereotyped ways are aware of the broader implications of this behavior.

In practice, of course, there are difficulties with this solution. Many people believe sex-role stereotypes are true, and they do not care to be confused by the facts. Others just simply do not believe there really is a problem with sex-role stereotypes in this day and age. What can you as an individual do? As a first step, we suggest you work on *consciousness raising*—increasing your awareness of the problem. Try observing yourself and others for a few days and make a list of stereotype-perpetuating behaviors. Here are a few examples.

- Do your professors call on male students more than female students? (Men are more likely to say something worth listening to.)

- Do you or your fellow classmates address or refer to your male professors as *Doctor* or *Professor* and your female professors as *Miss, Mrs.,* or *Ms.?* (Real professors are men.)

- Do you tend to chalk your female boss's criticism of your work up to "hormones"? (Women are too emotional to be good supervisors.)

- If you are a parent, do you tend to be more tolerant of your son's lapses of good manners than of your daughter's? (Women are supposed to be polite.)

- Do you or your friends feel uncomfortable at the thought of going to a female dentist or general practitioner physician? (These are not appropriate professions for a woman.)

- Do waiters and waitresses automatically hand the check to a man when there are people of both sexes at the table? (Men pay when they eat in a restaurant with women.)

How many of these and other sex-role stereotype-perpetuating behaviors did you identify? Were you surprised? Can you imagine what a change would come over our society in this realm if large numbers of people undertook to change the behaviors on their own personal lists? As with social responsibility, individual behavior can make a real difference in this area.

## Gender Identity, Sex Roles, and Self-Concept

Most adults who are asked to provide self-descriptions will begin by identifying their sex, and many other aspects of their descriptions may be related to this one. For example, a woman who is 5 feet, 9 inches tall may say, "I am tall." A man who is exactly the same height may say, "I am short." The same height means different things to these two people because they are of different sexes. Five feet, nine is very tall for a woman in our society, both by statistical and by ideal standards, but it is well below the masculine ideal of 6 feet or more.

This tendency to describe ourselves relative to social expectations about our sex is even greater if we have a very strong sense of gender identity and accept traditional sex-role stereotypes. Such a man is likely to lead off a self-description with his occupation; "I'm a [doctor, mechanic, or salesman]. His wife likely will tell you that she is Mrs. so-and-so and state her husband's occupation. The role that gender and sex-role stereotypes can play in self-concept extends far beyond such superficial characteristics, however.

Do you describe yourself as too aggressive, not very domestic, or selfish? Then you probably are a woman, because it is women who are expected to be passive, domestic, and giving. By the same token, you probably are a man if you say you are too emotional, wishy-washy, or not good with your hands. Men are supposed to be controlled, decisive, and good at manual tasks.

Is it healthy for gender to play such a large role in the way we define our self-concept? There isn't any general answer to this question. It depends to a

# FACE OF THE FUTURE:
## The Age of Androgyny?

What do Grace Jones, Annie Lennox, Michael Jackson, and Nick Rhodes have in common besides the fact that all are well-known rock singers? All four of these personalities of the eighties have a look that is a blend of the masculine and the feminine. Physically, these stars are "gender benders," or, to use the accurate term, they are *physically androgynous*.

There is psychological androgyny as well as physical androgyny, and neither concept has anything to do with transsexualism, male or female impersonation, or sexual preference. Nor do they have anything to do with being a "feminine man" or a "masculine woman" (such people are referred to as *cross-typed*). **Androgyny,** whether physical, psychological, or both, simply means displaying both male and female characteristics.

A number of psychologists are coming to believe that psychological androgyny is healthier than strong gender identity because it frees people to express aspects of themselves that are not consistent with prescribed sex roles. Bem (1975), a leading spokesperson for this view, argues that this freedom would be enormously beneficial in coping with the demands of modern life. For example, it has been speculated that efforts to conform to traditional expectations that they be strong, decisive, and in control of their emotions make it difficult for men to manage stress effectively. As a result, they are more subject to ulcers, alcoholism, and coronaries than their female counterparts.

Arguments such as this have led to much research into androgyny. Among the findings are that (compared with strongly sex-typed individuals) people who are more androgynous (on tests designed to measure this orientation) are:

- Better able to express love behaviors (Coleman & Ganong, 1985).

- Seen as better same-sex friends (Baucom & Danker-Brown, 1983).

- Somewhat more adaptable to problem situations (Baucom & Danker-Brown, 1979).

- Somewhat less inclined to have marital problems (Baucom & Aiken, 1984).

Research findings such as these tend to support the argument that androgyny is psychologically healthier than strong sex typing, but it must be said that this research is controversial. Other researchers have questions about getting true measures of androgyny from a written questionnaire. In addition, many of the differences obtained between more and less androgynous subjects are very small. There also is a conflicting body of research that strongly links psychological adjustment and effective coping behavior with a masculine (rather than a feminine or androgynous) orientation (Jones, Chernovertz, & Hansson, 1978; Locksley & Colten, 1979).

At this time, we must say that the question of whether psychological androgyny is healthier and more adaptive than strong sex typing is still very much open. It may be that it is simply too early to gather enough evidence one way or the other; androgyny is a relatively new concept, at least on any scale. But there is much evidence of it to be seen. Many men and women wear similar hair styles and similar clothing. They play the same sports and compete with equal ferocity. Men are getting the message that it is okay to cry and women that they can express their anger. Women pursue careers with single-minded zest, and some men stay home and care for the children. It is too soon to say that the "Age of Androgyny" is here; however, the face of the future may be shaping up more in that direction.

considerable degree on how you feel about it. If your self-concept suffers because you fall short of a mythical "ideal man" or "ideal woman," or, alternatively, if you feel constrained by having to operate within such boundaries, accepting this standard probably does not contribute to your adjustment. Indeed, some psychologists are coming to believe that we all would be better off if we put such standards aside. There is more on this in *Face of the Future*.

## Summing Up ■

Your self-concept develops over time as you compare yourself with other people and with the standards and expectations of significant others in your life. This is an ongoing process that probably continues throughout life, although most psychologists believe that the earlier years are critical.

Many of the standards and expectations with which you compare yourself relate to your particular gender, and we call these sex roles. These roles are in a transition period in our society, and there is considerably more flexibility for the individual man or woman now than at any time in the past. At the same time, certain strong sex-role stereotypes persist, perpetuated by parents, teachers, and the media.

## SELF-CONCEPT, THE IDEAL SELF, AND SELF-ESTEEM

We have been examining your impressions of yourself, where these come from, and how they are affected by your gender, by sex roles, and by sex-role stereotypes. Your self-concept is entitled to all of this attention; it plays a vital role in your expectations for yourself and in your associated decisions and actions. So important is this influence that the self-concept often is like a prophecy. In the words of psychologist Sidney Jourard,

> When a person forms a self-concept, thereby defining himself, he is not so much describing his nature as he is making a pledge that he will continue to be the kind of person he believes he is now and has been (1974, p. 153).

Like Festinger, Jourard stresses the importance of *consistency* in our self-concept. We can all find examples in our own lives of how we try to be faithful to our self-concept and how this striving for consistency affects our behavior. Do you see yourself as shy? Then you probably avoid situations in which you would have to speak in front of a group of people. Do you believe that most people like you? Then you are likely to start conversations with strangers at the pool, the bus stop, or the grocery store. Do you feel that you are a failure? Then you may find, if you examine them, that you tend to set goals that are impossible to attain or you put little effort into your work so as to avoid providing yourself with contradictory positive information in the form of achievement.

This search for consistency is discouraging if your self-concept is predominantly negative. One young man taking part in a group discussion voiced this discouragement well:

I've always felt like a social flop, and I think now I can see that I keep setting myself up for social disasters. But I don't want to. I want to be comfortable with other people and to have a good time and to be popular.

## The Self and the Ideal Self

The young man just quoted is describing a discrepancy between his impressions of himself as he is—his self—and the way he wishes he were—his ideal self. The **ideal self** is a picture a person has of the way he or she would like to be. Most of us have such pictures, and some psychologists find formal measures of the discrepancy between self and ideal self to be helpful when people are dissatisfied with themselves or their lives. Such measures encourage people to be specific about the sources of their dissatisfaction; you can get an idea of how this procedure works by completing the form in *Test Yourself.*

Self-report measures, such as the self-concept checklist in *Test Yourself,* are very important to humanistic personality theorists. You remember that they believe it is the way *you* see yourself, not the way others (even psychologists) see you, that is important. There can be quite a difference, as we saw in the story about Sam.

Although Sam's description of himself and the descriptions others give of him do not fit very well, the difference probably would be less obvious if Sam were asked to describe himself as *others* see him. Most people are pretty accurate in their perceptions of how they appear to others (Mischel, 1972). Sometimes, as in Sam's case, this knowledge is distressing. Sam believes the competent image he gives others makes him a fraud. It would seem that he has low self-esteem.

## The Self and Self-Esteem

Your self is your *consciousness* of being a person who is separate from your environment. Your self-concept is your *description* of this self. Your **self-esteem** is your evaluation of your self-concept, that is, how highly you regard yourself. One very rough measure of self-esteem is how much difference there is between your self and your ideal self *(Test Yourself)*. In general, if you see yourself as more like your ideal self than not, you feel pretty good about yourself. On the other hand, a discrepancy does not necessarily mean that you evaluate the way you are negatively; it may mean only that you would like to be different in some way. For example, you may see yourself as intelligent but think it would be great to be still *more* intelligent.

Psychologists have studied self-esteem extensively because it affects so many aspects of a person's life. They find that people with low self-esteem tend to be more easily influenced by others, to do less well in school, to set lower goals for themselves, to be loners, and to have emotional problems (Wells & Marwell, 1976). Such people often have what we call an *inferiority complex*—a belief that they are not as good as other people.

## Changing Self-Esteem

Because low self-esteem can have such negative effects on the quality of life, there has been a good deal of interest in how it develops and what can be

## TEST YOURSELF
### Your Self–Ideal-Self Discrepancy

*Directions:* Read each statement. In the first blank space to the right, put the number (1–10) that indicates how well the statement describes you (1 = not at all like me; 10 = just like me). In the second space to the right, put the number that represents your *ideal evaluation* (the number you would like to be able truthfully to put in the first space).

|  | Self | Ideal | Discrepancy |
|---|---|---|---|
| I am a responsible person. | —— | —— | —— |
| I am a hard worker. | —— | —— | —— |
| I am a rational person. | —— | —— | —— |
| I am usually relaxed. | —— | —— | —— |
| I am intelligent. | —— | —— | —— |
| I am self-reliant. | —— | —— | —— |
| I am poised. | —— | —— | —— |
| I have self-control. | —— | —— | —— |
| I am tolerant. | —— | —— | —— |
| I get along with almost everybody. | —— | —— | —— |
| I am sexually attractive. | —— | —— | —— |
| I make strong demands on myself. | —— | —— | —— |
| I am a good person to have as a friend. | —— | —— | —— |
| I am depressed frequently. | —— | —— | —— |
| I like the way I look. | —— | —— | —— |

TOTAL ——

*SCORING:* For each statement, subtract the smaller number from the larger number (it doesn't matter which number is which). Put the result in the third space. Add up the numbers in this third column. This is your *self–ideal-self discrepancy* on the listed aspects of self-concept. The maximum discrepancy score is 135. The smaller your number, the less the discrepancy and the more like your ideal self you are.

done to change it. Most psychologists believe that it begins to develop early, and the dim view that teachers say many first graders already have of themselves would seem to support this assumption.

Children who enter school with low self-esteem are likely to behave in ways that communicate this opinion to others, and the reactions of these others to this behavior are likely to reinforce this low opinion. On the brighter side, the early school years may have a positive effect on sagging self-esteem because here, perhaps for the first time, children can compare themselves on a regular basis with a large number of others the same age. If you are a child, it is easier to feel successful in a world of children. Boys and girls whose only standards of comparison have been those of adults or older brothers and sisters may decide they aren't so bad on their own turf.

The way we look to others is an important part of self-esteem, but personal achievement also plays a significant role. School offers an opportunity to achieve or excel in ways that are new to most children, such as reading, learning to spell and write, acquiring mathematical skills, or learning to use a computer.

Children aren't the only ones who find personal achievement helps their level of self-esteem. Psychologists have found that something as simple as learning to swim can bring about a significant improvement in self-evaluations (Koocher, 1971). Adults who take up jogging, aerobics, or other exercise for fitness often report that new feelings of mastery over their bodies is a bigger payoff than the physical results. In fact, any new skill that gives you feelings of greater control over yourself and your life seems to be an effective boost to self-esteem.

It appears, then, that low self-esteem begins early but that there is no age limit on raising it again. Among the ways that seem to be effective in doing this are holding your own in comparison with your peers, learning a new skill, and acquiring mastery over some aspect of your life. These things don't automatically work, however. You can always find a way to belittle your accomplishments to yourself if you really are committed to an inferiority complex. As you know, some psychologists believe that these feelings of inferiority or worthlessness are deeply rooted in early experiences. Albert Ellis takes a different view.

> Anything you're good at contributes to happiness.
>
> *Bertrand Russell*

## Self-Esteem and Self-Talk

Ellis (1962) believes that many problems are the result of irrational beliefs about the world. These beliefs, he says, lead people to set standards for themselves that are so unrealistic they cannot possibly live up to them, and each failure gives self-esteem another knock. Ellis has identified a number of these beliefs; they are listed in Exhibit 5–4.

Ellis says that holding irrational beliefs leads people to "talk crazy" to themselves when interpreting their experiences. For example, suppose that you get back a major term paper with a grade of *D* and negative comments about your work on every page. If you hold irrational belief number 1, you will take this as evidence of your personal worthlessness instead of as feedback on one piece of work. This professor must think I'm a real turkey, you tell yourself. Or perhaps you hold irrational belief number 2. In this case, you can go from a *D* on one paper in one course to a feeling of I can't do anything right.

It is such irrational interpretations of experiences, not the experiences themselves, that Ellis and others believe do so much damage to self-esteem and effective behavior. One poor grade does not mean that you can't do anything right until you interpret it in light of the belief that you must be competent in all aspects of your life. To counteract such irrational thinking, Ellis developed what he calls *rational emotive therapy,* in which the therapist's job is to help

## EXHIBIT 5–4

### Irrational Beliefs That Lead to Crazy Self-Talk

1. I must be loved or approved of by everyone.
2. In order to feel worthwhile, I must be competent in every possible way.
3. People who are bad should be blamed and punished.
4. It is a catastrophe when things are not the way you want them to be.
5. People have little or no control over the external causes of the bad things that happen to them.
6. The best way to handle something that I'm afraid of or that is dangerous is to worry about it and dwell on it.
7. It is easier to avoid certain life difficulties and responsibilities than it is to face them.
8. I need to depend on others and to rely on someone stronger than myself.
9. Present behavior is determined primarily by what happened in the past.
10. The problems of others should upset me.
11. There is always a perfect solution to a human problem, and it is essential to find it.

*Note:* Adapted from *Reason and Emotion in Psychotherapy* by A. Ellis, 1962, New York: Lyle Stuart.

people think more rationally about their experiences. This process can be illustrated by a little imaginary conversation on the subject of your imaginary *D* grade.

YOU: *Oh, no, I got a D on my paper!*
ELLIS: *Not so good, eh? Did you give it your best shot?*
YOU: *Well, maybe not my best shot, but I did try my best.*
ELLIS: *Oh yeah? When did you start on it?*
YOU: *Well, not until a few days before it was due, but I did have a lot of other things to do and I had that awful cold . . .*
ELLIS: *So you think you did the best you could under the circumstances?*
YOU: *Pretty much, I think.*
ELLIS: *Well, then, that's the breaks. Sounds as if next time you have a paper coming up, you'll have to find a way to give yourself more time if you want a good grade. You know, allow for other classes and being sick and things like that.*

In this imaginary exchange, Ellis has taken a rational, problem-solving approach to analyzing what has happened to you. No connection is made between your grade and your likableness or worth as a person or your future life success. This rational approach is controversial as a way to help people in psychotherapy. As a way to keep things in perspective, however, it makes a lot of sense to examine the assumptions on which you make self-judgments.

The truth is that you cannot always succeed in what you want to do, nor is it likely that everyone you meet is going to like you (or vice versa). We all make bad decisions from time to time as well. None of these things is a disaster. None means you are worthless. And it is not very often that the effects follow you around for the rest of your life.

Feeling good about yourself seems to be a cornerstone of well-being and a considerable boost to effective behavior. If you were fortunate enough to have parents who helped you develop a strong positive sense of self-worth as a child, you got off to a good start. But self-esteem is fragile. It seems to be more responsive to being lowered than to being raised. For most people, continuing to think well of themselves takes vigilance, and boosting flagging self-esteem takes effort. Six specific suggestions that may help are presented in Exhibit 5–5.

**Summing Up** ■

**EXHIBIT 5–5**

## Ways to Boost Your Self-Esteem

1. Take responsibility for your own self-esteem. No one else can give it to you; that is why it is called *self*-esteem. Esteem from others is nice, but it is not a substitute; learn to set your own standards.

2. Avoid setting goals for yourself that are unrealistic; for example, I will get an *A* in every course this year. If you try to be perfect, you may be setting yourself up for failure and disappointment with yourself. Emphasize your strengths in setting goals; for example, I will get *A*'s in my major courses this year.

3. Make time to learn new skills once in a while. The old adage "nothing succeeds like success" is true when it comes to raising your opinion of yourself. Take up karate, learn to change the oil in your car, do your own typing until you are skilled with 10 fingers instead of only 2—anything that gives you a personal sense of accomplishment.

4. Cut down or cut out negative self-talk. Turn on the radio, make a telephone call, or go to a movie when you find yourself unable to stop obsessive thoughts about being a failure or being unloved.

5. Avoid constructing elaborate irrational scenarios about the implications and consequences of your behavior. Being turned down for a particular job position does not mean that the interviewer thought you were ugly or didn't like you. Nor does it mean that you will never get a job and will end up on welfare and a disgrace to your family.

6. Make a *strong, conscious effort* not to put yourself down to others, not even as a "joke." One of the saddest aspects of low self-esteem is that it is hard for others to like you if you don't like yourself. People who are always putting themselves down (even if they make a joke out of it) are a drag, and others will try to avoid them unless they too have a low opinion of themselves. And who needs friends like that?

---

■ *KEY WORDS AND PHRASES*

| | | |
|---|---|---|
| **androgyny** | **Ellis** | **Maslow** |
| **client-centered therapy** | **gender identity** | **need hierarchy** |
| **cognitive dissonance** | **humanistic personality theory** | **Rogers** |
| **conditions of worth** | **ideal self** | **self** |

*continued*

*continued*

## ■ KEY WORDS AND PHRASES

self-actualization

self-actualizing person

self-concept

self-esteem

sex role

sex-role stereotype

significant others

socialization

stereotype

unconditional positive regard

## ■ READ ON

*Beyond Sex Roles* (2nd ed.) edited by A. G. Sargent. St. Paul: West, 1985. A complete book of readings, exercises, and self-tests on what growing up male or female in our society means. In Sargent's words, "*Beyond Sex Roles* invites you to see yourself among your roles, obligations, expectations, rules, masks, and stereotypes, and to start to free yourself from inhibiting behaviors" (p. x).

*On Becoming a Person* by C. R. Rogers. Boston: Houghton-Mifflin, 1961. This classic textbook on the human potential for growth and creativity is so popular that it is still available (in paperback) at your local bookstore.

*The Kitchen Sink Papers: My Life as a Househusband* by M. McGrady. New York: Doubleday, 1975. An entertaining, thoughtful, and balanced account of a year-long, real-life role-reversal experiment. Mr. McGrady went the whole route: he shopped, he cooked, he cleaned, he took the kids to the dentist, he attended parent meetings at school on his own, and so on. His book tells those who have never been there (male and female alike) what it really is like to play the traditional housewife role in our society. Find it if you can!

## ■ REFERENCES

Baucom, D., & Aiken, P. A. (1984). Sex role identity, marital satisfaction, and response to behavioral marital therapy. *Journal of Consulting and Clinical Psychology, 52,* 438–444.

Baucom, D., & Danker-Brown, P. (1979). Influence of sex roles on the development of learned helplessness. *Journal of Consulting and Clinical Psychology, 47,* 928–936.

Baucom, D., & Danker-Brown, P. (1983). Peer ratings of males and females possessing different sex role identities. *Journal of Personality Assessment, 52,* 438–444.

Bem, S. L. (1975). Sex-role adaptability: One consequence of psychological androgyny. *Journal of Personality and Social Psychology, 31,* 634–643.

Brooks-Gunn, J., & Lewis, M. (1975). Mirror-image stimulation and self-recognition in infancy. Paper presented at the meeting of the Society for Research in Child Development, Denver, Colorado.

Cash, T. F., & Janda, L. H. (1984). The eye of the beholder. *Psychology Today, 118,* 46–52.

Coleman, M., & Ganong, L. H. (1985). Love and sex role stereotypes: Do macho men and feminine women make better lovers? *Journal of Personality and Social Psychology, 49,* 170–176.

Ellis, A. (1962). *Reason and emotion in psychotherapy.* New York: Lyle Stuart.

Festinger, L. A. (1957). *A theory of cognitive dissonance.* Stanford, CA: Stanford University Press.

Hall, C. S., & Lindzey, G. (1978). *Theories of personality* (3rd ed.). New York: Wiley.

Hall, R. M., & Sandler, B. R. (1984). A chilly climate in the classroom. In A. G. Sargent (Ed.), *Beyond sex roles* (2nd ed.). St. Paul: West.

Jones, W., Chernovertz, M. E., & Hansson, R. O. (1978). The enigma of androgyny: Different implications for males and females? *Journal of Consulting and Clinical Psychology, 46,* 298–313.

Jourard, S. (1974). *Healthy personality.* New York: Macmillan.

Koocher, G. P. (1971). Swimming, social competence, and personality change. *Journal of personality and Social Psychology, 18,* 275–278.

Locksley, A., & Colten, M. E. (1979). Psychological androgyny: A case of mistaken identity? *Journal of Personality and Social Psychology, 37,* 1017–1031.

Maslow, A. H. (1970). *Motivation and personality* (2nd ed.). New York: Harper & Row.

Mischel, W. (1972). Direct versus indirect personality assessment: Evidence and implications. *nal of Consulting and Clinical Psychology, 46,* 298–313.

Jourard, S. (1974). *Healthy personality.* New York: Macmillan.

Koocher, G. P. (1971). Swimming, social competence, and personality change. *Journal of personality and Social Psychology, 18,* 275–278.

Locksley, A., & Colten, M. E. (1979). Psychological androgyny: A case of mistaken identity? *Journal of Personality and Social Psychology, 37,* 1017–1031.

Maslow, A. H. (1970). *Motivation and personality* (2nd ed.). New York: Harper & Row.

Mischel, W. (1972). Direct versus indirect personality assessment: Evidence and implications. *Journal of Consulting and Clinical Psychology, 38,* 319–324.

Mussen, P. H. (1962). Long-term consequences of masculinity of interests in adolescence. *Journal of Consulting Psychology, 26,* 435–440.

Rogers, C. R. (1951). *Client-centered therapy.* Boston: Houghton Mifflin.

Rogers, C. R. (1961). *On becoming a person.* Boston: Houghton Mifflin.

Sadker, M., & Sadker, D. (1985). Sexism in the schoolroom of the 80s. *Psychology Today, 19,* 54–57.

Sullivan, H. S. (1953). *The interpersonal theory of psychiatry.* New York: Norton.

Thompson, S. K. (1975). Gender labels and early sex role development. *Child Development, 46,* 339–347.

Wehren, A., & DeLisi, R. (1983). The development of gender understandings: Judgments and explanations. *Child Development, 54,* 1568–1578.

Wells, L. E., & Marwell, G. (1976). *Self-esteem: Its conceptualization and measurement.* Beverly Hills, CA: Sage.

# 3

# Your Worlds

In Part 2 of *Psychology and Effective Behavior,* some of the more important personal characteristics that are created by a complex and lifelong interaction between your genetic/biological factors and your environment were examined. The purpose of that discussion was to encourage you to take a close look at yourself and how you came to be the way you are and how you might change in the future.

But you don't live in isolation. You have family, friends, neighbors, classmates, teammates, and co-workers. You go to school, to work, to the shopping mall, to ball games, to parties, to church, and to the beach. Television, newspapers, magazines, books, and movies make events, ways of life, and people in parts of the world you have never seen in person real to you. All of these are part of your social environment.

Part of achieving effective behavior is finding ways to meet your needs, accomplish your goals, and feel good about yourself that fit in with the expectations, opportunities, and constraints presented by your social environment. We took a broad look at that environment and the major ways it influences your behavior in Part 1. In Part 3, we explore some of the most important dimensions of that social world in more detail.

Chapter 6 takes a broad perspective on personal relationships—why they are so important to us, who we are likely to choose as friends, and how friendships are developed and maintained. In Chapter 7 the focus narrows to the intimate sexual relationships that can develop out of these friendships.

Chapter 8 takes a still narrower perspective, examining those few special love relationships and marriage. Finally, Chapter 9 opens the perspective up again to consider the social worlds in which you spend a third or more of your waking hours—the worlds of education and work.

The purpose of the discussions in Part 3 is to help you better understand your social worlds and the influence they have on your behavior and your continuing development as an individual. Special problems that may develop in these worlds are discussed in Part 5.

# Your Social World: Attraction and Friendship

In 1979, the editors of *Psychology Today* magazine invited readers to participate in a survey about friendship. Over 40,000 responses were received, making this one of the largest surveys of its kind ever. Participants were asked, among many other questions, to indicate how important each of more than 20 qualities was to them in a friend. The two *least* important qualities were similar income and similar occupation. The eight *most* important qualities are shown in Figure 6–1.

The *Psychology Today* survey tells us that the 40,000 people who responded valued trustworthiness, loyalty, and affection/warmth above all the other qualities they looked for in a friend. Where do we find people with such qualities, and why are these people so important to us? These are two of the questions examined in this chapter as we begin the process of exploring your relationships with the other people who make up your own special, individual social world.

## THE DEVELOPMENT OF YOUR SOCIAL SELF

**Attachment** is a term psychologists use to describe the bonds that people form with others. Most of us begin by forming attachments to our mothers (or substitute mothers), then to our fathers and/or other adults who care for us. Next, we move to friendships with playmates and classmates. As we grow older, we join clubs or groups and form personal relationships with members of both sexes. We may marry and have children as well. In short, we become very social beings.

Figure 6–1 **The Qualities People Want in Friends**

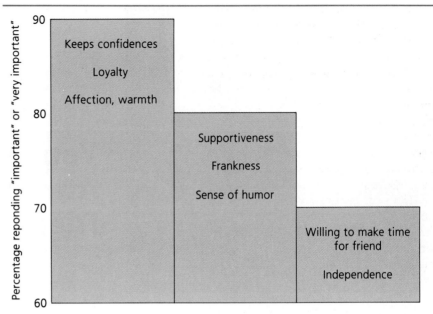

**Note:** Data from "The Friendship Bond," 1979, by M. B. Parlee and the editors of *Psychology Today, Psychology Today, 13,* pp. 43–55. Graph by author.

## The Importance of Attachment

Most infants form their first strong attachment to their natural mother or other caregiver, such as an adoptive mother or, in an increasing number of cases, a father. The utility of this attachment is clear; human infants are helpless. An adult provides them with comfort and protection as well as with the physical necessities needed to sustain life, grow, and develop into independently functioning persons.

This early attachment is simple. Developmental psychologists believe that both the form and reasons for attachment become more complex as we grow older (Bowlby, 1958). Being close to one or more important adults in his or her life is a child's first experience with social relationships. Such a relationship is rewarding in itself, and it provides a secure base from which to venture out and explore the world (and to which to return when that world is frightening).

As psychologists learn more about human attachment in the early years, they are accumulating knowledge about how the nature and strength of these attachments may affect later development. On the basis of this research, many have come to believe that there is a *critical period* for human social development, which lasts from birth until about the age of 3. They believe that what happens during this sensitive time has important and lasting effects because attachment seems to be the basis for later social interaction (White, 1975).

If attachment is the foundation for later social interaction with others, we might expect that infants who are not able to form secure attachments during this critical period would be more likely to have social difficulties as adults. As yet, researchers do not have enough evidence to say with any confidence that this is true. They do know, however, that the behavior of children who form strong bonds with others early on is different in some ways from the behavior of children who have formed only weak bonds with others.

Children who formed close attachments to adults as infants are called *securely-attached children*. Researchers have found that such children respond more positively to strangers when they are toddlers than do other children (Joffe & Vaughn, 1982). Securely-attached children also seem to be less hesitant about exploring the world around them, and they are more likely to be leaders among their peers in preschool (Waters, Wippman, & Stroufe, 1979). There also is evidence that girls who have close relationships with their mothers have closer relationships with other girls (Gold & Yanof, 1985).

In short, what psychologists know about attachment suggests that forming close bonds with others at an early age gets you off to a more sociable start in life. From this point of view, it makes sense that early attachments might affect satisfactory adjustment in later life. Many of our adult needs, such as needs for recognition, esteem, understanding, and sex, are dependent upon other people for fulfillment.

## Peers and Peer Groups

As an infant, you formed attachments to adults who cared for you. As you grew, you expanded your social horizons to brothers, sisters, toddler friends, and other adults around you, but this social world still was rather small. It expanded enormously when you entered a day-care center, preschool, kindergarten, or first grade. Suddenly you were in the midst of a group of children your own age with whom you interacted on a regular basis.

In a social developmental sense, **peers** are age-mates and **peer groups** are subsets of this larger grouping. When you entered school for the first time, your classmates were peers, but there were entirely too many for you to cope with all of them simultaneously. If you were a typical child, you managed relatively quickly to find a few special children with whom you felt comfortable. The basis for this first peer group formation may have been something as simple as sitting near one another in class or being in the same car pool.

Young peer groups usually are made up of same-sex members, and their role in the lives of children is very limited at first. Among 6- and 7-year-olds, who still are tied closely to home, peer groups may serve primarily as a source of friends to sit with at lunch or play with at recess. Older children spend more time with their peers, and similarity of interests becomes important. If you played Little League ball, for example, you probably spent much of your time in school with other members of your team or at least other children who were interested in sports.

### Peer Acceptance

Most children find a place for themselves in the complex social system that is school, and this peer acceptance is very important to later development. Psychologists find that children who are neglected or rejected by their peers at an early age often maintain this outcast role and go on to become lonely adults (e.g., Hojat, 1982).

It is well to remember that the entire population of the universe, with one trifling exception, is composed of others.

*John Andrew Holmes*

The quality of our early attachments to others can be important to later social adjustment.

**Peer acceptance** means having an acknowledged role in the same-age social system. This role most often is as a member of a particular clique or peer group. Thus, being accepted by such a group is doubly important. It provides you with friends and with a "place to be" in the overall scheme of things.

Peer acceptance becomes both more important and more complex as children grow older and peer groups begin to exert influence over their members. Little is required for an 8-year-old to be accepted into a peer group except dressing like the others and giggling at the same things. By age 10, expressing similar likes and dislikes and being willing to go along with group ideas about what to do with time are also part of the price of acceptance.

By the time children become teenagers, their peer groups are well-structured mini social systems. Do you remember your own? It had a dress code (although you probably didn't think of it in those terms), unwritten rules for behavior (norms), and penalties (called *sanctions*) for those who failed to conform to group expectations. Can you remember some of the dress codes and norms that you ascribed to in high school? How do they contrast with that nostalgia period currently in vogue—the 1950s?

In the 1950s it was critical to be "cool," and this meant wearing your hair in a certain style (a well-oiled duck tail for the "guys") and sporting the right clothes (long tight skirts and sweaters for the "gals"). Often, it also required expressing contempt for the "squares" who concerned themselves with good grades, teacher expectations for classroom behavior, and parental rules and regulations.

## Adolescent Peer Groups

Most psychologists agree that being accepted by a peer group is a critical stepping stone between the dependence of childhood and mature social relationships. Adolescents are ready to start forming their own opinions, tastes, and standards, yet few are ready to be completely independent. As a result, they turn to one another for support and guidance, and these groups have enormous influence on their members.

The influence that peers have on teenagers is a matter of great concern to many people. This concern stems from the fact that peer groups can, and do, influence members to behave in ways that are dangerous or illegal, or that cut off options for their futures. Fortunately, however, most of the vast energy that this powerful influence generates is expended in behavior that is at worst irritating to parents, teachers, and others.

Peer group influence is substantial, but before we leave this subject it should be mentioned that it is not the only source of influence being exerted on adolescents. Many psychologists believe that parents and teachers with well-defined standards that are fair and consistently enforced often are able to counteract the more negative effects of peer group influence in the long run. Finally, it also should be noted that vulnerability to social influence by peers is not something peculiar to teenagers. Most of us never outgrow our desire to be accepted by our peers. As a result, we do not outgrow our susceptibility to being influenced by them.

# Social Relationships and Stress

Adolescence can be a trying time; you are simultaneously too old and too young. You are too young to go with an unchaperoned group of friends to Florida or Mexico for the Easter vacation, but too old to pout when you are told no. You are too old to expect to have all your clothes washed and ironed for you, but too young to buy your own without an adult or an older brother or sister tagging along. In turning to one another during this trying time, adolescents may be wiser than they realize. There is some evidence that social relationships may serve as a buffer against some of the negative effects of stress.

In one well-known experiment in this area, psychologist Stanley Schachter (1959) found that undergraduate college women who were exposed to a high-stress situation created by the experimenter reported a strong desire for the company of others during a waiting period. This preference was more than twice that of the subjects in a low-stress situation. Interestingly, this was not true for men, and the effect was stronger for the women who were oldest in their families. Can you think of any possible explanations for this pattern?

Despite the fact that findings did not seem to generalize to everybody, Schachter's research opened up a new approach to the study of stress management. If people seek out others when feeling pressured, might not having close ties with others help reduce the experience of stress in the first place? At this time, the answer seems to be a cautious yes. Social support does appear to help many people feel less overwhelmed by certain kinds of stressful pressures, frustrations, and problems (Brownell & Schumaker, 1984).

The term **social support** refers to a complexity of positive effects that an individual may experience as the result of being part of a network of personal

> Without friends no one would choose to live, though he had all other goods.
>
> *Aristotle*

Dress standards adopted by adolescent peer groups often are a mystery to others, but they help the group to define its identity.

relationships. The people in this network may be friends, family members, neighbors, members of a church or social group, and/or anyone with whom an individual has personal contract and on whom he or she may call for help.

To date, researchers are not agreed on just how it is that social support and stress are related. One theory is that social support acts as a *buffer* against stressful circumstances and events; that it, it acts to reduce the perception of stress (Cohen & Wills, 1985). Another is that it acts in a more direct way to help people *cope* with stress when it is felt. Some psychologists are not convinced that it is actually the social support that has beneficial effects; they hypothesize that people with better social support networks are different from other people in being what is called a hardy personality (Kobasa, 1979).

The **hardy personality** takes control over his or her own life, sees life's problems as challenges, and makes commitments to goals and to others. Such people, researchers are speculating, may be more active in seeking social support and may be more successful in attaining it because they are so purposeful and optimistic. In other words, they are better equipped both to deal with stressful events and to marshall a social network to support them.

Whereas some psychologists work on the theoretical problem of the relationship between social support and stress management, others have identified a number of ways that social support may be of practical assistance to someone experiencing a stressful or potentially stressful situation (e.g., Schaefer, Coyne, & Lazarus, 1981).

First, other people can be important resources when the going gets tough; that is, they can offer *tangible support*. A friend who offers to drive you to a restaurant and treat you to a good dinner may do much to help you unwind from a frustrating week at work and avoid the buildup of pressure.

Second, members of a social support network can provide you with *information* to help you solve your problems or at least to realize that your situation or your fears are not unique. Imagine, for example, that someone with whom you are very much in love tells you suddenly that it is all over. You try to take it in stride but find yourself becoming obsessed with thoughts of this person.

Next, you find yourself calling your former lover (and then hanging up) and driving by places you used to go together. Alarmed, you begin to wonder if there is something abnormal about your behavior. This fear makes you anxious and nervous, and you have difficulty concentrating and sleeping. The whole problem gets worse.

Being able to talk to others who have gone through (or are going through) what you are experiencing may not reduce the pain, but it can eliminate your fears that what you are doing is strange and not normal. Your symptoms are not unique and they will pass. This knowledge may be sufficient to reduce the stress to a level that is manageable.

Third, social relationships offer *emotional support;* just being with someone who will listen and offer reassurance can help reduce feelings of stress. For all of these reasons, the active pursuit of social relationships is one stress management technique that works for many people. A variety of organized support groups have been formed throughout the country as well.

As the name suggests, **support groups** are groups formed for the purpose of providing mutual support to people coping with the same problem. The problem may be an alcoholic in the family, divorce, the loss of a child, unemployment, or any of a wide variety of other stress-producing conditions or events. Some of these groups are listed for you in Exhibit 6–1. Most have more than one chapter; you can find out if there is a group near you by looking in your local telephone directory or calling the number shown in the exhibit. You also may get in touch with your local mental health association, family service agency, or hospital health education office to find out about support groups for problems not listed. In addition, spaces are provided in Exhibit 6–1 for you to add groups that others in this class may know about.

Support groups are just that—groups whose members help to support one another through a bad experience (or, as in losing weight, a good but still stressful experience). They provide one another with emotional support and with information about additional resources for help. Such groups are founded on the premise that no one can offer more support or assistance to a person in a specific kind of stressful situation than someone who has been through it. Now some psychologists are wondering if there is a way to put this concept to work for formal mental health services (Kiesler, 1983). This possibility is discussed in *Face of the Future*.

## Summing Up ■

People are social beings, and a desire for the company of others begins very early in life. In the earliest days of social development, we form attachments to our mothers, fathers, or other adults who interact with us on a regular basis. When we enter school, social needs expand. Most children have a desire to be accepted by their peers, and research suggests that this acceptance is important to later life adjustment.

The need for peer acceptance usually peaks during the teenage years. Support from others in similar circumstances seems to help reduce stress as young people make the transition from child to adult. The same principle may extend throughout the life span; psychologists are coming to believe that social relationships play an important role in reducing perceived life stress.

# EXHIBIT 6–1
## Selected Social Support Groups

OVEREATERS ANONYMOUS
2190 West 190th Street
Torrance, CA 90504
(213) 320–7941

DRUGS ANONYMOUS
P.O. Box 473, Ansonia Station
New York, NY 10023
(212) 874–0700

DEPRESSIVES ANONYMOUS
P.O. Box 1777, Grand Central Station
New York, NY 10017
(212) 942–6540

DIVORCE ANONYMOUS
P.O. Box 5313
Chicago, IL 60680
(312) 341–9843

GAMBLERS ANONYMOUS
1543 W. Olympic Blvd. (Suite 533)
Los Angeles, CA 90015
(213) 386–8789

MOTHERS WITHOUT CUSTODY
Box 602
Greenbelt, MD 20770
(301) 552–2319

FRIENDS (specifically for stress)
c/o Roger Prescott
Box 389, 1325 South 11th Street
Fargo, ND 58107
(701) 235–7341

CHILDREN OF AGING PARENTS
2761 Trenton Road
Levittown, PA 19056
(215) 547–1070

NATIONAL GAY TASK FORCE
80 Fifth Avenue
New York, NY 10011
(212) 741–5800

PARENTS WITHOUT PARTNERS
7910 Woodmont Avenue
Bethesda, MD 20814
(301) 654–8850

NARCOTICS ANONYMOUS
16155 Wyandotte Street
Van Nuys, CA 91406
(818) 780–3951

GRAY PANTHERS (aging)
3635 Chesnut Street
Philadelphia, PA 19104
(215) 382–3300

ALCOHOLICS ANONYMOUS
P.O. Box 459
Grand Central Station
New York, NY 10163
(212) 686–1100

CANCER CONNECTION
H & R Block Bldg.
4410 Main Street
Kansas City, MO 64111
(816) 932–8453

NATIONAL ASSOCIATION
OF PEOPLE WITH AIDS
519 Castro, NO. 46
San Francisco, CA 94114
(415) 553–2509

BACCHUS of the U.S. (Boost
Alcohol Consciousness Concerning the
Health of University Students)
124 Tigert Hall
University of Florida
Gainesville, FL 32611
(904) 392–1261

NATIONAL SAVE-A-LIFE
LEAGUE (suicide)
4520 Fourth Avenue, Suite MH3
New York, NY 11220
(212) 492–4067

NATIONAL ASSOCIATION
FOR CHILDREN OF ALCOHOLICS
31706 Coast Highway, Suite 201
South Laguna, CA 92677
(714) 499–3889

AMERICAN ASSOCIATION
OF CITIZENS WITH DISABILITIES
1012 14th St. N.W., Suite 901
Washington, DC 20005
(202) 628–3470

AMERICAN ANOREXIA/BULIMIA
ASSOCIATION
133 Cedar Lane
Teaneck, NJ 07666
(201) 836–1800

NAME AND PURPOSE OF GROUP: _____
Address: _____
Telephone: _____

NAME AND PURPOSE OF GROUP: _____
Address: _____
Telephone: _____

NAME AND PURPOSE OF GROUP: _____
Address: _____
Telephone: _____

NAME AND PURPOSE OF GROUP: _____
Address: _____
Telephone: _____

# FACE OF THE FUTURE:
## Social Support as a Mental Health Service

It is estimated that somewhere between 15 and 35% of the population in this country is in need of mental health services at any given time. To supply such services, we have approximately 45 to 50 thousand people trained at the doctoral level. If all of these people devoted all of their professional time to working with those who need mental health services, they would be able to give each client about 2 hours a year. If everyone trained at the master's degree level were included as well, the time per client available would increase to perhaps 6 hours per person per year.

Of course, not all mental health professionals devote all of their time to clients. Many are involved in research, teaching, and administrative duties. No matter how we view it, the need clearly exceeds the professional help that is available, and the possibility that social support from family and friends might reduce some of this need is very exciting.

Putting social support to work for mental health is not a totally new concept if we consider group therapy a form of this strategy. But group therapy is a formal meeting conducted once (or a few times) a week by a mental health professional. Social support includes *informal* interaction and is available as needed. Research on social support raises the exciting possibility that it might be a *substitute* for professional help for some of those who need such assistance.

Psychologists do not as yet have much hard data on the effectiveness of social support, and considerably more research is needed before it can be established that formal organized efforts to get people with mental health problems involved with others is a viable way to help them with these problems (Lieberman, 1986). Even if it does appear that this might work, it most likely will work only for certain kinds of people. We would need to know more about who benefits from social support—older people, younger people, males, females, whites, minorities, people with serious problems, people with temporary problems, and so on.

There also are very practical considerations in using social support to help people with mental health problems. One question is how to get these people involved with other people. The research on the hardy personality (Kobasa, 1979) suggests that if they knew how to do this, they might not have the problems they have or at least not be as negatively affected by them. But the dilemma is not hopeless. Psychologists and other mental health professionals can start by helping individual clients understand the benefits of social support and explore ways they might find this for themselves. To take one example, going to church has been found to be a source of significant positive support for elderly women (Heller & Mansbach, 1984).

Other "involving strategies" that psychologists report have helped many people include doing volunteer work (hospitals, prisons, social service agencies, retirement or convalescent homes, boy's clubs, etc.), taking care of foster children or becoming a foster grandparent, joining social clubs or signing up for lessons of some sort, and even getting a pet! But research into how much such involvement reduces current symptoms of mental health distress or whether it can actually help people *avoid* mental health problems is still quite scarce.

When it comes to the possibility of a large-scale comprehensive effort to put social support to use as an assist to (or substitute for) professional mental health services, the questions are many and the problems are significant. But the potential is there and that is what excites many. Like crime, the scope of the mental health problem far exceeds our resources for dealing with it. The face of the future may see us all involved in an effort to help one another achieve better mental health.

# INTERPERSONAL ATTRACTION: THE FOUNDATION OF SOCIAL LIFE

At every stage of development, most people show a desire for the company of other people and a tendency to form bonds with certain of those others. This makes good practical sense. Your social interactions with other people provide you with stimulation, help you meet a variety of needs, provide you with models whose behavior you may imitate or avoid, and may serve as a buffer against some of life's stress. In this section, some of the major factors that play a role in who you choose to be members of your social network are considered.

## Social Interaction

**Social interaction** is the term psychologists use to describe your encounters and relationships with others. This is a complex process, so complex that society has developed an elaborate set of norms to help us deal with many of these situations. Norms, you will remember, are unwritten rules for behavior that grow out of social interaction. They are not fixed, but change as society changes. Not so long ago, for example, waiters and waitresses automatically gave the bill for a meal to the male member of a party of two. Some still do, but the norm these days is to place the bill tactfully in the center of the table or on the edge halfway between the parties.

Because norms grow out of social interaction and are highly sensitive to the social environment in which this interaction takes place, they differ from one part of the country to another. For example, New York City motorists use their automobile horns regularly and persistently. In many parts of the southeastern United States, by contrast, horns are not honked even when there is a flagrant violation of traffic rules or etiquette.

The fact that norms change over time and vary among different segments of society doesn't change the fact that they play a vital role in social interaction. Without norms, each situation would have to be dealt with individually—an impossible task given the complexity of our lives today.

Norms that tell you how to act in the bank, with a stranger on the telephone, or when another driver runs a yellow traffic light are norms about *encounters*—the brief social interactions in which you participate many times a day. What are the factors that determine whether or not you are sufficiently attracted to another person to pursue social interaction beyond an encounter? How do you select your friends, your lovers, and your marriage partner from among all the possibilities?

## Interpersonal Attraction

In the most general sense, the answer to the questions just posed is that you select your partners for special relationships on the basis of your attraction to them. **Interpersonal attraction** is a feeling of being drawn to another person. It includes physical attraction, but it goes far beyond this.

In the sense that psychologists use the term, you may be attracted to people who are not at all good looking, to members of the same or the opposite

> Be slow in choosing a friend, slower in changing.
>
> *Benjamin Franklin*

Most of our interactions with other people are brief encounters guided by social norms for behavior.

sex, to older people, people the same age, and to children. The question is: Out of all the people in the world you *might* be attracted to, what factors influence who you *are* attracted to and how do these operate? Three factors that psychologists have found to be especially important are proximity, similarity, and reciprocity.

## Proximity and Attraction

Other things being equal, the most important factor influencing your choice of partners for social relationships is geographical *proximity* (nearness). This may seem a strange idea, but it makes sense when you think about it. Being near to someone increases the opportunity to get to know him or her better. Getting to know someone better increases the basis for being attracted to him or her.

Think about the friends you have now. Where did they come from? How many are roommates, people who live or used to live near you, classmates who happened to be sitting near you in a class (grade school, high school, college, or other) the first day, people you work with, or people you have met in the course of your work? In each case, you had many other possible friendships to form, but the odds are good that the ones you made were with people who were physically closer to you at the time.

A classic study of the relationship between proximity and friendship was carried out by three psychologists who examined friendship patterns in a campus married housing project (Festinger, Schachter, & Back, 1950). The residents of this project were asked to name the other residents with whom they socialized most often. It turned out that almost all of the friendships were with next-door neighbors. Virtually no socializing took place between couples who lived even as short a distance as three apartments from one another.

Now, three apartments away isn't a very great geographical distance by most standards, but it is a greater distance than next door. This is an example of the concept of functional distance; when it comes to forming relationships, we are rather lazy, tending to take the easy path. *Functional distance* in this context means practical distance as evaluated by the extent to which a distance does or does not facilitate interaction. People who live next door to one another in many settings would have to go out of their way to *avoid* one another.

Functional distance and geographical distance are related, but not the same. For example, the couples in the married housing study would have had to go out of their way to interact with other couples three or four apartments away, so they tended not to form friendships with these people. How, then, do we explain the fact that some of their friends lived miles away? The friends who lived farther away were people they had normal contact with on a regular basis somewhere other than home. Their functional distance from these couples was less than it was from couples living several apartments away even though their geographic distance from the neighboring couples was less.

The pattern of results obtained in the housing study have been confirmed many times in other situations, including choice of a marriage partner. Even in this mobile day and age, people still are very likely to marry someone who grew up quite close to them (Ineichen, 1979). It appears that in the area of interpersonal attraction, familiarity does *not* breed contempt, with one exception: if your initial reaction to someone is quite negative, proximity probably won't help matters (e.g., Swap, 1977).

## Similarity and Attraction

Proximity makes it easier to get to know someone; it also is more likely that you will have something in common with people who live, work, study, or relax near you. Psychologists find that *similarity* of backgrounds, interests, values, and attitudes increases the strength of interpersonal attraction between people.

Physical proximity is one of the strongest influences on who we have as friends.

One of the most consistent findings in the study of interpersonal attraction is that attitude similarity increases attraction. In one well-known study of this relationship, 44 pairs of college student volunteers were matched up for a brief date on the basis of an attitude questionnaire filled out early in the school term (Byrne, Ervin, & Lamberth, 1970). Reports by these students after the date confirmed the researchers' prediction that those pairs who had been matched up to be similar in attitudes were more attracted to one another than those who had been matched up to be dissimilar.

At this point you may be wondering what happened to the old principle that "opposites attract"? Certainly, we all can point to examples of good friends or happily married couples who appear to be complete opposites. Does this invalidate similarity as a general principle of attraction? Well, yes and no. To some extent, it depends on the ways that people are different or similar.

When it comes to attitudes, relevant research leaves little room to doubt that it is similarity that increases attraction. The same is not necessarily true of personality characteristics, however. In this realm, complementarity may increase attraction. The rather shy, bookish young man may be attracted to the vivacious, outgoing young woman, for example, because her personality compliments his.

The *complementarity hypothesis* of interpersonal attraction is based on the idea that people tend to seek out in others those traits they find desirable, but lack themselves. There also can be something quite exciting about getting to know someone who is completely different. This excitement may fade, however, if differences become a source of disagreement or irritation or if one or the other party changes in some important way. The weight of the evidence seems to favor similarity as a more important force for *maintaining* a relationship, if not for beginning it (Murstein, 1982).

The importance of similarity holds up in the area of physical attractiveness as well. Some glamorous movie and television actresses may be married happily to physically unprepossessing men, but in general, relationships between people of about the same level of physical attractiveness seem to fare better (Murstein, 1972; Murstein & Christy, 1976). There is more on physical appearance and attractiveness in *For Discussion*.

## Reciprocity and Attraction

So far, we have seen that you are more likely to be attracted to people with whom you have regular contact and something in common. There also is some evidence that you will be more attracted to others who show in some way that they like you. For example, suppose a classmate whom you really never have noticed before comes up to tell you what a great class report you presented. Suddenly, you see this person in a whole new light; you are interested although you never were before. This tendency to return compliments or expressed feelings of interest or liking is called *reciprocity*.

There are some qualifications to the principle that we tend to be attracted to people who seem to like us. For one, this effect seems to be stronger if the other person is physically attractive and/or popular than if he or she is ordinary looking or not well liked (e.g., Sigall & Aronson, 1969). We also exercise a certain amount of judgment in reciprocity; if the other person is laying it on a bit too thick, the effort may backfire.

# FOR DISCUSSION:
## What Makes People Attractive?

In many aspects of life, first impressions tend to be lasting impressions, and the very first impression another person makes is a physical one. If this impression is positive, others will be attracted to that person. If it is not, they may not make the effort to get to know him or her better. In one experiment, for example, students attended a dance with blind dates they believed had been selected by computer (Riedel & McKillip, 1979). These students were given a great deal of information about their dates, but the only thing that predicted their desire to see the dance dates again was physical attractiveness.

Many studies have shown that good-looking people are seen by others as more intelligent, interesting, competent, sensitive, modest, kind, poised, and sociable than physically unattractive people (e.g., Dion, Berscheid & Walster, 1972). With the exception of intelligence (Moran & McCullers, 1984), they may *be* more likely to possess these characteristics. Attractive people are responded to favorably by others, and positive attention from others brings out the best in many people.

Since appearance is so important in our social lives, the question of what makes people appear attractive to others is an important one. Traditionally, it has been assumed that the answer lies in bone structure, coloring, body build, regular features, and other physical attributes. From this perspective, only a lucky few are "born beautiful"; the rest of us must learn to do what we can to improve on nature.

The idea that attractiveness is dependent upon actual physical attributes has helped to create and support a multibillion-dollar cosmetic industry, thousands of weight-loss and body-restructuring salons, and a great many plastic surgeon's practices, among other industries dedicated to helping people look more like some

*Continued*

## FOR DISCUSSION:—*Continued*

physical ideal. Yet psychologists who have studied the question of physical attractiveness have found that a number of factors that have very little to do with actual physical attributes are important influences on the way other people judge appearance.

- The expression on your face has a lot to do with whether people think you are attractive. In one study, people posed in sad expressions were judged less attractive than the same people posed in happy expressions (Mueser, Gru, Sussman, & Rosen, 1984).

- The company you keep affects the perception others have of your attractiveness. Geiselman, Haight, and Kimata (1984) found that ordinary-looking women were judged more attractive when seen in the company of very attractive-looking women than when seen with un-

attractive or other ordinary-looking women.

- Perceptions of appearance depend to some extent on the type of relationship between the people involved. Men and women interested in a long-term, meaningful relationship are more likely to see beauty in terms of attractive personality, character, and behavior characteristics. Those seeking a sexual relationship only are more likely to judge attractiveness on the basis of physical features (Nevid, 1984).

- The way other people evaluate someone affects your perception of attractiveness. In one experiment, students were shown old photographs of actors and actresses currently celebrated for their looks, along with photographs of nonfamous people that had been taken

about the same time. Students who were given the names of the people in the photographs judged the stars to be more attractive than the others; those who were told nothing about the people involved were as likely to put the stars into the "less attractive" pile as into the "more attractive" pile (Jewell, 1985).

What research such as this suggests is that beauty, as evaluated on the basis of others' first impressions of you, isn't even skin deep. Think about the people you find attractive. What are the attributes that make you see them that way? How important is physical attractiveness to you in your choice of friends or dates? Why do you think it is so important to most people?

## Beyond Encounters: Getting to Know Someone

You might think of proximity, similarity, and reciprocity as filters that screen out successively more and more people from serious consideration as partners in a personal relationship. Generally speaking, those who are left will be people with whom you are able to interact; who share your attitudes, values, and interests to some degree; and who appear to be attracted to you (as well as you to them).

The principle of reciprocity not only affects the extent to which we are attracted to someone else but also offers a suggestion about how we might get to know him or her better. Compliments, praise, or simply expressions of interest in a person to whom we are attracted are effective ways to open up communication if they do not sound insincere and are not too obvious. But what happens once we have gotten someone's attention?

### The Development of a Relationship

According to Levinger (1974), relationships move through a series of predictable stages. Prior to any contact, the parties are unaware of one another's existence and have *zero contact* (stage 1). The next stage is *awareness;* at this point, one or both people have seen the other, but no contact has been made (stage 2).

After awareness comes *surface contact* (stage 3). This is the stage at which encounters occur. The "small talk" that Levinger says characterizes this stage is important as a way to explore the similarity and reciprocity that increase interpersonal attractiveness. If this is mutual and fairly strong, the parties will see more of one another. Gradually, they will move from small talk to **self-disclosure,** which is sharing thoughts, feelings, and secrets about themselves.

## Self-Disclosure and a Developing Relationship

Psychologists have studied many aspects of self-disclosure, and their findings tend to be quite consistent.

- Under most conditions, women tend to be more self-disclosing than men (e.g., Jourard, 1971). This seems consistent with another finding about personal relationships: women tend to form closer same-sex friendships than men (e.g., Cozby, 1973).

- People who tell too much about themselves too soon tend to turn others off. These *early disclosers* are seen by others as less secure, less sincere, less mature, and more self-absorbed than late disclosers. The other party, especially if a man, has less interest in pursuing a relationship with an early discloser (Wortman, Adesman, Herman, & Greenberg, 1976).

- Both sexes seem to have standards about the time to share certain kinds of information (Berger, Gardner, Clatterbuck, & Schulman, 1976). Facts are

---

### EXHIBIT 6–2

## The Timing of Personal Information Disclosure

### Information Revealed at Early Stages
Facts
*Examples:* I was born in Nebraska.
This is the first time I've been to this club.
Preferences
*Examples:* The one TV program I never miss is the "Tracy Ullman Show."
I'll eat almost anything, but I really love Italian food.

### Information Revealed at Intermediate Stages
Strong Opinions
*Examples:* I believe women should be at home with young children.
Rock music is really awful. How can anyone like that junk?
Personal Information (mild)
*Examples:* I've never seen myself as very attractive.
Good grades are very important to me.

### Information Revealed Late or Never
Personal information (strongly emotional or negative)
*Examples:* I haven't had sex for over a year.
Being somebody is the most important thing in the world to me.
"Secrets"
*Examples:* I had an abortion a few years ago.
I was arrested for car theft when I was 16.

---

*Note:* Examples by author. Groupings and sequencing based on "Perceptions of Information Sequencing in Relationship Development" by C. R. Berger, R. R. Gardner, G. W. Clatterbuck, and L. S. Shulman, *Human Communication Research*, 1976, *3*, 29–46.

shared first; secrets may not come out for quite a long time. Examples of the various kinds of self-disclosures that tend to be made early on, later, and late, or never, are shown in Exhibit 6–2.

The pace at which two people go through the process of self-disclosure, as illustrated by the examples in Exhibit 6–2, can vary enormously. One pair may meet at a cocktail party at 5:30 P.M. and be telling one another their innermost thoughts by midnight. For another, the process may take months or even years. In either case, if the relationship survives this process, it moves, according to Levinger, to the *mutuality* stage of relationship development (stage 4). At this stage, the participants tend to think of themselves as "we." This we-ness may stop at close friendship, it may lead to living together, or it may lead to marriage.

**Summing Up** ■

Research tells us that we are most likely to develop personal relationships with people who are physically attractive to us, who live or work near us, who make it clear that they like us, and who have something in common with us. These relationships serve many purposes and meet a variety of needs. They develop through stages from encounter through increased interaction and self-disclosing communication. If things go well during these stages, we have a new friend.

## THE NEED FOR INTIMACY

We have many encounters in our daily comings and goings. Most of these are brief and we never see those who were involved again. Some lead to casual acquaintanceships, such as we have with neighbors, former classmates, or the person who cuts our hair. Such interactions meet social needs on a surface level, but most of us want something more than this. We have a need for some close sharing relationship—a need for intimacy.

A **need for intimacy** refers to a need for very close, personal, and meaningful interaction with another person on a physical, emotional, and/or intellectual level. Friendship is one of the ways that this need may be satisfied.

## Friendship

Friends are among our most valuable assets. They provide companionship, support, and a sounding board for ideas and decisions. They cheer us up when we do well and comfort us when we fail. They help us cram for the exam, lend us something to wear to dinner with the important client, come to get us when the car breaks down miles from home, and babysit with the children when we have an unexpected opportunity to spend a weekend at a famous resort.

We have examined some of the factors that make you more or less likely to be initially attracted to another person. We also have taken a brief look at one model of typical relationship development. What kinds of things make it more likely that a particular relationship will go through all of the stages and reach friendship?

## What Do You Look for in a Friend?

We are all a little different in terms of the characteristics and qualities we look for in our friends, but certain qualities do appear to be valued by many people. In the friendship survey (Parlee, 1979) discussed briefly at the beginning of this chapter, we saw that the most important qualities to many of us are trustworthiness, loyalty, and affection/warmth.

Qualities such as these and the others ranked high in the survey, reduce the likelihood of a one-sided or destructive friendship. Frankness increases trust. Supportiveness reduces competitiveness of the sort that leaves one friend feeling that he or she has to lose if the other wins something. Independence reduces the possibility of one friend dominating the other. A sense of humor helps any relationship over the rough spots.

Our preference for certain qualities in our friends is reflected in the results of research into the foundations of satisfying personal relationships in general. Respect for another's rights, awareness of another's needs, effective communication, and genuine caring all have been found to be important in building and maintaining any relationship (Knox, 1988). **Trust, in the sense of being able to depend on the other person to sustain these qualities, seems to be particularly important.**

How do you know if you trust the other person in a particular relationship? Eighteen statements defining behaviors that psychologists have found people believe indicate trustworthiness appear in *Test Yourself.* Although this test was developed initially to study trust in romantic love relationships (Rempel & Holmes, 1986), it can serve equally well for any intimate relationship.

---

## TEST YOURSELF
## How Much Do You Trust Your Friend?

*Instructions:* Read each of the following statements with a particular friend in mind. Decide how strongly you agree or disagree with each statement. Place the appropriate number from the scale below in the space to the **left** of the statement.

| | |
|---|---|
| Strongly Disagree = 1 | Mildly Agree = 5 |
| Moderately Disagree = 2 | Moderately Agree = 6 |
| Mildly Disagree = 3 | Strongly Agree = 7 |

Neutral = 4

_____  1.  I know how _____ is going to act. _____ can always be counted on   _____
         to act as I expect.

_____  2.  I have found that _____ is a thoroughly dependable person, especially   _____
         when it comes to things that are important.

_____  3.  _____'s behavior tends to be quite variable. I can't always be sure   _____
         what _____ will surprise me with next.

_____  4.  Though times may change and the future is uncertain, I have faith   _____
         that _____ will always be ready and willing to offer me strength,
         come what may.

_____  5.  Based on past experience, I cannot, with complete confidence, rely on   _____
         _____ to keep promises made to me.

____ 6. It is sometimes difficult for me to be absolutely certain that _____ ____ will always continue to care for me; the future holds too many uncertainties and too many things can change in our relationship as time goes on.

____ 7. _____ is a very honest person, and even if _____were to make un- ____ believable statements, people should feel confident that what they are hearing is the truth.

____ 8. _____ is not very predictable. People can't always be certain how ____ _____is going to act from one day to another.

____ 9. _____ has proven to be a faithful person. No matter who _____was ____ married to, she or he would never be unfaithful, even if there was absolutely no chance of being caught.

____10. I am never concerned that unpredictable conflicts and serious tensions ____ may damage our relationship because I know we can weather any storm.

____11. I am very familiar with the patterns of behavior _____has estab- ____ lished, and he or she will behave in certain ways.

____12. If I have never faced a particular issue with _____before, I occasion- ____ ally worry that he or she won't take my feelings into account.

____13. Even in familiar circumstances, I am not totally certain _____will act ____ in the same way twice.

____14. I feel completely secure in facing unknown situations because I know ____ _____will never let me down.

____15. _____ is not necessarily someone who others always consider reli- ____ able. I can think of some times when _____could not be counted on.

____16. I occasionally find myself feeling uncomfortable with the emotional ____ investment I have made in our relationship because I find it hard to completely set aside my doubts about what lies ahead.

____17. _____ has not always proved to be trustworthy in the past, and there ____ are times when I am hesitant to let _____engage in activities that make me feel vulnerable.

____18. _____behaves in a consistent manner. ____

*Scoring:*

Your final score is determined by the numbers in the right-hand column. To obtain these numbers, do as follows: For questions, 3, 5, 6, 8, 12, 13, 15, and 17, *reverse* your left-column score number, as shown below, and write the new number in the **right-hand column.**

| | |
|---|---|
| 1—change to 7 | 5—change to 3 |
| 2—change to 6 | 6—change to 2 |
| 3—change to 5 | 7—change to 1 |

4—leave as 4

Your scores for the remaining questions should be rewritten in the right-hand column *as is.* Your final trust score is the sum of the numbers in the right-hand column. If this score is over 110, you have a high trust in your friend. If you scored below 90, your friendship may be in trouble. Scores between 90 and 100 indicate a relationship that is sound, but has definite room for improvement so far as your confidence in your friend is concerned.

*Note:* Reprinted with permission from *Psychology Today Magazine* Copyright © 1986 (PT Partners, L.P.).

## EXHIBIT 6–3

### Being a Friend

We all want to *have* friends, but we do not always give much thought to *being* a friend. Here a few tips for taking care of the friendships you have and the ones you may make in the future.

**DO**

- **Be appreciative** of the things your friends do for you. Too often we take their thoughtfulness or helpfulness or support for granted. That may be "what friends are for," but everyone likes to hear thank you once in a while.
- **Keep in touch** even when you don't have anything special or exciting to say. A note or a telephone call "just to say hi" can mean a lot, especially if you and your friend are geographically separated.
- **Try to be alert to signals** that your friends need a little extra support. Not all of us are able to ask for what we need from others. The friend who struggles along with work, school, and two children may say, "I'm fine, honest," until he or she drops from exhaustion. Watch for things you can *do* as well as offering expressions of sympathy.

**DON'T**

- **Pretend** to like things you don't like, have more money than you really do, be single when you are only separated, or whatever. Friends feel betrayed when these things come out later. Honesty is the best policy for you as well; keeping up the pretense is wearing.
- **Be a user.** No matter how willing your friend is to be the one who always drives to where you are going, gives the party at his or her house, pays for the groceries when you eat together, lends you something to wear, and so on, avoid the temptation to become a user. It has a sneaky way of becoming a habit, and other friends are not so accommodating.

## Being a Friend

Psychologists know the qualities that most people look for in friends and they understand the dynamics of good relationships, but their discussions can seem rather academic. How can you demonstrate such qualities as loyalty, honesty, and caring to others when you feel them? How can you communicate respect and awareness of another person's needs? Each person has an individual style, but there are certain behaviors that generally work for or against good friendships. Some of these are described in Exhibit 6–3.

## Summing Up ■

Friends are special people. They provide companionship, support, and love. Surveys tell us that trustworthiness, loyalty, frankness, independence, and supportiveness all rank high as qualities we look for in a friend. All of these characteristics make it more likely that a relationship will survive the hard times as well as the good and the convenient.

The importance of friendship in our lives makes it well worth putting effort into making and keeping friends. Doing so requires learning to *be* a friend as well as to *have* a friend; it is an active process. Some people are so good at this that they seem to be able to satisfy all of their needs for intimacy through friendship. Most of us, however, want one special person to love as well, and most psychologists believe that the best kind of love has much in common with the best kind of friendship.

## ■ KEY WORDS AND PHRASES

attachment

hardy personality

interpersonal attraction

need for intimacy

peers

peer acceptance

peer group

self-disclosure

social interaction

social support

support groups

trust

## ■ READ ON

*Friendship: How to Give It, How to Get It* by J. D. Block. New York: Macmillan, 1980. A clinical psychologist uses the results of over 2,000 in-depth interviews to examine the subject of nonsexual friendship relationships. Sample chapter titles include "Sisterhood: Powerful or Treacherous," "Men and Friendship: Noble Companions or Companionable Competitors," and "Friendship and Fame."

*Just Friends* by L. B. Rubin. New York: Harper & Row, 1985. Given the importance of friendship, it is surprising how few books are available just on this subject. Rubin's examination of friendship and how it fits in with other relationships (family relations, lovers, and so on) may help you get to know this "neglected relationship" better.

## ■ REFERENCES

Berger, C. R., Gardner, R. R. Clatterbuck, G. W., & Schulman, L. S. (1976). Perceptions of information sequencing in relationship development. *Human Communication Research, 3,* 29–46.

Bowlby, J. (1958). The nature of the child's tie to his mother. *International Journal of Psychoanalysis, 39,* 350–373.

Brownell, A., & Shumaker, S. A. (1984). Social support: An introduction to a complex phenomenon. *Journal of Social Issues, 40,* 1–9.

Byrne, D., Ervin, C. R., & Lamberth, J. (1970). Continuity between the experimental study of attraction and real-life computer dating. *Journal of Personality and Social Psychology, 16,* 157–165.

Cohen, S., & Wills, T. A. (1985). Stress, social support, and the buffering hypothesis. *Psychological Bulletin, 98,* 310–357.

Cozby, P. C. (1973). Self-disclosure: A literature review. *Psychological Bulletin, 79,* 73–91.

Dion, K. K., Berscheid, E., & Walster, E. (1972). What is beautiful is good. *Journal of Personality and Social Psychology, 24,* 285–290.

Festinger, L., Schachter, S., & Back, K. (1950). *Social pressures in informal groups: A study of factors in housing.* New York: Harper & Row.

Geiselman, R. E., Haight, N. A., & Kimata, L. G. (1984). Context effects on the perceived physical attractiveness of faces. *Journal of Experimental Social Psychology, 20,* 409–424.

Gold, M., & Yanof, D. S. (1985). Mothers, daughters, and girlfriends. *Journal of Personality and Social Psychology, 49,* 654–659.

Heller, K., & Mansbach, W. E. (1984). The multifaceted nature of social support in a community sample of elderly women. *Journal of Social Issues, 40,* 99–112.

Hojat, M. (1982). Loneliness as a function of parent-child and peer relations. *Journal of Psychology, 112,* 129–133.

Ineichen, B. (1979). The social geography of marriage. In M. Cook & G. Wilson (Eds.), *Love and attraction.* New York: Pergamon Press.

Jewell, L. N. (1985). Stars in their eyes. Unpublished.

Joffe, L. S., & Vaughn, B. E. (1982). Infant-mother attachment: Theory, assessment, and implications for development. In B. B. Wolman (Ed.), *Handbook of developmental psychology.* Englewood Cliffs, NJ: Prentice-Hall.

Jourard, S. M. (1971). *Self-disclosure: An experimental analysis of the transparent self.* New York: Wiley.

Kiesler, C. (1983). A "top down" look at public policy. *APA Monitor, 14,* 5.

Kobasa, S. C. (1979). Stressful life events, personality and health: An inquiry into hardiness. *Journal of Personality and Social Psychology, 37,* 1–11.

Knox, D. (1988). *Choices in relationships* (2nd ed.). St. Paul: West.

Levinger, G. (1974). A three-level approach to attraction: Toward an understanding of pair relatedness. In T. C. Huston (Ed.), *Foundations of interpersonal attraction.* New York: Academic Press.

Lieberman, M. A. (1986). Social supports: The consequences of psychologizing: A commentary. *Journal of Consulting and Clinical Psychology, 54,* 461–465.

Moran, J. D., & McCullers, J. C. (1984). A comparison of achievement scores in physically attractive and unattractive students. *Home Economics Research Journal, 13,* 36–40.

Mueser, K. T., Gru, B. W., Sussman, S., & Rosen, A. J. (1984). You're only as pretty as you feel: Facial expression as a determinant of physical attractiveness. *Journal of Personality and Social Psychology, 46,* 469–478.

Murstein, B. I. (1972). Physical attractiveness and marital choice. *Journal of Personality and Social Psychology, 22,* 8–12.

Murstein, B. I. (1982). Marital choice. In B. B. Wolman (Ed.), *Handbook of developmental psychology.* Englewood Cliffs, NJ: Prentice-Hall.

Murstein, B. I., & Christy, P. (1976). Physical attractiveness and marriage adjustment in middle-aged couples. *Journal of Personalty and Social Psychology, 34,* 537–542.

Nevid, J. S. (1984). Sex differences in factors of romantic attraction. *Sex Roles, 11,* 401–411.

Parlee, M. B., & Editors of *Psychology Today* (1979). The friendship bond. *Psychology Today, 13,* 43–55.

Rempel, J. K., & Holmes, J. G. (1986). How do I trust thee? *Psychology Today, 20,* 28–34.

Riedel, S. L., & McKillip, J. (1979). Friends, lovers, and physical attractiveness. Paper presented at the annual meeting of the Midwestern Psychological Association, Chicago.

Schachter, S. (1959). *The psychology of affiliation.* Stanford, CA: Stanford University Press.

Schaefer, C., Coyne, S. C., & Lazarus, R. S. (1981). The health-related functions of social support. *Journal of Behavioral Medicine, 4,* 381–406.

Sigall, H., & Aronson, E. (1969). Liking for an evaluator as a function of her physical attractiveness and the nature of the evaluations. *Journal of Experimental Social Psychology, 5,* 93–100.

Swap, W. C. (1977). Interpersonal attraction and repeated exposure to rewarders and punishers. *Personality and Social Psychology Bulletin, 3,* 248–251.

Waters, E., Wippman, J., & Stroufe, L. A. (1979). Attachment, positive affect, and competence in the peer group: Two studies in construct validation. *Child Development, 46,* 348–356.

White, B. C. (1975). *The first three years of life.* Englewood Cliffs, NJ: Prentice-Hall.

Wortman, C. B., Adesman, P., Herman, E., & Greenberg, P. (1976). Self-disclosure: An attributional perspective. *Journal of Personality and Social Psychology, 33,* 184–191.

# Your Intimate World: Sex and Sexual Relationships

With the sexual revolution won
It's supposed to be so easy
To get a date, find your mate
Make wild love so pleasingly
So tell me why it's just so tough
To find the only one
Or even one who's joyous fun
With the sexual revolution won?
(Anonymous)

The sex drive is a basic biological urge; our bodies are programmed for it to enable us to reproduce ourselves. It would seem, then, that satisfying our sexual needs ought to be as simple as satisfying other biological needs, such as the needs for food and water. But sex, for most people, isn't just about biology. It is also about caring and closeness and sharing and commitment and expressing feelings. And it can be about anger and violence and power and manipulation and conquest and a host of other motives.

Many thought that the problems caused by the complexity of human sexuality would be solved if we would bring them out in the open, talk about them, and feel free to pursue our sexual natures without the taboos and restraints that so long surrounded this subject. But as the anonymous author of the poem says, this sexual revolution is won and it still isn't easy. To add to our difficulties, we've acquired some staggering social problems, such as the sexually transmitted disease epidemic of the late 1970s and 1980s. Most psychologists, doctors, and others concerned with sexual behavior and relationships believe that now, more than ever, there is a great need for better understanding of human sexuality and sexual behavior.

In this chapter, sex and sexual relationships are explored from several perspectives. First, sexual anatomy and functioning are reviewed. Next, attitudes toward sex and America's sexual revolution are examined in more detail. Then, some common problems arising in long-term sexual relationships are considered. Finally, we look at some of the special problems that people have either within or because of sexual relationships—sexually-transmitted disease, sexual dysfunctions, and unwanted pregnancies.

## SEXUAL ANATOMY, SEXUAL FUNCTIONING, AND SEXUAL BEHAVIOR

Were you a Terrible Teen? If so, it isn't surprising. After years of giving you dependable service (as long as it got plenty of the right food and rest), your body started playing tricks on you. If you were female, you developed breasts and hips, and finding clothes to fit became a lot more complicated. You may have "shot up" and found that you suddenly were several inches taller than most of the boys in your class. You also may have found yourself with skin problems for the first time in your life, and perhaps the menstruation cycle brought with it new feelings of depression and being fat.

If you were male, puberty was marked by the enlargement of the testes and penis and the growth of facial and body hair. Your voice began changing, perhaps embarrassing you by cracking at awkward moments. You too had a growth spurt; it probably lagged about 2 years behind that of your female friends and classmates, but you continued to grow for about 2 years longer than most girls.

The rate at which you passed through the stages of adolescent physical development may have been about the same as, or quite different from, that of your peers. You may have been your current full height by the time you

The physical changes that accompany puberty can be a source of stress and embarrassment to both sexes.

were 14 or continued to grow after entering college. You may have looked about as you do now by the time you were 16 or not blossomed out until you were 20. Nevertheless, once you passed through puberty, sexually you were an adult.

## Sexual Anatomy and Functioning

Your transition from child to adult capable of reproducing the species was a biological event of great significance. Although sexual curiosity and experimentation are natural in children, most of us do not experience strong physical attraction toward members of the opposite sex until our bodies are prepared for it. Love may be more than chemistry, but hormones certainly play a role.

Male hormones, called **androgens,** are produced in the testes starting about 8 weeks after conception. The most important androgen is **testosterone,** which together with other male hormones, promotes the development of male sex organs and represses the development of female sex organs. Prior to this time, the fetus is *undifferentiated*—that is, the sex chromosomes carry the genetic program for the hormones that will make it male or female, but this development has not yet begun. At puberty there is an increase in the level of testosterone, and this produces the rather dramatic external changes in male appearance described earlier. The fully developed male sexual anatomy is shown in Figure 7–1.

The **penis** is the male sex organ that transmits sperm to the female during sexual intercourse. This sperm is produced in the **testes,** which hang away from the body in a sac called the *scrotum* to maintain the required temperature for potency. During intercourse, the stored sperm travel from the testes through special ducts and canals up and over the bladder and back down into the *urethra.* From here, they are ejaculated during male orgasm. The urethra also carries urine out of the body, but a special valve makes it impossible for sperm and urine to mix.

Figure 7–1  **The Male Sexual Anatomy**

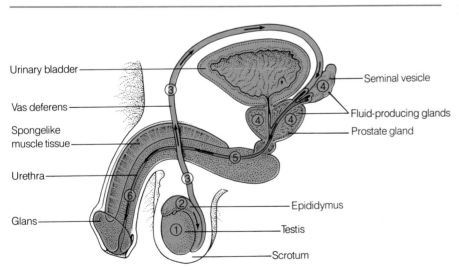

Female hormones are called **estrogens** and are produced by the **ovaries.** These hormones determine whether or not a female is able to become pregnant at any particular time, but they appear to have little effect on female sexual arousal. Unlike many female mammals who are sexually receptive only when their egg cells may be fertilized, human female sexual desire may occur at any time.

The fully developed female sexual anatomy is shown in Figure 7–2. The **vagina** is a tubelike cavity, normally some three to five inches in length, that expands to accommodate the penis during intercourse. It also serves as the exit canal for a baby in a normal delivery. The vagina is connected to the uterus by a small opening called a *cervix,* through which sperm must pass if fertilization is to occur. The uterus, in turn, is connected to the ovaries by means of the *Fallopian tubes.* Eggs, or *ova,* produced in the ovaries travel through these tubes, and it is here that fertilization occurs.

Female sexual pleasure is considerably less related to the reproductive process reviewed than is that of the male. While some would still argue that the only true female orgasm results from penile stimulation of the vagina, the facts contradict this belief. It is the **clitoris,** a small external organ that has no reproductive function, that appears to play the central role in female sexual stimulation.

Despite the numerous differences, there are some similarities in male and female sexual anatomy and functioning. The clitoris, like the penis, becomes engorged with blood and enlarged during sexual stimulation. The ovaries and testes serve similar functions, although ovaries are located inside the body and testes outside. Finally, males and female systems both produce male and female hormones.

## Sexual Behavior

Although *sex* means coitus (see Exhibit 7–1 for a definition of this and other terms in this section) to most people, there are number of other behaviors that

Figure 7–2   **The Female Sexual Anatomy**

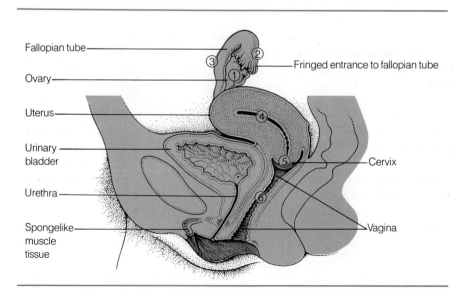

## EXHIBIT 7–1
## A Glossary of Sexual Behavior Terms

**Anal sex:**  A form of sexual intercourse in which the penis is inserted into the partner's anus and rectum.

**Coitus:**  The clinical term for sexual intercourse, in which the penis is inserted into the vagina.

**Cunnilingus:**  Oral stimulation of the female genitals.

**Ejaculation:**  Expulsion, by involuntary contractions, of semen from the penis.

**Fellatio:**  Oral stimulation of the male genitals.

**Foreplay:**  Physical contact and stimulation that leads to coitus.

**Masturbation:**  Self-manipulation of the genital area. Also called autoeroticism.

**Oral sex:**  Oral-genital contact between two persons, male or female, with or without orgasm.

**Orgasm:**  A series of involuntary tension-releasing contractions that occur in males and females at the climax of sexual arousal. Usually accompanied in the male by ejaculation.

**Petting:**  Mutual handling, stroking, or kissing of partners' bodies to enhance sexual excitement and arousal.

**Refractory period:**  A period of time following ejaculation during which the male is unable to experience another orgasm.

**Sex-tension flush:**  A red, measleslike blotchiness that may appear on the neck and chest during sexual excitement.

are part of sexual relationships. Petting long has been very common for members of both sexes. The primary differences today seem to be that it starts earlier and is enjoyed for its own sake rather than as a substitute for sexual intercourse.

Oral sex may be part of heavy petting or part of the foreplay for coitus. Both fellatio and cunnilingus also are engaged in for their own pleasure. Surveys suggest that a large percentage of couples practice oral sex, although it is somewhat more common among college-educated men and women (e.g., Belcastro, 1985). Anal sex is fairly common among male homosexual couples, and a small percentage of heterosexuals experiment with this form of intercourse.

Self-stimulation, or masturbation, a sexual activity that requires no partner, is a common practice among married and unmarried members of both sexes. Old ideas that this practice is harmful seem to have vanished. Almost all male adults and many female adults (percentages vary considerably from one survey to the next) report having masturbated to orgasm at least once (e.g., Petersen et. al., 1983; Story, 1985). Despite its frequency, most people do not discuss masturbation with their sexual partners. To this extent, former taboos are still with us. We no longer think it is wrong, but evidently we still feel a twinge of guilt when we continue to engage in masturbation even though we have a regular sex partner.

## The Sexual Response Cycle

Questionnaires and discussions about sex can tell us what people will say they think about sex and what they say they do about sex, but nothing about the experience itself. Until the 1960s, the only information of this nature available came from physicians, novels, or descriptions by participants. William Masters and Virginia Johnson (1966) moved the study of human sexual experience into the realm of science by observing activity directly.

Amidst a storm of controversy, Masters and Johnson filmed volunteers engaging in sexual activities in a laboratory that was equipped for recording a variety of physiological responses. (The pair decorated an entire wall of their famous institute in St. Louis with sarcastic cartoons prompted by their research.) In addition, they interviewed their subjects for more personal reactions. Observations and interviews with hundreds of men and women led them to propose the model of sexual response shown in Figure 7–3.

The Masters and Johnson model has four stages, the same four for men and women. The first is an *excitement phase*, during which the heart rate, blood pressure, and breathing rate increase. In women, nipples become erect, the clitoris expands, and the inner vagina lengthens and becomes lubricated. Men experience a rush of blood to the penis, which becomes erect. Either sex may exhibit a sex-tension flush, but it is much more common in women.

Figure 7–3 **A Four-Stage Model of Human Sexual Response**

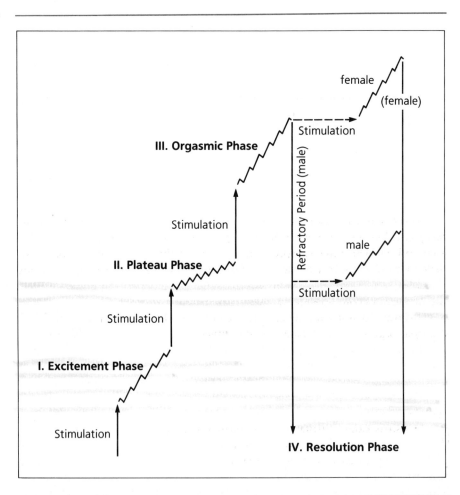

The physical arousal that characterizes the excitement phase is brought about in many ways. Some, such as kissing, petting, and other sex-play activities are behavioral and characterized by physical touching. Some, such as love or explicit sex talk and fantasizing are cognitive; stimulation occurs in the mind and is translated to the body.

In the second phase, the *plateau phase,* of the Masters and Johnson model, early responses, such as an increase in blood pressure and heart rate, are intensified in preparation for orgasm. The outer third of the vagina swells, the more easily to accommodate the penis, and the clitoris shortens. The penis enlarges even more and sometimes secretes fluid, which may contain sperm (one reason that it is possible for a woman to become pregnant during extremely heavy petting even though full penetration does not occur). The nipples of both men and women become erect and sensitive; the penis may become darker in color and a female's breasts may enlarge.

The third phase, the *orgasmic phase,* of the sexual response cycle is characterized by involuntary muscle contractions in the pelvic region of both men and women. The initial contractions are intense and occur at a rate of about five every 4 seconds. For men, they end with involuntary ejaculation of about a teaspoon of sperm; women may secrete excess lubrication at this time.

To describe orgasm as a series of contractions is to vastly underestimate the quality of the experience. Despite the physiological simplicity of this response, it often dims the participants' consciousness and perception of other events. Awareness seems to narrow down to a level that is exclusively physical. Both men and women report these sensations to be extremely pleasurable, although, as has often been noted, facial expressions and verbalizations during orgasm suggest the opposite.

A variety of myths has arisen about the orgasmic phase of sexual activity. These misunderstandings can confuse both sexes and reduce uninhibited enjoyment of sexual activity, turning it into a goal-oriented activity instead. A few of the more prevalent of these myths, together with the facts, are described in Exhibit 7–2.

Masters and Johnson's fourth stage of sexual response is called the *resolution phase*. During this period, physiological functioning returns to normal, but men and women differ sharply in the timing of this cool-down period. After male orgasm, there is a refractory period during which another orgasm is impossible (see Figure 7–3). This period varies considerably from one man to the next but becomes longer as men grow older.

Women do not experience a refractory period, and many are capable of multiple orgasms if stimulation is continued (see Figure 7–3). The fact that women are potentially multiorgasmic should not be taken as a standard, however. Not all women experience multiple orgasms, and the frequency of occurrence among those who do varies widely. Multiple orgasms also have been observed in men, but occurrence is rare and the capacity vanishes by age 30 (Pesman, 1984).

It also is quite normal for a woman not to experience an orgasm at all during a sexual encounter. Many researchers have confirmed that women typically take up to twice as long to reach orgasm as men. As a result, a woman still may be in the plateau stage when her partner is ready for a good nap. This difference necessitates some form of adjustment if the sexual relationship

## EXHIBIT 7–2

## Orgasm: Fact and Fiction

*Fiction:* Orgasm is a shattering, "earth-moving" experience.

*Fact:* Orgasms vary, even with the same partner, from relatively mild, pleasant contractions to an intense physical and emotional experience.

*Fiction:* Coitus without orgasm is harmful.

*Fact:* Men experience physical distress when intercourse does not terminate in ejaculation. Women also may experience physical discomfort, but it seldom is severe. For neither sex is intercourse without orgasm harmful.

*Fiction:* If a man is unable to bring a woman to orgasm without "artificial" (manual, oral, or mechanical) stimulation, he is a poor lover.

*Fact:* It is estimated that half of all women require some form of stimulation other than by the penis in order to achieve orgasm.

*Fiction:* There is a difference between female orgasm achieved as the result of vaginal stimulation by a penis and orgasm achieved by other means.

*Fact:* There may be a great difference emotionally and psychologically, but it has not been demonstrated that there is any difference physically.

*Fiction:* Simultaneous orgasm is the ultimate sexual experience.

*Fact:* Most couples find simultaneous orgasm exciting, but it is a rare occurrence. Experts say that setting this as a goal does more harm than good since it emphasizes performance instead of enjoyment.

is an ongoing one. Many women can derive considerable pleasure from sex without orgasm, but few of those who have experienced orgasms are willing to give up the experience entirely. (A few women never have experienced orgasm; see Exhibit 7–3.)

## Choice of a Sex Partner: Heterosexuality, Homosexuality and Bisexuality

It has been estimated that 75% to 80% of the male population and 85% to 90% of the female population are exclusively **heterosexual.** They choose their partners for sexual activities only from members of the opposite sex (e.g., Hyde, 1972; Story, 1985). An estimated 2% of men and 1% of women are exclusively **homosexual** (Huber et al., 1982). They are sexually attracted only to members of the same sex.

A few individuals are **bisexual.** They are attracted to and engage in sexual activity with members of both sexes on about an equal basis. There are no accurate figures on the extent of true bisexuality, but data suggest that some 25 million adult Americans have had both heterosexual and homosexual experiences (Zinik, 1985). Thus, we see that sexual preference is not a matter of heterosexuality *versus* homosexuality, but a continuum running from exclusively heterosexual through a mixed heterosexual/homosexual orientation to exclusively homosexual (Maier, 1984).

In our culture, heterosexuality is normal in the sense that it is the way most people are. True bisexuality seems to be relatively rare (although, as mentioned, we lack accurate information in this area). Homosexuality is common enough, yet different enough, to have attracted considerable research interest. Several findings about those who prefer sexual activities with members of their own sex may be summarized.

- *The causes of homosexual preferences are still speculative.* Genetic predispositions, certain patterns of upbringing, and the reinforcing effects of pleasant homosexual experiences in adolescence and early adulthood are among the factors believed to be relevant. It also has been found that a number of both male and female homosexuals have had extremely unpleasant experiences with members of the opposite sex prior to becoming homosexual (Coleman, Butcher, & Carson, 1984).

- *Homosexuality is not a mental disorder.* At various times in history, it has been regarded as sinful, criminal, a mental disease, an abnormal variation on the human theme, or all four. It was not until 1973 that homosexuality officially was erased from the American Psychiatric Association's list of recognized mental disorders. Despite this strong negative bias on the parts of others toward their choice of sex partners, there is no evidence that homosexuals, as a group, are any less well adjusted psychologically than heterosexuals, as a group (e.g., Bell & Weinberg, 1978).

- *There is no evidence that all, or even most, homosexuals want to be "cured."* The picture of the homosexual life as furtive, miserable, and degrading, where accurate, is to a considerable degree the result of negative social attitudes and pressures. It is this social stigma, not their homosexuality, that many want changed. *Reorientation therapy* is available for homosexuals who do wish to change their sexual preferences, but its success is by no means assured (Sturgis & Adams, 1978). Furthermore, many are coming to question this as an appropriate therapeutic goal (e.g., Davison, 1978).

Attitudes toward sex are to a significant degree influenced by the values of a particular culture (Levine, 1986). For a variety of historical reasons, homosexuality long has been regarded as unacceptable deviant behavior in our country. This is not so everywhere, and homosexuality is both more accepted and more widely practiced in other cultures today (Bales, 1986).

As more homosexuals in our culture have been openly proclaiming their sexual preferences and demanding an end to harassment, things have been changing in our society. Far more people than ever before seem to accept homosexuality as an alternative for others, if not themselves. But some people are concerned that **AIDS** (acquired immunodeficiency syndrome), the "gay disease," is going to undermine this social progress and bring about a return to "homophobia," an exaggerated fear of homosexuals.

AIDS is *not* a "gay disease." The AIDS virus isn't interested in an individual's sexual orientation; it is widespread among heterosexuals in Africa, the country where the virus is believed to have originated. It probably is chance that brought AIDS to us in a homosexual carrier rather than a heterosexual one, and it is worth repeating what you may have heard before. You do not "catch" AIDS as you "catch" a cold, and you cannot get AIDS from casual contact with a homosexual individual.

*Dear Miss Manners:*
What am I supposed to say when I am introduced to a homosexual "couple."?
*Gentle Reader:*
"How do you do?"
"How do you do?"

*Judith Martin*

## ATTITUDES TOWARD SEX

The need for physical closeness with another person goes deep in most of us. We express this need in various ways—by touching, hugging, patting, kissing, and engaging in sexual intercourse. A need for intimacy is not the only reason for sexual activity, however. There is sex for physiological release, for procreation, and for recreation as well, and all of these reasons are accepted as valid today. It wasn't always so, however. For much of our society's history, the prevailing attitude was that sex was basically for the procreation of children, at least where women were concerned. Men, believed to be fundamentally more physical creatures, were given more leeway to engage in sexual activity for physiological release. Sex as an enjoyable recreational activity for members of both sexes is a relatively newer idea.

Old attitudes toward sex are by no means dead, but they no longer represent the norm in our society. For a time at least, the pendulum actually had swung the other way. Sexual activity in or out of marriage for the sake of the physical enjoyment of the act became widely accepted. People who did not hold this view (or at least would admit that they did not) seemed to be in the minority (Hendrick, Hendrick, Slapion-Foote, & Foote, 1985).

## Behind the Revolution

The changes described took place in a relatively short time period that began in the 1960s. A number of factors played a part in this revolution. A major one was "the pill," a birth control method that freed women from fears of unwanted pregnancies for the first time in history. Reduced parental supervision as more mothers went out to work, increased availability of automobiles for privacy (or transportation to privacy), and relaxed supervision at many colleges and universities all contributed to a greater freedom to explore sexual horizons.

As opportunities for sexual activity became more numerous and fears of unwanted pregnancy became less powerful, sex for enjoyment became more acceptable. To many, if not all, sex became a natural part of regular dating relationships. The widespread commercialization of sex (which many believe, rightly or wrongly, got its biggest boost from Hugh Hefner's *Playboy* empire) also played a role in new attitudes toward sex. But this freedom to express our sexual selves more openly has not been without its costs:

> With this new set of standards, we are often unduly concerned about whether we are long enough, big enough, deep enough, tight enough, fast enough, slow enough, attractive enough, tall enough, or good enough (Napoli, Kilbride, & Tebbs, 1988, p. 293).

Such concerns mean that new attitudes toward sex have not represented freedom to some. They have felt pressured to be "sexy," to engage in casual sexual liaisons, to perform to some (mythical) standards for being "good in bed," and to profess an interest in sex that is wholly inconsistent with their true feelings and priorities. Among young people, this pressure often shows

Although the homosexual population in this country has been hit hard by AIDS, this is not a "homosexual disease;" many other people are at risk and so far as physicians know, anyone *can* contract AIDS.

itself in acute embarrassment at being a **virgin**—someone with no sexual intercourse experience.

## Where Do We Go from Here?

No one predicted current attitudes toward sex 30 years ago, and it is unlikely that anyone can say with accuracy where things will stand in the future. Some cautious speculations can be made, however, on the basis of certain trends that have been observed in a number of surveys about sex.

- *The majority of both men and women will have a premarital sexual relationship with at least one partner.* The clearest trend in surveys about sexual attitudes and practices has been the narrowing gap between men and women with regard to sex before marriage (e.g., Belcastro, 1985; Peplau, Rubin, & Hill, 1977). There is still, however, a slight tendency for *both* sexes to ascribe to the traditional line that it is more acceptable for men than for women (e.g., Kallen, Stephenson, & Doughty, 1983; Roper Organization, 1985).

- *The rate of extramarital sexual encounters will not rise significantly.* The gap between the number of women and the number of men who admit to having extramarital sexual encounters is narrowing (e.g., Tavris & Sadd, 1977). Attitudes toward infidelity, however, remain basically negative; the upper limit for men taking part in this practice has remained steady at about 50% for decades (Frank & Enos, 1983).

- *The "affection rider" will remain strong.* Both men and women continue to emphasize the role that strong affection should play in sexual relationships. There is little evidence that media emphasis on "fun sex" is bringing about any fundamental change in this attitude (Knox & Wilson, 1983).

- *The incidence of casual sex will diminish.* Disillusionment with uncommitted casual encounters, a trend toward more conservative values in society, and fear of sexually transmitted disease seem to be having their effects on the permissive attitudes of the 1970s (*U.S. News & World Report,* 1986). Some movement away from casual sex was seen by researchers well before AIDS reached its current proportions, but there seems little doubt that this disease will accelerate the movement back toward more conservative attitudes and practices. It is too early to say how long this will take and how far it will go.

The preceding conclusions are based on survey data, and whenever we deal with such data, we must keep in mind that people who respond voluntarily to questionnaires may be different in some significant ways from people who do not. This does not make such data worthless, however. In fact, when it comes to sex surveys, it may be that people who are willing to talk about their sexual attitudes and behavior are better indicators of what lies ahead in this area than people who are not. At the same time, we should always remember that *any* data based on questionnaire responses must be interpreted with caution; there is no way to know exactly how accurately people are answering the questions.

# SEXUAL ADJUSTMENT IN LONG-TERM RELATIONSHIPS

Changing attitudes toward sex have meant that many more people than previously have sexual relationships that are one-time encounters or short-lived affairs, but most people also become involved in a long-term or permanent commitment to another person at some time in their lives. No matter how good the sexual relationship that begins such commitments, things can change. Three problems that many couples face at one time or another are unequal sexual desire, boredom, and the effects of aging on sexual activity.

## Unequal Desire for Sexual Activity

More than 40 years ago, Alfred Kinsey and his associates published the results of their interviews with over 6,000 men and women on the subject of sexual behavior (Kinsey, Pomeroy, & Martin, 1948; Kinsey, Pomeroy, Martin, & Gebhard, 1953). One of the findings that was quoted often was that the majority of married couples in their 20s and 30s reported having sexual intercourse once or twice a week. This information caused great confusion. Couples having regular sexual relations more often worried that they were "oversexed." Couples whose sexual activity was less frequent worried that they had the opposite problem.

If the idea of evaluating the frequency of your sexual behavior on the basis of some national average sounds like nonsense to you, that is healthy. The right frequency of sexual activity for any couple is what is right for them. Problems arise, however, when one partner desires sexual activity more frequently than the other. Although, traditionally, the man has desired more sexual activity (e.g., Levinger, 1966), this seems to be changing. In a recent large-scale survey, the most frequent complaint women had about their sex lives was

Books and mechanical devices can help couples bring variety to their sex lives, but do not take the place of genuine affection and mutual consideration.

that their husbands did not want to make love often enough (Knupper & Enos, 1985).

Many factors can lead to partners getting out of sync with respect to sexual desire. Unusual stress at work or simply absorption in a career can reduce one partner's interest. So can the aftermath of childbirth or the exhausting care of small children. Illness or drugs can reduce sexual desire temporarily. Anxiety, hostility, anger, depression, and/or problems with the relationship also can have such an effect.

It is entirely normal for sexual desire in a long-term relationship to ebb and flow with state of mind, health, and life situation, but persistent inequality in desire for sex is likely to create serious problems. The unsatisfied partner feels frustrated and angry; the other partner feels pressured and guilty. Left unconfronted, these feelings can lead to extramarital involvement or other problems and eventually may lead to divorce.

What do you do about this problem? The answer varies according to the causes and the people involved, but any solution starts with getting it out in the open. Communication is vital, both for solving the problem and for maintaining some emotional intimacy while it persists. The longer couples avoid confronting this issue, the more difficult it becomes to talk about; and the more difficult it becomes to talk about, the more alone each partner may feel. If the situation persists, professional help may be necessary.

## Boredom

A lack of desire for sexual activity with one's partner may result from a reduced sex drive or from boredom with the "same old thing." Boredom also may be expressed directly in brief, perfunctory lovemaking or obvious preoccupation with other things during sexual activity.

The most frequent reason given for boredom with sex with the same partner is the predictability of the experience, yet the possibilities for variety seem virtually unlimited. Sexual activity at different times of the day, in different positions, in different places, longer foreplay, increased playfulness, and sharing of fantasies are among the avenues to be explored. Books of the how-to type and mechanical aids, such as a vibrator, also can add zest, provided these do not become ends instead of means for enriching the sexual experience.

Finally, some couples find that erotic material in books, magazines, and movies that describe and depict sexual encounters also stimulate the sexual experience. Such materials are highly controversial, however, and many people believe that they should not be made readily available. There is more on this issue in *For Discussion*.

### Extradyadic Relationships

Some couples believe that the solution to boredom with one's sex partner is to take other partners. The most common form of this solution is the **extradyadic relationship.** This term refers to a sexual encounter or relationship outside a steady, cohabiting, or marriage relationship. (When the individual involved is married, the older term *extramarital relationship* applies.) Experiences and opinions as to whether this is an adaptive solution vary widely. For every person who believes that outside sexual activity has been good for a

# FOR DISCUSSION:
## Erotica and Sexual Violence and Abuse

In July 1986, Attorney General Edwin Meese's Commission on Pornography released its final report on what it believed to be the connection between (a) sexually explicit material called erotica and (b) sexual violence and abuse of women and children, including rape, wife battering, and sexual crimes against children. (Pornography is a term that refers to erotic material with no socially redeeming value—as, for example, a moral or literary value. This designation is a matter of judgment, and the term *pornography* is not used here, although it is used extensively in the Meese report.)

The commission concluded that there is a causal link between erotica of a violent nature and aggressive behavior toward women. It also found a connection between sexually explicit material that degrades women (but is not violent) and sexual violence. It further stated a conviction that erotica that is neither violent nor degrading to women is not harmless, although there is no evidence that it is related to sexual violence or abuse.

The Meese report is in direct opposition to a 1970 report by the President's Commission on Obscenity and Pornography, which concluded that sexually explicit material was *not* a significant cause of sexual violence and abuse (Abelson, Cohen, Heaton, & Slider, 1970). Members of the Meese commission believe the difference lies in the fact that much more erotica is available now and it is far more violent and explicit than that available in the late 1960s.

The Meese report generated a storm of controversy. It is not based on any scientific study of the problem, but on a year-long process of reviewing the material and the sex-related goods and services that are available to the public, talking to the victims of sexual violence and abuse, and studying past academic reports on the question. Many believe that this approach simply is inadequate to show any causal link between erotica and violence. They argue that the facts that (1) there is more (and more violent) erotica available and (2) there are more crimes of a violent sexual nature do not mean that the first causes the second; scientific studies are needed to determine if there is a causal link.

Social scientists who do study the problem seem agreed that if there is a causal link, it probably is through the violence, not the sex. One researcher says of his laboratory studies on the question: "If you take out the sex and leave the violence, you get the increased violent behavior. . . . If you take out the violence and leave the sex, nothing happens" (Donnerstein, 1986). In addition, many social scientists believe that extensive involvement with erotica of a violent nature is a symptom, not a cause, of aggressiveness. But this is difficult to demonstrate, and even if it is true, it does not answer the question of whether the erotica may tip the balance to acting out aggressive impulses in a sexual context.

Almost any question about a connection between exposure to sexually explicit materials and sexual violence and abuse is difficult to answer in a manner that is both scientific and real. Not the least of the difficulties is the fact that in a realistic investigation much of the relevant data would be collected from the perpetrators of crimes. There is little reason to expect these people to be candid, even if they were accessible to interview.

As a result of this and many other problems, most people investigating the erotica-violence link reply on records (such as amount of erotic material sold in an area and number of reported sexual violence and abuse crimes) or on case histories or laboratory studies. What drawbacks do you see with these procedures from a scientific standpoint? Can you suggest a better way to study the question? What evidence would you want to have before concluding that there may be a connection? If you found it, what action do you think should be taken? Among the recommendations by the Meese panel:

- Enact federal laws to make it easier to seize the assets of those involved in the production, distribution, and sale of erotica of a violent nature and/or featuring children ("child pornography").

- Authorize the Federal Communications Commission to restrict porno cable TV shows and "Dial-a-Porn" telephone services.

- Enact a law to make willful possession of child pornography a felony.

- Persuade judges to give longer jail sentences to those who repeatedly violate existing laws in this area.

Do you agree with those who say such recommendations are simply a form of censorship? What would you recommend instead?

relationship, or even saved it, there is at least one who has found that one problem has been traded for another.

Counselors believe that an important source of the damaging effects extradyadic sex may have on a relationship is the deception that such activities require. One solution to this is for couples to agree that each has the right to his or her own private life, including relationships (sexual and otherwise) with other people. According to Nena and George O'Neill, authors of *Open Marriage* (1972), this agreement makes for greater individual growth and fulfillment. Since happier individuals are likely to have happier relationships, the idea makes sense in theory.

*Open Marriage* was published more than 15 years ago, and it is safe to say that the idea has not caught on as a major alternative to more traditional relationships. A big problem seems to be that it is rare to find two people who *both* want this sort of relationship (especially if it previously has been traditional), and the O'Neills stress that mutual participation is critical. Another problem with the open marriage concept (whether or not the couple is married) is the risk that one partner will fall in love with someone else. This also is a problem in clandestine extradyadic relationships, of course, and a minority of couples have tried swinging as a way to combat sexual boredom without running this risk.

*Swinging* involves both partners in controlled extradyadic sex. Usually, this takes place with another couple, or couples, of similar inclination at a party arranged for the purpose. The rules are that both partners participate and that there be no emotional involvement; for this reason, participants in swinging parties often are strangers who do not see one another again.

It has been estimated that about 10% of the population are engaged in swinging and/or open marriage at any given time (Thompson, 1984). We don't have much information about how well either serves its intended purpose, but it seems clear that neither is likely to become a common solution to the problem of boredom with a sex partner.

## Sexual Adjustment with Age

It is not true that people lose interest in sex when they get older, but it is true that age brings changes that affect sexual relationships. Studies of sexual responsiveness with age find that as men get older, they take longer and require more stimulation to achieve an erection and their refractory periods get longer. Women's vaginas become less elastic and lubrication decreases. Both sexes are slower to be aroused, and orgasms tend to be less intense (Rossman, 1978).

The physiological changes that accompany aging mean that sexual activity tends to decline for most people as they get older. In one study, the frequency of intercourse reported by men declined every year after the age of 46 (Pfeiffer, Verwoerdt, & Davis, 1972). It isn't only the age of the partners that affects sexual activity, however; the age of the *relationship* is relevant as well.

One of the most disappointing aspects of a long-term relationship to many couples is the decline in the intense sexuality experienced during the early days of being together. For example, although reported frequency of sexual intercourse between married couples has gone up substantially since the Kinsey survey, it still drops off with almost every passing year. In one study, couples married for a year reported having intercourse an average of fifteen times a month (Greenblat, 1983). This rate dropped to about six times a month after 6 years of marriage. Jasso (1985) studied couples married between 1 month and 25 years and found that the frequency of sexual intercourse decreased as the length of a marriage increased.

White hairs or not, you can still be a lover.

*Goethe*

The demands of work, housekeeping, and family can reduce the desires of one or both partners for sexual activity.

There are many reasons for the decline in rate of sexual activity as a relationship ages. Work and careers, the demands of keeping a household going, and other external factors play a role in this decline. So does satiation or fulfillment; most people do not have unlimited needs or desires for sexual intercourse.

The various changes that take place as a relationship ages require adjustments to established patterns of sexual activity, but they do not have to mean that the sexual relationship is less enjoyable. Nor do the physiological changes that accompany the aging of the partners have to mean that it is time to give up sex. Most reports find that men and women in their 70s still enjoy sexual intercourse as part of their relationships (e.g., Maier, 1984; Pfeiffer, Verwoerdt, & Wang, 1978).

It seems likely that the incidence of sexual activity among older couples will increase as a changes in attitudes toward aging and advances in health and medical care help people stay well and feel positive about their bodies longer. There is nothing about age that in and of itself means people lose interest in sex. Many older couples report feeling freer and less inhibited about sexual activity than in their younger days. And many women report that the experience is better because their older partners can more easily satisfy their preference for longer intercourse.

## Special Sexual Problems

The problems just discussed are common ones that many couples face to one degree or another if they stay together in long-term sexual relationships. The problems to which we now turn our attention are quite different. They can arise at any time in any sexual relationship from a long-term marriage to a casual one-nighter, and their solutions require special efforts that go beyond the mutual adjustment and accommodation that we have been discussing.

## Sexually Transmitted Diseases

In an earlier section, it was mentioned that many people are not wholly comfortable with the post–sexual revolution social environment. It also seems that we are paying another kind of price for this new sexual freedom. Health officials say that **sexually transmitted diseases** (STDs), such as syphilis, gonorrhea, herpes, and AIDS, had reached epidemic proportions by the mid-1980s. In 1984, for example, there were 27,000 new cases of one or another of these STDs reported *every day* (Seligmann et al., 1985). This seems incredible in an age of unsurpassed medical knowledge and availability of information on the subject. How much do *you* know about STDs? Check your basic knowledge in *Test Yourself.*

Many health officials believe that one reason for the rapid spread of STDs in the 1980s is that individual responsibility for being informed has not kept pace with the new freedom in attitudes toward sexual behavior. They stress the importance of knowing the facts even if you think you are in no personal danger from an STD; you may be able to help someone else. Consistent with this spirit, a summary of the most common STDs, their symptoms, and their treatments is presented in Table 7–1.

If you suspect that you or someone you know may have contracted an STD, or if you just wish to have more information, see your doctor or health department, or call the toll-free Operation Venus Hotline at 1–800–523–1885. If you are among the majority of people who are *not* infected, do your best to keep it that way. According to the U.S. Surgeon General's report (U.S. Department of Health & Human services, 1988), the following are among the behaviors most likely to put you at risk of AIDS and/or other STDS.

- Sharing drug needles and syringes
- Anal sex with or without a condom
- Vaginal or oral sex with someone who uses drugs or engages in anal sex
- Sex with someone you don't know very well (a pickup or a prostitute) or with someone you know has many sex partners
- Sex with someone who is exhibiting symptoms of an STD, such as a herpes breakout

The sexual behaviors listed put you at risk of one or more STDs, and the longer any or all of these behaviors are pursued, the higher the risk. Now, what about the other side of the coin; what is the "safe sex," we hear so much about?

The safest sex clearly is sex with one mutually faithful partner who is uninfected with any STD. Not everyone can achieve this goal, but everyone can achieve "responsible sex." If you are uninfected, *responsible sexual behavior* consists of limiting your partners, selecting them carefully (no casual sex), and

# TEST YOURSELF
## Do You Have The Facts about STDs?

A sexually transmitted disease (STD) is a disease that may be passed from one infected person to another through close sexual contact. The most common of these diseases are genital herpes, syphillis, gonorrhea, AIDS, and chlamydia. Test your knowledge of these diseases, and of STDs in general, by taking the following test. Cover the answer to each question until you have answered it, or have someone else read the questions to you.

1. T F Syphilis and gonorrhea are fairly rare these days.
   *False.* Almost 100,000 new cases of syphilis were diagnosed in 1984. Gonorrhea strikes over 5,000 victims a *day*.

2. T F AIDS is a male homosexual disease.
   *False.* The majority of AIDS victims in this country are male homosexuals, but the disease has spread widely among heterosexuals in other parts of the world and will do so in this country eventually if not stopped.

3. T F There is no cure for herpes.
   *True.* Once you have the virus, you never get rid of it, although the symptoms can be treated.

4. T F You can't have more than one form of STD at a time.
   *False.* It is possible to have *every* form of STD simultaneously.

5. T F *Chlamydia* is the name given to the fluid-filled sores that are one of the symptoms of genital herpes.
   *False.* Chlamydia is the fastest-spreading STD of the 1980s. It causes a puslike discharge from the penis of males, but most infected women show no symptoms. Complications for either sex include back pains, urination problems, and sterility.

6. T F Genital herpes usually is transmitted through sexual intercourse.
   *True.* But be aware that this is not the only way. If you or your partner has herpes, avoid *any* physical contact when symptoms—itching, burning, tingling, or sores—are present.

7. T F Genital herpes is painful and embarrassing, but not dangerous.
   *False.* Women with herpes have an increased risk of cervical cancer. Babies born to mothers with herpes may die, and survivors often suffer permanent nerve damage. Infected members of both sexes may become blind by transmitting the disease to the eye area.

8. T F STDs can be inherited.
   *False.* They are not hereditary in the usual sense, BUT they can be passed on to a child during birth if the mother is infected.

9. T F AIDS is contagious only after an infected person actually becomes ill.
   *False.* AIDS is contagious during the incubation period, which can last from 5 months to 5 years or more. In fact, researchers are beginning to suspect that carriers are *most* infectious during the early stages of the disease.

10. T F The initials HPV stand for a new STD that strikes hardest at girls in their teens and 20s.
    *True.* The human papillomavirus (HPV) strikes over half a million people a year (some estimates run as high as a million), most of them females in their late teens and early 20s. The virus may lie dormant for decades, and some types of HVP have been linked to cervical cancer.

11. T F You can avoid getting an STD if you or your partner always uses a condom (rubber) during intercourse.
    *False.* If properly applied and removed, a condom reduces your chances

of contracting an STD, but it is *not* a guarantee. Other measures recommended by health experts are that you wash your hands and genitals immediately after sexual relations, know your sex partners, and avoid promiscuous sexual activity. Your chances of contracting an STD go up with every casual sexual encounter.

## Table 7–1    The Most Dangerous Sexually Transmitted Diseases

### Acquired Immunodeficiency Syndrome (AIDS)

| | |
|---|---|
| *Symptoms:* | Weight loss, tiredness, fever, swollen glands, diarrhea, loss of appetite |
| *Risk Groups:* | Sexually active male homosexuals, intravenous drug users (extent to which AIDS will spread to heterosexual community controversial, but there are already cases) |
| *Treatment:* | Symptoms only |
| *Prognosis:* | Fatal |

### Chlamydia

| | |
|---|---|
| *Symptoms:* | Discharge from penis, burning during urination (men) Vaginal discharge, chronic abdominal pain, bleeding between periods (women) |
| *Risk Groups:* | Indiscriminant |
| *Treatment:* | Antibiotics |
| *Prognosis:* | Easily cured. If left untreated, may cause sterility in women. |

### Genital Herpes

| | |
|---|---|
| *Symptoms:* | Blisters in genital area form and become open sores. May be accompanied by itching, pain, fever, or headaches. |
| *Risk Groups:* | Indiscriminant |
| *Treatment:* | Symptoms only |
| *Prognosis:* | Can be controlled, but not cured. Women run risk of having cervical cancer and/or infecting newborn child. |

### Gonorrhea

| | |
|---|---|
| *Symptoms:* | Discharge from the penis, painful urination, pain in testes or abdomen (men). Vaginal discharge, painful urination or menstrual periods, bleeding after intercourse (women). It is not unusual, however, for there to be *no* symptoms. |
| *Risk Groups:* | Indiscriminant |
| *Treatment:* | Penicillin |
| *Prognosis:* | Usually can be cured, but a new penicillin-resistant strain (PPNG) is beginning to spread. |

### Human Papillomavirus (HPV)

| | |
|---|---|
| *Symptoms:* | Genital warts |
| *Risk Groups:* | Women in their late teens and early 20s (but anyone can get it) |
| *Treatment:* | Symptoms only |
| *Prognosis:* | Speculative; current treatments do not rid the body of the HPV virus, which can remain latent for decades. |

### Syphilis

| | |
|---|---|
| *Symptoms:* | Stage 1 (about 3 weeks after infection)—painless pimple, blister, or sore where germs entered the body. Stage 2 (about 6 weeks later)—hair loss, flu-type symptoms, rash. |
| *Risk Groups:* | Indiscriminant |
| *Treatment:* | Penicillin |
| *Prognosis:* | Can be cured, but has a very long list of possible complications including brain damage, heart disease, blindness, paralysis, mental illness, and infection of unborn children. |

Note: From a variety of sources on STDs in the late 1980s.

using a condom ("rubber") each time you have sexual intercourse. (If you have a partner who refuses to cooperate in using this protection, you are well advised to rethink your involvement with him or her.) It also is recommended that you wash your hands and genitals after each sexual experience.

Any individual who is already infected with an STD has the additional duty of telling any prospective partner about the condition and abstaining from any sexual activity at all during times when infection is likely. (So far as we know at this time, AIDS victims are infectious at all times. Those with other infections should get the facts from a knowledgeable medical source.)

## Sexual Dysfunctions

The term that is used to describe a sexual functioning difficulty that has physical symptoms is **sexual dysfunction.** The more common of these are described in Exhibit 7–3. Masters and Johnson (1976) believe that the origin of most of these difficulties lies in attitudes, fears, and inhibitions regarding sex. The idea that sex is dirty, the fear that one is sexually inadequate, or inhibitions about deviating from the standard man-on-top (so-called missionary) po-

---

**EXHIBIT 7–3**

## Common Male and Female Sexual Dysfunctions

### Male Dysfunctions

**Erectile dysfunction:**  The inability to achieve or maintain an erection of sufficient rigidity to allow for sexual penetration of any duration. *Most* men experience this difficulty at one time or another, but it seldom is prolonged or permanent.

**Premature Ejaculation:**  Inability to control the ejaculatory reflex, such that it occurs sooner than desired by one or both partners. "Too soon" is a matter of personal definition, of course. Hong (1984) found that the average duration of intercourse before ejaculation in men is about 2 minutes.

**Retarded ejaculation.**  Inability to ejaculate within the vagina (or sometimes at all). This disorder is relatively uncommon, and most cases are believed to be psychological in nature.

### Female Dysfunctions

**Vaginismus:**  A condition in which spasms in the muscles at the entrance to the vagina prevent male penetration. This disorder is relatively rare, and the success rate for treatment is high.

**Dyspareunia:**  A condition characterized by pain during intercourse. This problem frequently, although not always, has a physical basis and may be treated successfully by an experienced gynecologist.

**Orgasmic dysfunction:**  Inability to achieve orgasm by any means. Treatment of this disorder is difficult and must be tailored to the individual. Not to be confused with inability to achieve orgasm without direct clitoral stimulation, which is quite common and *not* a disorder.

**Female sexual arousal disorder:**  Lack of interest in sex and inability to feel sexual desire. This disorder, formerly called frigidity, may be primary (a woman never had any interest in sex) or secondary (previous interest in sex has disappeared). Lack of sexual desire may occur in men also, but as a disorder it is a more common problem for women.

sition during intercourse are among the issues they believe create anxieties that have physical consequences.

Beliefs that there is something shameful about sex or any position that differs from the missionary position are holdovers from a time when attitudes toward sex were quite different from what they are now. This does not mean that no one holds such beliefs now; they do and they teach them to others. In some cases, these older attitudes may lie behind sexual dysfunction, but many people who hold these beliefs do not experience physical problems of the type described in Exhibit 7-3.

The fear that one is sexually inadequate seems not to be a holdover from earlier attitudes about sex, but to have been *created* to a large extent by more recent ones. People who were happy to rid themselves of (or not adopt) old constraints on sexual activity found themselves with a new problem. In a world of apparent sexual sophistication where they needed to assume that a partner had had other partners, how did they measure up? Were they good enough? Were they as good as the other partners?

Despite all of the media hype that might lead us to think otherwise, sex is not an Olympic event. There are no bronze, silver, and gold medalists and there shouldn't be any losers. Satisfactory sexual experiences are not about winning and losing, but about mutual pleasure. If a partner continually compares you unfavorably to other lovers, it may be time to reexamine the relationship.

Fear that one does not measure up to some imagined standard for sexual performance is one of the costs that we have paid for more permissive attitudes about sex. But attitudes are not all that have changed in our society in the past generation. Changing male and female roles also are believed to be creating a share of the difficulties. Some evidence for this may be found in the sudden increase of reported male erectile problems during the turmoil of the 1970s "feminist revolution" (Burros, 1974).

So far, this discussion might lead you to think that sexual dysfunctions have more to do with society and individual attitudes than relationships, but of course this is not true. A poor or troubled relationship with the sex partner and/or a lack of skill or consideration on the part of one's partner often create difficulties. Finally, it should be mentioned that bad experiences with sex may lie behind such problems; many women who have been raped experience sexual dysfunction, for example.

Sexual dysfunctions often are devastating to the individual having the difficulty, and the accompanying guilt, confusion, and hurt feelings can play havoc with a relationship. With competent treatment, however, the majority of such problems can be cured. The first step is to have a thorough physical examination by a physician trained in this area to make sure that there is no physical basis for the problem. Occasionally, the symptoms turn out to stem from something as simple as medication being taken for another health problem. If no physical basis can be found, psychological help should be sought.

Psychologists and other professionals use different methods for treating sexual dysfunctions, but today most agree that (a) traditional psychological therapy is not very effective, and (b) sexual dysfunctions are more effectively treated as *relationship problems* rather than as individual problems. If you see someone for help with this kind of problem, you may expect treatment to consist of some combination of factual information, sensual awareness exercises, and the practice of certain nonintercourse sexual activities to reduce anxiety about sexual situations (Knox, 1988).

## Unwanted Pregnancy

A very different sex-related problem that faces some couples is unwanted pregnancy. Although this problem occasionally occurs when birth control methods believed to be safe fail, it is more likely to happen through ignorance, carelessness, or failure to take birth control responsibility (e.g., Byrne, 1982; Gerrard, 1982). In such cases, a couple must confront the issue of whether or not to have the child and take steps to avoid a repeat pregnancy until it is desired. One of these steps is being well informed on **birth control**.

A summary of the features, pros, and cons of the leading methods of birth control is featured in Table 7–2. This table is not intended to be a substitute for full information; it is merely a summary comparison. If you have any questions about any method—including the one you now use—or if you want more information, see your doctor, campus health clinic, Planned Parenthood office, or other health agency. Don't rely on what your friends tell you; what works for them may not work or be right for you.

Some unwanted pregnancies are more complicated than simply a failure to get and use up-to-date birth control information. In some instances a couple that is unable to decide whether they want a child or not play "baby roulette." They take no precautions during intercourse and leave the consequences up to fate. Some are delighted if a pregnancy occurs. Other couples find that they are dismayed; the timing is wrong or they are having personal or relationship problems or they have decided that they don't really want a family.

In other cases, an unwanted pregnancy is unwanted only by one partner. This is the case that has the potential to create the most serious problems, particularly if one partner has practiced deception. The assumption that the partner who does not want a baby will be won over once the deed is done is not a safe one. Couples with this problem are advised to seek professional counseling immediately.

There are three courses of action open to couples finding themselves faced with an unwanted pregnancy, however it has come about: (1) they may have the baby, and one or both may raise it; (2) they may have the baby and give it up for adoption; or (3) they may terminate the pregnancy through abortion. The second option is a traditional one, and the third has become more acceptable, although many people still have strong negative feelings about it.

In an effort to reduce the number of people having to make such difficult decisions about unplanned and/or unwanted pregnancies by encouraging them to be more responsible about preventing them, some high schools are beginning to experiment with a variety of educational programs to help students appreciate the realities of caring for a baby. In one, students, singly or in pairs, are given full responsibility for the care and feeding of a "baby" (a five-pound sack of flour in the original program) for some period of time. There is no way to structure any sort of analogous learning experience for giving up a baby or aborting a fetus, however.

Many people who thought adoption or abortion would be an acceptable option find, after the fact, that it was not. If you or anyone you know is considering one of these options, you are urged to get as much information—

## Table 7–2   A Summary of Birth Control Methods

| Method | How It Works | Possible Advantages | Disadvantages | Effectiveness if used properly |
|---|---|---|---|---|
| Birth control pill | ■ Prevents ovulation | ■ Regulates menstrual cycle | ■ Must be taken daily; may have unpleasant/serious side effects | 98%–100% |
| Intrauterine device (IUD) | ■ Fertilized egg cannot be implanted into the womb | ■ Don't have to think about birth control after the insertion of IUD | ■ May be expelled without knowledge; possible side effects | 98%–100% |
| Sterilization (male or female) | ■ Prevents fertilization | ■ One-time; don't have to think about birth control after the procedure | ■ Expense, possible emotional/psychological complications | 98%–100% |
| Abortion | ■ Removes embryo from womb | ■ Highly individual | ■ Expense, possible emotional/psychological complications | 98%–100% |
| Condom | ■ Prevents sperm from entering cervix | ■ Helps reduce danger of contracting STD | ■ Must be put on just before act <br> ■ May reduce sensory stimulation | 98% |
| Diaphram with cream or jelly | ■ Acts as barrier to sperm, chemically destroys sperm | ■ Use only if needed | ■ Must be put on prior to each act | 95+% |
| Vaginal foam with spermicide | ■ Destroys sperm | ■ May help reduce danger of STDs | ■ Messy, vulnerable to incorrect use which makes it ineffective | 80–95% |
| Withdrawal (before ejaculation) | ■ Prevents sperm from reaching ova | ■ No advance preparation required | ■ Unreliable, reduces sexual pleasure | 80–95% |
| Rhythm | ■ No intercourse at certain times | ■ No advance preparation required | ■ Ineffective for irregular cycles, Abstinence can create tension | 80–95% |
| Douching | ■ Washes out sperm | ■ Can be used after the fact if no precautions taken | ■ Messy, unreliable | Below 80% |
| Breast feeding | ■ Inhibits ovulation | | ■ Unreliable | Below 80% |

# FACE OF THE FUTURE:
## Sex in the Courtroom

Until recently, legal hassles involving voluntary sexual relationships between unmarried people were almost exclusively confined to patrimony cases. In most of these cases, a women attempts to prove that a particular man is the father of her child in order to claim financial support for the child and/or damages for herself. A number of celebrities, including Marlon Brando, Frank Sinatra, John Lennon, and Elvis Presley, have been involved in such litigation.

Things have changed. The 1970s saw a a significant rise in the number of lawsuits involving division of property, child support, and "palimony" (alimony for an unmarried former live-in) between couples who had never been married. To date, the disposition of these cases seems to depend considerably on the length of time that a couple has lived together. In general, the longer the time, the more likely it is that a financial settlement will be awarded.

The 1970s and 1980s also have seen changes in another area—litigation involving parties whose sexual relationship has been neither long-term nor live-in. Among the issues currently or previously being debated in the new area of **sexual liability** are the following:

- Does a man have financial responsibility for a child conceived as the result of deception by the mother (the woman lied about using birth control)?

- Is a woman entitled to financial support for a child conceived as the result of deception by the father (the man lied about being sterile)?

- Is a participant in a casual sexual encounter entitled to financial consideration if he or she contracts a sexually transmitted disease from the encounter?

*Continued*

both for and against each—as you can before making a decision. The local Planned Parenthood office is a good place to start. If at all possible, both prospective parents should be involved. As discussed in *Face of the Future,* special difficulties can arise when the two parties in a sexual relationship are not on the same side in coping with problems stemming from the relationship.

## Summing Up ■

Attitudes toward sex have changed significantly in the last 30 years. Freedom of sexual expression now is encouraged more than at any other time in our country's history, but this freedom has not been without its costs. Many people feel confused and anxious about sex and sexually transmitted diseases have become epidemic.

The scientific study of sexual behavior has helped to dispel many myths about sex and has formed the basis for helping many couples with sexual dysfunction. But long-term sexual relationships, like long-term relationships of any nature, require continuing adjustments, and many of these have little to do with the physical act of sex.

### *Continued*

None of these issues is new, but the willingness of people to talk about them in a court of law is. So far, the trend in the disposition of such cases is difficult to assess. A number have been dismissed; many judges seem to believe that protecting oneself against unwanted pregnancy and disease is a matter of individual responsibility. But the *right* to sue for damages stemming from a sexual relationship, however casual, has been established, and this opens up whole new possibilities for litigation (see Spake, 1985, for a discussion of these cases).

Is this a good thing? No one is sure. Increased responsibility for sexual behavior is a good thing, but having recourse to sexual liability lawsuits raises some complex moral issues. For example, what about the right of an unmarried woman to terminate a pregnancy against the biological father's wishes? And who is responsible for the extra expenses of raising a blind child born to the mother who contracted an STD from a man who did not tell her he had it?

What does seem to be certain is that sexual liability lawsuits have been admitted into our courts and there is no reason to think that they will go away. The evidence suggests just the opposite; at least twelve known herpes-related cases are currently on the court schedules in eight different states, and there can be no doubt that AIDS cases are coming. One suit to break the will of a wealthy man who left his estate to the live-in lover his family believes gave him AIDS is under way already.

---

## ▪ KEY WORDS AND PHRASES

AIDS

androgens

attitudes toward sex

birth control

bisexual

clitoris

erotica

estrogens

extradyadic relationship

heterosexual

homosexual

Masters and Johnson sexual
   response cycle

orgasm

ovaries

penis

pornography

sexual dysfunction

sexual liability

sexually transmitted diseases

testes

testosterone

vagina

virgin

---

## ▪ READ ON

*Babies and Other Hazards of Sex* by D. Barry. Emmaus, PA: Rodale Press, 1984. This gentle spoof of the hundreds of advice books for parents is fun even if your baby days are far behind you or far in the future. After you've read it, pass it along to some new parents; it makes a good antidote to the tons of conflicting advice they are getting!

*Love and Will* by R. May. New York: Norton, 1969. This classic book by psychoanalyst Rollo May is about putting love and sex back together again, a topic that is more, not less, timely 20 years later. May's book isn't for the timid; the reading level is high. But anyone who is serious about personal growth should find it well worth the effort.

*Sex and the Single Parent* by M. Mattis. New York: Holt, 1986. We hear a lot these days about being a single parent, but less about being a single person who must consider children when making decisions about his or her private life. The author of *Sex and the Single Parent* is a therapist who has worked with single parents for over 15 years on such problems as guilt about wanting a private life, how to handle casual lovers (don't let them sleep over), and what to do when the ex-spouse or his or her family tries to interfere in your social life for the "sake of the children."

## ■ REFERENCES

Abelson, H., Cohen, R., Heaton, E., & Slider, C. (1970). Public attitudes toward and experience with erotic material. In *Technical Reports of the Commission on Obscenity and Pornography* (Vol. VI). Washington, DC: U.S. Government Printing Office.

Bales, J. (1986). Explaining sexuality? Consider the Sambia. *APA Monitor, 17,* 18.

Belcastro, P. A. (1985). Sexual behavior differences between black and white students. *Journal of Sex Research, 21,* 56–67.

Bell, A. P., & Weinberg, M. S. (1978). *Homosexualities: A study of diversity among men and women.* New York: Simon & Schuster.

Burros, W. M. (1974). The growing burden of impotence. *Family Health, 6,* 18–21.

Bryne, D. (1982). Sex without contraception. In D. Byrne and W. A. Fisher (Eds.), *Adolescents, sex, and contraception.* Hillsdale, NJ: Lawrence Erlbaum.

Coleman, J. C., Butcher, J. N., & Carson, R. C. (1984). *Abnormal psychology and modern life* (7th ed.). Glenview, IL: Scott, Foresman.

Davison, G. C. (1978). Not can but ought: The treatment of homosexuality. *Journal of Consulting and Clinical Psychology, 46,* 170–172.

Donnerstein, E. (1986, July 26). Quoted in Sex buster. *Time,* pp. 12–21.

Frank, E., & Enos, S. F. (1983, Feb.). The love-life of the American wife. *Ladies Home Journal,* pp. 7.

Gerrard, M. (1982). Sex, sex guilt, and contraceptive use. *Journal of Personality and Social Psychology, 42,* 153–158.

Greenblatt, C. S. (1983). The saliency of sexuality in the early years of marriage. *Journal of Marriage and the Family, 45,* 289–299.

Hendrick, S., Hendrick, C., Slapion-Foote, M. J., & Foote, F. H. (1985). Gender differences in sexual attitudes. *Journal of Personality and Social Psychology, 48,* 1630–1642.

Hong, L. D. (1984). Survival of the fastest: On the origin of premature ejaculation. *Journal of Sex Research, 20,* 109–122.

Huber, J., Gagnon, J., Keller, S., Lawson, R., Miller, P., & Simon, W. (1982). Report of the American Sociological Association's task group on homosexuality. *American Sociology, 17,* 164–180.

Hyde, J. S. (1972). *Understanding human sexuality* (2nd ed.). New York: McGraw-Hill.

Jasso, G. (1985). Marital coital frequency and the passage of time: Estimating the separate effects of spouses' ages and marital duration, birth and marriage cohorts, and period influences. *American Sociological Review, 50,* 224–241.

Kallen, D. J., Stephenson, J. J., & Doughty, A. (1983). The need to know: Recalled adolescent sources of sexual and contraceptive information and sexual behavior. *Journal of Sex Research, 19,* 137–159.

Kinsey, A. C., Pomeroy, W. B., & Martin, C. E. (1948). *Sexual behavior in the human male.* Philadelphia: Saunders.

Kinsey, A. C., Pomeroy, W. B., Martin, C. E., & Gebhard, P. H. (1953). *Sexual behavior in the human female.* Philadelphia: Saunders.

Knox, D. (1988). *Choices in relationships* (2nd ed.). St. Paul: West.

Knox, D., & Wilson, K. (1983). Dating problems of university students. *College Student Journal, 17,* 225–228.

Knupper, G., & Enos, S. F. (1985, March). The men in your life. *Ladies Home Journal,* pp. 99–183.

Levine, M. (1986). Quoted in C. Turkington, Political 'pseudo-science' defines sexual pathology. *APA Monitor, 17,* 18.

Levinger, G. (1966). Systematic distortion in spouses' report of preferred and actual sexual behavior. *Sociometry, 29,* 291–299.

Maier, R. A. (1984). *Human sexuality in perspective.* Chicago: Nelson-Hall.

Masters, W. H., & Johnson, V. E. (1966). *Human sexual response.* Boston: Little, Brown.

Masters, W. H., & Johnson, V. E. (1976). *The pleasure bond: A new look at sexuality and commitment.* Boston: Little, Brown.

Napoli, V., Kilbride, J. M., & Tebbs, D. E. (1988). *Adjustment and growth in a changing world* (3rd ed.). St Paul: West.

O'Neill, N., & O'Neill, G. (1972). *Open marriage.* New York: Evans.

Peplau, L. A., Rubin, Z., & Hill, C. T. (1977).

Sexual intimacy in dating relationships. *Journal of Social Issues, 33,* 86–109.

Pesman, C. & the Editors of *Esquire* magazine. (1984). *How a man ages.* New York: Ballentine Books.

Petersen, J. R., Kretchmer, A., Nelles, B., Lever, J., & Hertz, R. (1983, March). The *Playboy* readers' sex survey. *Playboy,* p. 90.

Pfeiffer, E., Verwoerdt, A., & Davis, G. (1972). Sexual behavior in middle life. *American Journal of Psychiatry,* 128: 82–87.

Pfeiffer, E., Verwoerdt, A., & Wang, H. S. (1978). Sexual behavior in aged men and women. *Archives of General Psychiatry, 19,* 757–758.

Roper Organization (1985). *The 1985 Virginia Slims American women's opinion poll.* New York: Author.

Rossman, I. (1978). Sexuality and aging: An internist's perspective. In R. L. Solnick (Ed.), *Sexuality and aging.* Los Angeles: Ethel Percy Andus Gerontology Center at the University of Southern Claifornia.

Seligmann, J., Raine, G., Coppola, V., Hager, M., & Gosnell, M. (1985, Feb. 4). A nasty new epidemic. *Newsweek,* pp. 72–73.

Spake, A. (1985, July). Trial and eros. *Mother Jones,* pp. 25–28.

Story, M. D. (1985). A comparison of university student experience with various sexual outlets in 1974 and 1984. *Journal of Sex Education and Therapy, 11,* 35–41.

Sturgis, E. T., & Adams, H. E. (1978). The right to treatment: Issues in the treatment of homosexuality. *Journal of Counseling and Clinical Psychology, 46,* 165–169.

Tavris, C., & Sadd, S. (1977). *The Redbook report on female sexuality.* New York: Delacorte Press.

Thompson, A. P. (1984). Emotional and sexual components of extramarital relations. *Journal of Marriage and the Family, 46,* 35–40.

U.S. Department of Health & Human Services. (1988). *Understanding AIDS.* Rockville, MD: U.S. Public Health Service.

*U.S. News & World Report,* (1986, June 2). Sex, with care. pp. 53–57.

Zinik, G. (1985). Identify conflict or adaptive flexibility? Bisexuality reconsidered. *Journal of Homosexuality, 11,* 7–20.

# 8

# Your Special Relationships: Love and Marriage

In today's world, sexual relationships do not necessarily involve either love or marriage. They are private relationships, but not necessarily intimate ones, except on a physical level, and most people have a desire for intimacy with one special person that goes beyond the physical. They want to love and be loved, and most find that they also want to make a formal commitment to marriage at some point.

Love and marriage are the topics of this chapter. These special relationships, whether they occur together or not, are the most wholly intimate in our social worlds. Here we consider the nature of love, its relationship to marriage, and other reasons for marrying. We look also at adjusting to marriage and satisfaction with this relationship. (Problems stemming from love and marriage relationships are examined in Chapter 14.)

## LOVE

So far as love or affection is concerned, psychologists have failed in their mission. The little we know about love does not transcend simple observation, and the little we know about it has been written better by poets and novelists (Harlow, 1958, p. 673).

These words were written some years ago by psychologist Harry Harlow and there are those who feel it still is somewhat accurate. Psychologists understand more about love now, but they are still at a loss to explain certain phenomena. At the very top of this list is why you will fall in love with one *particular* person out of all of the dozens, or even hundreds, of possibilities.

This may be one aspect of human behavior that psychologists never can explain.

## Psychologists' Views of Love

The romantic love that remains one of the great mysteries of human behavior is only one kind of human love. We also love our parents and other relatives, our children, our friends, and even "humanity." The ancient Greeks gave us names for these different kinds of love that psychologists still use today. *Storge* describes the kind of love shared by parents and children, *philla* is a form of love that is like the deepest friendship, and *agape* is a selfless humanitarian love. The love that we call romantic love, they called *eros*.

Many of the psychologists who have studied love have studied romantic love, and they have a variety of views about what this love is. A *humanist view* sees the capacity to love and be loved as part of the fulfillment of human potential. By contrast, a *psychoanalytic view* of love emphasizes the role of drives (primarily sexual) and needs. In the humanist view, a good love relationship is the expression of a healthy personality. In the psychoanalytic view, it is a condition for developing one.

Two other contrasting views of love are the cognitive view and the behavioral view. A *cognitive view* emphasizes the role that thinking plays in being in love. From this view, certain beliefs about your loved one and your relationship are necessary for you to be in love. A certain amount of self-deception may be required to maintain these beliefs, supporting the old saying that "Love is blind."

According to the *behavioral view,* love is based on a set of conditioned responses that have been generalized to a particular person. Those who take this position believe that many of the behaviors we come to associate with love and loving are learned much earlier—long before we ever fall in love. Examples are being brought a present for "no reason", and having another person put your comfort, convenience, or preference ahead of his or her own.

These theoretical views of love may seem a bit dry to you. To most people, love is an emotion, pure and simple. Those who study love, however, find that it is anything but pure *or* simple. Among the feelings that people who say they are in love report having are happiness, joy, peace, fulfillment, and ecstasy. They also report feeling misery, uncertainty, pain, jealousy, depression, and even hate. Love inspires beautiful poems and great music. It also inspires revenge and murder. If love is an emotion, it is a complex one that is by no means pure.

The complexity of romantic love has led many to conclude that this is not a subject that psychologists can study in any meaningful way. Psychologist Robert Sternberg (1985) disagrees. He and his colleagues at Yale University have been exploring the nature of love for a number of years; they believe both that it can be investigated in a scientific manner and that it should be. Scientists who study love, they believe, may be able to make a contribution toward reversing the trend of failed relationships in our society.

### A Triangular Theory of Love

Sternberg and his colleagues began by trying to identify the nature of love. Is it a single, indivisible entity, or can it be understood better in terms of a set

Psychologists have many theories about love, but why you fall in love with one person and not another remains a mystery.

of separate aspects? After analyzing data from people who answered questions about love on special questionnaires, they concluded that the second explanation is more accurate. The following are among the many aspects of love that they identified.

- Having high regard for the loved one
- Valuing the loved one in one's life
- Promoting the welfare of the loved one
- Experiencing happiness with the loved one
- Giving emotional support to the loved one
- Communicating intimately with the loved one
- Receiving emotional support from the loved one
- Sharing oneself and one's things with the loved one
- Being able to count on the loved one in times of need

You can see that these aspects of love are not limited to romantic love. They fit any kind of love relationship, yet clearly not all such relationships are alike. The researchers went on, therefore, to investigate kinds of love. What makes romantic love different from infatuation or companionate love or the love of a child for a parent or the love of a parent for a child? These investigations led to what Sternberg calls a triangular theory of love.

The three sides of the triangle in the **triangular theory of love** are passion, commitment, and intimacy. Passion is the *motivational* component; it is characterized by physical arousal and an intense desire to be with the loved one. Commitment is the *cognitive* component. Sternberg describes it as both a short-term decision to love another person and a long-term commitment to maintain love. The *emotional* component is intimacy, which includes communication, support, and sharing.

Passion, commitment, and intimacy are the basic dimensions under which the various aspects of love, such as those just listed, can be grouped. Different love relationships may be visualized as triangles of different shapes, depending upon which of the three components are the most important in the relationship. In Figure 8–1, you see triangles representing three possible love relationships. Of Sternberg's three components, commitment is the most important in the love between a parent and a child, so this side of triangle *a* is the longest. Intimacy gets a significant, but shorter, side; and passion is missing, as shown by the dotted line for this component.

In a reverse of the parent-child relationship, intimacy is the strongest component of the best-friend love triangle *b,* with commitment making a shorter side. Passion again is absent. By contrast, passion is the dominating component in triangle *c,* which represents an infatuation relationship. Intimacy is moderate, but commitment is missing.

All in all, there are eight possible kinds of love relationships that can be described using Sternberg's three components. Trotter (1986) presents a detailed explanation with some interesting illustrations, or you may want to try out this method for yourself by drawing triangles of the important love relationships in your life.

Sternberg and his colleagues believe that their three-sided theory of love has potential for helping them understand love relationships, particularly romantic love relationships, more fully. One of the ways they have been using

In our life there is a single color, as on an artist's pallette, which provides the meaning of life and art. It is the color of love.
*Marc Chagall*

Figure 8–1 **The Triangles of Love: Some Examples**

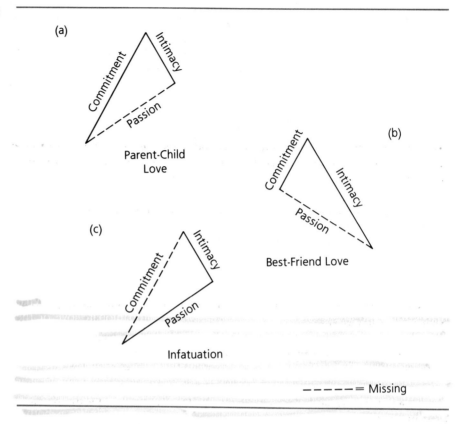

(a)

Parent-Child Love

(b)

Best-Friend Love

(c)

Infatuation

– – – – – = Missing

this concept in research is to examine how the perceptions that members of a couple have of their own triangles affect satisfaction with the relationship.

One of the most interesting aspects of this research concerns the comparison of (1) the way each half of a couple believes the other *actually* feels about him or her with (2) the way he or she would *like* the other person to feel (Sternberg & Barnes, 1985). What the investigators found was that a *match* between these perceptions is critical to satisfaction with a romantic relationship. If the triangle you would draw to describe the way you believe your partner in a romantic relationship *really feels* is not quite similar to the one you would draw to describe the way you *want* him or her to feel, you are likely to be dissatisfied with the relationship.

In this comparison, what is important is the way you *believe* your partner feels. This may or may not be the same as your partner would say he or she feels. Thus, this research points up yet again the importance of communication to relationships. If one partner is unable to express his or her feelings sufficiently well for the other to believe there is equal love, a potentially good relationship may be destroyed.

The work of Sternberg and his colleagues owes much to earlier investigators who developed and tested questionnaires to measure liking and love (e.g., Rubin, 1970). The particular contribution of the three-sided theory lies in its ability to generate specific research questions about love that may be tested in a scientific manner. For example, are romantic love relationships characterized by a triangle with three equal sides (equal measures of passion, commitment, and intimacy) the relationships that last? Do the triangles change in predictable ways as good relationships age? Answers to these and many other questions not only might enable counselors and therapists to find better ways to help couples with troubled relationships but also increase our understanding of the nature of love.

## How Do You Know If You Are in Love?

Walster and Walster (1978) define three conditions that must hold for a person to "fall in love." The first is that the culture must promote the ideal of romantic love. Certainly, our society gets full marks for emphasizing romantic love, and "falling in love" as a basis for marriage.

The second condition is that the "right person" comes along. In our mobile culture with its high value on romantic love and its relative freedom to explore relationship possibilites, it would be surprising if we *didn't* meet someone who at least appeared to be the right person. And, if you recall the cognitive view of love discussed earlier, we always can exercise a little selective blindness if the need arises.

Finally, Walster and Walster say that love requires a physiological arousal that is interpreted as love. So, you meet someone, are attracted to him or her, begin to see this person on a regular basis, and feel strong feelings. Could this be "it"? Are you really in love, or is it infatuation? How can you know for sure? You can't be sure, at least not in any objective sense. To most of us, the difference between love and infatuation is evident only after some period of time. If the feeling lasts, we call it love. If the glow fades quickly, we say it was infatuation.

You may have noticed that we have returned to the idea that people learn to give "emotion names" to feelings on the basis of certain aspects of the situation in which they occur. When it comes to love, there are a number of relevant factors that influence this labeling. One, already mentioned, is how long the feeling lasts. Another is your own attitudes and values. Some people just feel more comfortable calling strong physical attraction love rather than lust. Psychologists also know that people who are romantic by nature (place a high value on romantic concepts) are more likely to give their arousal the name of love than people who are not (Walster & Berscheid, 1971). Although there is no objective standard for being in love, psychologists have found that people who say they are in love tend to say very similar things about the experience and to report spending considerable time in similar behaviors, such as gazing into the loved one's eyes.

## Romantic Love in Perspective

Love is the single most popular theme for books, songs, movies, and plays. We hear so much about it that a natural conclusion is that we are missing something vital if we are not in love in the passionate, romantic sense. Certainly, this feeling can be quite wonderful while it lasts, but it seldom lasts very long. Romantic love seems to be something like a match. It gets relationships off to a blazing start, but it tends to burn out rather quickly. If the relationship is sound, however, it will survive the passage into a less intense phase of love that has been called companionate love.

**Companionate love** is characterized by trust, respect, appreciation, loyalty, and support as well as by heightened emotion. It is based on accepting another person as he or she really is (not as idealized) and on a caring that goes far beyond physical attraction (Berscheid & Walster, 1978). Some of the personal characteristics that seem to make people more ready for this form of love are described in Exhibit 8–1.

If you read the exhibit carefully, you may be struck by a similarity between the personal characteristics that make people more accepting and appreciative of companionate love and the characteristics that describe effective behavior. Control, independence, and realism are themes common to both.

As with the characteristics of effective behavior, the qualities that help a person enjoy companionate love exist on a continuum, and most of us are probably closer to the standards on some characteristics than others. It is nice to know, however, that efforts to become more effective in our individual personal lives will pay dividends in being more ready to share our lives with others.

You also may have noticed a similarity between the descriptions of companionate love and descriptions of friendship from the last chapter. The best friendship and love relationships seem to share the qualities of trust, acceptance, loyalty, support, and respect. It is with good reason that many people find friendship ripening into love after a time.

Since they are so similar, what makes friendship different from companionate love? A number of psychologists have been interested in this question. In one series of studies (Davis, 1985), the investigators concluded that love relationships are different in having higher levels of exclusiveness (no similar relationship with another party), fascination (preoccupation with the partner), and sexual desire. These authors also found love relationships to have a greater depth of caring about the other person and a greater capacity for strongly

## EXHIBIT 8–1

## Being Ready for Companionate Love

Most of us want to love and be loved in return, but this seems to come easier to some than to others. Some of the personal characteristics that make it easier to love and to maintain a successful love relationship are described below.

- *Good self-esteem.* There is considerable truth in the old saying that if you don't love yourself, you can't love another. People with low self-esteem are more likely to be looking to *be* loved than to love, and this works against companionate love.

- *The ability to meet your own basic needs.* Preoccupation with unsatisfied needs makes us insensitive to the needs of others. If you can get along on your own, you are more likely to be able to maintain a successful relationship with someone else.

- *Contact with reality.* An ability to see the situation as it really is, rather than as you wish it were, will make you better at relating to the needs, desires, and problems of your partner and your relationship.

- *Ability to deal with frustration.* Love requires giving and compromise and even sacrifice upon occasion. Putting yourself second can be frustrating, and those with low tolerance may give up too soon.

- *Reasonable expectations.* In love as in most things, if you expect perfection, you are likely to be disappointed.

positive emotional experience. On the down side, love relationships were found to have a greater potential for conflict, ambivalence, mutual criticism, and distress.

In summary, it appears that love is friendship plus and minus. It is plus a dimension of depth and strength of positive feeling that we seem to reserve for love relationships and minus a certain easygoing acceptance and tolerance that we seem better able to achieve in less intimate relationships.

## Summing Up ■

To most people, romantic love is one of life's supreme emotional experiences, a prize to be sought and to be mourned if lost. It is the favored subject of writers, musicians, and artists, and a favorite topic of conversation for many people, whether they are in love themselves or not. Everyone knows what love is—and no one knows. It is complex and elusive, and studying it in any scientific way is difficult.

Despite the difficulty, a number of psychologists have devoted their time to the study of romantic love. They find that people in love tend to describe the experience in similar ways that can be measured and that these measurements relate to other behaviors. Based on such descriptions, a recent theory of love proposes that it has three major components—passion, commitment, and intimacy—and that all love relationships may be described in terms of how much of each component is present. This theory holds promise for advancing research, but it leaves unanswered the fascinating question of why we fall in love with, and often marry, one particular person.

## MARRIAGE

Attitudes and beliefs about marriage have changed considerably in the past 25 years, and we can see these reflected in a number of social behavior patterns. First, people are marrying later. The median age at first marriage has been increasing since 1970 for both men and women (*U.S. News & World Report*, 1988). Women now tend to postpone marriage until sometime between ages 23 and 24, and men almost until 26, and this age at first marriage may continue to rise. Results of one 1980s survey of college undergraduate women, for example, indicated that most of these women intended to marry, but not until age 26 (Long, 1983).

People also are marrying more often. The number of divorces in this country climbed steadily from 1960 to peak in 1981 at a record 1.25 million (U.S. Bureau of the Census, 1984). After a 2-year decline, the rate has moved up again, but the majority of these divorced people remarry. About 75% of divorced women and 80% of divorced men marry again, usually within 5 years or less (Weingarten, 1985).

Finally, the sexes are living together without marrying in greater numbers than ever before. Four times as many unmarried couples were living together in the late 1980s as in the early 1970s (U.S. Bureau of the Census, 1984), but this cohabitation has by no means become a substitute for marriage. Nor does

*[handwritten margin note: marriage is a better deal for a man / like marries like (homogamy)]*

The qualities that make satisfying and rewarding friendships also form the basis for good companionate love relationships.

**singlehood,** described further in Exhibit 8–2, threaten it. Being single by choice is both more common and more acceptable than ever before; nevertheless, almost 90% of all men and women in this country marry at some point in their lives (National Center for Health Statistics, 1984).

## Reasons for Marriage

Why does marriage remain so popular despite the fact that the chances a marriage will fail are high and alternatives, such as singlehood and cohabitation, are more socially acceptable than ever? There are several very common reasons.

### Marrying for Love

Consistent with the emphasis that our culture places on the notion of romantic love, the most frequent reason given by both men and women who are asked why they married is that they were in love. In one large national survey (Pietropinto & Simenauer, 1979), some 56% of the women and 39% of the men

**EXHIBIT 8–2**

## The Single Alternative

According to the U.S. Bureau of the Census (1987), about 40% of adult Americans now are single. This is a whopping increase over a decade earlier and reflects in part the very high divorce rates of the 1970s and 1980s. But it also reflects the fact that Americans are delaying marriage until a later age, and an increasing number are making singlehood their life style of choice.

What is it like to be a one in a world of twos? Our society has a curiously ambivalent attitude toward single people. On the one hand, we envy their freedom to suit themselves in making decisions and enjoying a variety of relationships with the opposite sex. On the other hand, we expect this to be temporary.

People who stay single too long lead acquaintances, friends, and relatives to start wondering what is wrong with them. Is he gay? Is she frigid? There are different interpretations of "too long," but people who have never been married usually report that these suspicions begin to set in at about age 35 for women and 40 for men. We even have special, rather sexist, labels for these singles: he's a *bachelor;* she's a *spinster.*

In short, our society expects people to marry even if they don't stay married. So strong is this expectation that we make very little provision in a social way for singlehood as a life-style. Except for the very early and the very late years of our life spans, the world is set up for couples. And even if a single person feels at ease in this world (which many don't), the couples often do not feel equally at ease. A single may be at best awkward, and at worst a sexual threat to wives or husbands.

Our society also makes it difficult for many single people in an economic sense. Singles may not have the expense of a family, but they do not have a second income to meet living expenses either. They also may find it harder to get credit (especially women) and more difficult to get promoted in some work situations (especially men). In fact, they may even be paid less than married people for comparable work because they have no families to support. This is not legal, but a surprising number of people still believe that it is a reasonable consideration.

Despite a certain bias against singlehood, people do remain single by choice. The reason most often given is personal freedom—freedom to do what they want, when they want, and with whom they want within their own personal and financial limitations. Some people start out this way; it seems to grow on others. Says one 37-year-old unmarried psychologist:

> I always assumed I would marry, but there didn't seem to be any hurry about it. I've enjoyed a number of very good relationships and for a long time I considered the possibility of marriage with each. Then one day, to my complete astonishment, I realized that I no longer wanted to get married. The time for that seemed to have passed. I guess it is true that people do get set in their ways.

The greatest drawback most people see to singlehood is occasional loneliness or feelings of being left out of the mainstream of life. But living alone does not have to mean being alone. Many singles have stable relationships with others of like mind. Nor does living alone preclude having a family. An increasing number of singles, including men, are adopting children. The fact that agencies now allow them to do so is encouraging. It may take a while yet, but we are on the way to accepting singlehood as a life style choice.

who responded to the questionnaire gave this as their primary reason for marriage. (The researchers who conducted this survey did not speculate on the 17% difference between men and women on this response. Do you have any ideas?)

How do these marriages made in heaven work out? Rather well, it seems, provided that the partners are mature enough to survive the jolt when the passionate mutual absorption of courtship gives way to the realities of day-to-day life (Tavris & Jayaratne, 1976). Most divorces occur relatively early in marriage, usually within the first 5 years (South & Spitze, 1986). In addition, the divorce rate for very young people is much higher than that for the population in general (Booth & Edwards, 1985).

## Marrying for Companionship

The second most frequent reason people give for marrying is the desire for a companion with whom to share life's experiences. Among highly educated, older, or previously divorced individuals, this reason tends to take precedence over marrying for love (Long Laws & Schwartz, 1977).

Mutual and realistic expectations seem to be one key to the success of marriages entered into primarily for companionship. If one partner is marrying for this reason while the other feels very much in love, for example, there may be problems. In terms from the triangle theory of love discussed earlier, there will be a poor match between the way each partner believes the other feels and the way he or she wants the other to feel.

It also is important that expectations for the relationship be realistic. The desire for a companion to share our lives, our joys, our hopes, our fears, and our disappointments is strong in many of us, but this closeness is not guaranteed by marriage. Nor is it likely to be maintained at a constant rate if achieved. Closeness ebbs and falls as partners get involved with work, children, hobbies, or recreations the spouse doesn't share. So long as this is understood, accepted, and worked through if the outside interests of one partner interfere with the needs of the other, it does not have to damage a companionate marriage.

## Marrying for Children

Living together "without benefit of matrimony," as the saying used to go, is so common in our society today that it has ceased to elicit much comment. Nevertheless, the majority of Americans still believe that when a child is expected or desired, marriage is appropriate (e.g., Bower & Christopherson, 1977), and the majority of couples who cohabit do not have children (U.S. Bureau of the Census, 1987).

The mid-1980s saw a number of highly publicized births to unmarried celebrity couples such as actress Amy Irving and director Stephen Spielberg, and it seemed for a time that a new era was dawning. Interestingly, not only did these events not change the older, more conservative views of most of us where children and marriage are concerned, but almost all of these couples married within a short time after their offspring's arrival.

It seems that our culture places a firm and relatively unshakable value on marriage if children are involved, at least in principle (getting married and staying married being two different things). This value has a practical aspect as well as a moral one. Children are a heavy responsibility, and being a good parent takes a lot of time and energy. Children also are expensive; the estimated cost of raising a child through four years of college is over $200,000 (Olsen, 1983).

There is no particular reason, of course, why unmarried couples cannot share in raising a child in the same way as married couples, but the evidence says that they don't. Living together seldom is permanent, and if children are involved, it is the mother who traditionally is left with their care and support. Although things are changing in this regard, they are changing very slowly. So far, it is still true that unmarried fathers are far more likely than divorced fathers to disappear once the relationship with the mother has ended.

### Other Reasons for Marrying

Love, a desire for companionship, and children are the three reasons most commonly given for marriage, but they do not exhaust the possibilities. There is marriage for financial reasons, marriage because it is expected, marriage to get away from life with one's parents, and marriage to escape the responsibility of running one's own life.

Whatever the reason for marrying, marriage is alive and well, and most researchers in this area expect it to become even more popular. A trend toward more conservative life styles, combined with the growing menace of sexually transmitted diseases seem to be making marriage the "in" thing once again. In the next section we look at some of the factors that seem to increase the odds that the marriage will be satisfactory and will last.

## Marital Satisfaction

For many years a prevailing theme in jokes, movies, television programs, and other media reflections of our society was that marriage is an institution whose benefits go almost entirely to women and to which men must be coaxed or coerced. Things have changed considerably in the last two decades, and the idea that a woman must "catch" a husband is less prevalent (although still around). The interesting thing is that the idea that marriage really is for women did not receive much support from survey and research findings even when it seemed to be rather generally accepted.

- Most studies have found that married people of *either* sex report being more satisfied with their lives than single, divorced, or widowed people (e.g., Campbell, 1975; Jankowski, 1985).

- If only people who are married are considered, wives rate themselves as *less happy* than husbands (e.g., Rettig & Bubolz, 1983).

- Married women have higher rates of psychological disturbance than single women (e.g., Rubenstein, 1983), whereas the rate for married men traditionally has been lower than for single men (e.g., Knupper, Clark, & Roum, 1966).

Satisfaction, happiness, adjustment, and degree of psychological disturbance are some of the criteria that have been used to assess the responses of

The evidence does not support the stereotyped belief that the benefits of marriage go mostly to women.

men and women to marriage. By itself, each may sound a little vague, but there is nothing vague about the overall pattern of results in this line of research. Whatever it is called and however it is measured, women long have had a generally less favorable response to marriage than men.

Psychologists and sociologists believe that a major reason for this pattern of findings is the low-status role of the woman in a traditional marriage (e.g., Chafetz & Dworkin, 1984). For many years our culture emphasized the belief that women should find great satisfaction in love, marriage, and motherhood (while the emphasis for men has been on job satisfaction). For many women, the realities of their roles in traditional marriages may fall far short of expectations, leading them to feel cheated and dissatisfied with their lot.

Some support for this explanation may be found in the fact that there is evidence that the "happiness rate" for employed married women is greater than that for unemployed married women (e.g., Freudiger, 1983). This suggests that it may indeed be more the limitations of the traditional wife role than the actual fact of being married that gives us the observed differences in husband/wife satisfaction. As social changes continue to make it acceptable (and even expected) for married women, with or without children, to work outside the home, we may see a change in the pattern of less marital satisfaction for women.

## Increasing the Chances for Marital Satisfaction and Success

As the number of couples seeking marriage counseling (and divorce) has risen, psychologists have become increasingly more interested in what kinds of people seem to make happier and more successful marriages. A number of **marital success factors** have been identified.

- *Age:* Divorce rates are higher for couples who marry in their teens or wait until their late 20s or after (e.g., Booth & Edwards, 1985; Maneker & Rankin, 1985). The younger people have more stages of development to go through; their interests, values and attitudes are susceptible to change, and with each change the couple may move in different directions. People who wait to marry until their late 20s or older, by contrast, are more likely to marry someone who is quite different from themselves at the outset (e.g., Bitter, 1986).

- *Commitment:* A desire to *be* married as well as a desire to *get* married seems to be critical (e.g., Ammons & Stinnett, 1980). Our culture surrounds getting married with a variety of attractive features that can make it very romantic and appealing to people who have not given the matter much thought beyond the Big Day.

- *Emotional Health:* If one or both partners has serious emotional or psychological problems, the chances for a successful marriage are reduced (e.g., Renne, 1973). Consistent with the standards for effective behavior, the best marriage partners seem to be people who get along fine on their own.

- *Family History:* Couples whose own parents have made satisfactory marriages are more likely to achieve marital satisfaction (e.g. Pope & Mueller, 1979). The values of our parents have a strong influence on many of us.

*[handwritten margin note: mating maternity marrying of a higher social class]*

One of the factors that makes a difference in whether or not people are happily married is whether or not their parents were happily married.

In addition, people whose parents are happily married have models to imitate and vicarious experience with the rewards that a good marriage can provide, conditions facilitating social learning.

Age, commitment, emotional health, and family history are characteristics of the *individuals* involved that increase the likelihood of marital success. Certain aspects of the *couple as a couple* also are related to better marital adjustment and more satisfaction.

- *Financial Status:* Money does not buy marital happiness, but pressing financial worries are not conducive to a good relationship (e.g., Rosenblatt & Keller, 1983). The pressures of making ends meet may overshadow communication on other subjects, sharing, or enjoying time together.

- *Similar Backgrounds:* Psychologists have found similarity to be important in relationships, and this is as true in marriage as in friendship or dating (Kephart, 1977). Couples whose backgrounds are more similar than dissimilar simply are less likely to encounter basic life-style and value clashes.

- *Realistic Expectations:* Mutual and realistic expectations for marriage, including expectations about sexual fidelity, life style, and children, make success more likely. Marriages between people who have unrealistic expectations for the perfect relationship and/or different expectations about important aspects of the relationship are likely to encounter trouble (e.g., Farson, 1977).

- *Open Communication:* An established pattern of honesty and open communication increases trust and reduces the chances that small misunderstandings will grow into large grievances. A number of researchers have found that happily married couples differ from unhappily married couples in this regard (e.g., Yelsma, 1984), and the pattern seems to begin before a couple is married. Markman (1981) found that couples who described their communication as good before their marriage were happier with their marriages than other couples.

■ *Satisfactory Sexual Relationship:* Surveys find a tendency for more frequent sexual intercourse and marital happiness to go together (e.g., Thornton, 1977). This does not mean that the first causes the second, of course. It could be that couples who are happier experience more frequent sexual desire. Most likely, there is an interaction effect at work; that is, a more satisfactory sexual relationship serves to strengthen an already good relationship through the physical and emotional intimacy it provides.

By way of summary, trends from research into the factors that increase marital satisfaction and success have been turned into questions for this chapter's *Test Yourself.* Keep in mind that the findings behind these questions are based on statistics, and you are not a number, but a unique individual. *Test Yourself* can give you food for thought, but the results should not be considered any kind of mandate for making a decision about marrying or not marrying.

## TEST YOURSELF
## Are You Ready for Marriage with That Special Person?

*Directions:* Answer *yes* or *no* to each of the following questions. The more *yes* answers you have, the *less* likely it is that marriage at this time to this person will be a success. (Note: For this questionnaire, your "intended" may be anyone at all you choose so long as you know him or her well enough to answer the questions.)

|  | Yes | No |
|---|---|---|
| 1. Are you under the age of 20 or over the age of 27? | ___ | ___ |
| 2. Is your intended under the age of 20 or over the age of 27? | ___ | ___ |
| 3. Do you find being alone for any length of time uncomfortable? | ___ | ___ |
| 4. Do you and your intended have different ideas about religion? | ___ | ___ |
| 5. Have your parents been divorced? | ___ | ___ |
| 6. Have your intended's parents been divorced? | ___ | ___ |
| 7. Are there things about you and/or your past life that you do not want your intended to find out about? | ___ | ___ |
| 8. Do you and your intended come from noticeably different socioeconomic backgrounds? | ___ | ___ |
| 9. Have you known your intended less than a year? | ___ | ___ |
| 10. Do you find the idea of disagreements or fights with a spouse unacceptable? | ___ | ___ |
| 11. If you were to marry next week, would you or your intended have to give up some activity or goal, such as finishing college, for financial reasons? | ___ | ___ |
| 12. When you think of things you want to do in the future, does it seem that being married might get in the way? | ___ | ___ |

13. Are there things about your intended and/or his or her life-style that you don't like but won't mention?    ____    ____

14. Do you find yourself reluctant to discuss your feelings about children with your intended?    ____    ____

15. Is one of your primary reasons for considering marriage to escape from the problems and insecurities that often go with "dating" in today's social environment?    ____    ____

16. Do you feel dissatisfied in any way with your physical relationship with your intended?    ____    ____

17. Do you feel unable, for any reason, to discuss this problem with him or her?    ____    ____

**Note:** Questions taken from a variety of sources on the personal and life variables that affect the chances for marriage success and stability.

If you already are married, or have been married and divorced, you may want to return in your mind to the time before your wedding and take the quiz as things were then. Considering your personal experience, do you think that researchers are on the right track in their search for the important factors that affect marital satisfaction and stability? If not, what would you want to add or delete?

## Trial Marriages

Many of the individual and relationship factors that increase your chances for success in marriage are more likely to be present when you have known someone longer. Whirlwind courtships can lead to very successful marriages, but the odds are against it. Important differences often are disregarded, or they never have the chance to surface at all in the romantic excitement of love at first sight.

Knowing someone for a longer period of time does not guarantee knowing them well, but it usually helps. It also offers an opportunity to work through issues that might rock a marriage off its foundations. An increasing number of couples are coming to believe that a period of living together before making a commitment to marriage is vital for these very reasons (e.g., Kotkin, 1985). When cohabitation is for this purpose, we call it a **trial marriage.**

Can you, a tidy person, really stand living with that warm, wonderful, sensitive guy who also happens to be a slob? Can you, a man with traditional ideas about marriage, make a go of things with a bright, funny, loving woman who is committed to a career? One way to find out is to try.

Not all cohabitation is of the trial marriage variety, but a large number of people who live together say that they would like to marry one another eventually. Is this an effective strategy for increasing the odds that your marriage will be successful? Common sense would say yes, but the evidence does not support this expectation (Watson & De Meo, 1987).

Statistics tell us that your chances of being divorced when you have lived with your spouse before marriage are at least as great as if you have not. Indeed, they may be greater. One study of over 300 couples found that satisfaction with marriage was significantly *lower* for couples who had cohabited before marriage (DeMaris & Leslie, 1984). The authors suggest that people who live together before marriage may be different in some important ways from people who do not.

What kinds of differences might be involved? One possibility is that people who cohabit are people with very high expectations for marriage. They want everything to be perfect, and they see cohabitation as something like an insurance policy. But trial marriages do not seem to be a fair test. Perhaps the couples involved have too much at stake to make it so; they want to believe they have made the right choice of a mate, so perhaps they create a self-fulfilling prophecy that lasts until the wedding ceremony.

Another possibility is that people who enter trial marriages are undecided about marriage and hope to make up their minds by trying it out. Once together, they may find that factors other than their own attitudes toward marriage push them in that direction—splitting up to live apart again is a big nuisance, everyone expects them to marry eventually, they have made purchases and/or financial commitments jointly, and so on. Such people may more or less drift into taking the next step, forgetting why they were hesitant to begin with until after they are married.

All of this is speculative. Psychologists do not have much data on the dynamics of cohabitation, whether it is intended as a trial marriage or not. The following are among the questions that need to be answered.

Some couples believe that living together before marrying will help to increase the chances that their marriage will be a success.

- Do men and women enter into cohabiting relationships for the same reasons?

- Is the day-to-day relationship of cohabiting couples different in any significant way from that of married couples?

- Are there significant differences between people who live together and people who don't on such variables as age, education, and emotional maturity?

- Do people who cohabit before marriage try several partners, or is this a one-time phenomenon?

- If they try several partners, does the number relate to the success of a marriage when it does occur?

- How often does cohabitation lead to marriage?

## Adjusting to Marriage

Whether you live with someone with no expectations that the relationship will last, have a trial marriage, or take formal wedding vows, sharing your life with another person is not the same as living alone. You now have to consider someone else's needs, preferences, habits, expectations, and schedule. If you are married, you also must make decisions about money matters, children, and a variety of other issues you might let slide under a less formal arrangement. The exact nature of the adjustments varies from one couple to the next, but counselors find that several areas of adjustment problems are shared by most couples. Among these are adjustments regarding life style, finances, children, and marital discord.

### Life-Style Adjustments

Unless you have known someone long and very well, living with him or her is likely to produce some shocks. Has he always been such a neatnik? Doesn't she ever consider a quiet evening at home on a Friday or Saturday? Why has housework suddenly become such a big deal when it never was before?

**Life-style adjustments** involve reaching mutually agreeable decisions about how you will live as a couple. This means deciding about such mundane matters as who will take out the garbage and where the thermostat will be set as well as such exciting ones as where you will live and what kind of family car you will buy. These adjustments probably were easier when traditional marriages were the norm. As you can see in Exhibit 8–4, things have changed a great deal. It is by no means as clear who is going to do what these days as it once was. Sex roles currently are in a transition period, so male-female relationships, including marriage, also are going through a period of uncertainty.

These days, the couples involved have to work things out for themselves, and the process can be very disruptive if they are not prepared for it. One area in which many find themselves tripped up by crossed expectations is that of housework and child care. The couple who has agreed upon where to live, agreed that the wife will continue her career, and agreed that they want two children 5 years in the future may be surprised to find themselves fighting over who is going to vacuum the living room.

The woman in this scenario probably assumes that since she is working full time and contributing her income to the joint finances, her husband will

## EXHIBIT 8–4

## That Was Then, This Is Now: Life-Styles in the 1950s and 1980s

Although there always are exceptions, it still is possible to describe in a general way the differences between the life styles of the "typical" young American family of the 1950s with that we know today. Let's take a look.

| Area | 1950s | 1980s |
|---|---|---|
| Employment | ■ Husband supported family | ■ Both partners are employed |
| Homemaking | ■ Wife had full responsibility | ■ Husband expected to share chores |
| Child care | ■ Wife had full responsibility | ■ Husband expected to be an active coparent |
| Standard of living | ■ Within husband's income | ■ Up to or beyond dual income (no bank credit cards in 1950s) |
| Social life | ■ Arranged by wife, often with husband's career in mind | ■ Decided jointly; less likely to be career oriented |
| Leisure time | ■ Family oriented | ■ Fragmented; individually oriented |
| Meals | ■ Prepared by wife, usually "from scratch" | ■ Often eat out, take out, or microwave |

share the duties of maintaining a home. The husband probably is expecting to "help out"; equal responsibility is another matter. Study after study confirms that most of the housework in this country is done by wives regardless of their employment situation (e.g., Atkinson & Huston, 1984). More on this issue is to be found in *For Discussion*.

Psychologists, social workers, and others who work with couples having difficulties agree that mutual expectations are a critical factor when it comes to life-style adjustments. They recommend that you try to get important differences out in the open *before* you are married. Hoping that the other person will change his or her mind if you don't push it is a risky strategy. If *she* thinks you've agreed to go along with her and *you* think you can get her to change her mind later, there's trouble brewing. Compromises are much easier before the issue becomes immediate and takes on a win-lose dimension.

How much should you try to work out before you are married about how you will live after you are married? Alas, there are no guidelines. The most important thing seems to be to avoid making assumptions that your partner's expectations are the same as your own. At the least, talk things over in a natural way as the various subjects arise. For example, joint preparation of a cozy dinner for two before you are married might present an opportunity to explore how the two of you stand with respect to meal preparation and clean up on a permanent basis.

As you discuss the various aspects of living together, you may find that your expectations are similar and there is little reason to worry. On the other

## FOR DISCUSSION:

## WHOSE WORK IS HOUSEWORK?

Whose work is housework? Twenty-five years ago the question would not have arisen; everyone knew that housework was woman's work. But twenty-five years ago, that was the only kind of work most women did after they were married. Things are different today. Approximately half of all married women now hold jobs outside the home, and the percentage is much higher if only married women without children are considered.

The past generation has seen sweeping changes with respect to the role of women. Yet many married women today feel that what they have gained through these changes, most notably the freedom to have lives of their own and not live solely through their husbands' accomplishments, has a heavy price tag. Listen to Mary, a wife, mother of two, and clothing buyer for a department store chain:

Phil agreed before we were married that there was no reason for me to give up my career, and things went very well at first. We had enough money to eat out often, and sharing the housework in our tiny apartment seemed like fun. But then his career started booming and we bought a house and I had the children. Suddenly *my* career became just a way to meet the extra expenses. He seldom helps out at home because he works late almost every night and often works weekends as well. I don't work nights *or* weekends even though I could use the time. Somebody has to keep the house running and take care of the kids, and we can't afford live-in help. I seem to have ended up with two full-time jobs for the pay of one. Where did I go wrong?

Mary's husband, Phil, is an architect. His career took a sudden jump forward when his plans for a new shopping mall got the contract for his firm. Here is his side of the story.

It just never occurred to me that we would have these kinds of problems. I was always glad to help out at home in the early days. I still am when I have the time, but I just don't see the house or the kids as my responsibility. I wouldn't dare *say* that's "woman's work," but I do think that most men feel that way. And in my case, well, let's face it: Mary is very good at her job, but I make twice as much money as she does. If I start taking time away from work to do things at home, we'll all suffer.

Mary and Phil, like many married couples, assumed that they were in agreement about an important issue. As it turned out, they have very different ideas about where the responsibility for housework and child care lies. Mary believes that since she works outside the home, this should be shared. Phil is "glad to help out" if he has time, but believes the *responsibility* is Mary's, job or no job.

In this, as in other areas, attitudes have lagged behind social changes. Today's husband does chores his father would not have dreamed of doing, but don't be surprised to hear him say he is helping his wife with *her* work. Let's be fair, though. Women do their part to encourage this attitude. Mothers clean up after their sons, and few expect them to help with household chores to the same extent as daughters. Girls in college do their boyfriends' laundry; young career women rush home from a long day at the office to cook up cozy little dinners for their dates.

Looked at objectively, housework is just work, but who looks at it objectively? Do you? If you are married or cohabiting, how have you worked out this problem? Do you feel satisfied with this arrangement? If you live alone, what issues would you want to consider in trying to work out an arrangement in the future?

---

hand, you may encounter some surprises. Counselors say that now is the time to talk things over and try to reach a general understanding about life style and the responsibilities that will go with the one you choose. Some couples decide to formalize these discussions into a prenuptial agreement.

A **prenuptial agreement,** also called a marriage contract, often is for the purpose of keeping individual financial assets separate. The most well known form of such documents is that for the purpose of avoiding personal financial loss in property division or alimony should there be a divorce. But marriage contracts also may specify the rights and obligations of a marriage. Included are such issues as where and how the couple will live, whether there will be children and how they will be raised, how important decisions will be made, conditions for terminating the marriage, and, yes, who will have responsibility for what household chores.

We don't have much data on how many couples write marriage contracts, but the number probably isn't high for first marriages. The authors of one study reported that one-fourth of a sample of almost 300 students said that they would be interested in developing such a contract when they were ready to be married (Vander Mey & Rosher, 1981). Informal surveys of students by this author have found a figure of 10 percent or lower; the majority of students say that they don't think a contract is an appropriate basis for an intimate human relationship.

Interest in premarital agreements may be higher for people who have been married previously. These individuals usually are older and have had more time to accumulate substantial financial assets. They are more likely to have children whose security they want to protect, and they certainly are more aware of the possible pitfalls of marriage. If you fall into this group, or are curious about marriage contracts for any reason, a sample is provided in Appendix B.

## Financial Adjustments

In 1984, the *Ladies Home Journal* published a questionnaire asking readers for information and opinions about men and marriage (Knupper & Enos, 1985). Over 74,000 responses were received. One of the questions asked was what married couples argued about. The overwhelming answer—regardless of age, length of marriage, or financial status—was money.

Sharing your income, or just giving up some of your independence in making financial decisions, is one of the biggest adjustments you have to make when you marry. The potential for conflict may be greater if there isn't enough money, but arguments about financial matters are no respecters of income level. An argument over whether to go to Greece or Paris on a vacation can cause the same bitter feelings as one over whether to buy a television set or a washing machine.

As the *Ladies Home Journal* survey, many other surveys and studies, and perhaps your own experience make clear, most couples have arguments over money. Just as sex is not only about biology, money is not only about dollars and cents. Money is about security, power, values, keeping score on how we're doing relative to others, and a host of other motives. It is a rare couple who will not find some significant differences between themselves in this tangled set of issues, but disagreements do not have to be destructive. A first step to reducing the likelihood that financial disputes will damage your relationship is to set mutually agreed-upon financial priorities and goals.

Financial objectives do not have to be in the form of a strict budget, although many people find that useful, especially when money is tight. The main thing is to circumvent arguments of the "What do you mean there's no money for pizza?" type. Of course, this will only work if the partner paying the bills abides by the agreed-upon priorities. Deciding who will handle the money is a second step. Many couples take joint responsibility for financial matters, but there are still people who prefer not to have to pay bills. In the *Ladies Home Journal* survey, for example, 43% of the women reported that they handled family finances alone.

A third step in adjusting to the financial side of marriage and keeping its high potential for conflict within manageable limits is to agree to a rule about

## For Better or For Worse®                           by Lynn Johnston

arguments on this subject and resolve to stick to it no matter what. This rule is *Keep arguments about money about money.* The leap from money matters to character defects is all too short. The fact that last month's grocery bill was higher than the month before becomes proof that the person who buys the groceries is "trying to drive us to the poor house." The fact that a Club Med vacation is financially out of the question becomes proof that the person bringing home the check is a career failure.

Keeping arguments about money about money is not an easy rule to keep. Our attitudes toward money are complex and, as mentioned, often encompass quite different issues. To some people, money is to be spent; the future will take care of itself. To others, money is security; they can never accumulate enough, and they part with what they have reluctantly. To still others, money—making it, having it, deciding how it will be spent—is power.

Given this complexity, a potentially safe approach to financial disagreements is a problem-solving approach. One wants to buy a TV, but the other wants to buy a washing machine. That's a problem that can be solved by talking credit, cash flow, savings, and timing. Turning it into a free-for-all over his selfishness or her stubbornness violates the rule about arguments over money and will lead to what you'd expect—hurt feelings and entrenched win-lose positions for the next round.

## Adjusting to Children

Surveys usually find that the majority of young people express a desire for children at some time in the future (e.g., Stewart, 1986), and many couples marry expressly for this reason. Despite this commitment, they often are unprepared for the changes that children can make in a relationship. The most satisfactory adjustment is changed when two become three. A whole host of new issues arises, and old problems thought settled, such as how income will be spent, may come to life again.

The problems that arise when children are added to a marriage are likely to be less disruptive when couples are in basic agreement about child-rearing issues, but like arguments over money, they probably can't be avoided completely. Children change things. Schedules and routines are upset. Parents have less freedom and less time to spend together. Financial needs increase. New mothers and/or new fathers seem more interested in the child than in their spouse.

The list of adjustments that must be made when a family is begun is a long one, but a great many people find that the payoff for making them is enormous. To these parents, children are a source of satisfaction and pride that no other accomplishment can equal. Raising children together is a shared goal and doing it well is a shared victory. Nevertheless, there are few parents who would deny that children are still a source of stress. This reality is reflected in surveys of marital satisfaction, most of which find that it declines when children are born and stays low (at least in relation to childless couples) until they are grown (e.g., Glenn & McLanahan, 1982; White, Booth, & Edwards, 1986).

Research by psychologists, sociologists, and others into the factors that help parents cope with the stress in their new roles finds that self-esteem is critical to the husband's adjustment. For the new mother, satisfaction with her role in the marriage is the most important factor (Cunningham, 1985). These findings make sense. A father who is insecure can become jealous of the attention that his wife now bestows on the child. A mother who is unhappy with her role may build up resentment toward the child, her husband, or both.

The adjustments required by having a family have led an increasing number of couples to decide to remain childless. At the same time, more and more singles are making the opposite decision. Of the approximately one million adopted children in the United States, over 85,000 have been adopted by single women and over 26,000 by single men (Harden, 1985). An increasing number of women also are becoming unwed mothers by choice.

We have no statistics to tell us how many of the single people who have, or adopt, children would prefer to have a mate to help raise the child, but we do know that not all of them would. Comments by those who prefer to go it alone are surprisingly similar. Almost all mention a desire to avoid the negative effects that parental conflict has on children (Merritt & Steiner, 1984). Single parenthood is indeed a way to avoid this problem, but it creates other problems. Without a partner there is no one to share the work and the expense—or the joy and satisfaction.

The decision to have a child, with or without a mate to share the experience, is a decision that modern birth control methods place far more squarely upon the individuals concerned than at any time in history. In addition, our society's attitudes toward sex and human sexual relationships are more permissive than they ever have been. These factors (along with others) have combined to bring about associated changes in traditional ideas about families. With single women having and keeping babies by choice, single people of both sexes adopting children, divorced parents of both sexes raising children alone, and married couples deciding not to have children at all, the definition of *family* is broadening considerably in scope. There is more on these changes in *Face of the Future*.

## Adjusting to Marital Discord

The processes of making life-style and financial adjustments and adjusting to children are quite likely to involve disagreements. There are many other potential sources of disagreement between couples as well. Some of these will be

# *FACE OF THE FUTURE:*
## The New American Family

In the 1950s, anyone asked to describe a "typical American family" would most likely have depicted two parents and three children who lived in a single-family house and had one car. Mom stayed home and took care of the house and family. Dad went to a nine-to-five job, and when he came home the entire family sat down to dinner together. On weekends, they might go to a movie or visit the grandparents. In the summer, they might take a 1- or 2-week family vacation.

Not everyone lived this way, of course. Divorce, while not common, was not unheard of. Death, desertion, and unwed pregnancies also created some single-parent families. Some couples had more than three children, some less, and a few none. It wasn't unusual for wives to work until the children came, and some, because of financial necessity, continued to work after they began their families. But on the whole, the traditional family was the norm.

Things are quite different today. The Joint Center for Urban Studies at Harvard University estimates that by 1990 less than 15% of American families will be "normal" in the 1950s sense. Soaring divorce rates already have created an estimated 7 million single-parent families. The preferred family size has dropped to two children (Thornton & Freedman, 1983), and some sociologists believe that the family of the future will be a one-child family. There are a number of factors involved here. An important one is changing ideas about parenthood.

One of the ways in which the traditional American family differed from the families of today was in the extent to which parents became involved in their childrens' day-to-day lives. To a considerable degree, parents of the 1950s saw their role as providers, caretakers, and disciplinarians. Today's parents tend to see parenting as a much more active process. They are concerned with their children's intellectual, social, emotional, and academic development as well as with their physical development.

These concerns mean that today's parents spend more time and/or more money on their children; the more children there are, the less there is of both for each one. Concerns about personal freedom and growth and the increasing numbers of working mothers also are acting to limit family size. An estimated 50% of women with children under the age of 6 are in the labor force, and this figure jumps to 64% when the children are older than 6 (Robey & Russell, 1984).

Working mothers, more active parenting, and the more complex lives of children in today's world affect family life as well as the number of children a couple is likely to have. The majority of modern parents say they spend as much or more time with their children than their parents did, but this time is likely to be of a different sort. In particular, the amount of time the entire family spends together is less, although the time one parent and one or more children spend together may be greater (Rubenstein, 1985).

The active lives led by the members of many families today often mean that they are going off in several different directions at once. Mom is helping Mark with his math homework while Dad takes Lisa and her friends to a swim meet. Dinner may be take-out or microwave or "do it yourself." Family vacations are hard to arrange. Mom and Dad can't get time off at the same time, Mark wants to go with a friend to his parents' ski lodge, and Lisa has to be in town for swim-team practice.

In single-parent families the pattern is similar, if more frantic because there is no one with whom to share the load. Most single parents work, and scheduling can be a major problem. Single parents often feel guilty because their children do not have two

### *Continued*

live-in parents, so they pressure themselves to try to fill both roles simultaneously. In addition, many single parents have close personal relationships outside of the home that make a difference to family activities.

All of these changes mean that the "typical American family" with all that this implies about size, composition, and life style probably never again will be in the majority. But sociologists and others who study families emphasize that this does not mean the "death" of the family. Quite the contrary. They cite the growing number of single people adopting children as one kind of evidence that the desire for family life is a deep and abiding one.

What all of these changes do mean is that the face of the future encompasses a rich variety of family relationships that go far beyond the rather narrow roles typical of the 1950s. Included are many types of families virtually unthinkable 30 years ago. Among these are homosexual couples with children from earlier marriages, older women/younger men couples raising their children and/or her children from an earlier marriage, unmarried couples, and couples in which the woman pursues a career while the man stays at home with the children. The structure and roles may have changed, but the family is alive and well.

---

minor and blow over relatively quickly. Others will be major, and conflict may last for days or even weeks. Emotions accompanying such discord include anger, frustration, and depression. One or both parties may suffer hurt feelings that linger long after the argument or fight is over.

This **marital discord** is a source of great distress to many people. Like countless others before them, they believed that *their* marriage was going to be perfect. Discovering that they argue and fight just like their parents and their friends comes as a shock. Some begin to doubt that they have chosen the "right" person after all. Disagreements become more than disagreements; they become symptoms of something critically wrong with the relationship.

It is unlikely that there is any cure for marital discord. People are different, and when any two try to live together, these differences are bound to cause some disagreement. People also go through good and bad times as individuals. They have bad days and bad years (turning 30 or 40 seems to be vulnerable times for many), and the stress this puts them under makes them less able to overlook small annoyances.

Friends who live together seem to understand these things, but people in love often forget them. They go into living together with unrealistic expectations for perfect harmony, and they almost always are disappointed. A more realistic view helps to keep marital discord in perspective. All married people have arguments, and there is no reason at all for these to disrupt the relationship on anything but a temporary basis. Of course, understanding this does not make marital discord any more pleasant when it occurs, and many marriage counselors recommend that couples begin early to find ways to deal with conflict that keep it within bounds. You might look at this as setting **rules for disagreement.** There are several of these rules that may help.

■ *Get it out in the open as soon as it is reasonable to do so.* If you are upset about something, don't brood on it until you have really worked yourself into a rage. On the other hand, don't hit your spouse with an issue at a time when he or she can't deal with it (is on the way out of the house to work, for example).

■ *State the problem you are having* rather than hurling accusations at your spouse (who honestly may have no idea what is going on). For example: "I've been upset all day because you accepted that dinner invitation from your folks without asking me first," not: "I can't believe what a selfish, inconsiderate person you really are."

■ *Stick to the subject and to the present.* One of the most unpleasant aspects of marital discord is the way a small argument has a tendency to become a springboard to all kinds of other irritations and past grievances. A rule that you can't change the subject or generalize to the past can work wonders if you both stick to it.

■ *Don't go to sleep angry with one another.* This is an old remedy for marital disagreements and one of the best. You can't always resolve that disagreement in one day, but you can get over the anger and "agree to disagree" until further discussion. It is better to lose some sleep than to carry negative feelings about one another over into the next day.

Rules about fighting are one way to help keep disagreements in their place as problems to be solved. After all, you are both on the same side. The earlier in a marriage you set and begin to practice such rules, the better, because you have not had as much time to build up a history of grievances. It is never too late, however, and there are many professional counselors available to help you learn and practice the skill of "fighting fair" if you can't do it on your own.

## Types of Marriages

Different couples make their own individual adjustments in all of the areas we have been examining, and the result is a marriage style that works (or doesn't work, as the case may be) for them. Every marriage probably is a little different, but researchers in one well-known study of marriage styles have identified what appear to be five basic **types of marriage** (Cuber & Harroff, 1965).

■ *Conflict-Habituated.* As the name suggests, the conflict-habituated marriage is one in which the partners argue constantly. They have become used to, or habituated to, conflict; arguing is acceptable. These couples don't consider divorce an acceptable option even though they are basically incompatible.

■ *Devitalized.* This marriage is out of steam. Such couples don't argue; they don't do much of anything. Basically, they are bored with one another.

■ *Passive-Congenial.* There is little or no conflict in this type of marriage either, because the partners have little to do with one another. They are polite to one another, but their interests lie elsewhere (e.g., careers, children) and they do not put energy into the relationship.

■ *Vital.* These partners are involved with one another, and the marriage is important to their individual satisfaction with life. They try to work things out together.

In every marriage more than a week old, there are grounds for divorce. The trick is to find, and continue to find, grounds for marriage.

*Robert Anderson*

- *Total.* This is a vital marriage with a more complete sharing and emotional closeness. The partners make a point of spending a great deal of time together.

According to Cuber and Harroff, most marriages fall into one of the first three categories. Contrary to what you might expect, however, the researchers found that these couples were relatively content with their marriages. These styles represented their personal adjustments to being married, and they were adjustments with which both partners felt they could live.

## Summing Up

Reasons for getting married vary, but most people marry at some time in their lives. The popularity of marriage is supported by research that tells us that, on the whole, married people are more satisfied with life than unmarried people. There are some exceptions, however. Married women with children are somewhat more prone to psychological problems than their husbands, married women without children, and unmarried women. The arrival of children does not seem to affect men in quite such a dramatic way, but married men with children do seem to be somewhat less satisfied with marriage than are married men who have no children or whose children have grown and left home.

Whatever the circumstances, marriage requires adjustments of us all. Among the more important areas of this adjustment are those concerning life style, financial matters, and children. Sexual adjustments also may be required, even for couples whose sex life was mutually satisfactory before marriage.

## KEY WORDS AND PHRASES

| | | |
|---|---|---|
| adjusting to children | marital success factors | singlehood |
| companionate love | prenuptial agreement | trial marriage |
| life-style adjustments in marriage | psychologists' views of love | triangular theory of love |
| marital discord | reasons for marriage | types of marriage |
| marital satisfaction | rules for disagreement | |

## READ ON

*Living, Loving, and Learning* by L. Buscaglia. New York: Ballantine Books, 1982. A practical, realistic discussion by this popular author on learning to love yourself and others. One of the few down-to-earth discussions of love (not sex) you'll find.

*Finding Intimacy: The Art of Happiness in Living Together* by G. Zerof. New York: Random House, 1978. A refreshing practical approach to achieving positive intimacy with a partner. Questions at the end of each chapter help you examine your own relationship.

*Married People: Staying Together in the Age of Divorce* by F. Klagsbrun. New York: Dell, 1985. These stories of over 80 couples of all ages, walks of life, and areas of the country who have been married more than 15 years are both interesting and informative. The author found that all kinds of marriages can work and that staying together is a choice that is made over and over, not once; she describes her book as a tribute to that choice.

## REFERENCES

Ammons, P., & Stinnett, N. (1980). The vital marriage: A closer look. *Family Relations, 29,* 37–42.

Atkinson, J., & Huston, T. L. (1984). Sex role orientation and division of labor early in marriage. *Journal of Personality and Social Psychology, 46,* 330–345.

Berscheid, E., & Walster, E. (1978). *Interpersonal attraction.* Reading, MA: Addison-Wesley.

Bitter, R. G. (1986). Late marriage and marital instability: The effects of heterogeneity and inflexibility. *Journal of Marriage and the Family, 48,* 631–640.

Booth, A., & Edwards, J. N. (1985). Age at marriage and marital instability. *Journal of Marriage and the Family, 47,* 67–75.

Bower, D. W., & Christopherson, V. A. (1977). University student cohabitation: A regional comparison of selected attitudes and behaviors. *Journal of Marriage and the Family, 39,* 447–452.

Campbell, A. (1975). The American way of mating: Marriage *si,* children only maybe. *Psychology Today, 12,* 37–43.

Chafetz, J. S., & Dworkin, A. W. (1984). Work pressure similarity for homemakers, managers, and professionals. *Free Inquiry in Creative Sociology, 12,* 47–50.

Cuber, J. F., & Harroff, P. B. (1965). *Sex and the significant Americans.* Baltimore: Penguin.

Cunningham, S. (1983). Self-esteem, role satisfaction, and reduced stress in new parents. *APA Monitor, 14,* Dec., 16.

Davis, K. E. (1985). Near and dear: Friendship and love compared. *Psychology Today, 19,* 22–30.

DeMaris, A., & Leslie, G. R. (1984). Cohabitation with the future spouse: Its influence upon marital satisfaction and communication. *Journal of Marriage and the Family, 46,* 77–84.

Farson, R. (1977). Why good marriages fail. In J. E. DeBurger (Ed.), *Marriage today: Problems, issues, and alternatives.* Cambridge, MA: Schenkman.

Freudiger, P. (1983). Life satisfaction among three categories of married women. *Journal of Marriage and the Family, 45,* 213–219.

Glenn, N. D., & McLanahan, S. (1982). Children and marital happiness: A further specification of the relationship. *Journal of Marriage and the Family, 44,* 63–72.

Harden, T. (1985). More single men deciding to adopt children. *Suncoast Today,* Jan., 13.

Harlow, H. F. (1958). The nature of love. *American Psychologist, 13,* 673–685.

Jankowski, L. (1985). Marriage satisfying, 65% say. *USA Today,* p. A-1.

Kephart, W. M. (1977). *The family, society, and the individual.* Boston: Houghton Mifflin.

Knupper, G., Clark, W., & Roum, R. (1966). The mental health of the unmarried. *American Journal of Psychiatry, 122,* 841–851.

Knupper, G., & Enos, S. F. (1985, March). The men in your life. *Ladies Home Journal,* pp. 99–183.

Kotkin, M. (1985). To marry or live together. *Life Styles: A Journal of Changing Patterns, 7,* 156–170.

Long, B. H. (1983). Evaluations and intentions concerning marriage among unmarried female undergraduates. *The Journal of Social Psychology, 119,* 235–242.

Long Laws, J., & Schwartz, P. (1977). *Sexual scripts.* Hinsdale, IL: Dryden Press.

Maneker, J. S., & Rankin, R. P. (1985). Education, age at marriage, and marital duration: Is there a relationship? *Journal of Marriage and the Family, 47,* 675–683.

Markman, H. J. (1981). Prediction of marital distress: A five-year follow-up. *Journal of Counseling and Clinical Psychology, 49,* 760–762.

Merritt, S., & Steiner, L. (1984). *And baby makes two.* New York: Franklin Watts.

National Center for Health Statistics. (1984). Advance report of final marriage statistics, 1981. *Monthly Vital Statistics Report,* Feb. 29.

Olsen, L. (1983). *Costs of children.* Lexington, MA: Lexington Books.

Pietropinto, A., & Simenauer, J. (1979). *Husbands and wives: A national survey of marriage.* New York: Times Books.

Pope, H., & Mueller, C. W. (1979). The intergenerational transmission of marital instability: Comparisons by race and sex. In G. Levinger & O. C. Moles (Eds.), *Divorce and separation.* New York: Basic Books.

Renne, K. S. (1973). Correlates of dissatisfaction in marriage. In M. E. Lasswell & T. E. Lasswell (Eds.), *Love, marriage, family.* Glenview, IL: Scott, Foresman.

Rettig, K. D., & Bubolz, M. M. (1983). Interpersonal resource exchanges as indicators of quality of marriage. *Journal of Marriage and the Family, 45,* 497–510.

Robey, B., & Russell, C. A. (1984). A portrait of the American worker. *American Demographics, 6,* 17–21.

Rosenblatt, P. C., & Keller, L. O. (1983). Economic vulnerability and economic stress in farm couples. *Family Relations, 32,* 567–573.

Rubenstein, C. (1983). The modern art of courtly love. *Psychology Today, 17,* 40–49.

Rubenstein, C. (1985). What's become of the American family? *Family Circle, 98,* 24–39.

Rubin, Z. (1970). Measurement of romantic love. *Journal of Personality and Social Psychology, 16,* 265–273.

South S. J., & Spitze, G. (1986). Divorce determinants. *American Sociological Review, 51,* 583–590.

Sternberg, R. J. (1985). The measure of love. *Science Digest, 93,* 60–79.

Sternberg, R. J., & Barnes, M. L. (1985). Real and ideal others in romantic relationships: Is four a crowd? *Journal of Personality and Social Psychology, 49,* 1586–1608.

Stewart, S. A. (1986, May). They see an upscale, happy future. *USA Today, 13,* A-2.

Tavris, C., & Jayaratne, T. E. (1976, June). How happy is your marriage? What 75,000 wives say about their most intimate relationships. *Redbook,* pp 90–134.

Thornton, A. & Freedman, D. 1983. The changing American family. *Population Bulletin,* 38, No. 4.

Thornton, B. (1977). Toward a linear prediction model of marital happiness. *Personality and Social Psychology Bulletin, 3,* 674–676.

Trotter, R. J. (1986). The three faces of love. *Psychology Today, 20,* 46–54.

U.S. Bureau of the Census. (Yearly). *Statistical abstract of the United States, 1987* (107th ed.). Washington, D.C.: Author.

U.S. News & World Report (1988, May 30). Vital statistics: Late knot tying. p. 72.

Vander Mey, B. J., & Rosher, J. H. (1981). Marriage contracting: Sex role liberation? Paper presented to the Southern Sociological Society.

Walster, E., & Berscheid, E. (1971). Adrenaline makes the heart grow fonder. *Psychology Today, 5,* 46–50.

Walster, E., & Walster, G. W. (1978). *A new look at love.* Reading, MA: Addison-Wesley.

Watson, R. E. L. & DeMeo, P. W. (1987). Premarital cohabitation versus traditional courtship and subsequent marital adjustment: A replication and followup. *Family Relations, 36,* 193–197.

Weingarten, H. R. (1985). Marital status and well-being: A national study comparing first-married, currently divorced, and remarried adults. *Journal of Marriage and the Family, 47,* 653–662.

White, L. K., Booth, A., & Edwards, J. N. (1986). Children and marital happiness: Why the negative correlation? *Journal of Family Issues, 7,* 131–147.

Yelsma, P. (1984). Marital communication, adjustment and perceptual differences between "happy" and "counseling" couples. *American Journal of Family Therapy, 12,* 26–36.

# The Worlds of Education and Work

A leading business magazine asked a sample of MBA (Master of Business Administration) students about their career plans and expectations (Byrne, 1985). Here are some findings of this survey.

- Almost 90% of the sample expected to start at a salary between $25,000 and $50,000 a year. Only 4% expected their first salary to be below $25,000 a year.

- Over 30% of the sample expected to be making from $75,000 to $100,000 in 5 years.

- Seventy-five percent of the sample were willing to move at least every other year to advance their careers.

- Over 60% of the sample expected to start their own companies at some time during their careers.

Education is a traditional American route to job success, and the students in the *Forbes* sample believe that their master's degrees in business are going to pay big career dividends for them. They expect to be mobile and financially successful, and they plan to own their own businesses in the future. You may have your eye on a similar career pattern or something quite different, but what you share with these students is a commitment to education.

These subjects—education and work—are the focus of this chapter. For most of us, these worlds are where we spend a great deal of of our time for much of our lives. Here, we examine some of the basic issues in adjusting to, and making the most of, both worlds.

## THE WORLD OF EDUCATION

If you are reading this, you most likely are a student. As such, you spend some of your time attending class, doing assignments, and studying for tests. If you are a full-time student, you do the same for other classes. In either case, you have committed time to furthering your education beyond high school. Why?

### Why Go to College?

There are many things you might have done when you graduated from high school. You might have gone straight to work or maybe traveled around this country or Europe for a while. You might have joined a branch of the armed services. You might have attended a vocational training school or private training institution to become a computer technician, a travel agent, or a dental assistant.

Perhaps you did one of these things and now have gone back to school. In either case, you have chosen college. Why? There are a variety of answers to this question.

- *Because I wasn't sure what I wanted to do with my life.*
- *Because everybody expected me to go to college.*
- *Because I want to be an educated person.*
- *Because I want a better job.*

### Is College Worth It?

Some students find being at college difficult; they may be far away from home, they are having to compete with bright students from all over the state or country, and they often have limited financial resources. Quite understandably, they wonder if it is worth it. No one can answer that for those who go to college to buy some time or because it is expected, but let's look briefly at those who go specifically to get a better job or become an educated person.

Although many former college students complain that their educations did not prepare them well to perform their current jobs, the evidence suggests that completing college still is a wise investment. In one large-scale, comprehensive study of economic success, for example, a college degree (*not* "some college") was found to be a major determinant of income and occupational status (Jencks, 1979).

Does the prestige of the school matter in reaping these benefits? Certainly a degree from Harvard will be more likely to impress some employers than a degree from a relatively unknown college, but in general, prestige doesn't seem to matter as much as you might think. There is some evidence that students who have gone to the more prestigious schools are more satisfied with the experience, but there is little indication that they go on to be more successful in life (Astin, 1977).

If you think you might want to go on to postgraduate study, however, the situation may be different. Postgraduate selection committees at

> There is much pleasure gained from useless knowledge.
>
> *Bertrand Russell*

many schools are notoriously status conscious. In addition, the prestige of the graduate school you attend may be important to your future career. The better jobs in the legal field go to the graduates of the well-known law schools, to take one example. So if you have plans for a postgraduate degree, it is a good idea to begin now to investigate the status situation in your chosen field.

What about going to college for the purpose of becoming an educated person? This is a harder question because achieving this goal is highly dependent upon individual participation in the education process. If you don't make an effort, you won't get much of an education. Still, policies, teachers, and course offerings do play an important role, and those who make it their business to evaluate our country's institutions of higher learning are beginning to voice some serious concerns about the quality of what is being offered. There is more on this issue on *For Discussion*.

You have chosen college for your own reasons and have made your own choices about what to study. Despite the debate over what colleges should be teaching, the odds remain good that you can get what you want from the experience. If you hang in there and graduate, you will acquire knowledge and new skills; you also may make lifelong friends and have a better chance at economic success.

## Adjusting to College

Whether you go straight from high school or after a period away from school, going to college is an adjustment. If you return after a period of time, you may find it difficult to get back into the student role again. If you also hold a job and/or have a family, you will have to adjust an already crowded schedule. You may feel pressured and worry that your study skills are too rusty to keep up with the competition.

If you go to college straight from high school, you face a different set of adjustments, particularly if you go away to study. This may be the first time you have lived away from home. Chores, like the laundry, that seem to have gotten done by themselves there now have to be confronted. You also have to get yourself up for classes, clean your own room or apartment, and do something about meals.

College requires other kinds of adjustments as well. Many students go to schools that are much larger than their high schools and are swamped by feelings of being lost in the crowd or just another number. There is also the matter of making new friends. Unless you took a high school chum off to be your roommate, you may have to build your social life over from scratch. An important thing to remember when these things get you down is that you are not alone. Many of those laughing, seemingly confident people sitting around you in class feel the same way. Remember also that your school has a counseling center with people you can talk to if the pressures get too great.

Of course, you may be past all of this and feel quite comfortable with your college and your life there. There still remains the question of how you will do academically. It is surprising how many students go all the way through college and graduate without ever learning how to use their study time efficiently. Each assignment and test is like a new problem that must be solved.

It isn't uncommon to feel lost in the crowd when you go from a small high school to a large college, but the feeling usually passes.

## FOR DISCUSSION:
## WHAT IS EDUCATION FOR?

Recently, a humanities professor at a community college gave his students a short quiz on their knowledge of famous figures in science and the arts (Dawson, 1985). Among the answers he received were the following:

- Shakespeare is a 20th-century painter.
- Einstein painted the ceiling of the Sistine Chapel.
- Leonardo da Vinvi developed the theory of evolution.

These answers were not unusual. The professor has been getting much the same results for 8 years. He says that students who fail the test don't care. They believe such knowledge is trivial and does not affect their lives. They are at college to learn to do something that will help them make a living. In a recent survey by the Carnegie Foundation for the Advancement of Teaching, 73% of the high school students surveyed and 74% of their parents agreed that this is the primary purpose of a college education.

As life gets more competitive in every sphere, students like these are pressing colleges and universities to offer more directly useful courses of study. Many of these institutions are responding, and, as a result, some educators believe that the line between institutions of higher learning and vocational schools is blurring. Like the professor who gives the humanities test, they are concerned that the goal of *educating* people is being replaced by a goal of *training* people, a goal that has been called **vocationalism.**

One panel of prominent educators says flatly that the bachelor's degree has lost its intrinsic value (Association of American Colleges, 1985). What is wrong with it? It is watered down, they say, and fads are taking the place of these traditional educational values:

- Historical consciousness
- Appreciation of the arts
- Experience of the arts
- Study in depth, the "joy of mastery"
- Ability to understand numerical data
- A feeling of being at ease with science
- Capacity to make sound moral choices
- Reading, writing, speaking, and listening literacy
- Ability to think abstractly and perform critical analysis

Those who support the educational values listed believe that the purpose of education is to enrich people's lives—to broaden their interests, deepen their appreciation of life, raise their consciousness, sharpen their intellect, and, in the broadest sense, to ensure a better culture for all. Those who take the position that the purpose of education is to help people get better jobs (and not all of these are students, by any means) believe that the world is too competitive to afford the luxury of 4 years of "becoming educated." They point to cases of people with advanced degrees in humanities subjects like history and philosophy who have been forced to take jobs in steel mills and gas stations because they didn't have any "real" skills.

It is true that many employers now give preference to applicants with a college degree in a job-related subject even when the job really does not seem to require it. It also is true that jobs in the humanities are increasingly scarce. On the other hand, many people aren't going to college to prepare for a job; they are actively seeking to explore their intellectual potential and to become more informed and thoughtful individuals.

What do you think college is really for? How might our colleges and universities serve the needs and preferences of people with very different answers to this question? Remember that many of our schools are supported by public tax monies and must be responsive to the desires and demands of a wide variety of groups.

So regardless of your current level, it may be useful to spend time reviewing basic strategies for doing well in school.

## Doing Well at College

Going to college requires making academic adjustments. You weren't the first high school star or fast-track career person to find yourself being just another student. Nor were you the first to find that old study habits no longer seemed to be sufficient. The **study tips** in this section are basic—but easy to forget when you are feeling pressured. If you really are struggling, many colleges and universities have learning skills centers exactly for this purpose, and you should be sure to investigate this possibility on your campus.

## Make Time for Studying

If you are a student, you will have to make time for studying, whatever the other demands on your time. Put it on your schdule. It is fine to get in a little extra work during odd moments here and there, but you'll be constantly running behind if you rely on that method. A good solid hour of concentration when you are fresh and alert will do you far more good than four 15-minute sessions stolen from other activities.

A solid hour a day on one subject also will do you more good than 5 hours at once. With some exceptions, researchers find that *distributed study time* works better than *massed study time* (Gagné & Rohwer, 1969). For example, if you think you need to put in 10 hours of study for the biology test, it probably will be more effective to study 2 hours a day for 5 days than to set aside Sunday to study biology. (It also will be less demoralizing than spending an entire week dreading the dawn of Sunday!) A few more tips to help you perform better on tests are given in Exhibit 9-1.

## EXHIBIT 9–1
## IMPROVING YOUR TEST SCORES

*Read all the directions.*   Be especially alert for any time limits or penalties for guessing.

*Review the entire test before starting.*   This will give you a quick idea of its difficulty and will help you set yourself some time limits so that you don't get caught with 5 minutes to answer a 25-point essay question. It also will help you avoid using material in one question that is more relevant to a later one.

*Make notes.*   While reviewing the test, use the margin or back of the paper to jot down ideas for use as you begin to answer the questions.

*Answer all multiple-choice and true-false questions.*   Unless there is a penalty for guessing, you are better off answering all of the questions.

*Use common sense.*   If you think of a barely possible, but highly improbable, set of circumstances under which an otherwise false statement might be true, do not mark the statement as true. Most professors are *not* trying to trick you by using this tactic.

*Answer the question that is asked when taking an essay.*   If the question says *compare*, then compare. If it says *contrast*, then contrast. If it says to *explain the significance*, then do so. Avoid the trap of seizing onto a word and telling everything you know about it, unless the question specifically asks you to define the term.

*Outline answers if you run out of time.*   Most professors will give partial credit if you demonstrate knowledge of the material.

*Learn to spell.*   An essay exam full of misspelled words creates a poor impression and makes it difficult for the grader to attend to the meaning of what you have written. If spelling is difficult for you, get a small pocket dictionary for use on tests. (If you are afraid this will give the wrong impression, offer to let the professor or proctor leaf through it before the test begins.)

## Study When You Study

The point of scheduling study time is to get something accomplished, not to put in so many hours of time just to say you did. Be realistic and mark out study periods of a length that match your concentration limits. Then *study.* Don't watch T.V., do your nails, eat, talk on the telephone, do the laundry, or help the kids with their homework at the same time.

You may have to make some changes in order to be able to reserve your study time exclusively for studying. If you study at home and don't live alone, enlist the cooperation of your roommate, your parents, your husband or wife, or your children in letting you have this time undisturbed. If this isn't possible, go to your campus or public library. Try to set aside regular time for this and make it an understood part of your schedule.

When you get to the library, find a quiet place to work and do it alone. Group study, in which several people work together on the same subject or assignment, can be very useful; just studying in a group isn't likely to be. There are too many opportunities to do something else and too much distraction for effective concentration.

## Plan Ahead

It is 4 A.M. You pour your 12th cup of coffee and bend wearily over your typewriter. The term paper is due at 11 A.M. and you are only half finished. Sound familiar? Some people work like this all of their lives and seem to get by just fine. Most of us don't do our best work this way. When you are exhausted, your concentration suffers. Even your ability to type deteriorates when your body is overtired.

If you are a chronic procrastinator, try this exercise. The next time an assignment is made or a test is announced, add up the number of written pages to be turned in, the number of novel pages to be read, the number of text and note pages to be reviewed, or whatever specifically is involved. Now, divide this number by the number of days you have to get ready. Surprised?

Even if you only have a week to read a 300-page novel, that is just a little over 40 pages a day. Ten days to do a 25-page term paper is a mere two and a half written pages a day. Can't work that way? That's exactly how a great many successful authors do it—so many pages a day, every day. You probably can too if you discipline yourself until the habit is established. Once it is, you'll find you do it almost automatically.

Planning ahead means recognizing that upcoming events may affect your schedule as well as starting assignments or studying for tests in advance. If you are having a big night out Saturday night don't schedule important study time for Sunday morning. If you are going camping over the weekend with family or friends, put in some extra time the week before. Isn't a guilt-free, a book-free, weekend worth giving up something else during the week?

Frequently, students who don't plan use the excuse that the time it takes to plan could be put to better use. In the first place, planning isn't that complicated; once you get used to it, it takes very little time. In the second place, most nonplanners don's use their time efficiently anyway, and it is unlikely that planning time would be wasted time.

Another excuse for not scheduling study time and planning ahead is that this is constricting and takes the spontaneity out of life. If you use this ration-

In most cases, frequent shorter study sessions are more effective than one long crash session.

ale, keep in mind that you aren't being held to your schedule under pain of death. It is your schedule, after all. You are perfectly free to modify it or depart from it at will if something exciting comes up. If you go through the process of planning and stick to your schedule in a general way, however, you'll have more free time, not less.

## Reward Yourself

Studying takes time. To the extent that you set time aside for this purpose, use it well, and plan ahead so that you can fit your work into the scheduled time, your efforts should pay off well. You'll feel less pressured and make better grades. These benefits are not always felt immediately, however, so learn to give yourself little rewards as you go along. For example, if you try, and stick to, the "one day at a time" method of writing a paper (so that you are finished with no hassles on the day it must be turned in), celebrate! Give yourself and a friend or your family dinner at a favorite restaurant, buy that new tape you've been wanting, watch some extra television that evening, or take the kids to the park—whatever you would like to do to give yourself a small treat.

You can't reward yourself every time you stick to your schedule, of course; but promising yourself something special when you've successfully conquered a report, midterm, or class presentation will work wonders to keep you going. These rewards are immediate. They also are for the behaviors involved in the *process* of studying and/or preparing for an assignment or test, not for the *outcome* (grade) you receive. Professors don't see the effort and persistence you put into such work, but you do. If you've done well, that deserves some recognition even if the grade is not quite what you had hoped.

## Make a Good Impression

While you are in school, either full or part-time, you are in the role of student. Part of playing this role successfully is managing your study time and doing well on assignments and tests, but part of the student role is not played out at home or in the dorm or in the library. It is played in the classroom. What kind of impression do you make in this setting?

Sometimes, without meaning to, students give a false impression of themselves by the way they behave in class. Remember that professors can't see inside your head. They form their impressions of you by your behavior—what you do and say in class and how you perform on tests. The tips in Exhibit 9-2 will help you make an impression as the serious, motivated, responsible student you are.

## EXHIBIT 9–2
### Making a Favorable Impression in the Classroom

The following behaviors do not cost you anything or require you to hit the books for so much as an extra 5 minutes. Yet they considerably improve the odds that your professors will know you and think well of you. These same behaviors also pay dividends in what you get out of your classes and even how well you do on tests.

*Go to class.* Go on the first day, the last day, and the days before and after holidays. Go if it is raining or snowing. Go if you have a cold (but be considerate of your fellow classmates). Go if the professor is boring. Your absence is noticed more often than you think, and most professors believe that class attendance is a basic student responsibility. And even if a particular one doesn't care one way or the other (and/or gives confusing or noninformative lectures), you will still get a feel for what he or she thinks is important and for what is likely to be on the tests.

*Sit in the front of the room.* Professors notice and get to know students in the front, and being noticed in a positive way is what impression management is all about. You don't get ahead in life by fading into the crowd. Sitting in the front also can help you get better grades. There are fewer distractions, it is more difficult to yield to the temptation to do other things when you are under the professor's eye, and you'll find it easier to ask your questions if you don't have to shout them out. All of these factors can help you do better on tests and assignments.

*Be active.* Ask questions if you have them. Answer questions if the professor asks them and you know the answers. Volunteer to participate in demonstrations. Join in discussions. You'll not only be noticed and make a more favorable impression (unless your comments are obviously for show), but also the time will go faster and you'll get more out of the class.

*Never, never, never ask "Will this be on the test?"* At best, you will sound immature. At worst, you will establish yourself as so unmotivated that you are afraid you might learn something you don't have to. If part of the material is giving you trouble or just looks like it isn't all that important, see the professor privately and find some other way to approach the matter.

And while we're on the subject of questions not to ask, here is another. "Is it okay if I miss class tomorrow [next Thursday or the day before Thanksgiving or whenever]?" This question annoys more professors than not. If you have decided to miss class, it is responsible behavior to alert the professor to this fact and ask if there is an assignment you should know about. But don't ask for advance blessing on your absence.

*Meet your deadlines.* Don't ask for more time to do an assignment, extra time on a test, or a makeup exam unless you absolutely *must*. This gets you noticed all right, but not in the way that you want to be.

Psychologists call strategies for making a particular impression of yourself on others **impression management.** Is this dishonest? The truth is, you do it all the time. You try to make a good impression on dates. You go all out to impress job interviewers positively. You try to look good to your boss and to your child's teacher. You get out the best china and give the house a good cleaning when your mother-in-law is coming to visit. If you put your best foot forward with your friends, your prospective employers, your boss, your family, and others, why not with your professors?

**Summing Up** ■

There are many reasons to go to college. Whatever your own reasons and wherever you went, you found you had to make some adjustments. Some of these had to do with living away from home, some are adjustments in your social life, and some are alterations in your time management and study habits. Being a successful student also involves learning to present yourself as a responsible, interested, and motivated individual.

## THE WORLD OF WORK

Sigmund Freud once said that the two most important things in life are love and work. This is even more true today than in Freud's time, at least when it comes to the importance of work. At the turn of the century when Freud was writing, only about 5% of married women worked. Today the percentage is over 50. Teenagers also have entered the work force in greater numbers. Many high school students now take part-time jobs even when the economic status of their parents makes it unnecessary, a pattern virtually unheard of a generation ago. As a college student, you may work as well. You may be in your chosen occupation or just working to meet expenses. Either way, work is an important part of your life.

### Occupational Choice Factors

You may be attending college partially for the purpose of selecting an occupation. You may be there to prepare for one you already have selected. Or you may be going to school because you want to get ahead in the occupation of your current employment. If you already have chosen an occupation, there are many possible avenues by which you may have reached your decision.

A surprising number of people follow the occupation of a parent, sister, brother, or other relative. For others, the choice grows out of leisure-time interest. Perhaps you are studying to be a physical education teacher because you have always liked and been active in sports. Or maybe you got hooked on video games at an early age and plan to go into one of the computer-related occupations.

Some people choose occupations on the basis of what they were good at in school. In other cases, the choice is something of an accident. Perhaps the only part-time job you could find in high school was working in a clothing store, and as a result you became interested in retail management. At the other extreme, a few people seem to feel called at an early age to a particular occupation. Nurses, doctors, teachers, and ministers often report having had such an experience.

Despite the many possible ways people can choose an occupation, you may be undecided still. If so, you have lots of company. It isn't even unusual for college graduates to be uncertain of what they are going to do in life. What kinds of information might help them—or you—make this decision?

## What Are You Interested In?

By the time we are attending college, most of us have a pretty good idea of what interests us, or at least of what *doesn't* interest us. You've never taken a course in anthropology, for example, so you don't know about that, but you do know that you don't want to work in a math-oriented occupation.

Interests, both established ones and new ones, can serve as a guide to vocational exploration. One avenue open to you is to go to your counseling office and take what is called an *interest inventory*. These are questionnaires that allow you to compare your preferences and interests with those of people already employed in various occupations.

On the basis of your answers to a large number of questions about the kinds of things you do and don't like to do, your counselor can draw your interest profile. This is a graph that shows how your interests compare with the interests of those in different professions. It is important to remember that we are talking about interests here, not abilities. The fact that you have interests in common with brain surgeons, for example, does not mean that you would be a successful one.

If interest inventories do not provide any information about the abilities required to be successful in an occupation, why take one? You might look on it as a first step to help you narrow the field of possibilities. You are going to have the necessary abilities for at least one (and probably more) of the occupations that are suggested by your pattern of interests, and psychologists do have evidence that job satisfaction in later life is greater for people in occupations with compatible interest profiles (Super, 1985). This relationship reminds us that we do not choose an occupation in isolation; we choose a lifestyle as well, and interests are an important part of that decision.

## What Would You Be Good At?

Once you have a general idea of occupations that might be compatible with your interests in life, it is time to turn your attention to a realistic assessment of your abilities. **Abilities** are the basic physical, mental, and psychological characteristics you must have to be able to learn to do something. Perhaps you share a great many interests with professional musicians. Unfortunately, you also are tone deaf (lack a necessary physical ability), so a musical occupation is a poor choice unless you want to enter the business side of the field.

In sorting occupations of possible interest into those you might be good at, you are considering abilities, not skills. An ability is what it takes to learn to do something; for example, you can't learn to play a musical instrument well if you are, in fact, tone deaf. **Skills** are what you already can do. Perhaps you aren't tone deaf at all, but an accomplished pianist; that is a skill.

If you have the basic physical, intellectual, and psychological abilities, you can learn the skills. You may not know a thing about being an air traffic con-

People in various occupations that tend to have similar interests and studies find you are more likely to be satisfied with this work if you share the same interests.

troller, for example, but if you have good eyesight and hearing, the cognitive ability to process information and make decisions quickly, and tolerance for stressful working conditions, you can learn the necessary skills.

Your campus counseling office can help you get a better idea of your ability strengths and weaknesses, just as it can help you define your interests. There are many ability tests that will give you information about your reflex speed; coordination; visual and hearing acuity; and mechanical, mathematical, and verbal abilities. There are also tests that help you assess the likelihood of being successful in a particular occupation. For the fun of it, you may want to check out your potential for being successful in a management career by answering the questions in *Test Yourself.*

## TEST YOURSELF:
## Would You Be a Successful Manager?

*Directions:* Being a good manager requires problem-solving, decision-making, organizing, planning, and communication skills, as well as technical skills in a particular field. After reading each statement below carefully, place a check in the *yes* column to the left or the *no* column to the right of the statement. When you have finished, add up the number of answers in each column. The more *yes* answers you have, the better the chances that you would be successful in this occupation.

| YES | | | NO |
|---|---|---|---|
| ____ | 1. | I am good at getting to the heart of a problem and dealing with that rather than just tackling its symptoms. | ____ |
| ____ | 2. | I am creative when brainstorming, using the full power of my imagination as I formulate possible solutions. | ____ |
| ____ | 3. | In addition to considering the pros and cons of a solution, I take into account my "gut feeling" on a particular course of action. | ____ |
| ____ | 4. | I don't rush into decisions; I consider all pertinent facts and opinions beforehand. | ____ |
| ____ | 5. | I come to a decision within a reasonable period of time. | ____ |
| ____ | 6. | Once I make a decision, I am willing to accept responsibility for it. | ____ |
| ____ | 7. | I know how to break down long-range objectives into shorter-range goals. | ____ |
| ____ | 8. | When I am given an assignment, I stop to consider the various ways I could proceed before I begin. | ____ |
| ____ | 9. | I break down complicated projects into their component parts and perform each task in sequence. | ____ |
| ____ | 10. | I meet deadlines. | ____ |
| ____ | 11. | I am seldom guilty of wasting time. | ____ |
| ____ | 12. | I have learned not to be a perfectionist about small, unimportant details. | ____ |
| ____ | 13. | I am a good listener and observer of others. | ____ |
| ____ | 14. | I feel I have a good attitude about taking and giving constructive criticism. | ____ |
| ____ | 15. | I have gotten over the feeling that "if I want something done right, I have to do it myself." | ____ |

**Source**: From "Upward Mobility: A Comprehensive Career Advancement Plan for Women Determined to Succeed in the Working World" by the staff of Catalyst. Copyright © 1981 by Catalyst. Adapted by permission of Henry Holt and Company, Inc.

Management is a good example of a career that has been opened up to a considerable degree to women and minorities after years of domination by white males. As a result of the social changes that have brought more equal employment opportunity to this and many other fields, it is fashionable now-adays to say that people can be anything they want to be. A more accurate statement is that your choices are wider than at any time in history. They are not unlimited; ability is a fundamental constraint. You canot do what you lack the ability to do, no matter how much you might want to. And, as a general rule, the more your abilities are suited to your chosen occupation, the more successful and satisfied you are likely to be.

Your finances also are relevant to your choice of occupation. You simply may be unable to afford the long training required for some work. You also must consider the chances of finding a job in your chosen field; some already have more qualified people than jobs. A realistic choice of occupation involves consideration of future employment opportunities as well as interests and abilities. Finally, there are certain realities in the world of work that women and minorities should be aware of in considering choice of occupation. There is more on this in *Face of the Future*.

> Every calling is great when greatly pursued.
>
> *Oliver Wendell Holmes, Jr.*

## Where Are the Jobs?

In the past decade, service occupations have been growing the fastest, with computer-related occupations at the head of the line. For the immediate future, the hottest new jobs are predicted to lie in medical technology, computer graphics, robotics, fiber optics, telecommunications, energy, biotechnology, and training of people for all of these jobs of the future (Solorzano, 1985). Many of these jobs will be located in the West and Southwest and in Florida. These currently are the areas of greatest economic expansion, and this trend is expected to continue through the year 2000 (Naisbitt, 1985). This does not mean that you won't be able to find a job in your chosen occupation in another part of the country, but it does suggest that you should be prepared to be mobile if it is at all possible.

You can get more specific information about where the jobs are from your college placement office and from a variety of government publications at your campus or public library. Ask the reference librarian for assistance. You also will find useful information in business-oriented publications, such as *Business Week, Forbes, U.S. News & World Report,* and the *Wall Street Journal.*

## What Is the Work Like?

Once you have narrowed your search down to occupations in which you might be interested, for which you have the necessary abilities, and in which you may expect to find employment, you'll want to examine the work itself, working conditions, and compensation. A good place to start is by reading the literature about an occupation. One source book is the *Occupational Outlook Handbook* (Bureau of Labor Statistics), which will give you information about some 800 selected fields.

The view of an occupation you get from reading about it often will emphasize the positive features and gloss over the less attractive aspects. One way

# *FACE OF THE FUTURE:*
## Equal Employment Opportunity

It has been a quarter of a century since Title VII of the 1964 Civil Rights Act guaranteed equal employment opportunity to all citizens regardless of sex, race, color, religion, or country of national origin. The intent of this law is to prevent unfair discrimination in access to training, jobs, promotion, employment development, and other job-related opportunities.

In the work place, **unfair discrimination** means discriminating against people on the basis of some non-job-related characteristic. The two characteristics that have received the most emphasis are sex and race. We can expect the issue of age discrimination to loom larger as our population gets older, however.

Has the law worked? To an extent, the answer is a resounding yes. If we look at the number of women and minorities who now hold jobs that long were the exclusive province of white males, it becomes clear that a great deal has changed. For example, women now hold almost one third of all managerial and administrative positions as compared with less than one fifth in 1973. And the percentage of blacks in professional and managerial occupations now is approaching the percentage of blacks in the population.

Statistics like these are impressive, especially to those who remember how things used to be; but they do not tell the whole story. All together, women now account for almost 54% of the work force and the U.S. Census Bureau lists women as well as men in every one of its occupational categories. Nevertheless, as a group, women are concentrated in the lower-paying "pink-collar" jobs, such as nursing and clerical work. At present, the Census Bureau estimates that the lifetime earnings of a woman with 5 or more years of college will be only about 63% of that of a man with the same education.

Black citizens are in a similar situation. In 1980, to take one example, blacks not of Hispanic origin made up about 15% of the population of the state of Florida. Yet they held almost 25% of the lower paid jobs in the state, and their unemployment rate was four times the national average (EEO, 1980).

What do such facts and figures mean for the future? In general, they mean that you have a better chance now than at any time in history of gaining access to the occupation and job of your choice, whatever your sex and ethnic group. They also mean that if you are a white male, you may expect more competition, especially for those jobs traditionally regarded as a male preserve.

If you are a woman or a member of a minority group, the fact is that you still may expect to encounter discrimination in pay or difficulty in advancement in many fields. Things are changing, but the process is not complete. For the remainder of this century at least, pay and promotion opportunities for nonwhites and females will continue to lag behind equal access to jobs.

to round out this picture is to talk to someone who is (or has been) employed in the field. Among the things you would want to ask about are working conditions, day-to-day activities, requirements for getting into and advancing within the occupation, and potential status and earnings. Table 9–1 gives you a head start on this last point by presenting 1988 approximate average starting salaries for college graduates in a variety of occupations.

Table 9–1   **Average 1988 Starting Salaries for College Graduates in Selected Occupations**

| Field | Salary |
|---|---|
| Accounting | $23,000.00 |
| Agriculture | 19,000.00 |
| Advertising | 19,000.00 |
| Chemical Engineering | 31,000,00 |
| Chemistry | 23,000.00 |
| Civil Engineering | 25,000.00 |
| Communications | 18,000.00 |
| Computer Science | 28,000.00 |
| Education | 19,000.00 |
| Electrical Engineering | 29,000.00 |
| Financial Administration | 23,000.00 |
| General Business Administration | 20,000.00 |
| Home Economics | 17,000.00 |
| Hotel and Restaurant Management | 19,000.00 |
| Industrial Engineering | 28,000.00 |
| Journalism | 19,000.00 |
| Liberal Arts | 19,000.00 |
| Marketing—Sales | 21,000.00 |
| Mathematics | 21,000.00 |
| Mechanical Engineering | 28,000.00 |
| Physics | 24,000.00 |
| Retailing | 17,000.00 |
| Social Sciences | 19,000.00 |

*Note:* From a variety of sources. Data rounded to nearest thousand. Regional differences may be considerable.

Of course, the best information about an occupation is obtained by trying it. If you are in a position to do so, look around for a part-time or summer job in a field high on your list of possibilities. If you can't actually do the work, try to find a job where you can watch it being done and observe first-hand what the work and the working conditions are like. For example, you might be a hospital volunteer if you are interested in medicine, a file clerk in a bank if you want to see what banking is like, or a camp counselor if you think you might like to work with children.

Why go to all of this trouble? For one reason, psychologists have some evidence that people who take the time and effort to acquire knowledge about their chosen occupations have a better chance of getting a good job. In one study with college seniors and master's degree candidates, greater occupational knowledge was associated with (a) getting at least one job offer before graduation and (b) getting more job offers total than students with less knowledge about their chosen fields (Taylor, 1985).

Another major reason for becoming well informed about occupations you think may interest you is to increase the likelihood that you will be satisfied with your choice when you make one. For many people, *job satisfaction* is an important part of life satisfaction (e.g., Freedman, 1978). Finding out what an occupation is really like will give you a chance to assess whether or not it will meet your particular needs. Some of the aspects of work and working conditions that many people feel are important in this regard are listed in Exhibit 9–3. As you see there, and may know from your own experience, there is far more to job satisfaction than a good income.

It is possible to like your occupation and dislike your particular job in it, of course, but that is a problem that usually can be solved. It is more difficult to change your occupation once you have trained for it and gotten your foot on the ladder. Your age and financial obligations also may place constraints on a major occupation change once you have gotten into a field. In one survey, over 40% of the people responding said that they felt locked into their current occupations, and many were dissatisfied with them (Renwick & Lawler, 1978). There is a lot to be said for putting in time and effort to make a satisfactory choice the first time.

## Getting a Job

You have chosen an occupation, prepared yourself for it, and are ready to go. How do you find a job? The best way for you depends upon your particular circumstances, the occupation you have chosen, how well qualified you are, and who you might know who is working in the field. There are, however, some general guidelines for better and poorer ways to go about the process of finding a job.

### EXHIBIT 9–3

### Some Things People Want From Their Work and Their Working Conditions

Not everyone wants the same thing from work, but researchers who study job satisfaction find that certain aspects of work and working conditions are mentioned more than others (e.g., Brenner & Tomkiewicz, 1979). How many of the following are important to you? Does the occupation you are considering provide them? Are there factors not listed that you would be looking for?

**The Work**

Offers a sense of accomplishment
Allows for creativity
Is intellectually stimulating
Provides personal growth
Makes use of skills
Is important to the overall goals of the organization

**Working Conditions**

Job security
Good income
Opportunity for advancement
Comfortable working conditions
Congenial colleagues
Rewards for good performance

## Finding Prospects

If, for some reason, you were looking just for any job, your best bet would be to go around looking for "Now Hiring" or "Help Wanted" signs at business premises. Newspaper advertisements also offer such jobs, but your competition would be much stiffer. You also might find a job through an employment agency, but this would take longer and might cost you money (there are both fee and no-fee agencies in operation).

If you are looking for a particular kind of job in a particular occupation—the case under discussion here—you will have to go about things differently. Most companies don't hire for jobs that require specific preparation and training by putting a sign in the window. A few get into the classified ads, but, again, competition is fierce. Employment agencies also are likely to be disappointing. With some exceptions, the better jobs that they have to offer go to experienced people looking to *change* jobs.

So what *do* you do? Send out resumés to all of the organizations that you might want to work for? No, again. Some people do get jobs this way, but they are in the minority. Most companies will want a resumé as part of a formal application process, but they are unlikely to pay it much attention if they receive an unsolicited one in the mail. Here is what one expert on finding employment has to say about this strategy.

> The best way to find a job is to go out and visit company after company. The more people they [young people looking for a job] can see, the quicker they're going to get a job. What young people tend to do is stay home and wait for somebody to call them. It doesn't work (Challenger, 1984).

What companies should you go to? Sources of information are plentiful. Go through the books and brochures in your college placement office. Ask your friends and relatives. Look through the yellow pages of your telephone book to identify organizations that might have jobs in your area. Read the promotional material in the ads in *Time, Newsweek, Forbes,* and similar publications. And by all means use any contacts you might have; personnel managers estimate that as many as 40% of all jobs are obtained through personal acquaintance.

As you begin the process of looking for a job, keep in mind that you won't get one at many of the companies you visit. This doesn't have to mean that you have wasted your time. Experts recommend that you use job interviews as a way to get advice and information as well as to get a job. You may ask for feedback about your qualifications and communication skills (as displayed in your interview), suggestions for other companies to visit, or just advice for getting a job in your chosen field. Most professional personnel people are glad to help out interested, motivated job seekers in this way if they can.

## Doing Well at the Interview

Whatever else happens, you definitely may expect to have one or more interviews with a company before any job offer is made. You also may expect to get a good deal of advice from family and friends about how to handle these interviews, and don't be surprised if some of it is conflicting. For example, some people believe that it is vital to bone up on the facts and figures about a company before going to an interview and to ask questions about the company during the interview. Others say recruiters don't expect this, especially from applicants who are just coming out of college. Who is correct? It depends on the company, but it doesn't hurt to prepare yourself to some degree. The fact that you made this effort shows that you have initiative and motivation.

Conflicting advice reflects that fact that companies and interviewers differ considerably in what they expect and how they handle the interview process. The best general strategy probably is to think of these situations as another exercise in impression management. The impression you want to emphasize is that of a mature, poised, competent individual who would make a good employee. You don't have 10 or 15 weeks to work on creating this impression as you do in making a good impression on your professors, however. At best you have an hour or so. Some tips for making the most of that time are presented in Exhibit 9–4.

## EXHIBIT 9–4
## Making A Good Impression At A Job Interview

*Control your posture and body movements.* Don't slump, sprawl, constantly shift from one position to another, or cross and uncross your legs during the interview. On the other hand, don't be stiff as a board either. Use gestures when they are natural, but avoid nervous movements. Normal body movement is a sign of poise.

*Avoid being overly formal or overly familiar with the interviewer.* Do not address your interviewer by his or her first name unless invited to do so. Interviewers vary in their preferences, but keep in mind that you are a job applicant, not a colleague. At the same time, avoid going overboard with *sir* and *ma'am*. These forms of address tend to emphasize your youth if you are young and to make interviewers uncomfortable if you are their age or older.

*Vary your voice tone and facial expressions.* Show interest and expressiveness and avoid a fixed smile or speaking in a monotone. The interviewer is evaluating your communication skills as well as your training and technical skills.

*Maintain eye contact when speaking or listening.* Look away naturally when considering a question or if the interviewer is speaking to someone else, talking on the telephone, or looking through papers. A fixed stare can be as disconcerting as no eye contact at all.

*Don't put down former employers, professors, or co-workers.* If an interviewer questions your C grade in economics, for example, don't say, "I deserved a better grade, but that professor was really unfair." Mature adults take responsibility for their failures as well as their successes. And you don't want to give the impression that you have trouble getting along with people in positions of formal authority.

*Be assertive about your talents,* but don't imply that the company can't get along without you. It can. Be very careful about questions on the subject of what you would change if you were employed (unless the duties of the job for which you are applying include making recommendations for changes).

*Don't smoke,* even if the interviewer is doing so. A double standard often applies here. If the interviewer smokes, he or she is relaxed and at ease; if you smoke, you are nervous. If the interviewer should offer you a cigarette, decline with a polite "no, thank you." (Saying "I don't smoke" can be interpreted as a holier–than–thou attitude even if you don't mean it that way.) There is also the possibility that someone you would be working with is a militant antismoker even if the interviewer isn't. Don't risk it.

Many professional employment counselors believe that the impression you make in an initial interview can make or break your chances of getting a job offer. In most cases, the interviewer has seen, or will be seeing, other applicants. He or she is looking for a way to eliminate someone. The tips in Exhibit 9–4 will help reduce the odds that that someone will be you, but they don't guarantee it. One reality every job seeker must live with is that another applicant may have more impressive qualifications or simply hit it off with the interviewer better.

# Career Development

Even if you have not as yet decided what work you want to do, you have known for a long time that the decision was coming. You probably have thought about it a great deal and discussed it with others. For most of us, work is a big part of our lives for most of our lives. Many psychologists are interested in this long-term relationship that people have with work.

## A Model of Career Development

Models of **career development** such as the well-known one by Super and Hall (1978), are descriptions of the stages that most people go through in their relationships with work. Like the models of development discussed in earlier chapters, career development models describe general stages through which most people pass in a predictable sequence. The stages of Super and Hall's career development model are described in Exhibit 9–5.

Super and Hall's five-stage model is a general description of career development over a lifetime. It is a useful framework within which to consider individual behavior; the *establishment stage,* for example, can take a number of individual variations. You may take a job with a company at age 21 and stay there the rest of your life. Or you may move rather quickly from one company to another for a few years. You also may shift from one occupation to a related one during this period. All of these different patterns serve the same end— getting established and getting ahead in your career.

## Early Career Issues

The various career stages described by Super and Hall bring with them different career concerns. In the first real career stage, the *establishment stage,* career-oriented people are interested in work that allows them to show what they can do. They think in terms of frequent raises and rapid promotions as they meet the challenges.

Common sense tells us that not all first jobs are going to satisfy these desires. As one writer puts it:

> For every grad who starts with a plum job or a spot in a promising training program, there are many more who have to settle for the crummy ones (Bamford, 1986, p. 98).

*Crummy* may be too strong a word in most cases, but many people do find their first job in their chosen field disappointing in terms of the nature of the work and the opportunities for standing out and getting ahead. They feel

EXHIBIT 9–5 ■■■■■■■■■■■■■■■

## The Five Stages of Career Development

### The Growth Stage

Up until about the age of 14, most people try on the idea of various occupations, both mentally and through play activities. Some of the more popular occupations at this stage are police officer, firefighter, nurse, teacher, doctor, and astronaut. The realities of ability and suitability are not yet relevant. This stage is characterized by *fantasy*.

### The Exploration Stage

From about age 14 until some time in young adulthood, most people start considering a future career seriously. They get information about various occupations, consider career goals, and acquire some work experience on a part–time or summer basis. This stage is characterized by *trial–and–error efforts*.

### The Establishment Stage

Most people begin their work lives in earnest in young adulthood, concentrating on getting established and getting ahead. This stage is characterized by *growth*.

### The Maintenance Stage

Middle adulthood is the period during which most people hit their career strides. They know their work and do it well. This stage is characterized by *stability*.

### The Decline Stage

Beginning in late middle age, most people begin to slow down and reduce work activities, eventually stopping them altogether at retirement. This stage is characterized by a *shift of interests* away from occupations and toward family, hobbies, and leisure-time activities.

*Note:* Summarized from "Career Development: Exploration and Planning" by D. T. Super and D. T. Hall, 1978, *Annual Review of Psychology, 29;* pp. 333–372.

that anyone could do what they are doing; the job just doesn't seem to require the training, skill, and motivation they bring to it. In other words, they feel **underemployed.**

What should you do if you are experiencing the frustration of being underemployed? Should you stick it out for awhile or move on? How critical is that first job to your career anyway? In general, the first job is critical in the sense that it is like a freshman term at school. This is when you make the transition from one world to another and show that you have what it takes to get along in the work setting you have chosen.

The actual work you do on your first job may be less important to your later career than the extent to which you demonstrate effort, persistence, reliability, willingness, and the ability to work with others. Quitting after a few months, no matter how tedious the job, doesn't look good from this perspective, and most personnel people recommend that you stick it out at least a year—two if you can.

If you stay, you may find that you get more interesting work, more responsibility, and more autonomy as time goes by. Many people in organizations seem to believe that newcomers should serve a sort of apprenticeship before being allowed fully into the mainstream of activities. You may be able to speed up this process by finding your own challenges. Find a better way to do one of your routine tasks that saves money, for example.

If it doesn't seem possible to make your job more interesting, don't just mark time. Work on building your knowledge of the industry and the people in it. Read trade publications, attend conferences (on your own time and at your own expense if necessary), join professional groups, and take advanced night courses if you can. All of these activities will help to make you better qualified and more attractive to another company when you decide the time has come to move on. When you do, leave politely and professionally.

- Break the news to your boss first; don't let him or her hear it from someone else before getting it from you.

- Offer to train your successor to minimize disruption of routines.

- Give at least 2 weeks notice and more if you will be difficult to replace and/or your job requires considerable training.

- Try to leave at a time that doesn't put your boss or co-workers in a serious bind.

- When you give notice, mention the positive things you have gotten from the job you are leaving—how much you learned, what nice people you met, and so on.

- Be prepared to outline your reasons for leaving. Make these positive. Never, *never* bad-mouth the company, the job, or your co-workers. This serves no useful purpose, and it may come back to haunt you.

- Be prepared for a negative reaction to your announcement; don't be surprised into anger or defensiveness. If you've been open and aboveboard and followed the preceding guidelines, you have no reason to feel guilty.

## Middle Career Issues

Concerns about showing what they can do largely have vanished by the time most people have reached Super and Hall's *maintenance stage* in their careers. They know their work and do it well, and most have come to terms with their

Fantasies about what we will be when we grow up are an important part of the growth stage of career development.

personal limitations. Concerns at this stage tend to shift away from the nature of work and rapid advancement to issues involving change.

As people advance through their careers, things change. Jobs change. Organizations change. Even occupations change. Work that once was satisfying because it provided so much interaction with people may become more and more a matter of computers and paperwork. Younger people may be brought in to do the same work at bigger salaries because they have more education. Promotions come more slowly as you get older, and you may find yourself working for someone considerably younger than you are.

All of these changes have their effects. Some people worry that they are becoming outdated and will have to rely increasingly on younger colleagues for technical assistance. Others find themselves caught in tangled webs of political and social relationships resulting from reorganizations, changes in organizational goals, and/or mergers. The company they knew is gone, and they aren't sure where they stand in the new one. Many feel that they must run harder and harder just to stay in place.

Not all job situations change in ways that are unsatisfactory and unsettling. Many people grow and change with the job or company or occupation and continue to feel competent and secure. But some of these people find *themselves* changing, because the middle career years also tend to be the years during which many people question old values, needs, and priorities. The occupation chosen for its high salary and prestige, for example, now may seem superficial rather than glamorous. The fact that they know and can do their work so well seems boring rather than comforting. They are ready for new challenges.

> The harder you work, the luckier you get.
> *Gary Player*

## Changing Occupations

One way that people find new challenges is to start their own businesses in a related field; thus, the writer starts a magazine. Another way is to change occupations altogether, like the highly paid advertising executive who quit his firm to become a charter sailboat captain in Florida. Like many people at midlife, he felt he was losing touch with some important values. In particular, he regretted having missed so much of his childrens' growing-up years, and he was determined to enjoy his granddaughter to the fullest.

Not everyone who changes occupation does so out of a desire to change life direction. People also change occupations because they have new information or because their previous work experience has qualified them for a line of work they could not have entered previously. Experience, contacts, and more financial flexibility also make starting their own businesses attractive to many at midcareer. Finally, some people who change occupations at midlife are people who have been out of the work force, either voluntarily or involuntarily, for some period of time.

However an occupational change may come about, the point is that career development is a process. It is a *series* of decisions, not a single, final one. Although most people make their major career decisions and changes in their 20s and 30s, an increasing number are exercising their options later.

Making a career change can be scary, but it also can be exhilirating. When you leave the safety and security of one job or occupation to do something you would rather do, you are exercising full control over your life. You are doing something because you want to do it, not because you have to do it. To increase the chances that the change will be all you want it to be, career counselors recommend that you prepare for it. Before you make any move, you should have well-developed answers to each of the following questions.

1. What is it that I want out of a change?
2. What specific goals do I have for myself?
3. What are my available alternatives?
4. What are the constraints within which I must operate?
5. What do I need to do to make the change that meets both my goals and my constraints?
6. What kind of help will I need and where can I get it?

The following is one set of possible answers to these questions.

1. I want more responsibility and freedom of action.
2. I want to be *the* boss in a company.
3. I can start my own business, buy a going concern, or buy a franchise.
4. I have limited savings and one child still in college.
5. I need to investigate the kinds of businesses I might like and sources of potential financing.
6. I will need financial advice and small business management expertise.

(*Note:* There are many professionals and several public service groups that provide this help.)

The sample answers should make it clear that *planning* is essential to successful career change, as is *realism*. Table 9–2 presents a comparison of the occupations a sample of over 4,000 people over the age of 50 would *like* to change to and the percentage of older people *actually employed* in each occupation. The people who responded to this survey were not necessarily planning to make an occupational change; but if they had been, some of them would have been very disappointed. Their dreams just were not very realistic. The

**Table 9–2   A Comparison of the Jobs Older People Want and the Odds of Getting Them**

| Occupation | Percentage Who Would Like This Job | Percentage of Jobs Held by Older Employees |
|---|---|---|
| Counselors | 4 | Less than 1 |
| General office workers | 11 | 10 |
| Managers and administrators | 20 | 13 |
| Public relations workers | 3 | Less than 1 |
| Receptionists | 3 | Less than 1 |
| Secretaries | 2 | 3 |
| Social workers | 3 | Less than 1 |
| Teachers | 9 | 3 |
| Travel agents and guides | 4 | Less than 1 |
| Writers and editors | 6 | Less than 1 |

**Note:** Data from "The Jobs You Dream About" by C. Bird, Feb.–Mar. 1988. *Modern Maturity,* pp. 31–37.

feasibility of making an occupational change is limited by environmental factors as well as by personal ones.

Most people in midlife have financial obligations and other people to consider. Changing careers without a feasibility study and a realistic plan can create hardship and damage important relationships. Starting over, whether in your own business or a new job in a different occupation, changes the status quo. Even if you make the same or more money, you change the social environment.

It bears repeating one more time that when you choose a career, you also choose a life style. Different occupations have different patterns of social interaction, interests, values, and norms, and the ones in a new field can be quite different from what you are used to. You also are going to have to go through another period of learning the ropes, and this may take more time and effort than you have been devoting to work in your old occupation. All of these changes can affect those close to you as well as yourself.

## Summing Up

Most of us spend a significant portion of our lives at work, and this experience will be more fully satisfactory if we find an occupation in which we are interested and for which we have the abilities. Experts say that finding a job is a matter of persistent personal contact and that making a good impression at the job interview is vital; having good qualifications is not enough.

Over the course of your work career you probably will have many jobs, and you may have several occupations as well. Older onward-and-upward career development patterns are changing as more people make big changes in the middle years. Nevertheless, the importance of job satisfaction on a day-to-day basis suggests that time spent in making your initial occupation choice will be time will spent.

## ■ KEY WORDS AND PHRASES

| | | |
|---|---|---|
| abilities and skills | middle career issues | study tips |
| early career issues | occupational choice factors | underemployed |
| impression management | Super and Hall's career development model | unfair discrimination |
| improving test scores | | vocationalism |

## ■ READ ON

*What Color Is Your Parachute? A Practical Manual for Job-hunters and Career Changes* by R. N. Bolles. Berkeley, CA: Ten Speed Press, Yearly. The first edition of this book about finding a job was so successful that it has become an annual publication. The most recent edition will give you up-to-date and practical information about all aspects of job hunting, and the writing style is pleasant and humorous. There also is an extensive guide to other books and professional services relating to this subject.

*The Insiders' Guide to the Colleges* by the staff of the *Yale Daily News*. New York: Putnam's Sons, Yearly. This is intended to be a reference manual for prospective college students who want to know what the colleges *really* are like. Each entry has the usual facts found in college manuals, but it also has some comments by current students. This unique feature makes the book so entertaining that people buy it just for fun. It also is useful if you are considering a transfer, thinking about graduate study, or wanting to help someone who is making a decision about college attendance.

## REFERENCES

Association of American Colleges (1985). *Integrity in the college classroom.* Washington, DC: Author.

Astin, A. W. (1977). *Four critical years: Effects of college on beliefs, attitudes, and knowledge.* San Francisco: Jossey-Bass.

Bamford, J. (1986, July 14). Everyone has to start somewhere. *Forbes,* 98–100.

Bureau of Labor Statistics (1986–87). *Occupational outlook handbook.* Washington, DC: U.S. Dept. of Labor. (Revised every 2 years.)

Brenner, O. C., & Tomkiewicz, J. (1979). Job orientation of males and females: Are sex differences declining? *Personnel Psychology, 32,* 741–750.

Byrne, J. A. (1985, June). Some thoughts from the best and the brightest M.B.A.s. *Forbes,* 215–220.

Challenger, J. (1984, Aug. 6). Quoted in: What to do—and what not to do—when job hunting. *U.S. News & World Report,* 63.

Dawson, B. (1985, May 15). Quoted in: Ignorance is rampant, professor says. Associated Press.

Equal Employment Opportunity Commission. (1980). *Census of population.* Miami: Miami District Office of the EEOC.

Freedman, J. L. (1978). *Happy people.* New York: Harcourt Brace Jovanovich.

Gagné, R. M., & Rohwer, W. D., Jr. (1969). Instructional psychology. *Annual Review of Psychology, 20,* 381–418.

Jencks, C. 91979). *Who gets ahead? The determinants of economic success in America.* New York: Basic Books.

Naisbitt, J. (1985, Mar. 10). Scanning the job horizon. *Family Weekly,* 4.

Renwick, P. A., & Lawler, E. E. (1978). What you really want from your job. *Psychology Today, 11,* 53–65, 118.

Solorzano, L. (1985, Dec. 23). Jobs of the future. *U.S. News & World Report,* 40–48.

Super, D. E. (1985). Coming of age in Middletown: Careers in the making. *American Psychologist;* 405–414.

Super, D. E., & Hall, D. T. (1978). Career development: Exploration and planning. *Annual Review of Psychology, 29,* 333–372.

Taylor, M. S. (1985). The roles of occupational knowledge and vocational self-concept crystallization in students' school-to-work transition. *Journal of Counseling Psychology, 32,* 539–550.

# Basic Skills for Effective Behavior

**P**arts 1,2,and 3 of *Psychology and Effective Behavior* examined you, the forces that affect your behavior, and the social, work, and academic worlds in which you spend your time. In Part 4 we build upon this foundation and examine three basic skills for more effective behavior in those worlds: communication, decision making, and stress management.

Chapter 10 is devoted to the critical skill of communication. This is the way you interact with the people in your worlds, and the more skillful you are, the more effective and satisfying this interaction can be. Chapter 11 is about decisions and decision making. Decisions, big and small, are an integral part of everyone's

daily life, and no matter how good we get at making them, most of us believe we could do better.

Stress and stress management are the subjects of Chapter 12. This is one of the hottest topics of the 1980s as physicians, psychologists, and other researchers accumulate more and more evidence for the negative effects of stress on both physical and psychological health.

Part 4 is about basics, about acquiring and/or fine tuning necessary skills that can improve the quality of life for everyone. The emphasis remains on the central ideas of effective behavior, realism, and control.

# Communication and Communicating

**M**uch is said and written about the importance of communication to the quality of our lives and relationships, and you probably don't need further convincing. In addition to all of the communication about communication that you have received, you have considerable personal experience. Perhaps some of the following sound familiar.

YOU: *Have you seen my new white shirt anywhere?*
YOUR ROOMMATE: *Well, I didn't take it!*

YOUR FRIEND: *Where were you yesterday? I waited for over an hour.*
YOU: Yesterday? I thought it was today we were having lunch together.

YOU: *You look tired; how about if we make it an early night?*
YOUR COMPANION: *If you aren't having a good time, why don't you just say so?*

All of these exchanges are examples of communication gone wrong. You ask a straightforward question to get some information and you get a defensive reply. Your friend's message simply didn't get through to you. You show concern for someone's health and get accused of an ulterior motive. How do these things happen? Why is communication, which seems so simple, so difficult sometimes?

In this chapter you will learn that there is nothing simple about effective communication, but there is nothing mysterious about it either. Communicating effectively requires a set of skills, but they are behaviors that you can learn. The purpose of this chapter is to help you do so; the emphasis is very much on the practical.

## UNDERSTANDING COMMUNICATION

To understand the skills involved in communicating effectively, it helps to understand what communication is and what purposes it serves. It also helps to have a mental image of the communication process. Such a picture can be very useful when trying to identify or avoid communication problems.

## What Is Communication?

**Communication** is a process whereby the behavior of one individual or group (the **source**) transmits some message to a second individual or group (the **receiver**). Both the source and the receiver of a message may be a group, rather than an individual. In addition, the same person sometimes takes both roles, as when you "argue with yourself." We will keep things simple and concentrate on interpersonal communication, communication between two different parties. The basic process is diagrammed in Figure 10–1.

The first part of our definition of communication states that it is a *process*. This means that there is movement of some kind, as indicated by the arrows in the figure. This process is initiated by the source and may or may not be kept in motion by **feedback** (a reply to the first message) from the receiver. If the receiver does not transmit feedback, we say that one-way communication has occurred.

The second part of our definition of communication is that a **message**, or meaning, is transmitted by means of some behavior on the part of the source. This behavior is the **encoding** of the message. It may be verbal or nonverbal. Its observable form—a wink, a spoken sentence, a letter, or a picture, for

**Figure 10–1  A Model of Interpersonal Communication**

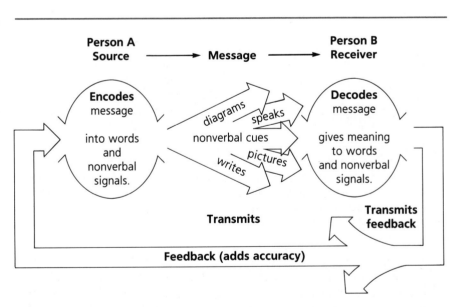

*Note:* From *Understanding Organizational Behavior* (2nd ed.) by D. D. Umstot, 1988. St. Paul, MN: West. Reprinted by permission.

example—is called the **communication channel.** The interpretation of the message by its receiver is the **decoding.**

Notice that our definition of communication says that *some* message, not *the* message, is transmitted. This is an important distinction. Your message, as decoded by your receiver, may not be the one you intended at all. We saw this in the opening example when you incorrectly decoded the message about lunch with your friend.

Sometimes, our receiver gets the wrong message because we send multiple messages that contradict one another. For example, you may tell your mother, in a voice close to breaking, that you are "fine, really." Now your mother has two messages: "I am fine" and "I am terrible." Which does she accept?

To complicate matters further, we send messages via our nonverbal behavior even when we are not trying consciously to communicate at all. If you are very tired today, for example, your eyes may keep closing during the lecture. You aren't trying to communicate with your professor, but he or she may get a message anyway—*Boring!*

## Effective Communication

**Effective communication is communication that is received and acted upon (decoded) as intended (encoded).** Looked at this way, it is obvious that the three exchanges at the beginning of this chapter are ineffective communication attempts. In each case, the effect of the message was not that intended.

What *was* the intent behind these communication attempts? Although interpersonal communication gets very complex with multiple levels of meaning and messages, the basic purposes of communication fall into a few categories (Jewell & Reitz, 1981).

■ *Communication to convey or elicit information.* Much of our communication is for the purpose of sharing thoughts, feelings, or ideas; giving someone facts; or asking others for such information by means of questions. This communication succeeds if the other party listens and understands and/or tells you what you want to know. Let's assume that when you asked your roommate about the shirt in the beginning of this chapter, you were asking for information. This communication attempt, as far as is described, was not successful because you didn't get the information.

■ *Communication to command or instruct.* When we order someone to do something or explain how to do it, this is communication to command or instruct. It succeeds if the other person acts accordingly. In the conversation we may assume took place between you and your friend, he or she set a time and place for you to meet for lunch. This was communication to instruct, but it was ineffective; you didn't show up.

■ *Communication to influence or persuade.* When we want someone to do something but either lack the authority to have it done or don't wish to sound authoritarian, we attempt to influence or persuade instead of to command or to instruct. The purpose of this communication is the same, however. Communication to influence or persuade succeeds if the other person acts accordingly. Remember when you attempted to influence your companion for the evening to go home early for a good night's sleep? He

Information is giving out; communication is getting through.

*Sydney J. Harris*

Communication to command or instruct is more acceptable to most people when the sender has some formal authority over the receiver.

or she took offense; the communication attempt seems to have been ineffective.

■ *Communication to clarify relationships.* Communication to clarify relationships is communication that conveys messages about status, authority, or social relationships. It succeeds if the receiver accepts the message and behaves accordingly. An example familiar to most people (from one side or the other) is when the exasperated parent says to the child who is demanding to know why she has to go to bed (or eat his vegatables, or whatever): "Because I say so, that's why." In other words, "I am the parent and you are the child and what I say goes."

Much communication is for the purpose of clarifying relationships. The boss who tells the subordinate "That will be all" is also saying "I am ready to end this meeting, and I can do so since I am in charge here." But much communication that *isn't* really intended to make a statement about a relationship may be interpreted that way. Your roommate appears to have thought you were saying you didn't trust him or her. Your companion thought you were saying you weren't enjoying his or her company.

Understanding the various purposes that communication can serve will make it easier for you to acquire the skills that will help you avoid being misunderstood; it always is easier to accomplish something if you know specifically what you are trying to accomplish. But there is more to effective communication than getting your message across. Effective communication is also communication that does not have undesired side effects.

## Undesired Side Effects of Communication

There are two major categories into which undesired side effects of interpersonal communication fall. One is communicating something you didn't intend as well as something you did. The other is communicating in a way that has negative effects on your relationship with your receiver. The first of these situations may be called surplus meaning, and the second relationship threats. Although each is discussed separately, keep in mind that they often go together. For example, it often is the unintended surplus meaning in a message that has a negative effect on your relationship with the receiver.

## Surplus Meaning

A communicated message that has more to it when it is decoded than it had when it was encoded has **surplus meaning.** For example, suppose your professor says to the class; "The suggested readings at the end of this chapter are good ones. I think you would get a lot out of them." Some students may interpret (decode) this as; "There will be questions on the exam from the suggested readings." If so, they have added surplus meaning to the professor's statement (assuming that he or she meant only what was said).

## Relationship Threats

How many times have you heard someone say (or said yourself) "It wasn't what he said, it was the way he said it"? Your tone of voice can offend a receiver and damage a relationship even when the message is not offensive. So can your choice of words. For example, we can speculate that your companion in the opening example might not have been offended if you had chosen your words more carefully and left out the part about looking tired. Most of us don't like to hear this in a social situation; it implies that we do not look attractive.

Timing also is critical when it comes to avoiding the undesired effects communication can have on the sender-receiver relationship. If you want to ask your spouse or a friend to drink less or not tell off-color jokes, don't do it in a social situation. He or she may not take this influence attempt very well under any circumstances, but you can be sure that embarrassing him or her in public will add to your problems. Clearly there are many ways in which poor communication skills may constitute **relationship threats.**

Learning the basic communication skills discussed in the next section will do much to help you minimize both surplus meaning and relationship threats in your messages, but you cannot always avoid these. As we will see, there is defensive listening as well as defensive speaking.

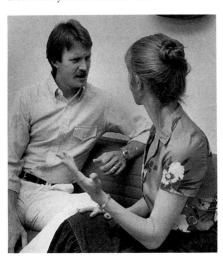

Your tone of voice, timing, or choice of words can make a message offensive to your receiver even when you don't intend it to be.

**Summing Up** ■

Communication is a process involving two parties—a source and a receiver. The behavior (including speech) of the source transmits to the receiver some message or messages, which may or may not be the one(s) intended. Effective communication is communication that transmits the intended message without the excess baggage of surplus meaning and without having negative effects on the relationship between source and receiver.

# BASIC COMMUNICATION SKILLS

In communication terminology, anything that interferes with effective communication is called **noise.** Noise may be actual physical sound, as when a poor telephone connection interferes with a conversation, but the concept goes far beyond this. Noise can originate with the source or receiver as well as in the channel. Noise also can be created by the social environment in which the communication takes place. A list of some possible kinds of noise from these various sources appears in Exhibit 10–1.

The list in the exhibit is a long one, but it does not include all of the possibilities. It is no wonder communicating effectively is so difficult; the sources of interference appear to be endless. Appreciating this fact is one step toward being a better communicator, because it will help you understand that good intentions seldom are enough when it comes to communicating effec-

## EXHIBIT 10–1

## Sources of Noise in the Communication Process

### Noise from the Sender

**Encoding the Message**
   Message is vague or ambiguous
   Message is incomplete
   Message is too long
   Message is indirect
   Message uses loaded words
   Message is in words receiver doesn't understand (e.g., jargon)
**Sending the Message**
   Timing is poor
   Receiver is wrong
   Form is wrong (e.g., written instead of verbal)
   Nonverbal behavior contradicts message
   Presentation contradicts message

### Noise from the Receiver

   Receiver is not paying attention
   Receiver is defensive
   Receiver perceives sender to lack credibility
   Receiver lacks ability or knowledge to decode message accurately

### Noise from the Physical Environment

   Too much distance between sender and receiver
   Message goes astray or to wrong receiver
   Actual sound that interferes with message transmission
   Poor reproduction or transmission (as scrambled TV reception)

### Noise from the Social Environment

   Norms in the situation
   Values in the situation
   Relationship between sender and receiver
   Presence of others during communication

tively with others. You also need behavioral skills and that is the purpose of this section.

## Choosing a Receiver

A communication skill so basic that it often is overlooked is that of choosing an appropriate receiver for a message. If you call home to say you'll be late getting in and your 6-year-old sister or 2-year-old son answers the telephone, you should ask for someone else or your message may not get through. If the expensive shorts you bought at the Uptown Boutique fell apart when they were washed, don't chew out the high school student who took your money and put it in the cash register; see the manager. If your roommate's mother made you a cake for your birthday, thank her, not your roommate.

Sometimes it isn't possible to communicate directly with the appropriate receiver. The driver of the car that cut in and nearly forced you off the road is long gone. You don't dare tell your boss how you feel about the dressing down he gave you at work because you really need the job. These are frustrating situations, and some people deal with them by taking out their feelings on a completely innocent third party. They snap at a co-worker or yell at someone when they get home.

Venting frustration on the wrong receiver, called *displaced aggression,* may bring temporary relief, but it also leaves a residue that can affect future communication. No matter how understanding and concerned someone may be about your problems, no one really likes being the target of displaced aggression. It is perfectly okay to tell someone else *about* an incident or encounter if you can't deal directly with the person involved, but find some other way to vent the associated negative emotions. For example, one young woman has found a way to deal with a hypercritical boss that is ideal for her. She goes straight from work to a local racquetball club and smashes away. Alternatively, she might hold imaginary conversations with her boss in which she says exactly what she thinks and reduces the frustration of not having her say.

## Choosing the Channel

When was the last time you sat down and wrote someone a real letter? Many of us would have to think about this question for quite a while before we could remember. This is the age of the telephone. As a communication channel, it is fast, it is convenient, and it provides instant information, gratification, and feedback. Because of these obvious advantages, the telephone has come to be a substitute, both for written channels of communication and for much verbal communication that used to take place face to face. Today it is not uncommon to have business dealings for years with someone you never have met in person. Nevertheless, really skillful communicators do not reach automatically for the telephone.

Skillful communicators understand that the channel of communication can have considerable influence on the effectiveness of the message. For example, telephone calls are fine for giving or receiving certain kinds of information or instructions, but they are usually inferior to face-to-face communication if your purpose is to influence or persuade (D'Aprix, 1982). This may be changing, however. As discussed in *Face of the Future,* new technology is bringing us some startling new options in telephone and related communication.

## *FACE OF THE FUTURE:*
New Ways of Staying in Touch

It is 11:30 P.M. You have been to a party in a downtown hotel, but you had to leave before it was over. As you walk down the deserted street toward your car, you see that you aren't alone after all. A shadowy figure wearing a ski mask steps from a doorway on the opposite side and crosses the street at an angle heading straight for you. You are about to be mugged! Quickly you punch some buttons on a small electronic device hidden in your pocket. Within seconds a police siren can be heard and a cruiser rounds the corner. Your would-be assailant takes off running.

Science fiction? No, reality. As of 1987, subscribers to the Geostar Satellite System were able to send messages, such as your distress signal, anywhere in the continental United States by means of a battery-powered transceiver that fits in the pocket (Black, 1984). The message is received by satellite, which scans the ground, finds the recipient (in your case the nearest police station), and relays the message complete with the sender's position. Developers say that Geostar is able to determine the sender's location within three or four feet and that delay time for forwarding the message is measured in microseconds.

Pocket satellite communication devices are only one of the new ways that advances in the field of telecommunications are finding for us to communicate with one another. Another new wrinkle is electronic mail (E-mail). This is correspondence—letters, personal messages, memos, orders, and so on—that shows up on your personal desk computer screen, not in your mailbox. Companies that have been experimenting with E-mail like its speed, convenience, and potential for reducing the glut of paper that circulates in many organizations. Privacy remains a problem, however. No one yet has come up with a code that insures no one will "read over your shoulder" electronically.

The ordinary telephone also is undergoing radical changes. We already have cordless telephones and telephones that can be programmed to talk to other telephones. A voice-activated telephone is also available. On spoken instructions, it will locate a number in its memory and then dial it. This might not be very important to most of us, but to the elderly, ill, or handicapped, it can literally be a lifesaver.

Perhaps the most exciting advance in telephone technology, however, is *televised*

---

The age of telecommunications described in *Face of the Future* is bringing exciting advances in communication to more and more people, but it does not change the fact that there are times when the telephone is not the best channel for a message. Skillful communicators know that the very choice of one channel over another can send a message of its own. For example, leaving your roommate a note saying "You owe me $15.00 for the groceries I bought last week" can imply that you are trying to avoid facing up to this issue in person. Writing a personal letter on a word processor to someone who has previously expressed the view that this seems impersonal may be interpreted as saying "Your preference is not as important to me as my convenience."

Often, your purpose in communicating is just to let someone know that you are thinking of him or her. A telephone conversation may be just fine, but it is possible that your purpose may be accomplished more effectively through

## *Continued*

telephone conversations. Researchers have been working for years to find a way for the participants in a telephone conversation to see one another. It isn't here yet for most of us, but the technology exists. With specially equipped rooms at both ends, it is possible for the parties to a conversation to send televised pictures of themselves simultaneously with speech. U.S. Sprint's Meeting Channel, one of the leaders in this area, expects to have at least 300 of these rooms in operation by the end of 1988 with service to 25 countries worldwide.

Most people in organizations realize that the telephone is not a replacement for face-to-face contact. As a result, companies incur heavy costs in travel expenses and time away from the job for their personnel to meet with suppliers, customers, advertisers, company staff in other locations, and others. **Teleconferencing** makes this travel unnecessary; participants in a meeting can look at one another face-to-face and get the nonverbal with the verbal communication, just as if they were in the same room. This service was very expensive at first, but technological advances have brought it down to surprisingly reasonable figures; it costs under $1,000 per hour to hook U.S. cities together, about $2,000 an hour to "meet" with Europe, and

about $3,000 per hour to teleconference with Japan (Elias, 1988).

What giant corporations have today, we in our homes often have tomorrow. Visual telephones in the home are only a matter of the time it takes to make them economically feasible. Most experts believe this will happen when glass wires, called fiber optics, have replaced the copper wires that form the backbone of our national telephone system. The glass wires are cheaper and far more efficient. One bundle of wires no thicker than your finger can carry almost a quarter of a million telephone calls at once.

Fiber optics are also the foundation for what is to date the most startling prospect of all in the way we communicate with one another. Scientists expect to be able to combine holography with telephoning in the not-too-distant future. Holography is a technique that uses lasers to project lifelike three-dimensional images into thin air. Combined with the telephone, it would bring the person you were speaking to right into the room. Visually, the holographic image would be indistinguishable from the real person; you could get up and walk around him or her and see the back. But if you try to hug or shake hands with the image, you'll feel only thin air. Now *that's* science fiction!

---

another channel. Your parents are happy to get a call, for example, but it takes more time and effort to write a letter or buy and send a card. The fact that you are willing to do so can be a very effective way to communicate caring.

In a similar vein, you probably can call the friend or relative in the hospital, but making time in your schedule to pay a personal visit helps the time pass more pleasantly for the patient and communicates; "You are worth this extra time and effort to me." Just as poor communication skills can damage relationships, so can good ones build, nourish, and sustain them.

## Encoding the Message

As defined earlier, encoding refers to the acutal words, symbols, gestures, or other physical means by which you transmit the message in your head through a channel. If you refer to Exhibit 10–1, you will see that there are several ways in which noise gets added to communication at this stage. Turning these around gives us the guidelines for more effective encoding presented in Exhibit 10–2 (Arnold & Feldman, 1986). If you follow these guidelines, you will have made your point clearly, precisely, completely, and in words your receiver understands. You don't need to keep belaboring it unless the receiver asks for clarification. Two other aspects of encoding for communication effectiveness, avoiding loaded words and being direct, require some discussion.

## Avoiding Loaded Words

Words that carry strong meanings of their own over and above their context are called **loaded words.** They push emotional buttons, and the reactions they elicit can create so much noise that the rest of the message is completely lost (Trippett, 1982). Some common examples are always, never, fair, dumb, and overreact. Exhibit 10–3 provides some examples of how the implications of such words can overwhelm any other message.

There are many loaded words in our language; you probably can think of some others to which you personally react. There also are loaded sentence frameworks, with number one on the list being "Your problem is . . ." What makes us react so strongly to such words and phrases? If you look back, you will see that they are all *evaluative*.

## EXHIBIT 10–2

## Encoding the Message

There are many ways that any particular message may be expressed, or encoded, to be sent to a receiver. The following guidelines will help you reduce the chances that the way you choose will add noise to the communication process.

*Be clear.* If you are going to be ready for your dinner guests at 6:30 P.M., tell them that. "Oh, anytime after six" opens you up to guests coming before you are dressed or showing up after the roast has turned to shoe leather. This is frustrating for you and embarrassing for them.

*Be precise.* Don't say "I'd appreciate it if you would make this place presentable while I am gone" if what you mean is you want your son, daughter, spouse, roommate, or whomever to make the beds and wash the dishes. People have different ideas about *presentable*.

*Be complete.* If you give directions to your home, give complete directions. Leaving out an "obvious" turn when the road forks or describing how to get halfway and then saying "just follow the signs from there" may send your friends, date, aunt and uncle, or study partner to the next town.

*Avoid slang or jargon unless you are sure your receiver will understand.* Are you a computer whiz who tosses around terms like *byte* and *software* and *compatibility* as part of your regular conversation? Did you know that there are many people who have no idea what these words mean? When it is important to get your message across, use ordinary words everyone will understand.

*Keep the message to a reasonable length.* Make it as long as it has to be to get the point across, but not so long that your receiver "tunes out." This is especially critical in written communication but applies to verbal channels as well.

**EXHIBIT 10–3**  ████████████████████████

## Look Out: The Words You Use May Be Loaded!

*A:*  Boy, that was really a good movie.
*B:*  Well, I thought it was pretty *dumb.*
Possible Message:   And you are pretty dumb if you liked it.

*A:*  I don't really feel like going out to dinner tonight.
*B:*  You *never* feel like going out to dinner.
Possible Message:   You are a boring old stick-in-the-mud.

*A:*  If you turn in your papers late, you will lose 10 points.
*B:*  But, that's not *fair.* What if you're sick or something?
Possible Message:   You are an insensitive person who ignores the needs of others.

*A:*  I don't like it when you talk to me like that.
*B:*  Don't you think you are *overreacting* just a little?
Possible Message:   You are immature or too sensitive.

*A:*  I'm really mad. I went to pick up my car and the station was closed.
*B:*  I *always* call before running off somewhere like that.
Possible Message:   I'm smarter than you are.

It is a very natural tendency to respond to the statements of others in terms of your own point of view; but when this comes across as judging someone else's point of view, there is often a defensive reaction. Some psychologists believe that this tendency to be judgmental is the major barrier to effective interpersonal communication (e.g., Rogers & Roethlisberger, 1952). One way to reduce or eliminate this barrier is to learn to avoid loaded words and phrases.

## Being Direct

One of the more difficult communication skills to master is that of being direct enough to accomplish your purpose without being so blunt that you raise defenses or damage relationships. As a result, many of us often resort to **indirect communication;** instead of saying what we really mean, we say something else and expect our receiver to break the code. For example, you tell someone who asks you to go to a concert on Saturday night that you already have other plans even though you don't. The truth is that you wouldn't consider spending any social time with this person, but you shrink from coming right out and saying so.

Is there anything wrong with this "little white lie"? Actually, this is a fairly standard and accepted way to deal with such situations in our society. From a communication viewpoint, however, it often is ineffective. The trouble with plausible excuses is just that—they are plausible. So this person continues to make suggestions for getting together and you continue to make excuses. After about the third time, you exclaim to yourself with exasperation; "Good grief, some people never take a hint!" True, some people never do.

Sometimes we use indirect communication not to avoid hurting someone's feelings, but because we have been taught that it is more polite or tactful to do so. This is especially true when we want someone else to do something. Thus, you say to your son or daughter, "Doesn't the trash truck come tomorrow?" instead of "Would you take the garbage out, please?" Such hinting around may work. Alternatively, your receiver may totally ignore what you are trying to say. In addition, hints annoy many people; if you want something from them, they would prefer you to ask straight out.

Of course it isn't true that it never is appropriate to use indirect communication. Social norms tell us otherwise. For example, it isn't a very good idea to ask directly at the end of a job interview; "Well, do I get the job?" Circumstances do alter cases, but your communication skill will improve if you are aware that encoding messages indirectly has the potential for a number of undesired effects.

When you encode your messages indirectly, you make your receiver guess at what you really are trying to say, and he or she may guess wrong. In addition, many people take exception to indirect communication, believing it to be manipulative and "gamey." Thus, you can damage a relationship or keep one from developing at all if you aren't careful. Finally, indirect communication can make you appear uncertain about your message or lacking in self-confidence. There is more on communication style in *For Discussion*.

## Timing Your Communication

You communicate with others for a reason, and if this purpose is to be accomplished, your receiver must be attending to the communication attempt. Often, this is no problem. You are engaged in a friendly conversation or a study session or an exchange of work-related information, and the other person is fully attentive and active. But this is not always the case.

Sometimes when you talk to other people, they don't seem to hear at all. In other cases you think that you were heard but find out later that the message went "in one ear and out the other." And sometimes an innocent question gets a loud no or a funny story sets off an impatient "Will you leave me alone?" These things can happen for many reasons, but you can reduce the chances that they will by increasing your communication timing skills.

One important aspect of timing is sending messages, particularly verbal messages, when your receiver's **receptivity** to them is greater, that is, when he or she is ready to listen and attend to you. In general, most people aren't very receptive to any sort of message when they are very busy, very tired, not feeling well, or upset for some reason. It isn't always possible to find the right time, but you can learn to avoid the following kinds of obvious blunders.

- Explaining to your father what he should have done after he has smashed his thumb with the hammer while trying to hang a picture
- Asking your friend what she thinks of your new dress while she is in the middle of trying to finish a term paper
- Waking up your roommate, who is in bed with the flu, to tell him about the great girl you just met
- Telling your spouse that you didn't get the raise when you are together in the car on the way to dinner with friends
- Interrupting your son or daughter's telephone conversation to tell him or her not to forget to wash the dishes when finished

## FOR DISCUSSION:
## Male and Female Communication Styles

*There's an old joke that goes:*

*Question:* What are the three fastest modes of communication?

*Answer:* Telephone, telegraph, tell a woman.

Well, you may be thinking, no one would laugh at that today. Wrong. Recently, a businessman was overheard telling his associates at a lunch meeting in a fashionable restaurant, "Don't worry about advertising. I'll handle it; I'll just tell my wife" (big laugh from all). This incident occurred early in 1988.

Is there any truth to the stereotype that women are the "talkative sex"? Perhaps, but if so, they've earned this label only while talking to one another. Study after study confirms that, in mixed-sex groups, males dominate the conversation. They also interrupt women far more than they interrupt other men or than women interrupt men or other women (West & Zimmerman, 1975). Many of these interruptions are for the purpose of changing the subject to a topic that men prefer; one investigator found that both men and women tend to regard topics introduced by women as tentative, whereas topics introduced by men are topics to pursue (Fishman, 1978).

These differences in who chooses the subject matter and who dominates the conversation are not the only differences researchers interested in male and female styles of communication find. Lakoff (1975), one of the leading investigators in this area, points out that the *way* men and women say what they say also differs considerably. In general, women's speech is characterized by a lack of confidence and assertiveness. This may be seen most clearly in their strong reliance on a questioning mode of interaction with others. Specifically, women tend to

- Ask more questions
- Turn statements into questions (e.g., I was thinking we'd have steak?)
- Start off a story or conversation with a question (e.g., Guess what? I . . . )
- Stick a question onto the end of a sentence (e.g., That was a good movie, don't you think?)

Questions serve to make what women say tentative in case someone might want to disagree with them. Other ways they provide themselves with these loopholes are by sprinkling their conversation liberally with qualifiers such as

- I could be wrong, but I . . .
- I guess I . . .
- I'm sorry, but I . . .

Communication researchers have a number of hypotheses about the source of these and other differences in male and female communication styles. Some think that women have internalized traditional sex-role-stereo-typed beliefs that women aren't likely to say anything very interesting or intellectually stimulating; they believe this themselves and speak accordingly. Others emphasize that the relatively powerless style used by women reflects the fact that the majority of women still occupy relatively powerless social positions (O'Barr, 1982). Some support for this position is offered by Gleason (1983), who found that male day-care workers (a low-status position) communicated in a style more like female day-care workers than like typical male speech.

Ayim (1984) sums up current thinking by many on this matter by concluding that female tendencies to be more polite and less assertive, as well as more supportive and less dominating in their speech merely reflects the reality in every other sphere of life in our culture.

Have you noticed these differences yourself? Can you give any examples from your own experience? Try conducting your own "listening poll" for a day or so and count the number of times males and females interrupt one another, ask questions, or add qualifiers to their statements. You can do this at home if there is a mix of sexes, at work, in any class that has sufficient class discussion, or even by watching television.

Did your mini research project confirm the tendencies communication researchers have identified? If so, what do you think is behind them? Do you agree with Ayim? Why or why not?

It is surprising how often we ignore the obvious when it comes to timing our communications. And sometimes we just can't wait even when we do realize that it is a poor time. Then, when our receiver does not pay attention, ignores or denies our request, or blows up and says "Get lost," we feel let down or angry or frustrated.

Another aspect of timing is understanding the principle of salience. In a communication context, **salience** means timing messages so that they are received close to the time when the information they contain will be relevant or must be acted upon. For example, if you tell your boss in February that you have to miss several days work in May, don't be surprised if he or she forgets and is annoyed when it happens. You want your boss to have plenty of notice, but February is too far from May; your message is not salient in February.

Finally, timing communication skillfully requires some planning if your receiver is supposed to act on your message in some way. If you want to squeeze in a dentist appointment while you are home for 3 days, you may be disappointed if you don't start trying to make the arrangement well in advance. It is surprising how much general frustration can be removed from life by planning around the possibility of busy signals on the telephone, your receiver being unavailable to take your message, or the mail arriving a day later than you thought it should.

## Making Your Message Stand Out

Sometimes we forget that a message must be noticed—heard, seen, or read—to be effective. A shouted "I'm leaving now" that fails to compete with the stereo is a verbal message that escapes attention. A note saying you won't be home for dinner that is stuck to the refrigerator with ten other little pieces of paper may not be seen. The message you leave on your friend's answering machine may not be heard for days. (The assumption here is that you want these messages to be received. If you don't, but you want to be able to say you *tried* to communicate, these may be effective strategies.)

Advertisers are very skillful communicators when it comes to messages that stand out. Among the tricks they use are loud music, speech that is faster than usual, speech that is softer than usual, and animation. Advertising material that comes through the mail may be brightly colored, larger than ordinary mail, or have URGENT or YOU ARE A WINNER stamped in large red letters on the front. You may not always appreciate these efforts, but the communication principles are sound.

## Soliciting Feedback

The model of the communication process in Figure 10–1 shows a *feedback loop* in the form of an arrow from the receiver of the message back to the source, but this loop is not built in. We do not always receive feedback, and some of what we do receive doesn't tell us what we want to know. Does "um" mean that your brother is giving you permission to borrow his car or not?

The skill of soliciting feedback in communication rests on not assuming that because you said it, wrote, it, or sent it the other person received and understood your message. No matter how effective you become at sending messages, things go wrong. Your receiver may appear to be listening, but actually may be thinking about something entirely different. Your letter may get lost in the mail, or the little note you wrote on your exam paper may be overlooked entirely by a professor who has 50 exams to grade.

Once you understand that you cannot assume automatically that your message has been received and decoded as you intended, you can exercise your judgment as to whether it is necessary to solicit direct feedback. A good rule of thumb is: If it is important, follow up on it. For example, if you are giving

Timing a message for a time when your receiver is ready and able to listen to you is an important communication skill.

a friend telephone directions to your new apartment, you might ask him or her to read them back to you. If you don't hear from someone in a reasonable time after leaving a message on an answering machine, call back. If you aren't sure the professor saw your note, ask.

We have discussed some basic communication skills. All have the same purpose—to reduce or eliminate noise that can interfere with effective interpersonal communication. None of these skills requires any special talents or individual attributes to master. All that is required is a basic understanding of the communication process and practice.

**Summing Up ▪**

## NONVERBAL COMMUNICATION

Up to now, the communication under examination is that which takes place through transmitted words, but much communication takes place nonverbally. **Nonverbal communication** refers to messages sent via posture, gestures, facial expressions, touching, voice tone, and other nonspeech behaviors that can be observed by those with whom we are interacting.

The different aspects of your behavior that send messages to others are numerous, and it has been estimated that as much as 90% of the communication in some situations may take place this way (Mehrabian, 1971). Some of these nonverbal messages stand alone. For example, you may raise your eyes heavenward to communicate to a classmate your exasperation when the professor keeps lecturing after the bell has rung.

Some nonverbal communication reinforces verbal messages. You may pound the table and raise your voice to add emphasis while verbally making an important point. Or you may slump back in your chair and close your eyes while describing the exhausting day you have had.

Nonverbal communication also can contradict verbal messages. Tapping your foot says hurry up to most people even if your lips are saying "I don't mind waiting." A sarcastic tone of voice can turn "That's wonderful" into a put-down. Many times, it is the perceived nonverbal message that is believed if there is such a contradiction (Mehrabian & Ferris, 1967). If you want to avoid the misunderstandings that can arise in such situations, it is a good idea to check out your interpretation. For example, you might say, "I noticed you looked at your watch just now. Would it be better for me to come back another time?" The other person then can confirm your interpretation or set you straight if it is inaccurate.

The importance and power of nonverbal communication are not new discoveries; actors and actresses always have made use of it. Widespread popular interest in the subject dates back only some 15 years or so, however. Since that time, a wide variety of books, articles, and even songs ("Body Talk," Fisher & Clyde, BMI) on the subject have appeared. What most of these discussions do not mention, however, is that nonverbal communication is a very imprecise language.

## "Reading Nonverbal"

The human mind is a wonderful thing. It begins working the moment you're born and doesn't stop until you have to speak in public.

*Anonymous*

Much of what we hear about nonverbal communication implies that various nonverbal behaviors have universally understood meanings and that we are going to miss out on many vital messages if we do not learn to "read" this language. In fact, this is a long way from the truth. With the exception of a few (mostly rude) gestures, most behaviors are ambiguous communicators that can be interpreted by others in a variety of ways.

Consider, for example, the behavior of sitting on the edge of a chair seat. Is this person interested in the conversation, uncomfortable in the chair, or signaling a desire to leave? Is the man wearing tinted glasses indoors ill at ease, trying to hide something, untrustworthy, or did he happen to forget his regular glasses? Is the woman who closes her eyes briefly while you are speaking to her ill, bored, tired, disgusted, or trying to rest her eyes?

The fact that nonverbal communication is subject to a variety of interpretations is easy to demonstrate, but it also is easy to overlook because this is such an interesting and exciting subject. For example, in one book the author tells us that each of the following is a sign that someone is lying to you—covering the mouth, touching the nose, rubbing an eye or ear, and scratching the neck (Pease, 1984). This is fascinating stuff, and it is easy to forget the author's caution that these signs are not *infallible* evidence of lying.

Of course, gestures and body language are not the only ways that people communicate nonverbally. Voice tone and emphasis also are important. You can get some idea of the power of emphasis by trying the following exercise: Let one or more of the members of the class say the following sentence, emphasizing a different italicized word or phrase each time.

*I really don't want to go to [this party] tonight.*

After each repetition, the other class members should write down the message they would get from this way of saying the sentence. How many different meanings did you find in this one simple sentence? Can you think of other examples in which emphasis or tone of voice might completely change the nature of the message that is received?

None of this means that you should ignore the nonverbal signals that others may be sending you, but it does suggest that you exercise some caution in acting on the basis of what you might have read that these behaviors mean. You very well could be wrong; furthermore, many people dislike being "analyzed" like this.

## "Speaking Nonverbal"

Since nonverbal communication is open to varying interpretations, it isn't surprising that mastering the art of using this language to your advantage can be difficult. The advice you get from the experts often is contradictory. For example, you will read one place that putting your hands in your pockets while giving a speech or presentation makes you appear insincere. Then you will read that letting your hands dangle by your sides while you make a speech or presentation communicates a lack of poise. Confused, you turn to still another article on nonverbal communication, and it tells you that using a lectern or table to place your notes and your arms on while you speak suggests to your audience that you are insecure. Now, just what are you supposed to do with your hands when you give that presentation in class next week?

How about relaxing? You already know that no matter what you do someone is likely to "read you wrong." And if what you say is interesting enough, most of your audience won't be paying attention to what you do with your hands. The same applies to many other situations. So have fun with body talk if you like, but don't get uptight about it. To help you out, Exhibit 10–4 presents four practical suggestions for "speaking nonverbal."

## SPECIAL COMMUNICATION SITUATIONS

The basic skills we have reviewed will serve you well most of the time, but several communication situations require closer examination. Here, we look at four of these: reducing defensiveness, giving and receiving feedback, assertiveness, and being a good listener.

## Defensiveness

In one of the imaginary communication exchanges that opened this chapter, you asked your roommate about a missing shirt. He replied as if you were accusing him of taking it, even though there was nothing in your words to suggest that is what you meant. This **defensiveness** created noise in your communication, and the original message got distorted by surplus meaning. How does this happen?

Messages may be distorted by defensiveness for several reasons. Perhaps there was something in your voice tone that added surplus meaning to what you said. Perhaps you and your roommate have had disagreements in the past about his using things of yours without asking. Perhaps he was just feeling out of sorts.

---

**EXHIBIT 10–4** ▮▬▬▬▬▬▬▬▬▬▬▬▮

### Four Rules for Nonverbal Communication

1. Try to rid yourself of any nonverbal habits that you know mean you are nervous. Examples include drumming your fingers, swinging your foot, chewing your fingernails, or twisting your hair.

2. Learn to maintain eye contact when speaking to others. If you are speaking to a group, make eye contact with a number of different members. It is perfectly possible to tell a whopping lie while looking someone in the eye, but most people still prefer eye contact because it communicates interest.

3. Act on any consistent feedback you receive about your nonverbal communication. If enough people tell you that you sound depressed when you aren't, for example, there probably is something in your voice tone you aren't aware of that is communicating this message. Try listening to yourself on a tape recorder or answering machine; you'll probably find the characteristic of your tone rather quickly.

4. Now, relax!

▬▬▬▬▬▬▬▬▬▬▬▬▬▬▬▬▬▬▬▬

## Sources of Defensiveness

In the example of the shirt, you can see that defensiveness on the part of a receiver of communication may arise because of (1) something the source says or does (e.g., your voice tone), (2) something in the relationship between the source and the receiver (your past disagreements over this matter), or (3) something about the receiver that has nothing to do with the source (your roommate's bad mood). To some extent, what you do about this problem depends on where it comes from. For example, you can't do much about this last problem except utilize your timing skills and avoid asking such questions when your roommate obviously is not receptive to them.

Receiver defensiveness that arises from something in his or her relationship with the source can be the most difficult to combat. A history of disagreements on a particular topic may make it almost impossible to broach the topic again without a defensive reaction. An argument over something entirely different may spread to generalized defensiveness. This, you may recall, often is a problem in marital communication. Overcoming this source of defensiveness can be a long process that involves resolving the problem behind it.

## Reducing Defensiveness

It isn't always possible to solve relationship problems that cause your receiver to listen defensively to what you say. When this seems to be the case, you may be able to reduce some of the defensiveness by being more careful about the *way* you say things. Sometimes, for example, a *negative question* will help. Thus, you might have asked your roommate: "I don't suppose you've seen my new white shirt anywhere, have you?"

A negative question gives your receiver the chance to respond with an easy no and if he or she takes it, you have avoided a defensive reaction for now. A word of caution, though. Don't get in the habit of phrasing every question this way. There are times when you don't want to give your receiver such an easy out. Also, negative questions can make you sound unsure of yourself if they are used habitually.

You have the greatest control over reducing defensiveness that stems from your own behavior as a communicator. One of the most effective ways is to get in the habit of owning your own feelings, opinions, and perceptions. As used in a communication context, *owning* means that you take verbal responsibility in your communications for what is going on with you. You don't blame or accuse or put the cause of your own feelings or problems on the other person, even by implication. The easiest way to learn to do this is to practice phrasing your messages with the words *I* and *me* ("I-words"), rather than *you*. Some examples of this and other communication behaviors that may reduce defensiveness in your receiver are shown in Exhibit 10–5.

Reducing the probability of defensive listening in others is a skill that becomes more well developed the more you practice it. The guidelines in Exhibit 10–5 will help, but don't forget the basic communication skills already discussed. Being sure that you have the right receiver, using the appropriate channel, being clear and direct, timing your message appropriately, and soliciting feedback will do much to reduce defensiveness as well.

## EXHIBIT 10–5 ▰▰▰▰▰▰▰▰▰▰▰▰▰▰▰▰

### Reducing Defensiveness in Interpersonal Communication

#### Use I-Words to "Own" Your Own Feelings and Perceptions

*Example:*   I am so angry with you! NOT
            You make me so mad!

*Example:*   I can't find the car keys. NOT
            What have you done with the car keys?

*Example:*   I'd really rather go to a movie than to the ball game. NOT
            You never ask me what I'd like to do.

#### Be Tentative Rather than Dogmatic When Dealing with Opinions or Uncertainties

*Example:*   That doesn't sound quite right to me. NOT
            You're wrong!

*Example:*   I believe that restaurant is closed on Sundays. NOT
            That restaurant is closed today. We'll have to go somewhere else.

*Example:*   I've always had better luck with foreign cars. NOT
            Anyone who buys an American car is just asking for trouble.

#### Don't Imply that You or Your Opinion/Experience Is Superior

*Example:*   I'm sorry you had trouble finding the place. NOT
            If you'd gone the way I said, you wouldn't have any problem.

*Example:*   I'd prefer red wine. NOT
            Oh, I never touch white wine.

*Example:*   Would you like some help? NOT
            Here, give it to me. I've done this a hundred times.

#### Don't Generalize from One Incident to Someone's Entire Personality or Behavior Patterns

*Example:*   I found a mistake here where you added up what I owe you. NOT
            I can't believe somebody your age can't add a simple column of figures.

*Example:*   This kitchen is a mess! NOT
            Look at this kitchen! You really are a slob!

# Feedback

The feedback loop in the basic communication process may be used to check that your receiver has gotten your message and understood it as you intended. Knowing when to solicit such feedback is a basic communication skill. But the word *feedback* has another common use in communication terminology; it often is used to refer to evaluations. Giving and receiving this kind of feedback is the topic of this section.

## Giving Feedback

There are many situations in which you are asked to give your informal evaluation of something that someone else owns, has said, or has done. For example, your friend may ask you what you think of the new car he or she has bought. A few such feedback situations are formal. If you become a manager or own your own business, you will have to make formal evaluations of the performance of your subordinates or your employees.

If you are like most people, you have little trouble with such situations unless honesty compels you to make a negative evaluation. Almost no one likes to give negative feedback, so we often take refuge in being vague, sidestepping the question, or simply not saying what we really think. If this is you, take heart. Giving useful feedback, whether positive or negative, is a skill like any other. Like any other skill, it also improves with practice.

Learning to give good feedback is well worth the effort. Most people will appreciate your directness and will come to trust your opinion. You will feel better about yourself when you are able to say what you think. And you will not have to deal with the consequences of *not* saying what you think (like going back to the same restaurant again and again because you can't bring yourself to say you don't like it). With practice, the guidelines shown in Exhibit 10–6 can help you achieve this happy state of affairs (Gibb, 1961).

You'll find these guidelines easier to follow if you learn to think of feedback as information. We seek this information from others to help us make decisions about our future behavior. Good feedback provides a guide to action; feedback that is indirect, vague, or focused on things a person cannot change does not. And if it is judgmental, completely negative, or unsolicited, it may be ignored completely by the receiver. It also may leave bad feelings that will affect your future relationship with him or her (Morris & Saskin, 1976).

## EXHIBIT 10–6

## Giving Good Feedback

*Be direct.* Hinting around and hoping that your receiver will understand what you mean doesn't do either one of you any good.

*Be descriptive, not evaluative.* Stick to your own reaction and your own feelings and opinions. For example; "I found it hard to concentrate after the first 10 pages" is a description of your response to a paper. "It's too long," is a value judgment, and another reader might disagree.

*Be specific.* To be useful, feedback must give the receiver information about what you reacted to positively and what you didn't. For example, "I like the style on you, but I think the color makes you look a little pale" is better than "I don't know, it just isn't you somehow."

*Be constructive.* A professor once received a course evaluation form on which was written "Dr. ____sweats too much." Criticizing something that is out of the receiver's control and/or is irrelevant to the feedback being sought serves no useful purpose. Emphasize things that can be changed if you give negative feedback.

*Be positive as well as negative.* Even if the feedback you must provide is mostly negative, find one positive aspect to mention; for example: "I can see that you worked very hard on this."

*Be quiet!* Don't give "feedback" that someone has not asked for (unless for some reason that is your job). There are times when others just don't want to hear it and that is their right. If you believe that it is important to speak up, ask the intended recipient if you may do so first.

## Receiving Feedback

Compared with giving feedback to others, receiving it ourselves seems a simple matter. But as is true of any communication attempt, there is a knack to soliciting feedback. Asking for this information usually means asking a question, and questions can be tricky things. If you want honest feedback of the kind described in Exhibit 10–6, you have to learn to ask for what you want to know.

Some questions are so vague that they are unlikely to give you any information at all. To see this problem in action, try this little test. Tomorrow, ask the first ten people you meet, "How do I look today?" At least nine, and probably all ten, are going to reply, "Fine." This isn't much help if what you want to know is what they think of your new haircut, outfit, lipstick color, or athletic shoes.

Other questions are not questions at all; they are traps, or setups, that close off the receiver's options in making a reply. Two communication researchers have identified eight different varieties of these **pseudoquestions** (Pfeiffer & Jones, 1974). Descriptions and examples of each appear in Exhibit 10–7.

Pseudoquestions are a form of indirect communication. We use these "questions" when we really want to say something else or get someone to agree with us. We also use pseudoquestions to solicit feedback when we aren't open to the real thing; when what we want is approval or praise. If the other person plays the game and tells us what we want to hear, all is well. If he or she takes our request for "feedback" as genuine and says something we don't want to hear, we get upset. In this sense, such questions are setups, and like all setups, they nearly always lead to hurt or angry feelings.

To sum up, when you want feedback, ask for it directly in a way that helps the other person understand what you want to know. If you want genuine feedback, don't ask a pseudoquestion. If you don't want any feedback, don't ask any question. There is no law that says you have to be open to feedback from others at all times and in all circumstances. Acting as if you want honest feedback and then getting upset or arguing with the other person's opinion when you get it almost always causes resentment and makes your receiver wary of giving you feedback in the future.

# Assertiveness

**Assertive behavior** is behavior that expresses your personal feelings or opinions or helps you accomplish your goals in spite of the disagreement or opposition of others. This is not the same as **aggressiveness,** which is hostile, injurious, or destructive behavior toward others. When you are assertive, you respect the rights of others, but do not allow yourself to be intimidated or inhibited by challenges, disapproval from others, or fears of "making a scene." Consider, for example, how you would feel in the following situations.

Do people edge ahead of you in line in the supermarket or the movie theater? . . . Do you patiently line up to check in for a plane while the person in front of you wastes five minutes of the agent's time asking about a flight a week later? Do you arrive on time for a dinner reservation, then stand there or get

## EXHIBIT 10–7 ▰▰▰▰▰▰▰▰▰▰▰▰▰▰▰▰▰▰▰▰▰▰

### Pseudoquestions

#### Co-optive "Question"

*Example:* Would you rather watch the news or "Miami Vice"?

*Real Purpose of Communication:* To limit receiver's responses to those acceptable to sender

#### Got'cha! "Question"

*Example:* Didn't we meet at that singles bar on 43rd Street?

*Real Purpose of Communication:* To trap receiver into an admission

#### Hypothetical "Question"

*Example:* If I were to ask you out, would you go?

*Real Purpose of Communication:* To probe or criticize on basis of answer

#### Imperative "Question"

*Example:* When are we finally going to have dinner?

*Real Purpose of Communication:* To put receiver on the spot by implying negligence

#### Punitive "Question"

*Example:* What right do *you* have to tell me it's no good?

*Real Purpose of Communication:* To punish or expose receiver

#### Rhetorical "Question"

*Example:* Isn't it time we went?

*Real Purpose of Communication:* To get agreement from receiver

#### Set-up "Question"

*Example:* But don't you think that all organized religion is wrong?

*Real Purpose of Communication:* To maneuver receiver into a vulnerable position

#### Screening "Question"

*Example:* Which dress do you think I should wear to the office party?

*Real Purpose of Communication:* To put responsibility for decision on receiver

---

*Note:* Examples by author. Question categories from "Don't You Think That . . . ? An Experiential Lecture on Indirect and Direct Communication" by J. W. Pfeiffer and J. E. Jones, 1974, in J. W. Pfeiffer and J. E. Jones (Eds.), *1974 Handbook for Group Facilitators.* La Jolla, CA: University Associates.

detoured to the bar while people who come in after you are seated ahead of you? And after being seated, do you wait and wait for a waiter to appear and take your order? (Cohn, 1984, p. 9)

Situations like these are awkward and frustrating. Dealing effectively with them requires skill in assertive communication. One psychologist offers three very practical techniques to help you start developing this skill. The ten word response, the broken record technique, and fogging (Buffington, 1985) are simple beginner's tools that can help you break the habit of allowing yourself to be intimidated.

The essence of the **ten word response** is to point out what is unsatisfactory to you in a situation and offer an alternative in ten words or less. For example, you might say to the person who broke in line in front of you, "You're out of order. I was next." Notice that you do not preface these eight words with "I'm sorry" or "Excuse me." You have no reason to be apologetic; it is the other person who is wrong. On the other hand, you don't get upset or hostile and demand to know, "Who do you think you are anyway?" The secret of the ten word response is that it leaves no room for such comments, which mark you as aggressive, not assertive.

There are times when even a nice strong assertive ten-word message of which you are very proud does not seem to work. Consider the salesperson who keeps hovering and commenting and suggesting even though you have said firmly that you will let him or her know if you require assistance. The **broken record technique** calls for you to repeat your assertive phrase in exactly the same calm, matter-of-fact tone as many times as it takes: "I'll let you know if I need assistance." The message that you will not be bullied and will not get into an argument on the subject should get through eventually.

The broken record technique works very well with strangers, but it is hard to use with people we know. A refusal to discuss the matter can be taken as a put-down by relatives and friends. A way around this problem is called fogging. As you might guess from its name, **fogging** is a way of clouding the issue so as to avoid a confrontation. For example, you might tell your mother, who is criticizing your husband, wife, live-in, or friend, "You know, you could be right." You have not argued with her or apologized for anything or made any other concession, but you have acknowledged her comments.

The ten word response, the broken record technique, and fogging are more difficult to bring yourself to try than they are actually to do. The secret to this, as to all communication skills, is practice. It gets easier every time, and before you know it, you will do it automatically without the sweaty palms or the racing pulse. If you are apprehensive, take your practice in the measured steps described in Exhibit 10–8.

## EXHIBIT 10–8 ▬▬▬▬▬▬▬▬▬▬▬▬▬
## Three Steps to Assertiveness

1. *Imagine a situation in which you would like to be assertive.* Now practice being so in your head. When you can do this comfortably without feeling embarrassed

2. *Role play the situation with a friend.* Have him or her be the line breaker or the salesperson who won't take a hint, and practice until you find yourself really "getting into it" and feeling in control. You also might want to swap roles so that you can be the person bugging you. This will give you a chance to say out loud all those things that you are worried such a person might say, and to work with your friend on responding to them. (Your professor may be willing to let your entire class work on this step together.) Now,

3. *Try out your assertiveness skills in public.* Start slowly with strangers you won't see again, like a waiter or waitress in a restaurant you don't go to regularly or that pushy guy at the airport who wants to bend your ear about religion or some cause when you are in a hurry. You may even want to start over the telephone if the opportunity presents itself. (How about those folks who call you at dinner wanting you to buy magazines or give money to a cause you've never heard of?)

Not all of the situations in which you would like to be assertive involve responding to what someone else is doing or has said. In some cases, it is a matter of being able to take the initiative. Instead of pestering you, for example, that salesclerk may be ignoring you—reading or holding a conversation with a co-worker while you stand there with a question or an item to buy.

The same assertiveness principles apply when you must take the initiative. Say your piece firmly, but in a matter-of-fact tone of voice. Don't be hostile, but don't be apologetic. It is all right to say "I'd like some help, please" if you feel more comfortable saying please, but avoid the temptation to preface your request with "I'm sorry to interrupt, but . . . " You have no reason to be sorry. The salesperson is being paid to assist customers.

Being assertive will feel strange at first if this has not been your style in the past, but the more often you try it, the more often it will work. And the more often it works, the more skilled you will become and the better you will feel about yourself. Learning to be assertive means freedom. You can ask the people next to you at the movies to stop talking or ask them to go to the lobby to do so. You can send the undercooked meat back to the restaurant kitchen. You don't have to buy things you don't want, or put up with pushy questions about your personal life, or be ignored by people who are paid to be helpful to you.

One word of caution, however. There are times when assertiveness may not be wise. These include situations in which the other person is overtly aggressive or intoxicated, or gives other signs of not being fully in control of his or her behavior. If you ever should feel that you might be in danger if you assert yourself, let it go!

## Listening

Up to now, we have been concentrating on skills to make you a better sender of messages. Much of the time, however, you are on the other end of the communication process; you are a receiver of messages, and communication skill in this situation means being a good listener. What does this skill include? There are at least three important aspects: receiving, hearing, and responding.

### Receiving a Message

The first rule of being a good listener is to attend to your speaker. Open your ears and your mind and reinforce your receptivity nonverbally by looking at the other person. If appropriate, put down what you are doing. Try not to interrupt.

If you are not receiving, you won't hear a message. One major block to reception is preoccupation, thinking about something unrelated to what your speaker is saying. Sometimes, circumstances dictate this distraction; the speaker has timed the communication poorly. For example, if someone is trying to tell you something while you are driving in heavy traffic, you may find it impossible to pay much attention.

Some preoccupation comes about because you think you know already what the speaker is going to say. Some occurs because you aren't really very interested. Some is because you are rehearsing what you are going to say next. However it comes about, it makes you a poor listener.

Good listening communicates "I am interested. I care."

## Hearing the Message

Being attentive and ready to receive a message is the first step; hearing is the second. **Hearing** means understanding what the speaker is trying to communicate. One barrier to this understanding is surface listening. In **surface listening,** we hear only the words spoken and take them at face value. For example, you come home quite late and your mother, father, or roommate says to you, "What do you mean by staying out until all hours? You have absolutely no consideration for others!"

If you start explaining the events of the evening or arguing that you are not an inconsiderate person or demanding to know why someone is waiting up for you, you have listened at the surface. Events surrounding this communication suggest that the intended message is more likely to be, "Thank heaven you're home. I've been worried!" As one writer describes it, when you listen to a message, "Listen to the music as well as the words" (Cross, 1978, p. 443).

Another barrier to hearing is selective listening. **Selective listening** means hearing only what you expect to hear or want to hear. It is listening with a filter or tuning in and out. The result is a distorted message or a partial message. For example, suppose that you ask a friend to pick you up after work because your car is in the repair shop. He says yes, which is what you want (and expect) to hear. The part you didn't hear (because you tuned out when you'd heard what you wanted to hear) was that he would not be able to get there until thirty minutes after your quitting time.

Listening to hear takes practice. Two hints for this practice are

1. Concentrate on giving full attention to the entire message; don't tune out when you think you have the point or know what is coming next.

2. Listen actively for overall content and feeling of the message. Don't jump to conclusions or make assumptions. Try to listen for tone as well as words.

People aren't sponges soaking up the meaning of everything to which they are exposed. Understanding others is an *active,* not a passive, process (Miller, Nunnally, & Wackman, 1975). Communicating to others that you have understood them (or tried) is part of this process.

## Responding to the Message

Your response to a message tells your speaker whether or not you heard and understood. Even if what was said wasn't very important, being a good listener is good for relationships. The following guidelines for responding will help you to show that you are listening and understanding.

- *Pause before you reply.* This covers the possibility that the speaker wasn't finished. It also communicates to the speaker that you really were listening and not just waiting for a chance to take over the conversational ball.

- *Acknowledge the speaker's message.* Completely ignoring what someone says can leave him or her wondering if you heard the message at all. It also may give the impression that you didn't think what was said (or the speaker) was worth bothering about with a reply. So even if a communication doesn't seem to require a reply, you will be a better listener if you acknowledge it in some way.

  There are all kinds of ways to acknowledge a message. You can say "That's interesting" or "I didn't know that" or "No kidding!" or even just "Um." Asking a question is a very good way to show not only that you did hear, but also that you are interested. A way that isn't very effective, although it is very common, is to begin relating something similar that you saw or did or thought or that happened to you: "That's like the time I . . ."

- *Don't play "I can top that."* Responding to a message by launching into an "I story" is *not* a sign of being a good listener. Your speaker is more likely to get a message that runs along the lines of: "That's all well and good, but what happened to *me* or what *I* thought or did is *really* interesting." If you want to share a similar experience or reaction with the other person, ease into it by acknowledging the other's message first.

- *Don't change the subject before your speaker is through with it.* Think about how you'd feel if your friend interrupted your description of a television program you had seen the night before to ask; "Do you think I would look good with short hair?" You probably would feel that your friend was not the slightest bit interested in what you were saying. You might also get the idea that *you* were not very interesting either, so watch yourself for this tendency if you want to be a good listener.

- *Check out your understanding of the message.* If you have doubts that you really have understood what someone is trying to tell you, check it out. A good technique to master is the **"say back" technique.** In "say back," you paraphrase what you thought your speaker meant and allow him or her to confirm or clarify (Rogers & Farson, 1955).

  *You:* So, you're thinking of adding economics as a minor instead of changing your major from math?
  *Your Friend:* No, what I meant is that I'm thinking of switching to economics and keeping math as a second major.

> You can listen like a blank wall or like a splendid auditorium where every sound comes back fuller and richer.
> *Alice Duer Miller*

To recapitulate, being a good listener means opening your ears and your mind to receive a communication, listening for the real message in context, and checking the meaning if you have doubts. Psychologists refer to this group of behaviors as **active listening.** Being a good listener also includes responding to messages in such a way that the other person does not feel cut off, put down, or unimportant. You can check your understanding of these concepts with the questions in *Test Yourself.*

## Summing Up ■

Mastering basic communication skills will help you through most communication situations, but some require extra effort. Overcoming defensiveness on the part of your receiver means understanding what might be giving rise to this reaction and doing what you can to avoid or reduce it. This may mean waiting until another time for communication, working through a problem that is getting in the way, or modifying the way that you send your message.

Giving feedback, especially negative feedback, without damaging your relationship with your receiver means learning to be descriptive rather than evaluative. When seeking feedback, you will be less likely to have problems if you learn to ask for what you want and avoid hints or pseudoquestions.

Being a good listener involves receiving, hearing, understanding, and responding skills. If you can master these, you will be a valued friend indeed; being listened to and understood is a need that almost all of us have. Like most communication skills, listening well is a message in itself. It says: "I think you are important enough for me to make an active effort to hear and try to understand you." (Active listening answers: *b, c, a, c, b, a*)

# TEST YOURSELF
## Are You a Good Listener?

*Directions:* Pretend that someone has spoken each of the sentences below to you and select the response that you think is most likely to communicate to that person that you really are hearing him or her. Answers appear at the end of the *Summing Up* section.

1. Oh, gosh! What time is it?
   a. Relax, it's early yet.
   b. It's 9:10 by my watch.
   c. Aren't you having a good time?
2. Sometimes, I feel like just quitting school completely.
   a. I know what you mean. It's like the time I wanted to leave camp.
   b. You can't do that!
   c. You sound pretty discouraged about things.
3. How do you like my new car? Isn't she a beauty?
   a. I'll say. Boy, are you lucky!

    b.  Yeah, now all you have to do is pay for it.

    c.  When I get a new car, it's going to be black with a red interior.

**4.**  I got a *B* on my psychology test.

    a.  A *B*? I though you were doing real well in that class.

    b.  Lucky you. I got a *C* on my biology exam.

    c.  Is that good news or bad news?

**5.**  Today is my birthday. How about dinner to celebrate?

    a.  No kidding. How old are you?

    b.  Hey, that's great! I can't make dinner, but how about lunch tomorrow?

    c.  Thanks, but I have plans. Maybe some other time.

**6.**  I'm thinking about breaking up with Karen.

    a.  That must be a tough decision to make.

    b.  Oh, Lord, what's she done now?

    c.  Good! I never did like her.

## ■ KEY WORDS AND PHRASES

| | | |
|---|---|---|
| active listening | fogging | relationship threats |
| assertive behavior | hearing | responding to the message |
| aggressiveness | indirect communication | salience |
| broken-record technique | loaded words | "say back" technique |
| communication | message | selective listening |
| communication channel | noise | source |
| decoding | nonverbal communication | surface listening |
| defensiveness | pseudoquestions | surplus meaning |
| effective communication | receiver | teleconferencing |
| encoding | receptivity | ten word response |
| feedback | | |

## ■ READ ON

*What Do You Say after You Say Hello?* by E. Berne. New York: Grove Press, 1972. Psychiatrist Eric Berne's analysis of communication in terms of parent, child, and adult ego states (transactional analysis) has been around for some time, but it still seems to have something of interest for almost everybody. His discussions of "crossed transactions" are useful to understanding more about how communication can go wrong no matter how hard you try.

*Straight Talk* by S. Miller, D. Wackman, E. Nunnally, and C. Saline. New York: Rawson, Wade, 1981. This book, based on the authors' successful Couple Communication Program, may help you learn to share your feelings (including anger), discuss problems, confront differences, and listen to others more effectively. It is long, but easy to read and filled with specific useful examples.

*Nobody's Perfect: How to Give Criticism and Get Results* by H. Weisinger and N. M. Lobsenz. New York: Warner, 1981. More on giving and getting feedback in a way that is constructive and leaves the self-esteem of both parties intact.

## REFERENCES

Arnold, H. J., & Feldman, D. C. (1986). *Organizational behavior*. New York: McGraw-Hill.

Ayim, M. (1984). Conflict and interaction in language: A study of male and female speech patterns. *Resources for Feminist Research, 13;* 19–20.

Black, R. (1984). The first pocket satellite phone. *Science Digest, 92,* 50.

Buffington, P. W. (1985, June). Are you assertive enough? *Sky,* 36–41.

Cohn, R. (1984, Dec. 9) How to get attention. *Parade,* 9–11.

Cross, G. P. (1978, Aug.) How to overcome defensive communications. *Personnel Journal,* 441–456.

D'Aprix, R. (1982). The oldest (and best) way to communicate with employees. *Harvard Business Review, 60,* 30–32.

Elias, C. (1988, Feb.). Strides in videoconferencing keep executives in office. *Insight,* 44–45.

Fisher, D., & Clyde, A. B. *Body Talk,* Coffee Shop Music, BMI.

Fishman, P. (1978). The work women do. *Social Problems, 25,* 397–406.

Gibb, J. R. (1961). Defensive communication. *Journal of Communication, 11,* 141–148.

Gleason, J. B. (1983). Men's speech to young children. In B. Throne & N. Henley (Eds.), *Language and sex.* Rowley, MA: Newbury House.

Jewell, L. N., & Reitz, H. J. (1981). *Group effectiveness in organizations.* Glenview, IL: Scott, Foresman.

Lakoff, R. (1975). *Language and women's place.* New York: Harper & Row.

Mehrabian, A. (1971). *Silent messages.* Belmont, CA: Wadsworth.

Mehrabian, A., & Ferris, J. (1967). Inference of attitudes from nonverbal communication in two channels. *Journal of Consulting and Clinical Psychology, 31,* 248–252.

Miller, S., Nunnally, E. W., & Wackman, D. B. (1975). *Alive and aware: Improving communication in relationships.* Minneapolis, MN: Interpersonal Communication Programs.

Morris, W. C., & Saskin, M. (1976). *Organizational behavior in action.* St. Paul, MN: West.

O'Barr, W. (1982). *Linguistic evidence.* New York: Academic Press.

Pease, A. (1984). *Signals: How to use body language for power, success, and love.* New York: Bantam Books.

Pfeiffer, J. W., & Jones, J. E. (1974). Don't you think that . . . ? An experiential lecture on indirect and direct communication. In J. W. Pfeiffer and J. E. Jones (Eds.), *Annual handbook for group facilitators.* La Jolla, CA: University Associates.

Rogers, C. R., & Farson, R. E. (1955). *Active listening.* Chicago: Industrial Relations Center, The University of Chicago.

Rogers, C. R., & Roethlisberger, F. J. (1952). Barriers and gateways to communication. *Harvard Business Review, 30,* 214–220.

Trippett, F. (1982, May 24). Watching out for loaded words. *Time,* 86.

West, C., & Zimmerman, D. (1975). Sex roles, interruptions . . . In B. Thorne and N. Henley (Eds.), *Language and sex.* Rowley, MA: Newbury House.

# 11

# Decisions and Decision Making

The telephone rings. You put down your book and answer it. "Hello?"
"Hi," the cheery voice of a friend says. "How about going out to dinner to-night?"
"Great!" you say. "Where do you want to go?"
"Well, why don't you choose this time? What sounds good?"
"Um, well, let me think. Gee, I don't know. My mind has gone blank."

**D**oes this conversation sound at all familiar? There are 20 restaurants within a five-mile radius and you can't come up with the name of a single one at first. Then they start coming back to you, but nothing sounds right. This one is too expensive. That one is too far away. A third is too dressy. You just heard a bad report about the food at a fourth . . .

Deciding where to go to dinner is not one of life's crises, but for a routine sort of decision it can be surprisingly difficult. There are many factors you might need to consider. How much money can you spend? How dressed up do you want to get? What kind of food sounds good? How crowded is a particular place likely to be?

If a simple matter like choosing a restaurant has so many aspects to it, complex decisions such as what occupation to pursue, which job offer to ac-cept, and whether or not to get married are likely to be far more difficult. In these cases, the list of factors you might need to consider is much longer, and you probably have to think about other people as well. In addition, these decisions have long-term consequences to you and others, unlike the decision about where to go for dinner.

You don't make big decisions every day, but you do have to make them. And you do make some decisions every day, even if they are no more compli-cated than where to go for dinner. If you are like most of us, you find yourself wishing from time to time that you could make these decisions better and faster or with more confidence and, perhaps, fewer regrets after the fact.

This chapter begins with a discussion of the three main elements of making decisions and then moves on to consider some ways that you can use this knowledge to make better decisions and live more happily with the results. To help you follow this discussion more easily, some basic decision-making terms are presented in Exhibit 11–1.

## ELEMENTS OF DECISION MAKING

Every situation that calls for you to make a decision, no matter how simple or complex, has three elements. The first is the decision itself. Is it a major one or a minor one? Is it simple or complex. Have you made similar decisions in the past, or is this a novel one? Is there a problem involved?

The second element is you, the decision maker. What are your needs, values goals, and priorities? How good are you at finding and evaluating relevant information? What is your personal decision-making style?

Finally, every decision is made under certain physical conditions and in a social context. Together, these make up the environment of the decision. Aspects of the environment that can have important effects are time pressures, the presence of others, social norms about acceptable choices, and pressures from friends, relatives, or peers. These and other factors are shown in Figure 11–1, which summarizes the three main sets of factors that influence decision making.

## THE DECISION

A **decision** is required of you when you must choose between one or more alternatives. The choices come in all forms—big ones, small ones, novel ones,

### EXHIBIT 11–1
### Decision-Making Terminology

**Bounded rationality:**   Cognitive, information, and social limits on perfect decisions

**Cognitive limits:**   The amount of information a person can deal with at one time

**Decision:**   The choice between two or more alternative courses of action

**Information processing:**   Organizing, evaluating, and drawing conclusions from information

**Maximizing:**   Choosing the alternative that provides the greatest return

**Problem:**   An obstacle to a personal or organizational goal

**Programmable decision:**   A decision that can be made by some set strategy or rule

**Risk:**   The possibility that an expected outcome will not occur

**Satisficing:**   Choosing the alternative that meets minimum criteria

**Subjective probability:**   A personal estimate of the likelihood of some event or outcome

**Uncertainty:**   A gap between the information available and perfect information

**Utility:**   The usefulness of an outcome as measured by some standard

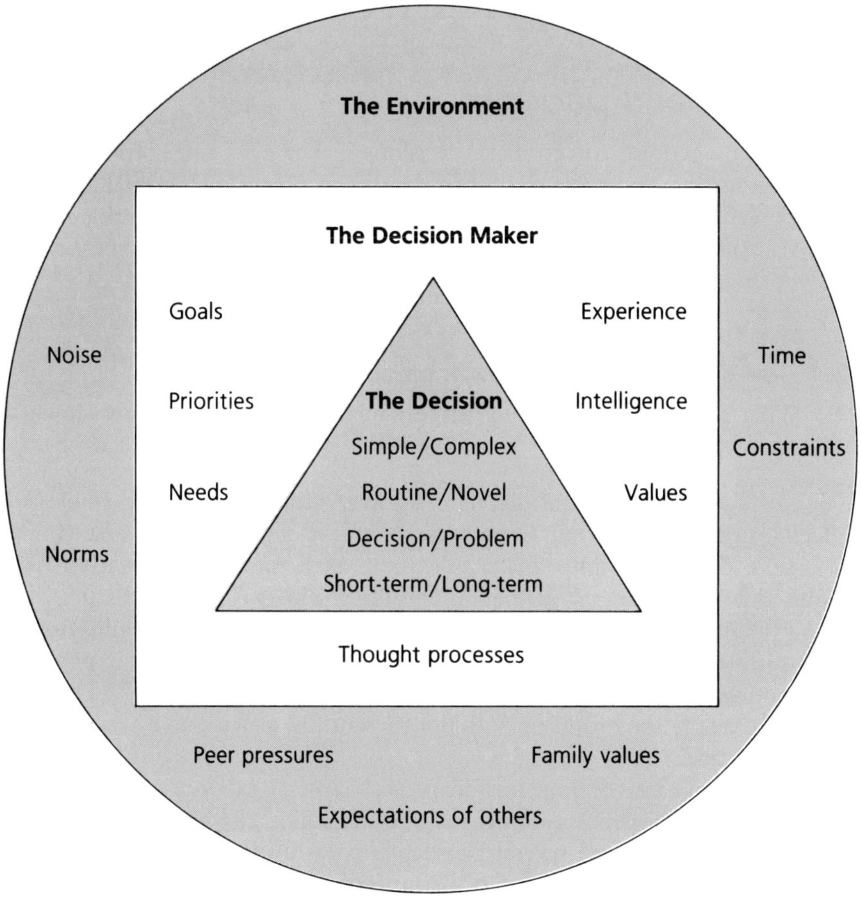

Figure 11–1  **The Three Elements of Decision Making**

**The Environment**

**The Decision Maker**

Noise

Norms

Goals

Priorities

Needs

Experience

Intelligence

Values

Time

Constraints

**The Decision**
Simple/Complex
Routine/Novel
Decision/Problem
Short-term/Long-term

Thought processes

Peer pressures          Family values

Expectations of others

routine ones, decisions that have long-term consequences, and decisions that don't matter much but still have to be made. It makes sense that we should put more time and effort into the big important decisions that have long-term consequences, but it doesn't always work this way. One business executive, known for her ability to make sharp decisions quickly, confessed that she often stood in front of her closet in an "agony of indecision" over what to wear that day.

Why do we make some decisions easily while others baffle us? Part of the answer to this question lies in individual characteristics, but certain aspects of the decision are relevant as well. One is the number of alternative courses of action that appear to be open. The business executive had only two alternatives from which to select a new store site, for example, but she had 11 suits, 13 dresses, 14 skirts, and 22 blouses in her closet.

Another characteristic of decisions that affects the way we see and respond to them is whether or not there is a problem involved. For example, deciding what new car to buy is a big decision, but if you have the necessary financial resources it isn't a problem. By contrast, consider the matter of failing a college course that you must pass in order to graduate. You have a decision to make—

what to do? But unlike choosing which new car to buy, this decision involves much more than selecting from among a set of known alternatives.

## Problems and Decisions

All problems require you to make decisions if they are to be solved, but not all decisions involve problems. **A problem is an obstacle to a goal.** To solve the problem, you must remove or reduce the obstacle to manageable size so that you can continue to progress toward your goal. To do this, you have to answer three questions:

1.  What is the obstacle?
2.  How did it get there (or what is causing it)?
3.  What course of action (alternatives) might remove it or cut it down to size?

Next, you have to consider the feasibility, desirability, and possible side effects of these alternatives. Eventually, you must choose one of these courses of action; that is, you must make a decision. Let's return to the matter of the required college course. Your hypothetical problem, as shown in Figure 11.2, is that failing the course blocks your goal of graduating on schedule. Among the possible causes of this problem are (1) you have not taken the necessary background courses, (2) you don't study enough, (3) you don't go to class regularly, or (4) the professor does not present the material in a way that you can understand.

The actual cause of your imaginary problem may be one, or some combination, of these possibilities, or it may be something else altogether. In every case, however, there are several alternative courses of action that you might take. For example, if the difficulty is the professor's presentation, you might (1) go to see him or her, explain that you are having difficulty, and ask for suggestions; (2) tape record the lectures and play them over as many times as necessary at home; (3) get a study group together and pool your knowledge,

Figure 11–2  **A Problem Is an Obstacle to a Goal**

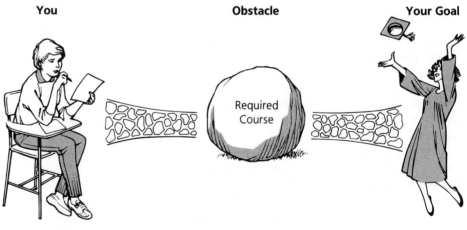

**You**                          **Obstacle**                          **Your Goal**

Required Course

or (4) drop the course and take it another time with another professor. Which is the right choice?

The example is hypothetical, so there isn't an answer; but the situation makes the point that problem decisions require more work than plain decisions, even important ones. If you fail to recognize a problem when you see it, you may have to keep making the same decision over and over.

As an example, let's consider the man or woman who is forever having to decide whether or not to keep seeing the current date. He or she claims to want a steady and meaningful relationship and feels it is a matter of finding the "right" person. It would seem that this individual might have a problem—perhaps he or she isn't very good at building relationships, for example. Until this obstacle is removed, our hero or heroine will be trapped on the same decision treadmill treating a problem as if it were a series of simple yes-no decisions.

## THE DECISION MAKER

The kind of decision to be made is an important influence on decision-making behavior, but different people make different decisions even when faced with the same choices. This is because individual characteristics of the decision maker play an important role in decision making as well. In this section we examine three that have particular importance: needs, goals, and cognitive processes.

## Needs and Decision Making

**Motivation** refers to the sum of the forces that energize, direct, and maintain your behavior (Steers, & Porter, 1983). Some of these forces are basic physical needs. For example, your body must have food to sustain itself, so some of your behavior is motivated by hunger. This can raise a whole series of decisions. Should you eat at home or go out? If at home, what should you have? If out, where should you go? Should you go alone or ask someone to join you? Of course, if your hunger is severe enough, things are simpler; you obtain whatever food is available most quickly.

Much of your behavior is motivated not by physical needs but by psychological ones. Among these may be needs for achievement, for the company of others, for respect, for power, for self-consistency, and for self-esteem. Such needs affect your values and priorities, and these play a big role in the standards you use for making decisions.

Let's suppose, to take an example, that you have a high need for achievement. You value accomplishment, so you will give priority to activities required to get things done. When you are faced with a decision about whether to go out on Sunday night or stay home and review for a test coming up on Monday, you probably will choose to study. You like to have fun, but your level of motivation for studying is higher in this instance because you have a high need for achievement.

Your psychological needs also affect your ability to evaluate information. In particular, a strong need can cloud your perception or bias your evaluation

The decision to devote a great deal of energy to work may be based on a high need for achievement.

of alternatives. In other words, needs can reduce your objectivity and your decision making may suffer. This is one reason many believe that computers are better decision makers than people; their judgment is unaffected by personal considerations. More on computers as decision makers may be found in *Face of the Future*.

## Goals and Decision Making

A **goal** is an end toward which people will exert effort. Some goals, like graduating from college, take a lot of effort and will be reached, if at all, far in the future. Others, like losing five pounds, also take effort, but don't take nearly so long. Some, like having all of the reading assignment completed before class, may take very little time. But however much effort is required or however far in the future they may be, goals help us to direct our efforts in a certain direction. And when we reach them, we feel a sense of accomplishment.

Of course, not all goals serve this purpose equally well. Some are too vague to be of any help in directing our activities. For example, the goal of "being somebody some day" doesn't offer much help. What does "being somebody" mean? How do you accomplish this? When is "someday"? How will you know when you've arrived? If goals are to be useful in helping us accomplish things, they must be *clear*. They also should be *measurable*; that is, they should specify how you will know when you attain them. We might restate the goal of "being somebody," for example, to read: "I want to be a company vice-president by the time I am 35 years old."

This brings us to a third characteristic of useful goals. They should be *attainable*. Pursuing unrealistic goals can create frustration and stress, and failure to accomplish them can damage self-esteem. You'll remember that one of the characteristics psychologists believe describes effective behavior is the ability to be realistic in judging your own capabilities and constraints. If you are

# FACE OF THE FUTURE:
## Computers to Solve Our Problems?

In 1985 the Arts and Entertainment cable television network ran a British-made four-part drama called "The Consultant." This consultant is a specialist in computer crime. He earns his living examining computer systems for vulnerable points. If he happens to discover a fraud already in progress, he exposes it and closes the loophole.

On one of his assignments, the consultant comes up against evidence of a well-established and lucrative fraud scheme in a large bank. Figuring out what is being done isn't so difficult; figuring out who is doing it takes a little longer. He perseveres, however, and eventually eliminates all possibilities except the head of the entire computer division—Mr. Alloway.

But Alloway is no ordinary criminal. Before the consultant can figure out how to get proof, a very large sum of money appears mysteriously in his personal bank account. Since he is—alas!—overdrawn, the deposit is used by the bank to pay off the deficit. Our hero knows what this means. He can't give the money back, and if he blows the whistle on Alloway, this "payoff" will implicate him in the crime. In addition, he is open to blackmail from now on.

What to do? The consultant turns to his faithful personal computer for the solution to the problem. Feeding in all the facts, he tells it, "Now you know as much as I do about the situation, honey. Tell me what to do." After a suspenseful moment or two, the answer appears on the screen:

### KILL ALLOWAY

The consultant is stunned. The perfect solution, but he never would have thought of it.

The computer that takes in available information, no matter how incomplete, sorts out the relevant from the irrelevant and comes up with the perfect decision alternative (which has completely escaped the poor human operator) is a favorite subject for writers of books, movies, and television scripts. Are there such machines? Can we look to computers to solve our problems for us?

The answer is no, not in the sense implied in "The Consultant." Despite the incredible feats of information processing that computers perform, none is capable of the cognitive leap made by "honey." Since the consultant didn't input murder as an alternative, it wouldn't have come out as the solution.

Today's computers make decisions of all kinds, ranging from which airport can accept an unscheduled landing by an aircraft running short of fuel to how many more copies of the latest Whitney Houston record to order for the record store. But these decisions are made on the basis of facts and criteria programmed in. The computer makes the most rational decision given the information it has.

Today's computers excel at information processing, not at thinking. Scientists working on the so-called "second-wave" of the computer revolution are hoping to change this. Their goal is AI—artificial intelligence that can mimic the decision-making capabilities of human beings. After years of false starts and overoptimistic promises, advances are being made; but current systems operate within strict limits, and it may be centuries before AI becomes a reality, if it ever does (Linden, 1988).

On balance, it seems a good thing that the face of the future does not as yet reveal machines that transcend our own human judgment, however irrational that sometimes may be. "Honey," unlike the consultant, does not have to live with the consequences of its decisions.

able to do this objectively, it may be perfectly realistic to aspire to be a company vice-president by age 35.

A large body of research leaves no doubt that both school and work performance improve when people have clear, measurable, and attainable goals (Locke, Shaw, Saari, & Latham, 1981). Such goals seem to increase productive effort and decrease irrelevant or counterproductive behaviors. Much the same principle applies to personal decision making. The clearer your goals, the less likely you are to get bogged down in a morass of extraneous information and impractical alternatives.

You can see this principle operating in the very simple situation of the restaurant choice described earlier. Your general goal is to have a meal in a restaurant with a friend. This leaves you to decide among all of the restaurants in the vicinity. A more precise goal of a good meal at a reasonable price will eliminate many of these alternatives immediately. You can eliminate still more if you specify quiet surroundings where you and your friend can have a personal conversation.

Having clear goals, whether for something as small as what you want out of an evening or as big as what you want out of life, helps you make decisions. Few of us have only one important goal at a time, however; and often if we do one thing, we accomplish one goal and give up another. For example, if you go to an expensive restaurant, you have an excellent meal in nice surroundings (meet that goal) and ruin your budget (fail to meet your financial goal of saving $100 a month). In other words, goals sometimes conflict with one another.

One day Alice came to a fork in the road and saw a Cheshire cat in a tree. "Which road do I take?" she asked. His response was a question: "Where do you want to go?" "I don't know," Alice answered. "Then," said the cat, "it doesn't matter."
*Lewis Carroll*

## Goal Conflict

Perhaps one of your major goals in life is to be successful in your career. Another is to have a happy marriage. Still another is to remain attractive and physically fit and active as you grow older. These goals, together with many other possible ones, have to do with different areas of your life, but the behaviors required to accomplish them may conflict. For example, the time required to get ahead in your career may leave you with insufficient time to pursue physical fitness activities. In other words, there is **goal conflict**. Psychologist Kurt Lewin (1935) described a number of different types of goal conflict.

When you are motivated to strive toward each of two goals that are both attractive but don't seem to be simultaneously attainable, you experience *approach-approach conflict*. Such conflicts are fairly common in day-to-day life. For example, you'd like to go out with Pat; you'd also like to go out with Chris. But if you date one, the other will look around for someone else. Or you've been looking forward to visiting your parents over vacation, but now your roommate has invited you to go skiing that week. Or you have two very attractive job offers in two different cities.

Approach-approach conflict can be frustrating. On the other hand, it isn't all that bad to have two *good* choices, and it often is possible to achieve the other goal at another time. As a result, the indecision that goes along with this type of conflict may be short-lived. Approach-avoidance conflicts are a different matter.

In an *approach-avoidance conflict*, the same goal has both attractive and unattractive features. Going to graduate school may be attractive to you, for example, since you enjoy learning and a master's degree would help you get a better job. These features pull you toward this goal (approach). On the other hand, graduate school requires 2 more years of studying during which you will have little free time and less money. These features push you away from this goal (avoidance).

Psychologists have found that people have a fairly consistent reaction to approach-avoidance conflicts. The further you are from attaining the goal involved, the more you are attracted by its positive aspects. The closer you get to it, the stronger the negative forces become and you back off. At some point, you have backed off far enough so that the positive aspects are once again stronger and the goal again looks attractive.

The relative strength of a goal as we are closer to it or farther from is called a **goal gradient** (Miller, 1944). As you may see in Figure 11–3, research data have demonstrated that the avoidance gradient is steeper than the approach gradient. This means that the negative aspects of a goal get powerful faster as you approach the goal than do the positive aspects.

The effect of the approach and avoidance goal gradients upon decision making is to create a form of indecision called *vacillation*—back and forth you go. First you will, then you won't. Let's suppose, to continue with our example, that you are in your junior year at college. Graduation is still some time away, and graduate school looks very attractive to you for the reasons mentioned. So you write to various universities for information and arrange to take the entrance examinations.

Taking the graduate school entrance examination brings you closer to this goal (in your mind), and you find yourself hesitating (tendency to avoid) as the negative aspects get stronger. But time passes, graduate school recedes into the future (the goal becomes farther away), and the prospect becomes more attractive again (tendency to approach is stronger). You begin submitting your application forms, and in due time letters of acceptance begin to arrive. Now you are much closer to your goal, and you begin to experience the avoidance forces again. Getting a job after graduation now looks more attractive. And so it goes, sometimes right up until the last minute.

Approach-avoidance conflicts create a good deal of anxiety and worry, which can be aggravated by the feeling that we are being indecisive, or "wishy-washy". It helps to try to put things in perspective. If the consequences of making a wrong decision aren't going to be too severe, give the pros and cons one last run-through and make a choice. If you are like most people, once you have committed yourself to one or the other course of action, you will tend to start seeing fewer negative sides and more positive sides to your choice, and the conflict will be reduced or eliminated (Frey & Rosch, 1984).

One hypothesis about why this cognitive shift occurs after we make a decision is found in Festinger's (1957) *cognitive dissonance theory*. Festinger postulates that people are made uncomfortable by ideas that are inconsistent with one another and are motivated to reduce or remove this dissonance. We met this idea earlier in our discussion of feedback from others that does not fit with an individual's self-concept.

In the present case, your knowledge of the negative features of your goal, going to graduate school, would be inconsistent with your decision to go. According to Festinger, this dissonance would make you uncomfortable, and

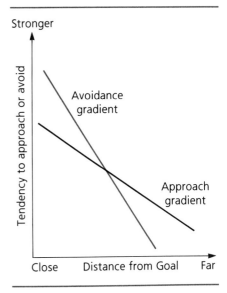

Figure 11–3 **Approach and Avoidance Goal Gradients.**

you would want to eliminate it. One way to accomplish this is to begin piling up the evidence for the decision you made (Festinger, 1964). As you focus on the positive aspects of your decision, the goal conflict disappears.

A third major type of goal conflict is the *avoidance-avoidance conflict* that occurs when you must decide between two equally unattractive prospects. Here, you are in the classic position "between a rock and a hard place." For example, let's say that you wake up feeling terrible, but you know if you don't go to work you'll have twice as much to do tomorrow. Stay home or go to work—either way you lose.

When faced with avoidance-avoidance conflict, a common strategy is to put off actually making the decision in hopes that the necessity for doing so will go away or that some new factor will appear to tip the balance. For example, you can always hope that while you lie in bed trying to decide what to do, your boss will call to find out why you are not at work. Then, when you explain, he or she will tell you not to worry; everything is under control, and someone else will carry your load until you are well again.

The most complex kind of goal conflict is the *double approach–avoidance conflict*. In this case, you must choose between two goals, each of which has positive and negative features. For example, perhaps you were accepted to two good graduate programs right away. One is at a very prestigious school. You believe it would help your career to go to this program, but you are not being offered any financial assistance. The other program is at a modest university, but you have been offered full financial support.

Now, you are in a double approach–avoidance conflict situation. Not only do you have the initial conflict about going to graduate school or not going, but each of your two choices has attractive and unattractive features as well. This situation is an enlarged version of the single approach–avoidance conflict, and it tends to elicit much the same response. You go back and forth until at some point you must choose, and then you start building your case to yourself for your choice.

## Cognitive Processes and Decision Making

Think wrongly if you please, but in all cases think for yourself.

*Doris Lessing*

Many people believe that more intelligent people make better decisions, but we have surprisingly little evidence that this is generally true (Reitz, 1981). Your cognitive processes, or *how* you think, seem to be more important than your IQ. One writer refers to the cognitive processes you bring to bear on decision making as your "mental software" (Vaughn, 1985). One aspect of this software is what is called a decision-making style.

### Decision-Making Styles

Psychologists who study decision making say that each of us has a **decision-making style,** or information-processing approach, that characterizes the way we go about making decisions. Researchers say this style varies primarily according to two factors. One is the amount of information used, and the other is the number of alternative choices developed (Driver & Rowe, (1979). If we consider the individual variations on both factors, we get the four basic decision-making styles shown in Figure 11–4.

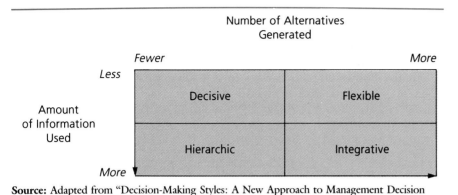

**Source:** Adapted from "Decision-Making Styles: A New Approach to Management Decision Making" by M. J. Driver and J. Rowe, 1979, in G. L. Cooper (Ed.), *Behavioral Problems in Organizations*. Englewood Cliffs, NJ: Prentice-Hall.

Figure 11–4 **Four Individual Decision-Making Styles**

In this scheme, *decisive decision makers* simplify the decision process. They use a relatively small amount of information to come up with a small number of alternatives. *Integrative decision makers* are at the opposite extreme; they collect a great deal of information and generate a large number of alternatives before making a decision. In between are *flexible decision makers* who generate many alternatives out of limited information and *hierarchic decision makers* who use a lot of information to generate only a few alternatives. Can you identify your basic style?

Your decision-making style can affect your confidence in your ability to make good decisions (Phillips, Pazienza, & Ferrin, 1984), the extent to which your decisions meet your goals (Harren, 1979), and your tendency to attack a problem head on or avoid it (Heppner et al., 1982). The psychologists who developed the classification shown in Figure 11–4 believe that most of us have a major decision-making style and a back-up style.

Driver and Rowe (1979) believe that we make better decisions when we use the style that best fits the demands of a particular decision situation. For example, integrative decision makers are more likely to come up with creative solutions to problems because they collect a lot of information and generate many alternatives. This would be a good style if you were trying to figure out how to support yourself and go to school at the same time. But integrative decision making is a waste of time if you are only trying to decide what movie to attend. In this case, a decisive style would fit the decision situation better.

# THE ENVIRONMENT OF DECISIONS

The nature of the decision to be made and your individual characteristics have important effects on your decision making, but decisions are not made in a vacuum. As we saw in Figure 11–1, they are made in an environment, or context, that has both physical and social aspects.

## The Physical Environment and Decision Making

Other things being equal, you will make more satisfactory decisions when your physical surroundings are comfortable and reasonably quiet and you are not pressed for time. Extremes of heat impair cognitive functioning (Fine & Kobrick, 1978), for example, and time pressures tend to make you overlook important information or weigh negative information too heavily (Simon, 1957).

There are times, of course, when you have no choice but to make a decision under hostile physical conditions. Deciding what to do when you are alone on a dark back road at night in the pouring rain with a flat tire and no spare is one such time. Fortunately, such situations do not arise too often. A little forethought usually allows you to tackle problems and make decisions in a reasonably comfortable physical environment, and you probably will make better decisions if you do not ignore this set of influences.

## The Social Environment and Decision Making

You may tend to think of your personal decisions as involving you and people close to you exclusively, but this often is not the case. For example, if you make the decision to drive 80 miles an hour on the freeway in order to get home more quickly, you are violating a law. If you are caught, a police officer will give you a ticket. If you have an accident at this speed, you may injure others. In both cases, people you do not know at all have become involved in your personal decisions.

Because your decisions do not always involve you alone, society places certain constraints on your decision making. Certain courses of action won't do, not because they won't solve your problem or accomplish your goal, but because they are illegal (like the decision to drive 80 miles an hour). Others seldom are considered because they violate those unwritten standards for appropriate behavior called norms. There is no law against reporting that you saw someone using notes during a closed-book exam, for example, but most students would not make that decision because it violates a strong student norm for sticking together.

Your social environment is created by other people—your relationships with them, their expectations, their behavior, the norms that grow out of these interactions, and the rules and laws of various segments of our society. This social environment places demands as well as constraints on your decision making. This means that others have expectations for what you decide, and your relationships can be affected if you ignore these expectations.

Most of you would not feel like free agents, to take one example, if you were making the decision about attending graduate school after you receive your bachelor's degree. Your parents might be strongly in favor of your continuing your education. Going straight to work would let them down, and, after all, they have been helping to pay the bills all these years. On the other hand, your girlfriend or boyfriend might want to marry when you graduate, or your spouse may be looking forward to buying a house or starting a family; going on to school lets down someone else who is important.

The constraints and demands that your social environment place on your decisions can be extensive. Many of these factors cannot be altered or gotten around, and they become sources of goal conflict. You can reduce some of this conflict by being selective about whose expectations you consider. What your girlfriend or boyfriend, spouse, or parents expect of you is relevant to your decision about what to do after graduation. But don't add to your problems

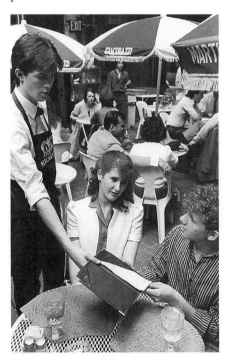

A social environmental norm that most people find difficult to ignore when making decisions is the one that says: "Don't make a scene in public."

by getting caught up in what people not directly involved are going to think of your decision.

> The decisions you make are affected by the nature of the decision, your motives and goals, the way you approach decision making, and the environment in which the decision is made. The social environment is particularly significant since it forces you to rule out some choices. In addition, expectations and pressures from others to do one thing or another can complicate matters.
>
> Understanding these basic elements of decision making can help you make better decisions. Appreciating the difference between ordinary decisions and decisions that involve problems can help you use your time more effectively. Knowing how your motives and goals affect the process can give you a greater feeling of control over your decision making. And understanding the influence of your environment offers guidelines for coping with demands and constraints. Now, we turn our attention to more specific suggestions for helping you improve your decision making.

**Summing Up** ■

## MAKING BETTER DECISIONS

There are two approaches that researchers take to the study of that process we call decision making. One is to look at it from the standpoint of how decisions *should* be made made. The other is to investigate how decisions really *are* made. Decision scientist Herbert Simon (1957) calls the difference between ideal and real decision making the difference between maximizing and satisficing.

**Maximizing** is a rational decision-making strategy that emphasizes making the *best* possible decision. By contrast, **satisficing** is making a "good enough" decision. We are forced to be satisficers most of the time because we lack the perfect information and the perfect objectivity to be truly rational decision makers. Nevertheless, the ideal model offers some guidelines for better decision making. In this section, we discuss defining the task and setting decision criteria, collecting information, and organizing and evaluating information.

## Defining the Task and Setting Decision Criteria

Decisions differ in scope, importance, immediacy, and whether or not a problem must be solved. A first step in improving your decision making is figuring out which sort of decision you have, that is, defining the task. If you have a decision that is going to affect you in important ways and/or for a long time to come or if you have a problem to solve, prepare to spend some time on the process. If you have a simple decision whose most important characteristic is that *some* decision must be made, don't agonize over it

While you are defining your decision task, it also helps to set the criteria by which you will evaluate the decision you make. Is there some goal you are trying to reach through this decision? Is timing important? Is your primary

Learning to make simple decisions without a lot of agonizing gives you more time and energy for the difficult ones when they come along.

criterion economic? Are you more concerned with being satisfied with your decision than with how much it costs? The best decision for you to make can vary considerably according to your criteria. Consider deciding where to spend your spring break vacation, for example. You've been asked to join some friends on a trip to the beach, but this could be expensive, If economic criteria are foremost, you won't select this option. If you'd really like to go, however, and being satisfied with your decision is more important than financial considerations, you may choose this alternative anyway.

There also could be other criteria involved in your decision. Perhaps timing is important. For some reason, you have to decide right now what you are going to do, and your friends' plans are still very tentative. In this case, you decide to rule out the beach. Or perhaps you want to catch up on some reading during the break, and you realize that this won't happen if you go with your friends. Whatever your situation, being aware of how you are going to measure the success of your decision will make the process of deciding easier and more effective.

## Collecting Information

A major difference between ideal decision making and real decision making is the amount and kind of information collected and used in the process. In order to maximize, you must have all the relevant information, and this seldom is possible. There is always a gap between the information you have and perfect information. This gap is called **uncertainty.**

Decisions made under uncertainty entail risk. For example, you can get quite a lot of information about the safety record of a certain make and model of automobile. But you cannot get this information for the current year or for any *particular* car, so you cannot get perfect information. When you buy an automobile, therefore, you are taking some risk.

A dislike for making decisions under conditions of uncertainty and taking the associated risks leads many people to believe that the more information they can get, the better the decision they can make. Research evidence does not support this belief entirely; too much information can reduce your decision-making effectiveness just as surely as too little (O'Reilly, 1980). There is more on information and decision making in *For Discussion*.

# FOR DISCUSSION:
## INFORMATION AND MAKING DECISIONS

The belief that the more information we have pertaining to a decision we must make, the better that decision will turn out to be is a widely held one. On the surface, it makes sense. You should be able to choose a better insurance plan if you have the facts about what the various policies you are considering are offering and what these features mean to you. The more you know about a particular company, the better you should be able to evaluate the probability of being satisfied with a job there.

But let's take a closer look at this commonsense assumption. Consider a very simple decision—what movie to go see tonight. Now, think of the information you might seek out to help you make a decision that will leave you feeling your money and your evening were well spent. Among the possibilities are the following:

- What movies are playing (within, say, a 30-minute driving radius)?
- What is each of these films about?
- What do reviewers say about each?
- What do your friends who have seen them say?
- Where are the theaters in which the films are playing?
- What are these theaters like (comfort, size of screen, etc.)?
- How much are tickets at the various theaters?
- What times do the various films begin?

Deciding what movie to see is one of those decisions upon which very little rides, but the example makes an important point about information and decision making. This is a simple decision situation with a finite number of known alternatives, and there is still an enormous amount of information that might be relevant. Now, consider what might happen if you did take the time to collect this information. It is quite likely that you would find that

- For every critic or friend who *liked* a particular movie, there was one who *disliked* it.
- The best movies are playing at the expensive, far-away theaters.
- Your favorite theater is playing a second-rate horror flick.
- The movie that sounds the best has been playing to sell-out crowds, and you might not be able to get in.

Even for such a simple decision, full information would make your choice harder, not easier. And for more complex decisions, both the amount of information you might seek and the problems of making sense out of it would be correspondingly more complex. To illustrate this complexity, let's assume for the moment that you are in the position of choosing your college major. (In reality, of course, many of you already have done so.)

Individually, or together with your classmates, make a list, like the preceding one, of all of the information

you could get that would be relevant to this decision. Keep in mind that you will have to consider personal needs, goals, interests, background, and career aspirations. You'll also have to look at such practical matters as what your college or university has to offer and what career opportunities are available in the various fields you are considering. Would you need to go to graduate school? Could you find the financial resources to do that?

Making this list should take a long time, because you are describing what perfect information for choosing a major would be. Now, when you have thought of all the possibilities, take a look at the list and see what information you actually used in making your decision if you already have chosen your major. What information did you get that you didn't need? What information did you not get that you did need? What information that might be relevant to this decision could you not use if you had it? Why?

The truth is that human beings have cognitive limits when it comes to information processing. We can deal with only so much information at a time. Different people have different limits, but when you reach yours (whatever they are), more information serves no useful purpose. You have reached information overload. Are you currently facing any decisions that seem to be in this state? If you are (or were), what suggestions do you have for getting out of your fix?

As the example in *For Discussion* illustrates, even a simple decision can generate **information overload,** more information than we can deal with at one time. When faced with too much information, people tend to divert their energies into trying to make sense of it instead of making use of it. The decision gets put off and put off again. Alternatively, the decision maker may just give up and make the same decision that would have been made with no information.

If it is possible to have too much information as well as too little, how do you know when you have the right amount? Here are a few useful guidelines (Reitz & Jewell, 1985).

- If all of the alternative courses of action you see open to you appear to be equally desirable or undesirable, you may have too little information. There usually is one factor, however small, that makes some of the alternatives more attractive than others.

- If you can't make heads or tails out of the information you have, you may have too much; certainly you need to get organized before seeking out more.

- If collecting information has become an excuse for not making the decision, it is time to stop.

## Organizing Information

The purposes of collecting information before making a decision are so that you can use it to identify possible alternatives you haven't thought of and/or pick the course of action that best meets your criteria. For information to serve these purposes, it must be organized in some way. Formal techniques for organizing information are called **decision aids.**

Figure 11–5 presents an example of a kind of decision aid called a *decision tree.* To illustrate how it works, let's assume that you are going to buy a new car. That decision is made. The one facing you now is what to do with your current vehicle. You see three alternatives: trade it, sell it yourself, or give it to your brother, who can't afford to buy a car. You have decided that your major criterion for evaluating this decision will be financial.

To use a decision tree to organize information relevant to a decision about what to do with your old car, you must know several things.

1. You must know the alternatives; these you have established (trade, sell, or give away).

2. You must know your decision criterion; this you also have established (financial).

3. You must be able to estimate the likelihood (the *subjective probability*) of certain relevant future conditions. In this case, you are concerned with whether or not your current car will be sold and how much financial gain you will make from the sale. Given your financial criterion, you rule out giving the car to your brother. This leaves you the alternatives of trading it or selling it yourself.

The future condition if you trade your car is that it definitely will be sold (to the dealer); the probability of a sale if you make that decision is 1.00. Your gain will be the $1,500 the dealer has offered you in trade. The future condition if you sell your car yourself is that you will make more money. You believe you can get $2,500, but a sale at this figure is not guaranteed; you estimate the probability to be about .75.

Using all of the information described, you create the decision tree shown in Figure 11–5. With this organization, you can see the estimated outcomes of the two viable alternatives under the relevant future conditions. These tell you that your best bet, given your established criterion, is to try to sell your current car yourself before buying a new one. If you succeed, you are $375 (less any costs of advertising or other expenses) ahead.

Both the example and the decision tree in Figure 11–5 are simple, but the principle may be expanded as long as you have (or can estimate) the required input information. Obviously, this requirement limits the utility of the decision tree to certain kinds of decisions, but there are many other such aids available (Pitz & Sachs, 1984). All of them are tools for helping you evaluate alternatives in terms of the criteria you have set and the information you have available. Decision aids help you organize information; they make a decision

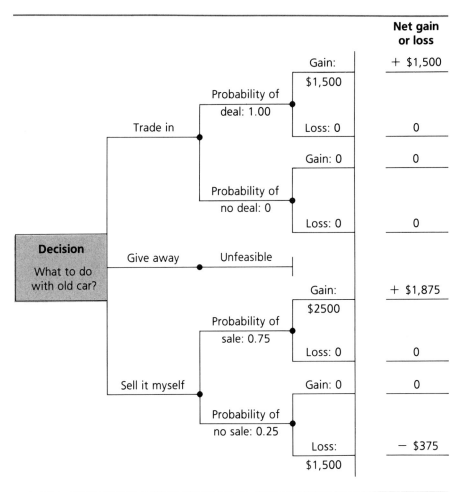

**Figure 11–5 An Aid to Organizing Information: A Decision Tree**

for you only in the sense that this organization may reveal one alternative to be clearly superior given your criterion.

There may be times when you find the course of action identified by organized information to be one you *don't* want to take. This information is helpful too. It suggests that you may want to reevaluate your decision criterion. In the case of the car, for example, an economic standard may not be what you want after all. In the final analysis, the good feelings that will come from helping your brother out may be more important to you.

**Summing Up** ■

Most people lack the time and cognitive abilities to be perfectly rational decision makers. Instead, we seek to satisfice, to find a decision that is good enough rather than ideal. To do this, we need some relevant information, but not too much, organized in such a way that we can make sense out of it by the decision criteria that we have set. Then comes the big moment—we make a decision and commit ourselves to a course of action. In the last section of this chapter, we take a look at what happens next.

## LIVING WITH YOUR DECISIONS

You don't get feedback as to how good a decision is until after you have made it. In some happy cases, it is clear that the alternative chosen was right for you. In others, it seems that another choice would have served just as well. And in

The decision to have a family involves very hot cognitions; the issues are emotional, important, and have long-term consequences for all parties.

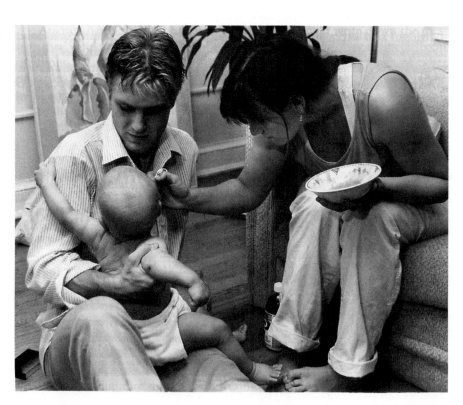

some cases, feedback leads you to the conclusion that you made the wrong choice.

## Postdecisional Regret

When a decision does not seem to have been the right one (or during that uncertain period when it is too soon to know), you may suffer from what is called postdecisional regret. **Postdecisional regret** refers to doubts about your choice or a wish that you had made a different decision.

When decisions can be reversed or made again or have no long-term personal consequences, postdecisional regret should be slight and short-lived. If the movie you chose was a bomb, you are only out a few hours and a few dollars, and you can always go another time to see the one you decided against.

Some decisions are not so easily dismissed, however. They have long-term or important personal consequences, and they can't be redone, or undone, easily. Examples include choosing one job offer or college over another, getting married, and starting a family. Robert Abelson (1963) has referred to our thoughts about such vital issues as *hot cognitions*. When your decision making involves such issues, you are particularly susceptible to strong postdecisional regret. Did I do the right thing? Should I have waited? How am I going to get out of this if it doesn't work?

Hot cognitions also make you more vulnerable to being influenced by negative information, including the negative opinions of others. In short, the more personal and important a decision, the shakier you may feel about it. This makes sense. The problem is that because such decisions *are* so important, you want to be more, not less, confident about your choice.

Postdecisional regret is a source of stress, and the more important the issue, the more stress is likely to be felt. Doubts about your decisions also can leave you vulnerable to self-fulfilling prophecies. If you wish strongly that you had taken the other job, for example, you may be more likely to find things wrong with the job you did take. This could affect your work performance in a negative way so that you don't get the first expected promotion. As a result, you are even more negative about the job, and the first thing you know, your prediction that you made the wrong decision has come true.

Because postdecisional regret can have a number of important negative effects, psychologists Janis and Mann (1977) believe that learning to anticipate sources of this regret is critical. They have devised a method they call the decisional balance sheet to help people to learn to do this. This, like a decision tree, is a decision aid although quite a different one since it allows you to include psychological factors.

## The Decisional Balance Sheet

Janis and Mann identify four major types of consequences a decision can have for you.

1. Utilitarian gains/losses for you (self)
2. Utilitarian gains/losses for others
3. Self-approval or disapproval
4. Approval or disapproval from others

The utilitarian gains and losses are what you or others get out of a decision in a tangible sense. In the example of what to do with your old car, the financial considerations of the various choices fall into this group. If you sell or trade your car, you (self) will gain by the amount you receive for it, and your brother (other) will lose by the value of the car (which may be much more than monetary).

A **decisional balance sheet** is a written summary of the various kinds of gains and losses that you anticipate will follow your major decision alternatives. An example appears in Table 11–1. The decision situation shown is a

## Table 11–1  An example of a Decisional Balance Sheet: To Smoke or Not to Smoke

| Anticipated Consequences | Alternative 1 Stop Smoking | | Alternative 2 Keep Smoking | |
|---|---|---|---|---|
| | + | − | + | − |
| *Utilitarian Gains and Losses for Self* | | | | |
| 1. Smoking relieves tension. | | − | + | |
| 2. Smoking helps me concentrate/do better work. | | − | + | |
| 3. Smoking makes me less energetic. | + | | | − |
| 4. Smoking is hazardous to my health. | + | | | − |
| 5. Smoking is pleasurable. | | − | + | |
| 6. Smoking is making my own decision. | | − | + | |
| *Utilitarian Gains and Losses for Others* | | | | |
| 1. I am relaxed/more pleasant when smoking. | | − | + | |
| 2. People close to me would suffer if I became ill from smoking. | + | | | − |
| 3. My cigarette smoke bothers other people. | + | | | − |
| 4. If I try to stop, I'll be irritable and a pain to be around. | | − | + | |
| *Self-approval or -Disapproval* | | | | |
| 1. I like the image of a cigarette smoker. | | − | + | |
| 2. I'm embarrassed that I have to smoke. | + | | | − |
| 3. I'm foolish to ignore warnings about cigarettes. | + | | | − |
| *Social Approval or Disapproval* | | | | |
| 1. People think I'm foolish to continue to smoke. | + | | | − |
| 2. People close to me disapprove of my smoking. | + | | | − |
| 3. People think I lack the character to quit. | + | | | − |

**Source:** Entries in table adapted from "Decisional Balance Measure for Assessing and Predicting Smoking Status" by W. F. Velicer, C. C. DiClemente, J. O. Prochaska, and N. Bradenburg, 1985, *Journal of Personality and Social Psychology, 41*, pp. 1279–1289.

two-alternative one facing many people—stop smoking or keep smoking. The decisional balance sheet calls for you to try to anticipate the positive and negative outcomes of both of the major alternatives. Doing this in formal written form makes it difficult for you to gloss over the negative aspects of a preferred alternative or to disregard the positive aspects of an unpreferred alternative. If you are a smoker, you will understand this perfectly. You *should* quit, but you don't *want* to quit, so you tend to minimize both the personal risks of smoking and the benefits of quitting.

Janis and Mann believe that this anticipation of outcomes is an important function of the balance-sheet technique. If you use this aid as intended, you will have a better idea of how well you have collected and evaluated relevant information. A reasonably full sheet tells you that you have done your homework. Other things being equal, you are less likely to experience painful postdecisional regret if you feel you have done a good job analyzing the situation.

In addition to serving as a check on your information collecting, the balance-sheet technique helps to prepare you for possible negative consequences of your decision. The consequences still will be negative, but the impact should be less severe. For example, smokers are warned that when they quit they may expect a 2- to 3-week period of persistent coughing as their lungs begin to clean themselves out. Knowing this doesn't make the experience any less unpleasant, but it may make it less likely to destroy the commitment to stop smoking. Janis and Mann call this effect of advance warning the **inoculation hypothesis.**

There is some research evidence that the inoculation hyposthesis has validity and that a careful decisional balance sheet reduces postdecisional regret and increases commitment to a course of action (e.g., Hoyt & Janis, 1975). Maybe you'd like to try this technique for yourself. A blank form is provided in *Test Yourself.* Use it to make an analysis of some decision you must make in the future. Or you might want to reanalyze one you made in the past to see if you might have done it differently.

## Changing Your Mind

We have been examining the matter of living with decisions after they are made. This tends to be much easier if you believe you really have thought the decision through and aren't suffering consequences that were totally unexpected. In many cases, however, you don't have to cope with postdecisional regret; you simply can change your mind about the decision.

Changing your mind about a decision you have made is in itself a decision, and it can be a difficult one to make. Like other decisions, this one will have gains and losses for you and possibly for others. It also will have some associated approval or disapproval from yourself and others. This involvement of others sometimes makes us feel that we must live with a decision even though we don't want to and, strictly speaking, don't have to. For example, you may realize as soon as you have accepted a job offer that it isn't really what you want. Or perhaps the job you really wanted came through shortly after you accepted another one.

This is an awkward situation to say the least. Deciding what to do is a matter of weighing the relative costs and benefits of the two alternatives— change your mind or don't. Many people would simply bite the bullet and go

> Like all weak men, he laid an exaggerated stress on not changing one's mind.
> *W. Somerset Maugham*

# TEST YOURSELF:
## The Decisional Balance-Sheet Technique

I want to decide between _____ and _____

| *Anticipated Consequences* | Action 1 | | Action 2 | | Action 3 | | Action 4 | |
|---|---|---|---|---|---|---|---|---|
| | + | − | + | − | + | − | + | − |
| A. *Utilitarian Gains/Losses, Self* | | | | | | | | |
| B. *Utilitarian Gains/Losses, Others* | | | | | | | | |
| C. *Self-approval or -Disapproval* | | | | | | | | |
| D. *Social Approval or Disapproval* | | | | | | | | |

**Source:** Form from *Decision Making: A Psychological Analysis of Conflict, Choice, and Commitment* by I. L. Janis and L. Mann, 1977. New York: Free Press.

ahead with the first job because they would feel that the inconvenience to the first company (loss to others) and the disapproval of those in it for saying no after saying yes (disapproval from others) would not be worth the gains to themselves (having the preferred job).

There also could be significant self-disapproval that would tip the balance further toward sticking with the original decision. Changing your mind after you have put time and energy and thought into a decision is another way that cognitive dissonance may arise. On the one hand, there is the fact that you have accepted a job you decided would be satisfactory. On the other hand, there is the fact that you don't really want it. If you have a strong need to be consistent, these two facts can't exist side by side without making you very uncomfortable. You disapprove of your own behavior, so you stick with your first decision to achieve consistency and eliminate the discomfort.

Although it is necessary to consider the effects on others when changing your mind, it seldom is wise to let these considerations be the only ones if there are important consequences to you as well (as in the example). One measure of effective behavior that has been emphasized repeatedly is control. If you stick with a decision solely out of concern for what others will think if you don't, you are giving up some of this control.

Every situation will be a little different, but a good rule to follow is to give yourself permission in advance to change your mind once a decision has been made if it is possible to do so. At the same time, make a rule that you won't change your mind without weighing the consequences as best you can foresee them. The decisional balance sheet can be helpful here since "change my mind/don't change my mind" is a two-alternative decision.

**Summing Up** ■

Making a decision involves choosing one course of action from among two or more alternatives. But making this choice does not end the matter; you have to live with it once it is made. Doubts that you have made the right decision create postdecisional regret, which can cause stress, reduce commitment to a decision, and lead to negative self-fulfilling prophecies. A decisional balance sheet is a decision aid to help you reduce these doubts by focusing your attention on the major positive and negative consequences of each alternative before you make the decision.

You also have the right to change your mind once a decision is made. This itself is a decision, and if the consequences are important, you will feel happier about making it if you try to follow the basic rules for good decision making.

---

## ■ *KEY WORDS AND PHRASES*

| | | |
|---|---|---|
| decision | goal gradient | postdecisional regret |
| decision aid | information overload | problem |
| decision-making style | innoculation hypothesis | satisficing |
| decisional balance sheet | maximizing | social environment and decision making |
| goals and decision making | motivation and decision making | uncertainty |
| goal conflict | physical environment and decision making | |

---

■ *READ ON*   *Decision Making: A Psychological Analysis of Conflict, Choice, and Commitment* by I. L. Janis and L. Mann. New York: Free Press, 1977. This integration of experimental, field, clini- cal, and historical knowledge of decision making has become a classic. The reading level is not low, but the style is easygoing and many of the examples are fascinating. If your current job or hoped-for career involves making important decisions, this is must reading.

*Overcoming Indecisiveness* by T. I. Rubin. New York: Harper & Row, 1985. A different perspective on decision making—that of a psychiatrist. Among the topics Dr. Rubin discusses in his easy-to-read little book are establishing priorities, recognizing pseudo-decisions, and removing decision blocks.

## ■ REFERENCES

Abelson, R. P. (1963). Computer simulation of "hot' cognition. In S. Tomkins and S. Messick (Eds.), *Computer simulation of personality*. New York: Wiley.

Driver, M. J., & Rowe, A. J. (1979). Decision-making styles: A new approach to management decision making. In G. L. Cooper (Ed.), *Behavioral problems in organizations*. Englewood Cliffs, N. J.: Prentice-Hall.

Festinger, L. (1957). *A theory of cognitive dissonance*. Evanston, IL: Row, Peterson.

Festinger, L. (1964). *Conflict, decision, and dissonance*. Standford, CA: Stanford Univeristy Press.

Fine, B. J., & Kobrick, J. L. (1978). Effects of altitude and heat on complex cognitive tasks. *Human Factors, 20,* 115–122.

Frey, D., & Rosch, M. (1984). Information seeking after decisions: The roles of novelty of information and decision reversibility. *Personality and Social Psychology Bulletin, 10:* 91–98.

Harren, V. A. (1979). A model of career decision making for college students. *Journal of Vocational Behavior, 14,* 119–133.

Heppner, P. P., Hibel, J., Neal, G. W., Weinsteing, C. L., & Rabinowitz, F. E. (1982). Personal problem solving: A descriptive study of individual differences. *Journal of Counseling Psychology, 29,* 580–590.

Hoyt, M. F., & Janis, I. L. (1975). Increasing adherence to a stressful decision via a motivational balance-sheet proceedure: A field experiment. *Journal of Personality and Social Psychology, 31,* 833–839.

Janis, I. L., & Mann, L. (1977). *Decision making: A psychological analysis of conflict, choice, and commitment*. New York: Free Press.

Lewin, K. (1935). *A dynamic theory of personality*. New York: McGraw-Hill.

Linden, E. (1988, Mar. 28). Putting knowledge to work. *Time,* 60–63.

Locke, E. A., Shaw, K. N., Saari, L. M., & Latham, G. P. (1981). Goal setting and task performance: 1969–1980. *Psychological Bulletin, 90,* 125–152.

Miller, N. E. (1944). Experimental studies of conflict. In J. M. Hunt (Ed.), *Personality and behavior disorders*. New York: Ronald Press.

O'Reilly, C. A. III (1980). Individuals and information overload in organizations: Is more necessarily better? *Academy of Management Journal, 23,* 684–696.

Phillips, S. D., Pazienza, J., & Ferrin, H. H. (1984). Decision-making styles and problem-solving appraisal. *Jouranl of Counseling Psychology, 31,* 497–502.

Pitz, G. F., & Sachs, N. J. (1984). Judgment and decision: Theory and application. *Annual Review of Psychology, 35,* 139–163.

Reitz, H. J. (1981). *Behavior in organizations* (rev. ed.). Homewood, IL: Irwin.

Reitz, H. J., & Jewell, L. N. (1985). *Managing*. Glenview, IL: Scott, Foresman.

Simon, H. A. (1957). *Models of man*. New York: Wiley.

Steers, R. M., & Porter, L. W. (1983). *Motivation and work behavior* (3rd ed.). New York: McGraw-Hill.

Vaughn, L. (1985, May). How to make smarter decisions. *Prevention,* 71–75.

# 12

# Stress and Stress Management

Y ou go to your biology class as usual on Monday morning, and to your dismay, your professor announces that the next test has been moved up. Instead of being a week from Wednesday, it will be on this Wednesday. You panic. You haven't even opened the book! Your heart starts beating faster and your hands begin to sweat. As soon as you are able to leave class, you bolt for the library and begin to cram for the test. You spend the afternoon and evening in the library, cut your classes the next day, and continue to study for biology. About five o'clock, you collapse over the desk; you can't do any more. You are exhausted.

What happened to you in our imaginary story is that a change in your environment—the rescheduling of an exam by a professor—sent your body into a general stress reaction. The change was a threat to your well-being, and your body mobilized its resources to try to help you meet the challenge. You were energized to step up the study pace and keep it up without rest until finally you went too far and your body protested.

This experience may have happened to you in reality. You may also have had similar responses to other sudden changes or unexpected events in your life, such as a broken relationship or a death in the family. Even if you know they are coming, such changes can create stress. In this chapter we examine the meaning of stress, some common stressors, and the ways that your body and your mind react to these threats. We also consider some of the factors that affect your sensitivity to stressors. Finally, we look at ways of coping with stress that have been found to be effective for most people.

## WHAT IS STRESS?

Stress is nothing new, but the intense interest people have in the subject today has come about only in the past decade or so. During this period of time, psychologists, physicians, and others working in this area have had a problem defining stress in a clear and measurable way that is acceptable to everyone. The major difficulty is that people look at stress in two opposite ways. Some take the position that stress is a *reaction* to a stimulus event (such as your driven study behavior when the biology test was changed). This point of view is reflected in the phrase "I am stressed out." The speaker means that he or she is experiencing the negative effects of continual efforts to adapt to stressors.

Others think of stress as the *stimulus* itself, in this case, the change in the test date. Here, the phrase "I am under great stress" will serve to illustrate. This speaker means that he or she has much with which to cope, but there is no indication that it has become too much as yet.

A recent view of stress is that it is not one or the other (a stimulus or a reaction), but a *relationship* between an individual and what is happening in his or her environment (Lazarus, DeLongis, Folkman, & Gruen, 1985). This view is illustrated in Figure 12–1.

The straight line in the center of the figure is an **adapted state;** this is your usual state as your life runs along day to day. The lower wavy line represents the state of the external environment to which you are adapted. You are not affected by small changes out there (waves in the line), but once in a while something big happens. We could say, for example, that point *a* is where the biology professor announced the change in the exam date.

In a similar fashion, the upper wavy line in Figure 12–1 is your internal environment. You are adapted to the routine fluctuations in this environment that go with changes in your physical and emotional states, but sometimes a bigger change occurs. Point *b,* for example, might be the great frustration that built up when you couldn't find a parking place, were late for your dental appointment, and had to wait an extra hour.

As you see in the figure, changes in the internal environment (point *b*) or external environment (point *a*) press on your adapted state; if you are to maintain it, you must make some physical, mental, or psychological adjustment. We can say then, that **stress** is a significant departure from an individual adapted

Figure 12–1  **Stress as an Interaction between an Individual and the Environment**

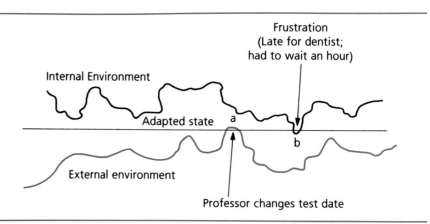

state. This definition incorporates both the stimulus and the response views. It allows both specific stimuli (such as the professor's change of exam date) and individual responses (such as a slow building of frustration as many little things go wrong) to fit the definition of stress. It also recognizes that positive things as well as negative things can create stress.

Events and conditions that have the potential to create those departures from the adapted state that we call stress are **stressors.** We have seen that these can be external or internal. Let's take a closer look at these two sources of potential stress.

# Environmental Stressors

There are many events, conditions, and changes in your environment that have the potential to upset your usual adjustment. Some, such as extremes of temperature, uncontrollable noise, and time pressure, are in the physical environment. Many of those who study stress, however, concentrate on the role of various common life events as stressors. Most of these events are significant primarily for the changes they create in a person's social environment. *Test Yourself* lists a number of such events that often happen to people in college.

Notice that many of the events shown in *Test Yourself* are positive. Stress researchers have found that happy events can make demands on us just as unhappy events can. For many, it is change itself that causes difficulty. Negative changes and events do seem to be related more strongly to subsequent psychological difficulties, however. This is especially likely to be true if the change or event is perceived to be out of the individual's control (Stern, McCants, & Pettine, 1982). The death of a loved one, for example, is both negative and beyond control, and it is for these reasons that such an event is almost a universal stressor.

You also may have noticed that most of the items in *Test Yourself* are major and important events and changes, but you know from your own experience that little things can get to you as well. An unexpected traffic jam on the way home, a long wait in a restaurant for dinner, a lost set of keys, that stubborn five pounds that simply refuses to come off—all of these can feel like a threat to your well-being under the right circumstances. For many of us, these *daily hassles* create some of the more significant internal psychological stressors in our lives (DeLongis et al., 1982).

# Psychological Stressors

In the last chapter we discussed the conflict that can occur when you are attracted simultaneously by two different goals (approach-approach conflict), when you have to choose between two equally unattractive goals (avoidance-avoidance conflict), or when you are both attracted to and put off by a goal (approach-avoidance conflict). These conflicts are psychological stressors; they interfere with the status quo and make demands on your adjustment. Two additional categories of psychological stressors are frustration and pressure.

### Frustration

You know that when you can't have or accomplish something you want, you feel frustrated. **Frustration** is the blocking of goal-directed behavior. It creates

# TEST YOURSELF
## The College Schedule of Recent Experience

*Directions:* Multiply the number of times (up to a maximum of four) each of the events listed has happened to you in the past year by the number of points shown, then total.

| POINTS | EVENT | TOTAL POINTS |
|---|---|---|
| 50 | Entered college | _____ |
| 77 | Got married | _____ |
| 38 | Had trouble with boss | _____ |
| 43 | Held job while attending school | _____ |
| 87 | Experienced death of spouse | _____ |
| 34 | Underwent major change in sleeping habits | _____ |
| 77 | Experienced death of a close family member | _____ |
| 30 | Experienced major change in eating habits | _____ |
| 41 | Changed or chose college major | _____ |
| 45 | Revised personal habits | _____ |
| 68 | Experienced death of close friend | _____ |
| 22 | Found guilty of minor law violation | _____ |
| 40 | Had outstanding personal achievement | _____ |
| 68 | Was pregnant or fathered a pregnancy | _____ |
| 56 | Saw major change in health/behavior of family member | _____ |
| 58 | Had sexual difficulties | _____ |
| 42 | Had trouble with in-laws | _____ |
| 26 | Had major change in number of family get-togethers | _____ |
| 53 | Experienced major change in financial state | _____ |
| 50 | Gained a new family member | _____ |
| 42 | Changed residence or living conditions | _____ |
| 50 | Experienced major conflict/change in values | _____ |
| 36 | Experienced major change in church activities | _____ |
| 58 | Had reconciliation with significant other | _____ |
| 62 | Fired from work | _____ |
| 76 | Was divorced | _____ |
| 50 | Changed to a different line of work | _____ |
| 50 | Had major change in number of arguments with significant other | _____ |
| 47 | Had major change in responsibilities at work | _____ |
| 41 | Spouse began or stopped work outside home | _____ |

| 42 | Had major change in working hours or conditions | _____ |
| 74 | Underwent separation from significant other | _____ |
| 37 | Experienced major change in type/amount of recreation | _____ |
| 52 | Experienced major change in use of drugs | _____ |
| 52 | Took on mortgage/loan less than $10,000 | _____ |
| 65 | Had major personal injury or illness | _____ |
| 46 | Had major change in use of alcohol | _____ |
| 43 | Had major change in social activities | _____ |
| 38 | Had major change in participation in school activities | _____ |
| 49 | Had major change in independence/responsibility | _____ |
| 33 | Took trip/vacation | _____ |
| 54 | Became engaged to be married | _____ |
| 50 | Changed to a new school | _____ |
| 41 | Changed dating habits | _____ |
| 44 | Had trouble with school administration | _____ |
| 60 | Underwent termination of engagement/steady relationship | _____ |
| 57 | Underwent major change in self-concept or self-awareness | _____ |

FINAL SCORE _____

*Source:* Adapted from "The Influence of Recent Life Experiences on the Health of College Freshmen" by M. B. Marx, T. F. Garrity, and F. R. Bowers, 1975, *Journal of Psychosomatic Research 19,* p. 97. Copyright 1975 Pergamon Press plc. Reprinted with permission of publisher and authors.

tension that can be a stressor. There are many ways this might happen. In some cases, something about you yourself is standing between you and your goal. For example, you may be too shy to speak to the attractive person in your English class whom you would really like to know better.

At other times, external conditions block your goals and create frustration. You can't get promoted at work, for example, because the position to which you aspire is held by a young person who has been there only a short time. Or perhaps you have been trying to save money for a down payment on a home, but inflation always seems to be one step ahead of you. Sometimes a particular individual seems to be blocking your goal deliberately. For example, a professor will not give you work to make up for your poor performance on the first exam, and this means you can't possibly get an *A* in the course as you had planned.

Another way frustration can occur is when you can't get something you want because you can't find it, not because there is something in the way. Many people report being frustrated by an inability to find someone with whom they can have a meaningful relationship. Others know they want more from work than they are getting but are unable to figure out what kind of work and job would be more satisfying.

Source: *New Woman Magazine*, April 1985.

Finally, frustration can occur because you set unrealistic goals or push yourself too hard for perfection. You have decided to achieve a straight *A* average, and the first *B* convinces you that you will be a failure for life. You are going to have the perfect relationship or marriage, and the first problem that arises gives you the feeling that you have lost it all. Because you have set goals that you are not likely to be able to achieve, you have set yourself up for frustration. If your tolerance for this is low, you have added stressors to your life.

## Pressure

Another potential psychological stressor is perceived **pressure**—pressure to change, speed up, accomplish, or finish. The qualifier *perceived* is important here. Some people do not notice or respond to attempts from others to apply pressure. Most of us have known the student who does not react to parental pleas and threats to raise his or her grade point average. On the other hand, some people feel pressure when an observer would say none is being exerted. Another student, for example, might feel enormous pressure to do well because his or her parents are paying all of the college expenses.

The fact that our second student's parents are glad to pay for college and have never suggested that there is any sacrifice involved is not relevant to this discussion; the student *perceives* this state of affairs as pressure. Such differences in the perception of pressure are one of the ways in which people differ with regard to sensitivity to stressors.

Not all pressure results from the perception of demands from external events or conditions. Some originates from within the individual. Common sources of internal pressure are guilt, ambition, and insecurity. These feelings have the same effect as perceived external pressure; the individual experiences stress.

Personal relationships can be particularly potent sources of both internal and external pressure in your life. You want to be with people you care about and help them out if they need it, but friends have a way of needing help at inconvenient times and wanting things that create conflict for you. They may exert pressure deliberately to try to get you to do what they need or want, or, like the student in the example, you may feel these things simply because of the situation; you are a friend and friendship carries certain obligations.

Special relationships may create even more pressure in this way. In addition to perceived obligations toward the other person (whether he or she is demanding anything or not), such relationships can take so much time and energy that you get behind in other areas of your life. This adds pressure to speed up the pace so that you can do all that you must do and still have time for what you want to do—be with that special person.

## Summing Up ■

Stress upsets the status quo of your normal adapted state and makes demands on you to adapt to the new situation in some way. Some of the stressors that bring this about lie in the external environment; others stem from important changes and events that occur in your life. Some stressors, such as conflict, frustration, and pressure, are psychological in nature. They arise from the way you perceive and react to what is going on in your life.

A few stressors are physical; if you catch a bad cold, for example, you are likely to experience stress. This may be aggravated by pressure and frustration (psychological stressors); for example, the cold may keep you from doing some things you need to do so that you get behind in your schedule.

People differ in the extent to which they are sensitive to such stressors and in the ways they try to cope with them. There are, however, some common physical and psychological reactions to perceived stress.

## REACTIONS TO STRESSORS

In Figure 12-1 we see that now and again a stressor "gets to you" (points *a* and *b*). When this occurs, a number of things are likely to happen. In our opening story, you first had a physical reaction, then you raced off and attacked the task at hand with a high energy level. Finally, you burned out. This scenario is a typical one that first was described by pioneer stress researcher Hans Selye (1976).

### Physical Reactions: The General Adaptation Syndrome

Selye's studies of the physical changes that accompany stress led him to the conclusion that these changes follow a particular and common pattern, which he called the **general adaptation syndrome (GAS).** The GAS has three stages. The first is an *alarm stage*. Remember your first reaction to your biology pro-

People differ considerably in their reactions to potential stressors in the environment.

What does not destroy me, makes me strong.

*Friedrich Nietzsche*

fessor's announcement? Your heart began to beat faster and your palms began to perspire. There was a reason for this. In the alarm stage of the GAS your body is alerted to action to help you meet a challenge to your adapted state of well-being. This stage has been called the "fight-or-flight" stage; you do what you have to do to meet the challenge (such as study), or you run away from it (such as drop the course).

Among the physical changes that occur during the alarm stage are increased blood pressure and metabolism, the release of certain hormones, and cessation of digestive processes. In addition, the muscles tense up, the kidneys retain water, and the immune system shuts down. Your body has perceived a threat, and it has done what is necessary to enable you physically to meet the threat. In this case, you go to the library and put in a prolonged study session.

The second stage of GAS is called the *resistance stage*. You can think of this as a time during which you and your body try to adapt to the new state of affairs. In our example, this includes sitting in one place longer, concentrating harder, and going without food longer than is your usual practice in order to prepare for the test. During the resistance stage, your body works at high efficiency, but this pace can't last. If you have not managed to reduce or eliminate the perceived threat to your well-being before then, your body will enter the last phase. This is the *exhaustion stage*. In our example, you simply collapsed at some point and fell asleep.

One of the most interesting things Selye noticed about the general adaptation syndrome was that this reaction occurs whatever the cause. Much the same thing that happened to you over the test is likely to occur if you get a bad cold, lose your job, or stumble upon a poisonous snake while mowing the lawn. If you perceive the event as a threat, you will move into the GAS. Although recent and more sophisticated physiological research is leading scientists to believe that certain aspects of Selye's model will be modified in the future, it remains the baseline from which physical reactions to stress are studied.

## Stress and Illness

You probably have heard or read that stress makes you more susceptible to certain kinds of illnesses and diseases, such as heart disease, tuberculosis, allergies, and even cancer (Cooper, 1982). You may also have heard of (or experienced) various problems, such as ulcers, hives, asthma, and migraine headaches, that seem to be brought on by stress. These last health difficulties are called *psychophysiological* (formerly psychosomatic) problems. In both cases, many physicians believe that we are dealing to some degree with the effects of a prolonged GAS resistance stage.

Recall that the general adaptation syndrome involves substantial physical and physiological change. Muscles are tensed; if they are not relaxed, the result will be head or backaches. Fluid is retained, which can raise blood pressure if it lasts too long. Cessation of digestive processes will cause ulcers, constipation, and diarrhea eventually. Certain chemicals that are present in much higher doses than usual may damage organs or normal physiological functioning if the stress if prolonged. Shutdown of the immune system makes the body vulnerable to a variety of infections and diseases (which add more stress).

It isn't difficult to see how the same processes that allow you to fight when you encounter a threat to your well-being could make you ill if they are not utilized in the way they were intended. Prolonged or repeated stress with no release of the accompanying energy turns that energy inward. Although there is much we do not yet know about these matters, one thing is clear. Stress can make you ill, and if your ways of managing it are not effective, it is entirely possible that it can kill you (Engel, 1977). There is more on this in *Face of the Future*.

## Psychological Reactions

The general adaptation syndrome describes automatic physical and physiological reactions to stress. These are helpful in the short-term, but not so benefi-

## *FACE OF THE FUTURE:*
### Behavioral Immunology Opens New Avenues for Understanding Stress

A connection between stress and illnesses (such as colds) or diseases (such as cancer) has been a topic of discussion and speculation for many years. The body's efforts to cope with prolonged stress seem to wear down defenses, as Hans Selye observed more than 40 years ago. Selye, a pioneering stress researcher, noticed a reduction in immuno-system activities in response to prolonged exposure to physical stressors.

Your body's immune system is made up of billions of white blood cells, which are manufactured in the lymph system. These cells circulate throughout the bloodstream finding, neutralizing, and destroying antigens, such as viruses, tumors, and bacteria. Some of these cells, dubbed "natural killer" (NK) cells, can destroy directly and are believed to play an important role in the body's ability to ward off the spread of cancer.

**Behavioral immunology** is the study of the relationships between behavior and health. Recent studies in this field have found that exposing rats to an uncontrollable physical stressor reduces the ability of NK cells to kill tumor cells. Other studies with monkeys have revealed much the same effect when infant monkeys were separated from their parents, a stressor that is psychological rather than physical (see Maier & Laudenslager, 1985, for a review).

Animal studies have provided guidelines for researchers to explore the link between illness and stress in humans. Early results are extremely interesting. People who react to stress with anxiety and/or depression have reduced NK-cell activity; those who cope with stress without these reactions have immune systems that function even *more efficiently* than people who experience few life stressors.

The big question, of course, is how a purely psychological reaction, such as anxiety or depression, can produce changes in a purely physiological system. Researchers suspect a link with a group of brain chemicals that act on neurons (nerve cells) to reduce pain. Certain white blood cells are known to be equipped to receive these "natural opiates," and it is possible that this diminished sensitivity to pain also suppresses immune responses.

Scientists have chemicals that block brain opiate action. If anxiety and depression do indeed create physiological states that elicit the release of natural pain killers, it is possible that these chemicals can be used to prevent the associated impaired immune function. The face of the future may hold a whole new vista for the control of psychologically induced physical problems.

cial in the long term. Much the same is true of those psychological reactions to stress that we call defense mechanisms.

**Defense mechanisms** are psychological responses that cushion the blow when we experience stress. These reactions, most of which were first described by psychoanalyst Sigmund Freud (1959), are entirely normal and to a large degree unconscious. Some of the most common of these reactions are described in Exhibit 12–1.

As may be seen by the descriptions, defense mechanisms work through self-deception and distortion of reality. Most psychologists believe that this is not healthy in the long run, but it can serve as a temporary check on anxiety in the short run. Many people who have experienced the infidelity of a spouse, for example, report later that their initial reaction was one of denial. At first, they simply refused to admit that their husband or wife was involved with someone else; subconsciously, they were buying time to get used to the idea.

Obviously, denial is not going to be helpful in the long run because it blocks behaviors needed to deal with a situation. If carried to extremes, it can produce disorientation and severe psychological disturbance. Much the same can be said of the other defensive reactions listed in Exhibit 12–1. Most of us use these mechanisms from time to time to get us through. They are not coping mechanisms in any other sense, however.

Two psychological responses to stress that do appear to be positive coping mechanisms are displacement and ventilation. **Displacement** is channeling the emotional energy created by stress into a positive activity. For example, one woman found that visiting other patients in the nursing home where her mother had spent her last days helped her to deal with her grief over her mother's death. In trying to cheer others, she cheered herself.

**Ventilation** refers to verbally discharging the feelings that accompany stress. It is letting off steam in a fairly direct manner—talking, laughing, swearing, crying, or whatever it takes to work it through. This process can take a long time and may try the patience of friends and relatives sorely. Nevertheless, it is a mechanism for confronting, rather than hiding from or distorting, reality.

## Distress Versus Eustress

It is easy to get the impression from what we see and read about the subject that stress is not good for people and should be eliminated. This is not a completely accurate conclusion, however. The physical and psychological reactions to stress can have negative consequences; that is, they can cause *distress*. But stress creates some positive reactions as well as negative ones.

The central fact to remember about stress is that it creates energy. Distress results when this energy is not turned to positive purpose but is allowed to lead to exhaustion and defeat. But this same energy may be beneficial. For example, you may have found that the slight stress an upcoming exam creates helps you to "get up" for the exam. You can see now that there is a good reason for this. Stress mobilizes physical resources. If you can direct and control this energy, you can use it to your advantage. To put it another way, "It's O.K. to have butterflies in your stomach as long as they're all flying in formation" (Sizer & Whitney, 1988, p. 47).

Positive responses to stress are called *eustress* (pronounced "you-stress"). Some people become reliant on eustress to keep them energized. They adapt

## EXHIBIT 12–1 ████████████████████████████████
## Common Defense Mechanisms

**Denial:**  Reducing or eliminating a threat to well-being by refusing to acknowledge its existence
  *Example:* Not "seeing" the evidence that a wife or husband or other close partner is involved with someone else
  *Utility:* Protection from stress
  *Drawback:* Prevents or delays effective action

**Projection:**  Reducing stress by putting your own motives or responsibilities onto someone else
  *Example:* Accusing your best friend of being an alcoholic when he or she has several drinks because you are secretly afraid that you yourself are
  *Utility:* Puts any pressure that might result from your feelings or fears or lack of responsibility onto someone else
  *Drawback:* Prevents or delays effective action

**Fantasizing:**  A way of reducing stress by imagining things to be the way you want them to be instead of the way they are.
  *Example:* Reducing the stress of loneliness by fantasizing romance
  *Utility:* Serves as a pleasant escape from reality
  *Drawback:* Can become a substitute for real problem-solving efforts

**Intellectualization:**  Detaching yourself from involvement with a stressor by explaining it in intellectual, abstract terms
  *Example:* Becoming an expert on the clinical details of a disease that a loved one has contracted
  *Utility:* Can make it possible to keep on in the face of extremely stressful conditions
  *Drawback:* Can lead to reduced capacity to experience emotions if used habitually

**Regression:**  Escaping from a stressor by reverting to an earlier stage of development where less was expected of you
  *Example:* Going to the park for a softball game with the gang every night instead of studying for the upcoming bar exam
  *Utility:* Gives a temporary feeling that life is back under control
  *Drawback:* Prevents dealing with the stressors creating the need for escape

**Repression:**  Protecting yourself from the perception of *internal* stressors by suppressing them from consciousness (in much the same way that denial protects from *external* stressors)
  *Example:* "Remembering" only the events leading up to an automobile accident in which a friend was seriously injured and nothing about the accident itself (and your role in it)
  *Utility:* Repression is an effective way to reduce anxiety since the threatening stimulus has vanished from consciousness (although it is not forgotten).
  *Drawback:* Unlike the related response of intellectualization, repression does not allow for any effective action with regard to the source of stress. We cannot cope with what we do not see. This reaction is much like putting the whole problem into cold storage.

to the feelings of excitement and exhilaration that accompany stress and find it difficult to operate at a level most of the rest of us would call normal (Klausner, 1968). Such people have been called "Type T's" for *thrill seekers* (Farley, 1985).

Most of us are not thrill seekers, but by the same token, few of us would thrive in the complete absence of stress. Some level of stress keeps us energized and on our toes to meet both the ordinary and special challenges of life. What level? It is impossible to say what level of stress is good for you as an individual. One of the most consistent findings in the stress research is that people differ enormously in their reactions to stress.

## INDIVIDUAL AND SITUATIONAL DIFFERENCES IN REACTIONS TO STRESSORS

You know from your own observation and experience that there are considerable differences between people in the way they react to the presence of potential stressors. Noise offers a convenient example. Perhaps some of your friends work on their school assignments quite happily in the midst of pandemonium—the radio is on, the television is on, someone is talking on the telephone, and two people are having an argument about whose turn it is to wash the dishes. Others find such noise intolerable and feel enormous stress if they try to accomplish any studying under these conditions.

### Individual Factors Influencing Sensitivity to Stressors

If you are sensitive to noise when you study, you may find it difficult to understand how anyone can *not* notice and be bothered by these things. On the other hand, if such conditions don't bother you until they become really excessive, you may find yourself amazed that others can be so uptight. This difference is a difference in stress tolerance.

**Stress tolerance** is the amount of exposure to stressors you can tolerate before you experience stress. The thrill seekers have such a high level of tolerance that they seek out stress (but theoretically even they have a limit). For the rest of us, there are ample stressors available in the everyday nature of things, and a number of personal characteristics play a role in whether our tolerance for these is relatively high, medium, or low compared with that of other people.

#### Biological Factors

Although the processes are not very well understood at this time, it does appear that some people have a more "excitable" autonomic nervous system than others and so are more likely to experience stress in the presence of stressors than others (Eysenck, 1960). If you think you might be such a person, you may want to see your physician for information on how you might be tested for such sensitivity.

#### Personality

Research suggests that certain patterns of personality characteristics are associated with greater stress tolerance. Kobasa (1979), the psychologist who iden-

Any idiot can face a crisis—it's the day-to-day living that wears you out.
*Anton Chekhov*

Coping successfully with one stressful situation leaves you better prepared the next time you are exposed to stressors.

tified this pattern, calls it hardiness. The following characteristics describe Kobasa's **hardy personality**.

- He or she has a strong sense of commitment to some goal or goals. People who lack direction seem to be harder hit by stressors.
- He or she places a greater value on challenge than on security. Such people are more likely to see stressful events as an opportunity for constructive life changes.
- He or she has an internal locus of control (belief that the individual, not luck or chance, is primarily responsible for what happens). Such people feel more in control of their ability to cope with stress.

## Past Experience with Stress

Extremely stressful events that occur early in life seem to have long-lasting negative effects on stress tolerance. On the other hand, so does no experience at all with stressors. In general, it appears that experience in coping successfully with moderate stress is associated with greater stress tolerance (Weiten, 1986).

The relationship between the experience of past stress and current stress tolerance suggests that confidence in your ability to handle stress is an important factor in how much tolerance you have. The greater your confidence that you can handle such threats to your adjustment as they come along, the less likely you are to experience events and changes as stressful. To put it another way, your past experience affects your cognitive evaluation of a situation.

## Cognitive Evaluation of the Situation

People react to the same situations with an impressive variety of different responses and behaviors. This is because their reactions are based not so much on the "objective" facts of the situation as on their perception of what it means to them. Psychologists refer to this appraisal as the *cognitive evaluation* of the situation.

To return to our earlier example, we could speculate that your panic reaction to the changed test date was based on your evaluation of this situation as one of a kind that gives you trouble; you don't feel you work well under a short time deadline. To someone else who is used to doing everything at the last minute anyway, the professor's announcement may have resulted in little more than a brief "blip" on the day.

## Life Style

The way people live seems to play an important role in vulnerability to stress. Smoking, drinking, or eating to excess; getting too little sleep, exercise, or relaxation; and having limited social relationships and emotional outlets all seem to decrease stress tolerance. You may get an idea of the extent to which your life style helps to protect you from stress by answering the questions in *Test Yourself*.

---

## TEST YOURSELF:
## Life Style and Stress Tolerance

*Directions*: Answer each of the following questions on a scale of 1 (almost always) to 5 (never), according to how much of the time each statement is true of you.

|  |  | **Points** |
|---|---|---|
| 1. | I eat at least one hot, balanced meal a day. | _____ |
| 2. | I get 7 to 8 hours sleep at least four nights a week. | _____ |
| 3. | I give and receive affection regularly. | _____ |
| 4. | I have at least one relative within 50 miles on whom I can rely. | _____ |
| 5. | I exercise to the point of perspiration at least twice a week. | _____ |
| 6. | I smoke less than half a pack of cigarettes a day. | _____ |
| 7. | I take fewer than five alcoholic drinks a week. | _____ |
| 8. | I am the appropriate weight for my height. | _____ |
| 9. | I have an income adequate to meet basic expenses. | _____ |
| 10. | I get strength from my religious beliefs. | _____ |
| 11. | I regularly attend club or social activities. | _____ |
| 12. | I have a network of friends and acquaintances. | _____ |
| 13. | I have one or more friends to confide in about personal matters. | _____ |
| 14. | I am in good health (including eyesight, hearing, teeth). | _____ |
| 15. | I am able to speak openly about my feelings when angry or worried. | _____ |
| 16. | I have regular conversations with the people I live with about domestic problems (e.g., chores, money, and daily living issues). | _____ |
| 17. | I do something for fun at least once a week. | _____ |

18.   I am able to organize my time effectively.                                          _____

19.   I drink fewer than three cups of coffee (or tea or cola) a day.       _____

20.   I take quiet time for myself during the day.                               _____

TOTAL POINTS   _____

Subtract 20       _____

FINAL SCORE     _____

Your total "stress audit" score is obtained by adding up your individual scores and subtracting 20. Your life style is not having a negative effect on your stress tolerance if your score is below 30. If it is between 50 and 75, you are not doing all you can for yourself to help reduce your vulnerability to stress, and you may want to consider some fine tuning. The behaviors on this questionnaire help increase stress tolerance through basic physical and emotional health and fitness; if your score is over 75, you may want to consider some substantial changes.

**Source:** "Vulnerability Scale" from the *Stress Audit*, developed by Lyle H. Miller and Alma Dell Smith. Copyright ©1983, Biobehavioral Associates, Brookline, MA 02146. Reprinted with permission.

# Situational Factors Influencing Sensitivity to Stressors

The fact that there are significant individual differences in stress tolerance does not mean that the situation plays no role in the way people react. The severity of a stressor is an important factor, and stressful situations differ in their severity, depending upon the nature, number, duration, and predictability of the stressors involved.

## Nature of the Stressor

You will remember that stressors are all around us and within us as well (frustration, for example). Some of these create stress for almost everybody, whatever the individual stress tolerance. Divorce is one example. Some people cope with this more effectively than others, but it is an event requiring a major adjustment of practically everyone.

## Number of Stressors

We've all had "those days" when everything seems to go wrong. A week of such events, even if each alone is a small thing, can leave you frazzled and exhausted with trying to cope. Stressors appear to be cumulative; life's little hassles add up and it often is something very small that is the proverbial "last straw." You might cope effectively all term with a demanding class schedule, a difficult personal relationship, and a part-time job you don't like very much. Then one day, to your astonishment, you find yourself in a rage over a broken zipper in your tennis shorts.

## Duration of the Stressor

It is said that one measure of pain is how long it lasts, and this appears to be true of stressors as well. Any stressor that drags on can make stress more severe. For example, it probably would be more stressful for you to go all term wondering if you are going to pass a particular course that you need to graduate than it would be to find out early on that you were not going to. Prolonged uncertainty about something that is very important is highly stressful to most people.

### Predictability of the Stressor

Research also tells us stress is more severe when a stressor is unexpected than when we know it is coming. This seems to be true even if there is nothing at all we can do to prevent an event from occurring. In one well-known study, for example, it was found that unpleasant noise did not have a detrimental effect on task performance when subjects were expecting it (Glass, Singer, & Friedman, 1969). By contrast, those subjects who did not know when the noise was coming experienced frustration that interfered with their performance of the experimental task (proofreading some written work).

**Summing Up** ■

We have seen that there are important differences between people in their susceptibility to stressors. Biological functioning, personality, past experience, and life style are among the factors creating such differences. Stressors themselves also differ in severity, and this severity affects the way people react. In general, major changes in life, multiple stressors, those that last longer, and those that are not anticipated create more severe stress. We turn now from our discussion about stress to a discussion of some ways of dealing with stress.

## STRESS MANAGEMENT

Potential stressors are all around you, and that state we call stress is created when one or more of these impinges on your life to the point of upsetting your balance and requiring that you make some adjustment. There are basically five alternatives for accomplishing this adjustment. These are described in Exhibit 12–2.

As the term will be used in this chapter, **effective stress management** is a matter of finding ways to adjust to stress that reduce and/or eliminate discomfort when it occurs and help you control the extent to which you experience stress in the future. Of the five alternatives in Exhibit 12–2, only the first three have the potential for meeting these twin goals. Escaping the situation often is not practical and in any event does nothing for your future ability to handle stressors. Ignoring the situation may allow you to keep going under pressure for a time, but it does not qualify as effective stress management in any other sense.

In this section ways to change the situation, the appraisal of the situation, and the response to the situation that have been found to be effective in managing stress are examined. Cognitive strategies are ways to change your appraisal of the situation. Behavioral strategies include ways to change the situation and/or your response to the situation.

## EXHIBIT 12–2 ███████████████████████
## Basic Alternatives for Adjusting to Stress

**Change the Situation**

*Example:* Drop a course that is causing you too much difficulty.

**Change Your Appraisal of the Situation**

*Example:* Decide that it is okay to weigh five pounds more than your "ideal" weight.

**Change Your Response to the Situation**

*Example:* Work off your feelings about your unpleasant boss by playing tennis in the evenings instead of fretting and stewing and thinking of ways to get even.

**Escape from the Situation**

*Example:* Move out of the house you share with three other students to get away from the stressful noise and mess.

**Ignore the Situation**

*Example:* Take no steps to prepare for the upcoming graduate school entry test that will determine whether or not you get into the program you want.

# Cognitive Strategies for Managing Stress

**Cognitive strategies for managing stress** are ways to control both potential and experienced stress through the way you think about situations and the way you talk to yourself. Three such strategies that work for many people are evaluating the situation, controlling irrational self-talk, and making positive coping self-statements.

## Evaluating the Situation

The general adaptation syndrome is a set of automatic physical responses to a situation perceived as stressful. It is not based on a rational assessment of the way things really are. So a first step in managing stress effectively is to train yourself to think before you act. Try to evaluate the nature and extent of the perceived threat rationally. For example, you might have spared yourself an eventual collapse over your biology books if you had taken time to think about the situation.

If you had taken time to think, you might have realized that moving the test date up meant that two chapters now had been eliminated from the test material. So even though you had to study now instead of next week, you had less material to cover. In addition, you might have figured out that getting this test out of the way early was going to give you a free weekend to work on your English literature paper, so you really were coming out ahead.

A useful tool in assessing a situation rationally when you feel under stress is to train yourself to avoid oversimplification (Kelly, 1955). Explore the various sides of the situation and see if it fits into your former experience. For example, you may never have taken biology before, but you did have a lot of trouble with algebra in high school. So your trouble with biology isn't necessarily because the subject is an impossibly hard one that you will never master (an oversimplification). You eventually found a way to study for algebra that

> In times like these, it helps to remember that there have always been times like these.
>
> *Paul Harvey*

was effective, and you probably will succeed if you take the same basic approach to biology.

## Controlling Irrational Self-Talk

One of the the more striking effects of stress is the way it can make us forget our normal good sense. When you are experiencing stress, things get out of proportion and you see one disaster after another looming on the horizon. Your girlfriend breaks a date to study for a final exam, and suddenly you envision her marrying a guy you saw her talking to in the library. Your car starts making a funny noise, and the next think you know, the noise is fatal and the car can't be fixed, you have to drop out of school because you can't keep your part-time job to pay the tuition without a car, you drift from job to job, you are so demoralized you begin to drink heavily. . .

This sort of irrational self-talk is called **catastrophizing.** Its effect usually is to set off yet another stress alarm reaction since catastrophizing affects your cognitive evaluation of a situation. It is rather like saying to yourself; "Good grief, if I am this upset about things, the situation must be serious!"

To some extent, merely being aware that magnification of events far beyond their logical meaning is irrational helps to control the tendency. But being aware that you are being irrational does not necessarily help you to stop being so once you have begun. One approach to controlling catastrophizing when it occurs is to train yourself to think thoughts that are incompatible with the runaway thoughts.

Countering catastrophizing with incompatible thoughts is a suggestion made by Meichenbaum (1976) to lower the physiological arousal level associated with stress. To do this, you counter every irrational thought with one that

Evaluating the situation objectively before panicking helps to reduce the experience of stress.

is rational. For example, every time you think, "I can't stand this one more minute" (which, of course, isn't true), you counter with, "This is pretty bad, but I'm surviving and nothing lasts forever." It is important to do this consciously and systematically; say the counterthought out loud if you can bring yourself to do so. Your ears as well as your mind will help to impress the thought upon you.

## Making Positive Coping Self-Statements

Meichenbaum and his colleagues have applied the basic ideas of using self-talk to counter the irrational thinking that can accompany stress to a more comprehensive approach to stress management. They suggest that the way you talk to yourself can affect the way you prepare for a stressor, confront it, cope with your feelings about it, and use the experience to make future adjustment easier. Some specific examples are shown in Exhibit 12–3.

# Behavioral Strategies for Managing Stress

Research on stress makes it clear that feeling in control (or potentially in control) of the situation is one of the most important aspects of effective stress management (*Journal of Personality and Social Psychology*, 1984). When you have control, you know that things will not get out of hand. There is action you can take to prevent this from happening.

---

**EXHIBIT 12–3**

## Positive Talking Your Way Through Stressful Events

**Preparing for a Stressor**
> What is it I have to do?
> I can develop a plan to deal with it.
> Don't worry. Worry won't help anything.

**Confronting and Handling a Stressor**
> I can meet this challenge.
> One step at a time; I can handle the situation.
> Don't think about fear—just about what I have to do. Stay relevant.

**Coping with the Feeling of Being Overwhelmed**
> Keep focus on the present; what is it I have to do?
> It will be over shortly.
> It's not the worst thing that can happen.
> Just think about something else.

**Reinforcing Self-Statements**
> It worked; I was able to do it.
> It wasn't as bad as I expected.
> My damn ideas—that's the problem. When I control them, I control my fear.

---

*Note:* From ''The Clinical Potential of Modifying What Clients Say to Themselves. by D. H. Meichenbaum and R. Cameron, 1974, in M. J. Mahoney and C. E. Thorensen (Eds.), *Self-control: Power to the Person.* Monterey, CA: Brooks/Cole.

When you don't see anything you can do to exercise some control over a situation that affects you in some way, you are likely to feel angry, incompetent, and helpless. Cognitive strategies help you to avoid this by achieving control over what is going on in your head. **Behavioral strategies for managing stress** can help in this way as well. They also give you control over what is going on outside your head—over your body, your behavior, and, to some extent, the behavior of others. Three such strategies are reviewed here: exercise, time management, and assertiveness.

## Exercise and Stress

It is hard to pick up a newspaper or magazine these days without seeing an article on reducing stress. And no matter what other recommendations are made, somewhere in the list will be "regular exercise." Opinions vary somewhat, but the consensus seems to be that regular means at least three times a week for at least 30 minutes at a time (e.g., Mirkin, 1983).

If you are not physically active, you may wonder if exercise isn't overrated. Those who make it part of their lives will tell you in no uncertain terms that it is not. The following are some of the stress-management benefits they find in activities such as jogging, tennis, swimming, aerobics, or simple walking.

- *Exercise increases energy.* Other things being equal, the better shape you are in physically, the better you will be able to tolerate stressors and manage stress. Feeling tired or just "out of steam" makes everything look worse.

- *Exercise decreases fatigue.* In addition to raising your general energy level, exercise can have almost miraculous restorative powers when you do run short. It is particularly effective when your fatigue stems from nonphysical activities, such as wrestling with a complex problem or dealing with difficult people.

- *Exercise make you look better.* Dissatisfaction with the way they look is a chronic stressor for many people, and their failure to do anything about it adds to the problem. Regular exercise pays off very quickly, both physically and psychologically; sticking to it is constant proof to yourself that you do indeed have control over your life.

- *Exercise has a positive effect on your life style.* One of the unexpected benefits frequently reported by people who take up exercise is that drinking, smoking, and overeating seem to lose their appeal. Since giving up smoking, eating sensibly, and drinking in moderation improve your health, your ability to manage stress is improved. And the good feelings that go along with being healthy and in control also may increase your basic stress tolerance.

- *Exercise has long-term effects on health.* Regular exercise increases stamina and flexibility and may be important in warding off cardiovascular disease and skeletal-muscular problems. It also may help to slow what long has been considered a natural aging process; some believe that the physical symptoms we often attribute to getting older actually are the result of progressive disuse of our bodies (Maloney, 1984).

These benefits of exercise are broad ranging and cumulative; the longer you have made exercise a part of your life, the more you will benefit. But exercise also has short-term stress-management benefits because it allows you to work off the energy generated by the general adaptation syndrome the way nature intended—physically. Exercise helps you get rid of it before it has a chance to exhaust you or make you ill.

There aren't any rules for choosing an exercise program that will do all of these wonderful things. The one that is best for you is the one that you will stick with because you enjoy it. Many people find that trying out what their friends are doing is a good way to get acquainted with the possibilities. Two cautions are in order here, however.

1. If you have been a real nonexerciser, see a physician for a general physical examination before you begin and start slowly. A 15-minute walk every evening is a good and safe way for "couch potatoes" to work into an exercise program (Brandon, 1985).

2. The stress-management benefits of exercise are dramatically reduced if you become a goal-oriented fanatic about it. Pushing yourself to run farther, jump higher, swim more laps, or get through a longer aerobics routine each week may add to, rather than reduce, the stress you feel (although, to a point, you will still get some of the physical benefits). Unfortunately, many people seem to have become hooked in this way. There is more on this in *For Discussion*.

# FOR DISCUSSION:
## THE UPS AND DOWNS OF EXERCISE

The most visible evidence of America's craze for physical fitness is the jogger whom we meet on tracks, in parks, on crowded city streets, at the beach, in the suburbs—almost anywhere there is space to put one foot in front of the other. Despite this visibility, jogging actually lags well behind swimming, bicycling, and body building in popularity. Tennis, aerobic dancing, and roller skating also attract millions of participants. Business organizations are supporting this trend. General Electric of Fairfield, Connecticut, for example, gives its employees free exercise equipment and offers them t-shirts, shorts, socks, towels, and a laundry service.

Is all of this exercise good for you? The answer to that question depends to some extent upon whom you ask. Participants in these activities be-

lieve it not only is good, it also is essential to their fitness, health, and psychological well-being. Others are not so sure. They point out that "weekend athletes" trying to do it all in 2 days account for an increasing number of hospital emergency room cases.

At the other end of the spectrum, critics of the fitness craze note that exercise has become an obsession with many people who work out far beyond reasonable standards for nonprofessional atheletes (e.g., Hathaway, 1984). And one psychologist has found some evidence that jogging, one of the most abused forms of exercise, reduces sexual desire and activity (Blotnick, 1985). Do you know anyone who seems to be obsessed with exercise for the sake of exercise? What do you think might be some of the more important personal and environ-

mental factors producing this behavior?

It also is clear that physical fitness has become something more than exercise where many people are concerned. On television, lithe young women taking part in make-believe aerobics classes in revealing clothing pedal everything from soap to soft drinks. Men spying on these same classes have become a standard gag in the movies. Health clubs are said to be the new singles bars. Is all of this cause for concern? Some say no; others believe that the whole point of exercise—taking care of your body—has become lost in yet another form of obsession with sex. What do you think? Have you had any relevant experiences to share with the class? Where do you see all of this heading? Do you think it helps or hurts the physical fitness cause?

## Time-Management Skills

The one resource we all have the same amount of is time. Rich, poor, successful, down-and-out, whatever, everyone gets 24 hours in a day. But you know from your own experience that some people seem to do a lot more with it than others; many people seem to be perpetually behind. Perhaps you are in this last group. If so, you know that not having enough time makes you feel pressured.

Because not having enough time can create pressure and pressure can lead to stress, one effective stress-management technique for many people is to develop better time-management skills. These skills not only take the pressure off but also increase your sense of control and so increase your tolerance for future stressors. The steps to this control are (1) to identify and eliminate time wasters, (2) to identify and eliminate strategic errors in time use, and (3) to plan your time.

## Identify Time Wasters

Time-management experts often recommend that you get in the habit of making a "do list" of things that you need to accomplish each day (e.g., Minninger, 1984), but many people find that they seem to end up copying the same list over day after day. There just doesn't seem to be time to get to the items on the list. What are they doing instead?

In many cases, what they are doing instead of what they need to do or want to do is wasting time. Wasted time is time spent in activities that are both unenjoyable and inefficient/nonproductive. Each of us has our own ways of doing this, but some common time wasters are listed in Exhibit 12–4.

## Identify Strategic Errors

The second step to effective time management is learning to identify any strategic errors you may be making in the way you use your time. Strategic errors are errors in your basic approach to time use that stem from counterproductive assumptions. The two most common such errors are "It's got to be perfect," and "If you want something done right, do it yourself."

Consider two students, Dale and Joey. Dale plays "It's got to be perfect" and types and retypes every paper until there not only are no errors, there are no noticeable corrections. This makes for beautiful papers at the cost of many hours that could be put to other uses. Joey plays "If you want something done right, do it yourself" and is unable to let someone else take over the simplest task for fear it won't be done right. So Joey does the housework and the cooking and the shopping and the laundering in addition to holding a part-time job and being a full-time student.

Maybe you aren't a perfectionist, but a softie. "I can't say no" is another strategic error many make in their use of time. Do you find yourself helping a friend clean the garage on Saturday when what you had planned to do was catch up on some chores at home? Are you typing your son's paper because he didn't do it earlier and would have to miss a planned social event to do it now?

Breaking these time-wasting strategies is simpler than you might think. Ask yourself the question: What will happen if I don't do this right now?

## EXHIBIT 12–4
## Wasting Time: Recognize Yourself?

**Deciding what to wear:** The amount of time many of us waste in this activity is astonishing. We stand and stare at the closet, put on and take off half a dozen different things, or search frantically for the right shirt or a pair of stockings with no runs. If you are in this group, start planning ahead. Decide what to wear to work the night before. Check your wardrobe several days before a special event to make sure what you want is clean and in good repair.

**Worrying:** There is very little in life that is as great a waste of time as worrying. To the extent you can, follow the maxim "Don't worry—do." Even if doing won't fix what you are worried about, it will accomplish something. So instead of sitting and worrying about your appointment with the dentist tomorrow, clean the kitchen or write to your mother.

**Hunting for things:** Another biggie on the hit parade of time wasters is hunting for things—hunting for your car keys, the scissors, the notes you took at the library, or your other brown shoe. If you spend much of your time hunting, clean up your act. Clutter is fine if it doesn't bother you (or those you live with) or get in your way. If it is taking over your life, get rid of it!

**Reinventing the wheel:** Do you make three trips to the grocery store to get what you need to make one meal? When it is over, do you put the rinsed dishes in the sink and then rinse them again several hours later to put them in the dishwasher? Do you leave the permanent press clothes in the dryer until they have become so wrinkled that you have to iron them? All of these things fall into the category of reinventing the wheel—time-wasting and totally unnecessary duplications of effort.

Then, try a harder question: "What will happen if I don't do this at all?" If you answer yourself honestly, you will be surprised at how many times the answer is *nothing*. Sometimes the key to regaining control over your own time is as simple as realizing that it *is* your own time.

## Plan Your Time

When you stop wasting time doing things that don't get you anywhere, that you don't have to do, or that you don't have to do to perfection, you have some of those precious 24 hours to put to other purposes. The secret to using time management to help control stress is to use these and other hours to advantage so that you have time both for the things you must do and for the things you want to do.

Most people today live very busy lives, and we find it difficult even to remember everything that we are supposed to do without some kind of help. For some people, the "do list" mentioned earlier is sufficient. This is a running list of tasks to be accomplished in a particular day, week, or month. When you finish the task, you scratch it off the list, and many people find a small reward in watching this list grow shorter (before you laugh, try it yourself).

Other people need more help than a simple list of tasks. Some have very tight schedules with many appointments at specific times; other tasks must be fitted in between these set obligations. Some just don't have a feel for scheduling; they can't do it automatically in their heads as others can. People like these can benefit enormously from a *time budget*.

A time budget, like a money budget, allocates resources (i.e., time not sleeping) to various activities in such a fashion that there is enough for both obligations and enjoyment. One way to do such a budget is shown in Exhibit 12–5. As you see, you begin with a grid showing days across the top and waking time periods along the side. Most people find that a week is about the right period of time to include on this grid.

The first information that goes into the grid is those tasks or activities that you do regularly every day, such as eating, showering, and studying. Follow these entries with any set obligations, such as class attendance or work, that you may have (be sure to allow for travel time). Next add things you do at least once every week. If you don't have a regular time period for these, now is a good time to schedule one. Examples include doing the laundry, exercising, calling your parents, and buying groceries. You also might want to schedule in television programs that you especially enjoy.

Now, you have your basic time budget. To it, you add items from an ongoing list of things that you must do sometime fairly soon (say in the next 30 days), but not necessarily this week or at any particular time. Examples include having the car inspected, buying some new athletic shoes, checking out samples for the new carpet in the family room, beginning the research for the end-of-term project, and so on. You should try to balance these tasks so that you get some accomplished each day or week but still have blocks of leisure time available.

If you are new to scheduling your time, you may find that your first few efforts don't work very well. A common mistake is over scheduling yourself. Remember that your goal is to control your time, not the other way around. You wouldn't sit and make a deliberate plan to spend every penny of your income; you'd want some savings and some "slush" for unexpected emergencies or treats. The same principle applies with a time budget. You want to

## EXHIBIT 12–5
## Sample Time Budget

|  | Friday | Saturday |
|---|---|---|
| 7–8 a.m. | Up, shower, eat | |
| 8–9 a.m. | Study | Up, shower, eat |
| 9–10 a.m. | Study ↓ | Run vacuum, dust |
| 10–11 a.m. | Psychology class | Racquetball with Jo |
| 11–12 a.m. | ↓ | |
| 12–1 a.m. | Lunch with Marc | Home, lunch, call Mom |
| 1–2 p.m. | Work | Begin history paper |
| 2–3 p.m. | | |
| 3–4 p.m. | | Mall to pick up suit |
| 4–5 p.m. | | |
| 5–6 p.m. | ↓ | |
| 6–7 p.m. | Home, read mail | |
| 7–8 p.m. | Change, pick up Pat | Party at Sam's (7:30) |
| 8–9 p.m. | Dinner—library to work | |
| 9–10 p.m. | on paper | |
| 10–11 p.m. | | |
| 11–12 p.m. | ↓ | ↓ |

have time to do what you must do with some left over to do what you want to do and/or those things that come up unexpectedly (or occasionally, time to do nothing at all).

## Assertiveness and Stress

We come now to have very different behavioral strategy for managing stress and one that many people find more difficult than either exercise or time management. As noted in Chapter 10, assertive behavior is behavior that allows you to express your personal opinions or feelings or helps you accomplish your goals in spite of the disagreement or opposition of others. It is a major weapon against the stress that can be created by frustration and even pressure, if the pressure is being unfairly applied by another person.

When it comes to managing stress, the power of assertiveness lies in the control it gives you. Assertiveness allows you to put yourself in the driver's seat when others are infringing on your rights, pestering you with unwanted attentions or communications, or ignoring you when it is their role to assist you. So long as you feel you must suffer these actions in silence, you feel like a victim; and this can create frustration, which is a stressor.

A natural response to these situations is aggressiveness—verbal or physical hostility toward others. This seldom gets you what you want, it makes you look bad to others or yourself ("I'm as bad as he is"), and it does nothing to help you deal with such situations in the future. These factors are more likely to increase stress than to decrease it. Assertiveness, by contrast, often gets you what you want, impresses others and yourself with your confidence and self-control, and develops your confidence in your ability to handle such situations in the future.

If assertiveness is such a positive thing, why is it so difficult for so many people? The answer lies partly in the way most of us are raised, or socialized. We are taught at home, in school, and at church to respect the individual and be polite to others, even if they are not being polite to us. So strong are these values for many people that they will put up with all kinds of intrusive or inconsiderate behaviors from others rather than be thought rude. Think, for example, of some of the personal questions that people you have never seen before have asked you when they were your seatmates on buses, airplanes, or trains. If you are like most of us, you probably found yourself answering them.

Another part of the difficulty many of us have with being assertive is that doing so often requires violating a powerful social norm: Don't make a scene in public. Many people will put up with almost anything rather than be the center of attention in a restaurant, movie theater, line, or other public place by confronting another person about his or her behavior. This norm tends to be particularly strong in adolescence and young adulthood, the time when assertiveness skills first might be developed. As a result, many people find themselves not knowing what to do even if they have overcome their reluctance to make a scene.

Finally, some people shrink from assertiveness out of fear. This is not altogether irrational. People who will blatantly ignore your rights for their own benefit are people who are less well socialized than most of us. They don't share your respect for the individual or the value you place on politeness, and they do not feel bound by the same social norms. Such people can indeed be

Learning to be assertive is a valuable tool in your stress management repertoire.

frightening, and the better part of valor in some situations is just to get out of the way.

As a general rule, however, most assertiveness situations are not dangerous. The salesperson you tell to stop harassing you is not going to wait for you in the alley. The server who is giving you poor service is not going to poison your soup if you point out that this will affect his or her tip. The woman who pushes ahead of you at the airline ticket counter is not going to beat you up if you object. Learning to appraise such situations rationally is part of being effectively assertive.

## Other Resources for Managing Stress

Three approaches to managing stress that are effective for most people and that almost anyone—regardless of age, financial situation, or life situation—can use have been discussed. In addition to these stress-management techniques, certain other resources, if they are available, also may help reduce perceived stress or manage that which occurs.

- If you have a strong *social support network* of family and friends, you may find stressors easier to tolerate and stress easier to manage (Holahan & Moos, 1985).

- *Adequate financial resources* also help; not having enough money is a stressor in and of itself.

- Finally, *activity* seems to be an important stress-management tool. Work, school, sports, volunteer work, social activities, and so on can be stressors, but most people find having nothing to do even more stressful (e.g., Vigderhous & Fishman, 1978).

Other techniques for dealing with stress include biofeedback, meditation, and systematic desensitization. Unlike the techniques we have discussed, these methods seem to be effective with some people and not with others. In addition, each requires the assistance of someone trained in the technique, and it may be necessary to pay for this assistance.

**Summing Up** ■

Managing stress effectively has two aspects: one is to help you now, one is to help you in the future. Part of the secret for accomplishing this dual purpose lies in how you think about a stressful situation. Learning to evaluate it before panicking, to control irrational thoughts and ideas, and to make an effort to talk positively to yourself about your ability to handle things are all important.

Of course, how you think about stress is only part of the story. What you do also is important. Among the stress-management techniques that have been found to be effective for most people are engaging in physical exercise, gaining control of time, and learning to be appropriately assertive. All of these approaches are based on the concept of personal control, which is coming increasingly to look like the key to the whole question of why stress incapacitates some people, makes others ill, and serves as an energizer to still others.

## ■ *KEY WORDS AND PHRASES*

adapted state

assertiveness and stress

behavioral immunology

behavioral strategies for managing
    stress

catastrophizing

cognitive strategies for managing
    stress

defense mechanisms

displacement

effective stress management

exercise and stress

hardy personality

frustration

general adaptation syndrome (GAS)

pressure

stress

stressors

stress tolerance

time budget

time-management skills

ventilation

## ■ *READ ON*

*Your Perfect Right: A Guide to Assertive Behavior* (5th ed.) by R. E. Alberti and M. L. Emmonds. St. Luis Obispo, CA: Impact, 1986. Do you have difficulty asking for what you want? Do you find it impossible to say no to people who are soliciting money? Will you eat a poor meal rather than complain? The authors offer a practical program for learning to deal with such situations without stepping on the rights of others.

*Stress Breakers* by H. Lerner and R. Elins. New York: CompCare Publications, 1985. Some interesting and creative ways to go about breaking out of patterns that create the ex-

perience of stress. Examples include making a "worry list," planning ahead for insomnia, and talking to your favorite animal.

*Stress without Distress* by H. Seyle, M.D. New York: Harper & Row, 1976. Dr. Seyle's book, *The Stress of Life* (McGraw-Hill, 1956) is probably the most influential book ever written about stress, but it is highly technical and difficult for the nonprofessional to read. *Stress without Distress* is for the rest of us, a guide by this pioneer stress researcher to understanding the general adaptation syndrome and mobilizing it to our advantage rather than our disadvantage.

## ■ REFERENCES

Blotnick, S. (1985, June 17). Joggers are lousy lovers. *Forbes*, 222–223.

Brandon, B. (1985, April). Stress—the energy buster. *Essence*, 66–67.

Cooper, C. L. (1982). Psychosocial stress and cancer. *Bulletin of the British Psychological Society, 35,* 456–459.

DeLongis, A., Coyne, J. C., Dakot, G., Folkman, S., & Lazarus, R. S. (1982). Relationships of daily hassles, uplifts, and major life events to health status. *Health Psychology, 1,* 119–136.

Engel, G. (1977). Emotional death and sudden death. *Psychology Today, 11,* 114–115.

Eysenck, H. (1960). Classification and the problems of diagnosis. In Author (Ed.), *Handbook of abnormal psychology*. New York: Basic Books.

Farley, F. (1985, April 15) As reported by B. Leo, Looking for a life of thrills. *Time*, 92–93.

Freud, S. (1959). *Collected papers: Vols. 1–5*. New York: Basic Books.

Glass, D. C., Singer, S. E., & Friedman, L. N. (1969). Psychic costs of adaptation to an environmental stressor. *Journal of Personality and Social Psychology, 12,* 200–210.

Hathaway, B. (1984). Running to ruin. *Psychology Today, 18,* 14–15.

Holahan, C. J., & Moos, R. H. (1985). Life stress and health: Personality, coping, and family support in stress resistance. *Journal of Personality and Social Psychology, 49,* 739–747.

*Journal of Personality and Social Psychology*. (1984). *46,* Whole.

Kelly, G. A. (1955). *The psychology of personal constructs* (Vols. 1 and 2). New York: Norton.

Klausner, S. Z. (Ed.) (1968). *Why man takes chances: Studies in stress seeking*. New York: Doubleday.

Kobasa, S. C. (1979). Stressful life events, personality, and health: An inquiry into hardiness. *Journal of Personality and Social Psychology, 37,* 1–11.

Lazarus, R. S., DeLongis, A., Folkman, S., & Gruen, R. (1985). Stress and adaptational outcomes: The problem of confounded measures. *American Psychologist, 90,* 770–779.

Maier, S. F., & Laudenslager, M. (1985). Stress and health: Exploring the links. *Psychology Today, 19,* 44–49.

Maloney, L. D. (1984, Aug. 13). Sports-crazy Americans. *U.S. News & World Report*, 23–24.

Meichenbaum, D. (1976). Toward a cognitive theory of self-control. In G. Schwartz and D. Shapiro (Eds.), *Consciousness and self-regulation: Advances in research*. New York: Plenum.

Minninger, J. (1984). *Total recall*. Esmaus, PA: Rodale.

Mirkin, G. (1983). *Getting thin*. Boston: Little, Brown.

Selye, H. (1976). *The Stress of life*. New York: McGraw-Hill.

Sizer, F. S., & Whitney, E. N. (1988). *Life choices: Health concepts and strategies*. St. Paul, MN: West.

Stern, G. S., McCants, T. R., & Pettine, P. W. (1982). Stress and illness: Controllable and uncontrollable life events' relative contributions. *Personality and Social Psychology Bulletin, 8,* 140–145.

Vigderhous, G., & Fishman, G. (1978). The impact of unemployment and familial integration on changing suicide rates in the U.S.A., 1920–1969. *Social Psychiatry, 13,* 239–248.

Weiten, W. (1986). *Psychology applied to modern life* (2nd ed.). Monterey, CA: Brooks/Cole.

# Problems That Block Effective Behavior

In Part 4 of *Psychology and Effective Behavior*, we examined three basic skills that everyone needs to manage their lives effectively. But many people have special problems that make their behavior less than effective, and these special problems require additional understanding, skills, and, perhaps, special help as well.

In Chapter 13 of Part 5, some of the problems people have with controlling and managing their own behavior on a day-to-day basis are examined. Two areas in which control breaks down for many are weight control and the use of potentially addictive substances.

In Chapter 14 the focus shifts from problems people have with themselves to problems they have in their relationships with others. Social pressure, loneliness, and the breakup of intimate relationships are three common problems in this sphere of life. Chapter 15 is focused not on behavioral or social problems, but on depression and anxiety, more pervasive emotional and psychological difficulties.

# Behavior-
# Management
# Problems

**D**o you reach automatically for a cigarette if you wake up in the middle of the night and then wish you hadn't because it tastes so awful? Do you drink more at parties than you really want to? Have you been watching your weight gradually creep up year by year without seeming to be able to stop it? Problems like these are examples of ineffective behavior management, failures to meet our own standards and expectations for ourselves.

In this chapter the facts about eating habits, weight control, and the use of addictive substances, such as tobacco, alcohol, and other drugs, are examined. Then, some of the reasons people have problems in these areas and some of the alternatives for dealing with them are considered.

## THE USE OF ADDICTIVE SUBSTANCES

The word *addiction* means being devoted to a behavior to such an extent that breaking it causes physical symptoms (physical addiction) and/or stress, discomfort, or anxiety (psychological addiction). An **addictive substance** is any substance that has the potential for creating physical or psychological addiction. Such substances include tobacco, caffeine, alcohol, and a wide range of substances more commonly called drugs.

### Tobacco

About three fourths of all Americans have never smoked or have stopped smoking cigarettes. Still, this leaves over 50 million people puffing away. In 1984 they purchased some 600 *billion* cigarettes despite the extensive publicity about the dangers of smoking. Why do they (and perhaps, you) keep smoking? In this section we look at the facts about smoking cigarettes, the most common reasons that people give for continuing to smoke, and what seems to be involved in breaking the habit.

## The Facts

Many biological factors and life-style variables can be involved when a person becomes ill, and often it is impossible to say that one particular factor caused the illness. Nevertheless, some 90% of the studies carried out since the 1950s confirm that smokers run a higher risk of certain diseases than nonsmokers, and it is estimated that some 340,000 Americans a year die prematurely because they smoke (Mervis, 1985). Among the leading smoking-related diseases are lung cancer, heart disease, bronchitis, pneumonia, and emphysema, but smoking also affects many other organs and functions; for example, it

- Increases the risk of ulcers
- Suppresses immunity to infections
- Increases the body's tolerance for medication
- Reduces the oxygen supply to the brain
- Causes progressive hearing loss at low frequencies
- Interferes with estrogen production
- Increases the risk of sinus infection
- Interferes with normal sleep
- Suppresses the appetite for carbohydrates
- Reduces blood circulation to the hands and feet.

The health problems that can be created by smoking cigarettes aren't surprising from a physical point of view. Tobacco smoke contains a host of harmful ingredients including nicotine, tars (hydrocarbons), and carbon monoxide. *Nicotine* is one of the deadliest poisons known to medical science. Tars, similar to the tars used on roads, are well-known cancer-producing agents (*carcinogens*). Carbon monoxide is a waste product that can kill all by itself in concentrated dosages. Researchers also have found evidence that all of these substances may cause permanent genetic changes in human cells (*Science '86*, 1986).

In addition to its connection with various diseases, smoking cigarettes gives many people other health and appearance problems. Cigarette smokers may experience nausea, diarrhea, clammy skin, shortness of breath, and poor circulation. Smoking yellows teeth and causes bad breath, and dentists say it increases susceptibility to gum disease. Using tobacco in other forms, such as cigars, pipes, and tobacco plugs, may reduce some of these problems (along with some of the associated health risks of smoking), but it increases the risk of cancer of the mouth and throat.

If tobacco is so dangerous, why is it that some people can be heavy smokers all of their lives without developing any of the health/disease problems associated with it? And why is it that some people who have never smoked develop smoking-related diseases, such as lung cancer? Scientists know that the answer to these questions lies in individual biological differences, but at this time they cannot be more precise. Certainly, they are far from being able to predict who can "safely" smoke and who cannot.

## Why People Smoke

It seems very unlikely that many people in this country today are unaware of the dangers of smoking cigarettes. Nevertheless, an estimated 5,000 people a day light up for the first time. Most of these first-time smokers are young people; statistics make it clear that if you haven't started by the time you are 20, you are unlikely to do so. Those who study this problem believe there are a number of interrelated factors behind this phenomenon.

Being cool and fitting in are two traditional reasons for taking up smoking.

- Some young people are in a hurry to grow up. They believe that smoking makes them appear more sophisticated and mature, and the associated health risks seem too far in the future to be important.

- Our weight-conscious society leads some young people to take up smoking to help them control their eating.

- Many young people who smoke are imitating attractive older people in their lives who smoke. Among these models may be parents, older siblings, friends, or movie/television stars.

- Cigarette smoking is made to look attractive by cigarette manufacturers, who stress the social aspects of smoking in their advertisements. Some impressionable young people who feel on the fringes of things get the idea that smoking will help their social lives.

Some of the young people who take up smoking for these or other reasons quit; many do not. Let's examine some of the more common rationalizations for continuing to smoke in the face of the evidence of this behavior's ill effects.

- *Smoking relaxes me.* Many people who smoke say they do so because it is relaxing and it calms them down in tense situations. To some degree this may be true: at high levels nicotine triggers the release of natural opiates (called *beta-endorphins*). Nicotine is also a stimulant, however, triggering the release of a hormone called *epinephrine* into the body. Epinephrine increases the pulse rate and sends extra sugar into the bloodstream. This leads the smoker to feel a brief spurt of energy, but the long-run effect is fatigue.

- *Everybody does it.* If you watch old movies, you may be struck by the strong supporting roles played by cigarettes. The stars smoked in Westerns, in war movies, in musicals, and in romantic comedies. Smoking was "natural," sophisticated, and socially acceptable in real life as well. The time for this excuse is running out, however. Smoking is not just "not in" today, it is well on the way to being "out."

All over the country, nonsmokers are becoming increasingly assertive about their rights to clean air, and the late 1980s have seen a host of new antismoking regulations that go far beyond the provision of smoking/no smoking areas in restaurants. In 1988, for example, Northwest Airlines banned *all* smoking on *all* of its domestic flights, and more and more companies began imposing no-smoking regulations on their employees. As one professor of behavioral medicine put it; "This socially approved habit is going to go the way of the spitoon" (Pomerleau, 1988).

■ *I can't quit.* A few assertive souls will look you in the eye and say; "I like smoking and I don't want to quit." More, however, do want to quit but believe they cannot. "I've tried, but I can't quit" is probably the most common reason that adult smokers give for continuing to smoke. Among the physical symptoms they report when they try to quit are fatigue, headaches, insomnia, nervousness, heart palpitations, and constipation.

Is there any physical foundation for these withdrawal symptoms? Certainly. There are bound to be reactions when the body is deprived of *any* foreign substance to which it has adapted. In addition, after a long period of study and debate, in May of 1988 the U.S. Surgeon General's office proclaimed that cigarettes and other forms of tobacco are physically addicting. Research finds that nicotine affects brain-wave functioning, alters mood, and serves as a biological reinforcement for behavior in laboratory animals, three of the major criteria for calling a substance physically addictive (Edwards, 1986).

## Kicking the Habit

There is no doubt at all that the easiest way to get Americans to stop smoking is to keep them from starting. There are more and more programs being set up to get the message to young people *before* they experiment with that first cigarette. The I'll Never Start Program, co-sponsored by the American Cancer Society and public schools, begins in the third grade, and health officials do not think this is a moment too soon.

What of the millions who already smoke? We know that they can quit. Millions before them have done so already, and most have done so on their own without any formal program. It takes many people more than one try, however, and some do find that formal programs help. One researcher found that 75% of those who had tried to quit at least once before were still off cigarettes 3 months after the end of a stop-smoking seminar (Coelho, 1985).

There are many stop-smoking programs available for those who want to stop and believe they cannot do it on their own. An alternative to a formal program that still offers the smoker some assistance is chewing gum that contains nicotine. This gum, which can be obtained only by prescription, is a bridge between smoking and nonsmoking. Each piece contains the nicotine of two or three cigarettes. The smoker replaces the cigarettes with the gum (according to directions given by the physician), and after several weeks he or she has broken all of the habits that go with smoking. In other words, the psychological dependence has been broken, and it remains only to break any physiological addiction to nicotine.

Many people have used nicotine gum successfully; others prefer to quit without going through this intermediate stage. A basic program for changing smoking (and other undesired) behaviors, is outlined in Appendix A. This section closes with a word on the question of quitting versus cutting down.

From a health standpoint, there is no question that cigarette smokers should quit, and the sooner the better. The extent to which a smoker recovers from the ill effects of smoking is highly dependent on how much he or she has smoked before quitting (e.g., Bertram, Jones, & Rogers, 1981). To a degree, however, the damaging effects of smoking cigarettes also are related to how many cigarettes are smoked (and how strong they are). Researchers emphasize that every cigarette counts, so there *is* something to be gained from cutting down if you can't quit.

# Caffeine

Americans lead the world in the consumption of caffeine. It appears in many forms in our society, including chocolate candy bars and a number of over-the-counter medications. One ounce of milk chocolate, for example, contains 6 to 10 milligrams of caffeine; the headache medicine Excedrin has 65 milligrams per tablet. Most of this substance, however, is consumed in beverages. The caffeine content of some of the most popular ones is shown in Exhibit 13–1.

Almost everyone drinks one or more of the beverages listed in Exhibit 13–1 every day. If you are one of these people, you know that this isn't just because you are thirsty; these beverages have strong social links as well. Going out for a cup of coffee or a soft drink is a traditional way to take a work break or get to know someone. Offering a cup of tea expresses concern or sympathy, and there is nothing like a cup of hot cocoa with that special person when the fire is blazing and the weather is doing dreadful things outside. Yet, like so

## EXHIBIT 13–1
## The Caffeine Content of Some Favorite Beverages

**5 oz. cup of coffee**
Brewed: Average of about 130 milligrams
Instant: Average of about 75 milligrams
Very Strong or Expresso: Average of about 200 milligrams
Decaffeinated: Average of about 3 milligrams

**5 oz. cup of tea**
Brewed: Average of about 50 milligrams
Instant: Average of about 35 milligrams
Iced (12 oz): Average of about 70 milligrams
Decaffeinated: Average of about 2 milligrams

**12 oz. soft drink**
Regular: 40 to 60 milligrams depending on brand
Caffeine Free: trace

**Cup of hot cocoa**
Average of about 10 milligrams

many other things these days, some physicians now are telling us that we should cut down or give up these beverages altogether.

## The Perils of Caffeine

Research into the possible dangers of caffeine is newer than studies of smoking and health, but certain relationships are beginning to emerge. The clearest findings involve caffeine and your heart. **Caffeine** is a powerful central nervous system *stimulant* and as such can lead to increases in blood pressure and heart rate. Heart palpitations and irregular beating (called *arrythmias*) also have been associated with too much caffeine. One study, carried out at Stanford University, found that men 35 to 55 who are heavy coffee drinkers may have a higher risk of developing heart disease than those who are not (Bales, 1985).

Other possible physical effects of caffeine include heartburn and various other gastrointestinal problems, insomnia, aggravation of anemia (since caffeine interferes with the body's absorbtion of iron), and aggravation of fibrocystic breast disease. There also are studies that link the excessive consumption of caffeine with psychological problems. Anxiety and depression both seem to get worse when caffeine is consumed, as does the severity of panic attacks (Wells, 1984).

It bears repeating that the relationships between caffeine and the various problems mentioned are only *possible* links. Unlike smoking research, caffeine research is plagued by ambiguous, confusing, or inconsistent findings. One of the problems is that laboratory studies of caffeine use involve high doses that are considerably more concentrated than a person normally would consume. This makes it difficult to generalize the findings of these studies to daily caffeine consumption.

The alternative to laboratory studies, actual use studies, are more realistic, but results can be equally difficult to interpret. People who drink many caffeine beverages frequently have poor general nutrition habits as well. In addition, there is a moderate to strong association between caffeine use and smoking (Istuan & Matarazzo, 1984). Both of these factors mean that it often is impossible to say for certain that caffeine consumption by itself is implicated in a particular health problem.

Whatever the connection between caffeine use and other life-style practices, research is clear about one thing; it is excessive consumption of caffeine that may cause problems. Most physicians consider more than three cups of coffee or other caffeinated beverage a day (very roughly 250 to 300 milligrams of caffeine) excessive, but individual differences are substantial (Truitt, 1971). Among the clues that you are taking in too much are insomnia, the "jitters," chronic diarrhea, acid indigestion, and a frequent need to urinate, but all of these symptoms also can signal other health problems. See a physician promptly if cutting back on caffeine doesn't eliminate them.

If you decide to cut caffeine down or out of your life altogether, you may expect to experience certain withdrawal symptoms of which the most noticeable are headache and a general feeling of lethargy or sleepiness. These symptoms seldom persist for more than about a week, but it can be a hard week; it probably is best to schedule your decaffeination program for a time when withdrawal symptoms will not interfere seriously with your daily activities.

If coffee, tea, soft drinks, or other caffeine beverages aren't bothering you in any way that you can notice, the odds are that you can continue to enjoy

Excessive caffeine may harm you, but in moderation it serves to stimulate and energize some people.

them in moderation. There is even evidence that caffeine has some beneficial effects. Among these can be improved capacity for long-term intellectual effort, reduced aggressiveness, and greater alertness and energy (Foley, 1985).

# Alcohol

Alcohol is considered by most health experts to be the single most abused substance in our society. In this section, some of the major facts about alcohol and its effects are presented, and we'll take a look at who "drinks." We then consider some of the individual and situational factors associated with alcohol abuse and review treatment methods.

## The Facts

Most people who use alcohol regularly report experiencing a sense of warmth, relaxation, and well-being after a drink or two. Cares are temporarily forgotten, the world seems a friendlier place, and inhibitions that usually prevent them from relaxing disappear. All of these positive effects are summed up in the phrase "to party," widely used to mean getting a group of people together to socialize with alcohol at the center of the activities.

Partying implies stimulation and this is the initial effect that alcohol has on many people. Actually, **alcohol** is a powerful central nervous system *depressant* that is rapidly absorbed into the bloodstream and carried to the brain. There, it depresses judgment and impairs the activity of those brain centers that normally hold impulsive behavior in check.

People vary considerably in the amount of alcohol and the length of time it takes for the depressing effects of this substance to become noticeable. Among the factors that are relevant are body type, sex, age, and health. Nevertheless, there is definitely an upper limit. If the concentration of alcohol in your bloodstream (the blood alcohol concentration) reaches .40%, you will pass out. If it reaches 0.55%, you probably will die. A chart showing relationships between body weight, time, number of drinks, and intoxication (blood alcohol concentration of .10% or greater) is presented in Figure 13–1.

Scientists still don't understand exactly how alcohol works on the brain, but there are a number of observable physical and physiological symptoms of this action. Among these are reduced muscular coordination, impaired vision and speech, impaired sexual functioning in men, and memory lapses ("blackouts"). Alcohol also has a number of aftereffects, including headache, nausea, and fatigue. Some people experience these even if they have had only a moderate amount to drink.

In the long run, excessive consumption of alcohol is associated with a variety of health problems including nutritional deficiencies, reduced ability of the white blood cells to fight disease, and cirrhosis (destruction) of the liver. There also are long-term effects on appearance, the most common and noticeable of which are a redness of the face and enlarged veins on the nose.

The **physical effects of alcohol abuse** on the individual, unpleasant though they can be, are by no means the only concern when it comes to the abuse of this substance. There can be serious **behavioral effects of alcohol abuse** as well. Through its action on the brain, the excessive use of alcohol is associated with a number of behaviors that are destructive to both the drinker

Figure 13–1 **Time, Body Weight, Number of Drinks, and Intoxication**

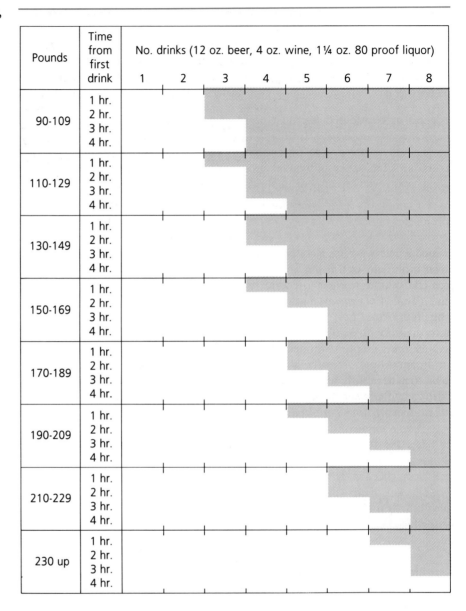

*Note:* Shaded area = .10% blood alcohol concentration (legal intoxication) or higher.
**Source:** Data from the California Department of Motor Vehicles (Pub. D. L606, 1987).

and others (Steele, 1986). For example, it is estimated that as many as 60% of the murders in this country are committed by intoxicated persons, and the figures for rape, assault, child abuse, and other crimes of violence are comparably high (National Council on Alcoholism, 1980; Pernanen, 1976).

Finally, there are **psychological effects of alcohol abuse.** These range from the slight lowering of self-esteem a social drinker might feel after drinking to excess at a party to acute psychotic disorders. The most well known of these psychotic reactions is *delirium tremens,* a short-term (3- to 6-day) disorder characterized by disorientation, hallucinations, acute fear, and marked tremors of the lips, tongue, and hands. Confinement and chemical therapy usually see the patient through an episode, but relapses are the rule.

*Korsakoff's psychosis,* another psychotic reaction to alcohol abuse, is characterized by memory impairment, lowering of moral and ethical standards, and reduced intellectual functioning. One of the most noticeable of its symptoms is the elaborate lies that the sufferer tells to fill in memory gaps and try to conceal the inability to think clearly. This disorder is more common among older alcoholics and seems to be primarily the result of the long-standing dietary deficiencies that tend to go along with alcohol abuse. Vitamin therapy is effective, but some permanent damage usually remains.

Of course, everyone knows that the destructive effects of alcohol we are considering are associated with alcohol abuse. Unfortunately, a great many people have very little knowledge of what this really means. **Intoxication** is defined legally as 0.1% alcohol in the bloodstream (approximately four drinks in an hour for someone who weighs between 130 and 170 pounds), but a practical definition of "too much" varies enormously from one person to the next. Alcohol abuse also often is defined in terms of drinking heavily for too long, but "too long" is a far shorter period than most people would guess. According to experts, 5 years is more than enough time to become a full-fledged alcoholic.

In addition to confusion about how much and how long one has to drink to be considered an alcohol abuser, there is considerable confusion about other attributes of this substance and about its use. You may test your "Alcohol IQ" in *Test Yourself;* the correct answers appear in *Summing Up.*

---

# TEST YOURSELF:
## What Do You Know about the Use and Effects of Alcohol?

*Directions:* Circle *T* if you think the statement is true or *F* if you think it's false.

1.  T  F    Alcohol is a stimulant.
2.  T  F    Alcohol is less dangerous than marijuana and other such drugs.
3.  T  F    Alcohol cannot produce a true addiction.
4.  T  F    The physiological withdrawal from alcohol is not dangerous.
5.  T  F    If you don't feel drunk, you have not had too much to drink.
6.  T  F    Exercise helps speed up the process of getting alcohol out of your body.
7.  T  F    You can't become an alcoholic if all you drink is beer.
8.  T  F    "Mixing" your liquor makes you drunk faster than sticking to one kind of drink.
9.  T  F    Black coffee helps to counteract the negative effects of alcohol.
10. T  F    Alcohol is part of the recognized treatment for certain diseases.
11. T  F    It is safe to drive about one hour after your last drink.

If you are like most people, you did not get all of the questions in *Test Yourself* correct. Despite all of the information available, people in general are not very knowledgeable about alcohol, either its negative or its positive attributes. Considerable attention has been paid here to the former, but a rounded discussion also will note that in moderation alcohol may have some benefits (Sizer & Whitney, 1988).

- For people who have difficulty eating because of stress-related tension, a small glass of wine taken a half hour before a meal may improve the appetite.

- People who eat too much for emotional or stress-related reasons may find it easier to reduce their food intake if they drink a small amount of wine before a meal. Again, it is the relaxing effect of the alcohol that is believed to be beneficial.

- There is some evidence that people who use alcohol in moderation over the course of their lives have a lower risk of heart attack than either nondrinkers or alcohol abusers. It is not entirely clear, however, that it is alcohol that is responsible. It may be that people in this group lead lives that are more social than others, allowing them a regular outlet for the release of tension.

## Who Are the Alcoholics?

There are many definitions of the term **alcoholic.** To the World Health Organization, an alcoholic is any person with life problems related to alcohol. The National Council on Alcoholism classifies as alcoholic only those persons exhibiting certain defined symptoms of alcohol abuse, such as consumption of a certain amount of alcohol per day. The American Psychiatric Association emphasizes the central role that alcohol plays in the life of an abuser; the alcohol-dependent person is one who exhibits at least three of the following behavioral symptoms over some period of time (American Psychiatric Association, 1987).

1. Alcohol often taken in larger amounts or over a longer period of time than the person intended

2. Persistent desire or one or more unsuccessful efforts to cut down or control substance use

3. A great deal of time spent in activities necessary to get the substance, take the substance, or recover from its effects

4. Frequent intoxication or withdrawal symptoms when expected to fulfill major role obligations at work, home, or school (e.g., does not work because hung over) or when use is physically hazardous (e.g., drives while intoxicated)

5. Important social, occupational, or recreational activities given up or reduced because of alcohol use

6. Continued alcohol use despite knowledge of having a persistent or recurrent social, psychological, or physical problem that is caused or made worse by the use of alcohol

7. Marked tolerance; need for increased amounts of alcohol to get the desired effect

**8.** Characteristic withdrawal symptoms if alcohol is not taken

**9.** Alcohol often taken to relieve or avoid withdrawal symptoms

You can see that standards for who will and who will not be called an alcoholic vary considerably according to who is doing the defining, but however it is defined, an estimated 10 to 15 million adult Americans have a "drinking problem." Who are these people?

Alcohol abusers come from all occupations and all social and economic conditions. Most of them are male, although women are moving up fast (Celentano & McQueen, 1978). It seems that the traditional higher rate of alcoholism for men has less to do with gender than with long-standing differences in behavior standards for men and women that now are changing.

A substantial number of today's alcohol abusers are teenagers; an estimated one-half million are between the ages of 10 and 19 (Ungaro, 1984). Many of these teenagers are college students, but a recent survey of over 6,000 high school students found that 30% of 11th graders used alcohol at least once a week and 5% used it daily (Needham, 1988). Comparable figures for 9th graders were 17% and 2%.

## Causes of Alcohol Abuse

The experience and research of physicians, psychologists, social workers, and others who are involved with the problem of alcohol abuse make it clear that there is *no one cause* to be singled out. Biological, psychological, and social factors all seem to play a part.

**Biological Factors**   Some researchers long have believed that there may be some genetic factor(s) that predispose certain people to become dependent upon alcohol. They know that it is possible to breed laboratory animals to prefer alcohol over other beverages (Segovia-Riquelma, Varela, & Mardones, 1971), and there are several kinds of evidence for biological predisposition in humans as well.

Alcohol abuse is particularly difficult to prevent since alcohol is the accepted center of so many social activities.

- There seem to be measurable individual differences in tolerance for alcohol that are biological in origin (e.g., Schuckit, 1980). Thus, people with a low tolerance may have a natural protection from alcohol abuse that those with a high tolerance lack.

- Children of alcohol abusers who are adopted by nonalcoholic parents have about twice the number of alcohol-related problems by their late 20s as adopted children whose real parents had no history of alcohol abuse (Goodwin et al., 1973).

- There is some evidence that children of mothers who consumed alcohol during certain critical stages of pregnancy are predisposed to alcohol abuse (Julien, 1978).

Findings like these are promising, but a solid link between genetics and alcohol abuse remains elusive. At this time, we can say only that biological factors almost certainly play some role, but the nature of that role is unclear.

**Psychological Factors**   Many investigators believe that it is not physical factors, but psychological ones, that distinguish the alcohol abuser from the nondrinker or the social drinker and the search for the alcoholic personality has been going on for some years. Coleman, Butcher, and Carson (1984) sum up the major findings of this research.

> Investigators have reported that potential alcoholics tend to be emotionally immature, to expect a great deal of the world, to require an inordinate amount of praise and appreciation, to react to failure with marked feelings of hurt and inferiority, to have low frustration tolerance, and to feel inadequate and unsure of their ability to play expected male or female roles. (p. 408)

This seems a clear psychological profile of an alcohol abuser until we realize that many people who have these same characteristics do not become problem drinkers and many who do not fit this pattern do. Some investigators believe that part of the answer may lie in the alcohol abuser's lower tolerance for tension or stress. Individuals with the characteristics described may be more likely to have such reduced tolerance, but not all of them experience high tension or stress in their lives. On the other hand, some people who do not fit the profile of the alcohol abuser may share the reduced tolerance for stress, and if it is present, they may resort to alcohol abuse to reduce it.

Tension and stress create anxiety, depression, and other unpleasant feelings. Schaefer (1971) believes that alcoholism is a conditioned response to coping with these feelings. However destructive the long-term effects of alcohol abuse, the immediate effects of taking a drink are relaxation and a reduced perception of stress (Levenson et al., 1980). When the individual does not drink, anxiety and other negative feelings are aggravated by physical symptoms of withdrawal. Thus, drinking becomes a self-reinforcing pattern of behavior that is very difficult to break because the negative consequences always come *after* the positive ones.

**Social Factors**   Although we know that certain individuals are more likely than others to become alcohol abusers, there still remains the question of what attracts them to alcohol instead of to some other way of dealing with their problems and the stress of daily living. Experts believe that a major factor is

Alcoholics Anonymous offers social support and informal counseling for alcohol abusers.

the long-standing connection between alcohol and social interaction in our culture (e.g., Pliner & Cappell, 1974).

The role of alcohol as a focus of social interaction is an important one in this country. Cocktail parties, end-of-term "beer blasts," champagne brunches, a bottle or two of wine with dinner, and bar "happy hours" are social traditions. "Getting together for a drink" long has been a way for businesspeople to cement deals, singles to begin relationships, and friends to catch up on the news. At this level, alcohol is very acceptable, and it is in such a context that most alcohol abusers begin to drink.

Of course, it is naive to say that our society's attitude toward drinking is the cause of alcohol abuse, but cross-cultural studies leave little doubt that it is a contributing factor. Alcohol abuse is almost unknown in Muslim societies where religious values forbid alcohol. At the other end of the spectrum is France, a country where alcohol is such an integral part of life that some workers take wine breaks instead of coffee breaks. France has the highest rate of alcoholism in the world.

To sum up, there seem to be certain types of people who for personality, life-situation, or biological reasons are more likely than others to find the effects of alcohol use reinforcing, and our culture provides ample opportunities for them to discover this fact in socially acceptable situations. This may not seem to be a very satisfying explanation for such a large individual and social problem, but it represents considerable progress in understanding the alcoholic. It wasn't all that long ago that those who abused alcohol were considered weak-willed at best and sinful at worst.

## Coping with Alcohol Abuse

A primary reason for concern with the causes of alcohol abuse is that assumptions about causes have implications for how the problem might be treated, or even prevented. Although we have learned much about alcohol abuse, we cannot say what causes any particular person to become dependent on this substance, and prevention is still far in the future. When it comes to treatment, however, the question of cause is somewhat academic. The *only* demonstrated cure is for the alcohol abuser to stop drinking. There are many approaches to bringing about this end; the ones reviewed here typify three very different perspectives on the problem.

**Alcoholics Anonymous**   **Alcoholics Anonymous,** or **AA,** was begun in the 1940s by two men in Akron, Ohio, who believed that the only person who really could help an alcoholic was someone who had gone through the experience. AA is a nonprofessional counseling and support group with a very simple premise: if you are an alcohol abuser, you cannot drink. Not now. Not next year. Not in moderation. Not ever. Members are encouraged to describe themselves as alcoholics even if they have not had any alcohol for many years.

AA meetings are open to everyone; there are no dues or fees. Most of each meeting time is devoted to open discussions of members' problems with alcohol. Those who no longer are drinking are encouraged to give testimonials to abstinence by describing their lives before and after they quit. (Only first names are used in these discussions.) The purpose of these meetings is to increase understanding of alcohol abuse, to share techniques for coping with it, and to provide mutual strength and support for abstinence. AA also has a "buddy system"; each member is assigned a particular person to call on at any time of the day or night when he or she feels particularly vulnerable to relapse.

There are no social rewards for drinking forthcoming from AA meetings and AA buddies. This is a group that continually emphasizes the down side of drinking. For this reason, it may be especially helpful to alcohol abusers who feel trapped in a life style that approves of, or encourages, social drinking. But AA is not the solution for everyone; it has a high dropout rate. Some people do not like the public exposure of the approach. Some need something more than support and peer counseling to cope with their problem. And some are put off by the evangelical style; AA is not affiliated with any church, but spiritual development is an important part of its philosophy. Some nonreligious AA groups have been formed recently, as have some nonsmoking chapters, but there is little information available about them at this time.

**Aversion Therapy**   AA helps people to stop drinking by offering an alternative social environment that does not reinforce the use of alcohol. A different way to counteract the rewards that maintain drinking is to make the actual experience unpleasant. **Aversion therapy** does this by pairing alcohol use with an aversive stimulus, such as an electric shock. After a time, the mere sight of alcohol will be enough to bring about the unpleasant reaction. Consistent with the principles of classical conditioning, the aversive stimulus itself no longer will be needed.

A variation of classic aversion therapy is use of the drug *antabuse,* which combined with alcohol makes a person seriously ill. Thus, taking an antabuse tablet is by itself a decision not to drink for a period of time (up to 5 days

A journey of 1000 miles begins with one step.

*Lao-Tze*

after one dose). Antabuse is inexpensive, it has no side effects, it is not addictive, and it never fails to work if used as directed. Many alcohol abusers have been taking it for years.

Aversion therapy or antabuse can be valuable aids to counteracting alcohol abuse because they attack the rewarding effects of that first drink. As noted, most alcohol abusers know that their behavior is destructive, but the negative effects are way out there somewhere and the rewards are immediate. Aversion therapy by itself, however, is unlikely to be enough. Everyone involved in the problem of alcohol abuse agrees that alcoholism is a way of life as well as a behavior. Eliminating it requires changing that life style (Marlatt & Gordon, 1980), so some form of psychotherapy usually is made part of an aversion therapy treatment.

**Psychotherapy**  Overcoming alcohol abuse is a two-part problem. One is to stop consuming alcohol so as to "dry out." The other is to stay sober, that is, to recover. Although a few researchers have experimented with controlled drinking for alcohol abusers (e.g., Lloyd & Salzberg, 1975), the evidence suggests that this may be a viable alternative for a tiny minority of abusers at best. Most people in this field believe, along with AA, that the only safe course is permanent abstinence.

Psychotherapy can help to support abstinence by providing a means for an individual to deal with the problems that lie behind his or her dependence. This therapy may be individual, but many professionals prefer to work with groups of alcohol abusers. In a group it is difficult for an alcoholic to hide from or rationalize the facts about himself or herself. Members also can support one another and help one another find new ways to cope with their problems. Other therapists prefer to have the "group" consist of the alcoholic and his or her family, believing that dynamics within the family often are part of the problem.

Research into the success of psychotherapy for alcohol abuse problems is difficult, and results are mixed (Brandsma, Maultsby, & Welsh, 1980). Estimates of the percentage of clients who continue to abstain from alcohol after therapy range from very low to very high depending on a number of factors. Among the ones that seem most important are (1) the motivation and self-esteem of the individual abuser, (2) how long the problem has persisted, (3) how severe it is, (4) how well the person understands it, and (5) the kind of environment he or she lives in (Miller, 1985).

> Self-conquest is the greatest of victories.
> *Plato*

## The Other Side of the Coin

Most experts consider alcohol the single most abused substance in this country, and the number of abusers is too large by any standard. Nevertheless, alcohol abusers are in the minority. There are many more people who do *not* have this problem than there are people who do. Many of these people use alcohol; they just don't abuse it. Some of the ways that the use of alcohol may be controlled in social situations are listed in Exhibit 13–2.

Today, many people are making a conscious effort to limit their consumption of alcohol by use of the kinds of strategies described in Exhibit 13–2. Increasing numbers also are making the decision not to use alcohol at all. If you are one of them, you already have discovered that this decision seems to

**EXHIBIT 13–2**

## Some Tips for Social Drinking

### As a Host or Hostess

- Provide nonalcoholic beverages as well as alcohol.
- Provide plenty of snacks if there is to be no dinner.
- Limit time available for predinner drinks if there is to be dinner.
- Limit noise from background music, too many guests, etc. (People drink more when they can't talk to one another.)
- Consider serving an alcoholic punch instead of the usual mixed drinks.
- Do not ask heavy drinkers to "tend bar."
- Keep an eye out for people drinking too fast and try to offer them an alternative (conversation, help with making coffee, etc.).
- Never, never try to "force" a drink on someone who declines your first offer. (Also, do not embarrass him or her.)

### As a Guest or Participant

- Eat before the party or get-together.
- Sip alcoholic beverages; drink water if you're thirsty.
- Order one drink at a time. Skip "happy hours," beer by the pitcher, and wine by the carafe. All tend to make you drink more than you really want.
- Never accept a drink you don't really want because someone else is buying (or pouring).
- Limit before-dinner drinks to one or two at the most. You'll enjoy the meal more.

bother some people, who may question you, tease you, or lecture you about your "holier-than-thou attitude."

This situation is an ideal one for practicing your assertiveness skills. You have as much right to decide not to drink alcohol as you do to decide not to drink grapefruit juice. You wouldn't feel called upon to apologize for and/or explain the latter decision, and you do not have to do so for the former. "No thank you," repeated as many times as it takes, is all you have to say to the individual who keeps urging you to have "just one to be social." "I don't drink because I don't want to drink" is a perfectly legitimate reply to the person who keeps questioning you about this behavior. The important thing to remember is to be calm, matter-of-fact, and firm.

If you don't drink, you also will have to respect the rights of those who do not join with you in this decision. It is not up to you to lecture them or try to change their behavior any more than it is up to them to try to change yours. If you have a family member or friend who abuses alcohol, however, your position is different; you cannot afford to ignore him or her.

Coping with the problems created by a loved one who abuses alcohol requires special skills. If you or someone you know is in this position, it is important to get help in learning these skills. The local public health office or any substance abuse facility can be of assistance. Many people also find Al-Anon, a support group for people who must cope with alcohol abusers, to be helpful.

# Other Drugs

A **drug** is any substance that alters normal functioning when taken into the body. This includes nicotine, caffeine, and alcohol, but to most people the term means something more exotic. They think of drugs as pep pills, marijuana, tranquillizers, or something that causes hallucinations. A "drug addict" is not someone who smokes or drinks, but someone who uses heroin or cocaine or pops pep pills.

Many of the substances thought of by most people as "real drugs" are illegal in this country, and most of the rest are *controlled substances* (legally obtained only by prescription). As a result, abuse of these drugs tends to attract more attention than the actual numbers might warrant otherwise. For example, it is estimated that there are about 225,000 heroin addicts in this country. (Because this is an illegal substance, it is difficult to get an accurate figure.) Certainly this is a matter for concern, but it still is a small number compared with the number of teenaged alcoholics, for example.

Another reason that the abuse of illegal or controlled substances gets so much attention is that so many young people are involved. The life style that accompanies this form of drug abuse, including criminal association and the possibility of death by overdose or contamination, seems especially tragic for those whose lives are just getting started. Although surveys in the mid-1980s suggest that teenage addiction is on the decline, the number of adult abusers seems to be on the rise (Thomas, 1986). There is no evidence that we can relax our efforts to understand and cope with this problem.

## Why Do People Take Drugs?

Drugs alter the way you feel. If you are in pain, they can make you stop hurting. If you are tired, they can pick you up. If you are depressed, they can cheer you up. If you are inhibited, they can give you the illusion of being a free spirit. If you are bored, they can give you exciting visions. If life is just too hard or the future appears hopeless, they can make everything seem easy and upbeat.

Viewed from this perspective, there is no mystery about why people take drugs. They take them to change the way they feel, but the effects are temporary. When the drug wears off, the pain or boredom or inhibitions or whatever are back and may seem even worse by comparison. For some people, the solution is to take more of the substance that made them feel better instead of trying to solve the basic problem. This substitute of a substance for coping behavior can get to be a habit that creates **psychological addiction,** a mental and emotional dependence on the altered state produced by a drug.

In general, psychological addiction is a far more serious problem than the widely publicized effects of physical dependence on drugs. **Physical addiction** has come about when a person's body must have a drug in order to function normally. If you will look at the drug summary table in Table 13–1, you will see that only two of the major categories of drugs—heroin and the barbiturates—have the potential for physical addiction.

Withdrawal from physically addictive substances causes unpleasant, painful, and sometimes dramatic physical symptoms, but only in the case of bar-

**Table 13–1  Drugs: Effects and Side Effects**

| Drug | Expected Effects | Addictive? | Common Side Effects | Possible Effects of Abuse, Prolonged Use, or Sensitivity |
|---|---|---|---|---|
| *Amphetamines* ("pep pills?") Benezedrine ("bennies") Dexedrine ("dexies") Methadrine ("speed") | ■ Wakefulness ■ Reduced appetite ■ Feelings of alertness, confidence | Physically: Not determined Psychologically: Yes | ■ Irritability ■ Restlessness ■ Insomnia ■ Loss of appetite | ■ Hallucinations ■ Violence ■ Psychosis ■ Suicide |
| *Barbiturates* Nembutal Veronal Seconal ("red devils") Tuinal ("rainbows") | ■ Reduced tension ■ Deep sleep | Physically: Yes Psychologically: Yes | ■ Irritability ■ Confusion ■ Depression | ■ Chronic drowsiness, slurred speech ■ Impaired memory, decision making ■ Brain damage, suicide |
| *Cocaine* ("coke," "snow," "rock," "flake") | ■ Euphoria, confidence ■ Decreased fatigue ■ Increased sex drive ■ Insensitivity to pain | Physically: Not determined Psychologically: Yes | ■ Sleeplessness ■ Mild anxiety/ depression ■ Severe headaches ■ Nausea | ■ Hallucinations ■ Damage to nose requiring surgery ■ Convulsions ■ Heart failure |
| *Heroin* ("H," "horse") | ■ Relaxation ■ Euphoria ■ Reduced anxiety | Physically: Yes Psychologically: Yes | ■ Lethargy ■ Loss of appetite ■ Distorted perceptions | ■ Criminal acts to support habit ■ Death by overdose |
| *LSD* ("acid") | ■ "Mind expansion" ■ Intensified feelings | Physically: No Psychologically: Yes | ■ "Bad trip" (frightening hallucinations) | ■ "Flashbacks" (distorted perceptions and hallucinations long after taking drug) ■ Psychosis |
| *Marijuana* ("grass," "pot") | ■ Relaxation/mood elevation ■ Increased awareness of sensation | Physically: No Psychologically: Yes | ■ Increased heartbeat ■ Nausea ■ Loss of coordination | ■ Anxiety/depression ■ Lethargy ■ Possible lung damage/possible genetic damage |
| *PCP* ("angel dust") | ■ Euphoria ■ Hallucinations | Physically: No Psychologically: Yes | ■ Distortion of reality ■ Slurred speech ■ Loss of motor control | ■ Extreme, senseless violence ■ Seizures ■ Coma/death |

biturates are these effects life-threatening. Barbiturates also are the most dangerous drug from the standpoint of overdose risk. With regular use, the dose needed to be effective increases far more rapidly than the body's tolerance. The more often a person uses barbiturates, the closer he or she comes to a fatal dose. Moreover, these drugs impair mental functioning, and the danger of an accidental overdose is substantial.

## Cocaine: The "In" Drug

Although barbiturates may be the most potentially lethal of the illegal or controlled substances, most experts consider the major drug problem at this time to be cocaine. When inhaled ("snorted") or smoked (in the form called "crack"), **cocaine,** a plant product, provides a feeling of confidence and euphoria. Users also report it increases their sex drive and decreases sensitivity to pain and fatigue. Conservative estimates put the number of regular users at around 8 million, but many experts believe that 25 million is a more accurate figure (Fisher, 1985).

Part of cocaine's popularity is due to the widespread belief that it is a relatively innocuous, nonaddictive substance. Neither belief is accurate. It is not innocuous; by the end of 1984, cocaine-related deaths were occurring at the rate of at least one per day, and the rate had reached two per day in major metropolitan centers by the following year (Taylor, 1986). Cocaine also is clearly addictive in the psychological sense and possibly in the physical sense as well, although this has yet to be established beyond doubt. Certainly, it is physically *dangerous*.

Not all of the popularity of cocaine is due to the effects of the drug itself. Because it was difficult to acquire until recently, its use had been concentrated among those in higher financial brackets. This group included many people in show business who found the particular effects of cocaine a useful crutch in an exhaustively competitive and demanding profession. As a result, cocaine acquired a reputation as a glamour drug—if you could get it and pay for it, you were traveling in heady company.

As cocaine has become less expensive and more readily available, it has moved into all segments of society. In the form known as crack, it is now a standard feature in the decidedly unglamorous urban inner-city neighborhoods. It remains to be seen what impact, if any, this will have on use in the upper income brackets. In the late 1980s, cocaine remains a growth industry.

## Marijuana

The publicity surrounding cocaine has tended to push concerns about marijuana into the background, but at one time this substance was at the center of the drug-abuse controversy. **Marijuana,** a drug prepared from the leaves and flowering tops of a plant that is grown quite easily in mild climates, was the in drug of the 1960s and 1970s. By 1981, the National Institute of Drug Abuse estimated that approximately one third of the people in the United States had experimented with marijuana at one time and that about 13% were still users (NIDA, 1981).

The usual way to take marijuana is in the form of cigarettes called "joints" or "reefers." It also may be cooked in food, with brownies being a favorite medium. However it is ingested, the general effect of the drug is a sense of relaxation and well-being. The world seems to be more meaningful and beautiful. Pleasurable experiences, such as sexual intercourse, seem to take on new dimensions. Marijuana also has a reputation for enhancing creativity, although most researchers find no evidence for this (e.g., Braden, Stillman, & Wyatt, 1974).

As may be seen in Table 13–1, marijuana use produces some unpleasant sensations, which occasionally are severe, but deaths related directly to the use of this substance are rare. In addition, both the psychological and the behavioral side effects tend to be less dramatic than those of other drugs. The "grass subculture" also seems to be different. There is little of the fast-track aura of cocaine or the crime and violence associations of many other drugs. For these and other reasons, many argue that this substance should be legalized. There is more on this issue in *For Discussion*.

## Recognizing Drug Abuse

One of the sadder aspects of drug abuse is that the people around the abuser often do not know there is a problem until it is far advanced. The following symptoms are some of the more frequent behavioral clues that suggest someone may be getting in over his or her head with drugs.

## FOR DISCUSSION:
## Should Marijuana Be Legalized?

Marijuana is far and away the single most used of the drugs that are illegal in this country. Its current popularity began in the 1960s when "grass" or "pot" use became a symbol of identity among people who shared a common rejection of prevailing social values and political actions. Many of those who use it today were not even born at that time, but marijuana has continued to attract users even as social conditions have shifted dramatically.

Although it shares illegal status with heroin, cocaine, and the hallucinogens, such as LSD, marijuana is different. Its primary effects are of relaxation and heightened feelings. It almost never produces the manic quality of a cocaine high or the blank mindlessness of the heroin fix or the terrifying visions of the hallucinogenic "bad trip." People react differently, of course, but compared with other drugs, the effects of marijuana seem almost gentle. Violence is rare, as are

the psychotic reactions that may accompany long-term use of other drugs.

Marijuana also is different in that, for whatever reasons, users seem to abuse it less than other drugs. Although some people become dependent on a day-to-day basis, more seem to reserve use of the substance for occasional recreational use. This tends to remove it from the mainstream of organized drug pushing (which encourages addiction). So does the fact that marijuana does not seem to be a particularly powerful "gateway drug" to the use of other drugs in the way that amphetamines seem to be.

Marijuana also appears to be less harmful than the two most widely used addictive substances, tobacco and alcohol. Although researchers have found evidence that long-term use may be associated with irritated lungs or lung cancer, heart problems, brain damage, a decrease in male sex

hormones, and, in some cases, the body's ability to fight disease, these links are still tenuous. Certainly, when compared with the destructive effects of cigarettes and alcohol, the *known* health hazards of marijuana are small. Yet the sale of marijuana is illegal while the sale of both tobacco and alcohol is legal.

Marijuana also seems to be less likely to disrupt the lives of users in the ways that alcohol does. While it is probable that regular marijuana use has broken up some families, led to the loss of some jobs, and been associated with some crime and fatal automobile accidents, these effects are not usual. By contrast, all are constant risks for the alcohol abuser.

What do you think? Are comparisons with other drugs, no matter how favorable, a valid basis for legalizing marijuana? What other arguments can you think of for such an action? What arguments can you think of against it?

- Lethargy
- Insomnia
- Dilated pupils
- Loss of memory
- Loss of appetite
- Increased perspiration
- Anxiety or suspiciousness
- Hyperactivity or "jitters"
- Runny nose and nosebleeds
- Sudden loss of interest in sex
- Sudden carelessness about personal appearance
- Lying, breaking appointments, breaking promises
- Inability to explain what happened to sums of money

By themselves, most of the behaviors listed could mean other things; important clues to drug abuse are sudden onset and marked departure from previous behavior. As with alcohol abuse, the skills needed to help someone with a drug problem do not come naturally. The first step is to get it out in the open. In some cases, it is only necessary for someone else to recognize the signs for the drug abuser to admit the problem and ask for help.

Many drug abusers will not admit a problem or ask for help, but even when one does, friends or family seldom can help him or her alone. There are some things they can do, however. One is to make sure that the individual understands that they do *not* endorse the drug habit but *are* on the abuser's side. Another is to become an information source; people who are abusing drugs often are unable or unwilling to find out the facts or where they can go for help.

## Over-the-Counter Drugs

When they hear the word *drug,* most people think of illegal or controlled substances, but this word also is used to refer to prescriptions and to self-medications of various kinds that are sold openly and legally for the relief of pain, acid indigestion, and other problems. It does not occur to most of us that there could be any harm in such preparations; would they be so inexpensive and so easy to get if there were?

The truth is that *no drug is harmless*. Any substance that alters bodily functioning can have dangerous side effects in certain people, and it is possible to overdose on many. The potential dangers of several of the most used over-the-counter preparations are noted in Table 13–2, but you should read the label for yourself whenever you buy such a preparation and heed all cautions and restrictions.

**Summing Up** ■

What do cigarettes, coffee, alcohol, Classic Coca-Cola, and sleeping pills have in common? All are substances whose use puts you at risk of psychological or physical addiction. The single most abused of these substances is alcohol (all of the statements in *Test Yourself* are false). The single most deadly for the largest number of people is tobacco, although many other drugs can kill through overdose, contamination, or indirectly through the associated life style.

Opinions differ as to what leads people to use and then abuse potentially addictive substances. What is clear, however, is that the cure for any such problem is to stop using the substance. Thus, most problems with these substances may be viewed as behavior-management problems, a view supported by the fact that most people who stop using drugs of any kind do it without assistance from a formal treatment program.

**Table 13–2  Some Cautions Regarding Over-the-Counter Drugs**

| Drug | Some Possible Problems |
|---|---|
| Aspirin | ■ Upset stomach |
| | ■ Drowsiness (if sensitive) |
| | ■ Damage to gastrointestinal tract, including ulcers |
| | ■ Iron-deficiency anemia (chronic use) |
| | ■ Can prolong bleeding (if combined with alcohol) |
| | ■ Possible factor in Reye's syndrome in children |
| | ■ Overdose is poisonous (especially in children) |
| Laxatives | ■ Can cause dehydration |
| | ■ Can lead to diarrhea and cramps |
| | ■ Can mask poor nutrition and lead to malnutrition |
| | ■ Associated with reduced mineral absorption from food |
| | ■ Can be habit forming |
| Appetite suppressants | ■ Elevated blood pressure |
| | ■ Headaches |
| | ■ Increased danger of stroke |
| Cold medications (with antihistamines) | ■ Severe impairment of ability to drive |
| | ■ Elevated blood pressure |
| | ■ Extreme excitability |
| Cough medicines | ■ Many contain up to 50% alcohol |
| Antacids | ■ Reduced mineral absorption from food |
| | ■ Can mask gastrointestinal disease |
| | ■ Aggravate high blood pressure (if contain sodium) |
| | ■ Cause overdose of calcium (if contain calcium) |

# EATING AND WEIGHT CONTROL

According to one expert panel, about one in five adults are 20% or more over their desirable weights and roughly 11 million are **obese**—40% or more over that weight (Hirsch, 1985). In this section we examine the reasons people are overweight, talk some sense about getting rid of excess pounds, and consider some of the psychological problems created by our society's widespread obsession with body weight.

## The Fattening of America

There always have been overweight people in this country, but the extent of the problem has increased dramatically in the last 30 years. Part of this shift may be attributed to standards for desirable weight, which were revised consistently downward for many years (thereby increasing the number of overweight people by default, as it were). Recently, more sophisticated analyses, which take age and distribution of body fat as well as height and frame size into account, have led to somewhat more realistic and higher recommendations (Cole, 1984), but the number of overweight people continues to climb.

What *is* your desirable weight, anyway? There are many height/weight charts available, but if you compare several, you probably will find that all give you different numbers. An easy rule-of-thumb estimate may be obtained as follows: Begin with 100 pounds for a height of 5 feet (110 pounds if you are male) and add 5 pounds for every inch over this height. For example, by this method, the desirable weight for a woman who is 5 feet 6 inches tall is 130 pounds; for a man of 5 feet 9 inches, it is 155 pounds.

Whether you use this quick formula or get your ideal weight from a chart somewhere, you may not be pleased with the number. You might say that weighing that amount would make you look too thin or too heavy, and you could be entirely right. *Your ideal weight has nothing whatsoever to do with appearance.* It is based on physical and physiological considerations including organ capacity and efficiency and human skeletal limitations.

### Why Are We Overweight?

The answer to this question seems obvious. We are overweight because we eat too much, right? Not entirely. Data indicate that Americans eat less than they used to. Moreover, there are studies that suggest that fatter people actually eat less on the average than slimmer people (Wood, 1985). It isn't just how much we eat, but what we eat, when we eat it, and how we live that put the pounds on.

A generation ago, most people ate regular, balanced, sit-down meals prepared at home. There were few fast-food restaurants as we know them today. Pizza delivery, microwave popcorn, and shopping-mall stores selling 25 kinds of fudge were still in the future. Most people also got plenty of exercise in the normal course of their daily activities. Since most families had only one automobile, bicycles, feet, and public transportation (reached by means of feet) had to do for many. Much of the physical work done in today's home and work place by machine was done by hand.

# FACE OF THE FUTURE:
## A New Perspective on Fat

Most people who are overweight are not really big eaters. They overeat in the technical sense that they eat more than their bodies require to sustain their particular levels of physical activity. For these people, losing weight is almost always a matter of stepping up the level of exercise and perhaps "watching" the intake of foods that are particularly high in calories and low in nutrients (e.g., potato chips). Restricting the overall amount of food usually isn't necessary or even desirable. When a healthy person eats less than required by his or her body to maintain efficient functioning, the body simply adjusts its needs downward, so eating less doesn't bring about weight loss.

Some people who are overweight *do* overeat. Some eat astonishing amounts of food at each meal; some eat less, but constantly. For many years, doctors and psychologists have believed that emotional and psychological problems such as anxiety, loneliness, insecurity, and depression were the primary causes of this overeating. An upset or unhappy person felt better after eating, but gradually, he or she also began to gain weight. As weight gain increased, guilt and other negative feelings about that were added to the problems that led to the original overeating. To relieve these feelings, it was necessary to eat more. And so the cycle was believed to go.

New research not only questions this cyclic premise but also suggests it may even be backwards. In other words, perhaps people don't get fat because they have problems but have problems because they get fat. This being the case, why *do* they eat so much? It is beginning to look as if the culprit could be biological in nature.

This new research is about **fat cells.** These are the cells in your body that are especially equipped to store fat. Everybody has these cells, but some people have more of them than others. If, as researchers are beginning to suspect, it is these fat cells that send "hungry messages" to the brain, people with more of these cells are more likely to overeat (Kolata, 1986). As they do, their fat cells become larger; obese people have fat cells two to two-and-a-half times as large as people of normal weight.

Dieting reduces the *size,* but not the *number,* of fat cells, so people with a great many of these cells find dieting much harder than those who have fewer. Adding to the problem is the fact that severe and/or persistent dieting plays havoc with the body's regulatory mechanisms. Studies with both animals and humans find that weight loss is slower with every attempt at dieting. Worse, weight gain is faster every time an obese person goes off a diet.

Does this mean that obese people must resign themselves to being fat? Not at all. As Albert Stunkard, a psychiatrist at the Obesity Research Center at the University of Pennsylvania explains it, what these new theories do is "explain why you have to try harder if the genetic and biochemical dice are loaded against you" (1986, p. 92). But if the theories prove correct, they may do far more than that. They will revolutionize the treatment of obesity for one thing, putting the emphasis on the body rather than the mind.

This better understanding of the nature of the problem also may give fat people back some of the self-esteem they lose because the world views them as too neurotic or weak-willed to be thin. This, in turn, may give them more strength to ignore the insistent clamoring of their excess fat cells for food.

Today, we eat on the run, snack frequently, and use cars to go everywhere except possibly to the mailbox. There seems to be a labor-saving device for almost everything, and we have television to take up any spare time this might leave us; we no longer even have to get up to change the channel! The net result of this hit-or-miss eating and vastly reduced physical activity is weight problems for many more people.

Of course, there are still people who would not be overweight if they didn't eat so much, but as you can see in *Face of the Future,* that problem isn't as simple as we used to think. Research is opening up some exciting new possibilities. Nevertheless, biology can account for only a limited amount of excess weight at best. Like all behaviors, eating habits are the result of a complex interaction of factors of which biology is only one.

## Eat It Today—Wear It Tomorrow: Dieting and Weight Control

**Dieting** is a term we use to mean cutting down on food intake and/or concentrating on certain foods to the exclusion of others. Millions upon millions of overweight individuals believe that there is some magic combination of amount and type of food that will make them thin, and they are making the authors of diet books rich in the pursuit of that illusion.

The authors of a leading book on nutrition have reviewed 16 of the best-selling diets on seven nutritional, psychological, and practical criteria (Whitney & Hamilton, 1987). They have given perfect scores to three of these: the New Canadian High Energy Diet, Weight Watchers, and the UCLA Diet (California Slim). Fasting and the Cambridge Diet received no points out of 100, and the popular Beverly Hills Diet only 10 points out of 100.

If you want to lost weight, you probably are safe with one of the diets that received a score of 100 points on the nutritionists' list, but you also should keep in mind that gaining weight is not a matter of "eat it today, wear it tomorrow." If it were, there would not be any slim people, much less thin people. It takes approximately 3,500 excess calories to gain one pound, and you gain a pound for every 3,500 more calories eaten than used up. Whatever you may have heard to the contrary, calories *do* count and counting them is a basic step in any weight-control program.

There are two ways that your body uses, or works off, the calories you consume. The first is to maintain essential bodily functions, such as breathing, heartbeat, and digestion. The rate at which your body expends energy (burns calories) to do this is known as your **basal metabolic rate (BMR).** This rate varies from individual to individual, but an average-sized adult requires somewhere in the vicinity of 1,400 calories a day to keep humming along. The extent to which you work off any calories over those required to maintain your body depends entirely upon the extent of your physical activity. The number of calories burned by some common activities and exercises is shown in Table 13–3.

As you see in the table, everything you do burns some calories, but what with the nonphysical jobs most of us have, labor-saving devices of all kinds, and the automobile, routine daily activities are not sufficient to offset the difference between food intake and BMR use for many people. Cutting down on

All the things I really like to do are either immoral, illegal or fattening.
*Alexander Woollcott*

**Table 13–3 Burning It Off—The Calorie Expenditure of Some Common Activities**

| Activity | Calories Burned per Half Hour |
| --- | --- |
| Aerobic dancing | 225 |
| Basketball | 200 |
| Bicycling, regular | 175 |
| Bicycling, stationary | 150 |
| Desk work | 75 |
| Ballroom dancing | 160 |
| Disco dancing | 250 |
| Driving | 75 |
| Eating | 60 |
| Golf | 120 |
| Handball | 450 |
| Hiking (with pack) | 150 |
| Ice skating | 225 |
| Jogging | 360 |
| Jumping rope | 400 |
| Lying still | 45 |
| Playing piano | 60 |
| Preparing a meal | 70 |
| Reading | 45 |
| Racquetball | 450 |
| Roller skating | 225 |
| Rowing | 190 |
| Sleeping | 30 |
| Snow skiing, cross-country | 275 |
| Standing | 70 |
| Swimming | 300 |
| Tennis | 210 |
| Typing | 55 |
| Walking | 100 |
| Washing/waxing car | 115 |
| Washing dishes (by hand) | 70 |
| Watching TV | 40 |
| Writing | 45 |

**Note:** Figures are averages for a person who weighs approximately 150 pounds and is not straining. If you weigh less, you work off less. If you "work up a sweat," you work off more.

intake doesn't take up all the slack unless intake is vastly over what is needed, because we have very efficient bodies. When we diet, they adjust to get by on fewer calories; in other words, the long-range effect of persistent dieting is that it simply adjusts the BMR downward. One theory of why this happens is the set-point theory.

The *set-point* is a hypothetical weight that your body is programmed to "defend." In theory, it works like a thermostat. If you take in more calories than you need to stay at this weight, your metabolism will speed up to burn them off. If you take in fewer, it will slow down to keep you from losing weight. The set-point theory is not regarded as fully confirmed because there are still many unanswered questions, but most of the evidence at this time suggests that it is on the right track (Hamilton, Whitney, & Sizer, 1985).

Does all this mean that there is no point in dieting? Sorry, but no. If you are more than a few pounds overweight, you almost certainly will have to restrict your food intake to get rid of the excess. What it does mean is that dieting is only half the story. The other half is exercise.

## Use It and Lose It: Exercise and Weight Control

If you eat less, you will lose weight, but your body also will begin adjusting to the lower intake. At some point, you will stop losing unless you cut your intake still further. Most doctors and nutritionists believe that if you go below the approximate 1,400 calories a day needed for body maintenance, you are risking malnutrition (Sizer & Whitney, 1988). In addition, you will put the weight back on at an even faster rate if you stop dieting. The key to avoiding this dismal scenario is to shift your *energy budget* so that you are taking in fewer calories than you are burning off. This is done by eating less (but still enough) and exercising more.

Results from a large number of studies in a variety of fields, including biology, medicine, and psychology, leave little room for doubt that exercise is an important part of effective weight control for most people. In combination with calorie control, exercise helps you to lose weight without starving yourself and it is also the key to not gaining it back. One specialist has estimated that adding enough exercise to burn off an extra 100 calories a day would make a difference of 10 pounds a year for most people if food intake were unchanged (Linder, 1984).

In addition to burning calories, regular exercise appears to lower the setpoint, that weight your body seems to "want" to maintain. Thus, many people find that over time they are able to eat more without gaining weight back. (Some people also find that exercising makes them less hungry, but this is a highly individual reaction.) Exercise also has a number of other health benefits. It tones muscles, increases cardiovascular (heart) capacity and efficiency, slows down bone mineral loss, and helps to counteract stress.

## Should You Lose Weight?

There is no longer any debate about whether you should exercise regularly. Unless your doctor has advised against it for specific medical reasons, you should (even if you do not want to lose weight). Whether or not you should make an active effort to lose weight is a more complicated question. The answer depends to a considerable degree upon how much overweight you are. People who qualify as obese run health risks that are every bit as serious as those run by smokers. The following are among the more prominent of these risks.

- Gout
- Diabetes
- Gallstones
- Kidney failure

Walking is the best possible exercise.
*Thomas Jefferson*

- High blood pressure, clots, and strokes
- Heart pain, heart "attacks," and heart failure
- Cancer of the uterus, breast, prostate, and colon

The health dangers of obesity are those associated with the breaking down of body tissue. The human body simply wasn't made to handle an overload of flesh for any length of time, and there are many ways it can break down under the strain. Not all of the problems associated with being overweight are physical, however. Our society places a high value on slimness, and obese people may be ridiculed, avoided, or exploited in their social worlds. They also are cut off from a number of activities and avenues of expression enjoyed by their slimmer peers. They have less to choose from in the way of stylish clothing, for example, and are less likely to be able to compete successfully in active sports.

The miseries and stresses of being overweight in a society that ascribes to the adage that "you can't be too rich or too thin" tend to create a vicious cycle. The more unhappy an overweight person becomes, the more he or she eats. Food becomes a substitute for other satisfactions, a substitute that makes the problem worse (Chernin, 1985). The way out of the circle is to lose weight;

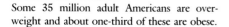

Some 35 million adult Americans are overweight and about one-third of these are obese.

those who can't do it alone will find many resources, including physicians, psychologists, and for-profit weight-loss programs, available to provide assistance.

This discussion is about people who are substantially overweight. It is worth emphasizing that most people who diet and worry about their weight are *not* obese. If you are in this group, you are five to seven pounds over the weight you would like to be. These are very difficult pounds to lose because it is your mind, not your body, that finds them excessive. We happen to live in a time when thin is in, but it wasn't always that way.

In former times, *plumpness* was a word used to praise feminine beauty. *Stoutness* in a man was a hallmark of success and prosperity. Nor was all of this in other centuries. Movie stars and "pin-up girls" of the 1940s would be considered overweight by today's standards. The extremely slim look considered ideal today is relatively new, and it may be on the way out again if we can use fashion models as any forerunner of the future. In the past few years, more and more successful models have the healthy look of a few "extra" pounds.

Of course, we would not want to return to times when actual overweight was considered beautiful. To a point, thinner is healthier. If you are one of those who feels there are only a few pounds standing between you and this goal, here are some tips for losing them. These are small changes in behavior, not a diet. If you follow them and get your exercise, you may never have to diet again (Allen, 1984).

1. Go to the grocery store only when you are *not* hungry.

2. Make a list and stick to it.

3. Make sure the list includes plenty of raw vegetables, crackers, yogurt, and cottage cheese for snacking. Throw out the potato chips, cookies, pretzels, doughnuts, ice cream, and other traditional snacks.

4. Let yourself eat desserts on weekends (or any two nights) to reward yourself from abstaining the rest of the time.

5. Don't eat after your main evening meal.

6. Find substitutes for sugar and salt.

7. *Make* yourself drink six to eight glasses of plain water a day. Your body needs it, and it helps to fill those hungry times between meals. Many people find that keeping a container of a day's water "ration" in the refrigerator or other convenient location helps them meet this goal.

These tips are for people who want to lose some weight even though no one would call them fat. There are a great many people in this category. A few of them, for reasons no one understands very well, lose all perspective on the issue. They become obsessed with being thin and unable to evaluate their own bodies objectively. Some become disgusted by food and won't eat at all. Others eat enormous amounts, then force themselves to vomit it up before it can be digested. We call these extreme forms of confusion about weight and the consumption of food eating disorders.

## Eating Disorders

In the fourth quarter of the 20th century, growing numbers of people are starving themselves in service to a distorted body image. They suffer from *anorexia nervosa,* an eating disorder estimated to have spread to 1 percent of

Many people, most of them women, have a distorted body image, seeing themselves as fat when no one else does.

the female population between the ages of 12 and 25 (*U.S. News & World Report,* 1982). Men also have this disorder, but it is relatively rare.

Anorexics are obsessed with being thin; they see themselves as fat even when they look emaciated and ill to others. The causes of this disorder are not well understood and the prognosis for recovery is not good (Franken, 1982). Most treated victims suffer relapses, and many, such as singer Karen Carpenter, die of the disease or complications brought on by malnutrition, such as dehydration and pneumonia.

*Bulimia,* another eating disorder, is estimated to be about four times as common as *anorexia nervosa.* Bulimics eat very large amounts of food (on eating "binges"), then self-induce vomiting or take laxatives to avoid gaining weight. Most do this secretly; actress Jane Fonda, now celebrated for her athletic body and physical stamina, confessed to having been bulimic for more than 10 years.

Unlike *anorexia nervosa,* bulimia is seldom fatal, but most bulimics suffer from digestive and dental problems. In addition, psychologists and psychiatrists find that the guilt associated with this bizarre behavior can lead to anxiety and depression that may persist long after the behavior has ceased.

Bulimia, like *anorexia nervosa,* is most common among adolescents, but both disorders tend to persist into later years once begun. So far as is known at this time, neither has a physical cause. Treatment is both psychological and medical (to deal with the physical results of the disorders) and professional help is essential (Schlesier-Strupp, 1984). Eating disorders do *not* fall into the province of self-management of behavior.

**Summing Up** ■

We live in a society that has a relatively high percentage of overweight people. Many qualify as obese and so leave themselves open to a number of physical, emotional, and psychological problems that their slim peers are less likely to have. Because our society places such a high value on slimness, there also are a substantial percentage of people who weigh more than they want to even though they are not overweight by health standards.

Researchers tell us that excess pounds (real or "imagined") are the result of what we eat, when we eat, and how we live, as well as how much we eat. Losing weight, then, is not just a matter of dieting. Dieting without exercise is unlikely to lead to real weight loss except in very obese people since our bodies are very good at adjusting to a lower intake of food. To a point, the less you eat, the less your body needs.

---

## ■ *KEY WORDS AND PHRASES*

| | | |
|---|---|---|
| addictive substance | aversion therapy | causes of alcohol abuse |
| alcohol | basal metabolic rate | cocaine |
| alcoholic | behavioral effects of alcohol abuse | controlled substances |
| Alcoholics Anonymous (AA) | caffeine | dieting |

| drug | marijuana | psychological addiction |
|------|-----------|------------------------|
| eating disorders | obese | psychological effects of alcohol abuse |
| fat cells | physical addiction | tobacco |
| intoxication | physical effects of alcohol abuse | |

---

■ *READ ON*

*Drugs: A Factual Account* by D. Dusek and D. A. Girdano. Reading, MA: Addison-Wesley, 1980. A readable book that covers historical, psychological, physiological, and legal aspects of the more common legal, illegal, and controlled drug substances.

*Learning to Change: A Self-Management Approach to Adjustment* by R. A. Martin and E. Y. Poland. New York: McGraw-Hill, 1980. This basic primer for applying principles of learning to the self-management of behavior is both interesting and useful.

*Getting Thin* by G. Mirkin, M.D. Boston: Little, Brown, 1983. Not a diet book, but a book about fat—where it comes from, how it can hurt us, and what it does for us (surprise!). The coauthor of *Sports Medicine* covers basic nutrition, physiological functioning, and facts and fallacies about weight loss in a form that serves as a useful reference book for anyone.

---

■ *REFERENCES*

Allen, A. (1984, Oct. 23). How to lose five pounds forever. *Woman's Day,* 91–94.

American Psychiatric Association. (1987). *Diagnostic and statistical manual of mental disorders, Third edition, Revised.* Washington, DC: American Psychiatric Association.

Bales, J. (1985). Effects of caffeine linked to personality, perception. *APA Monitor, 15,* 26–27.

Bertram, J. F., Jones, M. E., & Rogers, A. W. (1981). Does structural recovery of bronchial epithelium follow the cessation of smoking? Abstract cited in *Journal of Anatomy, 133,* 479.

Braden, W., Stillman, R. C., & Wyatt, R. J. (1974). Effects of marijuana on contingent negative valuation and reaction times. *Archives of General Psychiatry, 31,* 537–541.

Brandsma, J. M., Maultsby, M. C., & Welsh, R. J. (1980). *Outpatient treatment of alcoholism: A review and comparative study.* Baltimore: University Park Press.

Celentano, D. D., & McQueen, D. V. (1978). Comparison of alcoholism prevalence rates obtained by survey and indirect estimates. *Journal of Studies on Alcohol, 39,* 420–434.

Chernin, K. (1985). *The hungry self.* New York: Random House.

Coelho, R. (1985). Longest prior abstinence and cessation of smoking. *Psychological Reports, 56:* 468–470.

Cole, D. (1984, Dec. 23). Eating too much this season? Maybe not. *Family Weekly,* 5.

Coleman, J. C., Butcher, J. N., & Carson, R. C. (1984). *Abnormal psychology and modern life* (7th ed.). Glenview, IL: Scott, Foresman.

Edwards, D. D. (1986). Nicotine: A drug of choice? *Science News, 129,* 44–45.

Fisher, K. (1985). Cocaine concerns called well-based. *APA Monitor, 16,* 28.

Foley, D. (1985, June). Coffee and you. *Prevention,* 63–67.

Franken, R. E. (1982). *Human motivation.* Monterey, CA: Brooks/Cole.

Goodwin, D. W., Schulsinger, F., Hermansen, L., Guze, S. B., & Winokur, G. (1973). Alcohol problems in adoptees raised apart from alcoholic biological parents. *Archives of General Psychiatry, 28,* 238–243.

Hamilton, E. M. N., Whitney, E. N., & Sizer, F. S. (1985). *Nutrition: Concepts and controversies* (3rd ed.). St. Paul, MN: West.

Hirsch, J., M. D. (1985, Feb. 25). Quoted in: Gauging the fat of the land. *Time,* 72.

Istuan, J., & Matarazzo, J. D. (1984). Tobacco, alcohol, and caffeine use: A review of their interrelationships. *Psychological Bulletin, 95,* 301–326.

Julien, R. M. (1978). *A primer of drug action.* San Francisco: Freeman.

Kolata, G. (1986). Weight regulation may start in our cells, not psyches. *Smithsonian, 16,* 91–97.

Levenson, R. W., Sher, K. J., Grossman, L. M., Newman, J., & Newlin, D. B. (1980). Alcohol and stress response dampening: Pharmacological effects, expectancy and tension reduction. *Journal of Abnormal Psychology, 89*, 528–538.

Linder, P. (1984, Oct. 8). Quoted in A. Meyer: Latest diet craze—not for everyone. *U.S. News & World Report,* 57–60.

Lloyd, R. W., Jr., & Salzberg, H. C. (1975). Controlled social drinking: An alternative to abstinence as a treatment goal for some alcohol abusers. *Psychological Bulletin, 82.* 815–842.

Marlatt, G. A., & Gordon, J. R. (1980). Determinants of relapse: Implications for the maintenance of behavior change. In P. Davidson and S. Davidson (Eds.), *Behavioral medicine: Changing life styles.* New York: Brunner/Mazel.

Mervis, J. (1985). Policy institute tackles smoking behavior. *APA Monitor, 15,* 7.

Miller, W. R. (1985). Motivation for treatment: A review with special emphasis on alcoholism. *Psychological Bulletin, 98,* 84–107.

National Council on Alcoholism. (1980). *Facts on alcoholism.* New York: Author.

National Institute of Drug Abuse. (1981). *Trend report: January, 1978-September, 1980.* Data from Client Oriented Data Acquisition Program (CODAP) (Series E, No. 24). Washington, DC: U.S. Government Printing Office.

Needham, J. (1988, Mar. 25). Under the influence. *Los Angeles Times,* IX–1.

Pernanen, K. (1967). Alcohol and crimes of violence. In B. Kissin and H. Begleiter (Eds.), *The biology of alcoholism, Vol. 4: Social aspects of alcohol.* New York: Plenum.

Pliner, P. L., & Cappell, H. D. (1974). Modification of affective consequences of alcohol: A comparison of social and solitary drinking. *Journal of Abnormal Psychology, 83,* 418–425.

Pomerleau, O. (1988, May 30). Quoted in C. Gorman; Why it's so hard to quit smoking. *Time,* 56.

Schaefer, H. H. (1971). Accepted theories disproven. *Science News, 99,* 182.

Schlesier-Strupp, B. (1984). Bulimia: A review of the literature. *Psychological Bulletin, 95,* 247–257.

Schuckit, M. A. (1980). Self-rating of alcohol intoxication by young men with and without family histories of alcoholism. *Journal of Studies on Alcohol, 41,* 242–249.

Science '86 (1986). Currents. 8.

Segovia-Riquelma, N., Varela, A., & Mardones, J. (1971). Appetite for alcohol. In Y. Israel & J. Mardones (Eds.), *Biological basis for alcoholism.* New York: Wiley.

Sizer, F. S., & Whitney, E. N. (1988). *Life choices: Health concepts and strategies.* St. Paul, MN: West.

Steele, C. M. (1986). What happens when you drink too much? *Psychology Today, 20,* 48–52.

Stunkard, A. (1986). Quoted in G. Kolata: Weight reduction may start in our cells, not psyches. *Smithsonian, 16,* 91–97.

Taylor, R. A. (1986, July 28). America on drugs. *U.S. News & World Report,* 48–54.

Thomas, E. (1986, Sept. 15). America's crusade. *Time,* 60–66.

Truitt, E. B. (1971). The xanthines. In J. R. Dipalma (Ed.), *Drill's pharmacology in medicine* (4th ed.). New York: McGraw-Hill.

Ungaro, S. K. (1984, Oct. 2). Teen alcoholics speak out: What every parent must know. *Family Circle,* Oct. 2, 34–42.

*U.S. News & World Report* (1982, Aug. 30). Anorexia: The starving disease epidemic. 47–48.

*U.S. News & World Report,* (1985, Nov. 18). Teen drug abuse—The news is bad. 16.

Wells, S. J. (1984). Caffeine: Implications of recent research for clinical practice. *American Journal of Orthopsychiatry, 54,* 375–389.

Whitney, E. N., & Hamilton, E. M. N. (1987). *Understanding nutrition* (4th. ed.), St. Paul, MN: West.

Wood, P. D. (1985, Jan.). Eat more, play more—weigh less. *Executive Health Report,* 97–103.

# Relationship Problems

No one knows the reasons. The trend-setters know the rules: The watch—it is a Swatch, naturally—should be worn loosely around the wrist, never snug.

Socks should be pushed down around the ankles, never pulled up . . .

Oversized shirts, Levi 501's, antique brooches, black and anything from Benelton, the Italian clothing chain, is in. Neon, rhinestones and Jordache jeans are out . . .

To be avoided at all costs is looking like someone from out of town. "As soon as you see someone coming over the bridge wearing something you're wearing, you take it off," Ian Dallow said (Rimer, 1985).

The excerpt is from a news article about the mysteries of what's in and what's out of fashion with high school seniors, but it could as easily be about college students, yuppies, jet setters, corporate executives, grandparents, or any other social grouping. No one knows where these "rules" come from, but almost everyone is aware of them, and most of us conform to them to some degree.

Wearing your socks around your ankles is harmless enough, but there are times when pressure to conform to the expectations of others is not so easy to accept. This and other problems with being comfortable in your social world are discussed in this chapter. Self-consciousness, shyness, and loneliness, which are ongoing sources of difficulty for many people, are discussed first. Then, problems that can arise with peers, friends, and in special relationships with one person are examined.

## PROBLEMS WITH GETTING ALONG IN THE WORLD

Have you ever stopped to think about how much time you spend in the presence of other people? If you are a college student, you are surrounded by people in class, at the library, in the sorority or fraternity house, and at football games. If you work, you have co-workers and perhaps customers as well. There are people around when you shop, go to the bank, or attend a movie. Even if you don't have to interact with them, they are there, and this by itself is a source of discomfort to some.

## Self-Consciousness

We use the term **self-consciousness** to mean being overly aware of how we appear to others. People who are self-conscious are focused on themselves and are uncomfortable around others because they feel as if they and their appearance and behavior are continually being watched and evaluated.

Psychologists Fenigstein, Scheier, and Buss (1975) believe that there are actually three types of self-consciousness. Being overly aware of how we appear to others describes what they call *public self-consciousness.* Because of their belief that all eyes are on them, people who are high on public self-consciousness tend to be very concerned with their appearance, with wearing the "right clothes" and with behaving the "right way."

People high on public self-consciousness also are more likely than other people to make the assumption that something going on is relevant to themselves. Results of one study, for example, found that significantly more of the highly self-conscious students believed that a good or bad exam singled out by the teacher for comment (before the exams were returned) was their own (Fenigstein, 1984).

*Private self-consciousness,* by contrast, refers to a very high level of attention to one's own feelings and thoughts. This is a literal meaning of self-consciousness—consciousness of self. These people are what we call *introspective;* they are forever examining what is inside their heads. This isn't necessarily a bad thing; if you want to be a writer, for example, a high level of private self-consciousness probably is useful.

Fenigstein and his colleagues' concept of *social self-consciousness* is most like what we all tend to think of when we think of self-consciousness. This is a generalized anxiety in the presence of others. People with a high level of social self-consciousness often dislike parties and other social gatherings and sit in the back of the classroom hoping to be unnoticed. They are easily embarrassed and will go to great lengths to avoid a scene. This concern can override even their own health and safety, as the incident described in Exhibit 14–1 illustrates.

Of the three types of self-consciousness described, social self-consciousness probably causes the most suffering. Public self-consciousness may be useful in some ways, for example, to a politician. Private self-consciousness takes up a lot of time and energy, but it too may be helpful. For example, one study found that people with greater tendencies toward introspection had more sat-

**EXHIBIT 14–1**

## To Die of Embarrassment

The summer sky was clear blue; the air did not stir. At 8:00 A.M., it was hot as blazes. As usual on a summer Saturday, I was sitting on a shadeless concrete pool deck watching my children's swim meet. Two hours later, the sun sizzled, my head ached, and I was sick to my stomach. I couldn't concentrate on the banter of the other parents. I was gasping for breath. I realized I was heading for a heat stroke.

Did I ask for help? Seek out a lifeguard? No, I quietly left the pool deck and sat under a tree because I didn't want to cause a fuss.

Some of the swimmers asked if I was O.K. I lied, "I'm fine, just a little hot." One by one, my children, other swimmers, and the coaches came over. Each time I insisted, "I'm fine, really." The coach suggested a cool shower, but I declined. Why? I didn't want to walk past the spectators—other parents who were my friends—because I was afraid that I would throw up on the way to the bath house. I preferred to die of heat stroke rather than die of embarrassment.

*Note:* From "To Die of Embarrassment" by L. F. McGee, June 1985, *Savvy*, p. 80.

isfying intimate relationships with others (Franzoi, Davis, & Young, 1985). Can you think of any explanations for this finding?

People with high levels of social anxiety may be quite comfortable with family, friends, or a one-on-one special relationship, but more general social situations frighten them. Is there any cure for this problem? Some people find it helps to remind themselves frequently of two facts. First, the fears expressed in Exhibit 14–1 are unfounded; you don't die of embarrassment. Second, most of us are of far less interest to others than we imagine. So you may be a one-minute sensation if you give a really weird answer to a professor's question, but it won't kill you. And you can be fairly confident that no one but you will give the incident another thought when class is over.

Of course, knowing these things and believing them are not necessarily the same. Giving yourself permission to make a fool of yourself once in awhile (if that's the way it actually goes) is very freeing, but if you can't bear the thought you may want to seek professional help (Mereson, 1985). Extreme social self-consciousness has much in common with phobias, and psychotherapists have some very effective ways to deal with these.

## Shyness

Self-conscious people who suffer from high social self-consciousness and shy people have much in common. Both avoid putting themselves forward and tend to become anxious if put into the spotlight. Psychologists find that both typically have poor self-esteem and are fearful that interactions with others will confirm this low self-opinion. There do seem to be some differences, however. For one, self-conscious people tend to overestimate their interest value to others, whereas shy people are more likely to underestimate how interesting they are to others.

A second difference between shyness and self-consciousness seems to be in the extent to which it pervades an individual's life. If you are self-conscious (in the social sense), you are likely to avoid going into expensive shops for fear the clerks will turn up their noses at the way you are dressed. If someone honks a horn as you are driving in traffic, you probably assume this behavior was directed at you. You don't like going to the beach because you don't think you have a good body and you believe everyone will be looking at you. By contrast, shyness seems to be less pervasive.

**Shyness** may be thought of as a high degree of caution in interpersonal relationships. Shy people are uncomfortable about approaching other people and making contact with them, and they often feel anxious when they are actually in the spotlight, but they are less prone to feel that they are always being watched and evaluated. In fact, surveys indicate that most people who describe themselves as shy say they experience this only in certain situations (meeting a new group of people, for example). The idea that shyness is a deep-rooted personality trait is not supported by research (Zimbardo, 1977).

Psychologist Philip Zimbardo, who has made an extensive study of shyness, believes that most people can get over it. The keys, he says, are understanding the problem, building up self-esteem, and improving social skills. This last may be particularly critical since many people report that the fear of interacting with others is much greater than the actual experience.

If you are shy, you might want to make a pact with yourself that you will say hello to the people you come into contact with for a week or so. When you are comfortable with this, move up to initiating small conversations with people you interact with on a business basis—bank tellers, grocery check-out clerks, your server in a restaurant, to name but a few possibilities. If you have trouble getting started, watch and copy a friend who never seems to experience any difficulty interacting with strangers.

An unfortunate consequence of shyness can be loneliness.

You probably will be surprised at how quickly you improve your own social skills if you practice. But if you find that no amount of determination enables you to try out these exercises, you may want to get some help. Shyness is a real problem for many people; psychologists take it seriously even if others sometimes do not (Harris, 1984).

## Loneliness

An unfortunate result of both self-consciousness and shyness is that individuals with these problems may shrink from contact with others until their social lives become so small that they begin to feel lonely. *Social loneliness* is the loneliness that occurs when a person does not have a network of friends and acquaintances with whom to share life (Weiss, 1973). Since the obvious cure for social loneliness is to go out and meet people, those who are shy or overly self-conscious are caught in a vicious cycle.

Not all people who are shy or self-conscious are lonely, and not all people who are lonely are shy or self-conscious. *Situational loneliness* occurs when something about an individual's life circumstances is causing him or her to feel lonely. You may have experienced this when you first went to college and found yourself in a new environment away from your friends and family. Long illness, divorce, or a death in the family also can make you feel lonely for awhile.

Loneliness is more central to the lives of others. *Emotional loneliness* stems from a dearth of intimate relationships. This form of loneliness is not situational, and it is not the result of a lack of social contacts. People who suffer from emotional loneliness tend to have low self-esteem, to experience anxiety in interpersonal encounters, and to fear being rejected or hurt by others (Wilbert & Rupert, 1986). This fear may begin at quite an early age, and it can last throughout life.

Psychologists have studied loneliness for some time, and their findings contradict a number of common myths about this condition. They find, for example, that it is not old people who are more likely to be lonely, but those in the 18 to 25 age group (Meer, 1985). It also appears that more men than women may experience emotional loneliness, although women are more likely to admit to and discuss the problem.

Actually, most of us feel lonely at some time or other. Social loneliness is the easiest to combat. If you have this problem, a first step is to teach yourself to be comfortable with yourself. People who don't know what to do with themselves when no one is around or available for socializing are hard hit when some circumstance leaves them temporarily alone. Some suggestions for learning to be more comfortable with yourself are made in Exhibit 14–2.

If you take the suggestions in Exhibit 14–2 seriously, you'll quickly learn (if you don't know it already) that being alone and being lonely are not the same thing. Of course, no one wants to be alone all the time, and if your problem is social loneliness, it probably is an unnecessary condition. The world, especially a college campus, is full of social organizations whose members are all potential friends.

If you find yourself saying "yes, but . . . " to this and suggestions that may be made by others for enlarging your social horizons, you may need to reconsider your problem. If you feel unhappy with this aspect of your life but

**EXHIBIT 14–2**
## Being Alone and Liking It

Many people dislike being alone and will do almost anything to avoid it. Others have learned that this time can be enormously rewarding, and they look forward to having time with themselves. Here, in a series of graded steps, are some suggestions for learning to be alone and like it.

1. *Put "found time" to good use.* The next time your date or friend cancels out at the last minute, resist the temptation to call around for a substitute or to slump in front of the television watching something you don't even care about and feeling sorry for yourself. Use this time to do one of those things that you never seem to "have time" to get around to. Organize your closet or change the oil in your car or write that long-overdue letter. When you are just learning to be alone, it is important to be both active (so you don't brood) and productive (so that you experience the satisfaction of having accomplished something).

2. *Schedule time alone in your home when you know that your spouse, live-in, or roommate(s) will be away.* Eat when and what you want (and where you want), watch whatever you choose on television, or read in undisturbed luxury. What is important here is that you have *chosen* to be alone at this time.

3. *Go out somewhere alone at least once a week.* You can go to do the laundry, to the shopping mall, or to a movie—anywhere at all that you want or need to go and usually would not go alone. Keep practicing this step until you feel as comfortable about doing things away from home by yourself as you did with other people.

4. *Go out to eat alone once in awhile.* The ultimate challenge for learning to like your own company is eating alone in a nice restaurant. You can expect this to take some time; some people never do master it. Your goal is to feel comfortable and to be able to behave normally. You don't want to have to apologize to the hostess or maître d' for being "just one" or to carry a book to read while waiting for service and eating. Some tips: pick an interesting place to eat, make a reservation, and go at a time when there will be plenty of other people around (so you don't feel quite so conspicuous).

reluctant or unwilling to take any steps to change things, your loneliness may be emotional rather than social.

Emotional loneliness can be extremely difficult to cope with alone, especially if it has persisted for any length of time. A counselor or therapist will listen to you, help you to clarify your feelings, and perhaps make some suggestions you can feel comfortable with for changing things. He or she also is a safe person to practice having an intimate relationship with since the counseling situation is well structured and defined. A therapist won't take over your life (or your apartment), leave you for a more attractive man or woman, make fun of you, or say things deliberately to hurt you—all fears that contribute to emotional loneliness.

## Summing Up ∎

Most of us spend a great deal of time with, or just around, other people. If you are shy or self-conscious, this can be uncomfortable. Self-conscious people focus on themselves and often think everyone is watching and evaluating them. Shy people are anxious if they must make contact with others. Both of these problems with adjusting to the world can create social loneliness.

Emotional loneliness comes not from being alone, but from fear of close relationships with others. The emotionally lonely person often has many acquaintances, but no friends. This kind of loneliness often leads to depression and can be a forerunner of suicide; therefore, it should not be ignored.

# PROBLEMS WITH PEERS AND FRIENDS

Peers, you recall, are age mates and peer groups are groups of people in your own situation (and usually about your own age) with whom you identify. Being accepted by their peer groups is extremely important to adolescents; it often seems to be the most important thing in their lives. But most of us never really lose this desire to be insiders, whatever our age, and the price of this acceptance almost always is conformity to a group's norms.

You'll also remember that norms are unwritten rules for behavior that grow out of the social interaction of some group or grouping. Some late-1985 norms for dress for urban teenagers (a social grouping) are described at the beginning of this chapter. It would be difficult to say exactly where these dress norms come from; like weeds, they often seem just to spring up, and they are very powerful influences on the behavior of individuals. In this section we consider some of the problems that this influence can create. We also look briefly at a related problem—when friends ask too much of you.

## Peer Pressure and Influence

Most of us are members of several groups (a club, professional organization, or sorority, for example) and groupings (the members of a particular church, a class, the people on one floor of a dormitory). Some of these groups are more important to us than others. The important ones, which psychologists call **reference groups,** influence the way we think about things and the way we evaluate our own behavior. If you are on a sports team, for example, part of your self-evaluation of your own athletic ability rests on how well others on the team play. And your opinions on the role of sports in education are influenced considerably by those of other team members and coaches.

Reference groups are important to us; we want to stay in them and be accepted. They give us a niche in this big world and offer support, help, and solace when the world gets to be too much. But these benefits come with a price tag. Groups make demands on us in the form of asking for loyalty, participation, and conformity to group standards, or norms.

The price of being accepted by a group usually is conforming to its expectations for behavior.

### When the Group Wants Too Much

You've read stories about the strange or illegal or horrible things that people have done under the influence of some group to which they belong. Members of street gangs shoot members of other street gangs, members of campus social groups streak naked through commencement exercises, and teenagers go to school with blue hair.

Stories like these make the news, but it is important to remember that young people are not the only ones who must pay a price for acceptance into groups that are important to them. There is the woman executive who wears an unattractive hair style and unfashionable clothes so that she won't be "too feminine" to be accepted by upper management. There is the young salesman who doesn't like to drink or tell "dirty" stories but does both at sales meetings in order to be one of the gang. There is the member of the board of directors of the local country club who goes along with rejecting an Italian applicant even though he does not share the prejudices of the other members.

In short, expectations for conformity to groups in dress, behavior, and expressed opinions do not end when we turn 21 and/or leave school behind. And, like the country club board member, there invariably will come a time when there is a clash between your personal preferences, desires, or values and what the group expects. Then the question becomes: To what extent can you meet group demands without losing your personal integrity? Do you have to give in, and if you do, will you have to keep giving in until your personal identity is threatened?

There is a danger that this can happen, of course, but it doesn't have to. For one thing, groups need a certain amount of nonconformity in order to remain flexible enough to survive changing conditions. This means that you don't always have to conform, and playing the "devil's advocate" by explaining your reasons may perform a valuable function for the group.

For another thing, most groups tolerate some deviance from their expectations before you are at risk of being relegated to being an outsider. In addition, the extent to which you contribute something to the group affects the group's reaction. Hollander (1964) has offered a detailed analysis of the extent to which deviance from group standards is tolerated relative to that status of an individual in the group.

Hollander suggests that members of groups accumulate what he calls **idiosyncratic credits,** a sort of credit account for license to behave in individual, nonconformist ways. The higher an individual's status, the greater the credit he or she has available. Since a group's leader (informal or formal) tends to have the greatest status, this individual usually can get away with considerable deviance from group norms.

Other members of groups who may have relatively greater idiosyncratic credit accounts are people who make important contributions to the group functioning in some way. For example, a regular study group may have one member who ignores all of the group's informal rules. He or she doesn't bring copies of notes for other members, offer to let the group study in his or her apartment, get to meetings on time, or even attend all of the meetings. The group puts up with this, however, because this individual makes straight *A*'s and has exceptional ability to communicate insight on subject matter to other group members. In other words, there is a relationship between *competence* and the extent to which someone may deviate from group norms.

## Resisting Group Influence

**Conformity** is changing your behavior or a belief so that it agrees with those of some group (or grouping) of other people. The decision of whether or not to do this when you feel strongly that what the group wants of you is out of

It is very easy to forgive others their mistakes. It takes more gut and gumption to forgive them for having witnessed your own.

*Jessamyn West*

line is always a personal one. You take a risk if you decide not to, but as discussed, this risk may be less than you fear. Even when it is substantial, however, many people resist the attempts of groups to influence them to conform to expectations. Psychologists have been interested in this individuality for some time, and this line of research has identified a number of factors that make it more likely that resistance to group influence will be successful.

- *More intelligent people seem to be able to resist influence attempts more successfully.* In general, more intelligent people are more inclined to think for themselves on issues, although they also are more likely than less intelligent people to listen to attempts made to persuade them (Tedeschi & Lindskold, 1976).

- *Strongly held personal values seem to make it easier to resist attempts to make people conform.* A group is unlikely to get a deeply religious person to join them in shoplifting, for example, since that person feels strongly that stealing is wrong (Jewell & Reitz, 1981).

- *High self-esteem seems to make it easier to resist group influence attempts when people don't want to conform.* People with high self-esteem are less dependent upon the good opinion of others; thus, the ridicule or arguments that can come with deviating from expectations are less threatening (Nord, 1969).

- *A strong belief in one's own opinions, values, and competencies regarding the issue at hand makes it easier to resist pressures to conform.* This is especially true when the group standard seems out of line in some way (Kelly & Thibaut, 1969). Operating against this factor, however, is the power of group consensus.

## The Power of Group Consensus

Study the lines in Figure 14–1 carefully. Which of the three comparison lines is the same length as the standard line? The answer is obvious: comparison line number 1. But suppose 10 people before you gave the answer "line number 2." Would you stick to your opinion in the face of this *group consensus*? A surprisingly large percentage of people will not.

In the classic study of conformity from which the lines in Figure 14–1 are taken, subjects were asked to give their opinions about similarities or differ-

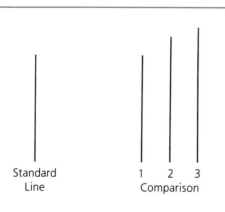

Figure 14–1   **The Lines from the Asch Study**

ences between various pairs of lines (Asch, 1955). It was arranged that the real subjects would give their answers after listening to a group of other "subjects" who really were acting on instructions from the experimenter (these subjects are called confederates). Upon occasion, all 10 of the confederates would give an answer that obviously was wrong (such as, line 2 is the same length as the comparison line). A full one-third of the time, the real subject then would give the same answer.

The results of the Asch study have been confirmed many times; group consensus can have a very strong influence on an individual's confidence in his or her own position. The demonstration is all the more impressive when you remember that the subjects in these studies did not know any of the members of the group to whose opinion they were conforming. Research results such as these may make it a bit easier to understand (if not approve) historical examples of mass conformity, such as the behavior of German citizens during World War II and the mass suicide of Jim Jones's followers in Guyana in the late 1970s.

What does all of this mean to you if a group is pressuring you to do or say or believe something you find is unacceptable? Well, the decision is still yours (that hasn't changed), but studies of conformity help us understand that it is indeed possible to be right when everyone else is wrong. If you feel strongly, stick to your guns. Much the same advice may be given when individuals are pressuring you, but like many other situations in life, there are skills for coping with this one.

## When Friends Impose

You know the scenario. You've finally finished dinner and dishes and settled down to watch your favorite TV show when Joe calls. He has run out of gas and wants you to stop by a service station, pick up some, and bring it to him. Then there is Diane, who wants to use your apartment with her boyfriend while you are away on vacation. Or Marty, who wants you to give up your first free Sunday in weeks to paint a bedroom. Or Jeff, who is only 17, who wants to use your driver's license to buy whiskey.

Friends are wonderful and what would we do without them? But sometimes, as in the incidents described, they can be a real pain. They ask you to do things that are inconvenient, illegal, or that you plain just don't want to do. But if you don't, what will happen to the friendship? And if you decide to refuse, how do you say no? These are hard questions and only you can determine the answers, but there are some questions you can ask yourself that may make it easier to figure out what your decision should be. The decision tree in Figure 14–2 puts these questions into a program that you can use for almost any request.

### How Do You Say No?

Suppose that you use the decision tree aid and come up with a no answer that you feel sure is the right decision? How do you say no to a friend? Let's look first at some ways *not* to say it.

■ *Don't apologize.* You have the right to turn down a request, even from a friend. Beginning your refusal with "I'm sorry, but . . . " makes it sound

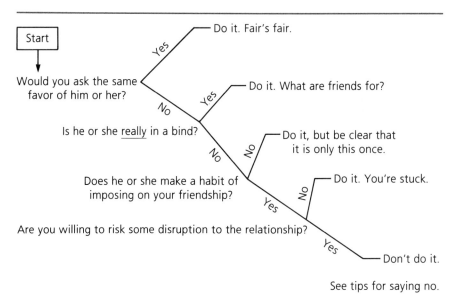

**Figure 14–2   Do a Favor—Or Not?**

Start

Would you ask the same favor of him or her?
— Yes → Do it. Fair's fair.
— No →

Is he or she <u>really</u> in a bind?
— Yes → Do it. What are friends for?
— No →

Does he or she make a habit of imposing on your friendship?
— No → Do it, but be clear that it is only this once.
— Yes →

Are you willing to risk some disruption to the relationship?
— No → Do it. You're stuck.
— Yes → Don't do it.

See tips for saying no.

as if you are uncertain about this and perhaps open to having your mind changed.

■ *Don't hang your refusal on an excuse.* The problem with excuses is that people are very good at finding ways around them. So if you tell Marty that you are busy on Sunday, Marty may find that Sunday is not the only day the bedroom can be painted.

■ *Don't pin your refusal on someone else or some external circumstance.* If you tell Diane that your landlord doesn't like for other people to stay in your apartment (otherwise, you'd be glad to let her and her boyfriend stay there), she may begin to argue with you. Your landlord doesn't have any legal grounds for objecting, anyway he won't know they are there . . . Unless you really *would* do it were it not for someone else or some circumstance, take the responsibility for your refusal. Otherwise, expect to have similar requests in the future.

Now, some tips on what *to do* when saying no.

■ *Learn to use the phrase "not willing."* This may be hard to do at first, but it will serve you well once you master it. For one thing, it makes it clear that you have thought about the request and made a conscious decision; you are not just refusing off the top of your head. *Not willing* also sounds more objective and less emotional than *won't*. Your friends may not like your decision, but they will know you thought about it.

■ *Say no to the request, not the friend.* By all means, tell Jeff that you are not willing to lend your driver's license to be used as a fake I.D. But if you value the friendship, leave out the part where you say; "Only a jerk would ask me to do something like that."

■ *Show that you understand and sympathize with the friend's plight even though you are saying no.* For example, you might tell Marty that you realize the

One of the joys of friendship is being able to help out when you are needed, even though there are some times when you'd rather say no.

painting would go much faster with two people and you hope she finds someone to help.

■ *Tell your friend what you* are *willing to do even if you won't do the favor asked.* For example, you might tell Joe that you don't want to go out but you will be glad to call a taxi company and explain the situation. If he doesn't have any cash with him, you can even offer to pay for the taxi if he'll come to your house.

All of these are tips for saying no, but there is something to remember if you say yes as well. If you agree to do what you are asked, do it with good grace. Certainly, you may tell the person asking that it is inconvenient and you are doing it only because he or she is a friend, but once you say it stop complaining. Nobody likes a martyr, and you may need a favor yourself someday.

## Summing Up ■

Groups can be a great source of fun, comfort, and support; but they expect you to pay for these benefits in loyalty, participation, and conformity to expectations. The question of how much of this conformity is too much is one that only you can answer. Pressure from friends can be even more difficult since these one-on-one relationships are the very cornerstone of the social worlds of most of us. There are, however, times when no is the right answer for you.

## PROBLEMS WITH SPECIAL PERSONAL RELATIONSHIPS

In previous chapters we examined marriage and other relationships of a personal, intimate nature and discussed some of the adjustments required of almost anyone in such a relationship. In this chapter, problems that people have with intimate relationships are examined from a more individual perspective. Among the more common of these problems are finding someone to love, jealousy and other destructive emotions, and saving (or abandoning) an intimate relationship.

### Looking for a Special Someone: Why Is It So Hard?

In 1970 only 29% of the population was single; by 1988 the percentage was about 40. There is no evidence that these figures reflect a rejection of the married state, however. Most people still want and expect to marry, even those who have had bad experiences before. But ironically, in this age of unparalleled interaction of the sexes, freedom of personal choice, and sexual permissiveness, finding that special someone seems more difficult than ever.

People give many reasons for not being able to find someone with whom to have a satisfying and lasting relationship. The following are among the ones mentioned most often.

■ *I'm not good looking enough.* Many people believe that it is their lack of physical attractiveness that stands between them and a good relationship.

While we do live in a society that seems obsessed with attractiveness, unattractive people get married every day. One possible explanation for this inconsistency lies in attitudes toward looks. A belief that they are all-important can lead those who weren't born good-looking to give up. The truth, of course, is that we all have good features, and we all have the potential to develop attractive personalities and to make ourselves interesting people.

Another aspect of the looks problem seems to lie in expectations. Many physically unattractive people adopt a sort of double standard. As one young man put it; "Yes, I'm fat. I know that. But that doesn't mean I want a fat girlfriend. I'm as entitled to a good-looking one as the next guy." No one is to say that he isn't as entitled as the next guy, but he may be reducing his chances for finding Ms. Right. Psychologists have substantial evidence that couples of about equal attractiveness are likely to get together and to have a better chance of forming a good long-term relationship (e.g., Berscheid & Walster, 1979).

- *I don't know what women/men want anymore.* Another stumbling block to special relationships is confusion about what the opposite sex wants in a partner. Both sexes feel they get contradictory messages. Men say that women want the best of both worlds; they want to be treated as equals when it suits them and to be dependent when it suits them. Women say the men want them to be warm, loving, and cater to their needs, but to be independent when it comes to financial matters and the day-to-day hassles of living.

The answer to dealing with sex-role conflicts and confusions in a relationship seems to be for the partners to work out how they will be with each other. This may or may not be how they are with the rest of the world. Who is going to do what (and depend on the other for what) is an issue that can be worked out between two people even though there does not seem to be any way to take a general position right now. The plain truth is that just about *everybody* is confused on this subject in these days of transition from old sex-role stereotypes.

- *I never meet any eligible men/women.* Another common complaint of people looking for someone special is simply that the people with whom they regularly come into contact are too old, too young, married, gay, or all of the same sex as themselves. Many people are in this situation, and the solution obviously is to look somewhere else. But where?

In the 1950s people who wanted to meet eligible potential relationship partners were advised to join a social club or go to church. In the 1960s they went back to school or joined a "cause." In the 1970s it was the bar scene; in the 1980s health and fitness clubs and singles resorts, cruises, and vacations are popular. "Lonely hearts clubs" have been around for a long time, and recently there has been an enormous growth in the dating-service industry. All of these possibilities have advantages and disadvantages, some of which are described in *For Discussion*.

## FOR DISCUSSION:

## LOOKING FOR LOVE

There are all kinds of ways to meet another person who might be a partner for a special relationship. These range from chance meetings in the produce department of the grocery store to carefully screened dates selected by a computer; the singles industry is estimated to be a $40 million–a-year business in the 1980s. Some of the pluses and minuses of various ways to meet people are as follows.

**Personal Advertisement in Newspaper or Magazine**

*Pluses:* Newspaper ads are cheap, get you a large response, and give you hours of entertainment reading the replies. And, surprisingly, many people report finding interesting and attractive dates in this way. The days in which only desperate, homely, or "weird" people put personal ads in the newspaper seem to be gone.

*Minuses.* Of course, there are still some pretty strange people out there, and this is the number-one drawback to this method of meeting people. Women who report using personal ads successfully recommend having a male friend as a safety backup for the first meeting.

**Dating Services**

*Pluses.* Dating services range from those that do some hand matching of men and women on the basis of a written questionnaire to those that do computer matching and those that use sophisticated video equipment and maintain "libraries" for their clientele. The major advantage of all three types is that someone else has done some screening for you. You are less likely to

find yourself going out with someone who is crazy about tennis while your favorite recreation is stamp collecting than if you make a date with someone you meet through a newspaper ad. Video dating services take the guesswork out of appearance as well. You sit down and watch video tapes of possible dates and identify those who appeal to you.

*Minuses.* Dating services can be quite expensive—up to $1,000 for a 12-month membership. And most offer no guarantees of dates. In the video arrangement, for example, the men or women you choose are shown *your* tape; if they aren't interested, you don't hear from them. Services that do offer a guarantee of so many introductions can get careless; if they don't have anyone on file who meets your preferences, they improvise.

**The Bar Scene**

*Pluses.* So-called singles bars have one great advantage: everyone knows why everyone else is there, which is a time saver. And a few drinks are considerably cheaper than a dating service.

*Minuses.* You'll meet lots of people in a bar, but most who frequent these establishments report that the odds of meeting someone with whom you are likely to have more than a casual encounter are low. And many people find the "meat market" atmosphere unpleasant.

**Singles Clubs**

*Pluses.* Singles clubs range from those sponsored by the local church to the elaborate Club Med organization,

which has resorts for singles all over the world. As in singles bars, you'll meet a lot of people and you can assume that those you meet are unattached (although you will be wrong occasionally). Singles clubs have activities, such as dancing, skiing, aerobics classes, and the like, and many people find they have a good time even if they don't meet anyone special.

*Minuses.* Some people who have tried them complain that local singles clubs are full of "losers." The big organizations, like Club Med, often have very interesting people, but ski trips, cruises, or resort stays don't come cheap. And some people find the atmosphere a little too demanding and competitive for comfort.

Have you tried any of these different ways to meet other single people? What were your experiences and reactions? Do you agree with the pluses and minuses described? Do you have some to add? How did you meet your current steady, spouse, or cohab? If you are unattached, how do you go about meeting new people with whom you might form a special relationship? Do you find that you, like many people, tend to keep looking in the same old places even when results are not as hoped or even bad? Do you have any idea why? When it comes to meeting interesting and compatible new people, do you think the problems of divorced people are different from those of others? Why or why not?

## Relationship Killers

Finding someone to love and be loved by can be difficult and so can maintaining a relationship when you do find someone. Three kinds of feelings that can sabotage a relationship at any stage are examined here: general hostility toward the opposite sex, jealousy, and a lack of trust in one's partner.

## Hostility

The point has been made a number of times that expectations for the behavior of men and women in our world are in transition. Many people find this confusing and some react to this confusion with feelings of **hostility**—antagonism or unfriendliness—toward the opposite sex. This hostility is not dislike of a particular person, but a more generalized feeling about all members of the opposite sex. Although the "war between the sexes" has been going on for centuries, it appears to have warmed up as a result of recent efforts to ensure equal opportunity and treatment for men and women ( Check, Malamuth, Elias, & Barton, 1985). Women who are striving for equality often see only one enemy—men. Men who are losing long-standing privileges that went with having been born male may react with resentment.

General feelings of hostility toward the opposite sex on the part of one or both partners obviously makes any relationship more difficult to maintain. The other person isn't just an individual; he or she is representative of an entire sex. The husband who leaves his socks on the floor is "just like a man," and the wife who cries during an argument is being a "typical woman." Such remarks can strike at the very core of self-concept and turn a routine argument into a pitched battled in which one's gender as well as one's behavior must be defended.

Not all hostility in relationships is of this general kind, of course. For many reasons, one or both members of a couple may build up hostility toward one another as the relationship develops. One or both also may use the other as a target of *misplaced hostility,* taking their hostility toward someone else (a boss, a former love or spouse, a parent) out on the partner. Whatever the source, hostility gets in the way of communication, working out problems, and just enjoying one another's company since one or both partners is seeing the other in a negative light.

## Jealousy

**Jealousy** is an emotional experience characterized by a feeling that your relationship is being threatened in some way by a person or persons outside of it. Symptoms range from mild agitation when your lover spends too much time talking to an attractive friend at a party to jealous rages that leave your self-control in shreds.

A curious feature of jealousy is that it often occurs independently of any deliberate act of the partner. You may have experienced a relationship that broke up because of your partner's persistent, and completely unfounded, jealousy. You didn't do or say anything to suggest that you were interested in someone else, yet your partner felt threatened by the mere fact that you talked to other men or women or mentioned one casually in conversation.

The fact that so many people seem to experience jealousy when there is no cause has led to a widespread belief that this emotion is a by-product of insecurity, immaturity, low self-esteem (or all three), and there is some evidence for this (e.g., Bringle & Evenbeck, 1979). On the other hand, people who have none of these characteristics admit to feeling a prod from the old green-eyed monster when a partner mentions a former love or ex-wife or husband in a positive way. Many feel jealous even if the former relationship was over 20 or 30 years before!

In short, jealousy is a strange creature that requires no external cause, leaps time barriers at a single bound, and visits most people at one time or another. A recent survey found single or cohabiting people more likely to report feelings of intense jealousy than marrieds or homosexuals, but almost no one claimed *never* to have had such feelings (Salovey & Rodin, 1985).

The effects of jealousy on the behavior of the jealous person vary, but common reactions include looking through the partner's personal belongings for "evidence," checking up on his or her whereabouts (calling during working hours, for example), dropping in at his or her home unexpectedly, listening in on telephone conversations, and making accusations of infidelity. Clearly, none of these behaviors is conducive to a happy relationship.

Chronic real jealousy almost always is destructive to a relationship. Being constantly under suspicion for something you aren't doing and haven't thought of doing gets old fast. It is difficult to go on feeling the same way about someone who seems to have so little faith in you or your commitment to the relationship. One reaction to this situation that many counselors have noted is involvement of the accused partner in an extradyadic relationship. The idea seems to be that if they are going to be accused of it, they might as well do it.

Other people react to chronic unfounded jealousy by leaving the relationship. Still others try to ignore it or to reassure the jealous partner. It is difficult to know what the best reaction might be since this emotion is someone else's. Some people just seem to be the "jealous type" and are capable of being jealous of children, same-sex friends, and careers as well as other possible romantic interests for their partners. There is some research evidence that these people suffer more self-esteem damage over loss of a partner to a rival or to rejection than those who do not tend to be jealous in love relationships (Mathes, Adams, & Davies, 1985).

The essence of jealousy is that some outsider is threatening a relationship with another person. To the jealous person, then, his or her partner is sufficiently desirable in some way to interest someone else. From here it is but a short step to the idea that a person who *isn't* jealous doesn't believe this is true. Such is the contradiction of human nature that a little pretend jealousy seems to be a necessary ingredient in many relationships.

## Lack of Trust

You may think of jealousy as not trusting your partner to remain committed to you and your relationship, and this is indeed one aspect of lack of trust. But trust in a relationship involves more than believing your partner won't be unfaithful. It also includes believing that he or she is dependable and reliable and will continue to behave in loving and caring ways. And trust requires sufficient faith to put yourself at risk in a relationship, to be open and leave yourself vulnerable. These three elements of **trust** have been called dependability, predictability, and faith (Remple, Holmes, & Zanna, 1985).

Trust in relationships is something that develops over time through mutually satisfying interactions and increasing confidence in a relationship. As trust grows, the relationship is strengthened. Faith seems to be particularly important in this process. Remple, Holmes, and Zanna found that couples who reported the greatest love and happiness with one another were also the

It is only possible to live happily ever after on a day-to-day basis.

*Margaret Bonnans*

ones who reported having the greatest faith that one partner would continue to care no matter what the future held.

Like hostility and jealousy, lack of trust in a relationship may be one-sided as well as mutual. Either way, there is a holding back that makes open communication and full sharing with the other person difficult or impossible. Even if this does not kill the relationship (leads to divorce, for example), such holding back erodes its quality and tends to lead to dissatisfaction and feelings that there must be something better. You might want to evaluate the trust you have in your current partner by filling out the questionnaire in Chapter 6's *Test Yourself* again, this time using the other half of your special relationship as the focus.

# When the Relationship Is in Trouble: Shape Up or Ship Out?

One of the most difficult decisions we ever have to make is what to do about a relationship that is in trouble. Do we do nothing and hope that things get better, try to fix things, or just get out? There is no one answer for everyone, but "wait and see" probably is the least attractive of the options for two reasons. First, things get better by themselves only under very special conditions—one partner gets over a very bad time that had nothing to do with the relationship, for example. Second, waiting and doing nothing are very difficult things to do since they make most people feel that they have no control over the situation.

Many couples with troubled relationships find that some kind of couples or family counseling helps them through the bad times. If you want to seek out such help, you should do a little homework and try to find a counselor who comes recommended by someone you trust. If possible, both you and your partner should attend the sessions, even if only one of you believes there is a problem. Going to a couples counselor alone may be personally beneficial, but the chances are slim that it will do much for your relationship problems.

Many of the problems that couples have can be worked out when the partners still care, but they can become insurmountable once one or both is trying only out of guilt or pity. (This often is the situation of a partner who wants out of a relationship because he or she has fallen out of love with the other.) A list of the most common problems people bring to couples therapy is presented in Exhibit 14–3.

The problems listed in Exhibit 14–3 are many and diverse. Some are quite serious. Special treatment may be required for one or both partners; and it still may be impossible to save the relationship, as for example, when the problem is alcoholism or spouse abuse. Most of these problems do not necessarily have to mean the end of the relationship, however. When they do, an inability to communicate well enough to work them through is a common theme.

## Communication in Special Relationships

Communication involves the way you look and move, your voice tone, your posture, your choice of what aspect of someone else's message to respond to, and a hundred other aspects of behavior as well as the actual words used. Even what we don't say communicates something to others. No wonder effective

**EXHIBIT 14–3**

## The Most Common Problems Taken to Couples Counselors

### Sex
- Lack of sexual desire
- Infrequent or no orgasm
- Pain during intercourse
- Vagina too tight for penetration
- Premature ejaculation
- Impotence
- No ejaculation
- Differences over how sex occurs:
  Too little foreplay
  Spouse crude in approach
  Oral sex
  Positions
  Too little affection
- Disagreement about frequency of intercourse
- Disagreement about when sex occurs
- Extramarital affair

### In-Laws
- Talking over the phone to in-laws
- How often in-laws visit
- Borrowing money from in-laws
- Living with in-laws
- How often to visit in-laws
- In-laws' dislike of spouse
- In-laws' interference in children's lives
- Loaning/giving money to in-laws

### Money
- Too little money
- Wife's job
- Husband's job
- Conflict over who buys what
- Gambling
- Borrowing
- Excessive debts

### Recreation
- No sharing of leisure time
- Desire of spouse for separate vacations
- Competition (egos may be hurt if one spouse is more athletic than partner)
- Disagreement over amount of money to allocate for vacation
- Spouse doesn't like family vacations
- Disagreement over what is fun
- Where to spend vacation
- How long to be on vacation

### Children
- Discipline of children
- Care of children
- Time with children
- Number of children
- Spacing of children
- Infertility
- Whether or not to adopt
- Rivalry for children's love
- Activities children should be involved in
- Sex education for children
- Distress at children's behavior
- Child abuse by one spouse
- Retarded, autistic, or otherwise handicapped child
- Stepchildren

### Friends
- Too few friends
- Too many friends
- Different friends
- Confidences to friends
- Time with friends

### Communication
- Don't feel close to spouse
- Rarely alone with spouse
- Spouse complains/criticizes
- Don't love spouse
- Spouse doesn't love me
- Spouse is impatient
- Too little time spent communicating
- Nothing to talk about
- Intellectual gaps
- Unhappiness with type of conversation
- Spouse is unhappy and depressed
- Arguments end in spouse abuse/violence

### Alcohol or Drugs
- Spouse drinks too much
- Spouse smokes too much marijuana
- Spouse takes too many pills
- Amount of money spent on alcohol/drugs
- Flirting as a consequence of drinking
- Influence of drinking/drug habits on children
- Violence as a consequence of drinking

### Religion
- Which church to attend
- Wife too devout
- Husband too devout
- Wife not devout enough
- Husband not devout enough
- Religion for children
- Money to church
- Observance of religious holidays and rituals such as circumcision
- Breaking of vows

*Note:* From *Choices in Relationships* (2nd ed.) by D. Knox, 1988. St. Paul, MN: West, Reprinted by permission.

communication between any two people can be such a complicated business. When the two people are emotionally involved with one another and have a stake in one another's lives, feelings and the history of the relationship can make things even more difficult. There are a number of common **couple communication problems.**

**Withholding Information.** Not telling one another things is a frequent source of couple communication difficulty. Whether it be something as ordinary as the fact that you have to work late on Friday night or as sensitive as unmet sexual desires, keeping back information that involves the other party can create problems. The reason for not sharing information may be as simple as "I forgot"; it is easy to overlook the fact that this can communicate "You aren't very important to me" or "I wasn't thinking about you." Failing to share more intimate matters until they become a problem may be result of embarrassment or shyness, but the effect can be: "Our relationship is less important to me than sparing my own feelings about discussing such matters."

**Poor Timing.**    Another common couple communication problem is poor timing. A cocktail party is not the time or place for one partner to air complaints about the weight the other is gaining, nor is a family get-together the time to discuss financial problems. Late at night when both partners are tired is a poor time to try to work out problems with the kids. First thing in the morning when you are rushing to get ready for work or school isn't the time to discuss sexual problems. Picking the wrong time to raise issues or just to convey information can blow a small matter out of all proportion and turn a serious one into a disaster.

**Not Listening.**    Failing to hear what the other person said may mean that one partner doesn't hear at all or that he or she doesn't listen for the real message. Both can convey a sense that the listener doesn't think the other person is very important, which is not true in many cases. Not hearing the real message also causes resentment and hurt feelings. The classic example is the following exchange.

> *One:* Do you still love me?
> *Two* (absentmindedly): Of course I do.

This exchange probably has been going on between couples since time began. Of all the meanings the question might have, the last answer desired is the one given. The listener was not hearing the real message, which may have been as simple as, "I'd like some attention paid to me."

**Not Talking.**    One of the most common complaints women have (although men have been known to make it as well) is that their partners simply don't converse with them. Said one, "If there isn't a question to be answered or an issue to be settled, he watches TV or reads or does work he brought home. It never seems to occur to him to just sit and talk."

The problem here is that language and intimacy are interwoven. Having conversations isn't enough to provide that special bond by itself, but it does keep communication channels open. Couples who are accustomed to talking to one another on a regular basis get to know one another better and feel closer. And because they are used to talking to one another, discussing personal issues comes easier.

Couples who are used to communicating with one another also find it easier to get back to basics if they begin to drift apart. One of these basics is keeping an eye on your partner's good qualities and deeds. A strategy many marriage and family counselors recommend is that couples make a point of telling one another something positive on a regular basis (Safran, 1982). This may be anything from "I have always liked your smile" to "You don't know how much I appreciated your picking the children up from playschool today."

Although people who communicate better with one another tend to have fewer problems and to be more successful in working out the ones they do

Couple communication is special—intimate, complex, and critical to the relationship.

have, good communication is not a universal cure for relationship distress. Some problems are too deeply rooted or have been around too long. Sometimes, one or both partners are unsure about the desire to remain in the relationship. In such instances, a trial separation may be helpful in clarifying issues, feelings, and directions.

## Trial Separations

Sometimes, relationships in serious trouble are helped by a "time-out" period, a **trial separation.** Whether this actually does any good or not depends upon a number of factors, including the motivation behind the separation. If one partner is using it as a way to start the process of leaving, it is likely to speed up the breakup of the relationship. Assuming, however, that both parties would prefer to save the relationship (or at least are uncertain about how they feel in this regard), there are some ways to increase the chances that a trial separation will help (Kiley, 1984).

- *Spend some time alone if you possibly can.* You've got some serious thinking to do, and you need to do it alone.

- *Don't look for someone new during the separation.* It won't help the old relationship to get involved with someone else, and the new one will get off to a bad start as well.

- *If you see your partner during the separation, avoid serious matters and try to have fun.* See if you can remember what attracted you to one another in the first place.

- *Set a goal for yourself to be accomplished during the separation.* Decide you will lose five pounds, take a course in photography, learn to use a personal computer, spend more time with your child, or whatever you would like to do. Separations solely for the purpose of letting the other person come to his or her senses seldom accomplish much.

It may be that no matter what you do, you find that you can't—or don't want to—save the relationship. Ending it can be as simple as walking away or as complicated as two divorce lawyers battling it out in court over financial settlements and child custody. Either way, it is unlikely to be easy. The breakup of a relationship is a major stressor for the most people, so be prepared with a plan to help you cope with these extra demands if that is your decision.

## DIVORCE: THE SPECIAL PROBLEMS OF ENDING A MARRIAGE

"Of all the horrendous things I've known, this divorce has been the worst." The woman who spoke these words has had a lot of experience with misfortune. Academy Award winner Patricia Neal's son is brain-damaged from an automobile accident, her daughter died of encephalitis at age 7, and she herself has fought back from a series of strokes that left her unable to walk, talk, or see. Yet she feels that the emotional desolation of her divorce from writer Roald Dahl after 30 years of marriage created the greatest stress.

The breakup of any relationship is painful, but the breakup of a marriage is in a category by itself. Married couples have made a public commitment to

Marriage continues to be popular, but so does divorce; there are approximately one million marriage dissolutions every year.

one another. They have a history together, their finances are intertwined, they have mutual possessions, and many have children as well. Breaking up a marriage is breaking up an acknowledged family unit in a public way. Outsiders, especially parents, tend to get far more involved than they do when unmarried couples split up. If, like Pat Neal's, the marriage is breaking up so that one partner may marry someone else, the emotional strain is increased. And the need to take care of practical matters, such as getting at least one partner established in a new place to live, may add to the burdens.

## Why Do Marriages Break Up?

The number of divorces in this country increased steadily during the 20 years between the 1960s and the 1980s to the present level of approximately one million per year. So common has divorce become that most people now assume that an unmarried person over 35 is a divorced person.

People marry for many reasons—for love, companionship, or financial security; to have a family; or just because it is expected. These marriages break up for many reasons as well. There probably are many couples who divorce for each of the issues listed in Exhibit 14–3, even though some of these would appear trivial. Psychologists, sociologists, and others who study the problem also believe that a number of factors in the social environment of this country play a role in our high divorce rate (Knox, 1988).

- *Changes in the role of the family.* Many of the religious, recreational, and educational functions of the family now are performed by outsiders. Since these will continue even if the family unit is broken up, keeping it together may seem less critical than it did formerly.

- *Employed wives.* Women are no longer economically dependent upon husbands to the extent they were when most did not work outside the home. Men whose wives work no longer must bear full financial responsibility for the support of their families if the marriage is dissolved. For both sexes, divorce is financially more feasible, even though it may lower the standard of living for one or both partners.

- *Fewer moral and religious sanctions.* Divorce has ceased to be a moral issue for most people as values have shifted in society. For a great many people, the right to individual happiness and fulfillment has become more important than older ideas of doing one's "duty" and staying married at all costs. Strong religious sanctions against divorce also have been relaxed. For example, the Catholic church no longer excommunicates divorced members who remarry.

- *Liberal divorce laws.* Divorce laws differ from state to state, and researchers find that states that make divorce relatively easy, such as California, have higher rates of divorce. Legal barriers won't stop those who are determined, but they seem to make a difference for many couples. Since it is easier to get a divorce in almost every state now than 30 years ago, many who might otherwise have stayed married have not done so.

- *The social acceptability of divorce.* One of the most striking social changes of the past 30 years has been the change in attitudes toward divorce. While it would not be true to say that no one disapproves anymore, most people today regard divorce as a normal, if unfortunate, event. Thus, a couple whose marriage is distressed can terminate it without fear of being considered deviant, as they once would have been.

These social changes may be summed up by saying there is a change in the **climate for divorce.** It is easier and more acceptable, and may appear to be a more reasonable alternative to couples having problems than trying to work them out would be. Although every couple has such problems, it does appear that some are more likely than others to abandon the marriage when they do. One psychologist has incorporated the factors that seem to make an important difference into the divorce proneness scale in *Test Yourself.*

If you are not married, you may want to answer the questions in *Test Yourself* anyway, using the person in your current special relationship instead of your spouse. This will help to give you some idea of the odds for staying together. Keep in mind, however, that whether you are married or not, that is all this test is about—odds. Couples who are very young, financially struggling, have been married before, married in the face of disapproval from others, and so on have a greater chance of being divorced. But this is a statistical chance, and relationships have a way of overcoming the odds.

## TEST YOURSELF:
## The Divorce Proneness Scale

This scale is designed to indicate the degree to which you are prone to get a divorce. There are no right or wrong answers. After reading each sentence carefully, circle the number that best represents your feelings.

1  Strongly agree
2  Mildly agree
3  Undecided
4  Mildly disagree
5  Strongly disagree

|  |  | SA | MA | U | MD | SD |
|---|---|---|---|---|---|---|
| 1. | My parents have a happy marriage. | 1 | 2 | 3 | 4 | 5 |
| 2. | My closest married friends have happy marriages. | 1 | 2 | 3 | 4 | 5 |
| 3. | My partner and I can negotiate our differences. | 1 | 2 | 3 | 4 | 5 |
| 4. | I plan to marry only once. | 1 | 2 | 3 | 4 | 5 |
| 5. | I am a religious person. | 1 | 2 | 3 | 4 | 5 |
| 6. | I will wait until my mid-twenties to marry. | 1 | 2 | 3 | 4 | 5 |
| 7. | I do not require a number of sexual relationships to be happy. | 1 | 2 | 3 | 4 | 5 |
| 8. | I think it best to marry only after I have known my partner for at least a year. | 1 | 2 | 3 | 4 | 5 |
| 9. | My parents approved of the person I married. | 1 | 2 | 3 | 4 | 5 |
| 10. | My partner and I have an adequate source of income to meet all of our expenses and some money left to play with. | 1 | 2 | 3 | 4 | 5 |

Scoring: Add the numbers you circled. 1 (strongly agree) is the least divorce-prone response, and 5 (strongly disagree) is the most divorce-prone response. The lower your total score (10 is the lowest possible score), the less your chance of getting a divorce; the higher your score (50 is the highest possible score), the greater your chance of getting a divorce. A score of 30 places you at the midpoint between not getting and getting a divorce.

*Note:* From *Choices in Relationships* (2nd ed.) by D. Knox, 1988. St. Paul, MN: West. Reprinted by permission.

# A Multitude of Divorces

Divorce usually is more complicated than splitting up nonmarital relationships because so many factors and other people are involved. Bohannan (1970) describes this complexity as the **six stations of divorce:** emotional, economic, legal, coparental, community, and psychic.

**The Emotional Divorce.**   The *emotional divorce* is the aspect of splitting up in which couples are withholding positive feelings from one another and emotion from the relationship. Love and other positive feelings begin to be replaced by indifference and/or antagonism.

**The Economic Divorce.**   Divorce has financial as well as emotional consequences. When joint resources are not sufficient to sustain both partners and any children at the same standard of living, financial matters can increase greatly both the stress of the experience and the negative emotions that may accompany the emotional divorce. This aspect represents the *economic divorce*.

**The Legal Divorce.**   The *legal divorce* is the public aspect of splitting up, and this can be difficult even in "friendly" divorces. Consulting lawyers, going to court, having your private difficulties discussed in front of a judge—all of these are painful emotional experiences for most of us.

**The Coparental Divorce.**   The *coparental divorce* is the aspect of divorce that involves children, a facet that has led many couples to abandon the whole idea and stay together for the sake of the children. Have they made the right decision? Unfortunately, there is no way to know. Research on this question consistently leads to the conclusion that children cope better with happy one-parent homes than with homes that are filled with the conflict between two parents (e.g., Hetherington, Cox, & Cox, 1978). It does not tell us, however, how the lives of children in *unhappy* one-parent homes compare with those whose battling parents stay together. Nor do we have any data on how the children of divorced parents might have turned out if the parents had stayed together.

The impact of divorce on children after it has occurred has been studied intensively. The findings tell us that the effects are long-term ones, but more severe at first. Anger and fear seem to be the most common first reactions; after that, what happens varies enormously according to the age, sex, past experience, and temperament of the child and the nature of the relationship between the ex-spouses (Dworetzky, 1984). Girls seem to cope better than boys, and "easy" children adapt more quickly than "difficult" children. There also is some evidence that divorce is easier for very young children to adapt to than for older children.

The fact that children adjust better to happy single-family homes than to unhappy two-parent ones does not mean that the children of divorced families don't have problems. They do, and the chances that they will have these problems are somewhat greater than for other children. One parent simply does not have the resources that two have, and certain aspects of the child's life may not get much attention. In addition, divorce often means a lower standard of living, a circumstance that seems to be associated with greater adjustment problems (e.g., Bane, 1976).

**The Community Divorce.**   When a couple is divorced, *they* become *him* and *her*, and friends and family often feel put into an awkward position. As a result, divorced men and women often find that their ex "got custody of our friends," and they are left to build a new social life in addition to coping with all of the other adjustments. Community ties also may be broken; the ex-spouses may feel uncomfortable about continuing to go to the same church, for example. The *community divorce* can be very painful.

**The Psychic Divorce.** Bohannan believes that breaking off psychologically from a former husband or wife and becoming a whole and autonomous person once again—the *psychic divorce*—may be the most difficult aspect of divorce. This adjustment seems particularly hard for people like Pat Neal who have been married for many years and/or did not seek the divorce. Being "Ed's wife" or "Mary's husband" is a role they have grown into; giving it up is traumatic.

## Adjusting to Divorce

Divorce may be less difficult for one partner or the other, but it seldom is easy. Recognizing this and being prepared for emotional, financial, and social adjustments can help get you through. Some specific suggestions that may help ease a difficult time are presented in Exhibit 14–4.

As suggested by the exhibit, there are things that people can do to make adjustment to divorce a little less painful than it might be otherwise, but ac-

---

**EXHIBIT 14–4**

### Ten Tips That May Help Ease Adjustment to Divorce

1. Avoid spending time with people who encourage you to pity yourself. You'll need some friends, but decide who you will tell what, and take it easy. Many people find it embarrassing later that they "fell apart" with so many of their family and friends.

2. Avoid jumping into another relationship immediately. You would not do so if your spouse had died, and the situation has its similarities; a relationship has "died."

3. Allow yourself to feel depressed, irritable, or impatient upon occasion. You cannot expect to escape such feelings, and although you don't want to wallow in them, it is important not to deny them either.

4. Avoid constant rehashing (to yourself as well as others) of the ex-spouse's faults, what went wrong with the marriage, and so on. It is a natural tendency, but adjusting to divorce requires looking forward, not back.

5. Take good care of yourself. Get your rest, exercise, and enough nutritious food. This is a high-stress time.

6. If you have children, avoid saying negative things about your ex-spouse, even if you know he or she is doing so. You will dislike yourself for it later.

7. Make a point of scheduling some fun into your life. Filling all of their time with exhausting activities so they won't have time "to think" is a mistake many make at this stage. You need relaxation as well as rest.

8. If you have to see your ex-spouse, try to keep the interaction matter-of-fact and stick to the subject. It's over now.

9. Try to keep alcohol consumption to a minimum for awhile. Alcohol is a depressant.

10. Consider getting professional help if you need it.

cepting the divorce emotionally as well as legally still may be very difficult. Psychologists who have studied divorced couples find that the degree of this acceptance depends on a number of factors, and these tend to be different for women and men. In one study of over 200 divorced persons, it was found that men who had initiated the divorce (or recalled it as decided upon mutually) were more accepting than men whose wives had initiated the divorce (Thompson & Spanier, 1983). Acceptance was not related significantly to this factor for women.

In the same study, men whose friends did not disapprove of the divorce were more accepting than other men, but friend approval or disapproval was not a significant variable for women. The acceptance of divorce by women was greater for those who recalled the last stages of the marriage as being less affectionate and more conflict ridden. More highly educated women also were more accepting than less educated women. Both sexes were more accepting of their divorces if they held a lower personal commitment to the idea of marriage itself.

Studies like these give us some useful insights into the dynamics of divorce, but there are still many questions. Of particular interest is the question of what factors, if any, differentiate couples who divorce from couples who are reconciled after a trial separation, during the waiting period for divorce, or even after the divorce itself. Do you have any ideas on this subject based on your own experience or that of people you know?

## Summing Up ■

Most of us would like to have a special someone in our lives, but finding him or her can be difficult. When we do, there are many traps for maintaining a mutually satisfying relationship. Hostility, jealousy, and lack of trust are particularly potent relationship killers, but the list of potential problems is a long one.

The decision about what to do when a relationship is in trouble is a difficult one. Some people ignore the problem, hoping that it will go away. Others try to get help from family, friends, or professional counselors. For still others, the answer is to get out of the relationship; but when the relationship is marriage, the issues can become complicated indeed. The lives of married couples are interwoven on many levels, and divorce affects relationships with family, friends, children, and the community as well as the couples themselves.

## ■ KEY WORDS AND PHRASES

| | | |
|---|---|---|
| climate for divorce | jealousy | shyness |
| conformity | loneliness | six stations of divorce |
| couple communication problems | reference groups | trial separation |
| hostility | self-consciousness | trust |
| idiosyncratic credits | | |

## ■ READ ON

*Getting to Yes: Negotiating without Giving In* by R. Fisher and W. Ury. Boston: Houghton Mifflin, 1981. A practical primer for negotiating differences. Sample chapter titles: "Separate the People from the Problem" and "Invent Options for Mutual Gain."

*Shyness* by P. Zimbardo. New York: Addison-Wesley, 1977. If you are shy, you will want to read this book by one of the foremost experts

in this area. Shyness isn't a deep-rooted personality trait, and it can be overcome.

*Rebuilding: When Your Relationship Ends* by B. Fisher. San Luis Obispo, CA: Impact, 1981. Life after divorce—from denial through loneliness, guilt, rejection, grief, and anger to new friendships, love, and freedom—is the focus.

## ■ REFERENCES

Asch, S. E. (1955). Opinions and social pressures. *Scientific American, 193,* 31–35

Bane, M. J. (1976). Marital disruption and the lives of children. *Journal of Social Issues, 32,* 103–117.

Berscheid, E., & Walster, E. (1979). Physical attractiveness. In L. Berkowitz (Ed.), *Advances in experimental social psychology* (vol. 71). New York: Academic Press.

Bohannan, P. (1970). The six stations of divorce. In P. Bohannan (Ed.), *Divorce and after.* Garden City, NJ: Doubleday.

Bringle, R. G., & Evenbeck, S. (1979). The study of jealousy as a dispositional characteristic. In M. Cook and G. Wilson (Eds.), *Love and attraction.* New York: Pergammon Press.

Check, J. V. P., Malamuth, N. M., Elias, B., & Barton, S. A. (1985). On hostile ground. *Psychology Today, 19,* 56–61.

Dworetzky, J. P. (1984). *Introduction to child development* (2nd ed.). St. Paul, MN: West.

Fenigstein, A. (1984). Self-consciousness and the over-perception of self as target. *Journal of Personality and Social Psychology, 47,* 860–870.

Fenigstein, A., Scheier, M. F., & Buss, A. H. (1975). Public and private self-consciousness: Assessment and theory. *Journal of Counseling and Clinical Psychology, 43,* 522–527.

Franzoi, S. L., Davis, M. H., & Young, R. D. (1985). The effects of private self-consciousness and perspective taking on satisfaction in close relationships. *Journal of Personality and Social Psychology, 48,* 1584–1594.

Harris, P. (1984). The hidden face of shyness: A message from the shy for researchers and practitioners. *Human Relations, 37,* 1079–1093.

Hetherington, E. M., Cox, M., & Cox, R. (1978). The aftermath of divorce. In J. H. Stevens, Jr., and M. Matthews (Eds.), *Mother-child, father-child relations.* Washington, DC:

National Association for the Education of the Young.

Hollander, E. R. (1964). *Leaders, groups, and influence.* New York: Oxford University Press.

Jewell, L. N., & Reitz, H. J. (1981). *Group effectiveness in organizations.* Glenview, IL: Scott, Foresman.

Kelly, H. H., & Thibaut, J. W. (1969). Group problem solving. In G. Lindzey and E. Aronson (Eds.), *Handbook of social psychology.* Reading, MA: Addison-Wesley.

Kiley, D. (1984). *The Wendy dilemma: When women stop mothering their men.* New York: Arbor House.

Knox, D. (1988). *Choices in relationships* (2nd ed.). St. Paul, MN: West.

Mathes, E. W., Adams, H. E., & Davies, R. M. (1985). Jealousy: Loss of relationship reward, loss of self-esteem, depression, anxiety, and anger. *Journal of Personality and Social Psychology, 48,* 1552–1561.

Meer, J. (1985). Loneliness. *Psychology Today, 19,* 28–33.

Mereson, A. (1985). When all eyes are on you. *Science Digest, 93,* 20.

Nord, W. R. (1969). Social exchange theory: An integrative approach to social conformity. *Psychological Bulletin, 71,* 174–208.

Remple, S. K. Holmes, J. G., & Zanna, M. P. (1985). Trust in close relationships. *Journal of Personality and Social Psychology, 49,* 95–112.

Rimer, S. (1985). *Teens know the rules of style.* New York: *New York Times* News Service.

Safran, C. (1982, Aug.). "Of course I love you" and other warning signals. *McCalls,* 142–143.

Salovey, P., & Rodin, J. (1985). The heart of jealousy. *Psychology Today, 19,* 22–29.

Tedeschi, J. T., & Lindskold, S. (1976). *Social psychology: Interdependence, interaction, and influence.* New York: Wiley.

Thompson, L., & Spanier, G. B. (1983). The end of marriage and acceptance of marital termination. *Journal of Marriage and the Family, 45,* 103–113.

Weiss, R. S. (1973). *The experience of emotional and social isolation.* Cambridge, MA: MIT Press.

Wilbert, J. R., & Rupert, P. A. (1986). Dysfunctional attitudes, loneliness, and depression in college students. *Cognitive Therapy and Research, 10,* 71–77.

Zimbardo, P. G. (1977). *Shyness: What it is, what to do about it.* Reading, MA: Addison-Wesley.

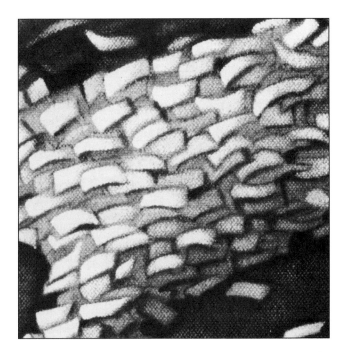

# 15

# Emotional and Psychological Problems

> There are so many things I should be doing, but I just don't seem to care. Sometimes I sit and stare into space for hours at a time. I cry a lot too.
> I feel like something is wrong, but I don't know what. There doesn't seem to be any reason for me to be afraid, but I am.

These statements are typical of those made by people who are suffering from depression and anxiety. These conditions may be initiated or aggravated by physical factors, life conditions, or relationships with others, but in many cases the external cause is not obvious. This can make such problems all the more distressing and set up a vicious cycle. Depressed people often get more depressed, for example, because there seems to be no rational reason for their feelings.

Outside of problems with other people (difficult relationships with the spouse, the boss, the children, and so on), anxiety and depression are the two most common problems that most psychologists, psychiatrists, and other physicians encounter. In this chapter these are examined in both their common everyday forms and in the more extreme forms that are recognized psychological disorders. The discussion begins with a description of these problems and then moves to a general consideration of the causes and more common methods of treating disorders characterized by anxiety and depression.

The line between a disorder and the normal experience of anxiety and depression is by no means fixed; disorders consist of *extremes* of feelings and behaviors that are otherwise perfectly normal. For this reason, it is important for you to develop an understanding of these conditions. Many people who suffer from anxiety and/or depression worry that they are "abnormal" when, in fact, their feelings are entirely within the normal range. At the other extreme, people sometimes suffer needlessly from anxiety and/or depression disorders, believing that there is nothing to be done for them (i.e., that they are "normal"). The more you know about these conditions, the better able you will be to evaluate your own behavior and feelings realistically.

# THE CONCEPT OF ABNORMAL BEHAVIOR

The kinds of problems discussed in this chapter's sections on anxiety and depression disorders often go by the label abnormal behavior. Literally, **abnormal behavior** is behavior that is "away from the norm," or the usual. This definition implies that there must be some standard of normal behavior; otherwise we would not know when someone's behavior deviated from the norm. There are such standards, but they are not quite as clear as that. In addition, there is some disagreement among psychologists and other mental health professionals as to just what the standard itself should be.

## Two Views of Abnormal Behavior

The two major sets of standards for normal behavior differ in their point of reference. In one view, society is the reference; behavior that is outside the norm for a particular society or culture is abnormal behavior. Ullman and Krasner (1975), two psychologists who support this view, believe that no behavior is abnormal if the majority of people in an individual's environment accept it.

To understand this *cultural view of abnormal behavior* better, consider the simple matter of showering one or more times a day. You probably see nothing unusual in such behavior; quite likely, you do it yourself. In other cultures, however, showering this often would be considered as abnormal as you would find washing your hands several times each hour. Washing is involved in both cases; it is only societal norms that make one behavior "normal" and the other "abnormal."

The other view of abnormal behavior takes individual well-being, rather than cultural norms, as the reference point. Psychologists Carson, Butcher, and Coleman (1988) adopt this view, which defines abnormal behavior as any behavior that impairs individual functioning or causes distress and harm to someone.

From this *individual view of abnormal behavior,* the same behavior may be evaluated quite differently when it is exhibited by two different people. You may have been a neat and tidy person all your life, for example. No one thinks anything about this. But your friend, who is also neat and tidy, becomes extremely upset and anxious when anything is out of place in his immediate surroundings. Unlike your own, his behavior appears to be normal.

Which view of abnormal behavior is correct? Is it best seen as deviation from a cultural standard or as deviation from individual standards of well-being? Since the focus of this book is individual effective behavior, the second

**GARFIELD**

Reprinted by permission of UFS, Inc.

view is more useful to us. Consistent with this view, the term *maladaptive behavior* will be substituted for the term *abnormal behavior*.

## The Use of Labels for Maladaptive Behavior

Schizophrenia, passive-aggressive, neurotic—these terms are both familiar and exotic. They are familiar because they have become part of our vocabulary in an age when a large segment of the population in our society has had some exposure to the terminology of psychology and psychiatry. They are exotic because they describe patterns of behavior that most people have not observed directly. In most cases, knowledge of these disorders comes primarily from books and movies, which have a way of playing up the dramatic and the bizarre.

One result of limited and distorted information about what certain labels for patterns of behavior mean is that these labels may be given more power than they deserve. *Schizophrenic* is not specific in the sense that *male* is, for example. Like men, people diagnosed as schizophrenic have certain things in common, but there is far less agreement about who should be called schizophrenic than about who should be called male.

So long as they are not considered to be specific and objective (which they are not), labels are useful in the study and treatment of emotional and psychological problems. They provide a common vocabulary for communication and they help psychologists and psychiatrists describe and organize information about these problems. The American Psychiatric Association publishes a standard guide to terminology and symptoms for psychological disorders called the *Diagnostic and Statistical Manual for Mental Disorders (DSM)*. The current volume of this publication is a revised form of the third edition, known as the **DSM-III-R** (American Psychiatric Association, 1987).

The *DSM-III-R* consists of over 250 diagnostic codes, and these are used by most professionals who treat people for emotional and psychological problems. For this reason, general *DSM-III-R* terminology is used in this chapter, although we won't concern ourselves with the technical details of specific diagnostic codes. It may help you get oriented, however, to take a look at definitions of some of the terms you may have heard in other contexts. These,

**EXHIBIT 15–1**

## Selected *DSM-III-R* Diagnostic Categories

**Antisocial Personality:**  Disorder characterized by a lack of moral or ethical development. Sometimes called psychopathic personality.

**Anxiety Disorder:**  Acute/chronic feelings of apprehension, fear, or dread.

**Borderline personality:**  Disorder characterized by instability, drastic mood shifts, and impulsivity. Such individuals are on the "border" of normality.

**Bipolar disorder:**  Disorder in which periods of depression alternate with periods of excitement and hyperactivity ("mania"). Formerly called manic-depressive disorder.

**Conversion disorder:**  Condition in which physical symptoms appear with no physical or physiological cause.

**Depressive disorder:**  Emotional state of dejection, loss of hope, feelings of unworthiness, and gloomy thoughts.

**Dissociative disorder:**  Disorder in which an individual becomes "dissociated" from himself or herself. (The most well known form is the multiple personality. )

**Hypochondriasis:**  Obsession with bodily functions and fear of disease.

**Paranoid disorder:**  A psychosis involving a systematic and organized delusion of some sort (often, but not always, of persecution).

**Passive-aggressive disorder:**  Nonactive (passive) behavior aimed at hurting or destroying someone or something.

**Phobia:**  Irrational fear that cannot be dispelled by the intellectual knowledge that it has no basis in reality.

**Psychosis:**  Severe disorder in which the personality is distorted and contact with reality is limited or nonexistent.

**Schizophrenia:**  A psychosis characterized by withdrawal from reality and severe disturbances of both thought and behavior.

together with the terms you will see in this chapter, are defined in Exhibit 15–1.

## Watch Out for Student's Disease!

Some of the disorders described in Exhibit 15–1 are discussed in the pages to come, but some cautions are necessary before beginning that discussion. First, you should keep in mind that these labels describe patterns of behavior that have certain features in common, but the specific manifestation of symptoms can vary enormously. Second, you must never lose sight of the fact that emotional and psychological problems exist on a continuum.

The continuum concept means that we must consider the degree, severity, and duration of unusual behavior patterns before putting labels on them; otherwise, there is a risk of confusing disorders with temporary symptoms of known origin. Some women have premenstrual symptoms that have much in common with certain maladaptive behavior disorders, for example. These symptoms are transient, however, and have a known cause. Extreme grief also can have much in common with certain recognized disorders, as can a number of other conditions including some reactions to medications taken for other purposes.

It bears repeating that at one time or another, most of us have feelings or manifest symptoms that, in other contexts, would indicate severe emotional problems or psychological disorders. As a result, you may recognize yourself on several occasions as you read through the remainder of this chapter. Don't panic and fall victim to student's disease.

**Student's disease** is a common affliction among medical and psychology students characterized by a conviction that they have the disorders they are studying. In the present case, you would be extremely unusual if you had never experienced any of the symptoms discussed. Emotional and psychological disorders are a matter of *degree,* not *kind* of feeling and/or behavior.

# ANXIETY

Most people have experienced feelings of anxiety at some time. If you are one of them, you know that anxiety feels like fear, but it is much less specific. You may not even be able to say what it is that you are afraid of. Alternatively, your fears may have to do with things that have not happened and may never happen. *Anxiety* is characterized by feelings of dread and apprehension. Unlike depression, it is typically a high-energy state. Physically, the experience has much in common with the experience of stress. Your body prepares to meet a threat. Your heartbeat increases, as does your respiration, and you are unusually alert, restless, and tense.

Because anxiety in the uncomplicated form that we will call normal anxiety, creates stress reactions, it is possible to cope with it by means of the same basic strategies. Eat properly, get enough sleep (if you are too "nervous" to sleep, then rest), and—you guessed it—get your exercise. Research reports are consistent in finding that people who exercise regularly suffer from less anxiety and shake it off more quickly when they do experience it (e.g., Francis & Carter, 1982).

In addition to physical effects, normal anxiety has a cognitive, or thinking, component, which we call *worry.* When you worry, you dwell on your fears that something you don't want to happen will happen or something you want to happen won't happen (or you just worry about worrying so much). A new approach to coping with these obsessive thoughts is discussed in *Face of the Future.*

Remember that the anxiety under discussion here is normal anxiety. It comes to most of us at one time or another, and while it is not comfortable, it usually goes away sooner or later. In most cases, it will be sooner if you take a basic stress-management approach to coping with it. Anxiety disorders, by contrast, are both chronic and extreme, and you can't count on them to get better by themselves.

## Anxiety Disorders

When anxiety responses are extreme and persist, they become **anxiety disorders** (formerly called neuroses). Some of these disorders are characterized simply by an unusually high level of chronic anxiety. Other forms of anxiety disorder involve maladaptive attempts to manage anxiety; the attempts are maladaptive because they end up creating more anxiety. The obsessive-com-

# FACE OF THE FUTURE:
## Managing Worry

The number of things we can find to worry about is unending. We worry about work, school, relationships, money, appearance, security, crime, world hunger, the whales, "the bomb," and so on down the list. Most of these worries concern what might or might not happen in the future. We are afraid something terrible *will* happen or something we want *won't* happen.

To psychologists, **worry** is "a chain of negative and relatively uncontrollable thoughts and images. . . . Worriers generate a series of catastrophic hypothetical scenarios and try to envision their implications" (Borkovek, 1985, p. 59). To put it another way, worry projects you into a fear-producing situation that has not happened and may not happen; it is the *thinking* part of anxiety.

Studies of fear in humans and other animals have revealed something very interesting. Both repeated short exposures to a fear-producing stimulus *and* very long exposures tend to extinguish the fear. It is exposure to a real or imagined feared situation in moderate doses (10 to 20 minutes) that prolongs the fear or makes it worse. Chronic worriers put themselves in this situation.

The thoughts of chronic worriers tend to shift at moderate time intervals between their worries and what is going on around them or what they are doing. The result of this alternation is that they worry enough to maintain their fears, but not enough to extinguish them. In addition, the anxiety their worries generate becomes associated with a wide variety of times and places since worry can occur under any circumstances.

One research group (Borkovek, 1985) tested the hypothesis that both nonworriers and "controlled worriers" (subjects who worried continually for 30 minutes before an upcoming task) would be less hampered by anxiety than subjects with a chronic worry pattern (15 minutes of worry followed by 15 minutes of relaxation). As they expected, the chronic worriers reported significantly more difficulty putting worrisome thoughts out of their heads and concentrating on the experimental task than did the other subjects.

The authors of this study have done follow-up research to investigate a major implication of their findings—if you worry, worry thoroughly for a limited time period and put such thoughts out of your head for the rest of the day. In other words, *isolate* the worry process so that it becomes associated with only a small number of other circumstances.

To date, results of training people to "take time out for worry" suggest that this technique reduces the amount of time worriers spend with their negative thoughts and fears by about 35%. More research is needed, but the technique is simple and safe, and you may want to try it out yourself. The steps, as identified by the psychologists who are doing this research, are as follows:

1. Observe your thinking during the day closely and learn to identify the early beginnings of worry.

2. Establish a half-hour worry period to take place at the same time and in the same place each day.

3. Postpone your worrying, as soon as you do catch yourself, until your worry period.

4. Replace the worrisome thoughts with focused attention on the task at hand or anything else in your immediate environment.

5. Use your daily worry period to think intensively about your current concerns.

pulsive individual, to take an example, may suffer extreme anxiety if he steps on a crack in the sidewalk and so avoids them. But the knowledge that he must do this "crazy thing" ends up making him even more anxious.

## Generalized Anxiety and Panic Disorders

One of the most common forms of anxiety disorder is called the **generalized anxiety disorder.** There is no identifiable stimulus for the anxiety that characterizes this disorder; the individual is said to be experiencing "free-floating anxiety." Since the source of the threat is unknown, such people must be constantly on their guard. As a result, they tend to be tense, oversensitive to what others do and say, and easily upset and discouraged. They find decisions very difficult to make, and they worry about almost everything. From time to time, this persistent elevated level of anxiety may bring on an anxiety attack.

An *anxiety attack* is a period of acute panic that can last as long as several hours. Symptoms vary but may include faintness, dizziness, sweating, shortness of breath, choking sensations, stomach upsets, and heart palpitations. A feeling of doom often accompanies anxiety attacks; the individual may be convinced that he or she is about to die.

## Phobic Disorders

Unlike those who suffer from generalized anxiety disorders, people with a phobic disorder know exactly what they are afraid of. A *phobia* is a fear of some object or situation that is so intense it interferes with daily life. In many cases, the feared stimulus is not dangerous at all; for example, some people have hematophobia—an exaggerated fear of the sight of blood. Other phobic objects, such as snakes, can be dangerous, but people with phobic disorders go far beyond natural caution.

Psychologists and psychiatrists have identified many specific phobias over the years. The most common ones are fears of high places, storms, snakes, doctors, injury, sickness, and death (Agras, 1985). Many people who have such fears live perfectly normal lives. It is only when a fear disrupts daily life to a considerable degree that it is classified as **phobic disorder.**

People with phobic disorders will go to any length to avoid the object or situation that they fear. Some who fear open places have not left home in many years. One woman with claustrophobia (fear of enclosed spaces) organizes her whole life so that she never has to use an elevator—not an easy thing to do in her hometown of New York City. A man with an exaggerated fear of being poisoned (toxophobia) eats nothing that his wife has not sampled first.

Most phobias appear to have been learned through direct personal experience with the object or situation, or by some indirect experience such as reading about or seeing the situation in a movie or on television. Others seem to have been learned through observation or social learning. Children often imitate important adults, and a parent who is intensely fearful of something may produce a child with the same fear. By time the child realizes that this fear is not normal (for example, most people are *not* afraid of doctors), it is too deeply rooted to be shaken off alone.

Persistent and extreme anxiety often is characterized by the fact that the fear has no identifiable cause.

Finally, some phobias seem to have developed because the outcome of "being afraid" is rewarding in some way. Fear gets people—adults as well as children—attention. Others show concern and often go out of their way to try to help the individual avoid the problem. One man with aviophobia (fear of flying) admitted to a therapy group that his fear served a very desirable purpose. Because he was afraid to fly, his grown children all came to visit him instead of the other way around. As a result of this fear, he had neither the expense nor the inconvenience of travel.

However a phobia originates, treatment comes closer to being standardized than that for most disorders, so it can be described in some detail. Almost all therapists use one of the **controlled exposure techniques** to treat phobic disorders. One such method is called *imaginal systematic desensitization.*

The first step in imaginal systematic desensitization is to train the phobic individual in a physical relaxation technique. There are a number of such procedures that might be used. The one employed by Wolpe (1969), the originator of the imaginal systematic desensitization technique, is based on the principles of "progressive relaxation" outlined by Jacobson (1938). Since this technique is easy and safe and can be effective as an aid to falling asleep or a way to calm yourself when you feel "uptight" or "jittery" for any reason, the steps are outlined for you in Exhibit 15–2.

Once the patient has mastered physical relaxation by the method described in Exhibit 15–2 or some other approach, he or she is taken step by step

## EXHIBIT 15–2
## Relax Yourself: Steps to Progressive Relaxation

The following steps will systematically relax all of your voluntary muscles. Try to empty your mind of any other thoughts and concentrate all of your mental energies on recognizing and relaxing physical tension.

1. Lie quietly and comfortably on your back and let your eyes close gradually.
2. Learn to recognize tension (contraction) in a muscle by bending or tightening the muscles in your right arm.
3. Concentrate on the sensation of tension in your arm; learn to distinguish this muscle tension from other sensations.
4. Focus on the fact that what you are feeling is the result of *doing something.* Your goal is the opposite—*not doing.*
5. Relax and let the muscle go limp. (Do not gradually release tension).
6. Continue to lie quietly without movement, but also without rigidity, for a half hour.
7. On the days to follow, go through steps 1–6 for these muscles (in the order given): left arm, right leg, left leg, trunk, shoulders, neck, brow, eyes, forehead, cheeks, jaws, lips, tongue, throat.
8. At the end of this time, you should be able to go through and systematically relax all of your muscles (stick with the order given) in one session. Do this regularly, at least once a day; just before going to sleep is a convenient time for many people. Once you have mastered the technique thoroughly, you can learn to release muscle tension as it occurs without the necessity for lying down.

*Note:* Adapted from *You Must Relax* by E. Jacobson, 1978. New York: McGraw-Hill.

through a list of stimuli associated with the phobia. This list, called an *anticipatory anxiety hierarchy* (alternatively, an avoidance serial-cue hierarchy) has been constructed by the individual with the help of the therapist. It begins with the least threatening aspect of the feared situation that the phobic person can identify and moves by steps toward full confrontation with the phobic object or situation.

The steps in this progression take place in the phobic individual's imagination (thus the term *imaginal* systematic desensitization). The therapist helps the person conjure up a vivid mental image; he or she then uses the relaxation training to relax in the presence of this image (Wolpe, 1969). When completely comfortable with this step, the individual moves on to the next one. Someone who is afraid of storms to the point of phobia (astraphobia), for example, might begin by imagining being out in that close, still atmosphere that often signals stormy weather on the way.

When symptoms of anxiety no longer appear at this first step, the next mental image might be of feeling the wind picking up and seeing leaves blowing slightly. Eventually, the individual will reach the point of viewing a fully developed storm in his or her imagination. The last step is being exposed to the real thing without experiencing severe anxiety.

Systematic desensitization can take quite a long time. There can be a long list of stimuli associated with the feared object or situation, and there may be considerable backsliding. A phobic individual might get 10 steps down the path, for example, then suddenly become anxious again at step 3. When this happens, it is necessary to go back. As the name suggests, the desensitization must be systematic so that anxiety is eliminated for all components of the phobia.

A different way to provide controlled exposure to a phobic stimulus is to tackle it directly, rather than mentally, with an emphasis on teaching the phobic individual behavior skills to master the situation. A study by Williams, Dooseman, & Kleifield (1984) illustrates this approach. In that study, subjects who were afraid of heights were accompanied to a tall building by a therapist. Together, subjects and therapists worked their way to the top of the building floor by floor. On the way up, the therapists guided the subjects through such intermediate goals to mastering their fears as approaching a window by a side wall rather than directly. This *reinforced practice* (or *mastery treatment*) was found to be more effective than simple gradual exposure to the feared stimulus.

Direct exposure to a feared stimulus, with or without mastery practice, appears to be more effective with people who have acquired their phobias directly. The imaginal systematic desensitization technique, by contrast, seems more effective with those who have acquired their fears indirectly (Ost, 1985). Both techniques have a good rate of success, but not all phobic disorders can be eliminated in this way. In some instances, the phobia is so severe that the individual is unable to get beyond the first step or two. Others become anxious at the mere thought of talking about the feared stimulus; they prefer to structure their lives around the phobia rather than seek treatment.

## Obsessive-Compulsive Disorders

*Obsessions* are unwelcome and uncontrollable thoughts. *Compulsions* are acts that an individual feels driven to perform. In **obsessive-compulsive disorders,** people feel compelled to think about something they don't want to think about and/or do something they don't want to do. Obsessive thoughts that disease is "eating away" one's internal organs or a compulsion to return home several times a day to check that the water faucets, stove, coffee pot, or other appliances are turned off are fairly common examples. People who suffer from this disorder understand that they are behaving irrationally, but they can't seem to stop.

Most of us have obsessive thoughts at one time or another. Perhaps you have spent several hours or even days replaying in your mind a scene with another person in which you didn't feel you came off your best. Most of us have compulsions as well; we call many of them superstitions. How many people do you know who absentmindedly toss salt over their left shoulders after spilling some or walk around, rather than under, a ladder? As with fears, these are common behaviors. It is when obsessions or compulsions begin disrupting life that they become disorders.

The symptoms of obsessive-compulsive disorders often seem as bizarre to the individual who has them as they do to others. Still, they cannot help thinking the thought, and anxiety arises to an unbearable level if they try to resist performing the act (Carr, 1971). Psychologists and psychiatrists find that people with this disorder tend to be perfectionists who are very cautious in their behavior. Most have been concerned with their ability to control their lives long before their symptoms appear.

## Somatoform Disorders

Anxiety is the interest paid on trouble before it is due.

*William R. Inge*

There are several varieties of **somatoform disorders,** all of which are characterized by physical symptoms of illness or injury that have no physical organic cause sufficient to account for the symptoms. In *somatization disorder,* the symptoms are extensive, chronic, and begin before the age of 30. The following are among the physical complaints that characterize this disorder.

- Nausea
- Diarrhea
- Dizziness
- Chest pain
- Loss of voice
- Blurred vision
- Abdominal pain
- Shortness of breath
- Difficulty swallowing
- Intolerance for many foods

Most of us have experienced some of the symptoms listed at one time or another; somatization disorder is suspected only in cases where an individual has 12 to 14 of these and/or other identified symptoms on a regular basis, and the conditions are severe enough to require medical attention (American Psychiatric Association, 1987).

Closely related to somatization disorder is *psychogenic pain disorder*. In this case, there is only one predominating symptom—severe and lasting pain. No organic basis can be found for this pain, although some patients have had illnesses or injuries in the past that they believe precipitated the problem. In true psychogenic pain disorder, however, this history is not an adequate physical explanation for the pain.

The third major somatoform disorder is *hypochondriasis*. "Hypochondriacs" are obsessed with their health and with fear of disease. Medical news, visits to doctors, and discussions of bodily functions play a large part in their lives, although most are actually in good health. Hypochondriacs seldom experience real pain, and they show few actual symptoms of illness; this disorder is characterized by an exaggerated *fear* of becoming ill.

As physical manifestations of psychological problems, somatoform disorders previously were called *psychosomatic disorders*. This term became used widely to mean "It's all in your head," however, and this is not true. A person faking physical symptoms is said to be malingering; the physical symptoms of people with somatoform disorders are real. The problem is that they do not respond to the standard medical treatment for such ailments.

Psychologically, somatoform disorders are believed to be maladaptive ways to deal with anxiety. They are treated in all of the ways that other anxiety-based disorders are treated, but the success of any form of treatment is likely to be temporary. People who are sick or in pain receive attention. Even if the family and current physician become weary of a person's constant complaints and health obsessions, there is always a new doctor or the neighbors or a stranger on the bus to lend a sympathetic ear.

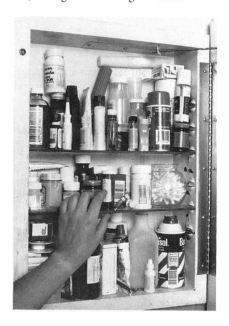

Hypochondriacs are obsessed with fear of disease, although most are in good health.

## Dissociative Disorders

The three forms of anxiety-based psychological disorders we have examined are the more common forms of this problem. **Dissociative disorders,** in which individuals cope with anxiety by escaping ("dissociating") from themselves, are rare. Examples of such disorders include amnesia (loss of memory), depersonalization (loss of a sense of self), and multiple personality.

It is unlikely that you will develop or encounter any form of dissociative disorder, but you probably have heard of multiple personality. Like many other people, you may believe that this is a form of schizophrenia. **Schizophrenia** is a psychosis (see Exhibit 15–1), and thus is beyond detailed discussion here; but it is a major mental health problem and one about which there seem to be an unusually large number of misconceptions. To help set the record straight, the more common misunderstandings—and the facts—about schizophrenia are presented in Exhibit 15–3.

# The Causes of Anxiety Disorders

Where do the exaggerated fears that characterize anxiety disorders come from? There have been a number of theories advanced, most of which tend to fall in line with the important theories of personality. For example, Freud believed that anxiety is a manifestation of a struggle between the ego and the id seg-

## EXHIBIT 15–3

## Schizophrenia: Fact Versus Falsehood

"Schizophrenia is the label applied to a group of disorders characterized by severe personality disorientation, distortion of reality, and an inability to function in daily life" (Atkinson, Atkinson & Hilgard, 1983, p. 470). It is the ultimate psychological breakdown and as such is surrounded by more erroneous beliefs than any other emotional or psychological problem. We will consider a few of the most common of these falsehoods.

**Falsehood:** *Schizophrenia* is another word for *multiple personality.*

**Fact:** Schizophrenia is a psychosis; multiple personality is not. People diagnosed as schizophrenic typically are unable to function on a day-to-day basis. Those with diagnosed multiple personality behave inconsistently, but each personality is a functioning entity.

**Falsehood:** Schizophrenics are violent and dangerous to be around.

**Fact:** Schizophrenics typically are withdrawn and seldom present a danger to others. The major exceptions are catatonic types when they are in the uninhibited, frenzied state that may be part of this condition and the paranoid type. Paranoid schizophrenia often is characterized by delusions of persecution, which may lead such individuals to attack others believed to be plotting against them.

**Falsehood:** Schizophrenia is a rare disorder.

**Fact:** About 50% of psychiatric hospital beds are occupied by individuals diagnosed as schizophrenic. In this country, about 6 out of every 1,000 people are treated for schizophrenia in any given year.

**Falsehood:** Schizophrenics are so crazy you can always recognize them.

**Fact:** Schizophrenia, like any other disorder, exists in many forms and to many different degrees. It would be difficult to overlook certain advanced symptoms, but others, such as distorted perceptions, are not at all obvious. And many of the characteristic thought disturbances (e.g., "I lost all of my green brain cells this week") are apparent only if the individual is engaged in conversation. Many "street people" are believed to be undiagnosed schizophrenics who escape attention because no one talks to them (and everyone expects such people to *behave* strangely).

**Falsehood:** Schizophrenia is inherited.

**Fact:** The rate of schizophrenia is higher for people who have relatives diagnosed as schizophrenic, and there is considerable evidence that some sort of *susceptibility* to this disorder is genetically transmitted. The actual disorder, however, is not inherited; environmental factors still play a significant role in whether or not potential for schizophrenia develops.

**Falsehood:** Schizophrenia is incurable.

**Fact:** About one third of diagnosed schizophrenics remain free of symptoms for 5 years after treatment, the clinical standard for recovery. Drug therapy helps a substantial number of others to adjust to life outside of hospitals or clinics. Only about 10% may be regarded as incurable, and most of these experienced an onset of symptoms at a very early age.

ments of personality. Carl Rogers, by contrast, saw it as caused by a discrepancy between an individual's true self and the standards of others that the individual is trying to meet.

If there is one theory about the origin of anxiety that can be said to be more generally accepted than others today, it is the view that anxiety is the product of faulty learning (Carson, Butcher, & Coleman, 1988). From this perspective, debilitating anxiety builds up when fears that were once quite specific generalize to a wide variety of situations. You saw this view in action in *Face of the Future*, which described attempts by psychologists to teach people to limit worrying to certain times and places so that it would *not* generalize.

Maladaptive attempts to control anxiety, such as obsessive-compulsive behavior, also may be learned. This could come about through the association of anxiety reduction (which occurred for some other, unknown, reason) with behavior that was occurring at the time. The faulty learning is the belief that it was the behavior (such as washing one's hands) that caused the reduction of the anxiety.

Finally, it should be mentioned that some anxiety has its origin in physical causes rather than psychological ones. You may recall from Chapter 13 that caffeine affects some people in this way. Illness also can create anxiety, and it need not be life-threatening to do so. Merely being incapacitated for some period of time while one's duties and responsibilities accumulate unattended can have this effect. For example, one student experienced a panic attack (the first she had ever had) when a serious bout of influenza made it impossible for her to study for an upcoming graduate school entrance examination.

## The Treatment of Anxiety Disorders

Statistics suggest that anxiety disorders are beginning to replace depression as the number-one mental health problem in this country (Tavris, 1986). Therapists use a variety of treatment methods, and there is evidence that anxious people who receive treatment are better able to function normally than those who do not receive treatment (Andrews & Harvey, 1981). It would be misleading to try to evaluate treatment methods in terms of their relative effectiveness, however.

The successful treatment of any psychological problem depends upon a number of factors, including the type of patient, how long the symptoms have been appearing and what form they take, and the relationship between the patient and the therapist. Within these limitations, a few cautious statements based on the literature relevant to the treatment of anxiety may be ventured.

- In general, phobic disorders respond the most readily to treatment, and the treatment of choice almost always is some form of desensitization. If the individual involved stays with the treatment for as long as it takes, most phobias can be overcome.

- By contrast, somatoform disorders have a poor prognosis; the symptoms of these disorders get sympathy for the sufferer, so the disorder is reinforced.

- If we consider only the reduction of anxiety *symptoms,* the treatment that works most quickly and effectively for the greatest number of people probably is medication, or psychopharmacological therapy (e.g., Bassuck & Schoonover, 1977). Two qualifiers must be added here, however. First, antianxiety medications have disruptive side effects for some people. Second, this treatment by itself does nothing about the *causes* of anxiety, and most therapists prefer to use these compounds in conjunction with some other form of therapy.

## Summing Up ■

Anxiety-based disorders take two forms. One, of which the generalized anxiety disorder is the most common, is characterized by a persistent high level of free-floating anxiety, which makes the individual tense, easily upset, and subject to occasional panic attacks. The other form is characterized by maladaptive behaviors, which are attempts to manage the anxiety. Phobic, obsessive-compulsive, somatoform, and dissociative disorders fall into this group.

Psychologists and other mental health professionals use a variety of treatment approaches for anxiety disorders. Phobias generally respond most consistently to treatment; at the other end of the spectrum are somatoform disorders. Chemical compounds are quite effective in relieving symptoms of anxiety but by themselves do nothing to eliminate the causes. At this time the most accepted explanation for the basic cause of anxiety is faulty learning, but the effectiveness of psychopharmacological therapy suggests that a biological susceptibility to anxiety reactions cannot be ruled out.

## DEPRESSION

Depression is the inability to construct a future.

*Rollo May*

Almost everyone has been depressed at one time or another, and the symptoms are remarkably the same. **Depression** is characterized by an overwhelming inertia; everything is just too hard. You can't seem to make a simple decision, initiate an activity, or take an interest in anything. If your fairy godmother finally appeared and said, "You can have anything in the world that you want," you couldn't think of a thing.

Depression is a normal reaction to stress, either directly or through the physical problems that stress may precipitate. It becomes a disorder only if it is out of all proportion to an individual's circumstances or if it lasts too long. Normal depression seems to be self-limiting; at some point you begin to feel better spontaneously.

The America of the late 20th century is crowded with potential stressors, many of which were totally unknown 30 years ago (such as the expectation that women will have careers as well as families). As a result, it is estimated that up to 15% of the population is feeling depressed at any given time (Rosenfeld, 1985). Because of this widespread occurrence, there are a great many books, magazine articles, and radio and television discussions of how to beat "the blues."

Most of the advice on how to cope with depression is well-meaning, and you will suffer no direct ill effects if you try to follow it. There are two possible indirect negative effects, however. First, if you try a suggestion for curing depression and it doesn't work, you can become even more depressed. What is wrong with you that this technique that works for "everybody else" doesn't work for you? Second, some psychologists are coming to believe that, within limits, the experience of depression is an adaptive state of affairs (e.g., Atkinson, Atkinson, & Hilgard, 1983) that should not necessarily be "beaten down" at all costs.

Depression good? How can that be? One reason is that we usually avoid many of the kinds of thoughts and feelings that accompany depression. They haven't gone away, however, and a period of depression serves to let them "out" where they lose much of their power. Depression also gives us a little "psychic vacation" from the demands of life; the temporary lack of interest in anything gives us time to restore a low psychic energy level.

The fact that depression may be serving a useful purpose is a good one to know, because the symptoms of depression can be very frightening. This does not necessarily mean that you simply must bear with it and wait for the depression to go away by itself, however. People differ widely in their tolerance for this condition, as in other respects. If you normally are a very "up" person, being depressed, even for a good reason, may be intolerable.

Because it is so common, most people have beliefs about depression and have developed ways to cope with it based on these beliefs. You can test your own knowledge and coping strategies in this area by answering the questions in *Test Yourself.* Keep in mind as you do so that this information and the entire discussion to this point have to do with normal depression, which is a temporary mood disturbance. Depression as a disorder is the next topic of discussion.

# Mood Disorders

**Mood disorders** involve extreme changes in mood—deep depression or wild elation or swings from one to the other. The two most common of these are the major depressive disorder and what is called bipolar disorder.

## Major Depressive Disorder

For practical purposes, the difference between normal depression and major depressive disorder lies in the extent to which depression persists and disrupts life rather than in the nature of the symptoms. Sadness, fatigue, insomnia (too little sleep) or hypersomnia (too much sleep), loss of interest in activities formerly enjoyed, and reduced ability to concentrate or make decisions are common symptoms of any depressed state.

In *major depressive disorder,* the symptoms of normal depression persist and dominate the individual's life. There is frequently a preoccupation with death, particularly suicide, as well. In severe cases, the person may enter a depressive stupor in which all interaction with what is going on around is terminated.

## Bipolar Disorder

The major depressive disorder is characterized by episodes of severe depression interspersed with normal moods. It is a *unipolar* disorder in which an individual's mood swings away from normal in only one direction (depression). A different problem is the *bipolar disorder* in which mood swings to the other extreme as well; there are episodes of manic behavior as well as episodes of extreme depression. (This disorder formerly was called manic-depressive).

The manic behavior of bipolar disorder is not the same as the genuinely happy, "up" behavior and optimism that it superficially resembles. The person having a manic episode appears euphoric and expansive, but this can turn to irritation in the blink of an eye. The major characteristics of this type of behavior are its pace and its lack of reality orientation.

---

## TEST YOURSELF:
## What Do You Know about Coping with Depression?

*Directions:* With the discussion covered, answer each question true or false by circling either *T* or *F*. Then read the relevant material, keeping in mind that answers are general and do not apply to every case and that the depression discussed is of the *normal* type that almost everyone experiences.

1.  T   F    Depression is caused by negative thinking. If you want to get over it, you have to think positively.
             *False.* The idea that positive thinking will give us what we want and solve all of our problems, including depression, is a popular theme in books and articles dedicated to self-improvement. This is a vast oversimplification at the best of times, and when you are depressed, it just isn't possible. If you were capable of thinking positively just then, you probably wouldn't be depressed.

2.  T   F    Exercise is a good antidote for depression.
             *True.* A major symptom of depression is inactivity, and doing something seems to be an important part of getting relief. Since most of us have difficulty thinking clearly while depressed, simple physical activities are the best, and exercise may be the most effective activity of all. Both personal reports and research consistently confirm that, among all of its other benefits, exercise also helps to dispel depression (McCann & Holmes, 1984).

3.  T   F    There are drugs that will control depression.
             *True.* There are two major classes of drugs that are effective in relieving depression, but drug therapy is *not* recommended for normal depression. Antidepressant drugs take up to 3 weeks or longer to work, and they have multiple side effects, some of which are dangerous.

4.  T   F    A few drinks with some friends will help you beat the blues.
             *False.* Alcohol is a *depressant.* If you are depressed when you start drinking, you'll probably be more depressed when you stop. The friends may not help either unless they are the kind who can be with you without trying to "jolly" you out of your mood.

5.  T   F    If you are depressed, go out and buy a new dress, stereo record, or something else you want.
             *False.* If you can afford it, the diversion of shopping for (and having) something new may be enough to snap you out of a mild funk. As a general strategy, however, shopping is not an effective cure for depression.

---

People having manic episodes have boundless restless energy. They move quickly, thoughts race through their brains, they talk a "blue streak," and they seldom sleep. They typically are full of grandiose ideas and schemes, most of which have no practical value. They also tend to be far more uninhibited than usual, saying and doing crude things and ignoring personal hygiene standards.

As is true for major depression, more women than men suffer from bipolar disorder, although men have more frequent manic episodes. For both sexes, this disorder begins at a relatively early age (25 to 40) and is associated with a higher suicide rate than other emotional disorders. Both the depression and the mania can be controlled chemically, but the matter is complicated by the fact that antidepressant compounds aggravate manic symptoms in some people.

## What Causes Mood Disorders?

You will not be surprised by this time to learn that mood disorders, like many other problems we have examined in this book, appear to be caused by a combination of biological, psychological, and external life-situation factors.

### Biological Factors

Although their role is a long way from being fully understood, the weight of the evidence leaves little room for doubt that a variety of biological factors, including inherited genetic predispositions, play a role in mood disorders (Nurnberger & Gershon, 1982). Adoption studies, much like those conducted in the areas of alcohol abuse and antisocial personalities, find the incidence of mood disorders to be disproportionately high among people whose adoptive parents did not suffer from such problems but whose natural parent(s) did (e.g., Cadoret, 1978).

Some researchers also believe that the observed tendency for women to suffer more than men from mood disorders suggests biological/genetic involvement in these disorders. There still are more questions than answers in this area (e.g., Mendlewicz, 1980), however. Newer research suggests that males and females actually may be about equal in their rates of depression, but learning and cultural factors create differences in the experience and overt expression of this mood.

More compelling evidence that biological factors are involved in mood disorders lies in the fact that the symptoms of these disorders can be reduced dramatically by certain chemical compounds. The effectiveness of antidepressant medications and other "mood compounds" has led many scientists to believe that both depression and mania may arise from disruptions to normal brain functioning (Zis & Goodwin, 1982). Again, however, there is no absolute statement that can be made at this time.

### Psychological and External Factors

There is a considerable amount of research to suggest that certain psychological characteristics place some people at higher risk of mood disorders (Depue et al., 1981). Among these are ambitiousness, extraversion, sociability, conventionality, and a high concern for the opinion of others. Of course, a great many people have some of these characteristics and never suffer from mood disorders. On the other hand, many people who do develop this problem have quite different characteristics. Biological predisposition may account for some of these differences; external life factors may account for others.

Research on the lives of people who experience mood disorders finds that, as a group, they have experienced a high incidence of stressful life events, such as the death of a loved one or the frustration of an important life goal (Paykel, 1982). There also is some evidence that status in life plays a factor. Major depression affects more urban than rural dwellers and has a disproportionately

In our society, more women than men report symptoms of major depression.

higher rate of sufferers among people of high educational and occupational status (Monnelly, Woodruff, & Robins, 1974). Do you have any ideas as to what explanations might lie behind such findings?

## The Treatment of Mood Disorders

At this time, it is estimated that about 40 to 60% of those diagnosed as having a mood disorder may expect a full recovery (defined as being free of symptoms for 5 years). This rate seems to be about the same whatever the type of treatment, although there is little empirical data to support claims for the effectiveness of traditional psychotherapy for these problems. Both psychopharmacological therapy and various cognitive and behavioral therapies appear to be more successful (Rosenfeld, 1985).

*Cognitive therapy* may be described briefly as an approach to changing behavior that focuses on changing thoughts or beliefs that may be causing (or reinforcing) the behavior. A cognitive-therapy strategy that seems to be effective in combating depression in some patients focuses on changing the inaccurate, negative thought patterns that characterize depression (Beck, Rush, Shaw, & Emery, 1979).

*Behavior therapies* focus on changing specific target behaviors by reinforcing desired behavior and extinguishing undesired behavior. Some therapists have found this method effective in treating depression. (Manic behavior almost always is treated with medication.) The general strategy is to reward (reinforce) behaviors that show attempts to cope effectively with life and ignore (extinguish) behaviors that are typical of the withdrawn helplessness of the depressed individual (Liberman & Raskin, 1971).

It should be emphasized again that some depression is a normal part of life, and the point at which it ceases to be normal and becomes symptomatic

Exercise is a safe and effective way to cope with normal depression provided that an individual is in generally good health.

of a mood disorder is impossible to specify in terms that will apply to everyone. But you know your own normal fluctuations in mood, and you also recognize unusual mood disturbances in your family members and close friends. These should not be a cause for panic, but neither should they be ignored; the risk of suicide is significant in all disorders involving depression.

**Summing Up** ■

Depression is a normal condition that most people experience at one time or another. If it is too severe, lasts too long, and/or seems to have no recognizable cause, it becomes a mood disorder. The most common form of mood disorder is major depression, but a minority of people experience episodes of manic behavior in alternation with depression. This bipolar mood disorder is difficult to treat effectively because the two sets of symptoms are polar opposites and treatments conflict.

The causes of mood disorders are not fully understood, but certain people are known to be more at risk than others. Woman report major depression symptoms more often than do men, for example. There is some question, however, as to whether the actual rate is higher for women or whether cultural factors make it more acceptable for women to express such symptoms. Some evidence for the second explanation may be inferred from the fact that more depressed men than women commit suicide, possibly because they suppress their symptoms and so do not get help.

People who lead outgoing, conventional lives and show concern for what others think of them also seem to be more susceptible to mood disorders. Finally, we know that depression runs in families, but the biological factors are far from clear at this time.

---

## ■ KEY WORDS AND PHRASES

| | | |
|---|---|---|
| abnormal behavior | *DSM-III-R* | phobic disorders |
| anxiety | dissociative disorders | schizophrenia |
| anxiety disorders | generalized anxiety disorder | somatoform disorders |
| controlled exposure techniques | mood disorders | student's disease |
| depression | obsessive-compulsive disorders | worry |

---

■ **READ ON**

*Abnormal Psychology and Maladaptive Behavior* by R. C. Carson, J. N. Butcher, and J. C. Coleman. Glenview, IL: Scott, Foresman, 1988. An excellent, comprehensive, and up-to-date summary of the field for the reader who is interested in learning more about the subject of abnormal psychology. This is a

text, and you are unlikely to find it in a bookstore, but your campus library or the professor of this course should be able to help you get a copy.

*Anxiety and Its Treatment* by J. H. Greist, J. W. Jefferson, and I. M. Marks. New York: Warner, 1986. A good, solid source book, available in paperback, for anyone who wants to learn more about the experience of anxiety and the ways that it may be relieved.

*Feeling Good: The New Mood Therapy* by D. Burns. New York: Signet, 1980. There are many books available on the subject of depression.

This one, by a student of depression expert A. T. Beck, reviews the problem of depression and covers its currently preferred treatment methods—chemical therapy and cognitive therapy—in detail.

---

## ■ REFERENCES

Agras, W. S. (1985). *Facing fears, phobias, and anxiety*. New York: Freeman.

American Psychiatric Association. (1987). *Diagnostic and statistical manual of mental disorders* (3rd. ed.), Revised. Washington, DC: Author.

Andrews, G., & Harvey, R. (1981). Does psychotherapy benefit neurotic patients? A reanalysis of the Smith, Glass, and Miller data. *Archives of General Psychiatry, 38,* 1203–1208.

Atkinson, R. L., Atkinson, R. C., & Hilgard, E. R. (1983). *Introduction to psychology* (8th ed.). New York: Harcourt Brace Jovanovich.

Bassuck, E. L., & Schoonover, S. C. (1977). *The practitioners guide to the psychoactive drugs*. New York: Plenum.

Beck, A. T., Rush, A. J., Shaw, B., & Emery, G. (1979). *Cognitive therapy for depression: A treatment manual*. New York: Guilford Press.

Borkovek, T. D. (1985). What's the use of worrying? *Psychology Today, 19,* 59–64.

Cadoret, R. J. (1978). Evidence for genetic inheritance of primary affective disorder in adoptees. *American Journal of Psychiatry, 135,* 463–466.

Carr, A. T. (1971). Compulsive neurosis: Two psychophysiological studies. *Bulletin of the British Psychological Society, 24,* 256–257.

Carson, R. C., Butcher, J. N., & Coleman, J. C. (1988). *Abnormal psychology and maladpative behavior* (8th ed.). Glenview, IL: Scott, Foresman.

Depue, R. A., Slater, J. R., Wolfstetter-Kausch, H., Klein, D., Goplerud, E., & Farr, D. (1981). A behavioral paradigm for identifying persons at risk for bipolar disorder: A conceptual framework. *Journal of Abnormal Psychology, 90,* 381–437.

Francis, K. T., & Carter, R. (1982). Psychological characteristics of joggers. *Journal of Sports Medicine, 22,* 386–390.

Jacobson, E. (1938). *Progressive relaxation*. Chicago: University of Chicago Press.

Liberman, R. P., & Raskin, D. E. (1971). Depression: A behavioral formulation. *Archives of General Psychiatry, 24,* 512–527.

McCann, I. L. & Holmes, D. S. (1984). Influence of aerobic exercise on depression. *Journal of Personality and Social Psychology, 46:* 1142–1147.

Mendlewicz, J. (1980). X-linkage of bipolar illness and the question of schizoaffective illness. In R. H. Belmaker and H. M. van Praag (Eds.), *Mania: An evolving concept*. New York: Spectrum.

Monnelly, E. P., Woodruff, R. A., & Robins, L. N. (1974). Manic depressive illness and social achievement in a public hospital sample. *Acta Psychiatrica Scandavicia, 50,* 318–325.

Nurnberger, J. I., & Gershon, E. S. (1982). Genetics. In E. S. Paykel (Ed.), *Handbook of affective disorders*. New York: Guilford Press.

Ost, L. G. (1985). Ways of acquiring phobias and outcome of behavioral treatment. *Behaviour Research and Therapy, 23,* 683–689.

Paykel, E. S. (1982). Life events and early environment. In E. S. Paykel (Ed.), *Handbook of affective disorders*. New York: Guilford Press.

Rosenfeld, A. H. (1985). Depression: Dispelling despair. *Psychology Today, 19,* 28–35.

Tavris, C. (1986). Coping with anxiety. *Science Digest, 94,* 46–51, 80–81.

Ullman, L. P., & Krasner, L. (1975). *Psychological approach to abnormal behavior* (2nd ed.). Englewood Cliffs, NJ: Prentice-Hall.

Williams, S. L., Dooseman, G., & Kleifield, E. (1984). Comparative effectiveness of guided mastery and exposure treatments for intractable phobias. *Journal of Consulting and Clinical Psychology, 52,* 505–518.

Wolpe, J. (1969). *The practice of behavior therapy*. New York: Pergamon.

Zis, A. P., & Goodwin, F. K. (1982). The amine hypothesis. In E. S. Paykel (Ed.), *Handbook of affective disorders*. New York: Guilford Press.

# 6

# Resources for More Effective Behavior

I n Chapter 1 effective behavior was defined as flexible, controlled, and productive behavior that allows us to feel good about ourselves and others as we move toward understanding ourselves and achieving realistic personal goals and good relationships. It has been stressed throughout this book that the primary resource you have for achieving and maintaining effective behavior is yourself. There are times in the lives of each of us, however, when our own abilities, skills, and energies seem inadequate to the task and we could use some help.

In this final chapter of *Psychology and Effective Behavior,* resources available to you if you believe you need some help, at least temporarily, are reviewed. There is nothing weak about seeking such help; rather, knowing when you have reached your own limits is an important part of being in control of your own life.

# 16

# Getting Help: Resources for More Effective Behavior

## Chapter Outline

■ You've tried talking to yourself, keeping busy, and pretending nothing is wrong, but you just can't shake off that feeling of vague anxiety that plagues you most of the time. For the life of you, you don't know what is wrong; you only know that *something* is.

■ You know you should lose weight. You've gone so far as to get a physical checkup and a diet from your doctor. But you have not stuck to it, and you have not lost any weight. In fact, you've gained some because the whole business is so frustrating.

■ You feel that your marriage is going off track somewhere. There seem to be more down or "blah" times than good times and more arguments than there should be. You've tried talking it over with your spouse, but you didn't feel any better afterward; in fact, you felt worse.

■ Life is going along pretty well. You don't have any big problems and you seem to be able to handle whatever comes along without feeling overstressed, but you know something is missing. You don't feel like you are expressing yourself or making full use of your talents or even that you understand yourself very well.

**D**o any of the preceding scenarios sound familiar? They depict common situations that lead people to look beyond themselves for resources to help them achieve more personally effective behavior. In the first instance, you are sure that you have some kind of problem, but you don't know what it is; you only know that you are unhappy. In the second, you know what your problem is and you know what to do about it, but you can't seem to do it. In the third, you've tried to do something about your problem, but it hasn't made you feel any better. In the last instance, you don't have any real problems; you just feel that you are capable both of giving to and getting more from life than you are right now.

People look for help outside themselves when they need relief, feel help-less, or want to expand and develop their potential. In this chapter some of the resources that are available to people who want or need help for any reason are discussed.

## SOURCES OF SUPPORT AND INFORMATION

The first line of defense for most of us when we find that we need some help is family and/or friends, and this social network is not a bad place to start. Even though such people are not professional helpers, they can help in several ways.

### Your Support Network

If you are lucky enough to have at least one good listener among your family and friends, you know that sometimes being listened to is all that is needed. "Getting it off your chest" is a tried and true remedy for some problems, such as experiencing a disappointment when you got your test paper back or having a "run in" with your children. In such cases, your family and friends have an advantage over professionals. They already know you and your situation, and you don't have to describe all of the background to your feelings before talking about them.

In addition to offering support, family and friends also are sources of vary-ing kinds of information that may be useful (Cutrona, 1986). Sharing your troubles may lead to the discovery that your friend or relative has had the same experience or problem. If you have been worried that there is something un-usual about your feelings, the knowledge that someone you know well has had the same experience may bring considerable relief.

Sometimes family and friends can give you information about what to do or where to go to get help or relief even if they have not had similar experi-ences. They may have read or heard about relevant services of professionals, or they may just know someone who knows someone. Finally, family and friends may give feedback about you and your behavior that can help you in making a realistic evaluation of your situation. For instance, if you ask, you may discover that those seven pounds you gained over the summer (the ones that have been depressing you so!) are not even noticeable to your husband or wife. Or you may find out that your parents don't feel at all that you let them down by not making the dean's list last term; they are still bragging about the times you *did* make it.

### Other Relationship Resources

Sometimes you don't feel that you can talk to people close to you about your feelings or a certain kind of problem. There could be many reasons for this. Perhaps you don't want to upset them with what may be only a minor problem or a temporary state. Perhaps you just don't want your family and close friends to know what is wrong. Perhaps they are part of the problem and you need to talk to someone more objective.

If you don't want to talk to any of the members of your immediate support network but feel you would like to talk to someone informally, there are other resources open to you. Most of us have relationships with many people that are personal without being especially close. The professor of this course is an obvious example. He or she has an interest in the problems that college students have and may be willing to listen or to suggest someone else.

Your rabbi, priest, or minister, if you have one, is another person who will be a good listener and may be trained specifically in counseling as well. Some people are able to confide in their family physician, a good neighbor, the family lawyer, or even their old third-grade teacher. A few people even seem to find it helpful to pour out their troubles to perfect strangers, perhaps because they can say what they need to say without having to consider the listener's feelings (since the listener does not know anyone involved).

Although some people may find temporary relief from problems by relating them to a stranger, the benefits of talking thing over with your seatmate on an airplane are limited. Strangers can listen to you, but they probably never will see you again, and they have little stake in really *hearing* you; most likely it is your story, not your feelings, that keeps their attention. In addition, it is quite likely that they will tell that story to the first person they meet off the airplane, and many people do not like the idea of being talked about in this way.

Finally, the process of opening up and talking about something that is bothering them is, for some people, sort of akin to opening a dam. Having

Most of us look first to a sympathetic friend or family member when we need someone to talk to.

taken the initial step, everything that has been held in comes pouring out, and the situation can get quite emotional. Having to put a lid on the emotions and leave the discussion unfinished because the airplane has touched down can be quite painful. If you prefer not to discuss your problems or feelings with someone who knows you (or cannot do so), you probably will be better advised to seek professional help.

As the term is used here, a professional is someone who is trained and certified or licensed, as appropriate, in a recognized profession. We are interested in professionals who specialize in offering help to people in coping with their problems or feeling better about themselves or more satisfied with their lives. Some of these are psychologists, some are physicians, and some have other specialities.

## PROFESSIONAL HELP

People who offer psychological help as a resource for more effective behavior believe this help can be achieved through psychological approaches. The usual name given to these approaches as a group is **psychotherapy,** which is defined by Strupp (1986) as "the systematic use of a human relationship for therapeutic purposes."

Although psychological approaches to helping people have in common the use of relationships as a way to accomplish this goal, there is considerable variation in specific working methods. Some years ago it was estimated that there were 36 different "schools" of psychotherapy (Harper, 1959), and there are many more today. To complicate matters, therapists who call themselves the same thing can vary considerably in what they actually do. It may help you, however, to be aware of the five broad categories into which most approaches can be placed.

## Insight Therapies

One of the earliest of the psychological approaches to helping people is based on the premise that we must have *insight* or understanding of our basic motivations and how we came to be the way we are if we are to experience relief from symptoms or change something about ourselves. As a result, **insight therapies** place considerable emphasis on personal history and development.

The most traditional form of insight therapy with us today is psychoanalysis and its various modifications. Psychoanalysts emphasize the importance of bringing buried thoughts and wishes that are causing internal conflict to active memory: "The discovery of the patient's unconscious conflicts comes bit by bit, as a memory surfaces here, a dream or a slip of the tongue suggests a meaning there," says Gleitman (1981, p. 720). It is the therapist's job to help the patient achieve insight by fitting all of these clues together. One of the more important tools in this process is interpretation.

There are other lesser-known therapies that fall into the insight therapy group; what they all have in common besides a belief in insight as the key to positive change is reliance on the therapist's role as the expert in the client-therapist relationship. People who are comfortable with this kind of relationship find it supportive, and many believe that the insight they gain into themselves and their behavior is extremely valuable. On the minus side, insight therapy does tend to go on longer than many other kinds of therapy (although you may stop at any time). This can make it an expensive experience, and hard evidence as to its long-term effectiveness is difficult to document.

## Humanistic Therapies

**Humanistic therapies** focus not on insight, but on *feelings*. They share a basic assumption that people have an inherent potential for growth and self-actualization and that this can be released through the exploration of feelings and greater acceptance of self. The *client-centered therapy* (Rogers, 1951) discussed briefly in chapter 4, is the most well known of these approaches.

As developed by Carl Rogers, client-centered therapy emphasizes the critical importance of the therapist's role in establishing a favorable climate for the client's exploration of true thoughts and feelings. The critical aspects of this climate are the therapist's acceptance of, understanding of, and positive regard for the client. There is little or no interpretation. Rather, the client-centered therapist relies upon restatement; he or she repeats, in different words and without any judgments, what the client seems to be saying. Thus, the client uses the therapist as a mirror to explore further and clarify his or her own feelings.

The goal of client-centered therapy is to help clients accept themselves, rather than trying to be what others think they should be (by suppressing their real thoughts, feelings, and attitudes). Rogers believed that reducing the incongruence between the true self and everyday experience (which usually includes hiding the true self) is what is required for a healthy personality, good personal relationships, and the elimination of such maladaptive experiences as anxiety.

Rogers was an extremely influential psychotherapist, and his approach opened the way for a large number of humanistic approaches. They differ in various ways from client-centered therapy, but all have in common what we

Client-centered therapy has had an enormous influence on the practice of psychotherapy.

might call a democratic philosophy; the therapist is a problem-solving *partner,* not an advice-giving expert. This approach is very comfortable for some people who find themselves able to relax and "open up" in this atmosphere in a way that is new to them, but it is not for everyone. The therapist's refusal to direct the sessions in a doctor-patient fashion makes some people very uncomfortable. Also, people who have definite behavior goals for therapy probably would prefer another approach.

## Behavior Therapies

A large and diverse group of therapy approaches emphasizes, not insight or feelings, but *behaviors*—actions that can be observed and recorded. Practitioners of **behavior therapies** share a belief that maladaptive behavior may be changed directly by restructuring its consequences. Although they do not, as a group, tend to be very much concerned with feelings, the self, and attitudes, most believe that changes in these areas *follow,* rather than precede, changes in behavior.

The basis for much of behavior therapy is the behavior-consequence link. Most concentrate on the *positive reinforcement* of desired new behavior along with *extinction* of undesired old behavior. We met an example of this approach in the last chapter; systematic desensitization is a process of systematically extinguishing fear responses and substituting relaxation responses in their place.

Helping people learn to control the conditions that tend to bring about a behavior (i.e., the antecedent conditions) also is recognized as important by behavior therapists. Spending time in settings that do not allow smoking (such as a movie theater or library) and removing all of the ashtrays from the home are two examples of suggestions that might be made to help a person whose goal is to quit smoking achieve this *stimulus control*.

In all but a few institutional settings or other unusual cases, the behavior therapy relationship may be thought of primarily as a *contractural* one. The client has behavior(s) that he or she wants to change; the therapist has the expertise for helping to bring this change about. Although mutual trust and respect are necessary, the personal relationship between therapist and client usually is not used so directly as a means of facilitating change as in insight and humanistic therapies. This well-defined situation is much more comfortable for some people than the more traditional therapy relationship, but the individual who does not have specific behavior-change goals is not likely to find it as helpful as another approach.

## Cognitive Therapies

As the name suggests, cognitive approaches to therapy are concerned primarily with *thought processes,* including how we perceive things, how we label things, and how we talk to ourselves. An important goal of cognitive therapists is to get clients to see, label, and talk about things in a realistic way, because they believe that many of the problems people have are the result of illogical beliefs and faulty thinking.

A "pure" cognitive therapist would have much in common with a therapist who relied on insight, since he or she, like the psychoanalyst, is interested in trying to help clients understand the causes of their problems. But many cog-

> There's only one corner of the universe you can be certain of improving and that's your own self.
>
> *Aldous Huxley*

nitive therapists also share the interest of behavior therapists in changing specific undesired or maladaptive behaviors. Because of this communality, we often find this group of approaches referred to as **cognitive-behavior therapies.**

Cognitive-behavior therapists seek to help people change their behavior by means of changing what they believe to be the irrational assumptions and illogical thinking patterns that cause the behavior. If this sounds familiar, it is because we already have met this approach twice in this book. Albert Ellis's (1962) *rational-emotive therapy* was discussed in connection with self-esteem, and Meichenbaum's *stress-inoculation therapy* (Meichenbaum & Cameron, 1982) was drawn upon to illustrate the role that positive self-statements can play in coping with stressful situations.

A third cognitive-behavior therapy approach is used by Beck (Beck, Rush, Shaw, & Emery 1979) to teach clients to combat depression. Beck's very effective approach is based on the assumption that depression results from illogical, negative thinking about oneself, the world, and the future. This thinking includes perceiving only those aspects of things that confirm negative beliefs, overgeneralizing on the basis of limited experience, magnifying the significance of negative events, and thinking in all-or-none terms (e.g., I have to be good at everything or I'm no good).

Beck's approach to treating depression (and other cognitive-behavior therapy approaches) involves three basic steps.

1.  Help the client identify and explore illogical thought patterns.
2.  Help him or her learn new ones that are positive, logical, and incompatible with the old ones.
3.  Help him or her put these ideas into practice to change behavior.

As you can see from these steps, the cognitive-behavior therapist-client relationship has elements of the partnership that characterizes humanistic therapies as well as some things in common with insight and behavior therapies. This combination of partnership relationship, insight, and specific behavior-change goals makes cognitive-behavior therapy a good choice for people who find other approaches too confining in one way or anther.

# Psychopharmacological Therapies

Psychotherapy is a form of treatment based on the assumption that psychological processes underlie the problem or concern that brings a person to a therapist, and this remains the most common approach to treatment. Some people respond very slowly or not at all to psychotherapy, however, and some professionals believe that an abnormal physical condition or biological functioning may be implicated in many of these cases. This will not be a new idea to you. The role that physiological and inherited biological factors may play in behavior has been discussed in almost every chapter in this book.

**Psychopharmacological therapies** (also called chemical therapies or medication therapies) treat psychological symptoms partially or entirely by means of controlled prescription drugs. In some instances, this treatment is used to calm or restore to reality severely disturbed individuals so as to make them accessible to psychological therapy. More often, it is used to control maladaptive symptoms, such as anxiety or depression, that are interfering with an in-

Table 16–1   **Drugs Used in the Treatment of Psychological Problems**

| Group | Examples | Used to Treat | Side Effects |
|---|---|---|---|
| Antipsychotic | ▪ Thorazine<br>▪ Mellaril<br>▪ Haldol | ▪ Extreme agitation<br>▪ Hallucinations<br>▪ Aggressive behavior<br>▪ Delusions | ▪ Long-term use may produce motor disturbances |
| Antidepressant | ▪ Pamelor<br>▪ Elavil<br>▪ Tofranil | ▪ Severe depression | ▪ Multiple side effects<br>▪ MAO inhibitors require dietary restrictions |
| Antimanic | ▪ Eskalith<br>▪ Lithonate<br>▪ Phi-Lithium | ▪ Manic behavior<br>▪ Depression that alternates with mania | ▪ Multiple side effects<br>▪ Can be toxic |
| Antianxiety | ▪ Librium<br>▪ Valium<br>▪ Xanax | ▪ Anxiety<br>▪ Chronic insomnia<br>▪ Tension | ▪ Lethargy<br>▪ Drowsiness<br>▪ Can be toxic<br>▪ Dependence a danger |

dividual's day-to-day life. As may be seen in Table 16–1, there are four major categories of compounds used for these purposes.

## Antipsychotic Compounds

The so-called major tranquilizers block a transmitter substance in the brain called dopamine. In so doing, they somehow reduce the intensity of severe psychological symptoms, such as hallucinations, and thus are quite effective in controlling the behavior of severely disturbed individuals. They do not bring about any cure, however; patients removed from the medication revert to their former state if there is no other form of treatment.

## Antidepressant Compounds

Antidepressants increase the concentrations of certain chemicals at locations in the brain that seem to be related to depression. The most common of the antidepressants are the tricyclics. Another group, called MAO inhibitors, are prescribed less frequently because they have more debilitating side effects. Some people are unable to tolerate either type of substance and both take several weeks to act even if tolerance is not a problem. Even then, relief from depression is not guaranteed; antidepressants do not work for some people. In those instances where they are effective, however, improvement tends to be dramatic.

## Antimanic Compounds

Lithium is a metal that has an ability to control manic behavior, such as that in the bipolar disorder. It also can be effective in reducing depression. In fact, researchers have found that regular doses of lithium actually can prevent the occurrence of symptoms in some cases, making it the first known *preventative* chemical therapy. A curious feature of this substance, however, is that no one understands how it works. It can have quite dramatic positive effects on behavior, but so far as scientists know, the lithium compounds used for psychological treatment have no physiological function.

## Antianxiety Compounds

There are several kinds of antianxiety medications but most patients are given one of the benzodiazepines. These are safe when used as directed and not combined with other medications without the advice of the physician. Like all antianxiety compounds, the benzodiazepines have a sedative effect, and it is this that is believed to be primarily responsible for the effectiveness of anxiety medications in reducing tension and anxiety.

Psychopharmacological therapy offers a convenient, effective, and relatively inexpensive way to alter debilitating moods and control certain symptoms of maladaptive behavior. Some mental health professionals believe it is too convenient, making it easy for people to ignore things about themselves or their lives that are creating their problems. Most psychiatrists (the only mental health professionals who may prescribe controlled medications legally) combine medication treatment with some form of psychotherapy, however. In addition, these medications have made it possible for many people who might otherwise have to be hospitalized to get on with living while having psychological treatment. Psychopharmacological therapy also holds potential for preventing and possibly curing certain diseases. More on this may be found in *Face of the Future*.

# Who Offers Psychological Help?

To this point, the terms *therapists* and *mental health professionals* have been employed in a rather general way. **Mental health professionals** are members of recognized disciplines whose primary purpose is to provide psychological services to people seeking such help. A brief summary of the major categories of professionals offering help that is primarily psychological in nature, together with the training they must have to do so, is presented in Exhibit 16–1.

**Therapist** is the word used to describe the professionals described in Exhibit 16–1. This term simply means a person who is trying to help another person in a way consistent with his or her particular training; in this discussion, that way is psychological. There are also many other people who are not professionals in the sense of our definition but who have special training and experience that make them valuable adjuncts or resources for certain kinds of problems.

- Psychiatric nurses
- Substance abuse counselors

## FACE OF THE FUTURE:
### A Chemical Cure for Alzheimer's Disease?

**Alzheimer's disease** is a disorder resulting from deterioration of the brain. Symptoms include decreased mental alertness and adaptability, increased self-centeredness and preoccupation with bodily functions, low tolerance for changes in routine or new ideas, periods of confusion and agitation, increased untidiness, and impaired memory and judgment.

Alzheimer sufferers also frequently exhibit paranoid delusions. Common ones include beliefs that someone (usually a relative) is trying to kill them, that internal organs are rotting away, that a spouse is having an affair, and that they are extremely poor. These and other symptoms typically appear so gradually that they are mistaken for "natural" aging until the disease is significantly advanced. By this time, the victim usually is well on the way to the terminal stage of Alzheimer's and death is only a matter of time.

Alzheimer's disease has been much in the news of late as doctors and psychologists have become increasingly aware of the real extent of the problem. It has been estimated that by the early 1980s, some one million Americans over 65 were suffering from this disease and as many as 40% of all nursing home residents may have Alzheimer's (Kolata, 1981). But it isn't just an old-age disease. Alzheimer's also strikes people in their 30s, 40s, and 50s, and when it does, the progress of the disease is speeded up considerably.

Certain biological factors, personality factors, and life stress are among the factors researchers believe are implicated in susceptibility to Alzheimer's, but the immediate cause is brain cell deterioration. Sufferers have lost up to 75% of the nerve cells in a part of the brain called the forebrain. This area produces a chemical that is vital to maintaining the brain pathways that support certain mental processes, including memory. This brain damage long has appeared to be irreversible, but new research is offering some hope of arresting Alzheimer's through chemical therapy.

The chemical produced by the brain cells Alzheimer's destroys is called acetylcholine. Researchers believe that if they can find a way to increase and maintain the level of this substance artificially, the progress of the disease's symptoms might be arrested or possibly even reversed. The brain is highly resistant to such tempering, but two promising chemical substances have been found.

One of these substances, physostigmine, blocks the action of a particular enzyme that is primarily responsible for the chemical breakdown of acetylcholine. The action of the other drug, naloxone, is less clear, but the administration of both substances has been associated with improved mental performance in Alzheimer patients.

All of this research is in early stages, and those who are involved with it emphasize that they are a long way from having a cure for Alzheimer's. Nevertheless, they are very hopeful that chemical therapy holds the key to a disease that, up to now, has been progressive, terminal, and particularly devastating to those close to the sufferer.

- Sex therapists
- Communication trainers
- Community mental health workers, such as those who staff crisis centers

It should be clear that the individual who decides to seek professional psychological help has many avenues open to him or her.

**EXHIBIT 16–1** ████████████████████████

## Mental Health Professionals Who May Help You Achieve More Effective Behavior

**Psychiatrist:**   An individual with an MD degree (in some cases a Doctor of Osteopathy degree instead) plus 3 years of residency training in a psychiatric hospital or mental health facility. About one third of the psychiatrists in this country have taken and passed the exam requirements for certification by the American Board of Psychiatry an Neurology. (You may recognize those who have done so by the term *Board Certified* among the list of a particular psychiatrist's qualifications.) Psychiatrists offer a varied range of services depending upon their particular interests and training, and they may prescribe drugs.

**Psychoanalyst:**   A psychoanalyst may also have an MD degree or alternatively, a PhD. In addition, he or she will have advanced training (4 to 10 years) in psychoanalytic techniques and will have undergone personal psychoanalysis. There is no licensing for psychoanalysts.

**Clinical psychologist:**   An individual with a PhD. or PsyD. in psychology with at least a 1-year internship of full-time supervised psychological assessment and therapy experience. Psychologists are licensed by the states in which they practice, and requirements vary considerably from state to state. A few clinical psychologists also are certified by the American Board of Examiners in Professional Psychology. Psychologists offer a variety of services according to their training and interests, including psychological assessment and therapy; they may not prescribe drugs.

**Counseling psychologist:**   A counseling psychologist has a PhD in psychology with special training in a student, couples, or other counseling setting. Counseling psychologists are licensed in the same way as clinical psychologists, but they usually do not work with the more severe forms of emotional/psychological problems. they may not prescribe drugs.

**Psychiatric social worker:**   An individual with a 2-year master's degree and specialized training in mental health settings. (A few psychiatric social workers have PhDs.) These professionals are licensed in some states and not in others; they also may be certified by the Academy of Social Workers. Psychiatric social workers provide a variety of services including psychotherapy, but they may not prescribe drugs.

## Who Seeks Psychological Help?

There is no typical client for the kinds of assistance offered by psychiatrists, counselors, and other professionals. Some people go because they need help in dealing with feelings of distress, some for help coping with a particular problem, and some for assistance in personal growth and development. Some don't go out of choice; they have been committed to a psychiatric facility, sent for evaluation and/or therapy by some legal entity (such as a court), or persuaded into seeking help by a concerned friend, family member, or employer.

Studies of people who voluntarily seek professional help with handling their lives find certain patterns. Women are far more likely than men to enter into these relationships, and people from upper socioeconomic groups more often seek help than those from lower brackets (Lichtenstein, 1980). Studies of college students who seek counseling find that they typically have more stressful life events than those who do not (Rubio & Lubin, 1986) and fewer alternative resources, such as close family ties or intimate friends (Goodman, Sewell, & Jampol, 1984).

What these studies do *not* find is that individuals who seek professional psychological help are more disturbed than other individuals. People seek out professional help for a variety of reasons, and many who do so appear to others to have no problems at all. So if you are considering such help, remember that no one is going to make any judgments about whether your concerns are serious or important or not. These professionals are a resource if you want to make use of them. Whether or not their help is effective depends on a number of factors, however.

## Does Psychological Help Help?

Many people who seek psychological help find their lives better for it; others don't. What makes the difference? It might seem that it would depend primarily on the training, experience, and, above all, method, of the individual providing the help. Despite the apparent common sense of this idea, the evidence does not support it (e.g., Frances, Sweeney, & Clarkin, 1985; Shapiro & Shapiro, 1982).

What seems to be critical to the outcome of therapy is the therapist's *relationship* with the client, and the ability to form a trusting and supportive relationship does not appear to be related in any predictable fashion to training, approach, or personality (Parloff, Waskow, & Wolfe, 1978). The therapist's characteristics seem to be important primarily if they matter to the client. For example, the sex of the therapist is relevant to someone who finds it difficult to talk to a man, or, alternatively, to a woman. There also is some evidence that a *match* between client and therapist on certain personal characteristics may be relevant to a good experience in some cases (Hunt et al., 1985; Foon, 1986).

What the client brings to a helping situation is in many ways as important to a successful outcome as what the therapist brings. Usually, the client who wants to receive help and expects to receive help will. You can see the sense in this. These individuals are more willing to be an active participant in the process, and some cooperation on the part of the client is recognized by almost all professionals as essential if there is to be any progress. The old stereotype of the passive patient who goes in to be cured by the psychiatrist does not apply any more (if it ever did).

Assuming that everyone involved is ready, able, and willing, does psychotherapy work better than efforts to deal with our problems ourselves (no psychotherapy)? The weight of the evidence available is that therapy is superior to no therapy in most cases (e.g., Bergin & Lambert, 1978; Paul, 1966; Smith & Glass, 1977). There can be substantial variation in the size of the effects, however. Dramatic improvements are rarer than modest improvements, and a very small number of people seem to get worse (Bergin, 1967). One explanation for this last outcome is that the therapy somehow disturbed an individual's equilibrium (which might have been maladaptive, but kept him or her going) without finding any way to help achieve a new balance.

The odds are very much against the possibility that you might be one of those people who deteriorates in psychotherapy. It has helped many people, and the chances that you will be one of them are quite good. One of the things

Encounter groups provide experiences in which the individual may "try on" new thoughts, feelings, and actions.

that you can do to raise the odds even further is to be quite selective in your choice of a therapist.

## Shopping for a Therapist

Suppose that you have decided that you want to seek out professional psychological help. How do you go about it? A logical first step is to visit any facility for this purpose available on your college or university campus. Your search may end there; many of these centers are staffed with highly trained and experienced professionals who have a special interest in the problems of students. If for any reason you cannot get what you want or need here, finding a therapist who is right for you should be at least a four-step process. Although this discussion is centered on individual psychotherapy, the steps are the same if you are looking instead for a group therapy situation or couples/family counseling.

■ *Ask around for recommendations.* The best sources of information are people you know who have used the services of a psychological professional. You might ask the staff at the campus counseling center, family members, friends, your doctor, the professor of this course, or someone at a local hospital, clinic, or telephone hotline. Even if no one has personal experience, someone will know someone who does. Use the yellow pages of your telephone book cautiously; keep in mind that these are paid advertising listings.

■ *Check out credentials.* Once you have a tentative list, do a little nosing around. Find out how long those on your list have been in the area or on the job, what degree(s) they have, and whether or not they are certified and/or licensed (your yellow pages may be useful for this last purpose since

Life itself remains a very effective thera-pist.

*Karen Horney*

many professionals list this information). Your local or school librarian can help you find appropriate professional listing reference material, or you can call your state psychological association. Doctors, nurses, teachers, and members of the clergy in your area also may have useful information concerning professional reputations.

■ *Call and ask questions.* Whether or not you are able to get the information you want about a prospective therapist from another source, you can get some from his or her office. You can ask about this person's approach, what kind of degree he or she has, whether or not the practice is limited to certain kinds of problems, and so on. If you meet with an unwillingness to answer such questions, steer clear. A responsible professional will not hesitate to tell you what you want to know and to instruct any office personnel to be receptive to questions as well.

■ *Make an exploratory visit.* Make an appointment with the most likely prospect on your list and keep it with the idea that it is exploratory. Ask any questions you haven't had answered as yet and see how comfortable you feel, both with the answers and with the person. Summarize your problem briefly and ask how the therapist would go about helping you. This is a big decision for you, and most professionals are not offended at the idea of being looked over. In addition, most are very busy, and you do not have to feel any obligation of any kind to return if you do not want to.

If all of this sounds like "shopping around" to you, it is. Not only is there nothing wrong with this, most of the professionals who offer psychological help to others strongly recommend it (Gilbert, 1985). A good relationship with your therapist is critical to a good therapy experience. You can't have this relationship with someone you don't feel is being straight with you or someone whose approach you don't trust or someone you dislike personally. Mental health professionals know this and are no more interested in undertaking a failure than you are.

Despite the acceptability and common sense of shopping around for psychological help, many people are reluctant to do so. There are several possible reasons for this, but an important one is that asking for this kind of help is difficult for many of us; it takes a fair amount of courage and determination just to locate someone and show up for the first appointment. (It may be especially difficult to make the effort if the problem is depression.) Who wants to go through it a second or even a third time? Nevertheless, you should promise yourself that you won't make a second appointment with your first professional if there is anything at all about the situation that puts you off. Make whatever effort it takes and keep looking. It's worth it.

## What Can You Expect?

Assuming that you find someone you like and whom you feel can help you in the way that you want, what can you expect to happen if you go "for therapy"? A lot depends on the individual therapist, but it is possible to outline a general idea of what to expect from the **experience of therapy** no matter what the approach. As in the previous discussion, these remarks apply generally to group and couples/family counseling as well as individual psychotherapy.

- *You may expect to be asked a number of questions and possibly to take some tests.* Some of these questions may come from a secretary or clerk who also may ask you to fill out a personal information form. Such forms typically ask you how you heard about this therapist and how you will be paying the bill (if applicable) in addition to standard questions about name, address, and occupation. The therapist will ask you questions about your background, what prompted you to seek assistance, and what you hope or expect to get from the experience.

  A therapist also may ask you to take one or more tests for the purpose of psychological assessment. These usually are personality tests, but some professionals also believe that intelligence, attitude, value, and/or interest test results are valuable aids to getting to know you better (and so being able to be of more assistance). If you have come to therapy as part of a couple or family, you (and the others) may be asked to complete questionnaires about your relationships in addition to or instead of the other kinds of tests. Most of the tests are paper-and-pencil; a few are given orally.

- *You may expect to sit facing the therapist in a comfortable chair in a pleasant room.* (If you are in a group, you probably will be part of a circle of chairs.) The days of lying on a couch are gone forever. It is likely that your therapist won't even sit behind a desk, since many believe that this sets up a communication barrier between the two of you. Many therapists will allow you to smoke if you feel you must, even though there may be no ashtrays in sight. If this is of concern to you, be sure to ask at the initial meeting.

- *You may expect to talk more than you listen.* Whatever the approach, you can expect to be the one doing the talking most of the time, although what you talk about will vary. Psychoanalysts encourage you to talk about whatever comes to mind at the time. A behavior therapist will want you to focus on the specific behavior(s) that you want to learn or change. A humanistic therapist will encourage you to express and explore your feelings. If you are in a group, you may be expected to talk about your reactions to other group members. In all cases, talking freely and completely about your problem is essential if the therapist is to be of any assistance to you. If you feel that you must withhold certain information from him or her, you probably are in the wrong place.

- *You may expect to have what you say recorded in some fashion.* Therapists see many people, and they cannot rely on their memories to provide them with the pertinent information at each meeting. Most make tape recordings or written notes during each session. (A few wait until you have left to make these notes, but they do make them.) This material is completely confidential, and professionals take this confidentially *very* seriously, so you needn't be alarmed by the fact that what you say is being recorded or written down. You also should know that as a consumer of psychological services, you have the right to be shown the contents of your file upon request.

- *You may expect to be shown the door politely, but firmly, at the end of the designated time period.* Some people are surprised and hurt to discover that their session is ended precisely on time (most run 50 minutes) no matter what is happening. This is understandable; if you don't expect it, it is a shock to hear a therapist say "Well, I'm afraid our time is up for today"

Sigmund Freud and his psychoanalytic theory of personality are what many people think of when they think about psychotherapy, but many other kinds of psychological help are available.

when you feel you are in the midst of an emotional crisis or an important breakthrough. So before it happens to you, realize that this is the way it most probably will be. Almost all therapists are very busy, and they must limit the time they give to each individual.

There also is another reason for limiting therapy sessions to a relatively short, set period of time. The fact that there is a limit discourages time-wasting "small talk" and focuses energy on the problem. The fact that the time is relatively short decreases the likelihood that what can be a very heavy, intense experience will have incapacitating effects on the rest of the day. A great many people who see therapists squeeze these appointments into busy schedules; they cannot afford to take a long rest period to recover from them.

■ *You may expect to do some "work" on your problems between sessions*. It is difficult to make any lasting change in either yourself or your life in 50 minutes once or even three or four times a week, and it is very likely that the therapist will give you tasks to carry out between sessions. These can range from taking notes about your feelings and reactions in certain situations to trying out specific new behaviors. You do not really *have* to do these assignments, of course, but you reduce your chances for a successful therapy outcome if you do not.

■ *You may expect to pay your bills promptly*. A therapist friend in private practice once said, "For some reason, many people seem to think there is something low and money-grubbing about asking the clients of psychological services to pay their bills. The attitude seems to be that these people have enough problems without our hounding them for money as well."

This therapist is not the only one to encounter such an attitude; it is not uncommon. As a result, those who are responsible for keeping agencies, hospitals, private practitioners, and others open for business tend to be tough on financial matters. Don't be offended; it isn't personal and the rules are not always inflexible. Feel free to check into the possibility of an "easy payment plan" if you like a particular therapist, but forsee difficulty making full payment after each visit.

And while we're on the subject of money . . .

## A Word about Cost

You may be wondering if psychological help costs too much for you. Certainly, it can be expensive; it is possible to pay up to $150 or more for 50 minutes with a popular psychiatrist. It also is possible to get good psychological services free if you are unable to pay. Most services fall somewhere in between these two extremes, and many professionals and agencies use a sliding scale, where the rate is adjusted according to ability to pay. In addition, many health insurance policies cover such services partially or completely; check your plan or that of your parents (if relevant) for the details of this coverage.

An interesting question is whether there is any relationship between the effectiveness of psychological services and whether or not you are paying for them. One argument is that if you are paying, you try harder in order to justify the financial commitment. The opposite side of the coin is that you may try less hard (or not at all) if you are paying for service because you feel that you can pay in money instead of effort.

Feelings on this issue can run quite high and lead to heated arguments among practitioners. The research evidence on the question is inconclusive; some studies have found no difference in pay versus no-pay situations (Subich & Hardin, 1985); other researchers have found differences, most of which tend to support the no-pay argument (Yoken & Berman, 1984). This could be because clients who pay have higher expectations that are more likely to be unattainable. Or it could simply be that clients think that people who do not charge them for their services are doing what they do out of more humanistic motives (although someone is paying them, even if it is not the client).

Although research results show a tendency to favor the no-pay therapy situation (so far as client evaluations of effectiveness is concerned), the trend is not a particularly strong one. Many researchers feel that more investigations are needed if we are to increase our understanding of the nature of the relationship between paying for therapy and therapy outcomes (Herron & Sitkowski, 1986). For practical purposes, the important thing is for you to be aware that you can afford psychological services if you want and need them.

## Saying Good-bye

You probably have heard about people staying "in analysis" (psychoanalysis) for years and years, up to 10 or more. The thought of making such an extensive commitment to some sort of helping relationship scares some people off, but it need not. In the first place, such long-term therapy is the exception rather than the rule. In the second place, you are free to terminate the relationship whenever you decide to do so, including, as mentioned, after the first visit.

Assuming that the first and subsequent visits go well and you see a particular therapist on some regular basis, how do you know when it is time to leave him or her behind? The answer is: when you have achieved your goals or, alternatively, when you feel you have not made any progress toward these goals in a reasonable period of time. You have several sources of information about this. You can ask your therapist and your family and friends, as well as yourself, what evidence they see that you are achieving your goals. You then can evaluate all of the information collected and make your decision.

That decision may be that you are ready to go back to managing on your own, that you want to stay in this relationship a while longer, or that it is time to look for help elsewhere. Don't be shy about making the last decision. As is true in any other type of human relationship, some helping relationships don't work, even though they may start out in a promising way.

This brings us to an unhappy subject, but one that must be mentioned. This is the matter of unethical behavior on the part of a therapist. There are no accurate statistics on this problem, but it is known that some clients have been deceived, exploited, and/or harassed by therapists in emotional, sexual, and financial ways. These cases make sensational reading when they become public; but the vast majority of therapists are *extremely* conscious of their responsibilities, and the chances that you will encounter an unethical one are remote. Nevertheless, this remote possibility is yet one more reason (to add to many others) for following the steps to selecting a therapist outlined earlier.

**cathy**®                                                                    **by Cathy Guisewite**

**Source:** Cathy © 1985 UNIVERSAL PRESS SYNDICATE. Reprinted with permission. All rights reserved.

## Summing Up ■

Family and friends who will listen are the first resource most people turn to if they are having problems or feeling dissatisfied with their lives. The help that such people can offer sometimes is sufficient. If you want to look further for professional help, there are many trained and experienced people who offer a variety of psychological services. You are advised to shop around to find one you feel comfortable with and one you can afford.

## OTHER RESOURCES

To this point, the focus has been on traditional resources for help with managing your life effectively—family, friends, and professionals who offer help that is primarily psychological in nature. Our discussion would not be complete, however, without some mention of other resources that have proved valuable for some people. These include self-help materials of various kinds, intensive group experiences, religion, biofeedback, and hypnosis.

There are people who believe that making use of the kinds of resources listed is of itself evidence of an inadequate ability to manage one's own life effectively. This point of view stems from the fact that these options so often are presented as *the* answer to life problems. Vulnerable people can become "converts" who accept this premise and believe that they need look no further for happiness, success, and self-fulfillment. Unfortunately, this promise seldom is fulfilled since life is rarely that simple. In addition, some of these approaches can leave people worse off—emotionally, psychologically, and/or financially— than they were before.

Of course, extreme reactions and/or damage are not inevitable consequences of using the resources we will be considering in this section. There is nothing about such approaches that in and of itself interferes with effective behavior as we have defined it; it is a matter of perspective. These are outside resources that may or may not be useful to you. As such, they may be used in much the same way as you might use a friend or psychologist—as a resource to help you get on with the business of controlling your own life effectively. Four of these resources—intensive group experiences, religion, biofeedback, and hypnosis—are reviewed in this chapter. Self-help books are discussed in Chapter 1.

## Intensive Group Experiences

The term **intensive group experience** refers to a variety of group meeting approaches that share an aim of promoting human psychological growth. Such groups are not to be confused with group therapy, which, as the name suggests, is psychological therapy in a group setting. Although this distinction may be blurred in the case of any particular group, it is an important one. Intensive group experiences are a resource for people who want to add something specific to their lives; most have a particular agenda and goals that are the same for all participants. Thus, they lack the individual emphasis of traditional therapy, where goals typically are determined by individual needs and problems.

The most common form of intensive group experience is the **encounter group** in which a number of participants spend time once a week or over a long weekend (marathon session) confronting one another in an intense way. The focus of this confrontation is behavior in the group as well as expressed thoughts, feelings, and experiences. The purpose is to strip away masks and pretenses and force awareness of real needs and feelings. For each participant, other group members are there to serve as both critics of disabling self-deception and supporters of honesty and insight.

Encounter-group sessions can get quite emotional, and not all of the emotions are positive. The group may "gang up" on one participant if they feel that he or she is not being honest or is resisting involvement or feedback. Alternatively, they may reject a participant entirely. Either can be quite devastating, leaving the individual damaged by the group experience rather than enriched. People in this category are referred to as *casualties*.

What about other members? Do encounter groups accomplish their goals? What is probably the most well known and comprehensive investigation of this question was carried out some years ago. In their study of 117 encounter groups, Lieberman, Yalom, and Miles (1973) concluded that roughly one third of the participants showed positive changes after the experience. An additional 18% showed negative changes, and about half of these were casualties.

Results of this and more recent analyses of encounter groups make it clear that such experiences are not for everyone. Almost half of the participants seem to get very little from them (or at least little that researchers can measure), and some actually are harmed by the experience. The leadership of such groups is critical in this respect, both in screening prospective members and in dealing with destructive group processes. A major function of group leaders in any group with a psychological focus is to serve as a "safety net" for participants (Lakin, 1986). You are strongly encouraged to avoid encounter groups whose leaders have no formal training and/or make no effort to determine whether or not you are a suitable candidate for the experience.

Another popular intensive group experience is *transactional analysis,* or TA. The goal of TA is to help people become more accepting of themselves and others and to stop playing destructive games with one another. This is accomplished not through the freewheeling confrontation of the typical encounter group, but through structured discussion and communication exercises developed by a psychiatrist (Berne, 1964) as a therapy method within the humanistic tradition. Some professionals still use it in this way, but most participants in TA groups are not signing up for therapy; they want to learn more about human communication and stretch themselves as people in the process.

## Religion

Many writers and social commentators have noted that the 1980s have been a time of increased church and temple attendance and greater interest in religion and religious values. Some believe that this represents a backlash against the "me-firstism" of the 1970s, a preoccupation they are convinced has been stimulated by the increased popularity of psychotherapy (Schumer, 1984).

Returning to abandoned religious beliefs and practices does seem to be more common today, and many people find this to be a valuable source of support, values, and direction. Others are turning to religion or spiritualism for the first time in hopes of finding something that will add to their lives or help them manage their problems. This isn't new. It happened in the 1960s when thousands of people turned to Eastern religions, and it happened in the late 1970s when thousands more made impassioned conversions to "born again" Christianity.

Not everyone who turns to religious sources of personal help joins organized churches or religious movements. Some find meaning in observing practices that are part of certain religions. Among these are transcendental meditation (from the Hindu religion); yoga (also from the Hindus); and the study of a philosophy, such as Zen (from Buddhism and Taoism). The benefits of such practices, like the benefits of any religion-oriented involvement, are highly individual and almost impossible to study in a scientific manner. There is some evidence, however, that they are effective in helping some people cope with stress and anxiety (e.g., Delmonte, 1985).

The ultimate use of religious resources for personal help lies in what one author calls *radical departures* (Levine, 1984). By this, he means departing an established life pattern to take up residence and allegiance to a radical religious group, such as the Hare Krishnas, the "Moonies," or the ill-fated followers of Jim Jones (900 of whom committed mass suicide in Guyana in the late 1970s). In Exhibit 16–2 a psychologist who "infiltrated" a Moonie community for 12 days describes the people he found there.

After reading Knapp's description, it is not difficult to see why radical religious groups are highly controversial. The life style looks very unattractive to most of us, and many outsiders are convinced that it would be necessary to trick or brainwash people into joining such groups and coerce them into staying in such environments. According to mental health professionals who work with ex-members, there is some truth to this allegation; casualties suffer emotional, financial, and occasionally, physical damage from the experience. It is very difficult to put such reports in perspective, however, since no one really knows how many people have joined these groups voluntarily and remain within them quite happily.

**EXHIBIT 16–2**

## One View of the "Moonies"

- Complies with all commands of superiors.
- Ceases all but the most cursory communication with nonmembers.
- Emits happy behavior all the time.
- Views any personal reinforcers as selfish and sinful.
- Contributes all personal property to the organization.
- Engages in deceptive solicitation of funds.
- Works 16–18 hours a day without pay.
- Recruits new members to do the same.

*Note:* From *Shine on, Hollow Moon.* by T. J. Knapp and L. C. Robertson. Unpublished manuscript.

Given this lack of information, the fairest statement to make about radical departures would seem to be that they help some people achieve a way of life they believe is better by changing their environments. Within these new worlds, they have new standards and they move toward achieving new goals in new ways. We may question the degree to which these standards and goals facilitate traditional views of effective behavior, but we must remember that not everyone accepts these views.

# Biofeedback

**Biofeedback** (for biological feedback) is an equipment-assisted method for training people to be able to exercise some control over such bodily processes as blood pressure, heart rate, muscle contraction, and temperature. As usually carried out, there are three steps.

1. A reading is taken of the subject's target response, such as heart rate.
2. This reading is converted electronically to a sound or visual signal.
3. This signal is transmitted ("fed back") to the subject in some way.

The biofeedback is a basis for training the subject to influence the response in a desired fashion. For example, some people have used this training to control tension headaches. As they see the signal that the forehead muscle that causes such headaches is beginning to contract, they use training in muscle relaxation to counteract the tension (Qualls & Sheehan, 1981). Over time, they learn to recognize the signs on their own without the equipment. Successes in training people to control certain brain-wave activity, reduce accelerated heart rates, raise the temperature of a finger, control bowel and bladder incontinence, and decrease blood pulse rate also have been reported (Miller, 1985).

Biofeedback is exciting because it opens up the possibility for voluntary control of processes long believed to be beyond such control. Researchers are optimistic that it may add yet another tool to those available to fight stress and related physical, emotional, and psychological problems. It has no known negative side effects, and if you have the opportunity to try it (perhaps in a research lab at your college or university), you can do so with safety. Biofeedback is not a proven ticket to a better life as some of the publicity in recent years would suggest, however, and it is expensive if you pay for it yourself.

## Hypnosis

**Hypnosis** is a technique dating back some years that traditionally has been used by psychotherapists (primarily psychoanalysts) as a way to gain access to hidden feelings and memories. This is accomplished by putting a client in a hypnotic trance, usually through some combination of relaxation and verbal suggestion.

Today, hypnosis sees independent use as a way to help people with specific behavioral problems through what is called posthypnotic suggestions. A *posthypnotic suggestion* is an idea about how an individual will behave in the future that is "planted" through verbal suggestion by the hypnotist while the hypnotized person is in a trance. For example, it may be suggested to a smoker that she will find the mere thought of smoking disgusting in the future. Or an overweight man may be told that his appetite will diminish sharply.

Most people considering hypnosis probably are drawn to it in hopes of getting quick results for some behavior problem, such as smoking, overeating, or insomnia. Does it work? It can, but not for everyone. An estimated 10% of the population cannot achieve a trance at all, and a large percentage of the remainder achieve one too shallow to be effective (Hilgard, 1982).

Even people who can achieve the necessary hypnotic trance do not necessarily follow posthypnotic suggestions (Hilgard, 1986); so if you are intrigued by hypnosis, go into it optimistically, but realistically. And be sure that you consult a trained professional with a responsible reputation. As with the other sources of possible help we are reviewing in this section, hypnotism attracts its share of those looking only to make a fast buck from other people's problems.

## Summing Up ■

There is a variety of resources available that lay claim to helping people with specific problems and/or to promoting psychological growth and development. There is no reason at all for any of these to work *against* effective behavior, provided that you do not believe them to be universal cure-alls and provided that you are assisted by responsible, experienced individuals. There are many such people offering these services, but there also tends to be more room for the irresponsible in this area than in professional psychological and medical circles. Don't be afraid to examine credentials or ask for more information about training; it is your responsibility as well as your right.

## PUTTING IT ALL TOGETHER

The subject matter of this book has been you—how you came to be the way you are, what kinds of factors influence your behavior in your day-to-day life, some problems you may encounter in the process of moving in the direction you want to go, and some emotional and psychological disturbances that can get you off track. In this final chapter, we reviewed resources for getting outside help if you need it. In the course of all of these discussions, you have been presented with a great deal of information, and the time has come to put it all together. In closing, then, here are four simple guidelines that sum things up.

1. *Study yourself.* Give some conscious thought to your strengths and weaknesses, your talents and interests, your goals and ambitions. You may even wish to make some notes. If there are things you want to change or just things you need to do if you are to work toward your goals, develop a plan. Use this book and any other resources you may have available. Whatever your age, this is the time in your life to equip yourself for the future.

2. *Work on accepting yourself as a valuable human being.* There may be some things you would want to change, but there are also some you don't want to change (as well as some you can't change). Make a conscious effort to be proud of the things you like about yourself. Also be willing to accept your feelings; the fact that you have unpleasant emotions sometimes doesn't make you a bad person. It just makes you human.

3. *Become involved with other people.* If you aren't already, make an effort to get yourself involved with others as a friend, helper, teammate, co-worker, study partner, or whatever. We are all social beings, however much we may try to go it alone. If you aren't too sure of how to go about this, consider doing some volunteer work in a hospital or becoming a Big Brother or Big Sister or finding some other way of showing concern for the welfare of others. This not only gets you involved but also makes you feel good about yourself.

4. *Remember that you have the ability to control your own life.* There is not *one* key to effective behavior, but if there were it probably would be a sense of control over your own life. Although life circumstances or the actions of parents, professors, bosses, spouses, children, and other people can make you feel that you don't have very much of this control, the fact is that almost everyone has the ability to control his or her own life. Many people are just out of practice. If you have been one of them, perhaps you now have some ideas (and the resolve) for putting yourself back in the driver's seat. If you need some help to do this, get it. That is part of being in control.

Good luck and good-bye.

> You only live once—but if you work it right, once is enough.
>
> Joe E. Lewis

---

## KEY WORDS AND PHRASES

| | | |
|---|---|---|
| Alzheimer's disease | experience of therapy | mental health professionals |
| behavior therapies | humanistic therapies | psychopharmacological therapies |
| biofeedback | hypnosis | psychotherapy |
| cognitive-behavior therapies | insight therapies | shopping for a therapist |
| encounter group | intensive group experience | therapist |

### ■ REFERENCES

Beck, A. T., Rush, A. J., Shaw, B., & Emery, G. (1979). *Cognitive therapy of depression: A treatment manual*. New York: Guilford Press.

Bergin, A. E. (1967). An empirical analysis of therapeutic issues. In D. Arbuckle (Ed.), *Counseling and psychotherapy: An overview*. New York: McGraw-Hill.

Bergin, A. E., & Lambert, M. J. (1978). The evaluation of therapeutic outcomes. In S. L. Garfield and A. E. Bergin (Eds.), *Handbook of psychotherapy and behavior change: An empirical analysis*. New York: Wiley.

Berne, E. (1964). *Games people play*. New York: Grove Press.

Cutrona, C. E. (1986). Objective determinants of perceived social support. *Journal of Personality and Social Psychology, 50,* 349–355.

Delmonte, M. M. (1985). Meditation and anxiety reduction: A literature review. *Clinical Psychology Review, 5,* 91–102.

Ellis, A. (1962). *Reason and emotion in psychotherapy*. Secaucus, NJ: Lyle Stuart.

Foon, A. E. (1986). Effect of locus of control on counseling expectations of clients. *Journal of Counseling Psychology, 33,* 462–464.

Frances, A., Sweeney, J., & Clarkin, J. (1985). Do psychotherapies have specific effects? *American Journal of Psychotherapy, 39,* 159–174.

Gilbert, S. (1985). Sizing up psychotherapy. *Science Digest, 93,* 30.

Gleitman, H. (1981), *Psychology*. New York: Norton.

Goodman, S. H., Sewell, D. R., & Jampol, R. C. (1984). On going to the counselor: Contributions of life stress and social supports to the decision to seek psychological counseling. *Journal of Consulting Psychology, 31,* 306–313.

Harper, R. A. (1959). *Psychoanalysis and psychotherapy: 36 systems*. Englewood Cliffs, NJ: Prentice-Hall.

Herron, W. G., & Sitkowski, S. (1986). Effect of fees on psychotherapy: What is the evidence? *Professional Psychology: Research and Practice, 17,* 347–351.

Hilgard, E. R. (1982). Hypnotic susceptibility and implications for measurement. *International Journal of Clinical and Experimental Hypnosis, 30,* 394–403.

Hilgard, E. R. (1986). A study in hypnosis. *Psychology Today, 20,* 23–27.

Hunt, D. D., Carr, J. E., Dugadakis, C. S., & Walker, E. A. (1985). *Psychotherapy, 22,* 718–721.

Kolata, G. B. (1981). Clues to the cause of senile dementia: Patients with Alzheimer's disease seem to be deficient in a brain neurotransmitter. *Science, 211,* 1032–1033.

Lakin, M. (1986). Ethical challenges of group and dyadic psychotherapies: A comparative approach. *Professional Psychology: Research and Practice, 17,* 454–461.

Levine, S. V. (1984). Radical departures. *Psychology Today, 18,* 20–27.

Lieberman, M. A., Yalom, I. D., & Miles, M. M. (1973). *Encounter groups: First facts*. New York: Basic Books.

Lichtenstein, E. (1980). *Psychotherapy: Approaches and applications*. Monterey, CA: Brooks/Cole.

Meichenbaum, D., & Cameron, R. (1982). Cognitive-behavior therapy. In G. T. Wilson & C. M. Franks (Eds.), *Contemporary behavior therapy: Conceptual and empirical foundations*. New York: Guilford.

Miller, N. E. (1985). Rx: Biofeedback. *Psychology Today, 19,* 54–59.

Parloff, M. B., Waskow, I. E., & Wolfe, B. (1978). Research on therapist variables in relation to prognosis and outcome. In S. L. Garfield and A. E. Bergin (Eds.), *Handbook of psychotherapy and behavior change: An empirical analysis*. New York: Wiley.

Paul, G. L. (1966. *Insight vs. desensitization in psychotherapy: An experiment in anxiety reduction*. Stanford, CA: Stanford University Press.

Qualls, P. J., & Sheehan, P. W. (1981). Electromyograph biofeedback as a relaxation technique: A critical appraisal and reassessment. *Psychological Bulletin, 90,* 21–42.

Rogers, C. R. (1951). *Client-centered therapy*. Boston: Houghton Mifflin.

Rubio, C. T., & Lubin, B. (1986). College student mental health: A person-environment interactional analysis. *Journal of Clinical Psychology, 42,* 205–212.

Schofield, W. (1964). *Psychotherapy: The purchase of friendship*. Englewood Cliffs, NJ: Prentice-Hall.

Schumer, F. (1984, Apr. 15). A return to religion. *New York Times Magazine,* 90–94.

Shapiro, D. A., & Shapiro, D. (1982). Meta-analysis of comparative therapy outcome studies: A replication and refinement. *Psychological Bulletin, 92,* 581–604.

Smith, M. L., & Glass, G. V. (1977). Meta-analysis of psychotherapy outcome studies. *American Psychologist, 32,* 752–760.

Strupp, H. H. (1986). The nonspecific hypothe-sis of therapeutic effectiveness: A current as-sessment. *American Journal of Orthopsychiatry, 56,* 513–520.

Subich, L. M., & Hardin, S. I. (1985). Counsel-ing expectations as a function of fee for service. *Journal of Counseling Psychology, 32,* 323–328.

Yoken, C., Berman, J. S. (1984). Does paying a fee for psychotherapy alter the effectiveness of treatment? *Journal of Clinical and Counseling Psychology, 52,* 254–260.

# Behavior Modification: The Self-Management of Behavior

In this book we have discussed a variety of behaviors that many people want to add to or eliminate from their lives. Examples include increasing study time, getting regular exercise, decreasing food intake, decreasing alcohol intake, and eliminating cigarette smoking. In this section, a general behavior modification plan that you can use to bring about self-management of such behaviors is outlined. Keep in mind, however, that genuine obesity, eating disorders, and behavior problems complicated by life-threatening physical additions (such as dependence on barbiturates) and/or serious life-style complications (such as alcohol abuse) require professional assistance. This program is not intended to be a substitute for that help.

## REINFORCEMENT: THE BASIC PRINCIPLE

Most of what you do and know and are has been learned as a result of the outcomes of your behavior. The basic principle of this form of learning is quite simple: Behavior is shaped by its consequences. Behavior that persists has been rewarded in some way in the past; that is, it has been positively (or negatively) reinforced, or strengthened, by what followed it.

What this basic principle means is that you are getting something you want (or avoiding something you don't want) by your accustomed behavior patterns, or at least you did at one time. For example, you may have begun cleaning your plate and asking for seconds at meals because it pleased your mother (you received a reward in the form of praise and approval.) You don't live at home anymore, but you still eat seconds. This is the kind of behavior pattern we call a habit.

Habits are difficult to break because they have become so automatic. The rewards that built up the behaviors in the first place are no longer present, or they are no longer noticed and savored to the same extent. The individual may not be fully aware that he or she even is eating a doughnut, smoking, or having a fourth beer.

Many of the behaviors that people want to change fall into the habit category. Others are habits people would like to acquire. Either way, the steps to bringing about the change are the same:

1. Chart the target behavior.
2. Chart the situation.
3. Break (or establish) the links.
4. Set up intermediate goals.
5. Reward yourself for successful goal accomplishment.

Two possible behavior-change goals are used to illustrate these steps. The first is the elimination of smoking, and the second is the establishment of an exercise program that includes three 30-minute sessions per week.

## Chart the Target Behavior

Whether you want to increase some behavior, such as exercise, or eliminate some behavior, such as smoking, the first step is identify the *target behavior* quite clearly. Vague statements about attitudes, undesirable personality traits, or so-called character flaws won't do. If you want to quit smoking, your target behavior is "stop smoking cigarettes." If you want to establish an exercise program, it is "exercise 30 minutes three times a week." In neither case is it anything like "becoming a more disciplined (or healthier) person."

Once you have defined your target behavior clearly, you must keep track of the extent to which you now perform it. If you are trying to change a habit, such as smoking, this step may be difficult. Nevertheless, it is crucial since this record tells you exactly what you are up against. It also provides the baseline from which you measure the success of your behavior-management program.

To establish the baseline for your target behavior, you must keep track of the behavior for some period of time without making any effort to change your usual pattern (which we will call your typical response rate). This step may be difficult; having decided to change something, you will want to get on with it. But resist the temptation to cheat, and simply write down the number of times you perform the behavior in a given time period (at least a week is recommended). At the end of this time, make a day-by-day chart or graph that will give you a clear picture of where you start with respect to your target behavior. A chart for a hypothetical smoker is shown in Figure A–1. He or she currently does not exercise at all, so the response rate for this behavior is zero and there is no chart to be made.

## Chart the Situation

The frequency with which you perform the target behavior is the baseline from which you will measure your success, but if your program is to be a success, you need some additional information. The next step is to analyze the context in which the target behavior occurs. This context includes time, place, pres-

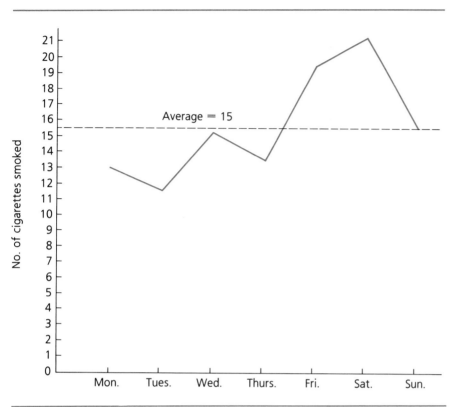

Figure A–1   **Charting Smoking Behavior**

ence/behavior of others, and the way you felt. Part of the record for one day in the life of our smoker is shown in Exhibit A–1. Again, there is no comparable record for exercising since the response rate for this behavior is zero at present.

## EXHIBIT A–1
## Analyzing the Stimuli for Smoking

| Time | Place and Activity | Other People Present | How I Felt/ Why I Lit Up |
|------|-------------------|---------------------|-------------------------|
| 9:30 A.M. | Kitchen/eating | No one | Always smoke with morning coffee |
| 10:30 A.M. | Desk/studying | No one | Thought it would help me concentrate |
| 12:00 P.M. | Restaurant/having a glass of wine | Jim, Jane | They were smoking, so I did too—social |
| 12:45 P.M. | Restaurant/finishing a good meal | Jim, Jane | Always smoke after a meal |
| 1:00 P.M. | Car/driving in heavy traffic | No one | Nervous—big test this afternoon |
| 1:45 P.M. | Desk/reviewing notes for midterm | No one | Thought it would help me study |

Information like that in Exhibit A–1 tells you what kinds of conditions, called stimuli, are associated with your target behavior and what kinds of outcomes might be reinforcing it. Notice, for example, that our smoker lights up when doing mental work, when eating or drinking, and when seeing others smoking. Some of these cigarettes seem to be for a purpose ("thought it would help me study"); others clearly are habit ("always smoke after a meal").

## Break the Links

The next step in the program to eliminate smoking is to begin breaking the links between the target behavior and the situations in which it tends to occur most frequently. We call this step *environmental management* (or stimulus control); you are going to use what you know about the context of your behavior to arrange external conditions so that they will help you eliminate—not elicit—the target behavior. Some suggestions to help our smoker accomplish this environmental management include the following:

- *Make a public announcement of your intention.* Ask your family and friends to help you by reminding you of it if you start to light up in their presence. Commit to *thanking,* not hassling, them for the reminder and immediately put the cigarette out. If you stick to this, you will be breaking the link between smoking and the presence of others.

- *Spend as much time as you can in places that prohibit smoking.* Use the non-smoking section of the library, go to the movies, or visit friends who ask you not to smoke in their homes. This is a general strategy for breaking the *habit* of smoking.

- *If you typically smoke while drinking certain beverages, switch for awhile.* Drink tea instead of coffee, club soda with lime instead of white wine, or water instead of soft drinks. Make a bargain with yourself that you can't smoke with these new drinks so that you don't substitute one link for another.

- *Set up competing responses.* These are behaviors that don't go with the target behavior ("compete" with it). Do you smoke while writing papers, letters, or reports? Type them instead. If you don't know how to type, now is a good time to learn. If that isn't possible, try to do these activities in a place where you can't smoke or when a nonsmoker who has agreed to help you can be around. When that can't be arranged, try chewing sugarless gum or sucking on hard sugarless mints. If all else fails, take a shower while the urge passes. Water is one of the would-be ex-smoker's greatest allies.

   Smoking is a particularly hard habit for most people to break and you may want to give your program a boost by using the nicotine gum that was discussed in Chapter 13. This gum serves both as a competing response (in the same way as any other gum) and as a way to manage your addiction to nicotine; see your doctor for detailed information (this is a prescription-only substance).

- *Set up a series of rules for yourself about where you can smoke and stick to them.* You might start, for example, with your car. You'll not only cut down your smoking right away, you'll be a safer driver and your car will smell better.

You can use these same principles to add a behavior, such as regular exercise. The key is to arrange things so that your surroundings "call up" the desired behavior.

- *Make a public announcement of your intention.* Ask your family and friends to ask you about your progress at intervals and commit to thanking them when they do (rather than getting defensive if you haven't progressed as far as you'd hoped when they ask).

- *Pick a form of exercise and a time of day that you can do it that are as free from built-in excuses as possible.* For example, if you are a slow starter in the mornings, don't decide that you will go out and jog at 6 A.M. If you live in an area that has hard winters and/or extremely hot and humid summers, don't start with jogging at all (unless you can afford to buy one of the devices for doing so inside). It also probably is better not to decide you will work out in a gym or sports club on the other side of town.

  Keep in mind that your objective at this step is to try to "outsmart yourself" by arranging circumstances so that there is no easy way out of exercise. You may find this easier at first if you select an activity that you can do in your home, regardless of weather, traffic, and so on. One possibility is to look into the variety of records and videotapes for home aerobics. You can find these for both men and women and at all levels of difficulty. Once exercise has become a habit, you can branch out with different activities at different times of the year and so on.

- *Do not do nonphysical things that you really enjoy during your selected exercise period even if it is an "off" day.* You want to set up an association between your selected time and physical exercise such that when this time rolls around you find yourself thinking more or less automatically about exercise. To look at it another way, you want to avoid setting up a significant difference between your use of this time on exercise days and on other days so that you do not think of exercise as interfering with something you'd rather be doing. This means that while you are getting started, you will be better off performing some physical chore during this time than talking on the telephone to a friend, watching television, reading a novel, or whatever.

- *Purchase (or select from your wardrobe) appropriate clothing and wear it only for your exercise.* Again, you are trying to build links; in this case, you want to think "exercise" when you see this clothing. If you wear a sweatsuit or shorts set that you often wear to the park when you walk the dog or to class or wherever, the link is weak or nonexistent.

These are just a few of the elements of stimulus control for someone who is trying to add exercise to his or her life. Your particular situation should suggest other arrangements to you. For example, if your telephone rings often, you might want to make a rule that under no circumstances will you stop exercising to answer it (you might want to alert your family and friends first). If you live with someone who also would like to begin exercising, a joint program might be effective.

## Set Up Intermediate Goals

Many ex-smokers report that they reached their goal by using principles of environmental management, such as those described, to quit "cold turkey." Not all smokers can quit this way, however, and many other behaviors cannot be changed this way. For example, you might set a goal of exercising 30 minutes a day, but you are out of shape and know that you won't be able to do this immediately.

Many behavior-change programs require setting *intermediate goals* that move you in the direction you want to go. If you want to add 30 minutes of exercise to your day, your first intermediate goal might be to exercise for 10 minutes every other day for a week. Then you might move to 15 minutes for one week, and so on. When you could handle 30 minutes every other day, you would start adding short segments on the alternate days until you had reached your goal. These intermediate goals allow you to work in steps, or successive approximations, toward your goal.

If our smoker decides to take this intermediate-goal approach, he or she will reduce the number of cigarettes allowed by one every few days, once a week, or whatever seems to be a realistic goal.

## Reward Yourself

Smoking, drinking, overeating, not exercising, and other behaviors that people want to modify are behaviors that already have rewards attached to them (otherwise they would not persist). To change them, you have to cut down the number of times you do them (or don't do them, as the case may be) and so cut down the number of associated rewards. At the same time, you must build up rewards for the new behavior. What you are trying to do is gradually shift the rewarding conditions from one behavior pattern to the desired one. This process is called *behavior shaping*.

Behavior shaping works by setting up rewards for each of the successive approximations to your goal. Make a bargain with yourself that you can have something or do something that you want *only* if you achieve your current intermediate goal. The possibilities are almost endless, depending entirely upon what you like and how imaginative you are. One high school student helped himself to study more, for example, by making watching television contingent upon meeting each day's study goal. If he made it, he could watch TV in the evening; if he didn't, he couldn't.

The high school student decided to go it alone in setting up his reward system, but it also is possible to enlist the aid of a friend, child, spouse or other person at this step. One former smoker, for example, got her husband to agree to take her out to dinner at the restaurant of her choice every Saturday night that marked the successful accomplishment of that week's goal.

"If-then" bargains, such as those the high school student made with himself and the smoker made with her husband are *reinforcement contingency statements:* If I do (don't do) _____, then I can _____. Obviously, it is possible to cheat when you set up your own reinforcement contingency statements, and this may be another reason for enlisting aid at the beginning of your program. Remember, though, that this is a *self*-management approach to changing behavior. If you cheat, you cheat on yourself. If you stick to the new rules, you get credit for the change.

A blank form listing the steps to go through to change a behavior of your choice is provided in *Test Yourself* to help you give this self-management a try. You don't have to undertake anything major. In the past, students have used this program to "train" themselves to stop nail biting, watch less TV, write home more often, be more punctual, be neater, drink fewer cola beverages, and remember to make the appropriate entries in a checkbook. Although the basic process requires rewarding yourself in an external, concrete manner, you will find that rewards begin to come internally as well as you increase your control over your own behavior.

## TEST YOURSELF
## Steps in the Self-Modification of Behavior

1. **State target behavior.** My target behavior is: _____

2. **Chart current response rate for target behavior.** The average number of times I do/don't (circle one that applies) this behavior each day/week/month (circle one that applies) is: _____

3. **Chart conditions under which behavior occurs:** The most important stimuli and rewards for this behavior are:

_____     _____
_____     _____
_____     _____
_____     _____
_____     _____

4. **Describe ways to change your environment to help you change your behavior** (from number 3 above).

a. _____
b. _____
c. _____
d. _____

Use as many lines as necessary; the more of the stimuli supporting the behavior you want to change that you can eliminate, the faster you will progress.

5. **Set up intermediate goals.** By the end of each day, every other day, or _____,
I will _____
Time: _____     Goal 1: _____
Time: _____     Goal 2: _____
Time: _____     Goal 3: _____
Time: _____     Goal 4: _____
(Use as many intermediate goals as necessary to reach your final goal.)

6. **Set up rewards for yourself.** For each intermediate goal that I reach, I will _____

_____

(You may want to state a different reward at each stage.)

7. **Keep track of your progress.** Make a chart showing each goal and time period and mark it in some way to show that you have made it. This will be a visible reminder that you are getting your behavior under control, and the feelings of accomplishment will serve as another reward.

# A Sample Marriage Contract

**P**am and Mark are of sound mind and body, have a clear understanding of the terms of this contract and of the binding nature of the agreements contained herein; they freely and in good faith choose to enter into this PRENUPTIAL AGREEMENT and MARRIAGE CONTRACT and fully intend it to be binding upon themselves.

Now, therefore, in consideration of their love and esteem for each other, and in consideration of the mutual promises herein expressed, the sufficiency of which is hereby acknowledged, Pam and Mark agree as follows:

### Names

Pam and Mark affirm their individuality and equality in this relationship. The parties believe in and accept the convention of the wife accepting the husband's name, while rejecting any implied ownership.

Therefore, the parties agree that they will be known as husband and wife and will henceforth employ the titles of address: Mr. and Mrs. Mark Stafford, and will use the full names Pam Hayes Stafford and Mark Robert Stafford.

### Relationships with Others

Pam and Mark believe that their commitment to each other is strong enough that no restrictions are necessary with regard to relationships with others.

Therefore, the parties agree to allow each other freedom to choose and define their relationships outside this contract and the parties further agree to maintain sexual fidelity each to the other.

### Religion

Pam and Mark reaffirm their belief in God and recognize He is the source of their love. Each of the parties have their own religious beliefs.

Therefore, the parties agree to respect their individual preferences with respect to religion and to make no demands on each other to change such preferences.

439

### Children

Pam and Mark both have children. Although no minor children will be involved, there are two (2) children still at home and in school and in need of financial and emotional support.

Therefore, the parties agree that they will maintain a home for and support these children as long as needed and reasonable. They further agree that all children of both parties will be treated as one family unit and each will be given emotional and financial support to the extent feasible and necessary as determined mutually by both parties.

### Careers and Domicile

Pam and Mark value the importance and integrity of their respective careers and acknowledge the demands that their jobs place on them as individuals and on their partnership. Both parties are well established in their respective careers and do not foresee any change or move in the future.

Therefore, the parties agree, however, that if need or desire for a move should arise, the decision to move shall be mutual and based on the following factors:

(a) The overall advantage gained by one of the parties in pursuing a new opportunity shall be weighed against the disadvantages, economic and otherwise, incurred by the other.
(b) The amount of income or other incentive derived from the move shall not be controlling.
(c) Short-term separations as a result of such moves may be necessary.

Mark hereby waives whatever right he may have to solely determine the legal domicile of the parties.

### Care and Use of Living Spaces

Pam and Mark recognize the need for autonomy and equality within the home in terms of the use of available space and allocation of household tasks. The parties reject the concept that the responsibility for housework rests with the woman in a marriage relationship while the duties of home maintenance and repair rest with the man.

Therefore, the parties agree, to share equally in the performance of all household tasks, taking into consideration individual schedules, preferences, and abilities of each.

The parties agree that decisions about the use of living space in the home shall be mutually made, regardless of the parties' relative financial interests in the ownership or rental of the home, and the parties further agree to honor all requests for privacy from the other party.

### Property; Debts; Living Expenses

Pam and Mark intend that the individual autonomy sought in the partnership shall be reflected in the ownership of existing and future-acquired property, in the characterization and control of income, and in the responsibility for living expenses. Pam and Mark also recognize the right of patrimony of children of their previous marriages.

Therefore, the parties agree that all things of value now held singly and/ or acquired singly in the future shall be the property of the party making such acquisition. In the event that one party to this agreement shall predecease the other, property and/or other valuables shall be disposed of in accordance with an existing will or other instrument of disposal that reflects the intent of the deceased party.

Property or valuables acquired jointly shall be the property of the partnership and shall be divided, if necessary, according to the contribution of each party. If one party shall predecease the other, jointly owned property or valuables shall become the property of the surviving spouse.

Pam and Mark feel that each of the parties to this agreement should have access to monies that are not accountable to the partnership.

Therefore, the parties agree that each shall retain a mutually agreeable portion of their total income and the remainder shall be deposited in a mutually agreeable banking institution and shall be used to satisfy all jointly acquired expenses and debts.

The parties agree that beneficiaries of life insurance policies they now own shall remain named on each policy. Future changes in beneficiaries shall be mutually agreed on after the dependency of the children of each party has been terminated. Any other benefits of any retirement plan or insurance benefits that accrue to a spouse only shall not be affected by the foregoing.

The parties recognize that in the absence of income by one of the parties, resulting from any reason, living expenses may become the sole responsibility of the employed party and in such a situation, the employed party shall assume responsibility for the personal expenses of the other.

Both Pam and Mark intend their marriage to last as long as both shall live.

Therefore the parties agree that should it become necessary, due to the death of either person the surviving spouse shall assume any last expenses in the event that no insurance exists for that purpose.

Pam hereby waives whatever right she may have to rely on Mark to provide the sole economic support for the family unit.

## Evaluation of the Partnership

Pam and Mark recognize the importance of change in their relationship and intend that the CONTRACT shall be a living document and a focus for periodic evaluations of the partnership

The parties agree that either party can initiate review of any article of the CONTRACT at any time for amendment to reflect changes in the relationship. The parties agree to honor such requests for review with negotiations and discussions at a mutually convenient time.

The parties agree that, in any event, there shall be an annual reaffirmation of the CONTRACT on or about the anniversary date of the CONTRACT.

The parties agree that, in the case of unresolved conflicts between them over any provisions of the CONTRACT, they will seek mediation, professional or otherwise, by a third party.

## Termination of the Contract

Pam and Mark believe in the sanctity of marriage, however, in the unlikely event of a decision to terminate this CONTRACT, the parties agree that neither shall contest the application for a divorce decree or the entry of such decree in the county in which the parties are both residing at the time of such application.

In the event of termination of the CONTRACT and divorce of the parties, the provisions of this and the section on "Property; Debts; Living Expenses" of the CONTRACT as amended shall serve as the final property settlement agreement between the parties. In such event, this CONTRACT is intended to affect a complete settlement of any and all claims that either party may have against the other, and a complete settlement of their respective rights as to property rights, homestead rights, inheritance rights, and all other rights of property otherwise arising out of their partnership. The parties further agree that in the event of termination of this contract and divorce of the parties, neither party shall require the other to pay maintenance costs or alimony.

## Decision Making

Pam and Mark share a commitment to a process of negotiations and compromise which will strengthen their equality in the partnership. Decisions will be made with respect for individual needs. The parties hope to maintain such mutual decision making so that the daily decisions affecting their lives will not become a struggle between the parties for power, authority, and dominance. The parties agree that such a process, while sometimes time consuming and fatiguing, is a good investment in the future of their relationship and their continued esteem for each other.

Now, therefore, Pam and Mark make the following declarations:

1. They are responsible adults.
2. They freely adopt the spirit and the material terms of this prenuptial and marriage contract.
3. The marriage contract, entered into in conjunction with a marriage license of the State of Illinois, County of Wayne, on this 12th day of June, 1984, hereby manifests their intent to define the rights and obligations of their marriage relationship as distinct from those rights and obligations defined by the laws of the State of Illinois, and affirms their right to do so.
4. They intend to be bound by this prenuptial and marriage contract and to uphold its provisions before any Court of Law in the Land.

Therefore, comes now, Pam Hayes Carraway who applauds her development which allows her to enter into this partnership of trust and she agrees to go forward with this marriage in the spirit of the foregoing PRENUPTIAL and MARRIAGE CONTRACT.

_____

Pam Hayes Carraway

Therefore, comes now, Mark Robert Stafford who celebrates his growth and independence with the signing of this contract and he agrees to accept the responsibilities of this marriage, as set forth in the foregoing PRENUPTIAL and MARRIAGE CONTRACT.

_____

Mark Robert Stafford

This contract and covenant has been received and reviewed by the Reverend Ralph James, officiating.

_____

Ralph James

Finally, comes Karen James and Bill Dunn who certify that Pam and Mark did freely read and sign this marriage contract in their presence, on the occasion of their entry into a marriage relationship by the signing of a marriage license of the State of Illinois, County of Wayne, at which they acted as official witnesses. Further, they declare that the marriage license of the parties bears the date of the signing of this PRENUPTIAL and MARRIAGE CONTRACT.

_____

Karen James

_____

Bill Dunn

_____

_Note:_ From _Choices in Relationships_ (2nd ed.) by D. Knox, 1988. St. Paul, MN: West. Reprinted by permission.

# Name Index

## Y

## Z

# Subject Index

group
  consensus, 363–364
  encounter, 423
  peer, 137, 139, 361
  deviance from, 362–363
  influence of, 139, 361–362
  psychological experience, 423–424
  reference, 361

## H

habit, 431–432
hardy personality, 140, 305
hearing message, 263–264
heterosexuality, 164
hierarchical decision maker, 279
hierarchy
  anticipatory anxiety, 391
  need, 108–109
holography, 247
homosexuality, 164–165
hormones, 159–160
hostility in relationships, 369
hot cognitions, 287
housework, 204
humanistic
  theories of personality, 107–111
  therapy, 409–410
hyperactivity, see attention-deficit
    disorder
hypnosis, 426
hypochrondriasis, 393

## I

id, 88
ideal-self, 125–126
identity
  crisis, 92–94
  gender, 118–119
idiosyncratic credits, 362
imaginal systematic desensitization, 390–
    391
imposition from friends, 364–366
impression
  at job interview, 228–230
  first, 115
  in classroom, 220
  management, 221
incongruence, 111
indirect communication, 249–250
inference, 14
inferiority complex, 126

information
  and decision making, 282–286
  overload, 284
innoculation hypothesis, 289
insight
  defined, 6
  therapies, 408–409
integrative decision maker, 279
intelligence
  and cognitive development, 56
  and decision making, 278
  and peer pressure, 363
interpersonal attraction, 144–151
  and appearance, 148–149
  and proximity, 145–146
  and reciprocity, 147
  and similarity, 146–147
  defined, 144
intensive group experience, 423–424
interest inventory, 222
internalizer, 83–84
intimacy
  and friendship, 151
  and triangular theory of love, 187–188
  need for, 151, 185
intoxication, 330, 331
introspection, 356
introversion, 80, 81
irrational beliefs, 127

## J

jealousy, 369–370
job, see occupation or work
job satisfaction, 226–227

## K

Korsakoff's psychosis, 331

## L

law
  of behavior, 15
  of effect, 63
learned helplessness, 12
learning
  -based therapies, 410
  classical conditioning, 58–60
  defined, 58
  discrimination, 61, 96–97
  generalization, 61, 96
  observational, 66

operant conditioning, 61–65
  social, 66–67
  theories of personality, 94–101
life style
  adjustments in marriage, 201–204
  and career choice, 222, 235
  and drug use, 339, 342
  and stress, 306–307
  changes in since 1950, 202, 345, 347
  single, 193
listening, 262–265
loaded words, 248–249
locus of control, 82–84
loneliness, 359–360
love, 185–191
  and friendship, 190–191
  and marriage, 192, 194
  aspects of, 187
companionate, 190
conditions for romantic, 189
kinds of, 186
looking for, 366–368
psychologists' views of, 186
triangular theory of, 186–189

## M

maladaptive behavior, 385–386
major depressive disorder, 398
management test, 223
manic-depressive, see bipolar disorder
marijuana, 341–342
marriage, 191–210
  adjustments to, 201–209
  age at, 14, 191
  and family life style changes, 202,
    207–208
  and extramarital relationships, 169–
    171
  contract for, 203–204, 439–443
  discord in, 206, 208–209
  reasons for, 192–194, 195
  satisfaction with, 195–196
  statistics, 191
  success factors, 196–198
  trial, 199, 200–201
  types, of 209–210
marriage contract, 203–204, 439–443
mastery treatment, 391
masturbation, 161
maturation
  and behavior, 25–29
  and sexual activity, 159

# Fine Art and Photo Credits (continued)

**Part III,** page **133,** "Spring" by Ben Shahn, 1947, Albright-Knox Gallery, Buffalo, New York. Details reproduced for chapter opening art for chapters 6, 7, 8, and 9

## Chapter 6
**138,** Sybil Shelton/Monkmeyer Press Photo Service; **140,** Gayle Zucker/Stock, Boston; **145,** Robert Capece/Monkmeyer Press Photo Service, 146 Hugh Rogers/Monkmeyer Press Service

## Chapter 7
**158,** Paul Conklin/Monkmeyer Press Photo Service; **166,** Pat F. Jones/Berg & Associates; **168,** Frank Siteman/Stock, Boston; **172,** Hazel Hanrin/Stock, Boston

## Chapter 8
**186,** Michael O'Brien/Archive Pictures; **192,** Jeffry W. Meyers/Stock, Boston; **195,** Hazel Hanrin/Stock, Boston; **197,** Mark Antman/The Image Works; **200,** Michael Kagan/Monkmeyer Press Photo Service

## Chapter 9
**215,** Paul Conklin/Monkmeyer Press Photo Service; **219,** Earl Dotter/Archive Pictures, Inc.; **222,** Dean Abramson/Stock Boston; **232,** James Holland/Stock, Boston

**Part IV**, page 237 "Three Acrobats" by Charles Demuth, Amon Carter Museum, Fort Worth, Texas. Detail reproduced for chapter opening art for chapters 10, 11, and 12

## Chapter 10
**242,** Michael O'Brien/Archive Pictures, Inc.; **243,** Mimi Forsyth/Monkmeyer Press Photo Service; **252,** Peter Vandermark/Stock, Boston; **263,** Irene Bayer/Monkmeyer Press Photo Service

## Chapter 11
**274,** Barbara Aper/Stock, Boston; **280,** Michael Kagan/Monkmeyer Press Photo Service; **282,** Jean-Claude Lejeune/Stock, Boston, **286,** Paul Conklin/Monkmeyer Press Photo Service

## Chapter 12
**299,** Cary Wolinsky/Stock, Boston; **305,** Dick Wade/Berg & Associates, **310,** Bohdan Hrynewych/Stock, Boston; **318,** Laimute E. Druskis/Stock, Boston

**Part V,** page **321,** Katherine Mahoney, illustrator. Details reproduced for chapter opening art for chapters 13, 14, and 15

## Chapter 13
**325,** Gale Zucker/Stock, Boston; **328,** Peter Menzel/Stock, Boston, **333,** Sylvia Plachy/Archive Pictures, Inc.; **335,** Courtesy of Mercy Hospital Medical Center, Des Moines, Iowa; **350,** Berg & Associates; **351,** George S. Zimbel/Monkmeyer Press Photo Service

## Chapter 14
**358,** Christopher W. Morrow/Stock, Boston; **361,** Lionel Delevingne/Stock, Boston; **365,** Hazel Hankin/Stock, Boston; **374,** Michael O'Brien/Archive Pictures, Inc.; **375,** Mike Rizza/Stock, Boston

## Chapter 15
**389,** Gale Zucker/Stock, Boston; **393,** Yvonne Alsip, **399,** David S. Strickler/Monkmeyer Press Photo Service; **400,** Mimi Forsyth/Monkmeyer Press Photo Service

**Part VI,** page **403,** "Survivors" by John Minton, 1954, National Gallery of Canada, Ottawa. Detail reproduced for chapter opening art for chapter 16

## Chapter 16
**407,** Rhoda Sidney/Monkmeyer Press Photo Service; **409,** Mimi Forsyth/Monkmeyer Press Photo Service; **417,** Paul Conklin/Monkmeyer Press Photo Service; **420,** Historical Pictures Service